BUSINESS COMMUNICATION

POLISHING YOUR PROFESSIONAL PRESENCE

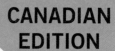

CANADIAN EDITION

BUSINESS COMMUNICATION
POLISHING YOUR PROFESSIONAL PRESENCE

Barbara Shwom

Northwestern University

Lisa Gueldenzoph Snyder

North Carolina A&T State University

Liz Clarke

Centennial College

With contributions from
Julia M. Lewis Satov and Julie Hamilton

PEARSON

Toronto

Editorial Director: Claudine O'Donnell
Acquisitions Editor: Jennifer Sutton
Marketing Manager: Euan White
Program Manager: Emily Dill
Project Manager: Susan Johnson
Developmental Editor: Lise Dupont
Production Services: Mohinder Singh, iEnergizer
   Aptara®, Ltd.

Permissions Project Manager: Alison Derry
Photo Permissions Research: Melody English, Integra
Text Permissions Research: Renae Horstman, Integra
Interior Designer: Anthony Leung
Cover Designer: Anthony Leung
Cover Image: Life On White/Getty images
Vice-President, Cross Media and Publishing Services:
   Gary Bennett

Credits and acknowledgments for material borrowed from other sources and reproduced, with permission, in this textbook appear on the appropriate page within the text.

Original edition published by Pearson Education, Inc., Upper Saddle River, New Jersey, USA. Copyright © [2015] Pearson Education, Inc. This edition is authorized for sale only in Canada.

If you purchased this book outside the United States or Canada, you should be aware that it has been imported without the approval of the publisher or the author.

Library and Archives Canada Cataloguing in Publication

Shwom, Barbara Lynne, author
   Business communication: polishing your professional presence/Barbara Shwom,
   Lisa Gueldenzoph Snyder, Liz Clarke.—1st Canadian edition.
   Includes index.
   ISBN 978-0-13-342766-0 (paperback)
   1. Business communication.   2. Business writing.   I. Snyder, Lisa Gueldenzoph, author   II. Clarke, Liz, 1963–,
   author   III. Title.
   HF5718.S47 2015
   651.7

                                                                          C2015-906526-7

2   16

ISBN 13: 978-0-13-342766-0

DEDICATION

To our husbands for their continued patience, and to our families for their enduring support.

To our students for helping us be better teachers by challenging us to learn more every day.

To our colleagues in our universities, in the Association for Business Communication, and in business for providing valuable feedback and insight.

—Barbara and Lisa

To my students, who inspire me, teach me, and lead me into new ways of thinking about communication, technology, culture, and diversity.

To my mother, the late Betty Clarke, who was the best teacher I've ever known.

To Letta, Vonda, Florence, Janet, Helen, George, and Charlie. My first instructors in diversity.

To Freddie, my co-pilot throughout the preparation of this manuscript. Yes, we can go for a walk now.

—Liz Clarke

ABOUT THE AUTHORS

Barbara Shwom

Barbara Shwom, Ph.D., is Professor of Instruction in Writing at Northwestern University, where she teaches in the Weinberg College of Arts and Sciences, Kellogg School of Management, and McCormick School of Engineering and Applied Science. For more than 30 years she has designed and taught communication courses that have influenced this textbook, including *Writing in Organizations, Communicating Complex Data, Engineering Design and Communication*, and *How to Become An Expert in Roughly 10 Weeks*. Professor Shwom's teaching at Northwestern has been recognized by both an outstanding teacher award and an appointment as a fellow of Northwestern's Searle Center for Teaching Excellence. Professor Shwom has gained industry experience as the managing principal of Communication Partners, a consulting practice that works with clients from a range of industries, including biotechnology, high-tech research and development, pharmaceuticals, management consulting, market research, financial services, engineering, and consumer products. Professor Shwom's research interests include evolving genres of business communication, visual communication of data, and methods of persuasion. In addition to many articles, she is also the co-author of a textbook on graphics and visual communication for managers. She currently sits on the editorial review board of *Business Communication Quarterly* and has served as president for both the Association for Business Communication and the Association of Professional Communication Consultants.

Lisa Gueldenzoph Snyder

Lisa Gueldenzoph Snyder, Ph.D., is a Professor and Chairperson of the Department of Business Education in the School of Business and Economics at North Carolina Agricultural and Technical State University in Greensboro. In addition to business communication, she teaches classes in computer applications and ecommerce. She earned a doctorate in Higher Education Administration from Bowling Green State University in Ohio, where she also received a master's degree in Business Education. Her Bachelor of Science in Business Education is from Northern Michigan University.

Dr. Snyder is widely published in journals, such as the *Business Communication Quarterly, Journal of Business Communication, Business Education Digest, The Delta Pi Epsilon Journal*, and *NABTE Review*. She has made over 150 presentations at local, regional, and national professional development events, workshops, and conferences. Dr. Snyder received the Meada Gibbs Outstanding Teacher Award from the Association for Business Communication and the Distinguished Alumni Award from the Business Education program at Bowling Green State University. She has also received the Innovative Instructional Practices Award from Delta Pi Epsilon, the Distinguished Service Award from the Ohio Business Teachers Association, and the Collegiate Teacher of the Year Award from both the North Carolina Business Education Association and the Southern Business Education Association. Dr. Snyder is also an active member of the Association of Business Communication, Delta Pi Epsilon, and National Business Education Association.

Liz Clarke

Liz Clarke, MBA, has been a full-time faculty member at the School of Business, Centennial College, since August 2000. Professor Clarke is also the Coordinator for the Business Administration: Leadership and Management Advanced Diploma Program at the school. Over the last 15 years, Professor Clarke has focused on emerging educational and business technologies as well as trends in business communications across a variety of both graduate and undergraduate programs and courses. In 2014, she represented Centennial College at the coveted biennial CASE (Canadian Academics Studying Europe) conference. Hosted by the University of Applied Sciences and Arts, Northwestern Switzerland, CASE 2014 concentrated on European law, banking, governance, and migration and took place in Paris, Strasbourg, Stuttgart, Zurich, and Olten. In 2012, Professor Clarke was nominated—by her students—for Centennial College's prestigious Wicken Teaching Excellence Award.

Professor Clarke has over 25 years' experience working with clients in a wide range of industries, including research, financial services, information technology (IT), supply chain and logistics, and education, including the Ontario Institute for Cancer Research, the Ontario College of Art and Design, Armstrong Partnership LP, CIBC, the Canadian Urban Transit Association, and the Toronto Region Research Alliance. In 2015, she is a member of the International Association of Business Communicators (IABC).

Professor Clarke holds a Master of Business Administration from the Rotman School of Management, University of Toronto, where she graduated with Dean's List Honours. She completed an Honours Bachelor of Arts degree at Brock University, where she won the J.H. and J.F. Harding Prize honouring Excellence in Theatre and Dramatic Literature (English).

BRIEF CONTENTS

PREFACE xvii
SUPPLEMENTS xviii
ACKNOWLEDGMENTS xix
VISUAL WALK-THROUGH xx

PART 1 | Establishing Context and Basics

1 Becoming a Successful Business Communicator 2
2 Managing the Communication Process: Analyzing, Composing, Evaluating 26

PART 2 | Working with Others

3 Who Am I? Understanding and Adapting Interpersonal Communication Styles 64
4 Who Are You? Understanding Intercultural Communication and Workplace Diversity 94
5 What Are the Tools and What Are the Rules? Communications Technologies in the Workplace 128
6 How Can We Be Better, Together? Collaboration and Productivity 160

PART 3 | Delivering Effective Messages

7 Communicating Routine Messages and Building Goodwill 190
8 Communicating Persuasive Messages 222
9 Communicating Bad News Messages 256

PART 4 | Researching, Proposing, Reporting, and Presenting

10 Finding and Evaluating Business Information 286
11 Preparing Business Reports and Proposals 326
12 Preparing and Delivering Business Presentations 382

APPENDIX A Communicating Your Professional Brand: Social Media, Résumés, Cover Letters, and Interviews 431

APPENDIX B Questions to Ask about Key Communications Technologies 447

APPENDIX C Formats for Business Documents 453

APPENDIX D Documentation and Reference Styles 463

GLOSSARY 479

REFERENCES 485

INDEX 493

CONTENTS

PREFACE xvii
SUPPLEMENTS xviii
ACKNOWLEDGMENTS xix
VISUAL WALK-THROUGH xx

PART 1   Establishing Context and Basics

1   Becoming a Successful Business Communicator 2

LO 1.1   Why should you study business communication? 4

Effective business communicators have a competitive edge in the job market 4
Communication skills will help you, and your employer, succeed 5

LO 1.2   Why is business communication challenging? 7

Business communication is a complex process 7
Barriers often block successful communication 8
Context adds to the complexity 9
Multiple audiences have different needs 9
Social media expands communication opportunities and responsibilities 10

LO 1.3   What characteristics do successful business communicators share? 10

Effective communicators are strategic 10
Effective communicators are professional 12
Effective communicators are adaptable 16

LEARNING OBJECTIVES IN REVIEW 22 • KEY TERMS 22 • REVIEW QUESTIONS 22 •
CRITICAL THINKING 23 • DEVELOPING YOUR COMMUNICATION SKILLS 23

2   Managing the Communication Process: Analyzing, Composing, Evaluating 26

LO 2.1   Why should you spend time analyzing? 28

Analyzing the purpose focuses the message 28
Analyzing the audience helps you meet their needs 30
Analyzing the content ensures a complete message 31
Analyzing the medium helps you choose the best delivery option 32

ETHICS   Ethics in Communication: Using O-A-R 34

LO 2.2   What is involved in composing? 34

Practising strategic time management 35

TECHNOLOGY   Boost Your Brainpower: Become a Single Tasker 36

Organizing the message 37
Drafting the content 40
Designing a professional format and delivery 41

LO 2.3   How does evaluating improve your communication? 46

Revise content: Improve effectiveness 46
Edit for style and tone: Project a professional image 49

CULTURE   Considering Culture in Business Communications 51

Proofread to increase your credibility 52
Review feedback to improve your communication strategy 54

LEARNING OBJECTIVES IN REVIEW 57 • KEY TERMS 57 • CASE STUDY 58 • REVIEW QUESTIONS 59 •
CRITICAL THINKING 59 • DEVELOPING YOUR COMMUNICATION SKILLS 60

PART 2   Working with Others

 Who Am I? Understanding and Adapting Interpersonal
Communication Styles 64

 Why do you need to understand communication styles? 66
Understand that styles are adaptable 66
Define and understand your communications comfort zone 67

CULTURE   How Can You Optimize Your Personal Communication Style at School?
At Work? 69
Learn to adapt: Get out of your comfort zone 70

ETHICS   Photography and Audio and Video Recordings: Just Because You Can,
Does It Mean You Should? 71

TECHNOLOGY   Has Facebook Made You Fumble? Beware the Impact of Social/
Mobile Technologies on Face-to-Face Business Etiquette 73

 What listening skills will help you communicate better with others? 74
Hearing accurately 75
Comprehending and interpreting 76
Evaluating 79
Responding 79

**What speaking strategies will encourage others to listen to you and
understand what you are saying? 80**
Focus on your audience 80
Share the conversation 81
Use clear, unambiguous language 81
Support your message with appropriate nonverbal communication 81
Avoid upward inflection 82
Avoid language that triggers a negative response 82
Be aware of gender-specific communication styles 84
Apply ACE to support interpersonal communication skills 85

LEARNING OBJECTIVES IN REVIEW 87 • KEY TERMS 87 • CASE STUDY 87 • REVIEW QUESTIONS 89 •
CRITICAL THINKING 89 • DEVELOPING YOUR COMMUNICATION SKILLS 89

 Who Are You? Understanding Intercultural Communication
and Workplace Diversity 94

 **Why do we need to study intercultural communication and workplace
diversity? 96**
Understand the impact of culture and diversity on communication 97
Know that each individual is unique 98
Develop a mindset of cultural intelligence 98

 What do you need to know to improve your cultural intelligence? 100
Understand how cultures differ 100

ETHICS   Speak My Language: Learn and Preserve Your Languages 102
Integrate communication style and culture: The Lewis model of cultural types 105
Be aware that common language does not equal common meaning or culture 106
Develop strategies that help you communicate interculturally 107

 How can you make your communications inclusive? 109
Develop a mindset of inclusion 109
Learn the art of respectful inquiry 116

CULTURE   When the Questions Say More Than the Answers 117
Use ACE to navigate diverse and intercultural situations 119

LEARNING OBJECTIVES IN REVIEW 121 • KEY TERMS 121 • CASE STUDY 121 • REVIEW QUESTIONS 123 •
CRITICAL THINKING 123 • DEVELOPING YOUR COMMUNICATION SKILLS 124

5 What Are the Tools and What Are the Rules? Communications
Technologies in the Workplace 128

LO 5.1 **Why is an understanding of communications technologies important? 130**
Understand media richness theory (MRT) 130
Consider a few basics about using communications technologies 131
Ask important questions about technology tools 134

LO 5.2 **What are the main functions of communications technologies? 136**
Use distribution tools to share information 136
Use networking tools to discuss, build community, and expand connections 140

TECHNOLOGY When Complaints Go Viral 142
Use collaboration tools to work virtually with others 142

CULTURE Assumptions and Access 146

LO 5.3 **What are the "best practices" of experienced virtual communicators? 146**
Email 146
Conference calls 148
Virtual meetings and videoconferences 150
Webinars (mass audience) 151
Social media 151

LEARNING OBJECTIVES IN REVIEW 154 • KEY TERMS 154 • CASE STUDY 154 • REVIEW QUESTIONS 155 •
CRITICAL THINKING 155 • DEVELOPING YOUR COMMUNICATION SKILLS 156

6 How Can We Be Better, Together? Collaboration and Productivity 160

LO 6.1 **How do you communicate effectively as part of a team? 162**
Create a team charter 162
Give the team time to develop 164

ETHICS Team Dynamics = Team Ethics? 165
Plan for effective meetings 166
Be a valued team member 167

LO 6.2 **How can working on a team help you develop leadership skills? 169**
Identify and practise key leadership fundamentals 169
Use conflict management to help develop leadership skills 170

LO 6.3 **What are some key aspects of high-performance team collaboration? 175**
Enhance productivity with virtual best practices 175

TECHNOLOGY Social Collaboration: Taking the Team Online 177
Develop the "c factor" in your team 178

CULTURE The "Second Hour": Creating a "C Factor" Team Culture 179
Use a peer coaching model for feedback 180

LEARNING OBJECTIVES IN REVIEW 184 • KEY TERMS 184 • CASE STUDY 184 • REVIEW
QUESTIONS 185 • CRITICAL THINKING 186 • DEVELOPING YOUR COMMUNICATION SKILLS 186

PART 3 Delivering Effective Messages

7 Communicating Routine Messages and Building Goodwill 190

LO 7.1 **How do you compose messages containing questions and requests? 192**
Decide between a direct or an indirect message 192
Provide reasons for the request 193
Adopt the receiver's perspective and include audience benefits 193
Conclude with gratitude and a call for action 195

How do you compose informational messages? 197

Reply to questions with a direct answer 197
Respond to customer requests by creating goodwill 197
Highlight key points in confirmation messages 199
Organize routine announcements so they are easy to skim 199
Format instructions so readers can easily follow the steps 200

ETHICS Is Blind Courtesy Copy (BCC) Like Spying? 201

Use your own templates to save time and reduce errors 203

TECHNOLOGY Raise Efficiency and Accuracy with Clipboard Manager
Software 204

 What kinds of messages build goodwill in business relationships? 204

CULTURE Routine Messages and Corporate Culture: How Can You Get It Right? 205

Thank you messages 206
Congratulatory messages 207
Sympathy messages 208
"For-your-information" messages 208

 How can you use social media to build goodwill in business? 210

Provide quick responses to questions and concerns 210
Build "real-time goodwill" by creating community with social media 211

LEARNING OBJECTIVES IN REVIEW 214 • KEY TERMS 215 • CASE STUDY 215 • REVIEW QUESTIONS 217 •
CRITICAL THINKING 217 • DEVELOPING YOUR COMMUNICATION SKILLS 218

8 Communicating Persuasive Messages 222

 How can the ACE process help you persuade your audience? 224

Analyzing helps you plan your message 224
Composing implements the persuasive plan 228
Evaluating helps you review the draft for effectiveness 228

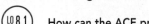 **What are the basic elements of persuasion? 229**

Building credibility 230

CULTURE Adapting Persuasive Appeals 231

Constructing a logical argument 231
Appealing to your audience's emotions 234

ETHICS Is Being Persuasive Like Being Dishonest? 235

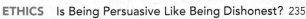 **What types of business messages require persuasion? 238**

Recommendations for action 239
Sales messages 240

TECHNOLOGY Composing a Persuasive Recommendation
with Presentation Software 242

Social media: Indirect persuasion 246
Persuasion helps you motivate others 246

LEARNING OBJECTIVES IN REVIEW 250 • KEY TERMS 250 • CASE STUDY 250 • REVIEW QUESTIONS 252 •
CRITICAL THINKING 252 • DEVELOPING YOUR COMMUNICATION SKILLS 252

9 Communicating Bad News Messages 256

  How does the ACE process help you deliver bad news effectively? 258

Analyzing and planning bad news messages 258

TECHNOLOGY Can You Email, Text, or Tweet Bad News? 262

Using effective strategies to compose bad news messages 263
Evaluating bad news messages 268
Checking cultural assumptions about delivering bad news 269

CULTURE   Gaining Intercultural Perspective on Bad News 270

 What types of bad news messages are common in business? 271

Denying customer claims 271

Acknowledging mistakes or problems 272

ETHICS   To Apologize . . . or Not to Apologize 273

Communicating negative change 273

 How can you control the spread of bad news through social media? 275

Having a plan in place 275

TECHNOLOGY   From Hashtag to Bashtag 275

LEARNING OBJECTIVES IN REVIEW 279 • KEY TERMS 279 • CASE STUDY 279 • REVIEW QUESTIONS 281 •
CRITICAL THINKING 282 • DEVELOPING YOUR COMMUNICATION SKILLS 282

PART 4   Researching, Proposing, Reporting, and Presenting

10 Finding and Evaluating Business Information 286

 How do you determine what information you need? 288

Analyze the research question and topic 289

Identify audience concerns and needs 290

Establish the scope of the research 291

Define research activities 291

CULTURE   Blurred Lines? 292

Develop a work plan 293

 How do you conduct and evaluate research in print and online sources? 295

Gather relevant print and electronic files 295

Search the web strategically 295

TECHNOLOGY   Going beneath the Surface of the Web 297

Use an online index or database to find articles and business data 298

Use a library or bookseller to find relevant books 299

Follow leads in reliable sources 299

Evaluate your sources for credibility 299

 How do you conduct and evaluate primary research? 300

Conduct survey research to gather information that is easy to compare 302

Conduct interview research to gather in-depth information 306

Conduct observational research to understand how people act 308

ETHICS   How to Be an Ethical Researcher 309

 How can you use social media in your research? 310

Search for experts 311

Post questions to your network and beyond 311

Share information 311

Gather anecdotal evidence 312

 How can you effectively organize the results of your research? 312

Build your reference list as you research 312

Organize documents and notes on your computer and "in the cloud" 313

Organize your findings by research questions 315

LEARNING OBJECTIVES IN REVIEW 319 • KEY TERMS 320 • CASE STUDY 320 • REVIEW QUESTIONS 321 •
CRITICAL THINKING 321 • DEVELOPING YOUR COMMUNICATION SKILLS 322

11 Preparing Business Reports and Proposals 326

 LO 11.1 **How can ACE help you write a business report? 328**
Analyze to understand the purpose and report type 328
Analyze to understand the audience's needs 328
Analyze to choose the best medium 329
Compose your report to meet audience expectations 329
Compose using an objective and easy-to-read style 330
Evaluate by reviewing on your own and getting feedback from others 331

 LO 11.2 **How should you structure typical business reports? 332**
Progress reports 332
Travel reports 332
Formal reports 332

TECHNOLOGY Using Software Features to Help Format Formal Reports 335

 LO 11.3 **How do you prepare an effective proposal? 350**
Understand the problem and propose a well-balanced solution 351
Identify the appropriate type of proposal 351

 LO 11.4 **How do you properly respond to a request for proposal? 354**
Structure an RFP proposal like a formal report 354
Follow specified guidelines when responding to RFPs 355
Use proposal-writing software to increase efficiency 358

CULTURE Proposals for a Non-Canadian Audience: Extra Research Is Required 359

 LO 11.5 **How do you integrate visuals into reports? 360**
Choose the best form of display: table or graph 360
Choose the best type of graph 360
Design graphs and tables to communicate 363
Integrate data displays within the text 365

ETHICS Representing Data Ethically 366

 LO 11.6 **How should you document your research? 368**
Determine what needs to be documented 368
Prepare the documentation 369

LEARNING OBJECTIVES IN REVIEW 372 • KEY TERMS 372 • CASE STUDY 373 • REVIEW QUESTIONS 374 •
CRITICAL THINKING 374 • DEVELOPING YOUR COMMUNICATION SKILLS 375

12 Preparing and Delivering Business Presentations 382

 LO 12.1 **What do you analyze when planning a business presentation? 384**
Analyze your purpose and outcome: Why? 385
Analyze your audience: Who? 385
Analyze your message: What? 386
Analyze your setting: Where? 387
Analyze your medium options: How? 387

 LO 12.2 **How do you compose the presentation? 388**
Identify the type of presentation 388
Organize the content 388
Create a storyboard 393
Develop a template 395
Design individual slides 397

Evaluate your slides in a practice session 398

TECHNOLOGY   PowerPoint Tip: Use Hyperlinks to Customize Presentations 405

Create effective handouts 405

 How do you deliver and evaluate the presentation? 407

Set the stage 407

CULTURE   Meeting Audience Expectations 408

Control your body 410
Use your voice effectively 410
Present your visuals effectively 411
Coordinate with your team 411

ETHICS   Plagiarism or "Repurposing"? 412

Evaluate the audience's response 413

 How do you handle questions and answers? 413

Plan for a question-and-answer (Q&A) session 414
Answer questions skillfully 415

 How do you adapt your approach for online presentations? 416

In a live online presentation, manage the audience experience 416
In a podcast, provide content that offers lasting value 417

LEARNING OBJECTIVES IN REVIEW 421   •   KEY TERMS 422   •   CASE STUDY 422   •   REVIEW QUESTIONS 426   •
CRITICAL THINKING 426   •   DEVELOPING YOUR COMMUNICATION SKILLS 427

APPENDIX A   Communicating Your Professional Brand: Social Media, Résumés, Cover Letters, and Interviews 431

APPENDIX B   Questions to Ask about Key Communications Technologies 447

APPENDIX C   Formats for Business Documents 453

APPENDIX D   Documentation and Reference Styles 463

GLOSSARY 479

REFERENCES 485

INDEX 493

PREFACE

Mastering the skills needed for proficient and professional business communication has never been more challenging than it is now. Students are confronted with a dizzying array of technologies that can facilitate messaging, but can these technologies help people communicate? To further complicate matters, many postsecondary students find themselves seated in real or virtual classrooms with people who may speak quite varied versions of the common language of instruction: English. On the other side of the real or virtual podium stands the university or college instructor. Across the postsecondary spectrum, instructors are faced with culturally diverse classrooms, reflecting decidedly nonhomogeneous English language skills. Often, fewer resources are at hand to support instructors in helping students become more polished communicators.

How can students and instructors make sense of this complex communications environment? Why should they bother trying?

Some old-fashioned truths about the Canadian workplace remain. Employers continue to rank strong verbal and written communication skills among the most highly desired qualities of their employees (see Chapter 1 for employer data). Being polished and professional in your messaging, be that via Twitter, Skype, or a face-to-face presentation, is critical to every business-related employment situation. Mastering this wide range of skills will go a long way toward ensuring a graduate's current and future employability, regardless of his or her primary area of study.

This text reflects a distinctly Canadian approach to communication studies. After acquiring the simple yet powerful ACE framework in Chapter 2, students are led on a journey through self-discovery and self-awareness of their current communication style in Chapter 3. Chapter 4 builds on this self-knowledge by exploring the impact that culture and diversity have on one's communication preferences. Together, these three chapters give students the foundational tools they need as they venture further into a review of communications technologies in Chapter 5. Once students understand the need to analyze, evaluate, and compose their messages, are cognizant of their preferred communication style and the styles of others, and can choose between the best available technologies to facilitate messaging, Chapter 6 leads them into putting these elements together as team members and leaders. In the contemporary Canadian workplace, all of these skills are vital to an employee's long-term success.

For readers who want concrete examples of how the key elements of each chapter support success in the workplace, look no further than the unique "@ Work" features that bookend each chapter. At the opening of each chapter, students learn about real communication challenges that confront professionals across all walks of life. Seemingly harmless choices can have deep "real-world" ramifications. At the close of each chapter, the problem identified at the opening is solved using the ACE framework as well as the techniques and concepts discussed in the chapter. Real business professionals + real-world problems + real content-based solutions = real learning.

Social media, as well as mobile and other emerging technologies, provides an astounding array of options for both business professionals and postsecondary learners. How can one possibly make sense of channel selection when a new option appears on the horizon almost daily? In this text, a discussion of communications technologies is incorporated into each chapter. In the same manner that ACE provides a simple yet powerful framework for messaging, Chapter 5 teaches students to match their purpose with one of three activities: distributing, networking, or collaborating. Chapter 5, in concert with the more detailed Appendix B: Questions to Ask about Key Communications Technologies, teaches students to ask evaluative questions about technologies that have not even been developed yet, thus allowing students to leverage new technologies for the most applicable communication purpose.

A detailed yet forward-thinking approach to technology, a deep exploration of one's own communication styles and the styles of others, a respectful yet thought-provoking look at cross-cultural communication and diverse workplaces, and a pragmatic toolkit on collaboration are the elements that combine to make *Business Communications: Polishing Your Professional Presence* the most dynamic, current, and engaging Canadian text in its category.

SUPPLEMENTS

At the Instructor Resource Centre, http://catalogue.pearsoned.ca, instructors can easily register to gain access to a variety of instructor resources available with this text in downloadable format. If assistance is needed, our dedicated technical support team is ready to help with the media supplements that accompany this text. Visit http://247pearsoned.custhelp.com for answers to frequently asked questions and toll-free user support phone numbers.

The following supplements are available with this text:

- **Instructor's Resource Manual.** Revised for use with the Canadian Edition by Denise Blay, Fanshawe College, this manual includes a variety of handy resources for instructors.

- **Test Bank.** Revised by Bruce Watson, Southern Alberta Institute of Technology. Students learn better when they are held accountable for what they have learned. That is why we developed a bank of questions in multiple-choice, true/false, and essay format.

- **TestGen® Computerized Test Bank.** This is a powerful assessment generation program that helps instructors easily create and print quizzes and exams. Questions and tests are authored online, allowing ultimate flexibility and the ability to efficiently create and print assessments any time, anywhere.

- **PowerPoint Presentations.** Revised for the Canadian Edition by Liz Clarke, Centennial College, these visual aids display, summarize, and help explain core information presented in each chapter. All of the PowerPoint slides have been updated for consistency and to reflect current content in this new edition.

ACKNOWLEDGMENTS

A WORD OF THANKS

The US authors, Barbara Shwom and Lisa Gueldenzoph Snyder, created the initial text with great wisdom, experience, and skill. I am grateful to have had such amazing material as my starting point.

Lise Dupont and the team at Pearson Canada, including Jennifer Sutton, Emily Dill, Susan Johnson, and Mohinder Singh, have shown fantastic patience, resolve, and determination to get this important book out to students in Canada. I am grateful for their support.

Many thanks to Julia Satov, who graciously shared her wisdom and creativity with me in the development of the Ethics and Culture boxes that appear throughout the book.

Thank you to Julie Hamilton, who jumped in and showed considerable talent and perseverance in the overhaul of Chapters 10 and 11.

A huge thank you to the @ Work professionals who have patiently stuck with this process through many iterations. You are learning heroes in this book!

- Marc Edwards
- Amy Elder
- Mark Federman
- Marzena Gersho
- Kathleen Leslie
- Wendy Kam Marcy
- Farzana Mawani
- Jeff Plotnikoff
- Courtney Rivington
- Adrienne Rosen
- Carolyn Swadron

Thank you to Catherine Town and David Pritchard for being interviewed for this book. Your input has been invaluable.

Enormous gratitude to my friends and family who heard, often more than once, that I was "on a deadline" and had to work on "the book" instead of doing something, ironically, infinitely more communicative. I promise to bring my now rusty interpersonal skills back up to speed as quickly as I can.

SPECIAL THANKS TO REVIEWERS

Several instructors, some of whom didn't want to be mentioned by name below, reviewed the entire Canadian manuscript; others provided feedback on key sections. We are grateful to everyone for their input and advice, which helped to ensure the content is both relevant and realistic.

- Trevor Arkell, Humber College Institute of Technology and Advanced Learning
- Bob Basil, Kwantlen Polytechnic University
- Denise Blay, Fanshawe College
- Kathlyn Bradshaw, Algonquin College of Applied Arts and Technology
- Bonnie Feigenbaum, Concordia University
- Katharine Ferguson, Seneca College of Applied Arts and Technology
- Ange Frymire (Fleming), Kwantlen Polytechnic University
- Marcia Gunter, Seneca College of Applied Arts and Technology
- Wendy Keller, Concordia University
- J. P. Lamarche, Algonquin College of Applied Arts and Technology
- Hugh MacDonald, University of Toronto
- Marian MacDonald, Niagara College of Applied Arts and Technology
- Peter C. Miller, Seneca College of Applied Arts and Technology
- Heather Peace, Algonquin College of Applied Arts and Technology
- Robin Potter, Seneca College of Applied Arts and Technology
- Melanie A. Rubens, Seneca College of Applied Arts and Technology
- Tanya Stewart, Fleming College of Applied Arts and Technology
- Christian Venhuizen, Simon Fraser University

VISUAL WALK-THROUGH

We have created a book that effectively presents core communication competencies in 12 chapters.

Part One: Establishing Context and Basics (Chapters 1 & 2)

Part One addresses the basic communication competencies of business communication and introduces the ACE (Analyzing, Composing, Evaluating) framework.

Part Two: Working with Others (Chapters 3, 4, 5, & 6)

Part Two takes students through the process of understanding their own communication style and preferences to understanding that others also have styles and preferences. In some cases, style and preference can be influenced by culture and by the diversity of the stakeholders participating in communication. Then students explore the various technologies that can facilitate (or impair) communication. The last chapter in this section, Chapter 6, puts all these elements together in a practical review of good collaborative practices in the workplace.

Part Three: Delivering Effective Messages (Chapters 7, 8, & 9)

This section reviews professional approaches to routine and goodwill messages, persuasive messages, and "bad news" messages.

Part Four: Researching, Proposing, Reporting, and Presenting (Chapters 10, 11, & 12)

More formal business documents, the research that can go into preparing them, and the skills needed to present them are reviewed in the final section.

Appendices

- Appendix A: Communicating Your Professional Brand: Social Media, Résumés, Cover Letters, and Interviews
- Appendix B: Questions to Ask about Key Communications Technologies
- Appendix C: Formats for Business Documents
- Appendix D: Documentation and Reference Styles

Get the Best Results from Your Communication

At the heart of the book is a flexible communication process called ACE, which stands for Analyzing, Composing, and Evaluating. ACE applies to any situation, from simple email messages to formal business presentations. As you go through the book, you continue to acquire knowledge about how to apply this framework and why it is important.

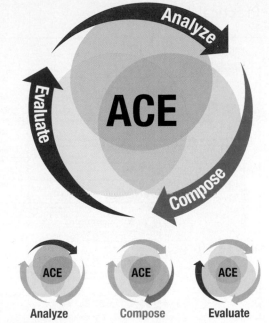

Analyze

Evaluate

ACE

Compose

ACE — Analyze

ACE — Compose

ACE — Evaluate

Wendy Kam Marcy
Cofounder and Lifestyle Blogger,
Hip + Urban Girl's Guide
Director of Marketing,
Adfluent Media

Photo courtesy of Wendy Kam Marcy and Geoff Marcy.

@ WORK

How can we keep it together when we are so far apart?

What started out as a hobby blog in 2010, Hip + Urban Girl's Guide (HUG), quickly grew to become a popular women's lifestyle website. We cover food, style, travel, and local events in Toronto. We also work with various public relations agencies and brands to promote their products and events through our site and social media.

Now in its fifth year, HUG is a successful small business with an international support team. My business partner and cofounder lives in Los Angeles, I live in Toronto, and our guest bloggers are scattered throughout the city. The agencies we work with and clients we represent are primarily in Canada. My accountant is in Edmonton and I have a business advisor/mentor in San Francisco.

Everything happens so fast in the digital world. Assignments often arrive on our desk with extremely tight turnaround times. How do we successfully juggle multiple campaigns, accommodate everyone's schedules (without inconveniencing one another), keep track of deliverables and deadlines, and manage all the different time zones?

Check the end of this chapter to find out how Wendy uses ACE to professionally manage all these important stakeholders, decisions, and action plans!

@ Work Business Profiles

The "@ Work" sections in the Canadian Edition highlight contemporary business professionals who are implementing the core concepts of each chapter. Each chapter opens with a real-life problem scenario, and each chapter closes with a solution that includes the implementation of ACE as well as core chapter concepts.

Wendy Kam Marcy
Cofounder and Lifestyle Blogger,
Hip + Urban Girl's Guide
Director of Marketing,
Adfluent Media

Photo courtesy of Wendy Kam Marcy and Geoff Marcy.

@ WORK

At the beginning of this chapter, Wendy described her complex working relationships with internal and external partners spread across a wide geographic area. How does Wendy use ACE to manage her choices?

Clear, thoughtful, and timely communication is the key to making everything flow seamlessly in the blogging business.

- **Analyze.** When a pitch arrives by email, my business partner and I analyze each request. Typically, we know right away if the campaign is a "fit" for our audience and if it is worth our time to pursue it. We look at immediate profitability, the potential for an ongoing business relationship, and any other opportunities a new campaign might open up.

  With this information we reply to each other via email with our thoughts. Usually we are in agreement, but there are times when one of us needs to persuade and sell the other person on the idea. When this happens, we discuss further by phone or Skype.

  Once we accept the campaign, we determine how we should proceed:
  - Should we continue correspondence by email?
  - Would it be better to schedule a teleconference with the agency/client?
  - Should we meet the agency/client in person?

  We make this decision knowing that some people communicate effectively electronically whereas others prefer face-to-face interaction. From experience, when it comes to the initial client briefing, it is best to do it in person when possible. This is especially true for larger projects. Having the decision makers in one room (or in one real-time video-conference) allows for more fluent communication, proper introductions, and a stronger foundation of trust.

- **Compose.** Our typical order of operation is as follows.
  1. A briefing with the client to discuss objectives
  2. The creation of a marketing strategy and an execution plan
  3. Gaining approval and signoff from the client

  As one can see, the other cofounder and I would find emailing all this information back and forth very tedious and time consuming. We typically find it more productive to communicate in real time over the phone or via Skype, where we can share screens and prepare documents in real time.

  As cofounders, we also have to make decisions on who is going to write the post, which social channels to leverage, and how to prioritize other content. The entire team has to ensure we are all on the same page by constantly engaging with one another. Opportunities for our team to meet in person are rare, so we rely heavily on virtual tools to collaborate and check in with each other. Spontaneous communication needs to occur regularly.

- **Evaluate.** Our team stays organized and well prepared using cloud-based tools like Google Drive. We are able to share and evaluate draft work and make corrections in a single document. This is all accessible anytime, anywhere, with a single login using a Gmail account.

  When the team needs a status meeting to review or evaluate our work, we use Google Hangouts. Regardless of where my team members are located or what device they prefer to use, I can hold videoconferences and even livestream meetings. This tool allows me to keep a history of my Hangouts, so I can always reference past conversations.

The Google suite of products, Skype, FaceTime, and other tools are all very powerful collaborative communications tools that make it possible for long-distance teams such as ours to stay productive. It is pretty remarkable how we have managed to run a successful, creative business with minimal face-to-face interaction!

Practical Advice

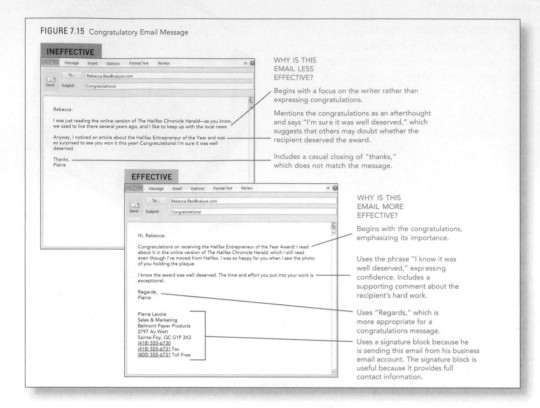

FIGURE 7.15 Congratulatory Email Message

WHY IS THIS EMAIL LESS EFFECTIVE?

Begins with a focus on the writer rather than expressing congratulations.

Mentions the congratulations as an afterthought and says "I'm sure it was well deserved," which suggests that others may doubt whether the recipient deserved the award.

Includes a casual closing of "thanks," which does not match the message.

WHY IS THIS EMAIL MORE EFFECTIVE?

Begins with the congratulations, emphasizing its importance.

Uses the phrase "I know it was well deserved," expressing confidence. Includes a supporting comment about the recipient's hard work.

Uses "Regards," which is more appropriate for a congratulations message.

Uses a signature block because he is sending this email from his business email account. The signature block is useful because it provides full contact information.

Review the Results

Targeted examples are provided throughout the book that highlight core communication skills, such as:

- Analyzing your audience and making choices about the best way to communicate with that audience
- Identifying and understanding interpersonal communication styles
- Navigating situations that require competency in communicating across cultures and with diverse audiences
- Composing a clear message
- Evaluating communication in ways that improve efficacy and readability

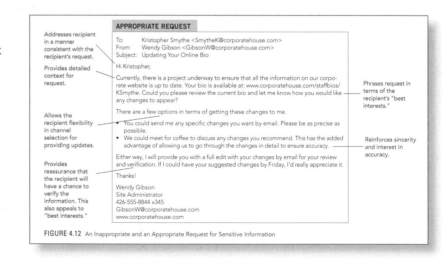

FIGURE 4.12 An Inappropriate and an Appropriate Request for Sensitive Information

Ethics, Technology, and Culture

As you move through the book, you will see the topics of ethics, technology, and culture integrated throughout. In addition, some chapters provide in-depth focus on these topics. To build your skills in ethics, technology, and culture, you will also find end-of-chapter exercises that challenge you to think critically about these topics.

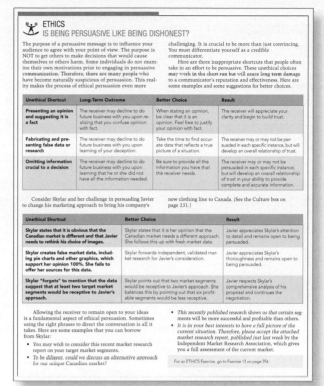

Learning Objectives

The book's main headings are structured as numbered learning objectives. These questions are answered in subheadings throughout the section.

Learning Objectives Summary

The end-of-chapter "Learning Objectives in Review" and "Developing Your Communication Skills" are also grouped by both the learning objectives and the subheadings. This structure helps you focus on the key points of the chapter, assess what you know, and complete exercises that polish your skills.

End of Chapter

Learning Objectives in Review

LO 6.1 How do you communicate effectively as part of a team? *pages 162–169*
- **Create a team charter.** Define goals and deliverables, and identify and agree on process issues and team expectations.
- **Give the team time to develop.** Be patient as the team progresses through the normal stages of development (forming, storming, norming, and performing).
- **Plan for effective meetings.** Create agendas and distribute minutes.
- **Be a valued team member.** Make a commitment to the team, create a collaborative working environment, and support team decisions.

LO 6.2 How can working on a team help you develop leadership skills? *pages 169–175*
- **Identify and practise key leadership fundamentals:** Overcommunicate, reinforce team objectives, and create a supportive climate.

- **Use conflict management to help develop leadership skills.** Identify the types and causes of conflict and select the appropriate management response.

LO 6.3 What are some key aspects of high-performance team collaboration? *pages 175–183*
- **Enhance productivity with virtual best practices.** Start with a face-to-face meeting and be fully prepared and present during online meetings.
- **Develop the "c factor" in your teams.** Make sure your team has social time with each other, and develop a strategy for sharing speaking time equally during meetings.
- **Use a peer coaching model for feedback.** Set up a coaching triangle, where goals are set, criticism is avoided, and feedback is sought.

Review Questions

REVIEW QUESTIONS

1. Why is analyzing your purpose important to composing an effective message? Is the purpose always the same as the desired outcome?

2. Explain the difference between the primary audience and the secondary audience, and provide an example of a message that would have audience benefits for both.

3. What is the difference between primary research and secondary research? Describe a business communication situation in which you would want to research both sources of information to support your message.

4. Why is it important to consider your audience when deciding the medium for delivery?

5. What is the difference between direct and indirect message organization? When would you use each?

6. Explain how reviewing feedback helps you improve your communication strategy.

Case Study

Each chapter concludes with a case study that places you in a realistic scenario and poses questions related to the content of the chapter.

CASE STUDY

Developing Better Interpersonal Communication Skills

This case study will help you review the chapter material by applying it to a specific scenario.

Joe was really looking forward to his first day at work as a senior application developer at BahlTec. He had left his job as an application developer at AxeWorks, a rival company, to accept this new position. At AxeWorks, Joe was part of a development team of 12 people responsible for creating new biometric apps for mobile devices. At BahlTec, he would be in a senior role with a larger, more experienced team working on a variety of apps and projects. He was excited about this opportunity.

Known for quietly producing quality work, Joe worked well with his colleagues at AxeWorks. He was accustomed to doing a lot of communications tasks online, either through the integrated instant messaging system on his computer desktop screen or via email. He met with co-workers once a week to identify problems and brainstorm solutions. The meetings were productive and very "on task" with very little social time. Each meeting had an agenda and someone taking notes that were distributed by email within a few days. Joe and his teammates would sometimes socialize outside of work, often stopping on the way home for a beer or meeting at

BUSINESS COMMUNICATION
POLISHING YOUR PROFESSIONAL PRESENCE

1 Becoming a Successful Business Communicator

Rawpixel/Shutterstock

LEARNING OBJECTIVES

(LO 1.1) Why should you study business communication? *pages 4–7*

Effective business communicators have a competitive edge in the job market

Communication skills will help you, and your employer, succeed

(LO 1.2) Why is business communication challenging? *pages 7–10*

Business communication is a complex process

Barriers often block successful communication

Context adds to the complexity

Multiple audiences have different needs

Social media expands communication opportunities and responsibilities

(LO 1.3) What characteristics do successful business communicators share? *pages 10–21*

Effective communicators are strategic

Effective communicators are professional

Effective communicators are adaptable

Marc Edwards,
B.Sc., MBA, PMP

Project Specialist, Health
Information Management
at Region of Peel, Ontario

@ WORK

"If at first you don't succeed . . ."

Photo courtesy of Mark Edwards and Shane Guadeloupe.

I was involved in a massive technology upgrade program with an objective of updating computers and applications for over 5,000 staff! As you can imagine, such an initiative can breed numerous instances where communication problems can arise.

One such problem occurred during the upgrade for a small group who uses specialized computer systems that are completely different than those used by the rest of the organization. Because of the level of specialization involved, this group's upgrade was continuously delayed until their machines were failing and productivity began to lag. The situation was getting critical.

I communicated the severity of the situation to the business analyst who was working with me on this project. We realized that we needed more detailed information about the computer systems and their use. When I finally met with the client group, they were confused and angry. Apparently, another business analyst had already asked this group similar questions, and those questions were practically the same as ones that had been asked by another analyst months ago! Clearly, something went very wrong with our team's ability to gather and share information.

Check out the info box at the end of this chapter to find out how Marc uses a technique called ACE (Analyze, Compose, Evaluate) to solve problems like this!

Introduction

Do you text, tweet, or use Facebook to keep in touch with friends and family? Do you have conversations with friends and acquaintances at lunch or dinner? Do you email professors with questions, or gesture to friends across the room to wait for you? If so, without even thinking about it, you are engaging in the complex process of **communication**: planning, creating, delivering, and interpreting messages.

The communication skills you have already developed will be valuable to you after you graduate. However, your current skills may not be sufficient to meet many of the challenges of communicating in the workplace. In your career, you will be required to use many different communication skills to succeed. For example, you will need to

- persuade people,
- explain decisions,
- solve problems,

- ensure that everyone shares the same understanding of a problem or plan, and
- maintain productive working relationships.

This book is designed to help you develop a set of best practices you can use to meet these challenges, no matter what career you pursue. It will also help you learn how to adapt to new technologies, new audiences, and the new levels of responsibility you will face as you progress in your career.

Think of this first chapter as a preview of the book. It will help you understand how you will benefit from studying business communication, why being a business communicator is challenging, and what skills you should be able to demonstrate when you complete this course.

Communication The process of planning, creating, delivering, and interpreting messages both verbally (through writing and speaking) and nonverbally (through gestures and symbols).

3

(LO 1.1) Why should you study business communication?

Studying business communication will offer you many benefits. Two primary benefits stand out. First, being a first-rate communicator will give you an immediate competitive edge over most people who do not possess solid communication skills. Second, being an effective communicator contributes to your long-term professional and personal success.

Effective business communicators have a competitive edge in the job market

The Canadian Council of Chief Executives (CCCE) produced a preliminary survey report in January 2014 on the skill needs of major Canadian employers (CCCE, 2014). The skills requirements for entry-level hires are noted in **FIGURE 1.1**.

Similarly, a report issued by the Canadian Association of Career Educators and Employers in 2013 supports these results in even more detail. Over 900 employers were surveyed, representing sectors like finance, insurance, retail, healthcare, professional services, telecommunications, and natural resources. Respondents were asked to rate 20 skills that a newly graduated job candidate should have. As you can see from **FIGURE 1.2**, communication skills feature prominently throughout the entire list (P. Smith & Lam, 2013).

Employers who recruit on campus value "hard-working team players who solve problems through analysis and communication" (P. Smith & Lam, 2013, p. 11). As one chief executive officer (CEO) noted in response to the CCCE survey, "Our entry-level employees are expected to gain experience and technical knowledge on the job and through training. However, core competencies such as initiative, communication skills and resourcefulness must be present during the selection process" (CCCE, 2014, p. 7).

This book will help you acquire the vital people skills, relationship-building skills, and communication skills that employers find critical to their hiring decisions. What are communication skills, exactly? Employers typically identify many communication-related skills as being important, such as the ability to do the following:

- Build productive and collaborative relationships with co-workers and external business partners
- Communicate clearly and efficiently, in writing and verbally, with people within the organization as well as with external audiences
- Obtain, validate, and process detailed business information (e.g., perform research accurately and ethically)
- Create and edit written reports and other business documents

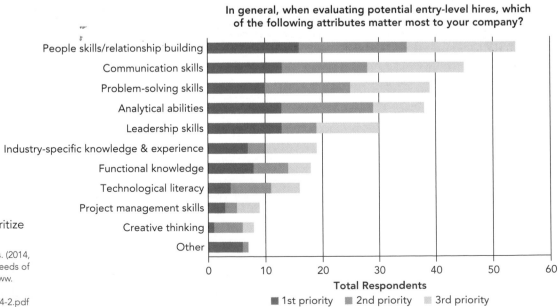

FIGURE 1.1 Canadian CEOs Prioritize Skills for Entry-Level Hires

Source: Canadian Council of Chief Executives. (2014, January). Preliminary survey report: The skill needs of major Canadian employers. Retrieved from www.ceocouncil.ca/wp-content/uploads/2014/01/Preliminary-report-on-skills-survey-Jan-20-2014-2.pdf

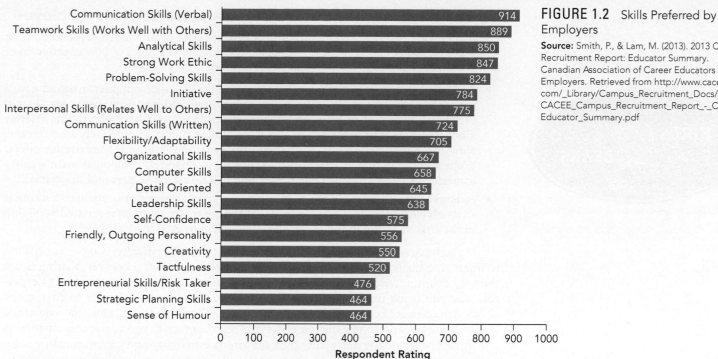

FIGURE 1.2 Skills Preferred by Employers

Source: Smith, P., & Lam, M. (2013). 2013 Campus Recruitment Report: Educator Summary. Canadian Association of Career Educators and Employers. Retrieved from http://www.cacee.com/_Library/Campus_Recruitment_Docs/2013_CACEE_Campus_Recruitment_Report_-_Career_Educator_Summary.pdf

- Use appropriate and ethical visuals to represent data and other key concepts
- Be persuasive and influence others

Ironically, although these communication skills are widely considered important, employers have trouble acquiring and retaining sufficient numbers of employees who possess a high level of competence in these skills. A 2015 survey of employers in British Columbia revealed serious concern with regard to finding employees able to communicate orally, demonstrate functional literacy, and collaborate with others (Conference Board of Canada, 2015). In 2013, a similar report in Ontario found employers having these same difficulties (Stuckey & Munro, 2013). **FIGURE 1.3** shows these results.

Bad news for the workforce may be good news for you. It means you have an opportunity to stand out in the crowd. If you are able to develop and hone the skills you learn in this course, you will be a valuable asset to your employer. This will lead to the second benefit: your professional and personal success.

Communication skills will help you, and your employer, succeed

Strong communication skills are highly valued in the workplace. Thus, developing proficiency in this area can enhance your professional and personal success in a variety of ways.

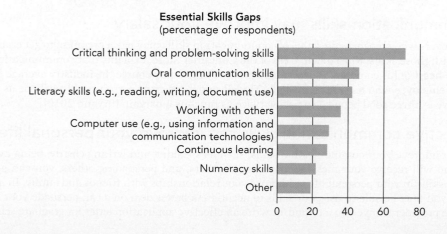

FIGURE 1.3 Skills Gaps Identified by Employers in Ontario (2013)

Source: Stuckey, J., & Munro, D. (2013, June). *The need to make skills work: The cost of Ontario's skills gap.* Conference Board of Canada (Chart 14, p. 27). Retrieved from www.collegesontario.org/Need_to_Make_Skills_Work_Report_June_2013.pdf

Courtesy of David Pritchard, President of Birds and Beans.

Communication skills will make you a more valuable employee

Companies want excellent communicators because effective communication is profitable: It *saves* money and it *makes* money. Consider the following examples of how effective communication contributes to both savings and revenues:

- Birds and Beans, a Canadian wholesale and retail coffee supplier, uses an email newsletter, Facebook, and Twitter to reach new and existing customers. David Pritchard, president of Birds and Beans, states that "until recently, the newsletter alone had a great impact on sales. We'd see a sales 'bump' immediately after release. Now the email newsletter, Facebook, and Twitter combine for maximum effect. What I know is that if I coordinate these three channels religiously with quality content, my sales grow. If I don't, they don't" (D. Pritchard, personal interview).
- Federal Express improved the readability of a ground-operations manual, making it so much easier for employees to read that the company saved an estimated $400,000 in the first year due to increased efficiency (Hackos & Winstead, 1995).

If you have solid writing skills and the ability to think critically, you can contribute to improving the bottom line and, thus, impress your employer. However, writing is not the only communication skill that makes you a more valuable employee. As a salesperson, you can bring in more sales if you know how to listen effectively to customers' needs, demonstrate how a product or service meets those needs, and close the sale at the end of a conversation. As a customer service representative, you can retain customers and attract new ones by answering their questions efficiently and communicating solutions to their problems. As a team member who collaborates well with other team members to solve problems, you may be able to bring a product to market earlier, increasing the opportunity to sell the product.

If you work at a managerial or executive level, you may have the opportunity to influence how your organization communicates with employees, investors, and the general public. That communication can directly impact the organization's success. For example, research by a global consulting firm found that companies that are highly effective at communicating also experience greater employee satisfaction and productivity as well as greater confidence by investors. As a result, these companies financially outperform their peers more often than companies that communicate less effectively (Towers Watson, 2011).

Expertise with **social media** can also benefit your company. Effective communication through social media improves employee satisfaction and builds brand awareness to reach more customers (Harte, 2009). Additionally, if you run your own small business as an entrepreneur, your communication abilities will be especially critical because you will be responsible for most, if not all, of your company's communication (Mitchelmore & Rowley, 2010). David Pritchard of Birds and Beans notes that "the two biggest referrers to our website are Facebook and Twitter, so managing these accounts regularly and with quality information is critical. When you run a small business, you need to be sure that you can either perform this task yourself or hire people whom you can trust to do this professionally. Entrepreneurs and their staff need a wide range of skills, including effective communications and the ability to stay on top of the demands of social media" (D. Pritchard, personal interview).

Communication skills may improve your salary

Employers who recognize the value of communication skills may pay a premium to get employees with those skills. Kip Tindell, CEO of the Container Store, explains that communication is at the heart of his company's success, and he is willing to pay double the industry average for a great employee who has the right skills. Tindell said, "one great person could easily be as productive as three good people," so paying twice as much is a bargain (Bryant, 2010).

Effective communication skills can improve your personal life

If you improve your communication skills, such as speaking and writing clearly, being aware of who will receive your message, listening to others, and persuading others, you can apply these skills in your personal life to improve your relationships with friends and family. In addition, you may be able to use your skills to negotiate a better deal on a car, persuade your cellphone provider to give you a refund, or write an effective application letter for graduate school.

Social media Web-based applications, such as blogs, Facebook, and Twitter, designed to promote social interaction.

These benefits confirm that studying business communication and practising your skills will generate a positive return on your investment of time and energy.

(LO 1.2) Why is business communication challenging?

Why do so many students graduate without sufficient communication skills? Some students do not take business communication courses. Others may take a course but not devote enough time to understanding what communication involves because they think it is an "easy" class. However, even for a dedicated student, communicating well in business is complex.

Business communication is a complex process

In business, communication is typically goal oriented. The goal may be to ask, instruct, inform, persuade, or reach agreement. To achieve that goal, communicators and their audiences send messages back and forth until the sender and receiver achieve a shared meaning.

However, reaching a shared meaning is not as easy as it sounds. As the transactional model of communication in **FIGURE 1.4** illustrates (Barnlund, 1970), the person initiating the communication, the sender, must first determine what he or she wants to say and then **encode** it by putting it into words, images, or action. The sender then has to select a **medium** or **channel** to transmit the message, such as a face-to-face conversation, telephone call, email message, text message, or social networking post. (You will learn more about choosing the best medium or channel for a message in Chapter 2: Managing the Communication Process, and Chapter 5: What Are the Tools and What Are the Rules? Communication Technologies in the Workplace.) Determining the best way to phrase the message and the best medium to use requires that you understand the **audience**, the individual person or people for whom a message is intended, and the **context**, the set of circumstances in which you are communicating. The receivers' prior knowledge, experience, or expectations may affect the way they **decode** the message, which involves interpreting and attaching meaning to the words, images, and actions.

Not all messages are decoded correctly. **Barriers** may stand in the way of effective communication. For example, assume you need a cost estimate for a project and email your co-worker requesting information: "How many hours will it take to write the Putney User Manual?" If your co-worker does not know the purpose of your message, she may decode it incorrectly. If she thinks you want just a general sense of how long the project will take, she might reply with, "It will take about a week if I work on it along

Encode To translate the meaning of the message into words, images, or actions.

Medium or Channel The method you use to deliver your message (e.g., face-to-face meeting, telephone, email, text message, website, or other).

Audience Anyone who receives a message and for whom a message is intended. The audience can be one person or many, depending on the number of recipients.

Context A set of circumstances that influences the purpose of communication, the best medium to use to communicate the message, and how receivers interpret a message.

Decode To interpret the words, images, and actions of a message and attach meaning to them.

Barrier An obstacle that gets in the way of effective communication.

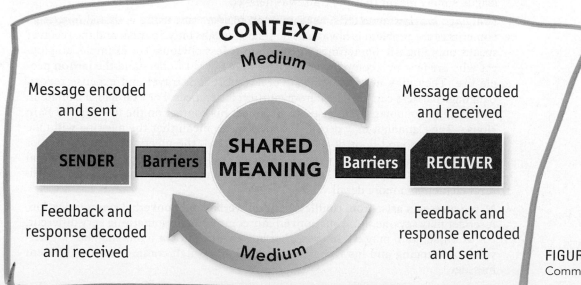

FIGURE 1.4 Transactional Model of Communication

with my other projects." This answer will not help you develop a cost estimate. The ambiguity of your message and your co-worker's lack of understanding are two of the many barriers that can block effective communication.

You may be able to recognize miscommunication by the **feedback** you receive from your audience. Feedback is any form of verbal or nonverbal response to a message. In this case, feedback may simply be a quick email that answers the question: "I estimate the project will take 50 hours." Other forms of feedback include requests for clarification or the addition of new ideas to think about: "Did you want to know how many total hours the project will take for budgeting purposes, or did you want to know when I think we can get it done, so that you can commit to a deadline?"

If the answer adequately addresses the sender's intended meaning, the exchange may be over. However, if the response indicates a difference in understanding, more clarification and additional communication may be required. Communication then becomes an **iterative process**. One message leads to another message, which can lead to another. The sender becomes the receiver, and the receiver becomes the sender, each encoding and decoding messages. By communicating back and forth, the sender and receiver ensure they understand each other, create shared meaning, and experience successful communication.

Barriers often block successful communication

Barriers can occur at any point in the communication process. For example, imagine that you emailed a co-worker to offer information for inclusion in a proposal. However, she does not read the email before the proposal is due and the information is not included. Choosing email as the communications channel was a barrier to communication. If she receives and reads the email, but does not understand the information provided, ineffective wording was the barrier.

Consider how all of the following possible barriers can interfere with the successful communication of even a simple message:

- *Physiological barriers* arise from a receiver's physical state. If you are speaking with someone who has hearing loss or a migraine headache, he may not be able to listen effectively.
- *Psychological barriers* arise from a receiver's attitudes toward the message or toward the sender. If you compliment someone who does not trust you, he may interpret that compliment as a subtle criticism. When you are upset, your emotions act as a barrier to effective communication.
- *Semantic barriers* arise from language that is difficult to understand or open to multiple interpretations. If a colleague rushes late into a meeting and says to you, "I was held up at the train station," you might ask if the robber had a gun, when your colleague simply meant that the train was delayed.
- *Language barriers* arise from senders and receivers not using a shared language. Sometimes the problem is obvious: The sender speaks only Spanish and the receiver speaks only English. Sometimes the problem is less obvious. For example, employees who are new to a company or industry may not yet understand the **jargon** people use. They may not know that a T&E report is a travel and expense report. Language barriers can also arise from cultural differences. For example, a Canadian travelling to London may be instructed to meet his contact on the first floor of Bain House. The Canadian may decode the message to mean that the meeting will take place on the ground floor of a large home. Instead, the meeting will be one floor above the ground floor (what people in Canada call the second floor) in a traditional office building. Chapter 4 will explore English language variants and Canadian cultural elements in more detail.
- *Mixed messages* arise from conflicts between verbal and nonverbal communication. A sender may say one thing but nonverbally communicate something very different. For example, John may tell his boss that he can stay late for a meeting, but his nervous foot tapping and his repeated glances at his watch communicate a different message.

Feedback Any form of verbal or nonverbal response to a message.

Iterative process A process or cycle that repeats, often with additional elements or improvements.

Jargon The specialized language of a specific field.

Context adds to the complexity

Communication is also challenging because it takes place in a specific context. If you are not taking context into consideration, interpreting meaning will become very difficult. Context influences the purpose of communication, the choice of medium to use to communicate, and the nature of the receiver's interpretation of the message.

As an example, assume you work in the software development department of your company and you want to persuade your supervisor to let you work with the marketing team to create a brochure for a new software product. You may not be successful if you merely state, "I'd like to work with the marketing team to create the brochure." Your supervisor may understand that message, but it will not persuade her. To determine how to achieve your goal, you will need to consider a range of contextual variables:

- What are the goals of the project?
  - If the goals are aligned with outcomes you are responsible for, you can use this information to help you persuade your supervisor.
- Who else is working on the project, and what can you contribute?
  - If there is a skills or knowledge gap in the existing team, you can use this information to offer your skills and knowledge to fill this gap. This is a persuasive argument.
- Does your supervisor like interdisciplinary work teams or does she prefer groups to work separately?
  - Knowing your supervisor's working style will help you make an appealing case.
- How does your supervisor prefer to receive messages: in person or by email?
  - Knowing communications preferences will help you choose the right medium to approach your supervisor.

Once you have considered these variables, you have a better chance of creating a message that will be both understood and persuasive.

Multiple audiences have different needs

Although the transactional model of communication in Figure 1.4 provides insight into the communication process, it does not capture all the complexities of communication in a dynamic business environment. The model depicts communication as happening between two people. However, in the workplace, communication typically occurs among multiple people who encode and decode messages differently and who have different contexts, backgrounds, concerns, and agendas.

Imagine working in an auto parts manufacturing company with team members from different departments: engineering, design, marketing, sales, project management, shipping, and accounting. You are all trying to solve the fortunate problem of having more orders for auto parts than you can fill. With eight people in the meeting, there may be eight different personalities, each with a unique communication style and goal. Some people may be willing to communicate freely, whereas others may become silent. All the team members presumably want to do what is in the best interest of the company, but each member may have a different point of view about what that is. Sales managers want to meet the needs of current customers and also gain new customers. They may not be thinking about the quality of the auto parts. Project managers, by contrast, may be more interested in maintaining the quality of the auto parts than rushing to meet the needs of current and new customers.

To solve the problem of meeting high demand while maintaining quality, the team members need to listen carefully to each other, negotiate a solution, document agreements, and inform both the CEO and the workers about the company's solution and new priorities. If the team decides the best solution is to limit new orders, sales managers will need to communicate carefully with disappointed customers to maintain goodwill. If the team decides to rush and create more auto parts to fill orders, managers need to determine how to ensure product quality.

Chapters 3, 4, 5, and 6 will offer more insight into collaboration and productivity within teams.

Social media expands communication opportunities and responsibilities

With the growth of social media and mobile communication devices, business communication is no longer limited to business hours and business locations. Businesses communicate all day every day, with audiences they may never meet in person.

Organizations are increasingly working to dialogue with customers, clients, and partners through blogs and social networking sites. Social media can create a community of people who communicate about brands to increase product awareness. Such conversations offer businesses two important benefits. First, they help companies collect customer feedback and gain customer insight (March, 2012). Second, they lead to sales: People who engage in social media are more likely to purchase from the brands they follow and recommend those brands to others (eMarketer, 2010).

Getting these benefits, however, requires that employees write, talk, and listen differently than they would with traditional media. Companies must post new content frequently to keep "fans" returning to a page. The top 50 brands on Facebook post an average of 38 times per month, while brands such as National Geographic, iTunes, and MTV post more than 100 times per month (Tobin, 2011).

(LO 1.3) What characteristics do successful business communicators share?

As the previous sections show, being an effective communicator is challenging. Fortunately, most people have at least one communication strength that they can build on. You may have solid writing skills or highly tuned listening skills. You might be very persuasive. However, to reach your full communication potential, you will need to develop additional strengths. The best business communicators share the key characteristics illustrated in **FIGURE 1.5**. These characteristics help businesspeople effectively deal with communication challenges. The remainder of this chapter previews these characteristics, which you will continue to develop throughout the course and throughout your career.

Effective communicators are strategic

Communication strategy A plan for what and how you are going to communicate to ensure your message achieves your purpose.

The best communicators always have a **communication strategy**: a plan for what and how to communicate to ensure that their message achieves its purpose. Strategic communicators are always making decisions, asking themselves these questions:

FIGURE 1.5   Characteristics of Effective Business Communicators

- What do you want to accomplish with your message? What is your goal?
- Who is your audience? With whom should you communicate to accomplish your goal?
- What content will your audience need? What content will help you accomplish your goal?
- What medium or channel should you use:
  - a face-to-face meeting?
  - video or teleconference?
  - email?
  - presentation?
  - instant message?
  - webinar?
  - report?
  - blog?
  - text?
  - a combination of multiple channels?
- How should you organize the message to state your main point and effectively support it?

As these questions suggest, to be a strategic communicator you must be purposeful, audience oriented, and often persuasive.

Purposeful

When writing or speaking in classes, you probably have a **purpose** and an intended **outcome**. These elements define what you want the recipients of your message to know, do, or feel about the subject of your message. Your purpose might be to ask a question about the instructor's lecture, further explain a point by contributing an example, or simply impress the instructor with your knowledge. You will achieve the intended outcome if you get the answer, have others understand your explanation, or get a smile from the instructor.

Similarly, business communication is effective when it has a clear purpose and achieves an intended outcome. For example, when you write a cover letter for a job, the letter is effective if you get an interview. Other features of effective communication, such as grammatical correctness, clarity, and conciseness, will also help you achieve your purpose.

Consider the two versions of an email in **FIGURE 1.6** by Zack Kramer, a business major and a member of his university's chapter of Students for a Cleaner Environment. The two emails appear to have similar purposes: to get information from a civil engineering professor for one of the club's projects. As you read the two versions, ask yourself which one is more likely to get Zack what he wants.

Audience oriented

Communication involves more than self-expression. Effective business communicators understand that their messages must reach and influence their audience, the individual person or people for whom a message is intended. Being able to reach an audience requires first that you read and listen with care so that you can understand audience concerns. It then requires that you compose messages that address those concerns and are easy to read.

Reading and listening provide you with insights into what is important to the audience. For example, when a professional communicator gets an email making a request, she replies only after reading it carefully to identify why the writer is making the request and what kind of answer he needs.

Once you understand your audience, creating an audience-oriented message requires answering two questions:

1. **What content will your audience need or want?** Your communication should address the questions on the audience's minds and anticipate the possible objections.

2. **How can you make the message easy for your audience to understand?** You will increase the chances that people will accurately read or listen to the message if you organize it for easy comprehension.

Purpose The reason for communicating.

Outcome The result of your communication. What you want the recipients of your message to know, do, or feel about the subject of your message.

FIGURE 1.6 Two Versions of an Email Message

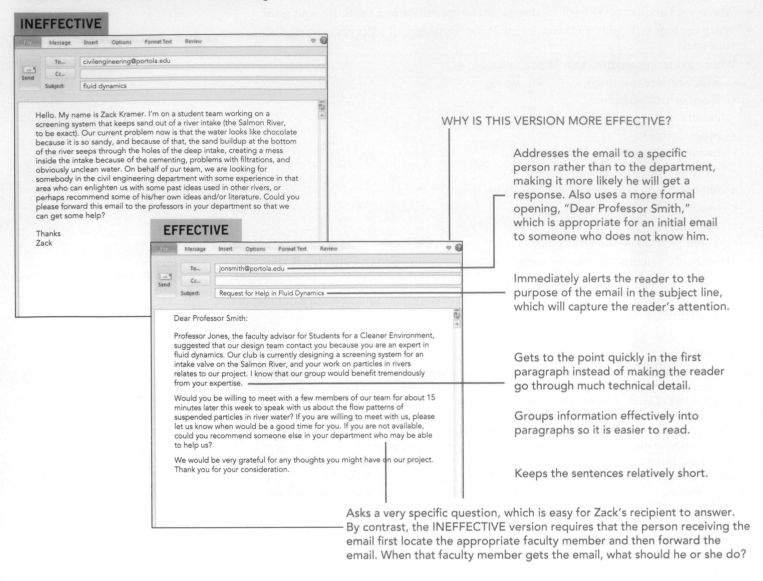

WHY IS THIS VERSION MORE EFFECTIVE?

Addresses the email to a specific person rather than to the department, making it more likely he will get a response. Also uses a more formal opening, "Dear Professor Smith," which is appropriate for an initial email to someone who does not know him.

Immediately alerts the reader to the purpose of the email in the subject line, which will capture the reader's attention.

Gets to the point quickly in the first paragraph instead of making the reader go through much technical detail.

Groups information effectively into paragraphs so it is easier to read.

Keeps the sentences relatively short.

Asks a very specific question, which is easy for Zack's recipient to answer. By contrast, the INEFFECTIVE version requires that the person receiving the email first locate the appropriate faculty member and then forward the email. When that faculty member gets the email, what should he or she do?

FIGURE 1.7 illustrates two versions of a business memo. To evaluate whether these memos are audience oriented, try reading them in two steps. First, glance at each memo for about 10 seconds to see what stands out and to determine which version is easier to read. Then, read each memo more carefully to identify which version more clearly provides reasons and explanations that will be compelling to the audience.

Persuasive

When you want to influence people's thoughts or actions, your message needs to be persuasive. **Persuasion** is the process of influencing your audience to agree with your point of view, recommendation, or request. In your daily life, you often need to communicate persuasively. You may be persuading people to accept a proposal or recommendation, give you a refund, agree with your argument, donate money to a charity, become a customer, or remain a customer . . . the list goes on and on. The more persuasive you are, the more effective your communication will be. (You will learn more about persuasion in Chapter 8: Communicating Persuasive Messages.)

Effective communicators are professional

Professionalism refers to the qualities that make you appear businesslike in the workplace. Professionalism is expressed by your actions, your attire, your wording in an email, your body language during a meeting, your tone of voice on the telephone, and

Persuasion The process of influencing your audience to agree with your point of view, recommendation, or request.

Professionalism The qualities that make you appear businesslike in the workplace.

FIGURE 1.7 Two Versions of a Business Recommendation

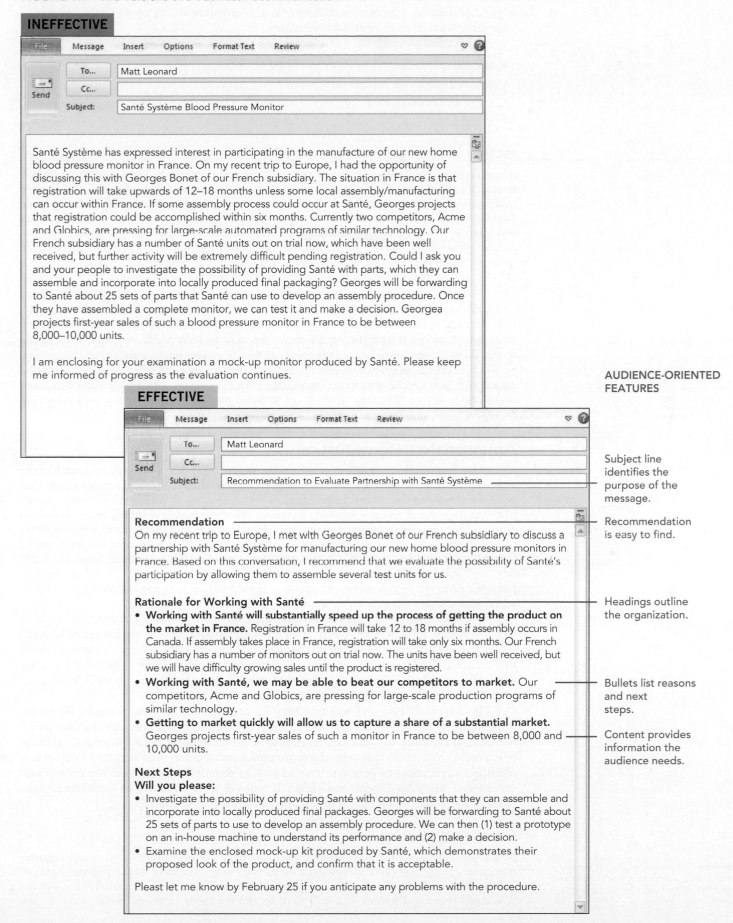

INEFFECTIVE

To... Matt Leonard
Cc...
Subject: Santé Système Blood Pressure Monitor

Santé Système has expressed interest in participating in the manufacture of our new home blood pressure monitor in France. On my recent trip to Europe, I had the opportunity of discussing this with Georges Bonet of our French subsidiary. The situation in France is that registration will take upwards of 12–18 months unless some local assembly/manufacturing can occur within France. If some assembly process could occur at Santé, Georges projects that registration could be accomplished within six months. Currently two competitors, Acme and Globics, are pressing for large-scale automated programs of similar technology. Our French subsidiary has a number of Santé units out on trial now, which have been well received, but further activity will be extremely difficult pending registration. Could I ask you and your people to investigate the possibility of providing Santé with parts, which they can assemble and incorporate into locally produced final packaging? Georges will be forwarding to Santé about 25 sets of parts that Santé can use to develop an assembly procedure. Once they have assembled a complete monitor, we can test it and make a decision. Georgea projects first-year sales of such a blood pressure monitor in France to be between 8,000–10,000 units.

I am enclosing for your examination a mock-up monitor produced by Santé. Please keep me informed of progress as the evaluation continues.

EFFECTIVE

To... Matt Leonard
Cc...
Subject: Recommendation to Evaluate Partnership with Santé Système

Recommendation
On my recent trip to Europe, I met with Georges Bonet of our French subsidiary to discuss a partnership with Santé Système for manufacturing our new home blood pressure monitors in France. Based on this conversation, I recommend that we evaluate the possibility of Santé's participation by allowing them to assemble several test units for us.

Rationale for Working with Santé
- **Working with Santé will substantially speed up the process of getting the product on the market in France.** Registration in France will take 12 to 18 months if assembly occurs in Canada. If assembly takes place in France, registration will take only six months. Our French subsidiary has a number of monitors out on trial now. The units have been well received, but we will have difficulty growing sales until the product is registered.
- **Working with Santé, we may be able to beat our competitors to market.** Our competitors, Acme and Globics, are pressing for large-scale production programs of similar technology.
- **Getting to market quickly will allow us to capture a share of a substantial market.** Georges projects first-year sales of such a monitor in France to be between 8,000 and 10,000 units.

Next Steps
Will you please:
- Investigate the possibility of providing Santé with components that they can assemble and incorporate into locally produced final packages. Georges will be forwarding to Santé about 25 sets of parts to use to develop an assembly procedure. We can then (1) test a prototype on an in-house machine to understand its performance and (2) make a decision.
- Examine the enclosed mock-up kit produced by Santé, which demonstrates their proposed look of the product, and confirm that it is acceptable.

Pleast let me know by February 25 if you anticipate any problems with the procedure.

AUDIENCE-ORIENTED FEATURES

Subject line identifies the purpose of the message.

Recommendation is easy to find.

Headings outline the organization.

Bullets list reasons and next steps.

Content provides information the audience needs.

your attention to correct grammar and proofreading. However, professionalism goes beyond projecting a professional image. It also involves living up to the standards of your profession, including ethical standards.

An effective professional communicator is

- an active listener,
- appropriate to the situation,
- clear and concise, and
- ethical.

Active listening

Being an effective listener is often even more important than being a perceptive reader. Research suggests that people in school and in the workplace spend much more of their communication time listening than they do speaking, reading, or writing. Too often people assume they listen well simply because they hear things every day. However, *hearing is not the same as listening*. **Active listening** is a learned skill that requires you to focus on the speaker, make sense of the information that he or she presents, and, when possible, provide feedback about the information to ensure you understand it correctly.

An active listener works to interpret meaning to understand both what a person is saying and why that person is saying it. An active listener will perceive emotional cues and body language. For example, if a person's voice sounds strained, she may be nervous or concerned about the information she is communicating. If a person is using defensive body language, such as crossing his arms, he may feel skeptical or upset, even if his words do not convey that same meaning. If you develop effective listening skills, your co-workers and customers will communicate with you more frequently and more fully. As a result, you will be able to communicate with them more effectively. (You will learn more about active listening in Chapter 3: Who Am I? Understanding and Adapting Interpersonal Communication Styles.)

Appropriate to the situation

Different situations require different behaviour. For example, if you have lunch with friends, you may not think to stand up when a new person joins you at the table or to introduce that person formally to the others. In addition, you may assume it is okay to tell your friends funny stories about another student. However, during a business lunch, professionalism requires that you observe etiquette and actively participate in conversations without disrespecting others. Etiquette errors become barriers that interfere with how the audience of your message perceives you. (You will learn more about online etiquette in Chapter 5: What Are the Tools and What Are the Rules? Communication Technologies in the Workplace. Detailed guidance on behaviour and etiquette in face-to-face business situations is available within the online support materials provided with this text.)

Professionalism is as important in writing as it is in speaking. For example, assume you just found out you have to cancel your evening plans because your marketing team needs to finish a new client proposal before an 8 a.m. meeting. You may want to email this message to your team: "hey guys, i hope you didn't get too wasted last night, cuz we gotta pull an all-nighter tonite to get that project done by 8 a.m. or we'll be in deep trouble! i'll order pizza. what should I get?"

The informal style and wording may be appropriate for your friends. However, informality in the workplace can be a problem because someone can forward your email to others at the company. The challenge is to be professional in your work email without being overly formal. In this case, the more professional email uses standard English and eliminates references to personal lives as well as negative references to the project and supervisor: "Hi, John, Deepa, and Elaine: It looks as if we will have to work late tonight to meet the 8 a.m. deadline. I'll order a pizza for us. Any requests?"

Clear and concise

In school, you may have developed a wordy writing style to fulfill word-count requirements in assignments like a 500-word essay. You may also have developed the habit of writing complicated sentences to sound sophisticated and well educated. If you have developed these bad habits, you will need to change them to sound professional in the

Active listening A process of focusing attentively on what a speaker says, actively working to understand and interpret the content and then responding to acknowledge understanding.

INEFFECTIVE	EFFECTIVE
Hi, Ahmad. This is Don. The meeting yesterday went on for two hours after you left and there was a lot of discussion about the new pricing system and how it will affect our sales and marketing campaign. No one could really agree about what the impact will be, which isn't surprising since we didn't have your charts to review, and we never agree about anything right away, so we decided to hold another meeting on Friday, which you are welcome to come to but you don't really have to. But what we do need from you are the sales projections for the four regions, which you never got a chance to present yesterday. Can you get those to Mary by Friday morning? Also, if you don't plan to come and there's anything else you want us to discuss, let me know.	Hi, Ahmad. This is Don. I'm sorry we didn't have a chance to discuss your sales projections at the meeting yesterday. We've scheduled a new meeting to discuss them at 2 p.m. on Friday. Could you let me know if you are available to attend? If not, please get the sales projections to Mary by noon on Friday so she can distribute them at the meeting. Thanks.

FIGURE 1.8 Two Voice Mail Messages Illustrating Different Levels of Professionalism

workplace. In business, people value clarity and conciseness. **Clarity** is the quality of being unambiguous and easy to understand. Clear communication has only one possible meaning. In addition, it uses simple words in well-constructed sentences and well-organized paragraphs. **Conciseness** means that a message uses no more words than are necessary to accomplish its purpose. Clarity and conciseness are valued in business because time is a scarce resource. Your audience will understand a clear and concise message faster than a wordy and complicated one.

Consider the two versions of a voice mail message in **FIGURE 1.8**. The ineffective message is long and unorganized. The effective message is short and to the point.

Ethical

As a professional, you are likely to face a number of ethical dilemmas that are difficult to resolve. **Ethics** refers to the principles you use to guide decision making, leading you to do the right thing. However, the right thing is not always immediately obvious, and making the wrong decision may put your career, your colleagues, your customers, or your company at risk.

Ethical choices in communications tend to be related to one of the following:

- Sharing too much information at the wrong time or with the wrong audience
- Witholding information from decision makers or customers
- Offending members of an audience by choice of language or tone
- Providing inaccurate or misleading information

You will know you are struggling with an ethical dilemma if you find yourself contemplating the **headline test**. How would you feel if a communication choice made by you resulted in a negative headline in the business section of a major news site? For example, assume your supervisor asks your team to prepare a persuasive presentation to support her recommendation that your company implement a recycling program for computers and mobile devices. Such programs often mean that electronic devices are upgraded more frequently, at a slightly increased cost to the company. Most of your research supports the move because it will ensure essential computer devices are upgraded regularly while preventing dangerous and toxic computer waste from entering local landfill sites. You are convinced that the slightly increased costs will be offset by increased productivity because all employees will have updated devices that will run faster with more current software. However, you do not have time to do more research because your supervisor is presenting the information tomorrow. Here is your ethical dilemma: Should you mention the potential risk of increased costs? Or should you ignore this potential risk and present the strongest case you can to support the recycling program? After all, your supervisor has asked you to put together a strong argument

Clarity The quality of being unambiguous and easy to understand. Clear communication uses relatively simple words in well-constructed sentences and well-organized paragraphs.

Conciseness Using no more words than necessary for a message to accomplish its purpose.

Ethics The principles used to guide decision making and lead a person to do the right thing.

Headline test A quick method of assessing the ethical impact of a communication choice by visualizing the action and its outcome as part of a publicly accessible news story featuring the individual who made the choice and the organization he or she is employed by.

Canadian and Global Business

Canada's Business News Source   Thursday, May 5, 2016

Unexpected Losses in Q3 for ABC Co.

Management Assistant Failed to Define Risk of "Green" Program

In a strong attempt to "do the right thing," ABC Co. unwittingly fell victim to inexperience.

Sheila Sykes, a newly hired management assistant, has been identified as the researcher who failed to share important details to the financial downside to ABC's newly launched "Evergreen" computer recycling program.

Substantial Upside Remains...
Productivity identified as key gain

ABC could have mitigated their losses if they had known to
- train employees in a timely manner an upgraded hardware
- train employees in a timely manner on speed improvements of upgraded software
- captured newly-available process improvements with revised process mapping

Colleagues Ask For More Details
Make Cost/Benefit Explicit, Board Advises

1. Provide downside early.
2. Evaluate risks.
3. Leverage productivity gains.

madhouse/Fotolia

FIGURE 1.9   Sample Headline Test

because management currently appears to be motivated to become more environmentally responsible.

Picture the headline in **FIGURE 1.9** with your name in the article that follows. This scenario highlights two kinds of ethical challenges:

1. **Your responsibility to tell the truth.** If your presentation gives the impression that moving forward with the recycling program will not result in increased costs, you would not be living up to that responsibility.

2. **Your responsibility to your supervisor and your organization.** If your supervisor wants a change that you believe may pose some risks, you face a difficult dilemma. In general, it is better to present the entire truth, both the measurable benefits and the possible downsides, of a situation. This allows decision makers to have all the information they need to arrive at a balanced decision.

Effective communicators are adaptable

The business world evolves continually. This requires you to adapt both as an employee and a communicator. Think of all the changes that occur during a typical business career. For example, a person who began to work for IBM in the mid-1980s joined a company whose key business was building and selling stand-alone mainframe computers for large corporate clients. IBM basically had one product to make and one product to sell to one kind of customer. Communication with those clients and with colleagues took place by phone calls, letters, memos, and face-to-face meetings.

However, in a few short years the world changed dramatically. IBM employees saw the company's one product being overshadowed by the personal computer and

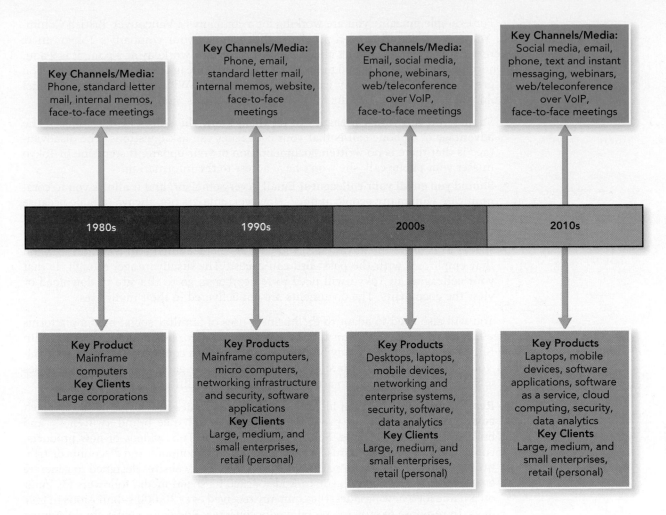

FIGURE 1.10 IBM as an Example of Adaptation in Business and Communication

networks. The Internet was rapidly growing as both a means of communication and a business platform. Clients began looking for software solutions, not hardware products. So IBM changed its focus from being a product provider to a service provider. **FIGURE 1.10** provides a timeline view of some of the shifts this major corporation has had to face.

These kinds of huge transformations continue today. Before 2003, Facebook and social networking did not exist. It is impossible to predict how business will change in the future and how communication will change as a result. Only one thing is certain: More change will come, and as a business communicator you must learn to adapt. Three specific areas of adaptation to focus on are

- new technologies,
- new cultures, and
- new ways of working with others.

Keep current with technology and social media

Technology changes so quickly that the hardware and software applications you use now will likely be outdated by the time you reach the workplace. New options and new challenges will arise. To take best advantage of technology, communicators continually need to address three questions:

- What is the best technology for the task?
- How can I use technology to enable more effective communication?
- How can I avoid unexpected problems that a new communication technology might create?

For example, imagine you are working for a company in Vancouver, British Columbia. You are collaborating on a project with a team in your company's Tokyo office, where the time zone is 16 hours ahead. At the end of your workday at 5 p.m., it is 9 a.m. the next day in Tokyo. You need to update your Tokyo colleagues about your progress on the project for the day so they can continue the work. What technology or channel should you use to do this? As the following analysis shows, no technology is perfect:

- **Should you call your colleagues to let them know the status of the project?** The advantage of a phone call is that your colleagues can ask questions. The disadvantage is that there is no written documentation of your update. If someone in Tokyo misses your phone call, she won't have access to the information.

- **Should you email your colleagues?** Email is very efficient, and it allows you to communicate with many people at once. However, email is not always reliable because there may be network delays or someone's spam filter may block your message.

- **Should you upload your documents to the company intranet or shared "cloud" space?** This offers the advantage of having all the documents in a central location that employees with the password can access. The disadvantage, though, is that your colleagues in Tokyo will need to remember to go to the site to download or view the documents. The documents are not delivered to their mailboxes.

You will also need to adapt to the business uses of familiar social media platforms as well as social media platforms that are used primarily for business, such as LinkedIn and SlideShare. You may already be using social media to connect with friends, broadcast your current activities, share pictures, and even play games. However, businesses use social media strategically to accomplish a number of different goals:

- **Reach customers.** Think of all the ways that companies use social media to reach customers, promote their products and services, enhance brand awareness, and build a community of fans. Some examples are YouTube videos of new products, community discussion boards on corporate websites, coupons and discounts distributed through Facebook fan pages, and promotions on websites designed to generate customer interest. When Eastman Kodak asked its social media followers for input on a name for a new product, the company received over 20,000 submissions in four days. In response to growing social media coverage, Kodak created a chief listening officer position to serve as an "air traffic controller" of the company's incoming and outgoing social media communications (Selling Power TV, 2010).

- **Provide customer and employee support and education.** Many companies use YouTube to provide product training to customers and employees. Potential customers also have access to the videos and comments from current customers. This education and validation build consumer confidence and can have a positive impact on sales and customer loyalty.

- **Find new employees through** *social recruiting.* Social media outlets such as LinkedIn and Facebook are excellent places to publicize jobs and search for new employees (CareerBuilder.com, 2012; McDonnell, 2010).

- **Strengthen employee satisfaction.** The ecommerce company Shopify developed a social collaboration site it calls Unicorn where employees post their ideas and accomplishments (see **FIGURE 1.11**). When employees read something on Unicorn that they think is a particularly worthwhile idea, they can vote to reward the innovator using a pool of funds that the company has set aside for this purpose. Shopify has found that this use of social media increases employee communication, creativity, collaboration, and satisfaction (Graham, 2011).

By being adaptable to changes in technology, businesses are creating communication opportunities and strengthening their connections with employees, customers, and the general public.

Able to work with many cultures

In 1971, Canada was the first country in the world to adopt multiculturalism as an official policy. . . . Canadian multiculturalism is fundamental to our belief

FIGURE 1.11 Social Media Used for Internal Communication

Source: Screenshot from Shopify.com "A Peek at Unicorn: Our Internal Software Used to Improve Employee Communication, Collaboration and Compensation" by Mark Hayes, August 2, 2011.

that all citizens are equal. Multiculturalism ensures that all citizens can keep their identities, can take pride in their ancestry and have a sense of belonging. . . . The Canadian experience has shown that multiculturalism encourages racial and ethnic harmony and cross-cultural understanding. . . . Canada's laws and policies recognize Canada's diversity by race, cultural heritage, ethnicity, religion, ancestry and place of origin and guarantee to all men and women complete freedom of conscience, of thought, belief, opinion expression, association and peaceful assembly.

. . . With no pressure to assimilate and give up their culture, immigrants freely choose their new citizenship because they want to be Canadians. As Canadians, they share the basic values of democracy with all other Canadians who came before them. At the same time, Canadians are free to choose for themselves, without penalty, whether they want to identify with their specific group or not. Their individual rights are fully protected and they need not fear group pressures.

Our diversity is a national asset. (Citizenship and Immigration Canada, 2012)

As Canadian workplaces become more diverse and companies become more global, the chances increase that you will communicate with people from many countries and backgrounds, including people who are not native English speakers. Even people who are very adept at English may come from **cultures** that approach business and communication differently than you do. People demonstrate their culture through values, ideas, attitudes, and their approach to communication. By increasing your awareness of cultural differences and keeping an open dialogue with your colleagues, you can adapt your behaviour as needed.

Adapting your communications style does not apply only to international communication. People who differ in age, gender, sexual orientation, gender identity, and other types of diversity may also experience issues with communication. Even within the same country, younger people are likely to be less hierarchical and formal than their older counterparts. People who do not identify as heterosexual wish to be referred to with respect, as do people who may have experienced a gender transition in their lives. The modern workplace has within it many ways in which a person could, through inexperience, say the wrong thing, or even say the right thing the wrong way. Finding out how to manage a variety of these situations with grace and sensitivity will serve you well as you move through your business career.

Culture The learned and shared attitudes and behaviours that characterize a group of people. People demonstrate their culture through values, ideas, and attitudes.

Customer Service at Beaver Tails, Ottawa, Ontario

Collaboration The process of working together to achieve a common goal.

Collaborative

In business, although you will routinely have to communicate as an individual, many of your projects will be team based because they are too big to be completed by just one person. As a result, **collaboration** is a crucial feature of the workplace.

Being collaborative requires that you adapt to the working style of many different people. In addition, it requires that you coordinate, compromise, negotiate, and manage conflict. Consider the following scenario. You work for an airline and have been assigned to a cross-disciplinary team that is researching various ways to decrease costs. Your team has 30 days to complete its research and present its findings and recommendations to management. Think about all the decisions you need to make to coordinate your work:

- How to identify talents of team members and divide the research
- How and when to share information with each other
- What criteria to use to evaluate the options
- Which options to present to management
- How to organize your presentation
- How to divide the task of writing the presentation
- How to organize and deliver your recommendations to management

In the process of working together and making these decisions, you and your teammates are likely to experience disagreements and conflicts. Perhaps one teammate firmly believes, based on his research, that the best option for decreasing costs is to eliminate the lowest-volume routes that the airline flies, while another teammate argues that this option has hidden public relations costs.

As this scenario suggests, effective communicators need to know more than just how to research, write, and present. They also need to know how to coordinate work, manage conflicts, and negotiate agreements.

In summary, being a successful communicator at work is not as simple as you may first believe. An effective communicator needs to be strategic, professional, and adaptable. Also, a professional communicator is a perceptive and active listener. Practice is the key to gaining these competencies and developing a competitive edge at work and in other facets of your life.

**Marc Edwards,
B.Sc., MBA, PMP**

Project Specialist, Health
Information Management
at Region of Peel, Ontario

@ WORK

Photo courtesy of Mark Edwards and Shane Guadeloupe.

At the beginning of this chapter, Marc needed to find a solution to his team's challenges related to gathering and sharing information. Can ACE (analyze, compose, evaluate) help?

First, I **analyzed** the situation:

- I needed to identify *all* of the stakeholders of this project. Upon a careful analysis, I realized that the requirements had already been retrieved by an analyst in another part of the project. I made a note to create a stakeholder map for all future projects like this.
- Based on my improved understanding of our stakeholders, I reviewed and updated the project communication plan.

- I considered carefully which channel was acceptable to relay this message to the recipients. Given their frustration with the never-ending meetings that failed to produce results, I chose email. This would give them a record of my response and the action plan going forward.

Then, I **composed** a message to the group of computer users who had experienced the delayed upgrade:

- I made sure that the message crafted was sympathetic to the receivers' distress.
- In the message, I admitted my mistake and accepted responsibility for the miscommunication.
- I ensured that an action plan meeting their most immediate needs was clearly stated.

Finally, I **evaluated** the message before sending it:

- I reviewed it myself multiple times for tone, typos, and clarity.
- I asked two colleagues and my direct manager to review the message and provide feedback.
- I made sure that there was a feedback mechanism for the recipients to offer a response and to gauge the success of the message.

As a result, the upgrade team was able to restore a functional and respectful working relationship with this previously disgruntled group of computer users. More importantly, upgrades quickly took place and productivity soon resumed its normal levels. I learned more about stakeholder management and the value of a solid communication strategy for complex projects like this one.

End of Chapter

Learning Objectives in Review

(LO 1.1) **Why should you study business communication?** *(pages 4–7)*

- **Effective business communicators have a competitive edge in the job market.** Communication, the process of planning, producing, delivering, and interpreting messages, is regarded as one of the most important business abilities. Yet employers find too few people communicate well.
- **Communication skills will help you, and your employer, succeed.** Communication will not only help you find a job, but will also make you a more valuable employee and perhaps even increase your salary. Improved communication skills can help you in your personal life as well.

(LO 1.2) **Why is business communication challenging?** *(pages 7–10)*

- **Business communication is a complex process.** As the transactional model of communication demonstrates, communication involves many steps: encoding a message, selecting an appropriate medium, decoding the message, and providing effective feedback.
- **Barriers often block successful communication.** Successful communication requires overcoming physiological, psychological, semantic, and linguistic barriers.
- **Context adds to the complexity.** Prior knowledge and experience also affect someone's ability to understand your communication.
- **Multiple audiences have different needs.** Often you will communicate with more than one person, requiring you to think about each individual's context, background, concerns, and agenda.
- **Social media expands communication opportunities and responsibilities.** As companies find new uses for social media, they increasingly look to employees to provide content.

(LO 1.3) **What characteristics do successful business communicators share?** *(pages 10–21)*

- **Effective communicators are strategic.** Effective communicators are purposeful and design their communications to achieve a specific outcome. They are also audience oriented, considering what content the audience requires and also what organization, format, and language will make the content easy to understand. Finally, when their purpose requires it, they know how to be persuasive and influence the audience's thoughts and actions. Three useful techniques for persuasion are identifying benefits, providing reasons and evidence to support the main ideas, and anticipating audience objections.
- **Effective communicators are professional.** Professionalism refers to the qualities that make you appear businesslike. Business communicators appear professional when they listen actively and carefully, act in a manner appropriate to the situation, are clear and concise, and live up to the ethical standards of their profession.
- **Effective communicators are adaptable.** Being adaptable means being willing and able to change to meet new business needs. In business, communicators must adapt to remain current with technology, including social media, which changes very quickly. In addition, because business is increasingly global and values diversity, communicators must adapt to working with other cultures. Finally, since many business projects require teamwork and coordination with others, communicators must adapt their work styles to collaborate well with others.

KEY TERMS

active listening p. 14	communication p. 3	encode p. 7	medium p. 7
audience p. 7	communication strategy p. 10	ethics p. 15	outcome p. 11
barrier p. 7	conciseness p. 15	feedback p. 8	persuasion p. 12
channel p. 7	context p. 7	headline test p. 15	professionalism p. 12
clarity p. 15	culture p. 19	iterative process p. 8	purpose p. 11
collaboration p. 20	decode p. 7	jargon p. 8	social media p. 6

REVIEW QUESTIONS

1. What communication skills do businesses value?

2. In what ways can communication skills save money or make money for a business?

3. What are the elements of the transactional model of communication?

4. Name three types of feedback you might receive as part of the communication process.

5. Name three barriers to communication.

6. Define active listening. How does it differ from passive listening?

7. When you proofread your business writing, what should you check to ensure that it looks and sounds professional?

8. How does business use of social media differ from personal use?

9. Why are collaborative skills necessary in the workplace?

CRITICAL THINKING

1. The chapter recommends that communicators address potential audience objections. Describe a communication scenario, either from your personal experience or a business example, where you would expect the audience to have objections. What would the objections be, and how would you address them?

2. Imagine that you are trying to persuade a teammate to agree with an idea for a presentation and the teammate accuses you of being manipulative by trying to influence someone for your personal benefit. What is the difference between being persuasive and being manipulative?

3. Assume that your supervisor asked you to lie to a customer in an email about why a shipment is delayed. Would it be unethical for you to write the email if you believe it is wrong to lie? Conversely, would it be unethical for you to refuse to write the email if you believe you have a responsibility to your employer? How would you resolve this issue?

4. Imagine you have been asked to collaborate on a project with a colleague whose work style is very different from yours. For example, you like to plan carefully and follow a schedule, whereas your colleague is spontaneous. You like to write thorough drafts that require only minimal revision, whereas your colleague likes to write incomplete drafts and revise heavily later. Based on these differences, you think it would be more efficient and cost effective for the company to have you work on this project by yourself. Should you make that argument to your supervisor? What might be the benefits of collaborating? What are the drawbacks or collaborating?

5. Cross-cultural communication requires you to use clear language. What are some of the other challenges of communicating across cultures?

6. Students who are not used to writing professional emails sometimes make the mistake of composing them as if they were text messages. What are some key elements of text messages that you should avoid in professional emails?

7. Businesses use different social media tools for different purposes. Based on your knowledge of Facebook, LinkedIn, and YouTube, what are some of the ways businesses can use each tool?

8. Readers often judge a person's professionalism based on whether a document is spellchecked and free of grammatical errors. Do you believe this is a fair basis for making a judgment?

DEVELOPING YOUR COMMUNICATION SKILLS

(LO 1.1) Why should you study business communication?
(pages 4–7)

EXERCISE 1 Communication skills will contribute to your company's and your own success

Use an online job bank like Workopolis to search for job advertisements related to your career goals. How many of them include communication skills in their descriptions or requirements? Summarize your findings in a paragraph that outlines your career goals, two or three jobs you found, and the communication skills they require.

(LO 1.2) Why is business communication challenging?
(pages 7–10)

EXERCISE 2 Business communication is a complex process

Think of a time when someone "decoded" your message incorrectly and misinterpreted your meaning. Was there a barrier involved? If yes, what kind of barrier? Write a few paragraphs explaining the situation and the result. Use the transactional model of communication to explain the situation in detail.

EXERCISE 3 Social media expands communication opportunities and responsibilities

Choose a company that interests you. Search for it on Facebook, LinkedIn, YouTube, and Twitter. Based on what you find, write a message to your instructor explaining how the company uses each social media tool, whether you believe the company uses each tool effectively, and why or why not.

(LO 1.3) What characteristics do successful business communicators share? *(pages 10–21)*

EXERCISE 4 Effective communicators are strategic and persuasive

You are the manager of a large supermarket that borders a residential neighbourhood. A customer who lives nearby comes into the store and says, "I am completely out of patience with the trucks that make deliveries to your store. Deliveries start at 7 a.m. and end at 9 p.m. Early in the morning and into the evening, trucks are banging their trailers into the loading docks. And the engines! The drivers keep the trucks running while they're making deliveries. I can't talk with friends in my yard because of all the noise of the trucks. And it's not just the noise. The trucks also block the alley so I sometimes can't get out of my garage to get to work in the morning."

To respond, you could just choose to explain the situation. Clear reasons exist for each of the behaviours the neighbour is complaining about:

- Local laws have set truck delivery hours from 7 a.m. to 9 p.m. To accommodate all the deliveries, management needs to spread them throughout the day.

- The engines are on in refrigerator trucks because they run the generators that keep food from spoiling.

- The trucks block the alley for only a short time while they are waiting for other trucks to leave. Drivers politely move if they are asked.

However, suppose your main goal is to retain this "neighbour" as a customer and increase goodwill. In that case, you may choose to respond in a way that is more persuasive. Brainstorm content to include in your response. As you brainstorm, consider these persuasive techniques:

- Show that you understand your audience's concern.
- Address the objections.
- Show the benefits to the audience.

As part of your brainstorming, think of possible solutions to the problem. If you mention possible solutions, your response may be even more persuasive.

EXERCISE 5 Effective communicators are professional, clear, and concise

Select a business or professionally prepared message you received, such as a letter or an email from a company or institution. Identify specific content that can be revised to be clearer and more concise. Offer specific revisions based on the content presented in the chapter. Prepare to present your suggestions in class.

EXERCISE 6 Effective communicators are professional and ethical

Your supervisor is preparing a speech for the company's CEO to distribute to shareholders. She asks you to read the speech and provide feedback on how effective you think it will be. As you read the speech, you think you recognize some of the wording from a speech by a financial analyst you heard a few weeks ago on the news. You begin to believe that parts of your supervisor's speech are plagiarized. You wonder if you should tell her that you recognize some of that speech from another source, but you decide not to for two reasons: First, if you tell your supervisor the speech sounds familiar, she may get angry or insulted. Second, the speech was televised very late at night, so you believe it is unlikely that many people watched it. Evaluate the pros and cons of that choice. Is your choice ethical?

EXERCISE 7 Effective communicators are adaptable and stay current with technology and social media

You are planning to hold a conference call with three other people, and you are looking for a technology that balances expense and convenience. Three kinds of conference call services are available to you:

- **Option 1:** Everyone calls in to a toll-free number. Your credit card will be charged 4 cents per minute for each person on the

call. If people need to join the call late, they can do so without inconveniencing the rest of the participants.

- **Option 2:** Everyone calls in to a long-distance number. Each person pays whatever he or she would normally pay for a long-distance call. For two people, it will be free because their telephone service offers free long-distance calls. The remaining two people will each pay 7 cents per minute. They will need to be reimbursed. This option offers the same call-in convenience as Option 1.

- **Option 3:** You initiate a web-based conference call using Skype. This call will be free for everyone. However, all participants need to be available at the moment you call them. Otherwise, you will need to repeatedly redial their numbers until they are available. If, for some reason, any calls are dropped, participants will have no easy way to rejoin the conference call.

The technology choice must balance costs versus convenience. Which option would you choose and why?

EXERCISE 8 Effective communicators are adaptable and collaborative

You are working with a team of five colleagues to research and write a report recommending a new sales strategy for your client. Because you are a proficient writer, you are designated the lead writer on the project. Everyone else is preparing drafts except for one colleague, Emma Yamaguchi. Emma has recently transferred to Canada from the Tokyo office, and her English writing is weak. Your team thinks Emma is contributing quite a lot to the project with her statistical analysis, which is strong. Everyone is happy with the distribution of labour except Emma. She transferred to Canada to improve her written English, and now she finds she is not being given the opportunity. Fortunately, she confides in you and tells you that she would like to help with writing the report. How can Emma contribute in ways that will help improve her English writing but will not compromise the quality of the final product? Think of two or three ideas that you can suggest to the team and to Emma.

EXERCISE 9 Effective communicators are adaptable and able to work with other cultures

Reread Exercise 8. Assume that you suggested to Emma that she write one short section of the report, which another teammate can then edit. Emma writes her part, and you volunteer to edit that section. Emma gasps when she sees all your edits. She looks down and tells you she is ashamed to have submitted such poor-quality work.

You are shocked by her response because you thought you were helping her learn to write better English. As you read more about Japanese culture, you think that your response has made Emma feel embarrassed. How could you handle the situation differently in the future? What approach can you take that will make Emma feel comfortable rather than ashamed?

EXERCISE 10 Increasing cultural and diversity sensitivity

Divide into teams of three to five students. Select at least three cultures or identity groups not represented by anyone on your team. When you identify these groups, do not limit yourself to thinking about different countries of origin. Also consider the following:

- Region of the country (e.g., the Maritimes, Prairies, or Quebec in Canada)
- Ethnicity
- Age (e.g., people in their teens, 20s, 30s, 40s, and so on)

- Gender
- Sexual orientation
- Gender identity
- Disability

For each of the cultures or identity groups you have identified, list two or three "communication characteristics" or things to keep in mind when communicating with people of that culture or identity group. Illustrate each with a concrete example.

Prepare a class presentation of your findings. If the findings of different teams conflict, have a class discussion about why the teams drew different conclusions about a particular culture or identity group.

2 Managing the Communication Process: Analyzing, Composing, Evaluating

grafvision/Shutterstock

MyBCommLab® **Improve Your Grade!**

Over 10 million students improved their results using the Pearson MyLabs. Visit **mybcommlab.com** for simulations, tutorials, media share assignments, interactive lesson presentations, and other helpful learning apps.

LEARNING OBJECTIVES

(LO 2.1) Why should you spend time analyzing?
pages 28–34

Analyzing the purpose focuses the message
Analyzing the audience helps you meet their needs
Analyzing the content ensures a complete message
Analyzing the medium helps you choose the best
delivery option

(LO 2.2) What is involved in composing? *pages 34–46*

Practising strategic time management
Organizing the message
Drafting the content
Designing a professional format and delivery

(LO 2.3) How does evaluating improve your communication? *pages 46–56*

Revise content: Improve effectiveness
Edit for style and tone: Project a professional image
Proofread to increase your credibility
Review feedback to improve your communication
strategy

Farzana Mawani
Marketing and Communications Manager
Altima Healthcare Canada Inc.

@ WORK

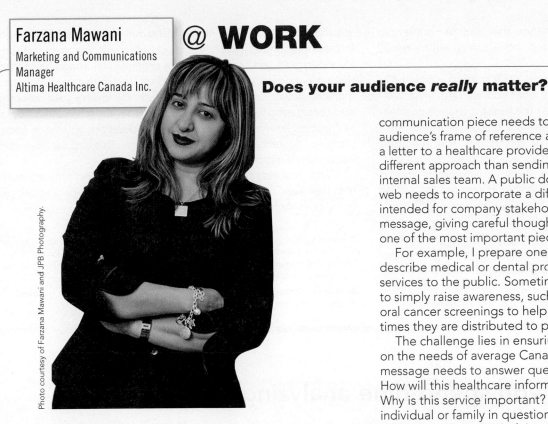

Photo courtesy of Farzana Mawani and JPB Photography.

Does your audience *really* matter?

One of the most important aspects of communicating, particularly in healthcare, is knowing your audience. Each communication piece needs to be customized to anticipate the audience's frame of reference and unique perspective. Sending a letter to a healthcare provider (e.g., a dentist) requires a different approach than sending an email reminder to your internal sales team. A public document that is published on the web needs to incorporate a different tone than a document intended for company stakeholders. Every time you send a message, giving careful thought to the intended audience is one of the most important pieces of the puzzle.

For example, I prepare one-page "info sheets" that describe medical or dental procedures to market those services to the public. Sometimes these one-pagers are used to simply raise awareness, such as to increase the uptake of oral cancer screenings to help decrease mortality rates. Other times they are distributed to promote limited-time offers.

The challenge lies in ensuring that these one-pagers focus on the needs of average Canadians. The composition of the message needs to answer questions from their perspective. How will this healthcare information have a positive impact? Why is this service important? How can this benefit the individual or family in question?

Find out at the end of this chapter how Farzana uses ACE to solve these communication dilemmas.

Introduction

Communicating in today's workplace is complex. You could face communication tasks that range from preparing simple emails to planning critical presentations to participating in online meetings involving people from around the globe. To help you adapt and thrive in these situations, you will learn a flexible communication process called ACE: Analyzing, Composing, and Evaluating. You can apply ACE in any situation, no matter how simple or complex. As **FIGURE 2.1** shows, each ACE step plays a unique role in successfully communicating a message.

Analyzing helps you make effective and professional decisions about each message you prepare and send. Before creating your message, you prepare by analyzing the following four important steps.

1. Determine your **purpose**. What is the reason for your communication? What is the outcome you want to achieve?

2. Analyze your **audience**. Who are the recipients of your communication? What are their concerns and interests?

3. Assess the **content**. What should be included? What is the substance of this message? Do you have all the content your audience needs? Have you included too much?

4. Choose the best **medium**. How will you deliver your message? What are your options? Should you communicate face to face, by phone, email, text message, Facebook, Twitter, or some other medium?

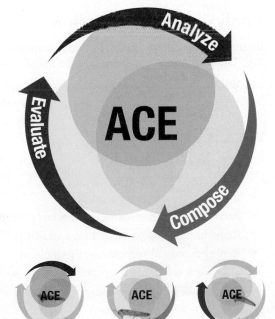

FIGURE 2.1 The ACE Communication Process

Analyzing The process of looking critically at four elements of your message: purpose, audience, content, and medium.

Purpose The reason for communicating.

Audience Anyone who receives a message and for whom a message is intended. The audience can be one person or many, depending on the number of recipients.

Content The substance of your message.

Medium The method you use to deliver your message (e.g., telephone, face-to-face meeting, email, text message, website, or other).

When you take the time to analyze the purpose, audience, content, and medium, your next step, composing, will be much easier.

Composing involves much more than putting words on a page or speaking them aloud. Use what you learned while analyzing to plan your message so it has the highest chance of effectively achieving your purpose. Determine the content you need and pay special attention to how you organize it. Your message must flow logically and make sense from your audience's perspective. Once you have this plan in place, you are better able to draft your message skillfully. If it is a written message, you will be able to format it appropriately so that your audience will easily understand it.

Evaluating is the process of reviewing your message with care and attention to detail. First, determine whether you have included all the content necessary to achieve your goal. If you have all the content you need, ask yourself if you have organized it well. Next, evaluate whether the word usage and style are professional and

appropriate to the task. Finally, consider whether the document format or planned delivery approach will make the message easy to understand and communicate a professional image. As part of the evaluating process, share your draft or practise your oral communication with others to get feedback. Reviewing your message and considering feedback may lead you to return to the first step of the process (analyzing) to reconsider the decisions you made about purpose, audience, content, and medium. This circular approach helps ensure effective communication.

This process may, at first, seem awkward and time consuming. However, once you are familiar with these steps you will get more consistent results with far less effort and in far less time.

Composing The process of drafting content, organizing it so that it is understandable from the audience's perspective, putting it into coherent sentences and logical paragraphs, and then designing a format or delivery approach that is professional and makes the communication easy to follow.

Evaluating The process of reviewing your communication to ensure it is complete, accurate, clear, concise, easy to understand, and error-free.

(LO 2.1) Why should you spend time analyzing?

Analyze

Many attempts to communicate fail. Usually these failures happen because the message senders did not think carefully about what they wanted the message to accomplish and how they wanted their audience to respond. Instead, in a rush to communicate, many people instinctively jump into composing their messages without adequate preparation. This section describes four important elements you should analyze before you start to compose: *purpose, audience, content,* and *medium.* Analyzing each element serves a distinct purpose.

Analyzing the purpose focuses the message

Before thinking about *what* you are communicating, analyze *why* you are communicating. Think about "why" from two points of view:

1. What is your purpose for communicating?
2. What is the outcome you would like to achieve?

What is your purpose?

Every business message should have at least one purpose. Here are some common purposes that business communications serve:

- *Inform* a client about a problem
- *Persuade* a supervisor to implement something new
- *Request* permission to extend a deadline
- *Report* financial information to a client
- *Propose* a solution to a problem
- *Create* **goodwill** with a co-worker or business partner

What outcome do you want to achieve?

Goodwill The positive relationship between you (or your company) and your audience.

Outcome The result of your communication. What you want the recipients of your message to know, do, or feel about the subject of your message.

Purpose statements alone are not enough to help you think clearly about the best content to use. As part of your analysis, identify your desired **outcome**. What do you want your audience to know or do as a result of the communication? **FIGURE 2.2** compares three purpose statements and related outcome statements.

PURPOSE	DESIRED OUTCOME
• To inform my client that I cannot take on a new project right now.	• My client will postpone the project rather than hire someone else to do it.
• To persuade my supervisor to approve a summer-hours work schedule.	• My supervisor will present the plan to upper management.
• To ask my supervisor for an extension on a project deadline.	• My supervisor will let me submit the project next Friday so I can finish it during the week.

FIGURE 2.2 Examples of Purpose and Outcome Statements

Why do you need to be able to clearly state the purpose and outcome, even if only to yourself? Clarifying both your purpose and desired outcome will help you make the best choices when it comes time to craft an effective message. For example, consider how you would address the first item in Figure 2.2. If you think only about your purpose, which is to inform your client that you cannot take on the project, you might draft a message that could cause your company to lose this project.

Consider the revision in **FIGURE 2.3**, which is designed to achieve both the purpose and the desired outcome.

Will the outcome require persuasion?

Persuasion is the ability to influence an audience to agree with your point of view, accept your recommendation, or grant your request. You will find it useful to consider whether achieving your outcome will require simply providing information or if it will also require some persuasion.

If your message is purely informative, no persuasion is necessary. For example, an email to all department employees about a room change for a meeting simply needs to provide clear and complete information, as shown in **FIGURE 2.4**.

However, many business messages require a persuasive approach. They need to influence a recipient either to agree with an idea or to take some action. For example, assume you want to convince your supervisor, Cherilyn Martins, to implement a summer-hours work schedule for your department. Your standard workday hours begin at 9 a.m. and end at 5 p.m. A flexible summer-hours schedule would allow employees to begin and end an hour earlier so that they could take advantage of the increased daylight and warmer weather during the summer. You propose that your department's workday

Persuasion The process of influencing your audience to agree with your point of view, recommendation, or request.

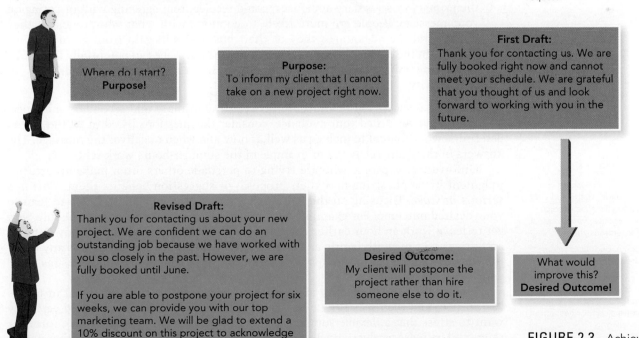

FIGURE 2.3 Achieving a Desired Outcome

PURPOSE	DESIRED OUTCOME
To persuade my supervisor to approve a summer-hours work schedule.	My supervisor will support the proposal and believe it is in the best interests of the department to adopt the plan. She will forward the proposal to upper management and request a meeting to discuss it, with the goal of having the proposal accepted in time to implement it for June 1.

FIGURE 2.5   Sample Purpose and Outcome Statements

hours begin at 8 a.m. between June 1 and August 31. Because you want to motivate action, this message clearly needs to be persuasive. **FIGURE 2.5** shows your purpose statement and desired outcome statement. With this desired outcome in mind, you can begin to analyze your audience to get a clearer idea of how you can influence her and achieve the outcome.

Analyzing the audience helps you meet their needs

Audience analysis may seem counterintuitive to you. After all, if you have something to communicate, shouldn't the message itself be the main focus? In fact, until you have carefully considered your audience, you cannot be certain that your message will be appropriate in terms of content, format, medium, or **tone**.

Here are three main elements to consider with regard to your audience:

- The **primary audience** is the direct recipient of your message, or in other words the person or people to whom your message is addressed. In our example, the primary audience is Cherilyn Martins.
- The **secondary audience** is anyone else who may receive a copy of your message or be influenced by it, usually from the primary audience. In our example, if Cherilyn Martins likes the idea of a summer schedule, she may forward your message to the vice-president of operations. Although you planned your message to be read by your supervisor (the primary audience), the vice-president becomes the secondary audience. **Audience benefits** are the advantages that message recipients (either within the primary or secondary audiences) could receive from agreeing with or acting on your message. People are more likely to go along with what you propose if they understand the advantages they or their business will gain from granting your request. In the case of the summer schedule, the audience can potentially benefit by improving employee morale, which usually leads to overall increases in productivity.

FIGURE 2.6 shows the relationship between the primary and secondary audience. Once you have identified your audience, consider the questions listed in **FIGURE 2.7** to determine what content to include as well as how and when to deliver the message. The answers in the figure relate to our example of the summer-hours work schedule.

Unfortunately, people who are trying to persuade others often make an error in judgment by emphasizing how their proposal or suggestion benefits them. *This is a serious mistake.* Focusing on the benefits to you is easy but is less likely to lead to your desired outcome. For example, by implementing a summer-hours schedule, you get to leave work an hour earlier each day and you have more time to enjoy outdoor activities and time with family and friends. These outcomes do not suggest any benefits for your supervisor or company. Therefore, those benefits are not persuasive to your audience.

The challenge is to identify audience-focused benefits, like those listed in Figure 2.7, item 6, and then *select the ones that will be most effective*. You would certainly want to stress that a flexible summer schedule may improve morale, reduce turnover rates, and increase productivity. However, you may choose to leave out the other potential benefits. It will be difficult to prove that quarterly sales figures will increase, and it

FIGURE 2.4   Informational Message: No Persuasion Needed

L_amica/Fotolia.

Tone   The image your language projects about you based on how the message "sounds" to the audience. Tone in writing is similar to your tone of voice (e.g., friendly, angry, positive, negative, formal, casual, professional, unprofessional, courteous, rude).

Primary audience   The person or people to whom your message is directly addressed.

Secondary audience   People whom the primary audience may communicate with or influence, based on the content, format, or tone of your message. The secondary audience may receive a copy or hear about your message without you knowing.

Audience benefits   Advantages the recipient gains from agreeing with or acting on your message.

would be unwise to suggest that summer hours will improve employees' perceptions of your supervisor. Your supervisor (the primary audience) may find this a valid reason to change the work schedule, but the vice-president (your secondary audience) may not.

Analyzing the content ensures a complete message

In addition to analyzing your purpose, desired outcome, and audience, you also need to analyze your content requirements. Do you know enough about the situation to compose your message? Do you have convincing and credible evidence to support your main ideas? Do you need to do additional research?

For example, assume you have identified a list of potential benefits for the summer-hours plan illustrated in Figure 2.7, as well as a list of questions your supervisor may ask. Before composing, you will need to gather additional information. You may be able to get information from *internal sources* such as company reports, databases, and experts. Or you may have to consult *external sources* such as industry journals, web-based search tools, or experts outside your company. For

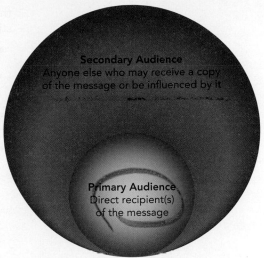

FIGURE 2.6 Primary and Secondary Audiences

1. **What does the primary and secondary audience already know?**

   My supervisor and upper management already know about the structure of our current workday, so I do not need to explain that.

2. **What information does the audience need to know—and why?**

   Both audiences need to know what I mean by "summer hours," how summer hours will work in our department, and how the change will affect the productivity of the department during the summer months.

3. **When does the audience need this information?**

   My supervisor needs the information soon so we can gain support from upper management in time to implement the change for June 1.

4. **How will the audience react to this information?**

   I don't know how my supervisor or upper management will react, so I will try to anticipate potential problems and provide solutions.

If the purpose is primarily persuasive, also consider these questions:

5. **What questions or objections will my audience have?**

   My audience may ask these questions:

   - How will we ensure that someone is available to answer phone calls after 4 p.m. if all employees ask to start and end their day earlier?
   - When workdays begin and end earlier, will we have to rearrange lunch hours and breaks? How will we handle that?
   - Will there be additional costs?
   - Has this plan worked well in other departments or companies?
   - Will anyone think this schedule is unfair?
   - Is there any evidence to support the benefits?

6. **How will my audience benefit from my idea or proposal?**

   - Providing flexible summer hours may improve employee morale, which may lead to the following additional benefits:
     a. reduced employee turnover rates
     b. increased employee productivity
     c. increased quarterly sales figures
   - Providing flexible summer hours may improve employees' perceptions of my supervisor.

FIGURE 2.7 Audience Analysis Questions

the purposes of our example, the following types of research would provide you with strong content:

- **Investigate existing company information.** Learn whether other departments in the company have implemented summer hours. You may call or email other managers, contact your human resources office, or research the company's employee handbook.
- **Survey employee opinions or perceptions.** Learn the degree to which employees will support the summer schedule by conducting a survey.
- **Research external sources of information.** Learn whether other companies offer a summer-hours schedule and if it provides tangible benefits. You can conduct **primary research**, which involves collecting your own original data. For example, you might call the human resources departments of other local companies. A more efficient method might be to look in libraries or online sources for **secondary research**, which is information other people have collected. For example, the *Canadian HR Reporter* (www.hrreporter.com) offers many recent articles and surveys on flex hours as adopted in the Canadian workplace (Hunter, 2012).

While it may be tempting to postpone some of this time-consuming research, your initial communication with your supervisor will be stronger if you can show that you have done some preliminary research and have evidence to support your proposal. More detailed information about finding and evaluating sources is available in Chapter 10.

Analyzing the medium helps you choose the best delivery option

You can use several methods to communicate a message. For example, you can send an email, write a text message, have a face-to-face conversation, or publish your message through a social media site. **FIGURE 2.8** lists many common methods of communication and identifies the advantages and disadvantages of each.

Making a smart and effective choice about the best medium to use is challenging. For example, if you need to send detailed financial data to your supervisor, you might choose to present that information in a spreadsheet and attach it to an email that summarizes the data. However, if the spreadsheet requires a more detailed explanation, a face-to-face meeting will be more effective. In many cases, selecting the medium actually means choosing more than one medium and then deciding how to proceed. In the case of sending detailed financial information to a supervisor, you may decide to meet face to face and follow up by sending a meeting summary and spreadsheet attachment via email.

Social media has expanded the number of medium options available, and companies are finding creative ways to use them. For example, when the software company Red Hat debates a company decision, managers invite employees to voice their opinions and make suggestions on an internal social media site called Memo List. Roughly 100 employees post opinions each day, and Red Hat's president, Jim Whitehurst, reads every post to gain insight from his employees' perspectives. Although Whitehurst typically makes the final decision, he values the role of social media in promoting deeper understanding: "Once you make a decision, you get flawless execution because everybody's engaged. They know what you're doing and they know why you're doing it" (Bryant, 2012). You might use social media in a similar way to begin a departmental discussion about summer hours to give employees an opportunity to express their point of view and contribute critical information to the decision-making process.

Making a decision about which media to use to communicate and exchange ideas also has an ethical component. What if the ideas under discussion could violate an employee's privacy or inappropriately distribute unauthorized intellectual property? Check out the **ETHICS BOX** for an introduction to these concepts as they apply to business communications.

Primary research Collecting your own original data.

Secondary research Searching published reports, articles, and books for information other people have collected.

MEDIUM	ADVANTAGES	DISADVANTAGES
Face to Face *(one-to-one conversation)*	• Allows personal explanation targeted to an individual • Provides for immediate feedback in the form of non verbal cues, such as facial expressions, gestures, and posture	• Is not efficient for disseminating information to many people • Is not usually permanently documented (recorded)
Meeting *(several people)*	• Disseminates information to many people • Provides for immediate feedback • Is documented by minutes	• Can be difficult to schedule • Is time consuming—takes employees away from assigned duties
Telephone	• Allows personal explanation targeted to an individual • Allows short messages to be delivered via voice mail if individuals are not at their desks • Can provide for immediate feedback if the person answers the phone	• Is time consuming if individual calls need to be made to several people • Is not usually permanently documented (recorded)
Text Message, Instant Message	• Allows quick communication • Creates a permanent record (if saved)	• Is not efficient if message is long, complex, or sensitive • Does not ensure immediate feedback
Email	• Allows quick communication • Disseminates information to one or many people • Creates a permanent record if saved or printed	• May not be a private and secure medium for sending sensitive content • Does not ensure immediate feedback because not everyone checks email regularly
Memo *(printed hardcopy to audiences within the organization)*	• Can accompany original documents or forms that need signatures • Can be used for employees who have no access to email • Creates a permanent record	• Incurs costs to copy to many people • Is delivered more slowly than email • Does not provide for immediate feedback
Letter *(formatted on letterhead and either mailed or emailed to audiences outside the organization)*	• Projects a more "official" or formal image than email • Can accompany original documents, such as forms with signatures • Can be emailed as an attachment for fast delivery • Creates a permanent record	• Incurs cost of letterhead and postage • Takes at least a day to deliver unless emailed as an attachment • Does not provide for immediate feedback unless emailed as an attachment
Newsletter *(printed hardcopy, html-designed email, or attachment)*	• Disseminates a lot of information to many people simultaneously • Creates a permanent record	• Incurs cost to copy and distribute by mail • Does not provide for immediate feedback
Website	• Makes information available to anyone with access • Can be password protected to limit access • Enables combinations of text, video, and audio through podcasts, MP3 files, webcasts, webinars, and web-conferencing tools • Is easy to keep up to date • May provide for feedback (wikis)	• Is not effective with audiences who have limited Internet access • Requires the audience to access the site • May not reach the audience • Does not provide for immediate feedback • May not provide a permanent record, unless web files are archived
Social Media: Networking Websites *(e.g., Facebook, LinkedIn)*	• Allows you to communicate to a community of people who have linked with you and expressed an interest • Allows interactive communication • Is easy to keep up to date	• Requires the audience to access the site • May not reach the audience • May reach unintended audiences
Social Media: Wikis, Blogs, and Microblogs *(e.g., Twitter)*	• Disseminates information to many people simultaneously • Encourages discussion • Is easy to keep up to date • Allows interactive communication • Provides a complete record	• Is not effective with audiences who have limited Internet access • Requires the audience to access the site or actively request messages be sent to them • May not reach the audience

FIGURE 2.8 Selecting the Best Medium to Communicate Your Message

ETHICS
ETHICS IN COMMUNICATION: USING O-A-R

Ethics are a set of values or beliefs we use to govern our-selves. Our ethics are based on moral ideals of what is believed to be "right" and "wrong" and inform and influence the way we interpret information, think, and act. A culture can follow a set of understood ethics. Therefore, living or working in a "multicultural" society means that we are also in a "multiethical" world. Ethics are not always governed by law, nor are they always explicitly stated. Yet ethics strongly influence relationships and business practices. Effective business communications can become complex because you need to consider what is "ethical" by legal, business, and sociocultural standards.

Therefore, considering ethics in your communications is extremely important. What may seem appropriate in one situation may not be appropriate in another situation. In business, recognizing when events, actions, or behaviours are potentially unethical is a critical skill to have.

When is it an ethical issue?

Here are some questions to ask yourself:

- Could an email potentially cause harm to a group, community, or individual?
- Could a private meeting create uncertainty regarding influence, morality, or respect?
- Is this communication that I am preparing based on beliefs or on facts?
- If I hit "send" on this email, will my employer face potential legal considerations, such as an action under the Charter of Rights and Freedoms, provincial human rights legislation, or the Criminal Code?
- Am I using any information in this report that violates another person's privacy, uses their intellectual property, or violates a signed competition clause?

How do you begin to adopt appropriate ethical behaviours when doing business with so many different people in different situations?

Many experienced business professionals will tell you that learning to navigate through complex ethical issues is an ongoing task. Think of this as a lifelong learning project.

However, to simplify this process as you begin your career, consider observing, asking, and researching (O-A-R). Soon you will develop a keen internal sense of when you need to find out more before proceeding.

- **Observe:** Observing is the practice of "looking to learn." From our childhood through to adulthood, we look to others to gain insight into how we relate and communicate. Now apply this more specifically to ethics. How do the people around you whom you respect handle certain situations?
- **Ask:** Whether you are in the middle of a workday in your organization or in a grocery store, be willing to ask questions: "Should I include this attachment with this email if I am not sure of the source of the data?" "Is it appropriate to blind-copy my boss on this response?" Even when you feel the action is harmless, there may be a business practice that is observed in your organization that may not be the normal procedure elsewhere. There may also be other ethical expectations that you may not have considered or "observed" in this situation before.
- **Research:** Use trusted Internet sources and social media to research common business, cultural, and ethical practices. Many such resources will be able to alert you to expected behaviours and language. This can help frame the context of your meeting, team discussion, or conversation more professionally.

For an ETHICS exercise, go to Critical Thinking Question 6 on page 59.

This section has served as an introduction to the decisions involved in selecting a communications channel. This topic is covered in greater depth in Chapter 5 and in Appendix B.

LO 2.2 What is involved in composing?

Compose

Composing involves more than just putting your thoughts into words. Composing includes organizing the content so that it is understandable from the audience's perspective, putting the content into coherent sentences and logical paragraphs, selecting a medium that is professional, and then formatting your content in a way that makes the communication easy to follow.

Composing is certainly easier if you have effectively analyzed your communication situation before sitting down to write. However, even a simple and well-planned message benefits from *at least two drafts*. The first draft allows you to get your thoughts on paper. The second draft allows you to refine your thoughts and pay more attention to evaluating the language and grammar. More complex messages may require more drafts to make the message complete, clear, and persuasive. This section will help you think through some key elements of the composing process: deciding where and when to compose, organizing the message, drafting the message, and designing a professional format.

Practising strategic time management

When you write a short email or plan a quick instant message exchange with a colleague, you may not need to pay much attention to your environment. However, when you are preparing a complex report or presentation, or planning an important phone call, you must allow enough time to prepare and compose your message effectively. For example, if you will be making a brief presentation to a new client, you might decide to allocate four hours to prepare for the meeting. While you may be tempted to leave the task to the morning of the meeting, you could also divide the four hours differently. You could spend two hours preparing your presentation on one day and then one hour to rehearse the presentation in front of a friend or colleague the next day. Based on the feedback you receive, you could then spend the final hour developing your ideas and refining your approach.

Planning your composing time is most important when you prepare long documents or presentations. Although estimating how much time you need may be difficult at first, you may find it useful to estimate at least two hours per page of actual composing time. Work backwards from the due date. For example, assume that you have a five-page report due in 10 days. During the analyzing phase, you have collected the data you need. **FIGURE 2.9** is an example of how you could manage this challenge. This expanded process takes the pressure off cramming multiple types of tasks into several hours the day before the deadline and ensures that you have a fresh perspective every day.

One of the biggest enemies to managing time effectively is multitasking. Many people allow their mobile devices to interrupt them and control how they use their time. For example, if you have set aside 1.5 hours for editing and proofreading, yet you answer 12 text messages, post two status updates, and write three tweets during that time, your focus and concentration will be seriously affected. For more information on the impact of multitasking on your work, see the **TECHNOLOGY BOX**.

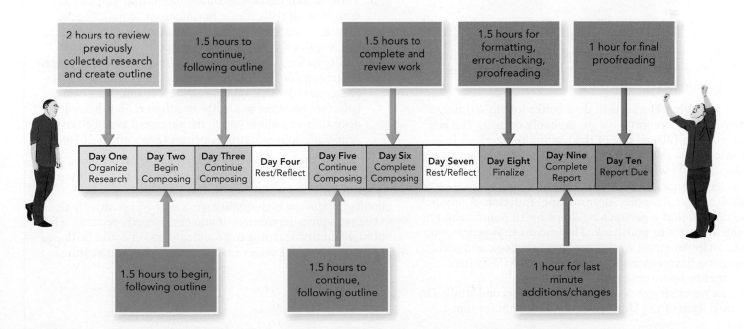

FIGURE 2.9 Managing Time (Analyzing – Composing – Evaluating)

TECHNOLOGY
BOOST YOUR BRAINPOWER: BECOME A SINGLE TASKER

How to Gain Time and Optimize Your IQ!		
Focus on one thing at a time and gain up to a 40% increase in productivity		
Optimize your IQ Studies show that "single tasking" can allow you to make optimal use of your IQ. Multitasking can lower your IQ by as much as 10 points.	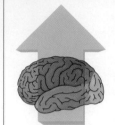	Multitasking can cause a drop in cognitive function, similar to the effects of missing a night's sleep.
Gain time While your co-workers will lose as much as 2.1 hours per day by multitasking (the equivalent of 546 working hours annually), single tasking can give you an employment edge: more time!		Effective analyzing, composing, and evaluating takes time, patience, and focus. Give yourself this extra time by single tasking your way through your work day.

Two employees, Hayley and Jayme, are working on a report that is due tomorrow at noon. Hayley has turned off all her notifications (phone, voice mail, email, Twitter, Facebook, instant messaging). Jayme has not. Consequently, Jayme is being interrupted about once every 90 seconds with information that *is not relevant* to her current task. Hayley is not being interrupted.

- Who do you predict will finish the report on time, without working late or coming in early tomorrow?
- Who do you predict will create a well-organized, readable report that will reflect well on her professional reputation in the workplace?

If you think Hayley will do a better job, in a timely manner, on her report, you are probably correct. The late Clifford Nass (2012), one of the leading researchers in chronic media multitasking, found that heavy media multitaskers (people who engage with three or more media at once) experience dramatically reduced cognitive processes, including executive (decision-making) function. A parallel study found that a person's IQ drops by 10 points when he or she attempts to multitask. This means that people who try to write an email while checking Facebook and text messaging have too many demands on their cognitive resources to perform optimally.

The psychologist who carried out the second study, Dr. Glenn Wilson of the University of London, notes that "unchecked infomania reduces workers' mental sharpness. Multi-tasking can be incredibly stressful on the brain [because] it impairs short-term memory and concentration. Those who are constantly breaking away from tasks to react to email or text messages suffer similar effects on the mind as losing a night's sleep" (G. Wilson, 2013).

What does this mean to the business communicator? The ACE model requires that you maintain sustained focus on specific tasks. It is hard to define your purpose, analyze your audience, do your research, organize your ideas, compose your message, revise for completeness/clarity/conciseness, edit, and proofread while being constantly interrupted or distracted.

Is it possible to become a "single tasker" in this age of interruptions? Yes. In fact, it is essential for maintaining productivity and quality. Here are a few basic guidelines:

1. **Prioritize.** One of the downsides of multitasking behaviour is that it programs us to believe we can achieve more in a day than is actually possible (Taylor, 2011). Select fewer daily objectives and prioritize them in order of importance and urgency. Following this process will allow you to be more productive, not less productive, as you will have fewer unfinished tasks at the end of the working period.

2. **Use the timer function on your mobile device.** Nass suggests creating 20-minute windows of working time, switching between two prioritized tasks (Lapowsky, 2013). For example, you can work for 20 minutes on a focused activity (like analyzing, composing, or evaluating) and then take a five-minute "connection" break to return texts, check your email, or look at Facebook. Be sure to remember to set the timer to alert you at the end of your five-minute break so you can return to your next working period.

3. **Turn "it" off.** Researchers have found that employees who turn off their media notifications (email, Facebook, Twitter, instant messaging, text messaging, and all other interruptions) have less measurable stress, a stronger ability to focus on one task at a time, and do less screen switching (Taylor, 2010). If you find this hard to accomplish, consider that an entirely new realm of software (Internet blocking productivity software) has been developed that will allow you to manage your connectivity in sync with your working priorities (*Economist*, 2010).

Here is the good news: Research shows that people who "are focused on a task indicate that they are happier than when their mind wanders" (Taylor, 2010). As an added bonus, producing high-quality work will add positively to your workplace reputation. If you consistently produce work of high quality, learning to be a single tasker could be one of the most powerful career management skills you acquire.

For TECHNOLOGY exercises, please go to Exercises 3 and 13 on pages 60 and 62.

FIGURE 2.10 Traditional Outline

OUTLINE

Proposal for Summer-Hours Work Schedule

PURPOSE: To propose that ABC Communication's Sales Department adopt a summer-hours work schedule between June 1 and August 31.

Introduction
- Statement of problem
- Proposed solution

Detailed Description of Proposed Summer-Hours Work Schedule
- Flextime options emphasizing core workday hours
- Suggested policies to ensure balanced staffing

Benefits (documented by primary and secondary research)
- Increased employee morale
- Reduced employee turnover rates
- Increased employee productivity

Implementation Plan
- Survey employees to assess flextime preferences
- Develop policies and procedures
- Create an assessment plan

Organizing the message

Composing is much faster and more effective if you make two decisions at the outset:

1. How will you organize the content of the message?
2. Where will you state your main point?

How will you organize the content of the message?

Whether you compose a short email or create a detailed presentation, every message you prepare needs an organizational structure that is logical and easy for your audience to follow. *Outlining* is a versatile and powerful tool that can help you get organized. An outline allows you to break a topic into major ideas and supporting details and then list that content in the order in which you will present it. For example, assume you researched information about summer-hour schedules and need to put together a report for your supervisor. **FIGURE 2.10** illustrates a traditional outline format for a long document, such as a report or proposal. Outlines like these may require several heading levels with multiple points under each topic.

Outlines for smaller efforts can be less elaborate. You do not need a detailed traditional outline format for brief messages, such as emails or short presentations at meetings. **FIGURE 2.11** illustrates two short outlines for brief communications situations. A

(A) NOTES FOR PLANNING AN EMAIL	(B) OUTLINE FOR DISCUSSION AT A MEETING
Notes for Email to Cherilyn SUBJECT: Update on Summer-Hours Schedule Proposal • Ask for feedback on attached rough draft • Briefly explain research gathered to date • Outline information to be included • Thank her for taking time to provide input	**Overview of Summer-Hours Schedule Proposal** 1. What is a flexible summer-hours schedule? 2. How will the company benefit from the schedule? 3. How will we avoid/overcome potential problems? 4. When/how will we implement the schedule? 5. How will we assess the schedule's effectiveness?

FIGURE 2.11 Short Outlines

FIGURE 2.12 Tree Chart Outline

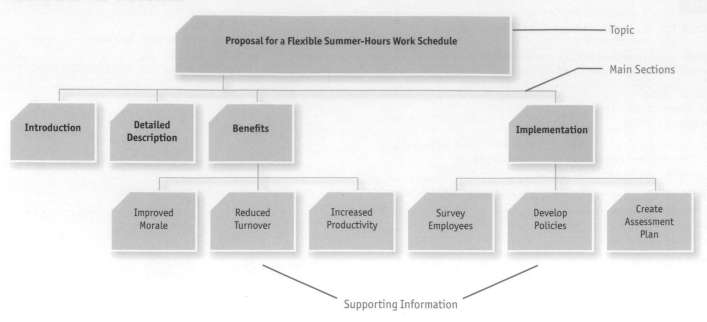

short informative email message may require only a few bullet points. Each bullet point will become a short paragraph in the email. Outlining the content for a short discussion during a meeting may require just a list of questions you will cover.

If you are a visual thinker, you might organize your communication using a *tree chart*, like that in **FIGURE 2.12**, which lets you see the hierarchical structure and connections between your ideas. This method is especially effective if multiple writers are collaborating on a single outline.

Where will you state your main point: At the beginning or the end?

Consider where you want to place the main idea. In basic informational messages (such as the message in Figure 2.4 on page 30), no persuasion is required. The main point may be the only content you include. However, in more complex, persuasive messages, you need to determine whether you want to state the main point directly at the beginning of the message or if you want to be indirect by building up to the point and placing it near the end of the message.

In many situations, being direct is a better choice. Audiences will become impatient if they do not know why you are communicating with them. To avoid this problem and help your audience understand your message quickly, use **direct organization** by stating the purpose and main idea of the message before the supporting details. Direct organization follows this sequence:

1. Present the main idea of the message in the first paragraph, or in the beginning of a long document.
2. Provide supporting information and related details in the middle paragraph(s).
3. Conclude the message with a call to action, any applicable deadlines, and contact information.

However, in certain circumstances, you may want to use **indirect organization**. This structure states the main idea *after* supporting information and related details. The indirect approach may be effective when you are communicating negative news to people who will not expect it, when you anticipate that your audience will be resistant, or when you need to provide an explanation before your main point makes sense. To organize the content indirectly, follow this sequence:

1. Open with a general or neutral statement about the topic that usually indicates the purpose.
2. Provide supporting information and related details in the middle paragraph(s).

Direct organization Stating the main idea of the message before the supporting details.

Indirect organization Building up to the main idea of the message after the supporting details.

FIGURE 2.13 Direct and Indirect Organization

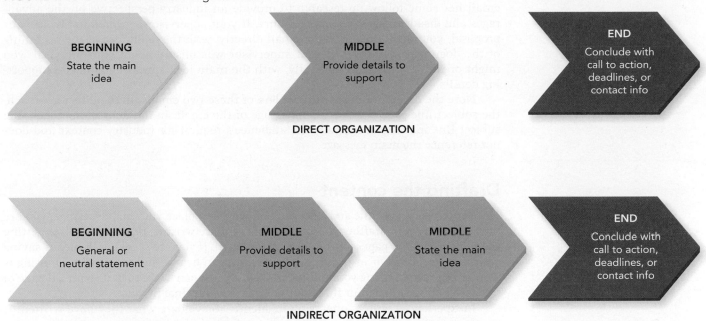

DIRECT ORGANIZATION

INDIRECT ORGANIZATION

3. Present the main idea of the message after the supporting details.
4. Conclude the message with a call to action, any applicable deadlines, and contact information.

FIGURE 2.13 illustrates this concept.

FIGURE 2.14 demonstrates the differences between the direct and indirect approaches to communicate research on flexible summer hours. Imagine that you presented the

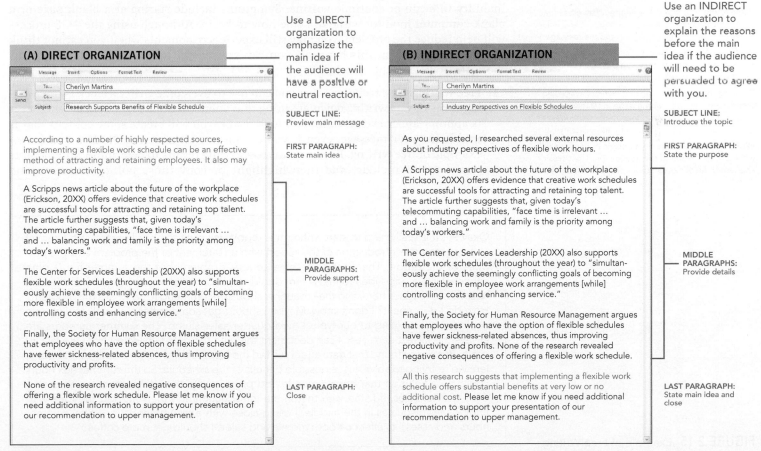

FIGURE 2.14 Examples of Direct and Indirect Messages

summer-hours proposal to your supervisor in a meeting. She might request that you email her some follow-up research to provide an industry perspective on the advantages and disadvantages of summer hours. If your supervisor appeared to favour your proposal, you might organize your email directly, with the main idea at the beginning of the document. However, if your supervisor was unsure about your proposal, you might organize your email indirectly, with the main idea appearing after the supporting details.

Note the difference in the **subject line** of these two emails. In the direct approach, the subject line previews the main message of the email. In the indirect approach, the subject line matches specifically the audience's request for industry context and does not reference the main message.

Drafting the content

Once you have an outline and a decision on where to place your main message, you are now ready to begin drafting your message. If you are writing, **drafting** involves getting the information on paper (or the computer screen). If you are speaking, it means saying your message aloud or in your head so that you can hear it and evaluate it. Drafting is a creative process. Using your outline as a guide, you can begin to draft with a degree of freedom knowing that your first draft will not be your final product.

Inexperienced writers often stop frequently to evaluate what they have written. If you feel a sentence has to be 100% perfect before you begin the next sentence, you are allowing your internal editor to take control. Writing and **revising** are different processes, and switching between them is inefficient and slow. These two activities require different mental processes. In contrast to the creative process of drafting, revising is a logical process that involves evaluating the effectiveness of your message in relation to your audience and purpose. Remember that by using the ACE system you have created ample time to evaluate and edit later. Ultimately, this will produce a higher-quality output in a shorter period of time.

Another barrier that many writers face at the drafting stage is **writer's block**: an inability to begin or continue writing. Symptoms include staring at a blank page or a blank computer monitor without a clue how to begin. Although using the ACE process will help reduce the problem, you may still experience moments when you cannot think of what to say. When this happens, you can try several techniques to unblock your thoughts, including the ones below:

1. **Free writing.** One technique that you can use to overcome writer's block is free writing. This means writing down anything that comes to mind regardless of whether it is appropriate or even meaningful. As a result, you will create some content that is usable for your message, even if you do not use all of it. See **FIGURE 2.15** for an example of free writing. Review your free-writing results to determine which points you want to include, and then highlight or copy those points into a second

Subject line The line in the header of an email that communicates what the message is about and influences whether the audience will read the message.

Drafting A creative process that involves getting information on the paper or computer screen before revising and editing it.

Revising A logical process that involves evaluating the effectiveness of your message in relation to your audience and purpose and then making changes in content, organization, or wording, as necessary.

Writer's block An inability to begin or continue writing, often as a result of procrastination. The stress of shortened deadlines can block creative writing skills.

> Okay . . . It is really hard to start writing this report as I can't think of how to start. I know I need to start the introduction of this report with a statement of the problem and the purpose of the report. There really wasn't a serious problem, but the summer-hours plan sounded like a good idea to me. A friend told me about it at his company, I mentioned it to some colleagues here, and they thought I should recommend it. So what's the problem? How do I describe it? I don't know. Maybe I should get some coffee. Oh well, low morale could be contributing to our typical third-quarter sales slump. The summer numbers are always the lowest each year. I can document this with the data I collected from the last 10 years. But since I found that data after I started the research, it shouldn't really be the problem we're trying to solve, just a possible benefit of the schedule. So the summer flex hours could be a solution that boosts morale and productivity, thereby potentially increasing third-quarter sales. If I start with that in the introduction and then support the idea with findings from sources in the middle, I could close with a recommendation to try summer hours and assess its effect on both morale and sales. I should get more coffee.

FIGURE 2.15 Example of Free Writing

document. Save all your original free-writing samples in a separate document in case you need to refer to them again.

Thinking aloud is similar to free writing except that you speak rather than write. Thinking aloud helps get your ideas "out in the air." Some writers find it useful to record their thoughts, play back the recording, and then type the most important points they hear. In fact, writers who struggle with awkward wording often find recording their thoughts to be an effective way to ensure that their business writing has a conversational, welcoming tone.

2. **Point form first.** If you feel challenged by grammar, try writing your thoughts in partial sentences or point form. You can structure entire sections of work this way, ensuring that your best and most important ideas are at least on paper. Once you have your most important ideas in point form, you can start a different kind of task: expressing your thoughts using effective and clear sentence structure and grammar. Completing the work in two stages (ideas first, then grammar) will help you ensure your best ideas do not get lost while you address the challenge of expressing them properly.

3. **Use an outline.** Writers who prepare an effective outline prior to composing find that their struggles with writer's block are significantly reduced. For example, you can begin by creating a word processing document with headings that match the outline you have created. Perhaps it is easier to start writing in the middle, with your research evidence. The magic of word processing allows you to start in a place that you find easier and work your way toward the more challenging parts. Many writers find openings and conclusions difficult. However, using a content outline within a word processing program gives you the option of completing these elements after you have built your confidence in the rest of the document.

Designing a professional format and delivery

After you have composed your message, arrange it into a professional format that is easy to read and understand. A document's format plays a role similar to your dress and behaviour in face-to-face communication. If the style looks professional, then it communicates to an audience that you are professional. If the format is difficult to read or confusing, then it undermines your credibility.

Although the specific techniques you use for designing your message will depend on the medium you choose, some consistent design principles apply to all medium options. For example, effective and experienced business communicators do the following:

- Start with a purpose-driven introduction
- Break their message into short chunks (paragraphs)
- Begin each paragraph with a strong **topic sentence** that identifies the main point or overall idea of the paragraph
- Use bullet lists for easy comprehension and skimming
- End with a specific conclusion, recommendation, or action item

The following sections provide examples of professional formats for email messages, letters, voice mail messages, and social media postings. Other chapters discuss methods of creating professional formats for longer, more complex documents, such as reports and presentations. For a comprehensive formatting guide, see Appendix C: Formats for Business Documents and online on MyBCommLab.

Email messages

Business email messages should focus on only one topic that is clearly identified in the subject line. However, devoting a message to one topic does not mean that the message should contain only one paragraph. Consider the two versions of the email message in **FIGURE 2.16**. Both versions contain the same information: The subject line and sentences are identical. However, the design is very different. Examine the layout. Which one looks more readable? Which one looks better organized? Which one looks more professional?

Topic sentence A sentence that identifies the main point or overall idea of the paragraph. It is usually the first sentence in a paragraph.

FIGURE 2.16 Poorly Designed versus Professionally Designed Email Messages

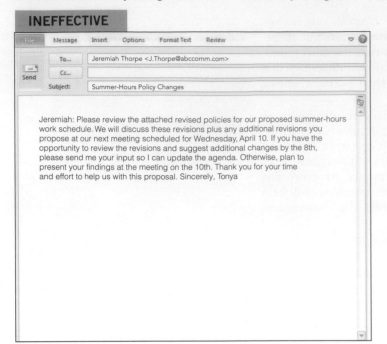

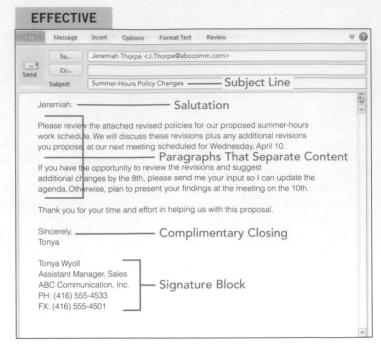

When you write longer emails, you can enhance the organization and design even further by using three important techniques:

- **Begin with a focused first paragraph** that identifies your purpose and previews your content. Strong first paragraphs are increasingly important as more people read emails on mobile devices with small screens. Those readers appreciate getting the core of the message without having to scroll down.

- **Use topic-specific headings** or paragraph titles that are short but include a key idea. For example, instead of using a generic heading like "Benefits," compose a **topic-specific heading** such as "Benefits of a Flexible Summer Schedule" that helps the audience understand the content of the paragraph.

- **Format important lists as bullet point lists**, with each item preceded by a dot or other simple shape. The content you are reading now is part of a **bullet point list**. Notice that the listed items have a **parallel structure**, which means that each bullet has the same grammatical structure. In this list, each item begins with a verb.

The email in **FIGURE 2.17** illustrates all three techniques.

Letters

Letters are generally intended for **external audiences**. A letter is considered more formal than an email. As a result, letters are sometimes used for **internal audiences** when the situation calls for formality. For example, you might receive a letter offering you a promotion, or you might write a formal letter of resignation if you were leaving a job.

When letters are sent in hardcopy on behalf of an organization, they are usually printed on the organization's letterhead. Letters can also be sent electronically (i.e., in softcopy) as email attachments. In fact, many companies use electronic letterhead templates so that letters attached to emails will look the same as printed letters. An attached letter maintains the formality of the message, while the email transmission takes advantage of the quick delivery and electronic documentation.

Several letter formats exist, such as block style, modified block, and simplified. However, block style, as shown in Appendix C: Formats for Business Documents and throughout this text, is the most efficient letter style and the one most commonly used in business. Block-style letters use no indentions or centring. Instead, all elements begin at the left margin, and paragraphs are separated with a double space. For guidelines

Topic-specific headings Section or paragraph titles that are short but include key ideas. They are often in the form of a short sentence and include a verb.

Bullet point list A vertically formatted list with each item preceded by a dot or other simple shape.

Parallel structure Writing that features a series of ideas in identical grammatical structure, making it easier to read and understand.

Letters Formal correspondence, generally intended for external audiences. Letters can be sent through postal mail or by email attachment for quicker delivery.

External audiences People outside your organization (clients, suppliers, partners).

Internal audiences People with whom you communicate inside your organization.

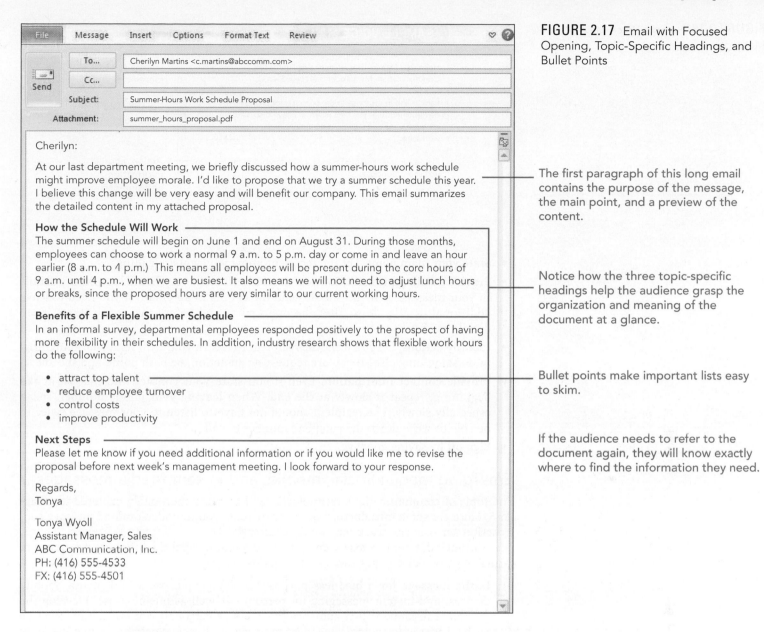

FIGURE 2.17 Email with Focused Opening, Topic-Specific Headings, and Bullet Points

The first paragraph of this long email contains the purpose of the message, the main point, and a preview of the content.

Notice how the three topic-specific headings help the audience grasp the organization and meaning of the document at a glance.

Bullet points make important lists easy to skim.

If the audience needs to refer to the document again, they will know exactly where to find the information they need.

about formatting letters and examples of modified block style, see Appendix C and refer to resources on MyBCommLab.

Voice mail messages

You may think it is odd to consider the design of oral communication, since design is a visual concept. Nonetheless, a savvy communicator designs voice mail messages with the same principles used in designing direct emails:

- Focus on one topic
- Keep the message short
- State the main point early
- Provide contact information

Take a few minutes to plan your message before dialing the recipient's number. Use the following advice to design a professional voice mail message. See **FIGURE 2.18** for a sample.

- **Greet the recipient** by name to personalize the message.
- **Identify yourself** and include your organization name and/or your position if the recipient is not familiar with you. Leave a callback number if you want the recipient to return your call. Concentrate on speaking slowly and clearly.

FIGURE 2.18 Sample Voice Mail
Message

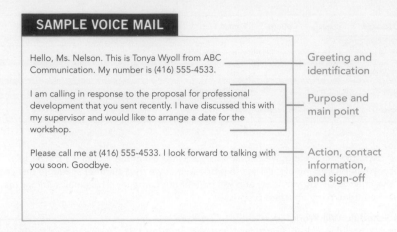

- **State your main point.** Let the recipient know why you are calling.
- **Provide details (optional).** Consider carefully whether you should leave many details in your message or if you should send the details in an email. If you need to leave additional details, do so after the main point and before the action items. Keep details brief.
- **Identify actions.** Do you want the recipient to return your call, send you something, or do something else? If you are requesting an action, be both polite and specific.
- **Provide contact information.** Even if you state your contact information at the beginning, repeat it slowly at the end. When leaving your phone number, speak especially slowly. The recipient should not have to listen to your message twice to be able to write down the complete number to call.
- **Sign off** by saying goodbye.

Emerging media: Social, mobile, and instant media messages

The topic of communications technologies will be more thoroughly explored in Chapter 5. Here are some introductory concepts to assist you in understanding message construction across a variety of technology channels.

Although different forms of emerging media require slightly different approaches to formatting and design, there are two key questions to consider:

1. **Is the message for a business purpose?** Many people use social media, mobile devices, and instant messaging for personal as well as business use. Develop the discipline to know which audience (business or personal) you are communicating with. If you are sending a business message, audience expectations may be quite different than if you were sending a personal message. Most social or personal messages do not require much planning. Any business message of any length, even 140 characters, requires planning and formatting.

2. **Who is your audience?** Many social media formats feature easy sharing and redistribution. Therefore, you need to keep both your primary audience (the direct recipients) and potential secondary audiences in mind as you craft your message. When you hear that a message, photo, or video has "gone viral," what this means in business language is that the primary recipients of a message shared their information with their own audiences, which is a vast and unpredictable secondary audience. Be sure that everything you send or post is constructed in a way that will, at best, reflect a positive image of you and your organization and, at least, not damage your personal image or your company's reputation.

Microblogs are short entries or updates on a blog or social media website, typically posted via a mobile phone ("Microblogging," n.d.). For example, a tweet is only 140 characters long (roughly two lines of text). How can you "design" a tweet? Twitter experts recommend making your tweets even shorter, less than 120 characters if possible. This will leave room for your followers to reply and quote you while remaining within the 140-character limit (TurkReno, Inc., 2011). If needed, use a link-shortening site, such as goo.gl or bitly.com, to cut down the character length of long URLs. Your tweets could,

Microblogs
(e.g., Twitter)
140 character max

- Use 120 characters or less to allow others to modify when resending
- Keep links/URLs short

FIGURE 2.19 Composing for Microblogs

Networking Sites
(e.g., Facebook, LinkedIn)
No character limit

- Keep posts shorter than 250 characters; these receive more shares, comments, and "likes"
- Use photos and links to videos to enhance interest
- Keep posts on topic (i.e., industry or skill related)

FIGURE 2.20 Composing for Networking Sites

potentially, reach a much wider secondary audience. **FIGURE 2.19** summarizes key tactics that will maximize the effectiveness of your microblog posts.

Networking sites, such as Facebook or LinkedIn, allow you to communicate with a wide audience, often based on individuals you have added or connected with as well as their networks. Therefore, over time these sites form groups or communities of people based on either your personal or business interests. Although there are few restrictions on the length of posts you can add to these types of sites, experts recommend that you keep your posts under 80 characters to maximize your readership (Geddes-Soltess, 2012). Facebook's own research shows that short postings (between 100 and 250 characters) receive 60% more shares, comments, and "likes." **FIGURE 2.20** summarizes the key tactics that will maximize the effectiveness of your networking site entries.

A blog posting offers the most social media space for you to develop and explore ideas. This could be a positive or a negative attribute. A disorganized, free-form blog post will not receive the same attention as a well-organized blog post. Therefore, make the extra space work for you and not against you. Take the same care as you would in designing an email, letter, or report: short paragraphs, white space, informative headings and subheadings, lists, and bold text all make posts more visually appealing and easier to read (Vandelay Design, 2008). **FIGURE 2.21** summarizes key tactics that will maximize the effectiveness of your blog posts.

Text messaging is ideal for sending extremely short, time-sensitive, information-based bursts of information. For example, if you need to clarify the location or time of a meeting that is about to take place, sending a text can be the perfect option. The **asynchronous** nature of texts allows recipients to answer when it is convenient for them to do so. However, texts are not the best media for transmitting complex or ambiguous information that requires deep discussion or debate. "It's in the area of customer relations, engagement, and interaction that text messaging holds the greatest potential to solve a range of critical business issues," says Naveen Gupta, chief product officer at RingCentral. "Yet, many businesses don't have a defined text messaging strategy" (Gupta, 2013). Until text messaging is more widely adopted for business use, it is best to use text messaging with clients and colleagues with whom you have an established working relationship. Meaning can be easily misinterpreted in this truncated medium. Therefore, it is inadvisable to use text messaging as the first point of contact with a potential business associate or client. **FIGURE 2.22** summarizes key tactics that will maximize the effectiveness of your text messages.

Asynchronous Refers to communication that takes place with a time gap between the sending of the message, the receiving of the message, and the response (e.g., email, regular mail, or text messaging).

Blogs

- Use blogs to present detailed and organized ideas
- Create opportunities for discussion and feedback from your audience
- Design using standard elements for business writing: headings, subheadings, bullet points, short paragraphs, white space

FIGURE 2.21 Composing for Blogs

Text Messaging

- Keep messages short, clear, and to the point
- Establish a professional tone by using "please," "thank you," and other courtesies
- Limit the use of short forms and emojis; use full words for clarity
- Get permission from business contacts before texting them

FIGURE 2.22 Composing Text Messages

FIGURE 2.23 Composing Instant
Messages

- Keep conversations short, clear, and to the point
- Establish a professional tone by using "please,"
  "thank you," and other courtesies
- Limit use of short forms and emojis; use full words
  for clarity
- Respect the other person's time management; ask
  first if they have time at that moment; respect the
  answer; book a better time to correspond online

With our workforce becoming more global and mobile, the use of instant, **synchronous**, screen-to-screen communication is becoming more widespread. It is an ideal way for teams or groups of people to "meet" and communicate across vast distances simultaneously. One of the key factors in planning a synchronous communication, such as instant messaging, is an awareness of the recipient's availability. While you may be motivated to have an instant messaging exchange with a business partner in another time zone or country, that person may not be available to chat at that moment. Therefore, plan to ask first if the person has time to have a conversation and, if he or she does not, plan to book an appropriate time to continue. **FIGURE 2.23** summarizes key tactics that will maximize the effectiveness of your instant messages.

(LO 2.3) How does evaluating improve your communication?

Evaluate

The final step in the ACE process is evaluating your communication to ensure it is complete, clear, concise, easy to understand, and error-free. This section describes four ways to evaluate your communication:

- Revise the content
- Edit for style and tone
- Proofread for errors
- Review feedback to improve your future communications

When preparing written communications, you need to plan to reread, revise, and edit before sending. Inexperienced business writers often skip the evaluating stage of writing because they believe it is more time efficient to treat their first draft as a final draft. Experienced business writers know that a first draft is rarely good enough. If you write your first draft quickly to get your ideas on the page, you may include incomplete thoughts, awkward sentences, and grammatical errors that computer editing tools such as spelling and grammar checkers may miss. In addition, by the time you get to the end of your first draft, you may have altered or reprioritized your original ideas. The evaluating phase gives you the opportunity to make those changes before you send the message.

By contrast, oral communication allows you to evaluate *while* you are delivering the message based on immediate feedback you receive from your audience. For example, imagine that you are making a point in a meeting. As you look around the room, you can gauge your audience's reaction and begin to adjust or revise your explanation on the spot.

The White House published this photo of
President Barack Obama editing a
speech.

Pete Souza/The White House/Getty Images

Revise content: Improve effectiveness

Even the best writers need to review and revise the content of a first draft. First drafts are opportunities for you to examine and think through your ideas. As you review the draft, you may see that you have left out an idea, changed your logic, or written a lengthy explanation because you did not understand your material well enough to be concise. As you reread your content, ask yourself these questions:

- Is it complete and well organized?
- Is it clear?
- Is it concise?

Synchronous Refers to communication that takes
place in "real time," such as a phone conversation,
meeting, or instant messaging exchange.

Completeness

As a first step in the revising process, reread the entire document from the audience's perspective. Think about the analysis stage of the ACE process (i.e., the purpose and outcome you identified for the communication) and the audience you defined. Ask yourself if the document has the right information and the right approach to achieve your goal. Here is a list of questions you can ask yourself:

- **Is your main point clear?** Underline your main point. Does it appear in the appropriate place in your document? If not, consider reorganizing so that the main point appears where it should. If you cannot find an explicit statement of your main point, add it to the draft document.

- **Have you provided all the information your audience needs?** Consider all the information you believe your audience will need to know. Then review your draft document, putting a mark next to each of these items. If any information is missing, revise. If you cannot imagine what your audience will need to know, ask friends or colleagues to provide feedback. Do they have any unanswered questions after reading your draft? If so, revise.

- **Are the benefits to the audience clear?** Your audience needs to know how to benefit from the information you provide. If you have not stressed this, revise.

- **Is the information well organized?** Read the topic sentences of each paragraph. Does each topic sentence identify the main idea of the paragraph? If not, revise. Does each sentence within the paragraph relate to the topic sentence? If not, revise. Does the progression from one topic sentence to the next seem logical? If not, reorganize and revise.

You will find it easier to revise if you spend some time away from your draft. Put it away overnight or for a few hours and then read it with fresh eyes.

Clarity

Clarity refers to using clear wording that an audience can easily understand. One of the first mistakes many new employees make is to try to impress colleagues, managers, and customers by using big words in long sentences. People are rarely impressed by writing that is long and difficult to understand, like the poorly worded sentences in **FIGURE 2.24**. The best business writing communicates its meaning as quickly and as simply as possible and does not attempt to impress people with vocabulary. The clearly worded sentences in Figure 2.24 intend the same meaning, but use natural-sounding language that is easy to understand.

Experienced business communicators also avoid **abstract wording**. Any language that refers to broad concepts with multiple meanings should be avoided. Consider the sentence "We need to examine the transportation situation ASAP." In this sentence, the terms "transportation," "situation," and "ASAP" (as soon as possible) are abstract.

What do they mean? A dictionary defines *transportation* as conveyance (carrying, moving, shipping, or hauling). Therefore, not everyone thinks of the same kind of transportation when they visualize the word. Similarly, the word "situation" is open to interpretation based on the reader's perspective or role. It could have a positive or a negative connotation. Does it mean that the transportation is delayed, has improved, or is too expensive? Does "ASAP" mean by today, by the end of the week, or whenever you have the time to do it? Using ambiguous wording results in miscommunication if your audience infers a different meaning than you intend. **Concrete wording** is specific. The more concrete the language is, the more likely it is that you and your audience will interpret the same message in the same way: "By tomorrow morning, we need to determine why shipments are leaving the warehouse two days late."

Clarity The quality of being unambiguous and easy to understand. Clear communication uses relatively simple words in well-constructed sentences and well-organized paragraphs.

Abstract wording Language that refers to broad concepts that an audience can interpret in multiple ways.

Concrete wording Language that is specific, making it likely that everyone will interpret it the same way.

POORLY WORDED	CLEARLY WORDED
• Please affix the appropriate amount of postage to the mailing package. • I sincerely appreciate your exertion on this critically important endeavour.	• Please put a stamp on the envelope. • Thank you for your work on this important project.

FIGURE 2.24 Using Clear Wording

FIGURE 2.25   Using Concise Wording

WORDY	CONCISE
• This email is in reference to our approval of your prior request.	• Your request has been approved.

• Attached herein are the agenda for this month's meeting, the minutes from last month's meeting, and the report we discussed last month and will review this month.	• Attached are the documents you will need for this month's meeting:
	  • the agenda
	  • the minutes from last month's meeting
	  • the report we will discuss

• If you have any questions, concerns, or suggestions, please do not hesitate to contact me.	• Please contact me if you have any questions.

Conciseness

In business communication, shorter is usually better. **Conciseness** refers to communication that is short and to the point, expressing ideas clearly in the fewest possible words. Whether your message is oral or written, a well-constructed, concise message saves the audience time. As entrepreneur Guy Kawasaki, managing director of Garage Technology Ventures, explains, schools "should teach students how to communicate in five-sentence emails and with 10-slide PowerPoint presentations. If they just taught every student that, American business would be much better off. . . . No one wants to read 'War and Peace' emails. Who has the time? Ditto with 60 PowerPoint slides for a one-hour meeting" (Kawasaki, 2010).

FIGURE 2.25 provides examples of how you can edit wordy phrases to be more clear and concise.

You can also make writing more concise by eliminating obvious fillers and any information that is not necessary or helpful to achieve your purpose. When you include extra words and unnecessary information, you waste your time as well as the audience's time. Consider the examples in **FIGURE 2.26**.

Concise wording also eliminates **redundancies**. Consider the examples in **FIGURE 2.27** (redundant phrases appear in red in the left column).

Conciseness Using no more words than necessary for a message to accomplish its purpose.

Redundancy Unnecessary repetition of an idea.

WORDY	CONCISE
• As you know, we met yesterday to discuss next year's budget. Based on the auditor's review, we recommended the following actions.	• Based on the auditor's review of our budget, we recommended the following actions.
• As your assistant manager, I am suggesting that we review our departmental procedures.	• I suggest we review our departmental procedures.
• There are three people who will attend the meeting.	• Three people will attend the meeting.

FIGURE 2.26   Eliminating Unnecessary Words

REDUNDANT	CONCISE
• Please refer back to the minutes from our last department meeting.	• Please refer to the minutes from our last department meeting.
• Advance planning on your project will allow our departments to combine together our resources and divide up the work to be done.	• Advanced project planning will allow our departments to combine resources and divide the work.
• The first issue we need to address is travel reimbursement. Travel reimbursement is an important issue to address because nearly 70% of our employees have expense accounts.	• First, we need to address travel reimbursement because nearly 70% of our employees have expense accounts.

FIGURE 2.27   Avoiding Redundancies

Edit for style and tone: Project a professional image

Effective business communicators evaluate their documents to ensure a professional style and tone. **Style** refers to *how* you express yourself rather than *what* you say. Do you use positive or negative language, big words or small words, long sentences or short sentences, strong active verbs or weak passive voice?

The style you choose will affect the tone of your communication. *Tone* is the image your language projects *about you* based on how the message sounds to the audience. Tone in writing is similar to your tone of voice when you speak. Your tone can be friendly or angry, positive or negative, formal or casual, professional or unprofessional, courteous or rude.

Many beginning business writers have trouble identifying tone in the passages they read and in establishing appropriate tone in their own work. This makes editing for tone quite challenging. As a rule, in all business messages keep your tone professional and courteous at all times. This is especially important when you are frustrated and angry. For example, when replying to an angry customer about a problem with a recent purchase, ensure that the tone of your message is polite and reassuring, even if this particular customer often complains or does not understand how to use the product correctly. If you choose to respond in an irritated or angry tone, that customer can, in this age of email, social media, text and instant messaging, choose to damage your reputation and your company's reputation. To ensure a professional style and tone, follow the guidelines below:

- Use positive wording
- Establish a conversational style
- Maintain the active voice as much as possible
- Avoid slang and clichés

Use positive wording

Effective business writers choose positive wording to communicate their messages, even in negative situations. *Positive wording* creates an optimistic, encouraging, and often more informative message. For example, consider the sentences in **FIGURE 2.28**. The sentences on the left are expressed as negative ideas. Note how, in each example, subtle changes in wording focus on the positive expression of the same ideas.

Use a conversational style

Business writing also should be *conversational* rather than academic. Academic writing often sounds too formal for everyday communication. A conversational writing style uses relatively short sentences and familiar words. When read aloud, the text should sound like the writer is talking with the audience. This style is especially important in social media messages where the goal is to create interaction and build a positive image for your corporate brand. Because they are so short, tweets are naturally conversational. To make blog posts conversational, experts suggest being personal in your writing, asking questions to promote a sense of dialogue, splitting up paragraphs for better flow, and proofreading out loud to hear how the words sound (Peters, 2012). To test the power of reading out loud, see the examples in **FIGURE 2.29**. Read the sentences on the left aloud. It is unlikely that you would speak this way in conversation with someone. The sentences on the right convey the same meaning but with a better conversational style.

Style How you express yourself.

NEGATIVE	POSITIVE
• We will not be able to approve a new budget until the analysis is complete.	• We will be able to approve a new budget when the analysis is complete.
• The board has not yet voted on the salary increases.	• The board will vote on the salary increases at the next meeting.
• If you do not sign the form before 5 p.m., we will not be able to fund your travel request.	• If you sign the form before 5 p.m., we will be able to fund your travel request.

FIGURE 2.28 Using Positive Wording

FIGURE 2.29 Using Conversational Style

TOO FORMAL	CONVERSATIONAL
• Henceforth all documentation is to be completed within two business days.	• Please complete all forms within two business days.
• As per your instructions, I have initiated discussions with the previously identified employees.	• I opened discussions with the employees you mentioned last week.
• This new policy will facilitate the implementation of more beneficial scheduling decisions.	• This new policy will let us schedule shipments more efficiently.

Use active voice

Voice refers to the relationship between the subject and verb in a sentence. In **active voice** sentences, the subject performs the action of the verb:

subject   verb

ACTIVE VOICE: The employees completed the project early.

In business writing and speaking, choose active voice for a clear and precise style of writing. Not only does the active voice enliven your writing, it allows you to give credit to individuals or groups who have achieved positive outcomes. See the examples below:

- Sandrine designed and implemented our department's winning strategy.
- The Eastern sales team set a new record for revenues last quarter.

In **passive voice** sentences, the subject does not act. Instead, the subject receives the action expressed by the verb:

subject   verb phrase

PASSIVE VOICE: The project was completed early.

Passive voice may be a better choice in a few special circumstances:

- **To avoid assigning blame.** To maintain a positive tone in your writing, avoid the appearance of assigning blame by using the passive voice:
  - Camilla misfiled the contract. (active voice, sounds like blame)
  - The contract was misfiled. (passive voice, sounds like a statement of fact)
- **To emphasize the most important word.** Use passive voice to highlight the most important word in a sentence. In the example below, the meeting scheduler's name is not as important as the meeting itself:
  - Roger scheduled the meeting for Friday at 2 p.m. (active voice)
  - The meeting is scheduled for Friday at 2 p.m. (passive voice)

The passive voice presents information diplomatically, and this can be appropriate in some circumstances. However, inexperienced business writers tend to overuse the passive voice in an effort to "sound businesslike." When possible, use the active voice to express your ideas more directly. One way to achieve this is to write your first drafts entirely in the active voice and then to reread and identify any areas where you need to be more cautious in your expression. Then you can rewrite only the ideas that require diplomacy in the passive voice. **FIGURE 2.30** provides an example of this technique. Active voice passages are shown in red, and passive voice is shown in green.

Eliminate slang and clichés

To communicate effectively in business, you need to use words that your audience will understand. **Slang** is nonstandard, informal language that may work well within a certain group but often excludes people from different countries, cultures, and social groups. Examples of slang include *cool, my bad, off the chain, plugged in,* and *go missing.* As you edit, eliminate all slang and clichés.

Clichés are commonplace and often overused phrases that have lost their force and meaning. Like slang, clichés are also very specific to cultures and languages, and they

Active voice A sentence structure in which the subject performs the action of the verb.

Passive voice A sentence structure in which the subject is passive and receives the action expressed by the verb.

Slang Nonstandard, informal language that may communicate well within a certain group but often excludes people from different countries, cultures, and social groups. This type of casual and colourful language tends to confuse others when translated.

Clichés Commonplace and often overused phrases that have lost their force and meaning.

FIRST DRAFT: ALL ACTIVE VOICE	SECOND DRAFT: REVISED (BLEND OF ACTIVE AND PASSIVE)
I am writing to apologize for the delay in presenting our report. John couldn't get the printer to work and, when it did work, the printer did not render Kumar's charts properly. So, Mona had to redo all the charts so that you could understand the data. We want to ensure that you have the clearest possible understanding of our research.	Please accept the delay in presenting this report. Technical issues prevented our original report from rendering properly. We are confident that this version is the clearest possible expression of our research. Thank you for your patience.

FIGURE 2.30 Using Active and Passive Voice

CLICHÉ	MEANING
Her proposal is all over the map.	Her proposal is disorganized.
The bottom fell out of that investment.	The investment lost money.
Hiring him was a bad call.	Hiring him was a bad decision.

FIGURE 2.31 Eliminating Clichés

may exclude international audiences. Would a businessperson who learned English in India or China understand the clichés in **FIGURE 2.31**?

If you speak to your classmates about their perceptions of "style" and "tone," you may soon discover that many people have a slightly different opinion on what is formal or informal, or professional or unprofessional. What you may be experiencing is a variation based on "culture." Your experience in future workplaces, either in Canada or abroad, will be similar. You will be around people with different cultural perceptions than your own and, often, you will need to adopt communications habits that are based on cultures dissimilar to your own. For an introduction to this idea, see the **CULTURE BOX**.

CULTURE
CONSIDERING CULTURE IN BUSINESS COMMUNICATIONS

Skylar is excited and a bit nervous as she starts her first week as an intern at the swanky uptown marketing firm Couture Ads. She arrives early on Tuesday morning and receives a voice mail message from the managing partner instructing her to receive their newest client, Simon Wu, who is arriving from Hong Kong today at noon. Skylar needs to arrange for a limo to pick Mr. Wu up from the airport upon his arrival. Skylar is anxious to impress her employer and hopes to be offered employment after her internship. She asks the interns' assistant to announce the client when he or she arrives. Skylar then begins to arrange a meeting back at the office for the marketing team to brief the client on his important project.

All Skylar's preparations are complete by 11:30 a.m., and she departs for the airport. However, Mr. Wu seems confused by being whisked back to the office and being placed immediately into a meeting. While he is too gracious to state that anything is wrong, Skylar senses that something is amiss.

Things to Note: In some business organizations, it is common practice (the business "culture") to greet clients at the airport. Expectations about working upon arrival may be the practice in Canada, but in other cultures a more informal welcome, like a lunch with partners or team managers,

may be more appropriate and culturally sound. "As a leader, you need to recognize the culture of the people you're working with" (McCarthy, 2009). In our diverse global network, considering the culture of both the profession as well as the person is an important skill to have in business communications:

> Culture is socially constructed. It is a set of implicit and explicit social expectations, values, and norms, shared between members of the same group. The characteristics of a culture include, but are not limited to: music, religion, traditions, etiquette, moral values, rules, gender roles, language, art, and history. Although cultural expectations, values and norms remain clearly identifiable, they evolve to varying degrees over time. Culture often connects to a strong value system, and governs how people relate, trust and exchange ideas. Therefore, because culture is a strong component of each individual's and group's identity, it is an extremely important consideration in business communications. (Satov, 2013)

For CULTURE exercises, go to Critical Thinking Question 7 on page 59 and Exercise 16 on page 63.

Proofread to increase your credibility

Proofreading is a critical step in the evaluation process. When you have analyzed, researched, and composed your written work, much remains to be done. If your work is full of misplaced pieces, your audience will focus more on those mistakes than on your intended message. Furthermore, your audience may assume that you lack attention to detail. Your communication efforts should enhance your reputation with your audience, but presenting work with errors will achieve the opposite effect.

Proofreading is like solving a puzzle. You need to find the errors that exist, rearrange or revise them, and put them in their proper place. To fully understand the importance of this, assume that your audience will find any misplaced puzzle pieces faster and more accurately than you will. When this happens, your credibility with your audience decreases. Here are some techniques that will help you present error-free work to your business audience. Check out **FIGURE 2.32** for a summary of the kinds of errors you will need to watch for.

Learn to recognize the five most common errors

Most writing errors fall into one of five categories: content errors, spelling and typographical errors, usage errors, grammatical errors, and format errors.

- *Content errors* **are mistakes in the substance of a message.** Content errors include incorrect or missing information. Pay special attention to
  - dates and days of the week,
  - locations and times stated,

Proofreading A systematic process of reviewing writing for errors.

FIGURE 2.32 Identifying Five Common Error Types

- lists of details,
- numerical data (look for misplaced decimals and commas),
- the spelling of names (both of people and organizations), and
- the accuracy of titles (e.g., president or CEO or both?).

You may be too familiar with the material to determine if content is missing. Get a second opinion! Ask a colleague to help you proofread and ask for specific feedback about information you should include.

- *Spelling errors* **result from a lack of knowledge about how to spell a word.** *Typographical errors* **are mistakes made in typing.** Typing too quickly often results in misspellings, transposed letters, and duplications. Spell checkers within word processing programs may help you proofread for spelling and typographical errors, but they will not find all your mistakes. For example, if you type the word "saw" instead of "was," the spell checker will not identify the word as incorrectly spelled. To catch these errors, look up the spelling of all words that you are not confident you have spelled correctly. Pay special attention to any information expressed in numbers, including addresses and phone numbers. Spell check will not be able to identify if numbers are incorrect.

- *Usage errors* **are errors in the way language is used.** For example, if you use the word "imply" when you mean "infer" or use the word "economical" when you mean "economic," you have committed a usage error. It is difficult to catch these errors when you proofread on your own because you chose the wrong words originally. Get a second opinion! Ask colleagues to help you proofread since they may be able to identify these types of errors.

- *Grammatical errors* **are violations of grammar rules.** These errors include sentence fragments, run-on sentences, shifts in tense, incorrect pronouns, and incorrect subject–verb agreement, to name but a few. Grammar checkers can help you identify some problems, but the automated tools will miss many critical errors. Furthermore, grammar checkers are known to offer weak corrections as alternatives. When errors are not properly corrected, they will reflect poorly on you. You need to identify and correct grammatical errors on your own and validate all suggestions offered by the automated tools.

- *Format errors* **are inconsistencies in design techniques within a document,** such as including both indented and block-style paragraphs, bullets that do not align correctly, and differences in font sizes or styles. These errors often occur when you cut and paste text from other sources such as documents or webpages. Correctly using word processing formatting techniques improves the professional design of your documents.

Check systematically for errors

To check systematically for all of these types of errors, follow these guidelines:

- **Read your work multiple times.** The errors listed in the previous section are different from each other and difficult to catch in one reading. If you proofread just once for all errors, you most likely will not find them all. Instead, focus on one type of error in each proofreading scan. You will be more successful in finding your mistakes.

- **Identify your own common errors.** Over time, you will come to recognize a pattern of common errors you make. Make a list of these errors and look for them in your drafts. For example, if you often misuse commas, proofread your draft once only for commas. If you also notice that you often use the word "there" instead of "their," proofread a second time just for those words. See **FIGURE 2.33**.

- **Read your work later.** If possible, put some time between your composing and evaluating stages. Too often, writers quickly compose a first draft and immediately try to proofread their work. Taking even a five-minute activity break can clear your thoughts and let you proofread with a fresh perspective.

- **Read your draft out loud.** Generally, people speak more slowly than they read. Reading your draft aloud slows your reading pace and helps you focus on the text and find more errors. Also, when you hear what you have written, you are more likely to identify a missing word or notice awkward phrasing and punctuation.

- **Read from the bottom up.** Some writers find it helpful to read from the bottom up. They start with the last sentence and read up the page sentence by sentence. This

FIGURE 2.33 What Are Your Most Common Errors?

backward approach slows your reading pace and lets you examine the information out of context to help you find typos and missing words.

- **Change it up.** Another effective technique for nonformatting mistakes is to temporarily change the font style and size before proofreading. This tricks your brain into thinking it is reading an entirely new document not written by you. Once you have found and corrected errors, you can revert to the original font size and type and examine for formatting problems.

- **Get a Second Opinion.** For a more objective perspective, ask a colleague to proofread your draft. Even the most experienced writers miss some of their own writing errors. Because you wrote the content and you know exactly what you meant when you composed the draft, your brain will fill in missing words or information as if it is actually there. An objective reader can often find errors that you have overlooked.

Take advantage of technology tools

Many word processors contain additional tools to help you evaluate, revise, and edit. For example, Microsoft Word includes a readability tool that assesses your writing based on sentence length and average word length. The analysis then assigns your writing a grade-level rating. Business writing should be short and simple, therefore most messages should be written at the Grade 8 level or less. The grade-level rating will increase when your style includes long sentences and **polysyllabic** words. See **FIGURE 2.34** for examples.

A **thesaurus** is a reference tool that provides synonyms and antonyms. **Synonyms** are words that have the same or similar meaning, such as "quickly" and "rapidly." **Antonyms** are words that are opposites, such as "clear" and "confusing." When you have trouble looking for the right word to express the meaning of your message, your word processing software's thesaurus can identify options. However, choose carefully among the words that you see in the thesaurus, and look up unfamiliar words in the dictionary before using them. Even when a thesaurus lists two words as synonyms, they may not have the exact same meaning. For example, a thesaurus could list the word "privilege" as a synonym for "benefit" (Princeton Language Institute, n.d.). However, if you were writing about "employee benefits," you could not simply swap the word "privileges" for "benefits." "Employee benefits" has a different meaning than "employee privileges."

Review feedback to improve your communication strategy

As discussed in Chapter 1, business communication is a two-way transaction. In its simplest form, you send a message and, whether you ask for it or not, you often get feedback that indicates how effectively you have communicated. This feedback may take the form of a smile, a puzzled look, a phone call asking for clarification, or compliance with your request. Even a lack of response is a type of feedback.

Polysyllabic Having more than one syllable.

Thesaurus A reference tool that offers alternative words, specifically synonyms and antonyms.

Synonyms Words that have the same or similar meaning.

Antonyms Words that have opposite meanings.

FIGURE 2.34 Examples of Reading Levels

INAPPROPRIATE	APPROPRIATE
Grade Level 12.3: Henceforth, all documentation is to be completed within two business days.	Grade Level 5.2: Please complete all forms within two business days.
Grade Level 14.8: As per your instructions, I have initiated discussions with the previously identified employees.	Grade Level 6.0: I began talking with the employees you mentioned last week.
Grade Level 16.6: This new policy will facilitate the implementation of more beneficial scheduling decisions.	Grade Level 8.3: This new policy will let us schedule shipments more efficiently.

You may receive more subtle feedback. Pay special attention to these cues. For example, if you receive no response to an email message, does that mean the audience did not believe a response was important? Did the subject line fail to capture the audience's attention? If you write a set of directions and your audience gets lost, does that mean they are poor readers, or that you included ambiguous information, or that you missed a step? What you learn from this feedback will help you make better decisions the next time you communicate.

To take full advantage of feedback, ask for it early in the communication process and use it to evaluate and revise your communication strategy. For example, when you share your summer-hours proposal with your supervisor, she may suggest that you reorganize your content, include additional possible disadvantages, or develop an assessment plan as part of the proposal. This feedback will require you to spend more time analyzing, composing, and evaluating, which may be disappointing if you thought the writing process was complete. However, it will lead to a more successful proposal. Ultimately, professional communicators develop the ability to seek out and take in feedback as part of their skills development and growth.

In summary, the ACE process will help you communicate more effectively by ensuring that you analyze, compose, and evaluate in a systematic way. In the following chapters, you will have an opportunity to apply this process to a range of business communications, from short, routine messages through complex reports and presentations. Short email messages may take only a few minutes to analyze, compose, and evaluate, while more complex communications will require more time. However, as you become a more experienced communicator, you will increasingly be able to go through each step of the process more quickly and effectively, regardless of the length or purpose of your communication. If you follow the process well, your messages will more likely achieve your purpose and project a professional image. **FIGURE 2.35** offers a summary of how ACE was used in this chapter to create the request for summer hours.

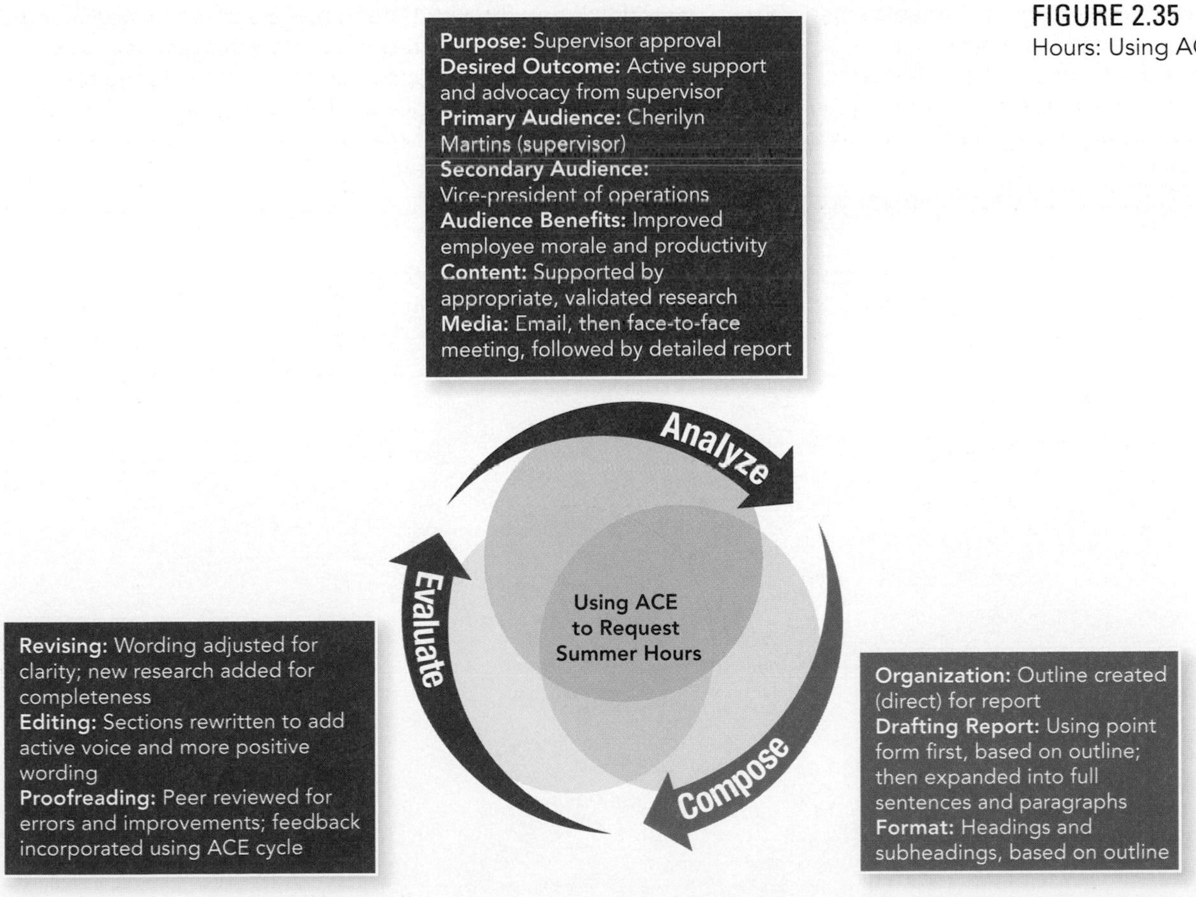

FIGURE 2.35 Request for Summer Hours: Using ACE

Purpose: Supervisor approval
Desired Outcome: Active support and advocacy from supervisor
Primary Audience: Cherilyn Martins (supervisor)
Secondary Audience: Vice-president of operations
Audience Benefits: Improved employee morale and productivity
Content: Supported by appropriate, validated research
Media: Email, then face-to-face meeting, followed by detailed report

Using ACE to Request Summer Hours

Analyze

Compose

Evaluate

Organization: Outline created (direct) for report
Drafting Report: Using point form first, based on outline; then expanded into full sentences and paragraphs
Format: Headings and subheadings, based on outline

Revising: Wording adjusted for clarity; new research added for completeness
Editing: Sections rewritten to add active voice and more positive wording
Proofreading: Peer reviewed for errors and improvements; feedback incorporated using ACE cycle

Farzana Mawani

Marketing and Communications Manager

Altima Healthcare Canada Inc.

Photo courtesy of Farzana Mawani and JPB Photography.

@ **WORK**

At the opening of this chapter, Farzana Mawani described the critical need to define both the purpose and the audience for each marketing message her company issues. Let's see how she uses ACE to help her!

The key to getting communication right is to ensure you are proceeding through the ACE process (analyze – compose – evaluate) with care.

- **Analyze.** To produce the one-page documents I mentioned at the outset, I need to make sure I fully understand my audience and their needs. Then, I need to research to find recent data in health or medical journals, the latest publications by experts in the field, or current industry best practices.

- **Compose.** The one-pagers need to be concise, accurate, eye-catching, and persuasive. They also need to be appealing to the general public as well as to healthcare professionals. The average person looking for health and dental information will not relate to a technical document filled with medical terminology and complex charts. My understanding of my audience tells me that the wording must be clear for the average reader, the tone must be as positive as possible, and the overall message must be organized in a logical, compelling way.

- **Evaluate.** I spend quite a bit of time in the evaluation process. All wording, data, and formatting must be error-free prior to publishing. A best practice is to have more than one person review and edit the final document to ensure any text or layout errors are caught and corrected. Even the most experienced writers can miss small errors in their work. As for design, I double-check to ensure each one-pager is graphically intuitive and aesthetically compelling. Visual components, including photos, objects, text layout, colours, typeface, logos, icons, and other elements, are carefully evaluated for best placement, size, formatting, and flow.

Ultimately, measuring audience response is the primary way to determine the success or failure of your message. If my audience has acted upon the message the way I intended, then I know my communication efforts have been successful. If not, then it's time to reevaluate each step along the process and adjust as required for better results next time. Every setback is an opportunity and a challenge to improve and refine the process. The most fulfilling moment is when all of the pieces of the puzzle come together, and everyone can see the picture.

Learning Objectives in Review

LO 2.1 **Why should you spend time analyzing?**
(pages 28–34)

- **Clarify your purpose and desired outcome.** Be able to state both your purpose and your desired outcome before you continue. Consider how you will maintain goodwill and determine whether your message will need to be persuasive.
- **Meet your audience's needs.** Think about what the audience needs to know. How will the recipients benefit from your message? What objections might they raise? Imagine receiving your message from the audience's point of view. Consider both the primary audience and secondary audiences.
- **Ensure your message is complete.** This step helps you determine whether you have enough information or need to conduct additional primary or secondary research.
- **Choose the most effective medium for delivery.** Understanding your purpose and your audience will help you determine which medium (email, letter, face to face, social media) will ensure that your message reaches your audience effectively.

LO 2.2 **What is involved in composing?** *(pages 34–46)*

- **Manage your time strategically.** Allow time for each stage of the composition. Avoid multitasking.
- **Organize the message.** This requires that you determine the overall structure of the communication. Long documents may benefit from using a multilevel outline. Short documents can start with a more informal outline. Decide where to state the main point. Messages can be organized either directly (main idea first) or indirectly (supporting details before main idea).
- **Draft the content.** This is a *creative* process. Save revising (a *logical* process) for later. Use strategies like free writing to avoid writer's block.

- **Design a professional format and delivery.** This requires that you consider formatting emails, letters, voice mail messages, and social media postings in a professional manner. When appropriate, use topic-specific headings to signal the structure of the document.

LO 2.3 **How does evaluating improve your communication?** *(pages 46–56)*

When you evaluate, you assess whether your communication will be effective and then make changes to improve it. You can evaluate in four ways:

- **Revising the content improves effectiveness.** Revising ensures your communication has the right information and approach to meet its goals. As you revise, look to see that your document is complete, clear, and concise.
- **Editing style and tone helps you project a professional image.** Use positive wording, a conversational style, and active voice. Eliminate slang, clichés, and unnecessary passive voice.
- **Proofreading increases your credibility.** To improve your proofreading skills, familiarize yourself with the different kinds of errors: content, spelling and typographical, usage, grammatical, and format. Systematically check for these errors, and take advantage of technology tools.
- **Reviewing feedback helps you improve your communication strategy.** You can ask for feedback that helps you revise a document, and pay attention to feedback you get in response to your finished communication. Using social media allows you to get continuous feedback both on your communication strategy and on your organization's brands and business.

KEY TERMS

abstract wording p. 47
active voice p. 50
analyzing p. 27
antonyms p. 54
asynchronous p. 45
audience p. 27
audience benefits p. 30
bullet point list p. 42
clarity p. 47
clichés p. 50
composing p. 28
conciseness p. 48

concrete wording p. 47
content p. 27
direct organization p. 38
drafting p. 40
evaluating p. 28
external audiences p. 42
goodwill p. 28
indirect organization p. 38
internal audiences p. 42
letters p. 42
medium p. 27
outcome p. 28

parallel structure p. 42
passive voice p. 50
persuasion p. 29
polysyllabic p. 54
primary audience p. 30
primary research p. 32
proofreading p. 52
purpose p. 27
redundancy p. 48
revising p. 40
secondary audience p. 30
secondary research p. 32

slang p. 50
style p. 49
subject line p. 40
synchronous p. 46
synonyms p. 54
thesaurus p. 54
tone p. 30
topic sentence p. 41
topic-specific headings p. 42
writer's block p. 40

CASE STUDY

Using ACE to Improve Communication Results

This case study will help you review the chapter material by applying it to a specific business situation.

Suppose your employer asks you to inform everyone in the customer relations department about an upcoming workshop on communication skills. You quickly create the flyer below and post copies on the break-room bulletin board and in the cafeteria. You send a copy in a document as a file attachment to all employees by email.

Although your department includes 60 people, only 4 people attend. How could using ACE help improve the communication results?

Communication Skills

Workshop

Wednesday, November 2 @ 2:30 p.m.

Training Room A

What Is the Desired Outcome?

Although your supervisor may have simply instructed you to tell the employees about the workshop, a desired outcome was implied. Your supervisor wants most employees to attend. Merely informing employees that the workshop exists will not make them attend. You need to persuade them.

What Content Does the Audience Need?

What will the audience need to hear to make them want to attend? To answer this question, you need to analyze the audience and anticipate their questions and objections.

All 60 employees from customer relations are busy. They also believe they are already good communicators. They are, after all, in customer relations. They will attend a workshop only if they are required to do so, if they believe they will benefit, or if they believe it will be fun. Here are some questions that will be on their minds when they hear about the workshop and some possible objections they may have to attending.

Possible Questions the Audience May Have:

- Is this workshop required?
- How long will the workshop last?
- How will I benefit from attending?
- Will my manager be upset if I don't attend?

Possible Objections the Audience May Have:

- I have too much work to do.
- I don't need to attend. I studied communication in school.
- A workshop won't help me get promoted.

QUESTION 1: *What other questions and objections can you anticipate? If you were going to* revise the communication, which questions and objections would you answer directly? How?

Which Medium Is Best?

You realize now that a flyer was not the most effective way to communicate about the workshop because some people simply walk past flyers without reading them. Furthermore, many people do not open email attachments without a compelling reason to do so.

QUESTION 2: *What are the advantages and disadvantages of the following other options: sending an email with an attachment to each employee, making an announcement in a department meeting, sending a tweet to an employee list, calling each employee, posting a notice to the internal community Facebook page, sending an email with the information in the message rather than as an attachment. Would a combination of these options be optimal? If so, which combination?*

How Can I Structure My Content?

You realize your audience may respond best to more than one exposure to the message in more than one medium. You decide to send an email with the information in the message, make an announcement at a department meeting, and post a note (based on the email) to the internal community Facebook page. Now you have the challenge of structuring the content. A draft of the proposed email message appears below.

QUESTION 3: *Review how the ACE process led to this improved message by answering the following questions.*

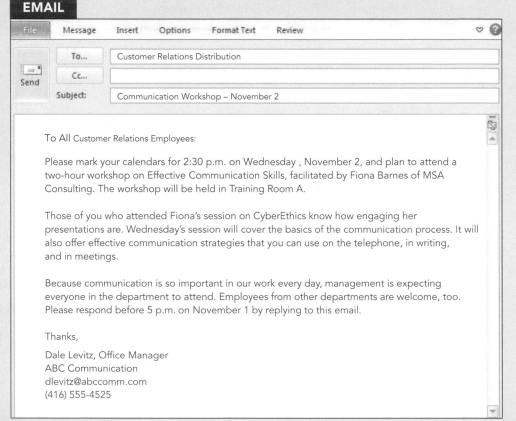

EMAIL

File   Message   Insert   Options   Format Text   Review

Send

To...   Customer Relations Distribution

Cc...

Subject: Communication Workshop – November 2

To All Customer Relations Employees:

Please mark your calendars for 2:30 p.m. on Wednesday , November 2, and plan to attend a two-hour workshop on Effective Communication Skills, facilitated by Fiona Barnes of MSA Consulting. The workshop will be held in Training Room A.

Those of you who attended Fiona's session on CyberEthics know how engaging her presentations are. Wednesday's session will cover the basics of the communication process. It will also offer effective communication strategies that you can use on the telephone, in writing, and in meetings.

Because communication is so important in our work every day, management is expecting everyone in the department to attend. Employees from other departments are welcome, too. Please respond before 5 p.m. on November 1 by replying to this email.

Thanks,

Dale Levitz, Office Manager
ABC Communication
dlevitz@abccomm.com
(416) 555-4525

Accompanies Question 3

Analyzing:

1. What information in the revised version addresses the need for persuasion?

2. How does the email message emphasize reader benefits?

3. What content appears in the email that was not included in the original flyer? Why is that content useful?

Composing:

4. Is the information in the email organized effectively? Explain.

5. What determines which information goes in which paragraph?

6. Is this email organized as a direct or indirect message? Why? Is this the correct choice? Why?

Evaluating:

7. In evaluating content, are there additional persuasive points you could add?

8. Does this email message use clear and concise wording as well as professional tone and style?

9. Which elements promote a conversational style?

10. When proofreading this email, which content elements would you proofread for accuracy?

11. Is the message designed well? Explain.

12. Would you keep the current subject line or would you revise it? Explain.

REVIEW QUESTIONS

1. Why is analyzing your purpose important to composing an effective message? Is the purpose always the same as the desired outcome?

2. Explain the difference between the primary audience and the secondary audience, and provide an example of a message that would have audience benefits for both.

3. What is the difference between primary research and secondary research? Describe a business communication situation in which you would want to research both sources of information to support your message.

4. Why is it important to consider your audience when deciding the medium for delivery?

5. What is the difference between direct and indirect message organization? When would you use each?

6. Explain how reviewing feedback helps you improve your communication strategy.

CRITICAL THINKING

1. Think about the last written assignment you completed. What percentage of your overall time did you spend on each element of the ACE process (analyzing, composing, and evaluating)? Will you change your approach in the future? Explain why or why not.

2. Analyzing your audience helps you compose effective messages. However, sometimes you may need to communicate with people you do not know. How do you learn about and analyze an unfamiliar audience?

3. Assume you work for a supervisor who generally prefers to receive email messages rather than have face-to-face meetings. Identify at least two circumstances in which you believe it would be better to request a meeting to discuss an issue rather than send an email. Explain your rationale.

4. Retrieve a recent email message that you wrote to someone other than your family and friends. Do you believe that the email portrays a professional image? If so, what elements of the email create that image? If not, what elements undermine that image?

5. Read three recent pieces of your writing (either emails or assignments). Begin to create your custom list of common errors. To help you develop your list, ask a friend to help you assess your messages, or seek assistance from your school's writing centre. How can you ensure you do not continue to make these errors in the future?

6. **(Work with a partner or in a small group.)** Take a look at the business scenarios given here. For each one:

   a. Decide with your partner or group whether or not this situation is ethically challenging.

   b. If yes, see if your group can define, in writing, why or how the situation poses an ethical challenge.

   c. Finally, write down the most appropriate response or behaviour that you would recommend in the situation.

   - I am considering giving a small gift to a potential client of our company.
   - When I called to ask for the manager or project lead, I asked if "he" was available.
   - Last night I showed the meeting agenda for today's strategy session to my friend who also works in this industry.
   - I was told I could pick anyone I wanted for this project, so I picked my favourite people.
   - Our company created a service that can't be used by people with a visual impairment.
   - Our new website launched last night in English only.

7. **"Convince Me" Tic-Tac-Toe!** A game to play with a partner. On a blank piece of paper, create the following Tic-Tac-Toe grid:

Greeting	Networking	Texting
Informal conversation	Colour Choices	Emails
Use of words	Body language	Phone Etiquette

a. One player chooses to be "X" and the other chooses "O."
b. Take turns with your partner.
c. You are allowed to place your mark over a square once you have convinced your opponent, *with an example*, that "culture" affects the concept in the box. For example, does culture have an impact on the colours people chose for designing documents or messages? If so, how? Give an example.
d. The first person to get three Xs or Os in a row (horizontal, vertical, or diagonal) wins!

DEVELOPING YOUR COMMUNICATION SKILLS

(LO 2.1) Why should you spend time analyzing? *(pages 28–34)*

EXERCISE 1 Improved communication: Knowing the purpose and the audience

You are part of a five-person team at work. The team's goal is to redesign the way in which customers apply for refunds. The team meets twice per week, on Mondays and Thursdays. The Monday meeting occurs online using appropriate meeting software, and the Thursday meeting is face to face. Typically, four out of five people show up for each meeting. In the four weeks you have been working together, you have not yet had 100% attendance, and this has hampered the team's progress. Your supervisor has asked you to reassess how your team communicates and to find a solution that will result in 100% attendance at each meeting. What do you need to know about your audience (i.e., the team) to proceed? Make a list of questions that you would need to have answered before you can propose a viable solution.

EXERCISE 2 Do you have everything you need for a complete message?

Your supervisor asks you to give a brief presentation at your company's annual sales meeting that analyzes sales trends for each of the company's three regions over four years. You collect the data about gross sales and then create the following exhibit:

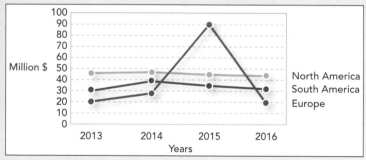

Accompanies Exercise 2

As you look at the graph, you realize it will raise questions during the presentation and that you should prepare answers. What questions and observations about sales do you think your graph will raise? What additional research would you do to answer those questions?

EXERCISE 3 Finding the most effective medium of delivery [Related to the Technology feature on page 36]

For each of the following scenarios, identify which medium would be the best choice to communicate your message. Select your choice from the list of medium options in Figure 2.8 on page 33 or other options you deem appropriate. Explain your reasoning.

a. Your employer leaves a message on your voice mail asking you to work overtime this weekend, but you plan to attend your cousin's out-of-town wedding. What medium would you use to explain why you cannot work overtime?

b. You are developing a new procedure manual for the sales associates in your department and need input on several issues from your department manager and training staff. What medium would you use to gather the input you need?

c. You ordered 14 boxes of 8 1/2" × 11" copy paper from a local office supply store, but you received 11 boxes of 8 1/2" × 14" legal paper. You call and speak with Karamjeet, an associate manager of the store. Within an hour of your call, he personally delivers the 14 boxes of standard copy paper to your office, carries the boxes into your supply room, and retrieves the boxes of legal paper. You are so impressed with Karamjeet's personal attention and quick service that you want to inform his supervisor. How do you contact Karamjeet's supervisor to praise his efforts?

(LO 2.2) What is involved in composing? *(pages 34–46)*

EXERCISE 4 Using your time effectively

Assume you are interning part time for a marketing company this semester while taking classes. Your supervisor's project team is working on an ad campaign for a new client that produces nutritional yogourt drinks. In preparation for the team's initial brainstorming session next week, you have been asked to gather preliminary information about the client's leading competitors. You have researched the three companies that currently dominate the market and have gathered sample TV ads, website screenshots, and print media sources. You need to create a five-page report that summarizes your research. The report is due in seven days. How much time do you estimate you will need to compose and evaluate this report? How would you spread that work over the seven days, considering that you also have school assignments and other commitments to manage? Create a timeline similar to that shown in Figure 2.9 on page 35 to plan how you could use your time.

EXERCISE 5 Getting organized!

Compare the following email messages. Email A is organized directly, and Email B is organized indirectly. Note that the only difference between these two messages is the placement of the main idea: "My analysis determined that Adaptive Solutions' website is more effective based on its ease of use, comprehensive content, and general appearance."

a. Under what circumstances would Nichole choose to write a direct message to Susan? Explain at least two circumstances.

b. Under what circumstances would Nichole write this same message indirectly? Explain at least two circumstances.

c. How would you revise each message to emphasize audience benefits?

EMAIL A – DIRECT

To... s.mcewen@fieldspatterson.com
Cc... Competitors' Website Comparison
Subject:

Susan:

As you requested, I compared the websites of our two main competitors: Creative Communications (CC) and Adaptive Solutions (AS). My analysis determined that Adaptive Solutions' website is more effective based on its ease of use, comprehensive content, and general appearance.

The AS website uses a consistent navigation format throughout. By contrast, the CC menus differ on several pages, which make finding specific information very difficult. Additionally, the AS website describes workshop topics, provides sample PowerPoint demonstrations, and links their handout examples. The CC site lists their workshop topics with a brief description of each, but does not provide additional materials. Finally, the overall appearance of the AS website is more professional. The content is well organized and the text is easy to read. I found it difficult to find information on the CC site and had a hard time reading the 10-point text.

Let me know if you need a more detailed analysis of these two sites. I look forward to working on our own company's web design team.

Best,
Nichole

Nichole Perkins, Consultant
The Fields-Patterson Group
50 Robson Street
Vancouver, BC V6E 1B0
www.fieldspatterson.com
PH: 604-633-2646
FX: 604-633-2601

Accompanies Exercise 5

EMAIL B – INDIRECT

To... s.mcewen@fieldspatterson.com
Cc... Competitors' Website Comparison
Subject:

Susan:

As you requested, I compared the websites of our two main competitors: Creative Communications (CC) and Adaptive Solutions (AS).

The AS website uses a consistent navigation format throughout its site. The CC menus differ on several pages, which make finding specific information very difficult. Additionally, the AS website describes workshop topics, provides sample PowerPoint demonstrations, and links their handout examples. The CC site lists their workshop topics with a brief description of each, but does not provide additional materials. Finally, the overall appearance of the AS website is more professional. The content is well organized and the text is easy to read. I found it difficult to find information on the CC site and had a hard time reading the 10-point text.

My analysis determined that Adaptive Solutions' website is more effective based on its ease of use, comprehensive content, and general appearance. Let me know if you need a more detailed analysis of these two sites. I look forward to working on our own company's web design team.

Best,
Nichole

Nichole Perkins, Consultant
The Fields-Patterson Group
50 Robson Street
Vancouver, BC V6E 1B0
www.fieldspatterson.com
PH: 604-633-2646
FX: 604-633-2601

EXERCISE 6 Moving past the first draft

Select a topic you are researching for a class or group project or use a topic assigned by your instructor. Use the free-writing technique to fill at least a page (typed and single spaced). Save this work, noting that it is a first draft. Save another copy of this work titled "second draft." Revise the "second draft" version into something more presentable to your instructor. Print both versions and compare. How did the freedom of the first draft influence the quality of the second draft? In what ways is the second draft improved? Do you need a third draft?

 How does evaluating improve your communication?
(pages 46–56)

EXERCISE 7 Sifting for meaning: Improving clarity and conciseness

Edit the following sentences to improve their clarity and conciseness:

a. Computer technology and its associated software applications in conjunction with the widespread usage of the World Wide Web have had the most profound and visible effects of any invention in modern history.

b. Technologies have dramatically impacted and modified our complex communication systems, exchanges of information, and our commercial endeavours.

c. As technology permeates nearly every facet of business entities, the question is whether today's college students receive adequate information and assistance as they prepare for the high-tech world of business.

d. A multitude of employers are now testing prospective employees prior to employment to determine if their information technology knowledge and skill levels will meet or exceed their technology expectations in terms of meeting their workplace needs.

EXERCISE 8 Trimming the excess: Removing unnecessary wording and redundancies

Edit the following sentences to eliminate unnecessary wording and redundancies:

a. You asked me to provide you with my recommendation for the new sales position, and I believe that Sarah Miller is the best candidate.

b. We combined together the proposals, and after close scrutiny of the results have come to the consensus of opinion that this project will be our first priority.

c. Foreign imports are an essential necessity in our business.

d. We respectfully and humbly extend our grateful thanks that your future plans have secured our company's good success.

EXERCISE 9 Project professionalism: Positive wording

Edit the following sentences to give them a more positive tone:

a. She will not do well on the employment exam if she does not review the company's procedures.

b. The committee will not make their decision until next week.

c. The employees will receive no bonus if they do not submit their performance evaluations on time.

d. I cannot attend the meeting if this report is not finished on time.

e. Because the construction plans were not delivered, we could not determine a timeline for completion.

EXERCISE 10 Project professionalism: Active voice

Edit the following sentences to change passive voice to active voice. (Note: You will need to supply a subject for the active verbs in some sentences.)

a. The proposal was written by the marketing team based on in-depth research.

b. The decision was made to extend overtime allowances by 10%.

c. Because two proposals were submitted, a meeting was scheduled to discuss the differences.

d. Positive feedback about the presentation was received from the clients.

e. The salary increase will be seen on your next paycheque.

EXERCISE 11 Project professionalism: Eliminating slang and clichés

Edit the following sentences by removing the slang and clichés (in italics) to clarify the meaning. If you are unfamiliar with the cliché, look it up online before editing.

a. Everyone in the department knows that the *buck stops here*.

b. She needs to *dangle some carrots* in front of her team to get anything done.

c. She has really been *a good soldier* about the change in leadership.

d. The union representative said that management needs to *sweeten the pot* if we want to end the labour strike.

e. He will be *swimming with the sharks* if he tries to present that proposal to the management team.

EXERCISE 12 Project professionalism: Improving reading level

Using Google Scholar (http://scholar.google.ca), find a paragraph that you find complicated and difficult to read. Copy and paste the paragraph into your word processing program. Using the software's assessment tools, or using an online tool you find through a web search, determine the grade level of the paragraph.

Rewrite the paragraph in a conversational style using simple words and short sentences. Determine the new version's grade level. Identify which version you believe is most effective and explain why.

EXERCISE 13 Project professionalism: Proofread for error reduction [Related to the Technology feature on page 36]

Type the following paragraph into any word processing program:

Do to recent security events, are technology upgrades our scheduled to be implemented at the beginning of next months. This change requires you to ask yourself what applications you current use and predicted those you may knee during the next fiscal year. How will you now what you what you might need in the future? That is a difficult question to answers. However, you're in put is necessary to assure that hour resources our used correct. Thank in advance for you're effort too improve this process.

Accompanies Exercise 13

Enter the words and punctuation exactly as shown. Highlight any errors that you see. Then run the application's spelling and grammar tools. Make a list of any (a) spelling errors that the spelling checker did *not* find and (b) changes the grammar checker suggested that would create an error. Do the results of this exercise change the methods you will use for proofreading in the future? Summarize your findings in an email message to your instructor.

EXERCISE 14 Revising and designing an email message

François and Darryl work for a product design firm in Montreal. This morning, François received a call from a client asking if he and Darryl could fly to Edmonton to consult on a new project. François and Darryl agreed, checked their calendars, and chose a 2 p.m. flight from Trudeau Airport the next day. However, when François called Air Canada to book two seats for the flight, he learned that no seats were available. He did a little research and decided that he would prefer to take a charter flight leaving from Saint-Hubert airport, switching planes in Winnipeg. See the following draft of François' email to Darryl on the next page. Revise this email to (1) use a direct organization, (2) arrange the material into effective paragraphs, (3) ensure all information is complete and clear, and (4) improve the subject line.

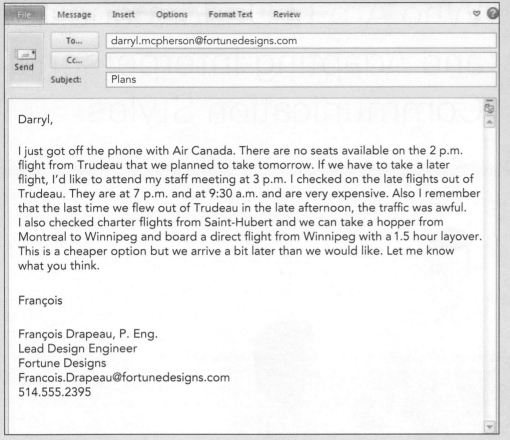

File	Message	Insert	Options	Format Text	Review

Send

To...   darryl.mcpherson@fortunedesigns.com

Cc...

Subject: Plans

Darryl,

I just got off the phone with Air Canada. There are no seats available on the 2 p.m. flight from Trudeau that we planned to take tomorrow. If we have to take a later flight, I'd like to attend my staff meeting at 3 p.m. I checked on the late flights out of Trudeau. They are at 7 p.m. and at 9:30 a.m. and are very expensive. Also I remember that the last time we flew out of Trudeau in the late afternoon, the traffic was awful. I also checked charter flights from Saint-Hubert and we can take a hopper from Montreal to Winnipeg and board a direct flight from Winnipeg with a 1.5 hour layover. This is a cheaper option but we arrive a bit later than we would like. Let me know what you think.

François

François Drapeau, P. Eng.
Lead Design Engineer
Fortune Designs
Francois.Drapeau@fortunedesigns.com
514.555.2395

Accompanies Exercise 14

EXERCISE 15 Revising and designing a voice mail message

Alex and Marika are planning to attend an 8 a.m. meeting with their boss to discuss a report they completed the night before. On the way to work, Alex gets into a car accident. The paragraph below is the voice message Alex leaves Marika to tell her that he will not be able to get to work in time for the meeting. He also needs to tell Marika where to find the photocopies of the report he made last night. Before Alex gets to the end of his message, the electronic "operator" interrupts and says: "If you are satisfied with this message, press 1. If you would like to record the message again, press 2." Alex realizes he should revise the message, and he presses 2. Revise this message for Alex.

> Marika, this is Alex. You won't believe what happened on the way to work today. I was driving down Sherman Avenue when a car ran a red light and hit me. I'm okay, but I'm at least 30 minutes from work and my car is undrivable. I can't leave anyway because the police officer is writing up the report really slowly, and I need to wait to get my licence back and to make sure the tow truck comes for my car. Then I'll need to get a taxi. I'm really glad I have my cellphone with me. Otherwise, I'd be in big trouble. I don't know when I'll get to work, so can you present our report at the meeting this morning? The photocopies are on Lucy's desk because . . ."

Accompanies Exercise 15

EXERCISE 16 Exploring cultural communication [Related to the Culture feature on page 51]

Review the Culture box on page 51. To answer the following questions, you may need to conduct some additional research. This could include searching for "intercultural business communications" online, interviewing classmates or professors from the relevant cultures, or reading materials available in your campus library.

a. Identify the specific cultural mistake or mistakes that Skylar made in her attempt to efficiently meet and transport Mr. Wu to the downtown office. How could Skylar have improved the outcome of this task?

b. Consider the exact same scenario, except that the incoming executive is Ms. Alejandra de Vieira from Spain. Should Skylar's response to this situation change? How?

EXERCISE 17 Impromptu presentations

Select one of the following topics and plan a brief one- to two-minute presentation that you organize directly. Begin with the main idea followed by supporting information and conclude with a short summary or wrap-up. Then select a second topic and plan a brief presentation that you organize indirectly. For this presentation, begin with supporting information, followed by the main point, with a brief summary or wrap-up at the end.

a. Describe your last experience travelling.

b. Describe your dream job.

c. Where do you see yourself in five years?

3

Who Am I? Understanding and Adapting Interpersonal Communication Styles

DragonImages/Fotolia

LEARNING OBJECTIVES

LO 3.1 **Why do you need to understand communication styles?** *pages 66–74*

Understand that styles are adaptable

Define and understand your communications comfort zone

Learn to adapt: Get out of your comfort zone

LO 3.2 **What listening skills will help you communicate better with others?** *pages 74–80*

Hearing accurately

Comprehending and interpreting

Evaluating

Responding

LO 3.3 **What speaking strategies will encourage others to listen to you and understand what you are saying?** *pages 80–86*

Focus on your audience

Share the conversation

Use clear, unambiguous language

Support your message with appropriate nonverbal communication

Avoid upward inflection

Avoid language that triggers a negative response

Be aware of gender-specific communication styles

Apply ACE to support interpersonal communication skills

Liz Clarke

College Professor and Communications Consultant

@ WORK

"What we have here is a failure to communicate . . ."

Courtesy of Elizabeth Clarke and Brandon Barre.

Some time ago I was placed on a cross-functional team with four other colleagues. Individually, we had each reached a certain level of success in our working lives. As a team, we were expected to complete a series of small internal problem-solving projects over 18 months. Our team looked like this:

- Rudy: Senior Production Manager, Professional Engineer
- Joseph: Financial Analyst, Chartered Accountant
- Samuel: Computer Programmer/Analyst
- Rajiv: Research and Development, Ph.D. in Chemical Engineering
- Liz: Project Manager, Communications Specialist

Between us, we had a wealth of knowledge, experience, and even wisdom. Anyone examining our qualifications on paper would have thought this team could easily tackle anything that we were asked to do.

The first six months were disastrous.

When we met to discuss our projects, we seemed to bring all our worst communication habits. If Rudy did not agree with the direction we were heading, he would distract the team with misplaced bits of humour and unrelated storytelling. Samuel would often stay silent while signalling hostility with his body language. His verbal input would come in short, sharp outbursts that always began with criticism of other people's contributions. Rajiv offered long, complex speeches that were burdened with details and analysis that few other people understood. As for me, I was frustrated with the level of detail Rajiv needed for his understanding of our work. My irritation showed in my disrespectful and dismissive responses to his input. I often encouraged Rudy with his attempts at humour, which was not helpful to the team. As for Samuel, I simply tried not to say anything that would upset him. When I did make my own contributions, I often found the others staring back at me with looks of confusion. I felt that there was something about my perspective on the problems we were attempting to solve that was not valued by the others. This made me try harder and harder to make my points. As someone who prides herself on having excellent communication skills, I felt a deepening sense of desperation and failure.

Joseph was probably the best-behaved member of the team, remaining quiet and still as he listened carefully to each team member's input. He would always attempt to summarize any progress we made while gently pointing us in some kind of useful direction. While his endless patience for our antics helped us survive the first part of our 18-month journey together, we certainly were not thriving as a productive and innovative team.

Wondering how Liz and her team addressed these interpersonal communication issues? Check out the @ Work box at the end of this chapter!

Introduction

Whether you work for a large company or a small one, you will interact with many people on the job: co-workers and teammates, supervisors and managers, suppliers and service providers, and customers and clients. You will work with them in person, on the telephone, and through online tools such as email and social media. Your ability to work well with people depends on your written, oral, and interpersonal communication skills.

Many employers are concerned that, as the world becomes more digital, people are spending less time developing their interpersonal communication abilities. This could signal a shift to people feeling more comfortable emailing and texting rather than talking with others in "real-time" conversations and discus-

sions (Turkle, 2012). While no one disputes the value of digital communication, it *cannot* replace conversations that encourage people to understand each other's point of view more deeply. In a face-to-face conversation you are presented with the opportunity to "listen" on multiple levels: tone of voice, facial expressions, body language, and other nonverbal signals. This kind of **synchronous** interpersonal communication will help you forge the positive and productive working relationships that are critical to business.

Synchronous Refers to communication that takes place in "real time," such as a phone conversation, meeting, or instant messaging exchange.

This chapter will help you understand your own preferred **communication style**. Once you know more about your own style, you can work on strengthening your interpersonal communication skills and improving your ability to work well with others.

Communication style The manner in which people interact with each other. The messages a person sends, intentionally and unintentionally, through spoken, written, and nonverbal communication.

(LO 3.1) Why do you need to understand communication styles?

Everyone has a preferred communication style. This style is unconsciously developed over time and can be influenced by family dynamics, cultural expectations, innate personality preferences, and a wide range of other factors. You can see a variety of styles in everyone you communicate with. Some people happily share every idea they have as they are having it. Others wait until their concepts are fully and completely formed and researched. Some people prefer face-to-face communication. Others are more comfortable putting some ideas down in writing and sharing only specific information face to face. Some people like speaking on the telephone, while others do not. Some people are naturally more formal in their style, while others are less so. The list of possible variables in communication style is nearly limitless.

How does this impact your working life? Consider the following scenario: Joe, an experienced technology manager, made an exciting career move from Company A to Company B. His new role in Company B was similar to his previous role, although he had a larger department and more responsibility. When he attended his first management meeting, he noticed a startling difference between meetings at his previous job and meetings at his new job. At Company B, everyone jumped in with their ideas, often interrupting each other. The meeting was loud and a bit disorganized, but a lot of information was shared and new ideas were generated. A participant in the meeting would have to be quite assertive to have his or her ideas heard in this environment. Unfortunately, although Joe was extremely experienced and capable, both as a manager and within his technology area, he was not an assertive communicator. He was accustomed to listening closely to others, considering carefully how to express his input, and finally offering his opinions and suggestions. Although he had some creative ideas to offer in the first meeting, Joe did not manage to contribute anything. Joe wondered if he could succeed within Company B with his communications **comfort zone** being so different than that of his new co-workers.

As you integrate into your future workplaces, you will find yourself facing situations in which communication styles are not matched. How can you make sense of this and move forward in a professional manner? Here are three concepts that will help:

- **Understand that styles are adaptable.** Not only does each individual have a preferred style, you develop multiple variations on that style over time as you are exposed to different situations and have more complex relationships.
- **Define and understand your comfort zone.** The more clearly you understand your communications preferences, the more adaptable you can be when you are presented with a completely oppositional communication style.
- **Learn to adapt.** When you find yourself outside your comfort zone, understand that you have an opportunity to learn where and how you need to adapt.

Understand that styles are adaptable

By the time you are ready for the workplace or for postsecondary education, you have developed multiple communication styles. For example, it is fair to say that a person communicates a specific way while in a spiritual or sacred space. Once removed from that space, that same person is likely to change his or her style while relaxing or chatting with friends. Similarly, many people find themselves making different choices when communicating with close family members than they might while meeting a new friend for the first time. How you speak with the principal of your secondary school is likely different than how you speak with someone who is a romantic attachment.

As Matthew MacLachlan, head of intercultural and communication skills training at Communicaid states, "If you were to pick a random topic, such as the weather or a recent film you have seen, and you discussed it casually with a few different people, you will most likely notice that even if your conversation covers the same topic, your style will vary

Comfort zone A term that describes preferred behavioural, cultural, or attitudinal characteristics that are familiar and known.

depending on the other person's position (your boss or work colleague), profession (lawyer, shopkeeper), relationship to you (relative, friend, someone you have just met on a street), age (a child, an older person) or culture (national, religious, etc.). . . . We tend to speak in different ways to different people" (MacLachlan, 2010). You will use different words, a different tone, and possibly different communications channels or media. Where you are and who you are with deeply influence how you naturally choose to communicate. You have already developed this natural ability to adapt your style to your surroundings and your audience (Turner & West, 2010). **FIGURE 3.1** illustrates the ways we have already learned to adapt our preferred communication style to a variety of situations and a variety of audiences.

As you begin to hone your communication skills, you can add to this communications toolkit by consciously acquiring comfort with new aspects of communication that you have not previously emphasized. By taking a business communications course, you are starting the process of adding "In My Workplace" to your version of the profile noted in Figure 3.1. Simultaneously, you are working on the skill of adaptability, which will allow you to be flexible and thrive in many diverse situations. You will work with people who have a wide variety of styles, strengths, and weaknesses. The purpose of adapting within a workplace is not simply to "fit in": The purpose is to find ways to communicate that maintain your professionalism in a variety of settings, while retaining the elements of your own natural preferences.

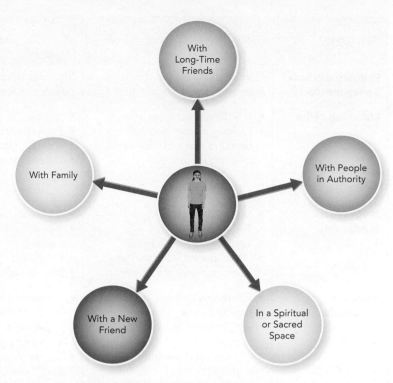

FIGURE 3.1 Natural Adaptation of Communication Style: Your Toolkit

Define and understand your communications comfort zone

There are a number of ways to begin to define yourself as a communicator. It is important not to rely entirely on just one type of input as you evaluate your approach to communication. You should begin now, at an early stage of your working life, to gather as much information about your own style as you can. Although you can start with the ideas presented here, continue to add to your self-knowledge throughout your career.

Access self-assessment tools

The study of interpersonal communication is a continually growing field and there are many self-assessment tools available. Wondering how you would score on a personality assessment? Check out our online personality assessment tool on **MyBCommLab** to identify your strengths and weaknesses as a communicator!

Your communication style is part of your personality. Credible and researched personality tests such as the Myers-Briggs Type Indicator test (MBTI), the Keirsey Temperament Sorter (KTS-II), and True Colors can generate results that will give you further insight into your communication style and how you can best respond when working with others who are either similar or different. There are also several online versions of these tests that you can search for and complete.

One of the key areas that these tests assess is the level of assertiveness displayed in interpersonal communications. **FIGURE 3.2** presents a spectrum of passive (nonassertive), aggressive (overassertive), and assertive behaviours.

Active listening, noted in the final section of Figure 3.2, will be examined more closely later in this chapter.

As you begin to assess your own style, you will naturally begin to observe the behaviours and the styles of others around you. Your objective is to cultivate your own assertive communication style that will allow you to be open and flexible in most collaborative situations. Concurrently, you will begin to see that some sources of conflict with collaborators can arise simply from stylistic differences in communication style. Conflict management will be covered in Chapter 6.

How does understanding your communication style and the styles of others help you succeed? Check out the **CULTURE BOX** for more information on this.

FEATURES	PASSIVE ➤	ASSERTIVE	AGGRESSIVE ➤
Primary attitude/ belief/motto	Don't make waves by expressing your true feelings.	My ideas have value. The ideas of others also have value.	Everyone should be like me.
Listening skills	• Is a distracted listener • Quickly adopts another person's point of view without offering input	• Is an active listener • Pays attention • May ask clarifying questions • Listens for answers to questions	• Is a poor listener • Has difficulty hearing another's point of view • Tends to interrupt • Waits for a chance to speak rather than listening
Nonverbal tendencies	• May sigh a lot • Tends to fidget • Voice has lower volume • Uses upward inflection even when not asking a question	• Uses natural gestures and posture • Attentive, interested facial expression • Favours direct eye contact • Uses an appropriate volume	• Points, shakes finger at others • Glares and stares • Has a critical, possibly sarcastic, tone of voice • Speaks quickly and loudly

Verbal tendencies	• Extremely indirect, using hedge phrases like:
	  • "(Statement), *don't you think*?" (e.g., "We should wrap up now, don't you think?")
	  • "(Statement), *isn't it*?" (e.g., "It is cold out, isn't it?")
	  • "... sort of ..."
	  • "... you know ..."
	• Usually agrees or stays neutral
	• May not speak until spoken to
	• Tends to hesitate
	• Is overly apologetic
		• Direct and clear, using phrases like:
		  • "What do you think of this idea?"
		  • "What are my options?"
		  • "What alternatives do we have?"
		• States observations without modifiers, labels, or judgments
		• Expresses him- or herself directly and honestly
		• "Checks in" on the opinions, input, and emotional state of others
		• Uses questions to draw out additional information or to encourage participation
			• Extremely direct, using phrases like:
			  • "You must ..."
			  • "You ought to ..."
			  • "You will ..."
			• Speaks in judgmental statements
			• Tends to treat his or her own opinion as fact
			• Unaware of emotional response of others
			• Uses questions to criticize and judge ("What are you doing THAT for?")

Conflict style	• Ignores or postpones conflict • Will withdraw from participating • May agree externally while disagreeing internally	• Negotiates, compromises • Confronts problems at the time they happen • Aims for a win/win outcome	• Will monopolize a debate • May turn a debate on ideas into a conflict between people • Offers only negative feedback • Accepts only his or her position (win/lose)

Moderating strategy	• Monitor your internal responses
	• Note when you are holding back
	• Learn one or two key opening phrases that will help you start expressing your ideas, such as:
	  • "I support your idea and I'd like to add to it in the following way ..."
	  • "Your evidence is very compelling, and I see why you support this idea. I have some additional evidence that needs to be considered. ..."
		• Monitor the internal and external environment
		• Continue to balance the need to self-express with the requirements of the audience
		• Watch for the limited occasions when a more passive or a more aggressive style is temporarily appropriate: Adapt!
			• Monitor external responses
			• Pay attention when people appear to pull away or fall silent
			• Learn to monitor body language, tone of voice, and facial expressions
			• Learn how to ask for the opinions of others in a respectful way, such as:
			  • "I have explained my idea. I know we have all been working on this problem. What are some other ideas?"
			  • "Thank you for listening to my input on this. I'm happy to hear what you have in mind."
			• Practise giving *only* positive feedback on other people's ideas
			• Develop and practise active listening skills

FIGURE 3.2 An Assertiveness Spectrum

Sources: Sherman, R. (n.d.). Understanding your communication style. Online Women's Business Center. Retrieved from www.au.af.mil/au/awc/awcgate/sba/comm_style.htm; Aw, A. (2014, February 24). Understanding different communication styles. IMA Management and Technology. Retrieved from www.ima-mt.com/understanding-different-communication-styles/; Scott, E. (2014, December 15). Reduce stress with increased assertiveness. About.com. Retrieved from http://stress.about.com/od/relationships/p/profileassertiv.htm; Counselling Service in France. (2012, September 11). Tell the difference between assertive, passive and aggressive behavior. Retrieved from http://counsellingservice.eu/tell-the-difference-between-assertive-passive-and-aggressive-behaviour

CULTURE
HOW CAN YOU OPTIMIZE YOUR PERSONAL COMMUNICATION STYLE AT SCHOOL? AT WORK?

Skylar spends three days a week at her internship placement and two days a week in classes at Provincial College. Skylar is an attentive student and is enrolled in the business program. She chose this program because the courses provide her with a variety of skills that employers need. Additionally, she really likes the internship requirement because she has no "hands on" experience in business. Skylar hopes this will give her an advantage in gaining employment after graduation.

Skylar understands that, in college, students are evaluated on assignments, tests, participation, and presentations. Her professors recognize her attention to detail and her high level of engagement with the course content. She is an exceptional student, yet her professors see her struggle with class participation. She does not seem to have any trouble making presentations, especially if she has time to prepare. However, taking the initiative to start a work group in class or to participate in lively classroom discussions seems to be a challenge. When working with people she knows well, Skylar is more comfortable participating actively in discussions. However, in a classroom full of strangers, Skylar often keeps her head down and avoids eye contact. When she is assigned to a work group, she always carefully considers what people say before she replies. This behaviour gives other students ample opportunity to speak up before Skylar has a chance. While Skylar does not think of herself as shy, she prefers online communication because it gives her time to weigh the details and organize her thoughts. Although she feels she has a lot to offer, being "quiet" in a Canadian classroom does not encourage Skylar's classmates and professors to think of her as a natural leader.

In her human resources class, Skylar learned that her Myers-Briggs personality type is ISFJ (Introverted, Sensing, Feeling, Judging). Skylar knows that personality types influence communication styles. In group work at school, she has started to wonder about the personality types of her classmates. She thinks about a student team in her communications class. If Jess is an ENTJ (Extroverted, Intuiting, Thinking, Judging), she is going to naturally take control of the team process. Perhaps this is her strength. Jess's style seems direct, often to the point of seeming stern. Skylar wonders if Jess is aware of others perceiving her as "stern." Danny might be an INFJ (Introverted, Intuiting, Feeling, Judging) or an INFP (Introverted, Intuiting, Feeling, Perceiving). Either way, he comes up with lots of creative ideas, even if following through is not his strong point. He will send emails in the middle of the night that take their group projects off in an entirely new direction. Trude has so much vitality and seems easily distracted, but perhaps she really is listening to the group interactions. Trude has a lightning-quick mind, but perhaps she thinks so fast she cannot respond immediately. Trude may be an ESFP (Extroverted, Sensing, Feeling, Perceiving). Regardless of which personality types these

classmates really are, Skylar has started to look for opportunities to identify strengths in herself and in others.

Provincial College has a lot of ethnic and cultural diversity. Although Skylar was born in Canada, both her parents are immigrants, each from different countries. Being of mixed heritage, Skylar has found it difficult to fit in with students who have grouped themselves by country of origin. However, when reflecting on communications and personality types, Skylar is objectively weighing her own cultural influences as well as the culture of her learning environment. Being mindful of the variety of communication styles needed to create a successful student team experience is similar to learning how to manage a variety of styles in the workplace. This is a kind of cultural awareness that students require to become successful in a dynamic, global business environment.

Once Skylar has identified a need to build up strengths that do not come naturally to her (like taking the initiative to ask questions in class), she begins to practise this one skill. She slowly builds up the courage to ask one question per class. Then she sets a goal of asking two questions per class. In time, Skylar expands her comfort zone in a way that will help her at school and in the workplace.

Can you do this too? Perhaps O-A-R can guide you:

- **Observe:** In your classroom environment, observe the culture of expectations. The professor (similar to a boss) will often explain the classroom etiquette expectations. These are unique to this classroom culture. You can observe how students interact with each other and how professors get a sense of the students from their interactions.

  Classroom culture varies throughout the world. In China, the professors often conduct lectures with students listening and taking notes. In Canada, students are often expected to interact with the professor and each other, demonstrating critical thinking and understanding. Employers expect new entry-level employees to be able to identify problems and find solutions, to take initiative, and to speak up when they have questions or concerns. These are skills that can be acquired and practised within a Canadian postsecondary learning environment.

- **Ask:** Ask a fellow student if he or she has experience with your professor. Can the other student describe the professor's style and expectations? This interaction may lead to conversations with other students that can, in turn, lead to positive team collaborations later on. Team projects are an important aspect of learning across cultures. Impressions about people based on your perception of their ethnicity does not tell the whole story.

  Similarly, in the workplace you can ask a colleague about his or her experience with a supervisor. Keep in mind that your colleague's perceptions will be influenced

(*continued*)

by his or her own personality and communication style. A supervisor who is seen by one person as "strict" may be seen as "focused" by another.

- **Research:** Review the course outline or syllabus (similar to instructions in a workplace) to see what key behaviours and skills receive marks. Are writing skills, critical thinking skills, or presentation skills rewarded? Are online interaction and discussion important? The emphasis on certain attributes contributes to a class culture.

When in the workplace, examine the areas of emphasis when you identify them. Does your employer value clear and direct communication? Do your work colleagues need lots of details to understand tasks? There is "culture" in every interaction: class culture, your own personal cultures, and team cultures. The more aware you are that you operate within many cultures, the more successful you will be.

For CULTURE exercises, go to Exercise 2 on page 89 and Exercise 21 on page 93.

Engage in reflective practices

Observation, both of yourself and others, is a key element in defining your communication style. The act of observing is only part of the task. You also need to reflect on what you are seeing. One key feature of reflective practice involves exploration through inquiry. Working from the chart in Figure 3.2, it is possible to develop a series of questions to ask yourself as you proceed through your daily opportunities to communicate with others. Some of these questions might include:

- Did I alter my word choices, my tone, or my body language for my audience?
- Did I ask others to offer their opinions? Did I listen after I asked?
- Did I listen actively, or did I "tune out" at times? What makes me "tune out"?
- Did my body language and facial expression match the intent of my message?
- Did I organize and express my ideas clearly?
- Did I ask nonjudgmental questions to clarify my understanding of the information I heard, or did I make assumptions that might not be correct?

To support your own observations, you can employ three additional strategies to enhance your ability to reflect:

- **Audio/video recording.** When you find yourself in a group setting, like a meeting or discussion with others on a project, ask for everyone's permission to record all or part of the session. When you review the recording, watch and listen with this list of questions in mind or questions that you may have developed based on your identified areas of strength and weakness. Consider what you may have been able to do differently if given a second opportunity. Identify areas of positive assertive moments and use them to build your confidence. Remember to erase all casual audio/video recordings once you have completed your review. To look more closely at the ethical implications of recording others, check out the **ETHICS BOX**.
- **Peer feedback.** Ask your peers (friends, other students, colleagues) for specific feedback on what they observe of your communication style based on your list of questions. Ask them to be as honest as possible. You may find some of their feedback difficult to hear at first. However, the insights you gain now may prevent you from making costly errors in the future as you are asked to collaborate on more projects with highly diverse teammates.
- **Instructor feedback.** Ask your instructors, whether for a communications course or any other course, for feedback on your communication style. You will gain valuable insight into how someone with some authority assesses your ability to communicate. Ask specifically if your level of assertiveness seems appropriate to the situations in which the instructor has observed you. Feedback from instructors who have worked in your industry of interest will be of particular value to you.

Learn to adapt: Get out of your comfort zone

The fact is, much of the balance of this chapter offers strategies for you to communicate differently than you may be accustomed to. Ultimately, you are working toward becoming an

⚖ ETHICS
PHOTOGRAPHY AND AUDIO AND VIDEO RECORDINGS: JUST BECAUSE YOU CAN, DOES IT MEAN YOU SHOULD?

Skylar's life is very full. She is constantly looking for ways to optimize her time and energies between her internship placement, her school obligations, and her family responsibilities. Often she wonders if she is really getting all the learning she could be out of her lectures because she is too exhausted to pay close attention.

A few weeks into her current semester, Skylar noticed a student sitting up near the front of her statistics class with a small digital recording device. After class, she asked this student, Bernice, about this practice. Bernice explained that she finds statistics very difficult. She asked the professor's permission to record the lectures and, later in the day, she plays back any sections that she needs to listen to again.

Skylar wondered if this might help her improve her understanding of her lectures. Perhaps this technique would help her study for exams. She asked her father if she could borrow the digital recorder he uses occasionally to record meetings, and he said she could have it for a week.

Like anyone with a new toy, Skylar delighted in recording every important lecture and meeting she attended. She did not want to draw attention to herself or distract the other people in the room, so she tried to keep this activity as low profile as possible. However, a few days into this new routine, Skylar had a rude awakening. She was in her human resources management class when the professor noticed the recording device on the desk in front of Skylar. The professor had been about to introduce a guest speaker but he stopped midsentence and addressed Skylar:

Professor: Excuse me, but is that digital recorder on?

Skylar: Yes, I am using it to record my lectures for study purposes.

Professor (irritated): You need permission from me, and from our guest speaker, and from each professor you record, before you can record audio or capture video of lectures or presentations. Also, all students must be made aware that their contributions during the class are also being recorded. Turn it off immediately.

Skylar was shocked and embarrassed. She fumbled with the recorder to turn it off as quickly as possible. Although she remembered Bernice mentioning that she had gotten permission from her stats professor to record those lectures, Skylar had no idea why her professor would be so upset at being recorded.

Almost everyone has a recording device in their pocket or bag these days. However, just because you *can* record an event or lecture does not mean you have permission to do so. Devices like smartphones and tablets have the ability both to capture images and to distribute recorded media via social networks. This is very different than the world that existed a few short years ago in which the recording and distribution of digital media was a much less common event. The laws that guide the use of such media are still evolving in jurisdictions around the world.

Ethically, it is best to assume that *most people wish to control the use and distribution of any photo or recording of their voice and image*. If you are taking photos for use in a publication, or recording sound for a podcast, or using video to document a meeting, you must do at least three things:

- Make all participants aware that they are being recorded.
- Inform the participants of the purpose and use you will make of the recording.
- Secure permission from each participant, preferably in writing, that they agreed to be recorded for the purpose that you describe.

While this might seem like a difficult and daunting task, remember that O-A-R can guide you:

- **Observe:** If you participate in public events at your college or university, you may notice that most official photographers are diligent about having students sign a waiver or release form for their image to be used in online, electronic, and print publications. Recognize that you may have been asked to provide such permission in the past, and this will help you prepare to have this conversation with your own future photo, audio, and video subjects.
- **Ask:** When in the workplace, ask your employers about their digital use policies for audio, video, and photographic recordings. Most established workplaces will have a waiver or release form on file. If they do not, you can quickly add value to your employer by researching and creating such a form for their use.
- **Research:** Look online, using search terms such as "video release form," "audio release form," or "image release form." Here is some sample text from Industry Canada's website:

[insert date]

I consent to the use of my name, portrait, picture or photograph as part of [insert title of Industry Canada communications product], which is being prepared by Industry Canada. This [publication/CD-ROM/DVD/other, as applicable] is slated for release in [insert month and year].

This [publication/CD-ROM/DVD/other, as applicable] will [insert brief description, e.g., "outline how the Department intends to meet its business priorities in the coming fiscal year"]. It will serve the following purpose(s): to [insert purpose(s) of the communications product, e.g., "engage employees and inform stakeholders"].

(continued)

I understand that this [publication/CD-ROM/DVD/other, as applicable] will be made available [online at [insert URL]/in print format/other, as applicable].

I agree that I shall have no claim against Industry Canada or against anyone accessing this communications product, whether online, in print or by any other means.

I confirm that I am over 19 years of age and that I have not given anyone the exclusive right to use my name, portrait, picture or photograph.

Signed,

_____

Name (print in block letters): _____

Date: _____

Sample Release or Waiver Form for Photography

Source: Industry Canada. (2013, June 6). Publishing toolbox: Sample release or waiver forms for photography. Page: E647-00492. Retrieved from www.ic.gc.ca/eic/site/pt-te.nsf/eng/00492.html

Viewing multiple release forms like this one will help you develop your own for yourself or your employer. Work with your employer's legal department to ensure your wording is effective and meets both legal and ethical obligations.

Professors usually find it flattering when students ask for permission to record lectures and, furthermore, may regard such students as behaving in a courteous and professional manner. Skylar learned from her oversight and sent an email to all her professors, asking their permission to use her recording device in their classes. Once they all understood, each one gave permission. Some asked that the lectures be erased immediately after the semester, and Skylar provided this agreement in a return email.

In the workplace, with the use of audio and video media becoming commonplace, it is critical that you protect yourself and your employer from ethical and legal entanglements. Make sure that you always have permission to take and use such recordings.

For an ETHICS exercise, go to Exercise 22 on page 93.

open, flexible, and asssertive communicator with *many possible variants* of your preferred communication style available to you at any given time, as noted in **FIGURE 3.3**. The better you are at adapting your style, the more valuable you will be as a collaborative co-worker.

Chapters 4, 5, and 6 will expand on these ideas further. Chapter 4 will help you explore the issues related to diversity and intercultural communications and their

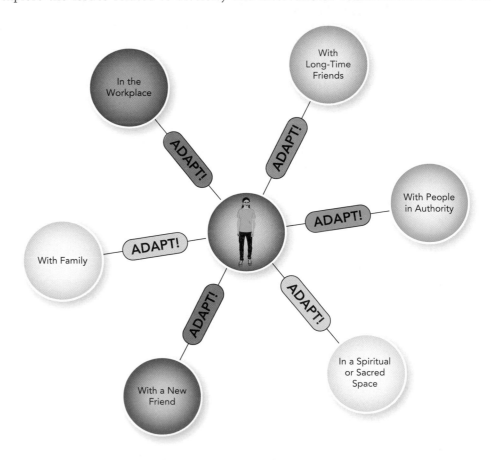

FIGURE 3.3 Conscious Adaptation of Communication Style: A New Toolkit

impact on communications style. Chapter 5 will help you learn to optimize a variety of technologies to create virtual collaboration space. Chapter 6 will synthesize all the related topics into a single chapter that reviews the communication best practices of successful teams.

The introduction to this chapter referred to concerns that employers have about the social and face-to-face skills of new employees. Check out the **TECHNOLOGY BOX** for some ideas on why this might be a concern and what you can do about it.

Hard skills Specific, "teachable" abilities that are usually measurable. Professional knowledge, tools, and techniques, such as driving skills, words per minute on a keyboard, accounting, math, or computer programming are examples.

Soft skills Skills that usually relate to one's ability to interact productively with others. Interpersonal skills, social skills, etiquette, and communication are examples.

TECHNOLOGY
HAS FACEBOOK MADE YOU FUMBLE? BEWARE THE IMPACT OF SOCIAL/MOBILE TECHNOLOGIES ON FACE-TO-FACE BUSINESS ETIQUETTE

Face-to-face interactions are often referred to as the "richest" form of communication. Many verbal and nonverbal signals are sent and received: Tone of voice, posture, gestures, facial expressions, and verbal content are all sent simultaneously. In contrast, communicaton that features any kind of technological intermediation is less "rich." Technology, be it telephone or texting or tweeting, removes much of the subtle but vital information we receive in face-to-face conversations. Therefore, people newly entering the workforce tend to have developed strengths in technologically mediated conversations but are lacking practice with face-to-face interactions.

McKenna Grant, editor of the college section of *USA Today*, recounts the story of a recent college graduate who took 17 interviews to land a job. This happened "not because he lacked the job skills required, but because he lacked the conversational skills required to navigate the job interview" (Grant, 2014). Dr. Susan Davis-Ali, founder of Leadhership1, suggests that "with verbal communication taking a back seat to non-verbal or limited-verbal forms of social media, many Millennials are literally losing their voices to texts, tweets and vines" (Grant, 2014).

College and university students focus naturally on acquiring valuable **hard skills**, from biomedical research to customer service to business management to construction engineering. While many believe that hard skills are of primary concern to employers, **soft skills** actually matter just as much if not more. Vital soft skill areas include the following:

- Clear and articulate oral communication
- Social skills and business etiquette to navigate both formal and informal business situations
- An ability to engage and motivate others
- Negotiation skills
- An ability to collaborate effectively and graciously

These soft skills are developed with practice, attention, and training in the face-to-face world. How can you develop these skills if your primary mode of communication involves a smartphone and a social media app? Here are some suggestions for your next casual social time with friends:

- **Stay present.** If you like using social media check-ins, do so before or after the event rather than during. Similarly, wait until after the event to post photos. By waiting, you can keep your focus on making memories you can share and discuss later.
- **Make it fun.** Turn the urge to check phones into a game. When you are out with friends, put all the phones in the middle of the table. The first one to reach for their phone has to pay a forfeit. Or the last one to pick up their phone gets their meal or refreshments paid for by the others who did use their phones. By making your friends self-aware of their phone focus, you will be helping them develop better social skills, too.
- **Conversation games.** There is a long oral tradition of storytelling and conversational game playing in many cultures. Generations of people learned to build social relationships while having fun with such games. When not looking at your phone, you could be playing one of the following games:
  - **Two Truths and a Lie:** Taking turns, each person in a conversation offers three pieces of information about themselves. They offer two true statements and one lie, without identifying which is which. The other conversationalists try to guess which information is true and which is not.
  - **Twenty Questions (Updated):** In the traditional game of Twenty Questions, one person thinks of an object and the other players ask questions that can be answered with a "yes" or "no." (These are called closed questions.) Traditionally, the first three questions are "Are you thinking of an animal? A vegetable? A mineral?" An updated version of this game restricts the potential object to technology, allowing the first few questions to be "Are you thinking of a device? An app? A game? Social media?"
  - **Call My Bluff:** Using a dictionary app on a phone (only for a moment), one player finds an unusual or obscure word. He or she shares the word and a definition of the word with the group. The player can choose to read the real definition or can make up a

(continued)

completely false definition. The other players have to guess whether the word definition is true or false. For every guess that is incorrect, the original player gets a point. This game has the additional bonus of expanding the vocabulary of all the players.

- **Free phone time.** When you gather with your friends, one person sets a timer for 55 minutes. Once this is done, everyone puts their phone aside and agrees not to check it. When the timer alarm goes off, you declare "free phone time" for five minutes, giving everyone in the group a few minutes to check their messages and social media. After phone time is over, another person sets their timer for 55 minutes and the process repeats.

While these exercises might seem unusual, the soft skills you need to master cannot be taught in a single course

or program. These skills are developed through the regular and mindful practice of social interaction. Beyond finding success in job interviews, solid working relationships are built on trust that is forged through face-to-face interaction. Even teams of virtual workers that are spread over a wide geographic range are encouraged to meet regularly face to face to develop working relationships (Reiche, 2013). To integrate into collaborative and healthy workplaces, and to achieve the successful career you are planning for yourself, you must devote energy to developing confidence in face-to-face interactions.

For a TECHNOLOGY exercise, go to Exercises 4 and 5 on page 90.

What listening skills will help you communicate better with others?

Every day, without thinking about it, you engage in an important communication skill: listening. In fact, research shows that college students spend more than half their communication time listening (Emanuel et al., 2008; Janusick & Wolvin, 2009). In the workplace, listening is widely considered to be one of the most important communication skills (Flynn, Valikoski, & Grau, 2008). Research suggests that, in a typical business day, regardless of profession, you will spend 45% of your time listening and 30% of your time talking. Yet 2% or less of business professionals have received any formal training in this essential communications skill (Llopis, 2013).

Decades of research show that listening is a complex process. Without strong, focused listening skills, people often mishear, misinterpret, and misunderstand (Wolvin, 2010). One common listening problem is **passive listening**. In business, passive listening leads to costly mistakes, unhappy employees, and customer complaints. Here are some examples:

- An employee does not pay attention to a customer reciting a mailing address and then sends a shipment of 1,000 computers to St. John's, Newfoundland, rather than St. John, New Brunswick. The shipping and return charges are extremely high, and the customer is angry because the computers haven't arrived.

- A manager does not listen carefully or ask follow-up questions when an employee says she is sick and needs to go home. The manager insists that the employee stay, which exposes the entire office to a contagious flu virus.

- The customer service team does not listen to or document customer complaints. This results in negative product and service reviews spread throughout many social networks that, in turn, result in a decrease in new customer acquisition.

As with any important skill, you cannot become a better listener without focus, practice, and attention. With study and training, you can become an active listener and significantly improve your communication skills. ~~Active listening~~ is the process of focusing *attentively* on what a speaker says, actively working to understand and interpret the content, and then responding to acknowledge understanding.

Passive listening Hearing the words being spoken without actively paying attention to their meaning.

Active listening A process of focusing attentively on what a speaker says, actively working to understand and interpret the content and then responding to acknowledge understanding.

In the study of language acquisition, whether first or subsequent languages, it is now understood that developing strong listening skills is a key component to developing full language proficiency (Bozorgian, 2012). Therefore, if you are someone who is working on improving your skills in English, time and attention to developing your ability to listen "in English" is a worthwhile investment of your time and energy.

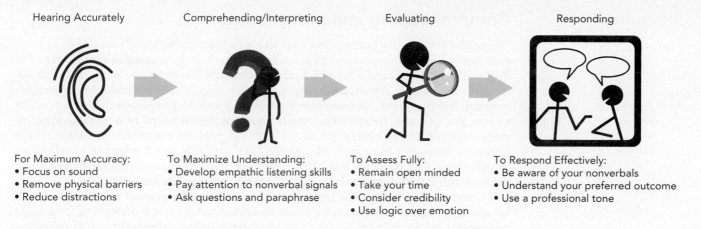

Hearing Accurately	Comprehending/Interpreting	Evaluating	Responding

For Maximum Accuracy:
- Focus on sound
- Remove physical barriers
- Reduce distractions

To Maximize Understanding:
- Develop empathic listening skills
- Pay attention to nonverbal signals
- Ask questions and paraphrase

To Assess Fully:
- Remain open minded
- Take your time
- Consider credibility
- Use logic over emotion

To Respond Effectively:
- Be aware of your nonverbals
- Understand your preferred outcome
- Use a professional tone

FIGURE 3.4 The Active Listening Process

These same skills are equally useful when you "listen" to written messages. Understanding the meaning of an email message, tweet, or social media posting can be as difficult as understanding the meaning of a conversation. As discussed in Chapter 2, tone in written messages is often present and needs to be considered when determining meaning. However, "listening" to tone in a written medium can be especially challenging for individuals who are in the process of becoming proficient in English. This skill takes practice and attention.

This section will help you develop four categories of active listening skills (Brownell, 2010):

- Hearing accurately
- Comprehending and interpreting
- Evaluating
- Responding

Check out the process diagram in **FIGURE 3.4**.

Hearing accurately

Listening typically starts with hearing: perceiving sounds and focusing on them. Sound is all around us. Therefore, listening requires that you first distinguish the sounds you need and want to listen to and concentrate on fully hearing those sounds.

Some barriers to hearing are physical. For example, you might have a temporary hearing problem, such as blocked ears from a head cold. Another significant physical barrier to hearing is the speed at which your brain can process what you hear. Dr. Pamela Cooper, vice-president of the International Listening Association, notes that effective listening "is just hard work. It takes a lot of energy to listen because we can process 400 words a minute in our brain but we speak at 125 words per minute. There are some time lags as we wait and we have a tendency to wander off. You really have to work hard . . . to stay interested and motivated to listen" (Cooper, 2013). This leads to a related barrier to listening: multitasking. As discussed in Chapter 2, if you choose to multitask while listening, your brain becomes engaged in a different task and you will not accurately hear what the speaker says.

The environment around you may also distract you from hearing well. Think about the last time you tried to have a conversation in a noisy restaurant or talk on your cellphone while standing at a busy intersection. You probably found it difficult to concentrate on what the other person was saying. At work, you may be distracted by ringing telephones, people passing by your desk, or noise from the next cubicle.

The key to hearing accurately is singular focus. Look at the speaker and concentrate on what he or she says. Make a comment or ask a question to keep yourself engaged. A benefit of this approach is that you earn the respect of the speaker by being attentive.

Comprehending and interpreting

You might very clearly hear someone speaking in Portuguese, Dutch, or Hindi, but you may not be able to comprehend all those languages. Listening **comprehension** refers to how well you understand what you hear. In culturally diverse workplaces, language differences can become significant barriers, but they are not the only obstacles to comprehension. You may have difficulty comprehending vocabulary or jargon that is unfamiliar to you. For example, imagine that you accompany a sick friend to a medical appointment. You hear the physician tell an assistant "The patient presented with acute febrile illness." Unless you have medical training, you probably won't comprehend that this means your friend suddenly had a high fever. You may also have difficulty comprehending something that is explained poorly, is confusing, or seems contradictory.

Interpretation is different from comprehension. **Interpretation** involves analyzing the content of what you hear, read, or see to determine its intended meaning. You might misunderstand a comment because you interpret it from a different frame of reference. For example, imagine you work in your company's Vancouver office and your colleague is meeting with clients in Montreal. Late in the evening, you receive an email from your colleague saying he needs information for a client meeting and he needs you to email it to him first thing in the morning. You could interpret that statement in two different ways. Does he want the information by 9 a.m. in Montreal (Eastern time), or by 9 a.m. in Vancouver (Pacific time)? If you interpret the statement from your frame of reference (Pacific time), you may be sending the summary too late (noon Eastern time).

Understanding what someone really means requires being empathetic and paying attention to the emotional content of messages, whether they are spoken or written. Being an empathetic listener does not come naturally to everyone. Both research and experience show that there is a wide range of individual differences (Brody & Hall, 2008; Spahn & Purses, 2012). Some people tend to pay attention to the literal content of communication. Others are skilled at focusing on the emotional content.

Consider this scenario: Kurt rushes late into a meeting with Sanjay and Erica. Sanjay asks Kurt if everything is okay. Kurt looks distracted and tense but says, "I'm okay." After Kurt leaves the meeting room, Erica comments that Kurt seemed very upset when he arrived. Sanjay responds, "There's no problem. He said he's okay." Sanjay focused on the content of the words, and Erica focused on the emotional meaning and the nonverbal signals she perceived.

Even if you are not naturally empathetic, you can train yourself to comprehend and interpret more effectively by "listening" to nonverbal communication and by verifying your understanding through questions and by paraphrasing.

"Listen" to nonverbal communication

Nonverbal communication refers to messages that are conveyed through something other than words. For example, tone of voice, facial expressions, gestures, body language, and other behaviours all contribute to creating the meaning of a person's spoken message. Consider how all these forms of nonverbal communication can help you better understand and interpret someone's meaning:

- **Emphasis and tone of voice.** Words carry different meanings depending on how they are said. Imagine someone speaking the simple phrase "I called him." Say that phrase three times, each time emphasizing a different word:
  - *I* called him.
  - I *called* him.
  - I called *him*.

    What three different meanings do those three statements convey? Now imagine saying those three words in an angry tone of voice and a happy tone of voice. Each time, you will be conveying a different meaning. You will benefit from paying close attention to tone of voice and letting it influence your interpretation of what you hear.
- **Facial expressions.** If someone says "hello" with a smile, you will interpret a very different meaning than if someone says "hello" with lowered eyebrows and a clenched jaw. While experts may disagree about whether facial expression is an unconscious reflection of emotion or a conscious technique that people use to

Comprehension Understanding what you hear or read.

Interpretation Analyzing the meaning of what you hear, read, or see to determine its intention.

Nonverbal communication Messages conveyed through means other than words, for example, tone of voice, facial expressions, gestures, and body language.

Surprise

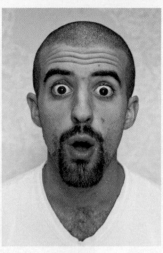
Shock

FIGURE 3.5 Surprise versus Shock
Source: William Perugini/Shutterstock.

convey meaning, most people agree that facial expression is an important element of communication (Ekman, 2007). Beware, though, of assuming that all people interpret facial expressions in the same way. In fact, research suggests that people from East Asia (e.g., China, Japan, and Korea) focus mainly on the eyes when they are reading facial expressions. By contrast, people from the West (e.g., Canada, Germany, and Mexico) focus on the entire face, including both the eyes and the mouth (Jack, Blais, Scheepers, Schyns, & Caldera, 2009).

As a result of this difference in perception, people from East Asia sometimes confuse surprise, shock, fear, and anger because these emotions are difficult to extract from the eyes alone. As shown in **FIGURE 3.5**, key differences in these emotions are reflected by the mouth.

The East Asian focus on the eyes is also reflected in their **emoticons**. As shown in **FIGURE 3.6**, in Western emoticons the face is represented on its side, and differences of emotion are represented by the mouth. In East Asian emoticons, the face is right-side up, and differences in emotion are expressed by the eyes.

EMOTION	WEST	EAST
Surprise	:-0	o.o
Sad	:-(	(;_;)

FIGURE 3.6 How Emoticons Differ between Eastern and Western Cultures

- **Body language, posture, and gestures.** You can uncover clues about a person's attitude toward what he or she is saying by observing body language. Is that person ashamed, proud, or uncertain? The speaker's posture, even their eye contact or lack of it, can help you interpret their attitude. In fact, you can often interpret attitude from body language without listening to any words.

Remember, though, that body language and gestures may be ambiguous. As **FIGURE 3.7** illustrates, you need to interpret gestures in the context of facial expressions. Both photos illustrate people leaning forward in a conversation. In the photo on the left, leaning forward with a smiling face communicates openness. On the right, leaning forward with a pointed finger and raised eyebrows communicates hostility and tension.

In addition, gestures must be interpreted within the context of culture. In Japan, it is a sign of respect to avoid eye contact and look down when an older or more powerful person is talking to you. In the United States, looking away when someone is talking is often interpreted as a sign of disrespect or guilt. Before reaching a conclusion about what nonverbal communication means, consider alternative meanings.

Ask questions and paraphrase to ensure understanding

In addition to "listening" to nonverbal behaviour, you can improve comprehension and understanding by asking questions and paraphrasing. Questions can be very straightforward. You can ask someone to repeat what he or she is saying, or you can offer two alternative meanings and ask which is correct. For example, you could ask your colleague, "By 'first thing in the morning,' do you mean Montreal time or Vancouver time?"

Paraphrasing is a little more complicated than asking for clarification. Paraphrasing involves restating what you hear in different words to ensure that you completely

Emoticons The series of characters used to represent facial expressions in emails and texts.

Paraphrasing Restating someone else's message in different words.

FIGURE 3.7 Nonverbal Signals Have Multiple Meanings

Blend Images/Shutterstock

HYPESTOCK/Shutterstock

GESTURE	DOES IT MEAN THIS?	OR THIS?
Leaning forward	Openness	Hostility
Eye contact	Friendliness	Anger
Lack of eye contact	Shyness, Respect	Guilt, Disrespect
Wrinkled forehead	Concentration	Anger, Frustration
Straight posture	Self-confidence	Rigidity

understand. Meaning has multiple dimensions. You might paraphrase in multiple ways to capture those dimensions. As **FIGURE 3.8** illustrates, you can paraphrase to ensure you understand the literal content, the ultimate intention, and the emotional content behind the speaker's statement.

Comment from the supervisor:
"I'd like all employees to take at least half of their vacation days by November 1."

CONTENT

Restate the message in different words to ensure you understand it.

"So you are saying that you want us to use our vacation days before the end of the year."

INTENT

Dig beneath the content to understand the reason for the statement.

"Are you concerned that too many people will want to take vacations in December?"

"Are you concerned that people are working too hard and need a break?"

FEELING

Confirm your understanding of the speaker's emotions.

"You sound frustrated that people seem to be saving their vacation time and burning out on the job."

FIGURE 3.8 Paraphrasing for Content, Intent, and Feeling

Evaluating

Once you fully understand what someone says, you **evaluate**. When you evaluate, you ask questions such as the following:

- Is this information accurate?
- Is it supported with credible evidence?
- Am I convinced? Why or why not?

As a listener, you may find it difficult to reach a fair evaluation of what you hear. There are many things that can impair your ability to evaluate fairly. A few of these impairments are listed here:

1. **Prejudgment of the speaker.** You may prejudge a speaker, especially if you find that speaker to be annoying or distracting. If you have had previous negative experiences with the speaker, you may give them a negative "**halo effect.**" This will mean that you are not listening to the content of the message as much as you are reacting emotionally, and negatively, to the messenger. You can miss valuable information and opportunities when you prejudge a speaker.

2. **Prejudgment of an idea.** You may prejudge an idea, especially if it is an idea you have already considered and dismissed. If you do not listen carefully to a speaker's rationale or explanation, you lose the opportunity to reconsider your previous evaluation.

3. **Jumping to conclusions.** You may jump to conclusions based on the beginning of a message and interrupt the speaker or tune out while you wait your turn to speak.

Making effective business decisions depends on your ability to clearly and objectively evaluate what you hear and read. For example, imagine that you own a children's clothing store. In a meeting with your employees, the assistant manager suggests that you open another store in an up-and-coming neighbourhood on the west side of the city. As evidence, she points to the growing population in the neighbourhood and the fact that the three new stores that opened in that neighbourhood appear to be doing very well.

Evaluating that proposal fairly requires that you remain open minded. Even if you live far away from the west side of the city and would prefer a closer location, you need to consider the business arguments. Evaluating fairly also requires that you critically analyze what you hear. Where has the assistant manager acquired the information about the success of other stores? Is that information source credible, or is this simply her opinion? Does the success of other new stores necessarily mean that a children's clothing store will succeed? To evaluate this, you will need data on how many children live in the area and what competition exists.

Clearly, evaluating what you hear can take a significant investment of time, energy, and focus. However, the cost of not taking appropriate time to evaluate can be measured in additional time correcting mistakes.

Responding

Responding has two roles in the listening process:

- You let the speaker know that you understand his or her points
- You initiate the next step in the conversation.

Some responses are designed to quickly stop any further exchange. Others will move the discussion forward. For example, a response such as "That's a ridiculous idea" may discourage further input, whereas you could encourage a speaker with a more tactful response: "That's interesting. How would that work?"

Responses can be verbal and nonverbal. You should assume that nonverbal messages communicate more powerfully than the verbal ones. To become a more effective responder, pay attention to the type of response you offer.

As **FIGURE 3.9** illustrates, you can respond to a speaker in many different ways. For example, you can ask a question, give your opinion or advice, disagree, or express empathy.

Evaluating The practice of critically reviewing and judging communication.

Halo effect A type of unconscious bias when receiving information in which a past impression of the speaker (or writer) influences the perception of his or her message. For example, if you like and respect a person, you will unconsciously perceive his or her messages in a positive light. On the other hand, if you dislike a person, you will perceive his or her messages in a negative light.

FIGURE 3.9 Five Ways to Respond

SPEAKER: *"The auditors are coming tomorrow to look at our books. We're not ready. I don't know what to do."*

YOUR RESPONSE OPTIONS	
Ask a Question	What do we need to do to get ready? How long do you think it will take?
Give an Opinion	I think if you have most of the documents they will need tomorrow, they can get a good start.
Give Advice	Let's try to reschedule the audit until next week.
Argue/Disagree	Actually, I think we are ready. We have completed everything on the checklist.
Express Empathy	It's nerve-wracking to get everything ready for a major audit. You're doing fine, and I'll be glad to help.

Hearing, comprehending and interpreting, evaluating, and responding are the key components of active listening. Developing these skills will help you better understand the meaning of the messages you receive. In addition, being an effective listener offers another important business benefit: The better you are at listening, the more carefully others will listen to you. As one organizational leader explains, "if people feel they were listened to, that their views were taken into account, that they had a chance to show you the world from their point of view, they're going to be much more likely to go along with a decision" (Hargie, 2011).

(LO 3.3) What speaking strategies will encourage others to listen to you and understand what you are saying?

Listeners and speakers are partners in the communication process. Just as listeners need to work hard to understand meaning, speakers need to work hard to engage listeners and make meaning clear. This section provides seven speaking strategies that you can use to communicate productively:

- Focus on your audience
- Share the conversation
- Use clear, concrete, unambiguous language
- Support your message with appropriate nonverbal communication
- Avoid upward inflection
- Avoid language that triggers a negative response
- Be aware of gender-specific communication styles

Focus on your audience

Many speakers fail to connect with the audience's interests or knowledge about a topic. Before speaking, take time to analyze your audience by considering the following questions:

- Why will they be interested in what you are saying?
- What barriers will prevent them from listening carefully?
- What questions or objections may they have?
- What is the best way to connect with them?

Imagine, for example, that you want to ask a co-worker to help you with a project, and you approach this person while he is concentrating on his own work. At the beginning of this conversation, he knows nothing about your project. He is focusing on something else, not on you. This may prevent him from listening carefully. Therefore, your immediate objective is to gain your audience's attention and focus in a polite and positive way that will lead to further discussion.

To achieve this, do not begin the conversation by describing the project in detail and then finally asking for help. Your co-worker needs to understand, quickly, why you have chosen to interrupt his work to speak to him.

Share the conversation

Have you ever noticed how some speakers are able to continue talking for a long time and will resist all attempts of other people to share the conversation? A one-sided conversation is really a **monologue**. A respectful interpersonal communicator will avoid monologues and instead share the conversation with others. When you have finished making your point clearly and concisely, invite your audience to respond or add to the conversation. You can do this by asking a question designed to move the conversation forward. It can be as simple as "What do you think?" Or it can be more situation specific, for example: "Has anyone else tried this approach in the past?"

Use clear, unambiguous language

Make your language as clear as possible. For example, imagine someone tells you, "Deliver the package next door." If you have offices on either side of you, it is **ambiguous** which office should get the package. You have a 50/50 chance of making a mistake. Similarly, if your supervisor says, "This project is your responsibility," you may assume "your responsibility" means that you have to do the project by yourself. However, your supervisor may mean that you are in charge of the project and need to assemble a team to get the work done. A more **unambiguous** way of expressing this would be to say, "It is your responsibility to assemble the team and the resources to deliver this project on time."

Pronouns, if not used precisely, can be ambiguous. Consider the word "they" in this statement: "I called the purchasing managers about the new vendors we want to use. They are too busy to meet with us for a few weeks." Who is too busy: the purchasing managers or the vendors? Although it is more effective to avoid ambiguous language in the first place, active listeners know to ask questions to clarify the meaning when they are unsure what the speaker meant.

Support your message with appropriate nonverbal communication

Many studies on the role of nonverbal communication have found that a speaker's body language, facial expressions, gestures, and tone of voice carry more weight than the speaker's words (Pentland, 2008). As a speaker, you can use nonverbal communication in two ways to enhance your communication:

- **Use body language and eye contact to engage your audience.** This means facing your audience and maintaining eye contact with them as you speak, keeping your facial expressions positive, and keeping your posture relaxed rather than stiff or clenched. You may also find it effective to mirror the body language of your audience. Research has shown that job candidates who demonstrate confidence and mirror the interviewer's gestures are more likely to get a positive response (Knapp & Hall, 2009).

- **Use gestures and facial expressions that complement your message.** In a conversation, your nonverbal communication can either conflict with a message or complement it. For example, if you say you are confident, but you fidget or frown while you speak, your audience will not have confidence in your words. By contrast, if you smile and use effective gestures, your audience will better sense your confidence. In addition, listeners remember what you say better when nonverbal signals reinforce your words.

Monologue A lengthy speech delivered by one person.

Ambiguous Having many possible interpretations or meanings.

Unambiguous Having only one clear interpretation or meaning.

Avoid upward inflection

English speakers are accustomed to hearing an **upward inflection** at the end of a sentence that is structured as a question. Imagine the question "Could you pass the salt, please?" As you thought of that question, you may have added a rising tone to the end of the sentence as the natural ending for a question.

Unfortunately, many people have adopted this speech pattern as a natural way of speaking, regardless of whether or not a question is being asked. This has also been referred to as "uptalk" or "upspeak." "Uptalk is the inability to utter a declarative sentence without curling up your voice at the end to signify a question," says Professor Hank Davis, faculty member in the Department of Psychology at the University of Guelph. "When I tell my students about this vocal habit, they often react as if they are hearing about it for the first time. Within days, they tell me: 'I see what you mean. I can't believe how much my friends and I do it'" (Davis, 2013).

People who adopt an upward inflection on their statements tend to sound immature, young, and insecure. Using uptalk will remove all sense of conviction and authority from your words.

It is possible to remove this pattern from your speech in the following two steps:

1. **Learn to recognize the pattern.** The first step in eliminating upward inflection from your speech is simply to recognize it. If you listen carefully to your intonation when you make statements, you will likely hear upward inflection more often than you expect. Another strategy is to video record yourself when you are speaking conversationally in a relaxed, casual setting. When you view the recording, close your eyes so you are not critiquing the visuals. Simply listen to the speech patterns. If you or your conversation partners are ending most of your sentences with an upward, rising intonation, then you have some work to do to sound more confident and authoritative.

2. **Become comfortable with a downward inflection.** If you remove the upward inflection, you need to replace it with a downward inflection. This takes some practice. A downward inflection does not mean a reduction in volume or pitch. It means ending your sentences in a declarative, confident manner. Carol Kauffman, director of the Institute of Coaching at the Harvard Medical School, in her video "Set the Tone for Trust" (Kauffman, 2014) demonstrates downward inflection in nearly every phrase of her three-minute discussion of tone. She describes the process as "creating **gravitas**," which is a dignified style of speaking that encourages the listener to take in what you have to say without being distracted.

Stephen Lewis, a Canadian politician, diplomat, and the former UN Special Envoy for HIV/AIDS in Africa, offers some excellent examples of the use of a downward inflection. When he speaks publicly, most phrases end in a downward or neutral inflection. Check out Lewis's 2010 inspirational and humorous speech on literacy called "Reading for the Love of It" (S. Lewis, 2010), and his 2013 television interview with Steve Paikin of TVO's public affairs show *The Agenda* (S. Lewis, 2013). He has trained himself to speak with authority and conviction. Part of that "sound of authority" includes a downward inflection at the end of most phrases.

One of the best examples of the constant use of downward inflection comes to us from someone south of the border: President Barack Obama. Samples include his inspirational speech to young entrepreneurs, published by Corporate Valley (Corporate Valley, 2013), and his 2013 Thanksgiving message, published by the *Wall Street Journal* (2013). After watching a few clips of President Obama's speeches, it may be difficult to imagine him ever using an upward inflection to ask a question. If you are determined to learn a downward inflection, you need to be comfortable ending all your statements with a lowered intonation.

Upward inflection A rising intonational speech pattern on the final syllables of a sentence, often indicating a question.

Gravitas An attitude of dignity, seriousness, and gravity.

Avoid language that triggers a negative response

Just as your choice of language can encourage listeners to pay careful attention, it can also evoke negative emotional responses. If you make your audience defensive or angry, they may refuse to pay attention to your ideas. The following four specific types of language can cause communication problems and negative feelings: biased language, provocative questions, accusatory language, and trigger words.

Biased language

Biased language suggests prejudice, prejudgment, or disrespect. When you use this kind of language, two things can happen. First, it can shut down the conversation. If you turn to a co-worker at a meeting and say, "Kevin, as our resident geek, tell us your opinion on whether we should upgrade our computer operating system," Kevin may not be open and honest about his ideas because you've labelled him as a "geek." Unbiased language would be, "Kevin, you're familiar with the pros and cons of the new operating system upgrade. Do you think we should implement it now or wait?"

Biased language can also encourage others to prejudge ideas without even hearing them through. Imagine introducing an addition to a meeting agenda in this way: "Clive wants a few minutes in the meeting to regale us with his latest and greatest idea." The word "regale," combined with "latest and greatest," suggests a sarcastic or mocking tone. This language diminishes Clive's idea, and it prejudices others against taking the idea seriously. Unbiased language is more respectful: "Clive has an idea he'd like to discuss."

Provocative questions

Typically, questions are a positive part of the communication process. Questions help you share information, uncover opinions, and confirm understanding. These genuine requests for information and opinion are *authentic questions*. In contrast to authentic questions, *provocative questions* are designed to annoy and inflame. For example, assume that after three days of work your information technology (IT) support professional says to you, "We've finally solved the problem with the online database." An authentic question would be, "What was the problem?" or "How did you figure it out?" By contrast, a provocative question might be "We have three days of bad data now. Why didn't you find the solution earlier?" This question is not designed to aid understanding or help the questioner learn anything useful. An exchange like this will only lead the IT professional to be defensive and negative.

Accusatory language

The provocative question "Why didn't you find the solution earlier?" is also an example of *accusatory language*. It focuses negative attention on the person ("you") rather than on the issue. **FIGURE 3.10** provides additional examples of accusatory language along with alternative phrasings. Notice that some of the alternative phrasings use what interpersonal communication experts call *"I" language*. "I" language focuses on how you respond to or feel about the other person's behaviour and focuses on your perception rather than assigning blame. This positive language, as contrasted with accusatory language, encourages people to listen to your point of view and respond.

Remember, however, that "I" is not always the best choice and that "you" is not always accusatory. If every sentence begins with "I," your audience will think you are egotistical. Conversely, many sentences that include "you" can be very positive, especially when you focus on audience benefits or offer a compliment (e.g., "You did a great job on that project.") (Bippus & Young, 2005).

INEFFECTIVE: ACCUSATORY LANGUAGE	EFFECTIVE: ALTERNATIVE PHRASINGS
We now have three days of bad data. Why didn't you solve the problem earlier?	I'm concerned that we won't have time to eliminate the bad data from our results.
Your instructions are confusing.	I got lost on step three of the instructions. Could you please explain further?
Your interpretation of this rule is wrong.	I understood the rule differently.
This is the third time this month you've been late.	I'm uncomfortable making excuses when people call for you. That's why I hope you can arrive on time.

FIGURE 3.10 Accusatory Language and Alternative Phrasings

Trigger words

Biased language, provocative questions, and accusatory language may trigger negative emotional responses (Schroth, Bain-Chekal, & Caldwell, 2005). Similarly, certain words or phrases may also trigger negative emotional responses. For example, some people get upset when they hear *absolutes*, words like "always" and "never," that are likely to be exaggerations: "You never get to work on time." "You always forget your keys." "No one ever answers the phone in this office." These absolute words, often combined with an accusatory "you," can create obstacles to effective communication. People will feel dismissed when they hear a phrase like "It's none of your business" or "That doesn't concern you." Although you cannot anticipate all the trigger words that might upset people, pay attention to emotional responses and avoid triggers when you recognize them.

Be aware of gender-specific communication styles

Men and women are often socialized to behave differently from each other and thus may develop different gender-related styles of communication (McHugh & Hambaugh, 2010). Neither style is better than the other. However, communication can break down if people are intolerant of other speaking styles or draw incorrect judgments about a speaker based on his or her style.

As sociolinguist Deborah Tannen points out, men are often socialized to value autonomy and independence, and therefore learn to communicate in ways that assert independence, power, and their place in the social hierarchy (Tannen, 1991). For example, in conversations, men tend to interrupt more than women do. In contrast to men, women are often socialized to value connections with other people and to communicate in ways that preserve equity and relationships (Wood, 2013). Thus, women tend to wait their turn to speak as an act of respect for the speaker. In addition, women more often minimize the assertiveness of what they say by using what linguists call *hedges*, *hesitations*, and *tag questions* (Palomares, 2009):

Hedge: I don't know if this is a good idea, but we could get an editor for our presentation slides.

Hesitation: Um, well, we could, uh, we could get an editor for our presentation slides.

Tag Question: We can get an editor, can't we?

FIGURE 3.11 Apply ACE to Support Interpersonal Communication Skills

Gender-specific characteristics may have negative results in conversation. Interruptions can easily lead to a communication breakdown, especially when men interrupt women. Men are often very comfortable with interruptions and interrupt right back, whereas women are more likely to get angry or feel silenced. Tag questions, hesitations, and hedges also cause problems. They lead some listeners to conclude that the speaker lacks confidence and thus does not deserve to be taken seriously (Blankenship & Holtgraves, 2005). However, by recognizing gendered characteristics of your own and others' language, you can avoid drawing incorrect conclusions about others and instead pay more attention to their ideas.

Apply ACE to support interpersonal communication skills

FIGURE 3.11 provides some ideas for applying ACE to the development of your interpersonal communication skills.

In summary, ACE can be applied to any communication challenge you face. In particular, taking the time to truly analyze yourself, your situation, and your audience will help you prepare properly for more professional messaging.

The interpersonal skills you learned in this chapter support your self-knowledge while expanding your listening and speaking skills. Chapters 4, 5, and 6 will continue to build on these foundational skills as you explore intercultural communications, diversity, and the role of communication in developing and supporting collaborative workplaces.

Liz Clarke
College Professor and
Communications
Consultant

@ **WORK**

Courtesy of Elizabeth Clarke and Brandon Barre.

This chapter opened with Liz Clarke and her team, who were struggling to communicate clearly and productively together. How did they find a way to resolve their communications issues?

Although we did not understand this explicitly at the time, we actually used ACE to work through these issues.

- **Analyze.** What we needed was an opportunity to step back and look at how we were communicating. We called a meeting in which we discussed our various communications issues. At this meeting, we discussed openly our discomfort with certain styles and our interpretations of each other's comments. I was saddened to learn that I had hurt Rajiv with some of my remarks. I know that Samuel was shocked to find out that we viewed him as hostile. As we began to understand that our communication styles were not received as we intended them to be, we each began to soften our words. As a natural outcome of this first discussion, we started to listen to each other with less judgment and defensiveness.

  Then, Rudy, Samuel, and I attended a workshop on the Myers-Briggs Type Indicator (MBTI, discussed on page 69). An MBTI mapping analysis of our team showed us that four members were clustered around strengths in appreciating detail, subtlety, and introspection. These were Rudy, Samuel, Rajiv, and Joseph. The fifth member, me, showed strengths in "big picture" planning, pattern recognition, and energetic interpersonal interaction. In other words, as I tried to communicate my planning and perspective to my colleagues, they were almost literally unable to understand what I was saying.

  I cannot overstate the impact this three-hour workshop had on our ability to understand why our team of successful, smart people had wandered so precariously into dysfunction. This analysis taught us two valuable lessons:

  - Everyone has their own style of communication and personality.
  - Each style has strengths and weaknesses.

  Our job, then, was to identify and leverage our strengths while helping each other improve on weaknesses.

- **Compose.** We "composed" our team differently from this point on. With about 12 months left on our various projects, we tackled them with renewed vigour. As each project started, I took on a planning role in terms of sequencing tasks as well as planning the structure and content of our report submissions and presentations. Joseph continued to synthesize our input and make detailed integrative

connections between our various contributions. Samuel gradually became more open and assertive, even allowing objective questions to be asked about his work. Rudy learned to ask insightful questions that helped him contribute more, and Rajiv learned to summarize and focus his verbal input, prioritizing the key points we needed him to cover.

As our work together continued, our team performance improved dramatically. By the time our last, culminating project arrived, we were almost a well-oiled machine. Almost.

Our last project involved the submission of a final report and a summarizing presentation. The audience would be all the other project teams who had been formed, like ours, to tackle a series of organizational problems.

As I began the work of planning and structuring the presentation, I realized that my role in the presentation would involve presenting a complex mathematical solution to one of the issues we had been tackling. Even though the presentation was a few weeks away, I felt myself grow clammy and cold with fear. While I am an experienced presenter and facilitator, my confidence in presenting anything complex with numbers is very low. This was especially true with this particular audience. In my mind, they were all much more advanced than I was with numerical analysis.

In our next team meeting, after I had outlined our proposed presentation structure and content, I took a deep breath and confessed my fear of the mathematical portion of the presentation. If I had revealed this weakness with this team 11 months earlier, I would have expected silence and then mockery. Instead, my team, who were all strong in their numeric skills, began to carefully brainstorm techniques to reinforce both my confidence and my communication of the complex mathematical problem I would be explaining. They helped me rehearse and revise this section, choosing the right sequence and vocabulary to ensure clarity and understanding in the audience. In short, they helped me "compose" this vital section of our presentation.

- **Evaluate.** In short, our last presentation together was fantastic and our most successful effort of the 18-month duration of our team. The audience was actively engaged throughout the hour, asking pertinent and relevant questions and productively debating the concepts and solutions we provided. My section, while not effortlessly delivered, showed me that I could be relied on to competently assist the audience in understanding complex mathematical solutions. My confidence in this area has improved enormously.

  After the presentation, the five of us sat together in the conference room. At first, there was stunned silence as we each seemed to be reflecting on the communication chaos we had created and the powerful and inspiring way we had, collectively, overcome it. Then, suddenly, we could not stop talking, each of us telling the others what a great job they did. At that moment, I felt like our team really could tackle any obstacle put before us.

  I have never forgotten this experience, both the despair and the struggles at the outset and the extraordinary way this collection of individuals evolved into a high-performing team. It was one of the most instructive and inspiring experiences of my life.

Learning Objectives in Review

LO 3.1 Why do you need to understand communication styles? *(pages 66–74)*

- **Understand that styles are adaptable.** Not only does each individual have a preferred style, you develop multiple variations on that style over time as you are exposed to different situations and have more complex relationships.
- **Define and understand your communications comfort zone.** The more clearly you understand your communications preferences, the more adaptable you can be when you are presented with a completely oppositional communication style. Access available self-assessment tools and engage in reflective practices (reviewing audio/video recordings, peer feedback, and instructor feedback with key critical questions in mind).
- **Learn to adapt: Get out of your comfort zone.** When you find yourself outside your comfort zone, understand that you have an opportunity to learn where and how you need to adapt.

LO 3.2 What listening skills will help you communicate better with others? *(pages 74–80)*

Use active listening techniques to ensure understanding. These include the following:

- **Hearing accurately.** This means eliminating distractions to focus on the speaker.
- **Comprehending and interpreting.** Fully understand what is being said by observing people's behaviour, "listening" to their nonverbal communication, being aware of tone of voice and emphasis, and paraphrasing.
- **Evaluating.** Judge what you hear objectively. Remain open minded, separate ideas from the speaker, and use sound reasoning.
- **Responding.** Let the speaker know you understand and initiate the next step in the conversation.

LO 3.3 What speaking strategies will encourage others to listen to you and understand what you are saying? *(pages 80–86)*

- **Focus on your audience** to analyze the audience's interests.
- **Share the conversation** by inviting others to speak.
- **Use clear, concrete, unambiguous language** to avoid misinterpretation.
- **Support your message with appropriate nonverbal communication** that reinforces your spoken message.
- **Avoid upward inflection** that will drain confidence from your speech.
- **Avoid language that triggers a negative response.**
- **Be aware of gender-specific communication styles.**

KEY TERMS

active listening p. 74
ambiguous p. 81
comfort zone p. 66
communication style p. 66
comprehension p. 76

emoticons p. 77
evaluating p. 79
gravitas p. 82
halo effect p. 79
hard skills p. 73

interpretation p. 76
monologue p. 81
nonverbal communication p. 76
paraphrasing p. 77
passive listening p. 74

soft skills p. 73
synchronous p. 65
unambiguous p. 81
upward inflection p. 82

CASE STUDY

Developing Better Interpersonal Communication Skills

This case study will help you review the chapter material by applying it to a specific scenario.

Joe was really looking forward to his first day at work as a senior application developer at BahlTec. He had left his job as an application developer at AxeWorks, a rival company, to accept this new position. At AxeWorks, Joe was part of a development team of 12 people responsible for creating new biometric apps for mobile devices. At BahlTec, he would be in a senior role with a larger, more experienced team working on a variety of apps and projects. He was excited about this opportunity.

Known for quietly producing quality work, Joe worked well with his colleagues at AxeWorks. He was accustomed to doing a lot of communications tasks online, either through the integrated instant messaging system on his computer desktop screen or via email. He met with co-workers once a week to identify problems and brainstorm solutions. The meetings were productive and very "on task" with very little social time. Each meeting had an agenda and someone taking notes that were distributed by email within a few days. Joe and his teammates would sometimes socialize outside of work, often stopping on the way home for a beer or meeting at each other's homes on the weekend for parties or musical jam sessions. He would miss his team but looked forward to his new work opportunities. He hoped he would not lose the friendships he had developed over six years at AxeWorks.

At BahlTec, Joe attended a team meeting on his first day. He was one of three senior application developers on a team of 20. He had never attended a meeting like it. Later that evening, he described the meeting to a friend as being "raucous, loud, and disorganized." It was his impression that everyone spoke at once and that no one listened. Someone wrote down the ideas discussed on a white board, but Joe was not sure if anyone actually took notes for distribution. There didn't seem to be a leader or facilitator. Although he was introduced to the group as a new senior team member, no one gave him background on the projects that were being discussed. He listened without being able to understand what he was hearing. When he tried to ask a question, no one heard him. Joe found his first meeting very frustrating.

After the meeting, one of the other senior application developers pulled Joe aside. Ted had worked at BahlTec for three years and noted the look of confusion and frustration on Joe's face. "You'll get used to it," he said with a smile. Ted introduced five people to Joe. These five people formed the project team that Joe would be leading:

- Sergio: application developer
- Portia: graphic designer
- Rae: application developer (interface specialist)
- Ming: application developer (integration specialist)
- Navjeet: hardware/device specialist

Joe asked if his team could meet right away, perhaps over coffee, so he could get updated on the projects they were working on. Everyone was available except for Sergio, who had a phone meeting booked with a client he was working with. Joe decided to meet with the remainder of the team. They headed out to the coffee shop in their office building.

Portia brought her tablet and, once they were seated, started to show Joe some of the screen shots of their projects. Joe took some notes and was able to ask some questions about the work. Rae texted on her phone while this conversation was going on, paying attention only when Joe asked her a question directly. Usually, Joe would have to repeat the question. Ming and Navjeet talked with each other, ignoring the other three, until Joe asked directly for their input on the projects Portia had been describing. Joe noticed that as soon as he began speaking with Ming and Navjeet, Portia began using an instant messaging app on her tablet, tuning out of his discussion with the other two team members.

At this point, Joe has begun to regret his career move. Although BahlTec is widely recognized as a leader in mobile application development, Joe has a hard time picturing how any work is accomplished with a culture of such poor interpersonal communication skills.

QUESTION 1: *What interpersonal communications issues are emerging in this scenario? Can you list and describe five?*

QUESTION 2: *If you were trying to help Joe understand what is happening in his first few hours of work in the new environment, what would you tell him?*

Setting Expectations

Joe set the next meeting for the next day at 9:30 a.m. The next morning, all the members of the team were ready at 9:30 a.m. in the meeting room except Sergio. Joe found Sergio at his desk, reading user requirements for his client's project. Joe expressed surprise that Sergio was not in the meeting. The conversation went like this.

Joe: Hey, Sergio. I'm glad you're here in the office. We are starting the meeting now and we don't want to start without you.

Sergio (Still reading the user documents, not looking up): Meeting?

Joe: Our team meeting.

Sergio (still not looking up): Oh. Didn't know about it.

Joe: I sent you the information in an email.

Sergio (still not looking up): Didn't read it. I usually don't go to meetings. I just submit my work online.

Joe: We need you in this meeting as we'll be setting up how our team will work together going forward.

Sergio (finally looking up): What?

QUESTION 3: *Identify what is going wrong in this exchange, using the topics discussed in this chapter.*

Joe suggests that the team begin by listing areas that need some improvement in performance. He writes the list down on the board as the team members call them out. The list includes the following:

- Timeliness of work completion
- Sharing of information
- Planning
- Deadlines and milestones

Joe notices that the team is focused on "what" they do as a team rather than "how" they work together. He adds to the list:

- Active listening skills
- Respectful interpersonal communication
- Responding to emails
- Punctuality
- Work standards
- Team goal and mission statement

QUESTION 4: *Would you add to or modify this list?*

Once Joe gets the team working on process issues, some interesting areas of friction are addressed and resolved. Ming always feels like he is waiting for information from other team members, but it turns out they have been uploading materials to the wrong FTP site. This causes Ming to send many unnecessary emails to track down his files. Rae's work could move faster if people agreed to simply check their email daily and send her a one-line confirmation response. Most of the team felt this was reasonable.

Sergio is very quiet during most of this discussion. He sits stiffly and distractedly stares out the window. Finally, he interrupts and mumbles that he is going to go back to his desk to work on his client's project. He gets up and leaves. Joe finds this behaviour very disturbing, but then he wonders whether Sergio's communication style is completely different than that of the rest of the team.

QUESTION 5: *Imagine yourself as a member of this team, at this meeting. Would you interpret Sergio's behaviour as simply rude and arrogant, or would you consider Sergio's nonengagement as a variance in communication or working style? Explain.*

Joe asks the team to say more about Sergio's work and style. It turns out that Sergio is highly valued by everyone because of his patience and care with intricate and highly detailed client requirements. Sergio's work tends to be the foundational work that everyone else builds on. Sergio then hands his work off to other specialists to refine and complete as he goes off to initiate another new, highly detailed client project.

This begins to make sense to Joe. Sergio relies on his client input more than he relies on communication exchanges with his teammates. Later that day, Joe meets with Sergio one on one to discuss Sergio's role and preferred style. Sergio had expected Joe to be irritated and angry. So when Joe approached Sergio with his analysis of the situation, Sergio was surprised and impressed.

QUESTION 6: *Does everyone on a cross-functional team need to have the same communication or working style? Why or why not? How would you handle working on a team with Sergio or, conversely, if you feel you are similar to Sergio, how would you handle working on a team that needs more social interaction than your comfort zone allows?*

REVIEW QUESTIONS

1. Describe two ways you can learn more about your communication style.

2. Describe two situations in which your communication style was different than the style of a co-worker or fellow student.

3. Name two barriers that interfere with hearing.

4. How does comprehension differ from interpretation?

5. What are three types of paraphrasing?

6. Describe how a person "listens" to nonverbal communication.

7. Describe the difference between asynchronous and synchronous communication.

8. How can you tell if a person is actively listening?

CRITICAL THINKING

1. Explain a situation, either at home, school, or work, in which you listened passively and neglected to hear important information. Describe the negative result and identify how you could have used active listening strategies to improve your communication process.

2. Designers of consumer products argue that to understand what customers really need, you have to do more than listen to what they say. You have to observe what they do. Why do you think there is often a gap between what people say and what they do?

3. Review the seven speaking strategies listed on page 80. Divide them into two lists: strategies that you currently try to use

when you speak and strategies that you typically do not use. Of the strategies that you typically do not use, identify one that you would like to begin using immediately. Explain why. Write a short story or description of a typical scenario in which you would use this strategy. What would be the desired outcome?

4. What words or phrases trigger a negative emotional response from you? If someone repeatedly uses one of your "trigger words," what are your options for responding? Which option would you choose?

DEVELOPING YOUR COMMUNICATION SKILLS

 Why do you need to understand communication styles? *(pages 66–74)*

EXERCISE 1 Understand that styles are adaptable

Consider a typical casual conversation about the weather. For example, imagine your city has had three days of sunny weather in a row, followed by a rainy day today. How would your style of discussing this casual topic change in each of the following scenarios:

- With your favourite instructor before class in the hallway?
- With your friends in the cafeteria, student centre, or pub?
- With your family over dinner?
- Online with your best friend in another city?
- On Twitter or Facebook or Instagram?
- With your parents, about to enter a sacred place or a place of worship?

Write a few paragraphs describing what changes in each scenario. Tone? Word choice? Body language? Length of conversation?

EXERCISE 2 Define and understand your communications comfort zone (a team or individual exercise) [Related to the Culture feature on page 69]

Search the Internet for three reputable, free, communications or personality style assessments. Options may include the following, although other options may be available at your time of search:

- www.16personalities.com
- www.keirsey.com
- www.newlineideas.com/communication-style-quiz.html
- www.prenhall.com/sal_v3_demo/wwo/q27.html
- www.cga-pdnet.org/en-CA/PDResources/Pages/10105.aspx

Take three such assessments and compare the results. How do they differ? Do they offer similar results? Do you feel the results accurately capture something about your style? Are you surprised by the results? What have you learned that might help you in communicating with others?

If in a team, discuss your results and how both self-knowledge and deeper knowledge of others can support your team's success.

EXERCISE 3 Learn to adapt: Get out of your comfort zone

In your next team meeting, do one thing differently than you usually do. For example, if you usually wait until after the meeting to email your suggestions to the team (i.e., you do not speak up in person during the meeting), try making one suggestion during the meeting. If you are typically full of suggestions and speak a lot, try holding back and listening more to others. Write a few paragraphs on what this experience was like. Do you feel a slight change to your style could help you be a better team member?

EXERCISE 4 Gain self-awareness of technology use [Related to the Technology feature on page 73]

Select a social occasion on which you are with five or more friends or family members. Create, on paper, a chart like this:

	1. Checked phone while having a conversation	2. Used keypad (texted, updated status, took photo) while having a conversation	3. Made a call while having a conversation	4. Stopped actively listening while doing 1, 2, or 3
(Your name)				
Friend 1				
Friend 2				
Friend 3				
Friend 4				
Friend 5				

Accompanies Exercise 4

Be sure to include your own name. Put a tick mark beside the name and under the column to note the behaviour when it occurs. Tally the results at the end of the event. Do these results surprise you? Do you think this behaviour has an impact on social skills in the workplace? Why or why not?

EXERCISE 5 Being present [Related to the Technology feature on page 73]

Select a social occasion in which you are with five or more friends or family members. Examine the strategies listed in the Technology box and try one or more of them to shift the perspective of the group toward being more present. Report back on the results. Did you notice a change? Was it enjoyable or difficult? Does "being present" in a social occasion help you practice for workplace interactions?

 ## What listening skills will help you communicate better with others? *(pages 74–80)*

EXERCISE 6 Hearing accurately

In each of the following situations, identify what you can do to improve the ability of listeners to hear accurately:

a. One member of your team has a hearing impairment and often misses key things that are said at meetings. Suggest at least four things that you and the rest of the team can do to make it easier for your teammate to hear well. Suggest at least four things your hearing-impaired teammate can do to hear you better.

b. At departmental meetings, your mind wanders when your boss is speaking because he has a monotonous tone of voice and rarely gets to the point. As a result, during the last two meetings you have missed important information. What can you do to improve your ability to hear what your boss says?

EXERCISE 7 Comprehending and interpreting

a. **Listening to tone of voice.** A speaker's tone of voice and emphasis provide clues about his or her attitudes and feelings. Imagine at least two different ways that you can say each of the following four statements. What are the different meanings conveyed by the different sets of nonverbal cues?

1. I didn't do anything wrong.
2. We need to talk now.
3. I'll give you my phone number after the meeting.
4. When did you come up with that idea?

b. **Paraphrasing to ensure understanding.** Learning how to paraphrase in multiple ways is challenging. Note the two conversational exchanges that follow, with paraphrases **highlighted in grey.** Identify which **grey** statements are paraphrases of content, intent, and feeling. Remember, when you paraphrase for content, you state your understanding of the explicit message. When you paraphrase for intent, you try to uncover why someone made that statement. When you paraphrase for feelings, you try to uncover the emotions in the statement.

1. Accounts payable: We keep getting invoices for partial shipments, and I can't figure out when a purchase order is completely filled. I can't pay an invoice for a partial shipment. The purchase order has to be closed out before we pay the invoice.

   Purchasing: So, you are saying that our computer system will not allow you to pay a partial invoice?

   Accounts payable: I don't know. The computer system might allow it.

   Purchasing: So, it's company policy not to pay partial invoices?

   Accounts payable: Well, it's not really a company policy. It's just so confusing to match these partial invoices with purchase orders. I'm never sure I get it right, so I don't think it's a good idea for us to do this.

   Purchasing: You sound like you might want some help with the invoices since you're spending so much time matching the invoices to the purchase order. Would you like me to match them for you? Because I wrote the purchase orders, I can do it more easily.

   Accounts payable: That sounds like a good idea.

2. Interviewer: What gets you excited about public relations?

   Interviewee: I've been thinking about public relations for a long time.

   Interviewer: Your goal has always been to go into public relations?

   Interviewee: Well, no. My original goal was to be a lawyer, and I worked as a paralegal for a few years, but there was really no career path, so I decided to do something else.

   Interviewer: So, you were frustrated and that led to a career change?

   Interviewee: Yes, exactly. I want to do something that allows me to be more creative and contribute more to an organization.

   Interviewer: You believe that public relations will make better use of your talents.

Accompanies Exercise 7b

EXERCISE 8 Evaluating

Your co-worker Bob is always complaining and makes only negative comments at meetings. He came into your office this morning to share a proposal he plans to make in a manager's meeting tomorrow. He proposes that the department change the hiring requirements so that all new hires have three years of experience in addition to a bachelor's degree. He claims that "a college education is not sufficient for the job." He supports his claim with this evidence: "The two newest employees, fresh out of college, have been making mistakes and cannot seem to learn the details of the job. We have no time to train them. We need to hire people who are already trained." He asks if you will support his idea at the meeting.

Your immediate reaction is "I don't know." You have made friends with one of the new hires, and you know from your own experience that it takes time to learn a job. You were hired right out of college too. You will need to evaluate this proposal critically before you take a stance. What steps would you take to evaluate what you heard?

EXERCISE 9 Responding

Assume you are working on a project with three other people. One of your teammates provides great ideas during team meetings, but consistently misses deadlines and provides only partial work. Her lack of follow-through has significantly slowed the project, and you are now concerned that your team will not complete the project on time. Your teammate says she will meet the next deadline. How could you effectively respond to her statement? Practise six different kinds of responses:

a. Ask a question.

b. Make a judgment.

c. Contribute an opinion.

d. Give advice.

e. Argue or disagree.

f. Express empathy.

Identify the one response you think is best, and be prepared to discuss your answer in class.

 What speaking strategies will encourage others to listen to you and understand what you are saying?
(pages 80–86)

EXERCISE 10 Focus on your audience

Imagine you receive a phone call from an actual friend or relative who asks you "How is school going?" or "How is your job?" Write a two-paragraph email to your instructor identifying how you will respond to this specific audience:

- In the first paragraph, identify the friend or relative you have in mind and explain what you think that person really wants to know in asking the question.

- In the second paragraph, explain how you will respond. What will you tell your friend or relative and why? What won't you tell him or her and why?

EXERCISE 11 Share the conversation

Observe a conversation at a meeting or between two or three people at lunch or dinner. Does any one person monopolize the conversation? If so, does that have any negative results? If the conversation is shared fairly, how long is each person's typical turn? How do people signal that they want to speak?

EXERCISE 12 Use clear, concrete, unambiguous language

Each of the following sentences contains at least one ambiguous phrase. Identify the possible ambiguity and rephrase the statement so that it has one clear, concrete meaning. Feel free to make up details if necessary.

a. You did a great job on that report.

b. Mary's job performance hasn't been satisfactory this year.

c. Our presentation needs to be perfect.

d. There are just a few small problems to clear up before signing the contract.

e. Clean up the conference room before the end of the day.

f. Let's talk after the project is finished.

EXERCISE 13 Support your message with appropriate nonverbal communication

Ask someone you do not know for directions to a nearby location, and pay attention to that person's verbal and nonverbal communication.

a. What is that person's verbal message? In other words, does the person provide directions, decline to help, or say something else?

b. What nonverbal elements support that message?

c. Are there any nonverbal elements that conflict with that message?

EXERCISE 14 Experience upward inflection

Search YouTube using keywords like "uptalk" or "upward inflection." View some samples of this speech pattern and listen for it. Does it sound familiar to you? Do you feel this is a pattern you have become comfortable using? Write a few paragraphs on your perception of upward inflection in speech.

EXERCISE 15 Avoid upward inflection

Open a file in the "notes" app on your mobile device, or create a paper version titled "Upward Inflection Observation." Make it look like the figure below:

	U.I. used for question	U.I. used in statement	U.I. used in middle of phrase	U.I. used at end of sentence
Classroom				
Cafeteria				
Pub				
Student Centre				
Bus/Subway/Train				
U.I. = upward inflection				

Accompanies Exercise 15

Pick a day that you know you will be around people for most of the day. For example, select a day when you know you will be in a cafeteria or other busy public place between classes or during a break. Spend the entire day, when you are not working or in class, just listening for samples of upward inflection around you. Note whether the situation was formal or informal, and whether the person speaking was asking a question or making a statement. Note whether the upward inflection happened at the end of a sentence or in the middle of a phrase. Once this is done, write about anything that surprises you about this exercise. Do the speakers you hear sound confident and sure of themselves, or do they sound hesitant? How might this speech pattern have an impact in the workplace?

EXERCISE 16 Avoid language that triggers a negative response

Read the following scenario and identify alternatives for the biased language.

Your first job after graduating is as an internal consultant with a small, local company. On your first day of work, the vice-president who hired you asks you to come to a meeting where he will introduce you to the head of every department in the company. As you stand up at the front of the conference room, the vice-president says, "I'd like to introduce the _____ who has been hired to help us." Imagine that the blank was filled in with each of the following terms (consider only the gender terms appropriate for you):

- Young lady/Young man
- Woman/Man
- Gal/Guy
- Expert
- Consultant
- Genius
- College girl/College boy

Which term(s) would you prefer the vice-president use to introduce you? What are the problems with each of the remaining terms? What kinds of bias, if any, do they represent?

EXERCISE 17 Be aware of gender-specific communication styles

Although there is no absolute "female" communication style or "male" communication style, researchers in sociolinguistics have identified a number of widespread differences between the way men and women typically communicate. In business, people need to accommodate different styles to work well together. In small groups (or as a whole class), discuss the following three scenarios. In your past experience, have you noticed these types of differences? What would you recommend the participants do to bridge the differences?

a. Ella and Michael are assigned to work on a project together. Ella goes to her supervisor to ask for clarification of details and to ensure she understands what the project requires. By contrast, Michael jumps right in and begins to work. He says he'll figure it out along the way. Michael tells Ella she's wasting time. Ella believes Michael hates to ask for help or directions.

b. In meetings, Richard illustrates his points with metaphors about war and sports: "I think we'll score a touchdown with this new product. But if we don't get it to market soon, the competition will outflank us." By contrast, Alice uses anecdotes and metaphors about relationships and home: "Our products are always the bridesmaids. This one will be the bride." Richard and Alice understand the other person's metaphors, but they are not comfortable with them.

c. At the monthly department meeting, Denise and James's manager asked for suggestions about how to research a client problem. Denise spoke immediately and began to make a suggestion. Before she had time to finish, James interrupted and said, "That gives me another idea," and he began presenting his thoughts. The conversation in the meeting then focused on James's idea. Denise waited for a break in the conversation to return to her point. She quietly tried to interrupt, but could not break the momentum of the conversation. She left the meeting feeling angry with James.

EXERCISE 18 Reflective practice

Select a recent team experience in which you participated for an organization or a class project. Consider your communication style in relation to the others on the team. In a few paragraphs, describe the following:

- Your assessment of your communication style. How have you assessed your style? What evidence do you have to support your description?
- Your assessment of the communication style of others on the team. How did you assess their styles? What evidence do you have to support your description?
- Do these styles work well together? Why or why not?
- What can be done to support or improve team communication, based on these assessments of communication styles?

EXERCISE 19 Improving active listening skills

In groups of four, assign one of these roles to each group member: Speaker, Listener 1, Listener 2, and Observer. Complete the following exercise:

- **Speaker:** Talk for two to three minutes about a problem you faced in a past job search or a concern you have about a future job search.

- **Listeners:** Use clarifying questions and paraphrases to understand the speaker's content, intent, and feelings. Consider nonverbal messages as you paraphrase.

- **Speaker:** After the conversation ends, describe the degree to which you feel satisfied that the paraphrasing represented meaning accurately.

- **Observer:** Point out specific examples of effective and ineffective techniques the listeners used.

- **Listeners:** Discuss how the paraphrasing and questioning felt. Was it difficult? Awkward? Useful in uncovering additional meaning? How did you pick up on nonverbal cues?

- **Each Individual:** Based on what you learned from this exercise, write an email to your instructor explaining the challenges and benefits of active listening. Use examples from the exercise to support your analysis.

Accompanies Exercise 19

EXERCISE 20 Analyzing trigger words

Work with a group of three or four classmates to analyze trigger words. Each person should identify at least two words or phrases that he or she reacts to negatively. Tell your team how you react when you hear the words you suggest. Also try to identify the source of this reaction. Does it result from your upbringing, your past experiences, or an association with a particular person? Summarize your team's discussion and prepare to report the most interesting insights to the rest of the class.

EXERCISE 21 Examining cultural differences [Related to the Culture feature on page 69]

Take a look at the pictures of different classrooms around the world shown in the link provided below. There are a variety of classrooms, from elementary schools to postsecondary schools.

www.theguardian.com/education/gallery/2012/sep/14/schools-around-the-world-children#/?picture=395983383&index=10

Look at each photo first. Then read the description provided. How does the description compare to your first assessment of the learning culture? If one adult person from each classroom were in your student work groups or in your workplace, how would you begin to understand their ways of learning and feeling included and valued?

EXERCISE 22 Recording and distributing images [Related to the Ethics feature on page 71]

Pooja was excited to have been asked to take photos during a weekend marketing and business strategy case competition. Teams of students from all over the province competed against each other by analyzing cases and presenting their solutions to a panel of judges.

By the end of the weekend, Pooja had about 200 candid shots to choose from for distribution online on the business school's website and as images within the quarterly printed business newsletter. There are images of students working hard while preparing and presenting their cases. There are some terrific shots of the judging panels, and some fun images of the gala dinner, the awards presentation, and the dance that followed. Some of the images at the dance show the faculty coaches looking more relaxed than usual, and Pooja is looking forward to getting these images circulated as quickly as possible.

As Pooja scrolls through her collection of images, something is bothering her. She feels like she has forgotten an important step.

What has Pooja forgotten? How can she remedy this situation at this point? What should she do in the future if she is asked to record images of others for publication?

4

Who Are You? Understanding Intercultural Communication and Workplace Diversity

Inti St Clair/Blend Images/Getty Images.

LEARNING OBJECTIVES

(LO 4.1) Why do we need to study intercultural communication and workplace diversity? *pages 96–100*

Understand the impact of culture and diversity on communication
Know that each individual is unique
Develop a mindset of cultural intelligence

(LO 4.2) What do you need to know to improve your cultural intelligence? *pages 100–109*

Understand how cultures differ
Integrate communication style and culture: The Lewis model of cultural types

Be aware that common language does not equal common meaning or culture
Develop strategies that help you communicate interculturally

(LO 4.3) How can you make your communications inclusive? *pages 109–121*

Develop a mindset of inclusion
Learn the art of respectful inquiry
Use ACE to navigate diverse and intercultural situations

Adrienne Rosen
President and CEO,
First International
Courier Systems Inc.

Courtesy of Dr. Adrienne Rosen and Philip Lapidus.

@ WORK

"Communication . . . a piece of cake?"

First International Courier Systems Inc. is an international logistics corporation based in Canada. We serve a niche market. Our services are available 24/7 as we deliver medical devices, organs for transplant, parts for grounded aircraft, and other time-sensitive deliveries across all time zones. Our standard operating procedure ensures that full details about every shipment are *carefully communicated every step of the way*. It is critical that the messages we send are clear, concise, and particular to our marketplace, keeping in mind that our marketplace is not a single geographic zone but a mosaic of cultures, religions, gender, and abilities.

I was once speaking on the telephone with a logistics trainee in Los Angeles. This individual was learning on the job at a medium-sized courier company. The shipment in question was an urgently needed part for an MRI machine at an emergency department. This trainee had never cleared customs with a shipment in the cargo sector, and we were taking him through the process, step by step. There was no immediate language barrier of particular note, and I thought I had made myself understood by him. I was very surprised when he called back to tell me that the shipment could not be cleared by customs until the federal Food and Drug Administration inspected the piece. Aghast, I asked why, given that it was a part for a medical device. I had made the mistake of telling him that *clearing customs was "a piece of cake,"* meaning that it was simple. I confused him. This shipment was significantly late because I did not consider that my use of language would be taken literally by this native English speaker.

This incident was a reminder to me that language is full of innuendos, double meanings, and expressions. The challenge, whether it's a phone call, an email, or a marketing piece, is to make our communications free from such expressions as much as possible. We must be careful to ensure that the recipients of any message are able to understand it without wondering about its true meaning.

Find out at the end of this chapter how Rosen uses ACE to solve these intercultural communication challenges.

Introduction

Ultimately, being an effective and respected business communicator means being able to build and maintain solid, high-functioning relationships with all types of people, be they at the next desk or halfway across the world. As you learned in previous chapters, knowing your audience is a key element of building a business message. In a business environment of great complexity, you must avoid harbouring a "single story" about your audience, be they business associates, partners, vendors, or customers.

What is a "single story"? In her compelling TED talk, *The Danger of a Single Story*, Nigerian author Chimamanda Ngozi Adichie suggests that a "single story" is what creates an uninformed and limiting perception of others. She recounts her experience of travelling to the United States to attend college at age 19. Her college roommate was surprised to hear Adichie's perfect English and was equally surprised to discover that Adichie knew how to use a modern, conventional stove. When asked to share her "tribal music," Adichie produced a Mariah Carey CD. Clearly, the roommate's "single story" of Adichie was one of backwardness and poverty. In the roommate's "single story," "there was no possibility of Africans being similar to her in any way . . . no possibility of connection as human equals," states Adichie (2009a). However, Adichie reflects that "if I had not grown up in Nigeria, and if all I knew about Africa were from popular images, I too would think that Africa was a place of . . . incomprehensible people, fighting senseless wars, dying of poverty and AIDS, unable to speak for themselves and waiting to be saved by a kind, white foreigner" (2009b).

Jeff Morgan 08/Alamy.

This chapter is about avoiding a "single story" perspective. In it you will learn how cultures differ, how diversity has an impact on communication, and how to develop strategies to communicate with confidence and professionalism in most settings and situations. In particular, you will learn how to

- develop cultural intelligence,
- develop a mindset of inclusion, and
- develop strategies to communicate interculturally and within diverse work environments.

Ron Glover, IBM's vice-president of global workforce diversity, had this to say:

We are seeing that culture now extends to areas of difference such as technical orientation, management style and other domains, which affect how we run the business and interact with others . . . When you begin to build a culture that is respectful and inclusive around things like race, gender and sexual orientation, the organization learns the skills to manage without assumption. (quoted in Brake, 2013, p. 13)

(LO 4.1) Why do we need to study intercultural communication and workplace diversity?

Workplaces are increasingly multicultural, and businesses are increasingly global. Therefore, learning about other cultures is no longer optional: It is essential. Your natural communications choices, from the words you use to the channel you select to the tone and timing of your message, are influenced by your **culture** as well as a variety of unique characteristics that make you an individual. Note that your business audience is made up of other people with their own cultural and social influences as well as their own unique individual characteristics. Therefore, not everyone will understand and respond to your communication choices in the way you would expect.

To some degree, learning about others (e.g., your audience) is a continuous process of creating a concept about what others are like and then rebuilding it based on new information. Terence Brake, president of TMA World and author of *Where in the World Is My Team? Making a Success of Your Virtual Global Workplace*, refers to these ideas about other groups as "tendencies," or tentative expectations, which are always open to modification based on the individuals you interact with (Brake, 2013). Therefore, it is a mistake to be trapped by rigid cultural **stereotypes**: oversimplified "single story" images or generalizations of a group. Although stereotypes may describe a generally observed cultural norm, if you assume everyone from that culture follows that norm, you ignore the fact that individuals are unique. As Richard Lewis, author of *When Cultures Collide*, states, "Such generalizations carry with them the risk of stereotyping as one talks about the typical Italian, German, American, etc. It is evident that Americans [and Germans] differ greatly from each other and that no two Italians are alike" (quoted in Hedderich, 1999).

Any time you hold an unverified set of assumptions about another person in your mind as truth, you are missing out on much of what makes that person valuable, interesting, and complex. Your unverified set of assumptions can contribute to a "single story" perception. Sometimes our "single story" originates from our assumptions that people are either completely like us or completely not like us. Neither of these perspectives is ever entirely true. **Ethnocentrism** is a conscious or unconscious belief that your own cultural norms are superior to all others and, further, that others wish to emulate your cultural norms. If you find yourself in a different cultural setting and your feeling is that "they are doing it wrong. Our way is better," you are experiencing ethnocentrism. Most people do not realize they are comparing cultures until they catch themselves doing it. Being self-aware about this tendency is critical to developing intercultural adaptability.

In a business setting, if you cling to a "single story" about others you risk seriously damaging relationships with inappropriate and offensive communications choices. You risk alienating, demotivating, and offending the recipients of your messages. Co-workers may refuse to work with you, which could negatively impact productivity. Business partners may refuse to complete contracts or repeat orders if your emails appear inappropriate to them. Employers may find you too risky to keep employed if you are unable to build and maintain relationships with all their valued stakeholders.

Culture The learned and shared attitudes and behaviours that characterize a group of people. People demonstrate their culture through values, ideas, and attitudes.

Stereotype A perception about an individual or group based on a belief that all people in a given group behave the same way.

Ethnocentrism A belief that your own culture is superior to all others.

There are many examples of stereotyping and ethnocentrism causing communications breakdowns that led to negative business consquences. The 1998 merger of two car manufacturers, Germany's Daimler-Benz AG and the American Chrysler Corporation, is a famous example of the destructive impact of such discord. The two organizations were challenged by vast cultural and linguistic differences that were never fully understood. These tensions eventually resulted in the two companies parting ways, at considerable cost to both (Bolchover, 2012). Closer to home, 2015 saw the abrupt end of Target's short-lived expansion from its US home base into Canada. As noted by the analysts at Kantar Retail, "Canadians are not Americans: Target did not fundamentally believe Canadians had significantly distinctive needs and expectations" (Chain Store Age, 2015).

Understand the impact of culture and diversity on communication

You may have heard the saying, "We cannot escape our culture." Culture describes learned and shared patterns in a society. People are shaped by the cultures they come from, and they develop a set of assumptions about how to act based on those cultural influences. For example, for many Canadians, the following statements are assumed to be true:

- If you have a 10 a.m. appointment, you should arrive a little before 10 a.m. to be on time.

- If someone makes a mistake, it is best to be honest (though polite) and point it out so that he or she has an opportunity to correct the mistake.

- To be efficient, it is important to get right to business quickly at a meeting.

- If you arc a man, it is a common courtesy to allow a woman to exit an elevator or go through a doorway first.

Not every culture subscribes to these codes of behaviour, however. For example, in the Swiss–German area of Switzerland, you would be rude to jump immediately to business at the beginning of a meeting. Similarly, Latin American cultures value getting to know the other person and building a relationship of trust. In Korea, a young woman would be rude to exit an elevator before an elderly man because respecting elders is highly valued in the Korean culture. Being time conscious is typically not part of many Canadian **First Nations** societies.

Organizational culture refers to an organization's expectations, philosophy, and values. Over time, any group of people who work together will evolve common attitudes, customs, and written and unwritten expectations that are powerful in guiding the behaviour of the group. Organizational culture is demonstrated in

- the ways the organization conducts its business and how it treats its employees, customers, and the wider community,

- the extent to which freedom is allowed in decision making, developing new ideas, and personal expression,

- how power and information flow through its hierarchy, and

- how communications are conducted, including
  - how and why meetings are held (e.g., the level of formality),
  - how emails are treated (e.g., whether they are readily answered or archived, how often "reply all" is chosen), and
  - how employees at a distance are incorporated into organizational operations and communications (e.g., via Skype, telephone, or other channels).

For example, in Learning Objective 3.1, page 66, there is an example of Joe, who moved from Company A to Company B and found the manner of holding meetings to be well out of his previous work experience. Company B's method put Joe out of his comfort zone, but that does not necessarily mean it was the wrong approach. This is an example of an employee being placed into a new organizational culture. The Case Study at the end of Chapter 3 could also be seen as an extended example of Joe struggling with a new organizational culture.

First Nations A term used to refer to the peoples who inhabited Canada from the earliest times, before colonization. There are currently over 630 recognized First Nations governments or bands across Canada, roughly half of which are in the provinces of Ontario and British Columbia. The total population is nearly 700,000 people (as of 2011).

Organizational culture The unique operational environment of an organization, as created by that organization's specific values, shared attitudes, beliefs, customs, and written and unwritten rules that have been developed over time; manifests in the ways an organization conducts operations, treats its employees, customers, and the wider community, as well as the extent to which freedom is allowed in decision making and personal expression.

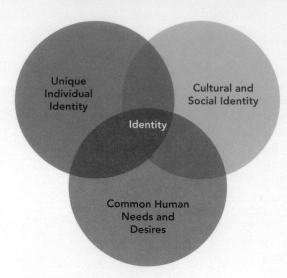

FIGURE 4.1 Three "Stories" That Create a Unique Identity

Know that each individual is unique

We work with individuals, not "members of groups." Earlier in this chapter, the author Chimamanda Ngozi Adichie suggests that we cannot limit our perception of others to a "single story" or a rigid set of assumptions about a "group" someone might identify with. Karim H. Karim, former co-director of the Institute of Ismaili Studies in London, England, and Carleton University professor, notes that almost everyone has a unique, multilayered sense of self:

> There are multiple kinds of identity that a person has—for many people, national identity is very different from ethnic and cultural identities. Focus groups that I have carried out with Muslims of various backgrounds over the last few years, as well as interviews that a doctoral student of mine has conducted with South Asians more recently, have demonstrated that most of these first- and second-generation immigrants felt equally comfortable with their religious, ethnic, cultural, and Canadian identities. . . . [T]he researchers of the study [did not] understand that most people have a multilayered sense of self. (Karim, 2009)

FIGURE 4.1 suggests that each person we meet and work with will have at least three "stories," three major influences on their sense of identity:

- **A foundation of common human needs and desires.** This includes some basic human qualities, such as love for one's offspring, gratitude for favours, anger at perceived injustice, and basic physical and psychological survival needs for shelter, food, companionship, acceptance and respect (Brake, 2013).

- **Cultural and social identity.** Your self-identity can originate from any group or groups you identify with. This can be a strong influencer for some people and a less strong influencer for others. People can cultivate behaviours, expectations, and beliefs when they identify with cultural groups or with socially identified groups, such as people living with disabilities or with gender dysphoria, or as part of a specific generation or age group, to name but a few possible group identities. It is possible for a person to identify with more than one group (Brake, 2013).

- **Unique individual identity.** There are elements of identity that each person develops that are uniquely their own: preferences (music, colour, food, personal style), personal beliefs based on experience that may conflict with cultural or social norms, and lifestyle choices, to name but a few possible individual traits (Brake, 2013).

Develop a mindset of cultural intelligence

When you understand that each person you meet has at least three "stories" that influence his or her sense of identity, you are much closer to developing a mindset of **cultural intelligence**. This mindset is critical to respectful communication in our diverse and globally active workplaces. Here are three keys to strengthening this crucial perspective:

1. **Always allow others to define themselves.** If you meet someone who appears to be different than you, let their stories unfold naturally. Do not make hasty assumptions. *Pay attention.* Find out which cultural, individual, or shared aspects of their identity are most important to them.

2. **Remain flexible.** Many sources on cross-cultural communication point to "adaptability" as a key skill. This skill was discussed at length in Chapter 3 and it continues to be important in an intercultural environment. *Pay attention.* If your method of connecting with others is not working, slow down and watch for new opportunities to learn and adapt.

3. **Keep all three "stories" in balance.** When you are unable to keep these "stories" in balance, your ability to communicate is deeply compromised. *Pay attention* to where you are placing your assumptions.

FIGURE 4.2 shows how our perceptions can sometimes become unbalanced if we ignore specific aspects of our audience's self-identity. This can lead to misunderstandings, mistrust, and the absence of actual communication.

Cultural intelligence A person's ability to adapt successfully when exposed to new cultural expectations.

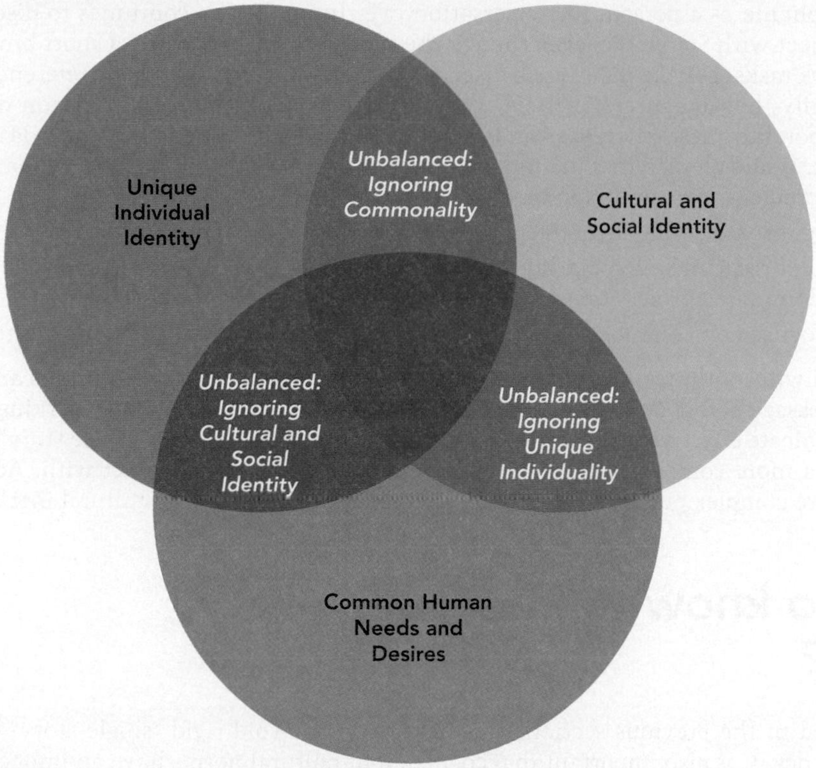

FIGURE 4.2 Three "Stories" Becoming Unbalanced

Note the three examples here that show why maintaining a balance between the three stories is crucial:

- **Khadeer meets Joyce,** an accomplished and skilled administrator who happens to be black and from the Caribbean. Khadeer only relates to her as he perceives her: someone of a different race and cultural background. His image of Joyce does not include her skills and experience in administration nor any common ground he shares with her. Therefore, in an inappropriate attempt to be friendly, Khadeer's communications with Joyce always include references to reggae music, jerk chicken, and warm weather. Instead of getting to know Joyce as an individual and rebuilding his mental image, Khadeer remains stuck on his inaccurate assumptions about her cultural and social identity. Khadeer has

  - ignored individual identity (Joyce as a skilled and experienced administrator),
  - overstated his stereotype (Joyce as someone of a different culture about which Khadeer has simplistic assumptions), and
  - ignored commonalities (Joyce as someone with the same education and industry experience as Khadeer).

- **Sophia meets Chris,** a talented web designer who has a hearing impairment. Instead of making small but important changes to her communication style, such as being sure to face Chris when she speaks, she carries on her normal, multitasking style. Sophia failed to ask Chris if he needed her to change her communication style. She ignored a key difference between them and assumed that Chris valued her usual fast-paced style. Sophia feels it is respectful to treat Chris "the same" as everyone else. However, her inability to respond to a key difference has the opposite effect. Chris feels slighted and his ability to keep pace with her is compromised. Sophia has

  - ignored individual identity (Chris cannot be a talented web designer if he cannot understand Sophia's instructions),
  - ignored a key social difference that needs to be respected (Chris as someone who needs minor accommodation to thrive in the workplace), and
  - overemphasized commonality (Chris as a fellow human being who is "exactly like" Sophia).

- **Rixon meets Stephanie,** his new co-worker and team member, and sees her only as a new financial expert on his project team. He does not exhibit any interest in

Stephanie as a person. In conversation over lunch, Rixon continues to discuss the project with Stephanie, even though they are both clearly taking a short break from work tasks. During their lunch discussion, Stephanie makes passing reference to her family (her daughter, Chrissie, and her same-sex partner, Leah). Rixon does not respond to these references and steers the conversation back to work-related matters. While pleased that her professional opinion is valued by Rixon, Stephanie feels ignored as a person. Rixon has

- ignored individualism (Stephanie as a person with a family life),
- ignored cultural/social identity (Stephanie as a successful woman in a male-dominated profession or as a person with a same-sex partner), and
- focused on commonalities (Stephanie as a member of the same project team).

You will continue to develop your ability to self-regulate your perceptions and adapt your message across cultural and diversity dimensions throughout your working life. To communicate effectively and respectfully, you need to step beyond a "single story" perception to a more complex understanding of the individuals you interact with. Achieving this more complex perception is critical to further developing your cultural intelligence.

(LO 4.2) What do you need to know to improve your cultural intelligence?

As noted in the previous section, it is important to avoid rigid "single story" cultural stereotypes. It is also important to recognize that cultural norms have an impact on the assumptions we make when we communicate.

The difference between a "cultural norm" and a "stereotype" is often debated. How can we say that we should avoid stereotyping while proceeding to use the concept of cultural norms to help us understand specific cultures? This would be a worthwhile debate to undertake in a classroom setting. Exercise 3 on page 125 is intended to help students explore this important question. In the meantime, it is useful to consider that respectful exploration of cultural norms prior to communicating with someone from a different culture can help you manage your expectations with regard to unfamiliar behaviours. Armed with a bit of basic information, you can more correctly interpret what you are experiencing. On the other hand, the use of stereotypes to generalize or judge values and behaviours different than your own is not respectful and does nothing to assist you in communicating in a professional manner. Your deepening sense of cultural intelligence will help you make this distinction.

Understand how cultures differ

In this section, you will explore specific *theories* on world cultures. These theories may help you understand the ways in which cultures may differ or intersect. **Keep in mind that these are theoretical models of cultural norms rather than absolute truths.**

Over the years, anthropologists, sociologists, and intercultural theorists have identified several dimensions of cultural differences. This section covers seven of those dimensions, all of which have implications for business communication.

High- vs. low-context cultures

Anthropologist Edward T. Hall first used the term **context** to describe how people deliver, receive, and interpret messages (Spencer-Oatey & Franklin, 2009). Hall proposed that countries exist on a continuum from high context to low context, as illustrated in **FIGURE 4.3**. In a *high-context* culture, such as China or Japan, communicators convey meaning not just by words but also by all the context surrounding the words: how something is said, the nonverbal behaviour of the communicator and audience, the history of the relationship between the two communicators, and even the silences in the conversation. In a *low-context* culture, such as in the English-speaking parts of Canada, communicators rely less on context and more on explicit language to communicate a message as clearly and unambiguously as possible.

Context A term that describes how people in a culture deliver, receive, and interpret messages. Low-context cultures rely on explicit language to communicate. High-context cultures derive meaning not just from words but from everything surrounding the words.

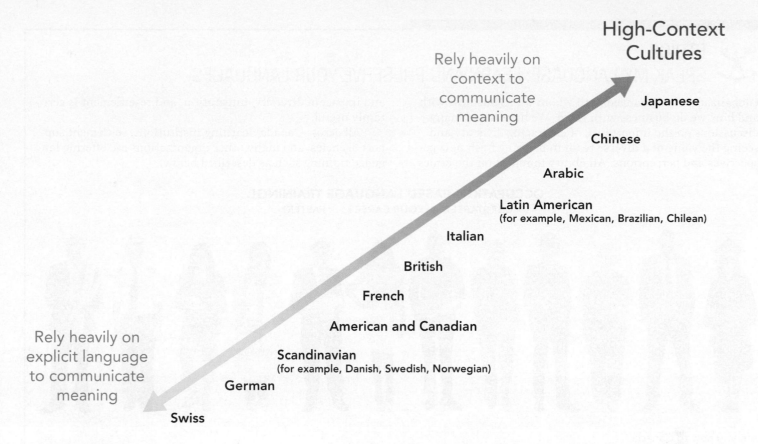

High-Context
Cultures

Rely heavily on
context to
communicate
meaning

Japanese

Chinese

Arabic

Latin American
(for example, Mexican, Brazilian, Chilean)

Italian

British

French

American and Canadian

Scandinavian
(for example, Danish, Swedish, Norwegian)

German

Swiss

Rely heavily on
explicit language
to communicate
meaning

Low-Context Cultures

FIGURE 4.3 Continuum of Low- to High-Context Cultures

Therefore, when working in a low-context setting, such as the English-speaking parts of Canada, occupation-specific language can be important. However, there is some debate as to whether this strong emphasis on language acquisition is fair or ethical to newly arrived Canadians. See the **ETHICS BOX** for an exploration of this topic.

Reflecting this difference, people in the United States and Germany typically value direct conversations that immediately get to the point. In contrast, people from Japan tend to rely on more subtle cues. If a Japanese businessperson wants to say "no," she may not actually use that word but may instead respond with silence or a reserved reply, such as "That is very interesting." She will rely on you to interpret the message correctly, based on the context of the communication.

Individualism vs. collectivism

Individualism versus collectivism is one of the key dimensions of culture identified by Dutch intercultural expert Geert Hofstede (Hofstede & Minkow, 2010). In an **individualistic culture**, people value an individual's achievements, satisfaction, and independent thinking. By contrast, in **collectivist cultures**, people put the welfare of the group or organization before their own individual interests. Obligation and loyalty to the group are more important than one's own achievement, and harmony is extremely important. Explore more of Hofstede's work at http://geert-hofstede.com.

Individualistic and collectivist values influence communication and business in a number of ways. In the United States, many companies reward individual leaders, such as CEOs and other executives, with multimillion-dollar bonuses for the companies' successes. By contrast, in more collectivist China, PepsiCo learned during its early years in that country that rewarding an individual leader was not an effective incentive. When one highly regarded manager chose to divide his bonus equally among his employees, PepsiCo changed its practice to reward an entire group when goals were met (Formula for success, 1992). Similarly, in collectivist cultures employees may be embarrassed if they

Individualistic culture A culture that values an individual's achievements, satisfaction, and independent thinking.

Collectivist culture A culture that puts the welfare of the group or organization before people's individual interests.

ETHICS
SPEAK MY LANGUAGE: LEARN AND PRESERVE YOUR LANGUAGES

Globalization has changed both whom we do business with and how we do business with them. We have heard many discussions on the importance of embracing diversity and seeing the value of a diverse team in bringing fresh new perspectives and perceptions. An ability to reflect on the ethics and impact of diversity, integration, and resettlement is certainly useful.

All across Canada, learning institutions, settlement support agencies, and many other organizations are offering language training such as described below.

OCCUPATION-BASED LANGUAGE TRAINING!
GET STARTED IN YOUR CAREER . . . FASTER!

Rawpixel/Fotolia

Are you new to Canada?

Employers are seeking employees who "speak their language". Occupation-specific workplace communication skills are critical to your success. Our courses will provide you with the language and workplace culture training required to communicate effectively on the job. *Sign up now!*

This fictional announcement was compiled based on a review of similar-type advertisements sourced from local media across Canada. These services exist to assist English language learners in adjusting to the low-context, language-heavy expectations within Canadian workplaces. However, to an extent these expectations can have consequences:

- They can perpetuate a perception that everyone who is new to Canada must make significant changes to their language and identity to succeed.

- They can suggest that full assimilation to Canadian culture is required for success.

- They can imply that certain aspects of identity need to be changed or suppressed to gain employment.

It would be hard to argue that it is not important to learn English, especially work-specific vocabulary, to achieve workplace success in English-speaking Canada. Does this mean that a person's first language is no longer a valued part of his or her identity? Perhaps, when arriving in Canada, an expanded definition of self is required. Dr. Vicki Bismilla found that "the creation of space for students' mother tongues in college classrooms is an ethical imperative since their mother tongues are integral components of their identities, and all of their prior learning and life experiences are encoded in their mother tongues. Overall the findings highlighted bilingual students' perceptions that their [first language] constituted an important scaffold for their learning of English. Students' comments also expressed their sense of the centrality of [first language] to aspects of their identity" (Bismilla, 2011). In a globalized economy, many languages are valued. A first language that is not English could help "scaffold" (or support) the acquisition of English if you are working with others of your original language group. Non-English languages are becoming more and more in demand in Canada as businesses and organizations expand their markets and business relationships across the globe.

Edward T. Hall, one of the pioneer researchers into intercultural communications, famously said the following:

> We should never denigrate any other culture but rather help people to understand the relationship between their own culture and the dominant culture. When you understand another culture or language, it does not mean that you have to lose your own culture. (E. Hall, n.d.).

A useful mindset to adopt is that strong spoken and written English provides additional, valuable skills in the Canadian workplace. These skills do not replace or supersede a first language.

Can O-A-R help you understand the role of language acquisition for employment?

- **Observe:** How can these implications affect a person's understanding of social class, identity, and self-perception? Do your own beliefs, values, or behaviours perpetuate this kind of thinking? Are you asking others, or being asked yourself, to give up valuable elements of identity in order to "fit in"? Or are you being asked to acquire a new language skill? This is deep reflection that you need to consider and revisit when seeking employment or, alternatively, when hiring others, creating teams, or building your own business.

- **Ask:** Informational interviews with any prospective employer or industry representative can assist you in learning about the practices and expectations of a firm. When considering a job offer from an organization, in addition to evaluating wages, hours, and benefits, it is wise to consider whether the values and ethics represented by the organization are in sync with your own.
- **Research:** Research any prospective employer thoroughly. Are there recent news articles related to ethics and employment? If so, how has your potential employer responded? Be sure to research a target company's corporate social responsibility strategy or vision. Business reputations, responses to ethical issues, and chosen marketing strategies should all contribute to a picture of the kind of values the organization represents. You can then decide if you and this organization are a "good fit" for a long-term, successful employment relationship. Should you be in charge of your own company or organization, follow the same process for researching future business partners. When you are in partnership with another organization, anything negative that tarnishes their reputation could also affect yours. Be sure to proceed with a long-term commitment only when you are sure that their values and yours are a match.

For an ETHICS challenge, go to Exercise 20 on page 127.

are singled out and praised for their accomplishments. In individualistic cultures, employees expect to be acknowledged for individual achievements. Although people in the United States tend to think of individualism as the norm, there are significantly more collectivist cultures in the world than individualistic cultures (ITIM International, 2009). US companies that respect these collectivist values and build business practices around them, as Pepsi did, can be extremely successful.

Power Distance

Power distance is the term Hofstede developed to describe how cultures perceive inequality and authority. In cultures with high power distance, organizations are very formal and hierarchical, with a clear separation between superiors and subordinates. People are granted respect based on their position alone. In high-power-distance cultures, people typically expect to conduct business with others of equal rank. To send a junior executive to meet with a CEO would be considered an insult to the CEO.

By contrast, cultures with low power distance believe in social equality and therefore have a more relaxed attitude about title and status. Seniority and age alone do not earn someone respect. Younger workers expect to be taken seriously and respected for the quality of their work despite their lower status. In low-power-distance cultures, people progress to a first-name basis much more quickly than in high-power-distance cultures.

Although there is often a correlation between power distance and context, this is not always the case. For example, French culture is relatively low context and direct. However, the French have more respect for formality and authority than people from other low-context cultures, such as Canadians.

Uncertainty avoidance

Uncertainty avoidance relates to how comfortable a culture is with ambiguity, risk, and change. Cultures that are uncomfortable with uncertainty tend to rely on rituals, rules, and codes of conduct that help make the future more predictable. For example, employees in these cultures tend to like clear guidelines that lead to a predictable result. These employees value learning by observation so that results are repeatable. By contrast, cultures that are more comfortable with uncertainty and ambiguity tend to like more flexible work environments that allow risk-taking and entrepreneurial behaviour. These employees value learning by doing, even though the result may be less predictable.

Robert Gibson, senior consultant for intercultural business competence at Siemens AG in Munich and a British national, offers the following example:

> *German colleagues often want a detailed agenda but I sometimes ask myself, why are we doing all this planning? I just feel like going in, doing something and seeing what happens. This can irritate them. For Germans planning provides security, a framework and a logical structure. The British tend to be more pragmatic, reacting to the situation rather than strictly following a plan. The key to dealing with this is to be aware of the differences. (Gibson, 2014)*

Power distance A characteristic of cultures that describes how that culture perceives inequality and authority.

Uncertainty avoidance A measure of how comfortable a culture is with ambiguity, risk, and change.

Attitudes toward uncertainty and ambiguity affect communication on many levels. Cultures that avoid uncertainty are often collectivist and tend to be cautious about integrating new people into a group. They also value harmony and consensus. Cultures that tolerate uncertainty are open to new people, new ideas, and risks.

Time orientation

In addition to cultural context, anthropologist Edward T. Hall introduced the terms *monochronic* and *polychronic* to describe two different cultural orientations toward time. **Monochronic cultures**, like the United States, most of Canada, and Northern European countries, value punctuality and efficiency. Meetings begin on time and are expected to follow a set agenda. Deadlines are usually strict. Although most monochronic cultures are also individualistic, some collectivist cultures, like Japan, also value punctuality and efficiency. In their view, keeping to an agreed schedule shows respect for the entire group. **Polychronic cultures** are more relaxed about time and punctuality. Polychronic cultures typically put people and relationships before schedules. In a meeting, participants may easily change the order of items on the agenda. While it is important for work to be completed, people may choose to spend time building a relationship over completing a task. In polychronic cultures, deadlines can often be adjusted.

Understanding the various approaches to time is crucial to maintaining smooth relationships. An American who lived for many years in both Denmark and Latin America said, "When you are invited to dinner at 7 p.m. in Denmark, this means you'll be sitting at the table at 7 p.m. When you are invited to dinner at 7 p.m. in Argentina, this means you'll be expected to arrive at around 8 p.m. The only thing they have in common is this: for both cultures, to arrive at 7 p.m. would be rude."

Holistic vs. Specific Thinking

How do you typically write down an address? In Western cultures, addresses move from the specific unit and street location, to the city or region, to a state or province, and then to a country. However, in Asian or Eastern cultures, addresses more typically are recorded by province, then city, then block, and finally gate or street number. This reflects a basic difference in thinking patterns between most Asian cultures and Western cultures (Matsuda & Nisbett, 2001). Western cultures (e.g., Canadian, American, British, and many Northern European cultures) tend to think specifically before considering context. Another way of describing this is that Western thinkers look deeply first at details (e.g., a specific location). Many Asian cultures (e.g., Chinese, Japanese, and Korean) tend to consider context first (i.e., the whole picture). Erin Meyer, renowned author in the field of intercultural communication in business, notes that, "In a *specific* culture, people usually respond well to receiving very detailed and segmented information about what is expected of each of them. If you need to give instructions to a team member from this kind of culture, focus on what that person needs to accomplish and when. Conversely, if you need to motivate, manage, or persuade someone from a *holistic culture*, spend time explaining the big picture and how all the pieces slot together" (Meyer, 2014).

Touch

Touch, as a nonverbal form of communication, varies widely across cultures. In some cultures, touch is an important way to show warmth, reassurance, and confidence. Touch is such a powerful form of communication that it is governed by cultural customs that establish who can touch whom and how. In Canada, the United States, and Great Britain, people informally touch each other less frequently than people in France or Costa Rica. Even within each culture's norms, however, individual comfort levels with touch can vary. A manager might feel comfortable using hugs to express support, but his or her subordinates might interpret those hugs as either a show of dominance or as sexual interest (Richmond & McCroskey, 2000).

In Western cultures, a handshake between business partners is a normal part of a business meeting. However, some cultures have prohibitions against men and women touching, even in this highly formalized way. In France, Quebec, Spain, and many other parts of Europe, it is common to "air kiss" on or near the cheek, regardless of gender, as a greeting or upon departure. It is wise to be prepared for this to happen and to recognize it as a gesture of warmth and courtesy.

Monochronic culture A culture that values punctuality and efficiency.

Polychronic culture A culture that has a relaxed attitude toward time and punctuality.

Integrate communication style and culture: The Lewis model of cultural types

In Chapter 3 we discussed communication styles and noted that everyone has developed a unique, preferred style. In a general way, the idea of "communication style" can be applied to cultures as well. In his book, *When Cultures Collide*, Richard Lewis outlines the results of his work on this subject. He cautions that this work should not be used simply to create clearer stereotypes of specific cultures. He states that "determining national characteristics is treading a minefield of inaccurate assessment and surprising exception. There exist excitable Finns, wooden Italians, cautious Americans and charismatic Japanese. There is, however, such a thing as a national norm" (Lewis, 2006). Lewis theorizes that there are three distinct types of "national norms":

- **Linear-actives.** Those who plan, schedule, organize, pursue action chains, and do one thing at a time.
- **Multi-actives.** Those who do many things at once, planning their priorities not according to a time schedule but according to the relative thrill or importance that each appointment brings with it.
- **Reactives.** Those who prioritize courtesy and respect, listening quietly and calmly to speakers and reacting carefully to the other side's proposals (R. Lewis, 2006).

   FIGURE 4.4 shows a diagram of the spectrums between these three different styles.
   FIGURE 4.5 provides some additional detail on the three types of "national norms" that Lewis identified.

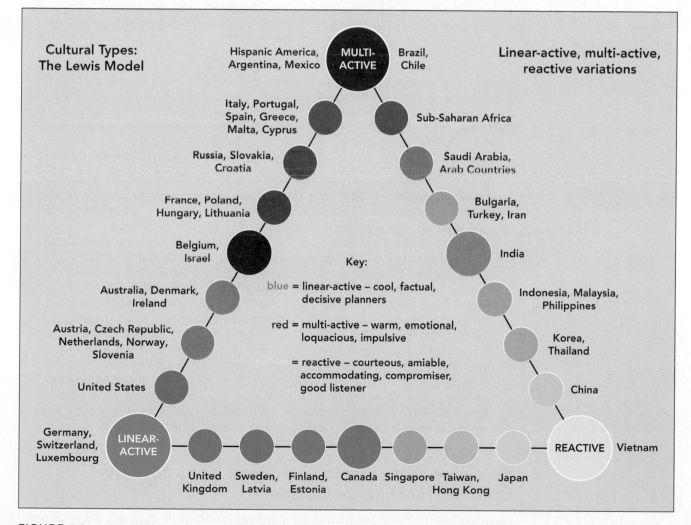

FIGURE 4.4 The Lewis Model of Cultural Types

Source: Richard Lewis Communications. (2015). Dowloaded from www.crossculture.com

FIGURE 4.5 Communication Styles in the Lewis Model

Source: Lewis, R. (2006). *When cultures collide: Leading across cultures* (3rd ed.). Boston, MA: Nicholas Brealey Publishing.

LINEAR-ACTIVE	MULTI-ACTIVE	REACTIVE
Likes privacy	Gregarious	Good listener
Talks half the time	Talks most of the time	Listens most of the time
Speaks on one topic at a time	Discusses several things at once	Reacts to input of others
Plans ahead, step by step	Plans grand outline only	Looks at general principles
Polite but direct	Emotional	Polite but indirect
Confronts with logic	Confronts emotionally	Never confronts
Sticks to facts	Feelings before facts	Statements are promises
Sticks to agenda	Interrelates topics	Thoughtful, summarizes well
Written word is important	Spoken word is important	Face-to-face contact is important
Restrained body language	Unrestrained body language	Subtle body language
Rarely interrupts	Interrupts frequently	Does not interrupt
Separates social/professional	Interweaves social/professional	Connects social/professional

This theoretical model maps out many possible cultures across these three spectrums. The advantage of such a model is that it gives you a rough assessment of the kind of cultural norms you may be interacting with when doing business across cultures. The disadvantage of such a model is that it can be misused to categorize cultures in a simplistic way. Also, some of the subtler differences between cultures are not captured. For example, the UK and Germany are quite close to each other on the Lewis spectrum. However, it is clear that there are important difference between these cultures:

What has it been like as a British national in Germany? When I came to Germany all those years ago I didn't think there would be massive differences between Britain and Germany. There probably aren't in the world context. When you go to China, you expect people to be different. The differences between Britain and Germany are more subtle. One of the main differences is in terms of communication style. Issues in Germany are often dealt with and understood in a very direct manner. For instance, the feedback I got after I ran a workshop was, "You use the word vielleicht *(perhaps) too much." That made me think. The word suggested to my German colleague that I wasn't sure what I was doing. To me it was a way of trying not to be too bossy, softening the instructions to get the group on my side. Or when a German says, "I gave a presentation in England and they said it was very interesting," I reply, "Oh dear." They are confused and then I point out that it may be that the British person was just being polite and didn't find it interesting at all. I like the saying "The Germans are too honest to be polite and the British are too polite to be honest." After nearly 30 years in Germany, I have got used to this direct communication and even find it quite refreshing. For many Germans, though, I'm still not direct enough. (Gibson, 2014)*

Be aware that common language does not equal common meaning or culture

Language is a powerful foundation for communication. It defines, usually with precision, what we mean to communicate. However, language can also be confusing, especially when we assume that same-language speakers ascribe the same meanings to words. A comparison of British English, American English, and common Canadian English bears this out. Canadians and Brits call the last letter of the alphabet "zed," while our American friends say "zee." A Canadian will wear a "toque" on his or her head in the winter to keep warm, whereas Brits and Americans wear a knit cap. Canadians and Americans use an elevator in tall buildings, but Brits use the lift. For more English words and phrases that are different in Canadian, British, and American cultures, see our handy chart on **MyBCommLab**.

Tone of voice and volume can leave different impressions. It would not be unusual for a Canadian to mistake a British speaker's soft tone and understated language as indications of the person being uninterested in the topic at hand. British and Americans often remark that Canadians use language that sounds apologetic. Each speak their native first language, English, but there are numerous variations among the three countries. There are, at minimum, 58 different countries that list English as their national language. Given that each country likely has multiple regional variations, a more accurate estimation would suggest that the variations on the use and meanings of spoken English could number in the hundreds.

Of course, non-English examples exist of this "same language, different culture" reality. For example, centuries ago the French language was exported to large areas of Africa and North America. The French spoken in modern-day France is quite different than the French spoken in the province of Quebec, Louisiana, or Senegal. Canadian French was deeply influenced by the origins and dialects of the original French settlers who came from the northwest or Norman areas of France.

Speaking of words with different meanings, what about business meals? Is lunch in Toronto the same as lunch in London, England? Or Montreal? What time should you show up to a dinner in France? Check out our handy reference chart on **MyBCommLab**!

Develop strategies that help you communicate interculturally

This chapter is intended to help you think about intercultural communications a bit differently than you may have in the past. Here are some additional strategies you can work on to improve your ability to adapt to a variety of intercultural communication situations:

- **Experience other cultures often.** This could mean travelling to a new part of your city that features a cultural community, or it could mean travelling to different parts of the world. People who have purposefully and thoughtfully had exposure to multiple cultures are far more open and adaptable to new cultural situations.

- **Employ your understanding of your own style.** Suppose, in your analysis of your own communication style in Chapter 3, you have learned you are direct, you speak quickly and with a slight accent to people outside your culture, and you often speak in incomplete sentences. By being aware of these tendencies, you will know that you should speak slower and make more of an attempt to complete your thoughts fully when you are trying to be understood across cultures.

- **Do your homework: Research!** If you know you are travelling to a certain area of the world or will be doing business with someone from that area, there are ample websites available to assist you with basic background, culture, and business practices for that area. Be prepared with some rudimentary knowledge.

- **Learn language basics.** If you will be doing business with someone who speaks another language, take the time to learn some basics in that language. See **FIGURE 4.6** for a list of basic concepts you should learn in other languages, as needed.

- **Talk less. Listen more.** Focus on the message and try not to be distracted by differences in accent and dialect. Listen to more than the words to ensure you understand the intended meaning. Listen for tone and emphasis (Beall, 2010).

- **Pay attention to the other person's nonverbal communication and, when appropriate, mirror it.** If you are doing business with someone from another culture, pay attention to how that person acts. Does she maintain eye contact? Does he shake hands vigorously? Also, pay attention to how closely people stand together to talk.

FIGURE 4.6 Useful Language Basics

Hello (or a greeting)	Goodbye	How are you?
Please	Thank you	You are welcome
Yes	No	Excuse me
I am sorry	Where?	Why?
When?	How?	Who?
Is there a washroom I could use?	Where is the meeting room?	Could I have your contact information?
What is your email address?	What time is it?	Where is the restaurant?

In the United States, a comfortable conversational distance ranges from four feet to seven feet. In northern Europe, the distance is half that much, close enough for a handshake. In Latin America and southern Europe, the distance is less, and in the Middle East the distance may be as close as one foot (Morrison, 2004). Watch for these signals and learn to moderate your own nonverbal behaviour to fit what you are learning through observation.

- **Default to extra formality and respect until you are sure of the cultural expectations.** Canadians are less formal than people from European and Eastern cultures. In situations where you might think people appear impersonal and distant, they believe they are behaving with propriety and decorum. To maintain formality and respect, address people by their last names ("Hello, Ms. Tsai") until they ask you to call them by their first names. Be polite and courteous. Avoid informality.

- **Avoid idiom, slang, and jargon.** Be specific with your choice of words when communicating with people from different cultures. Avoid **idiom** or **slang** because these phrases are difficult for other cultural or language groups to interpret correctly. Expressions such as "drive me up the wall" and "pass with flying colours" are culture specific. Similarly, avoid **jargon**. Even business jargon like "in the red" or "head-count" may be unfamiliar to your audience.

    Some slang has gradually receded from common use because it is offensive to some groups of people (Joseph, n.d.). For example, use of the following terms is becoming less common since they reinforce historical injustices or disrespectful stereotypes of Canada's Indigenous peoples. Therefore, do not use these colloquialisms:

  - Indian giver
  - Circle the wagons
  - Low man on the totem pole
  - Rain dance
  - Too many chiefs, not enough indians
  - Pow-wow
  - Indian summer
  - Indian time

- **Avoid humour.** Humour is extremely culture specific. It is easy to mistakenly offend your audience when you are trying to connect with them in a lighthearted way.

- **Speak more slowly than usual.** People who are unfamiliar with your dialect and accent will hear and understand you better if you talk relatively slowly and pronounce words clearly.

- **Request feedback to ensure understanding.** When speaking with people from different cultures, do not assume that smiling and head nodding mean they understand what you are saying. These nonverbal responses mean different things in different countries. Instead, ask friendly, open-ended questions that encourage people to give you detailed verbal feedback so you can ensure mutual understanding. For example, you can ask for others to summarize what they understand in their own

Idiom An expression that means something other than the literal meaning of its words.

Slang Nonstandard, informal language that may communicate well within a certain group but often excludes people from different countries, cultures, and social groups. This type of casual and colourful language tends to confuse others when translated.

Jargon The specialized language of a specific field.

way or perhaps to offer an example of the topic of discussion from their own experience. Avoid asking questions like "Do you understand?" A question like this is easily answered with a "yes," which does not help you get a clear sense of the person's level of actual understanding.

- **Smile.** Although it may sound like a cliché, smiling is a universal language. It expresses openness, friendliness, and willingness to communicate.

(LO 4.3) How can you make your communications inclusive?

The concept of **diversity** includes the idea of culture, but it also encompasses other elements. The HR Council for the Voluntary/Non-Profit Sector states that "diversity extends beyond race or ethnicity, religion, culture or newcomer status to include factors such as geography, language, politics, gender, beliefs, sexual orientation, economic status, abilities, skills and interests" (Community Foundations of Canada, n.d.).

For many Canadian businesses and organizations, **inclusiveness** is a key value. This means that many leading Canadian employers take the recognition of diversity very seriously.

Mediacorp, a human resources publications specialist, runs a Canada-wide competition each year for Canada's Best Diversity Employers. To make it to the Top 100 list in the diversity category, employers must have "noteworthy and unique diversity initiatives" that focus on making the workplace welcoming and positive for people who identify as disabled, as an Indigenous person or as a member of the lesbian, gay, bisexual or transgendered (LGBT) community (Mediacorp, 2014).

Employees, business partners, clients and customers, and other organizational stakeholders appreciate language that is respectful and inclusive. However, when we are not mindful of our use of language, we can speak without thought for how our language might exclude someone. This is why it is important to cultivate a mindset of inclusion.

Aside from inclusiveness being identified as part of a Canadian value system, ensuring that all employees and co-workers are treated with respect will have a positive impact on any organization's effectiveness and productivity. Employees who do not feel valued or respected in the workplace will experience reduced motivation, loyalty, and team cohesion. Employees who are treated respectfully can contribute their full energies to their workplace endeavours.

Develop a mindset of inclusion

The words you choose are rarely neutral. Language is closely tied to the style of the communicator and the context in which it is used. Inclusive communication respects and includes everyone. Therefore, you need to develop the ability to choose words that

- include rather than exclude,
- challenge and avoid stereotypes,
- are not burdened with extra meaning or connotations, and
- are not patronizing to individuals or identified groups.

It is important to review your word choices regularly. Different people prefer to be described in different ways. Ask people for their preferred descriptors and always honour individual preferences (University of Victoria, 2015).

Indigenous peoples of Canada

Before Europeans settled in North America, the land had been populated by groups of Indigenous peoples. Each group has their own language and cultural traditions that are distinctive from each other. When referring to or communicating with members of the Indigenous population, you must remember to refer to these cultures respectfully. Here are some basic guidelines (Joseph, n.d.; University of Victoria, 2015):

- Capitalize terms referring to specific Indigenous groups:
  - **Métis** (pronounced "may-TEE")

Diversity Any dimension that can be used to differentiate groups and people from one another, such as ethnicity, gender, gender identity, age, marital status, education, income, national origin, disability, sexual orientation, or religion.

Inclusiveness The quality or characteristic of including everyone and excluding no one.

Métis Mixed-race descendants of First Nations women and French men who self-identify as Métis and are accepted into the Métis Nation.

- First Nations
- Aboriginal peoples
- First Peoples
- **Inuit**
- "Indigenous" is preferred as being more reflective of a wider global community.
- "Aboriginal" is used in legislation to refer to Indigenous peoples of Canada. It is legally inclusive of Métis, First Nations, and Inuit.
- Some Indigenous people identify more closely with their tribal or linguistic group designation. There are over 630 recognized First Nations governments or bands in Canada. Be sure to find out if you are referring correctly to the appropriate group. When uncertain, ask. Major tribal groups include, but are not limited to the following:
  - Haida
  - Kwakiutl
  - Salish
  - Blackfoot
  - Anishinaabe
  - Mi'kmaq
- Research and use the correct Indigenous spellings for the names of tribes, bands, councils, and communities.
- Be prepared for decision-making processes to take quite a bit of time. Many First Nations councils prefer to operate by consensus.
- When a meeting is hosted by a First Nations council or organization, be prepared for everyone attending to be given an opportunity to speak and to be acknowledged. This means that meetings can run longer than you had anticipated.
- Avoid the word "native." This is an informal term used among members of Indigenous groups with each other and in some titles for social organizations, such as the Native Students Union.
- Avoid the terms "Indian" and "Eskimo," as these will be perceived as outdated or derogatory.
- Avoid imposing a timeline when working with representatives from First Nations groups. Many Indigenous cultures are more polychronic than monochronic. Instead, emphasize your willingness to listen and adapt.
- Expect less eye contact from an Indigenous audience and, similarly, be mindful of your own level of eye contact. Many Indigenous cultures find too much eye contact discourteous.
- Avoid overdressing for meetings with First Nations communities. This may send an unintended message of assumed power or authority.
- Be prepared for periods of unfilled silence during meetings with First Nations groups. Ensure that the last speaker has completely finished before you make your contribution.

People with physical impairments and disabilities

You will encounter classmates and work colleagues who may be living with some kind of physical disability. In some cases, the disability is visible (e.g., the use of a wheelchair or other device for mobility) and in some cases the disability is less visible (e.g., a hearing impairment or dyslexia). It would be a mistake to underestimate the degree to which people with disabilities can contribute to our economy and society:

> *According to the Royal Bank of Canada, people with disabilities have an estimated spending power of about $25 billion annually across Canada. People with disabilities also represent a large pool of untapped employment potential. (Ontario Ministry of Community and Social Services, 2015)*

As a general rule, most people who live with a disability prefer to be referred to with an emphasis on their individuality, skills, performance, or job duties and with minimal

Inuit A member of the Indigenous people of northern Canada. May also refer to the family of languages of the Inuit, also known as Inuktitut.

FIGURE 4.7 Useful Terms Related to People with Physical Disabilities

PREFERRED TERMS	PREFERRED USAGE	INAPPROPRIATE TERMS	INAPPROPRIATE USAGE
Person with mobility issues	Sam, our lead customer service representative, is someone who has mobility issues.	crippled wheelchair bound lame	Sam, the crippled fellow in customer service, is a team leader. Sam, the man who is wheelchair bound, is our lead customer service representative.
Person with a hearing impairment	Joyce brings unique skills, such as fluency in American Sign Language and a proficiency in lip-reading. Our store draws more customers with hearing impairments because they know they will receive top-quality service.	It is inappropriate to define a person by their disability rather than their skills. The term "deaf" is not necessarily inappropriate, but it can be used poorly.	Because she is deaf, Joyce connects well with our deaf customers.
Person with a visual impairment	Kiki's input was extremely valuable when we were designing a hazard-free office floor plan.	It is inappropriate to define a person by their disability rather than their skills. The term "blind" is not necessarily inappropriate, but it can be used poorly.	Because Kiki is blind, she has tripped over and bumped into a lot of poorly placed office furniture. She had a lot to say about our office redesign.

or no emphasis on their disability. A guiding principle would be to refer to the person first rather than identifying a person by their disability. If you feel it is necessary to refer to a disability, direct a respectful inquiry to the individual concerned to see which term is preferred. See **FIGURE 4.7** for some examples (University of Victoria, 2015).

In 2005, the Ontario government passed the Accessibility for Ontarians with Disabilities Act. This law stipulates that, among other actions companies and government agencies must take, websites must be designed to specifications that allow most people with a range of visual impairments to navigate and use the site. Sites must also be designed to be accessible to screen readers that read content "out loud" to users (Ontario Ministry of Community and Social Services, 2015).

People of diverse ethnicities

The Employment Equity Act (1998) refers to members of visible minorities as those who are "non-Caucasian in race or non-white in colour." This topic has been the subject of much discussion, and the concept of "race" is widely challenged as a valid scientific category. However, people who are visibly in a minority group because of their skin colour can face social and employment barriers that need to be addressed. Groups and individuals within these groups should be identified by the names they choose for themselves.

The use of the term "visible minority" is complicated, because minority status is relative. A person who is considered a "visible minority" in Canada may be considered part of a majority in other parts of the world.

Avoid stereotypes, generalizations, or assumptions about ethnic or "racial" groups. Try to be inclusive in the use of examples. Be aware that some references can, even unintentionally, extend to racial connotations (e.g., when the word "black" denotes negative attributes, such as a black mood, black magic, a black heart, a black day, or when the word "white" denotes positive attributes like virtue and purity: white knight, white rose) (University of Victoria, 2015).

People of diverse sexual and gender identities

The World Health Organization uses the term "sex" to refer to the biological and physiological characteristics that define men and women. In contrast, "gender" refers to socially constructed roles, behaviours, mannerisms, expectations, activities, and attributes. "Male" and "female" are sex categories, while "masculine" and "feminine" are gender

FIGURE 4.8 Inclusive (Preferred) versus
Noninclusive Terms

INCLUSIVE (PREFERRED)	NONINCLUSIVE (EXCLUSIONARY)
humankind	mankind
staffing the office	manning the office
ancestors	forefathers
working hours	man-hours
labour force	manpower
artificial or synthetic	man-made
sales representative	salesman
business professional or executive	businessman
flight attendant	stewardess
server	waitress
actor	actress
chair (of a meeting)	chairman
Ms.	Mrs. or Miss

categories. Aspects of sex (i.e., biology) will not vary substantially between different human societies and cultural groups, but aspects of gender may vary greatly. Always be guided by the stated preference of those concerned. Inclusive terms are usually preferred. Check out the table in **FIGURE 4.8** for some examples of inclusive and noninclusive terms.

This list is not intended to be a full list of possible terms. Look at the list carefully. When you use the noninclusive term, not only are you stating a role, status, or activity, you are also implying a gender assignment. When you imply a gender along with a role or action, you are implying an association between the gender and the role or action. Using inclusive language removes this association. In other words, anyone could perform the activity, regardless of gender.

In the case of marital status, it is best to use a neutral term such as "Ms." The use of "Miss" or "Mrs." denotes a specific marital status. Most interaction in the workplace does not require knowledge of an individual's marital status.

Take special care when using pronouns. When the sex or gender is unknown or a group is composed of both men and women, do not assume that the use of the masculine pronoun is appropriate. The usage of the masculine is not a neutral choice. Check out the table in **FIGURE 4.9** for some examples of biased and nonbiased usage.

You may encounter classmates or work colleagues for whom the traditional binary terms for male and female, masculine and feminine, are simply not applicable. The word "intersex" refers to people who, on a physical level, have a mix of typically male or female characteristics. The word "transgender" is a term used to refer to people who find the traditional concepts of gender to be limiting, confining, or inappropriate to their self-identity. Some people feel as though their biological sex (male, female, intersexed) and their socially constructed gender (masculine, feminine) do not match up. In these cases, when considering how to refer to these individuals in an inclusive manner, always be guided by the stated preference of those concerned (University of Victoria, 2015).

FIGURE 4.9 Using Pronouns Well

AVOID BIASED USE	IMPROVE WITH NONBIASED USE	FURTHER IMPROVE BY REWRITING TO REMOVE PRONOUN
If a fleet operator needs maintenance on a vehicle, *he* should contact *his* maintenance supervisor.	If a fleet operator needs maintenance on a vehicle, *he or she* should contact the maintenance supervisor.	Contact the maintenance supervisor if you need vehicle maintenance.
Each person should decide if *he* wants to come to the staff party.	All staff members should decide if *they* want to come to the staff party. *(Use a plural pronoun for a plural antecedent. Plural pronouns are gender neutral.)*	Please let us know if you will be attending the staff party.

Cathy LaRose, a senior manager for a luxury retail brand, recounts the story of hiring Judy, an 18-year-old repair technician, to provide service to high-end products:

She was highly skilled and very focused on developing her specific niche repair specialties. Judy worked for me for 10 years and was the most reliable and skilled technician on staff. After about 10 years of service, Judy transitioned from female to male. He wanted to be called "John" and, while everyone accepted the change, we all had to adjust our use of language, especially changing "she" to "he" consistently. It was a bit of an adjustment for everyone. Our store was the flagship location for our area. Many training sessions and location tours with staff from other regions would take place in our store. Although John no longer reported to me directly, I understand there were a lot of whispered questions about John from our out-of-town visitors. Many were confused by his gender change. The staff responded by stating that John remained the top repair technician and had simply and clearly communicated his need to be referred to as male. Responding to this need was really fairly simple and respectful of his request. In a way, the "transition" in language was far easier for staff and colleagues to manage than John's gender transition must have been for him to manage. (Cathy LaRose, personal communication, January 1, 2015)

People of diverse sexual orientations

In Canada, you should prepare for a full range of diversity in your classrooms and workplaces. You will work and study with people whose sexual orientation may be undefined, fluid, or different than your own. In terms of business communications, it remains important to be inclusive of everyone. As with other instances, always be guided by the stated preference of those concerned. When uncertain, make a respectful inquiry. Check out the table in **FIGURE 4.10** for some useful terms you may need relating to sexual orientation and relationship status.

Here are a few guiding principles to help you when you need to make communications decisions related to diversity:

- **Use names correctly.** Using a person's name is rarely, if ever, incorrect. If you are communicating in writing, be sure to spell the person's name correctly. If you are using a name in a presentation, check with the person to get your pronunciation as accurate as possible. If a person has a preferred name, you may wish to inquire about this. For example, some people named *Elizabeth* may prefer to be called *Liz* or *Beth*. Using a person's correct and preferred name avoids possible issues of gender or cultural identity. Asking and checking on these small details will indicate your interest in getting it right and will solidify your standing with your audience.

FIGURE 4.10 Useful Terms Related to Sexual Orientation and Relationship Status

WORD AND DEFINITION	SAMPLE USAGE	USAGE TO AVOID
Gay (adj.): Used to denote a homosexual orientation, usually applied to men but can be used to describe women or both men and women as a community	Our target market includes partnered gay men. The event downtown celebrated the contributions made by the gay community to the advancement of human rights.	As with any minority group, avoid slang or casual terms in business writing. Do not use this term as a noun. For example, the following usages would be **inappropriate**: Our target market includes partnered gays. The event downtown celebrated the contributions made by gays to the human rights movement.
Lesbian (adj. or noun): Used to describe a homosexual woman	We need sample data from single-parent families headed by lesbian women as well as those headed by heterosexual women. Let's make sure our focus group includes single women, both heterosexuals and lesbians.	As with any minority group, avoid slang or casual terms in business writing and speech.
LGBTQ (acronym): lesbian, gay, bisexual, transgendered, and queer/ questioning	The campus LGBTQ Social will take place next Friday at the Student Centre.	
Heterosexism (noun): An assumption that heterosexuality is the norm	Joan, I hope your partner is able to join us at the year-end celebration.	Joan, I hope your husband will be able to join us at the year-end celebration.
Partner (noun), spouse (noun), husband (noun, male), wife (noun, female): Terms used to refer to a person's life partner or spouse. Note that same-sex couples are allowed to legally marry in all parts of Canada. When in doubt, you can use the term "significant other."	Miriam, we hope your significant other can make it to the corporate launch dinner next week. Please RSVP and let us know. Bill, it was lovely to meet your husband, Jerry, at the fundraiser last week.	Miriam, we hope your husband can make it to the corporate launch dinner next week. Please RSVP and let us know. Bill, it was so nice to meet your friend, Jerry, at the fundraiser last week.

- **Use job titles.** Using a person's job title when referring to job duties is rarely, if ever, incorrect. At work, it is appropriate to refer to what someone does rather than your perception of who someone is.
- **Provide facts rather than assumptions.** Often, if you provide factual information to your audience they will guide you appropriately. This is more respectful than assuming your perspective on their needs is correct.

To get an idea of how all these guidelines apply, take a look at the email inquiry with two possible responses in **FIGURE 4.11**.

In the first response, the writer appears to have misunderstood the original inquiry. Some of his word choices and his tone could be taken as disrespectful. In this case, the writer's carelessness could mean a loss of valuable business.

The second response demonstrates a more appropriate approach. In addition to the specific changes in the text of the second response, notice how the writer avoids making any assumptions about the suitability of the facilities. In the first response, the writer implies that all other people with mobility impairments have been fine staying at that location. However, in the second response, the writer describes facts:

- Previous guests with mobility impairments have stayed there
- The property has been updated to provide access for people using wheelchairs
- Nuts are used in the kitchen

The writer provides concrete, factual information and allows the guests to decide what is suitable for their needs. This is a much more respectful approach.

To: Phil's Bed and Breakfast phil@philsbnb.com
From: Lucy Parker lucyp@othermail.com
Subject: Inquiring about accommodations

Dear Phil,

My partner, Pat, and I were happy to find your website and are interested in staying at your bed and breakfast. We would like to arrive on June 10 and depart on June 13.

We have a few questions for you:

- Is your house wheelchair accessible? Pat occasionally needs a wheelchair for mobility and would need to be able to enter and exit the house and the bathroom facilities using either a standard wheelchair or a mobility scooter. There were no photos of either the front door or the bathroom access, so it is hard for us to tell.
- I have a severe nut allergy. Bed and breakfast establishments often find it difficult to provide fully nut-free food. Is there a local restaurant that could provide a nut-free breakfast?
- We are interested in attending some social events in Forest City, which we understand is only 20 minutes from your location. In particular, we are thinking of attending the LGBTQ dance on June 11. Would we have access to our room, without causing too much disturbance, if we returned quite late that evening?

Thanks in advance for helping us out with these questions. We look forward to hearing back from you.

Lucy Parker and Pat Woods

INAPPROPRIATE RESPONSE

To: Lucy Parker lucyp@othermail.com
From: Phil's Bed and Breakfast phil@philsbnb.com
Subject: Re: Inquiring about accommodations

Dear Mrs. Woods,

I am glad that you and your husband are considering staying with us next June. Currently, those dates are available.

With regard to your questions:

- We have had crippled guests in the past, and they have had no trouble navigating the accessibility ramp to our back door nor have they had trouble using the bathroom facilities.
- Sorry to hear you are nut-allergic. My wife uses some nuts in our homemade granola, but I'm sure it won't be a problem for you if you just eat eggs instead.
- Since your disabled husband needs to use the back door entry, and the main floor bedroom is far from the other guests on the second floor, you will not be disturbing anyone with a late evening return on June 11. I don't know what an LGBTQ dance is or why someone in a wheelchair would go, but I hope it is fun.

My wife and I look forward to confirming your booking.

Sincerely,

Phil Dunning
Proprietors, Phil's Bed and Breakfast
(877) 987-6543
www.philsbnb.com
phil@philsbnb.com

Annotations (left margin):
- Inappropriate salutation as marital status was not indicated in original inquiry
- Offering sympathy rather than information
- Describes a person primarily by disability
- Provides his own name (Phil) but does not name his spouse, which is impolite.

Annotations (right margin):
- Possible erroneous assumption that "Pat" is male
- Obsolete and inappropriate term
- Assumption that what works for past guests works for all guests with mobility issues.
- Dismissive of problem identified; does not provide enough information.
- Poor attempt at humour that could be offensive.

FIGURE 4.11 Email Inquiry with Two Possible Responses

(continued)

APPROPRIATE RESPONSE

Refers to recipient as per original email

To: Lucy Parker lucyp@othermail.com
From: Phil's Bed and Breakfast phil@philsbnb.com
Subject: Re: Inquiring about accommodations

Dear Lucy,

Thank you for considering our bed and breakfast accommodations for your trip next June. Currently, those dates are available. We will hold the wheelchair accessible main floor room until a confirmation is received or until May 15, whichever comes first.

With regard to your questions:

- Previous guests who required mobility assistance have used the accessibility ramp at the back entrance. The main floor washroom facilities have been upgraded for wheelchair access as well. To assist your decision making, photos are attached with width measurements. Please let me know if you have additional questions.
- Some nuts are used in our homemade granola, and we cannot guarantee a nut-free kitchen. I will make some inquiries locally to see if a nut-free breakfast is available for delivery to our location. Please let me know if this is a suitable arrangement.
- Since you will be using the back door entry, and the main floor bedroom is the only one on that floor, you will not be disturbing anyone with a late evening return on June 11. The dance sounds like fun!

My wife Melissa and I look forward to confirming your booking.

Sincerely,

Phil and Melissa Dunning
Proprietors, Phil's Bed and Breakfast
(877) 987-6543
www.philsbnb.com
phil@philsbnb.com

Provides additional information to allow guests to decide.

Checks to ensure that assumptions are correct.

FIGURE 4.11 Email Inquiry with Two Possible Responses (*continued*)

Learn the art of respectful inquiry

In a cross-cultural, diverse workplace, there are several instances where learning how to ask the right questions can help you bridge gaps while earning the respect of others. Throughout the previous section, you read that you should be guided by the stated preference of others. How, exactly, do you find out how another person wishes to be addressed? Or how they wish to be referred to?

This is actually a variation of the earlier concept of "know your audience." Often it is possible that by being direct and respectful you can get the guidance you need.

What is a respectful question? According to Ned Parks, founder of New Directions Learning and Development, a respectful question "when asked, is not judgmental, accusatory, or threatening. It is a question that does not cause the person that answers it to recoil, hide for cover, or feel less than important" (Parks, 2013).

What do disrespectful questions sound, look, or feel like? A disrespectful question implies some kind of assumption, judgment, or bias. Often a question that asks for irrelevant or unnecessary information can be perceived as disrespectful. Check out the **CULTURE BOX** for a situational example.

Respectful questions should demonstrate, by tone and attitude, that you are genuinely asking for information that will help you understand your audience and their needs. Here are a few guiding principles to keep in mind:

- **Provide context.** Explain why you are asking. What kind of communication are you preparing and who is the audience? This will help the individual understand that you are not making a personal or inappropriate request.
- **Demonstrate "best interests."** Most people, regardless of how they identify, appreciate the ability to have some input into how information about them appears in print or on social media. If you phrase your request in a way that shows that you are

CULTURE
WHEN THE QUESTIONS SAY MORE THAN THE ANSWERS

Skylar's business program at Provincial College has an internship opportunity. This offers students with no previous experience in their field the opportunity to gain relevant work experience. Skylar has been given the opportunity to apply to CityScape Marketing for a three-month internship. To successfully acquire the position, she must be interviewed. Given her quiet nature and relative inexperience, this is a great opportunity for Skylar to hone her interview skills.

She is asked to arrange an interview time via email with Mr. Patrick Harris, the marketing manager for CityScape Marketing. Skylar sends a well-worded, error-free email to Mr. Harris. In response, she receives an email that is formal and polite. Mr. Harris asks about Skylar's time availability, program skills, and marketing career interests. After a few email exchanges, they set a date and time for the internship interview.

For the interview, Skylar is prepared and punctual. As soon as Skylar is introduced to Mr. Harris the interview begins. During the interview, Mr. Harris says three things that surprise Skylar:

- He comments, with surprise, on how well-spoken she is and then asks if English is her first language.
- He asks if she enjoys attending Caribana.
- He comments that she would fit in well with the culture of CityScape as all of the interns are women. He then tells a short story about his own start at the firm, as a junior manager, five years earlier.

Although the interview seems to end well, Skylar leaves the marketing firm feeling uncomfortable. She is puzzled that Mr. Harris would be surprised at her use of clear and precise language. She has never attended Caribana since her family has preferred to travel in the summers. She feels particularly concerned that "all the interns" at CityScape are women. She wonders if she would be considered for a junior manager's job in two years, after graduation, if the company only sees her as capable of an "intern" role.

What has unfolded in this interview? This is where O-A-R can guide you:

- **Observe:** If we were to observe Canadian business culture, we would see that women still occupy fewer management and senior-level positions. As of January 2015, *Canadian Business* reported that women occupy 20.8%

of corporate board seats in Canada. While this is a significant improvement on the 15.9% reported in 2013, the 2015 statistic places Canada slightly ahead of the United States (at 19.2%) but behind the United Kingdom (at 22.8%) and far behind the leader, Norway (at 35.5%) (Toller, 2015).

The statistics illustrate the slow progress of change. Some managers, like Mr. Harris, assume that women still start their business careers as interns rather than as junior managers. Mr. Harris has revealed the culture of the marketing firm through these comments. His remarks about her proficiency in English and her attendance at a local Caribbean festival are assumptions he made based on her mixed heritage.

- **Ask:** Many student interviewees feel overwhelmed, nervous, and vulnerable in the interview process. Be sure to prepare and rehearse a few key questions in advance. Knowing when and what to ask is an important skill. Here are some useful questions:
  - How would you describe the culture of this workplace?
  - What policies and practices are in place to ensure that this is an inclusive workplace?
  - Is it possible for me to advance in this company? Can you share with me examples of people who have started in this position and thrived in this environment?

- **Research:** Before attending your first interview, do some reading on the human rights legislation in your province. Most provinces have strict guidelines on what an employer can ask during an interview. Typically, questions that pertain to educational background, the job, and the job posting are fair and valid. Questions (and comments) related to cultural background, sexual orientation, marital status, age, and other elements of identity are usually prohibited. If you are knowledgeable in this area prior to the interview, you will be able to assess whether the employer is also knowledgeable and aware of his or her obligations in creating an inclusive and welcoming working environment.

For CULTURE exercises, go to the Case Study on page 122, the Review and Critical Thinking Questions on page 124, and Exercises 1–8 and 11–13 on pages 124–126.

attempting to achieve accuracy and clarity, you are operating ethically and in the "best interests" of the recipient.

- **Allow maximum flexibility.** Avoid asking for specifics like "Which pronoun should I use?" or "How should I refer to your partner, Jane, in the company bio?" Explain your dilemma more generally and allow the recipient to provide the information he or she feels will resolve your problem. See **FIGURE 4.12** for an example.
- **Frame your question as a request for assistance.** Most people respond well to a sincere request to help others understand. Questions that begin with a gently phrased

INAPPROPRIATE REQUEST

Using the female first name ignores the official request to use male references. A misguided attempt to appear friendly.

Fails to provide adequate context for the request. Without context, the reader would question the need for this information. This request would seem invasive.

To: Kristopher Smythe <SmytheK@corporatehouse.com>
From: Wendy Gibson <GibsonW@corporatehouse.com>
Subject: Updating Your Online Bio

Hi Krystal,

I hope you don't mind if I address you, between us, as Krystal. I have called you Krystal since we both started working here five years ago and it is a hard habit to break!

In any case, I need some information from you for a project I'm working on. Can you get back to me fairly quickly as I'm on a deadline?

- **Marital Status:** In the online bio that was updated before your gender transition, or whatever it is called, you are listed as married (to Steve) with three children. Is this still correct?
- **Pronouns:** I can't decide if you should be called "he" or "she" in the bio. Maybe I should I use "she" until six months ago and then switch to "he" for the more current items? For example, "She graduated from the University of Toronto with an MBA in 1995," and then "He was awarded the President's Gold Leaf Success Award in June 2015." Will that work?
- **Voluntary Service:** The online bio discusses your work with the ValleyBrook Business Association, but I wonder if, under the present circumstances, you would like this left out.

I'm working on these updates now. I'll just go with what I've got If I don't hear from you by Friday.

Thanks!

Wendy Gibson
Site Administrator
426-555-8844 x345
GibsonW@corporatehouse.com
www.corporatehouse.com

Ignores the recipient's request to be referred to as male. The decision is not Wendy's to make.

An unstated assumption that the recipient may feel embarrassed or ashamed. This is inappropriate.

APPROPRIATE REQUEST

Addresses recipient in a manner consistent with the recipient's request.

Provides detailed context for request.

Allows the recipient flexibility in channel selection for providing updates.

Provides reassurance that the recipient will have a chance to verify the information. This also appeals to "best interests."

To: Kristopher Smythe <SmytheK@corporatehouse.com>
From: Wendy Gibson <GibsonW@corporatehouse.com>
Subject: Updating Your Online Bio

Hi Kristopher,

Currently, there is a project underway to ensure that all the information on our corporate website is up to date. Your bio is available at: www.corporatehouse.com/staffbios/KSmythe. Could you please review the current bio and let me know how you would like any changes to appear?

There are a few options in terms of getting these changes to me.

- You could send me any specific changes you want by email. Please be as precise as possible.
- We could meet for coffee to discuss any changes you recommend. This has the added advantage of allowing us to go through the changes in detail to ensure accuracy.

Either way, I will provide you with a full edit with your changes by email for your review and verification. If I could have your suggested changes by Friday, I'd really appreciate it.

Thanks!

Wendy Gibson
Site Administrator
426-555-8844 x345
GibsonW@corporatehouse.com
www.corporatehouse.com

Phrases request in terms of the recipient's "best interests."

Reinforces sincerity and interest in accuracy.

FIGURE 4.12 An Inappropriate and an Appropriate Request for Sensitive Information

"Can you please help me . . . ?" are usually well received. For example, if you are unsure about the pronunciation of a name, you can phrase the request as follows: "I want to be sure to introduce you correctly at the staff meeting, but I'm unsure how to pronounce your name. Can you help me learn the pronunciation?"

When you are asking for sensitive information, your request should not include any assumptions you may have about your audience. Take a look at the two emails in Figure 4.12. Wendy Gibson is writing to clarify information posted on Kristopher Smythe's corporate bio on the website. Kristopher is a manager at Corporate House, an investment firm. Until recently, Kristopher was known as Krystal. However, six months ago he transitioned his gender identity from female to male. Employees at Corporate House were informed by the human resources department that Krystal should now be referred to as male. Wendy is in charge of keeping the corporate website updated. Wendy and Kristopher were hired in the same week several years ago and have attended many internal training sessions together. Wendy and Kristopher have always been friendly and have often sat together during these sessions.

The secret of our success in this community is very simple. We've learned a basic truth that evades so many in this broken world. We're all in it together. Our neighbour's pain is our pain; our neighbour's success is our success. (Calgary Mayor Naheed Nenshi, quoted in Elliott, 2013)

Use ACE to navigate diverse and intercultural situations

FIGURE 4.13 provides some ideas for applying ACE to your work within intercultural and diverse environments.

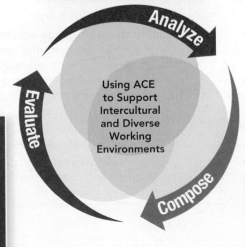

> Make no assumptions about your audience.
>
> Find out about language preferences of your audience.
>
> Balance all "three stories": yours and your audience's. Do not give undue weight to only one perspective.
>
> Research specific cultures carefully, reviewing the cultural intelligence points in this chapter.

> Analyze
>
> Using ACE to Support Intercultural and Diverse Working Environments
>
> Compose
>
> Evaluate

> Ask regularly for honest feedback from co-workers with "stories" that differ from yours.
>
> If unsure, default to extra formality until cultural expectations are clear.
>
> Remove attempts at humour, which can be misinterpreted.
>
> Speak more slowly than usual.
>
> Proofread for phrases or terms that may be inappropriate.

> Adjust your use of language based on your knowledge of your audience.
>
> Learn simple phrases in other languages to assist with relationship building.
>
> Use language that includes rather than excludes.

FIGURE 4.13 Using ACE to Support Intercultural and Diverse Working Environments

In summary, ACE can be applied to help navigate complex communications challenges such as those presented by diverse and intercultural workplaces. Take the time to honestly analyze your assumptions, the situation, and the audience to create messages that will win you valuable alliances and credibility.

The skills you learned in this chapter are wide-ranging and challenging. Chapter 5 will continue to build on these skills as you examine the role of communication technologies in supporting productive workplaces in a globalized business environment.

@ WORK

Adrienne Rosen
President and CEO,
First International
Courier Systems Inc.

Courtesy of Dr. Adrienne Rosen and Philip Lapidus.

At the opening of this chapter, Adrienne Rosen recounted a story in which an innocent phrase, "a piece of cake," was misinterpreted during a phone conversation, leading to unforeseen delays and other consequences. How has Adrienne used ACE to ensure this does not happen again?

How does Adrienne Rosen use ACE to craft her messages?

First, I take time to **analyze** each unique situation:

- **Who am I speaking to?** Avoid thinking about your audience in terms of your own set of beliefs.

- **Think of the word "culture" in more than one way.** We commonly analyze *our* message in terms of the cultural heritage of the person or place that is *receiving* our message. We forget that culture is also a word we use to define how we behave and think as a group. Look in *and* look out.

- **Do not make assumptions about your audience.** When in doubt, ask. Engage your audience. Listen. Record (i.e., write down) their responses and carefully consider the words they use.

Next, it is time to **compose** the message:

- **Use what you learned.** When communicating messages use the information you gleaned from analyzing your marketplace. Use the language that you heard, use the images that you have seen, and embrace the cultural thread that runs through it.

- **Check for organizational fit.** Ensure that the language that comes from you and your corporation matches and reflects what you are offering. Your corporate "tone" may need adjustment depending on your audience.

- **Be as literal in your word choice as possible.** Your communication should be clear, accurate, and fresh. Stay clear of "catchy phrases" because they may not be clear or meaningful to others. In fact, what is "catchy" to you could be insulting to someone else.

I then take time to consider and **evaluate** my messages:

- **Get feedback from diverse sources.** Have other team members from a diversity of backgrounds read or listen to the communication. If your team members are not all that diverse, get opinions from other areas of the company.

- **Double check language accuracy.** Have numerous people check and recheck grammar, spelling, layout, and images. Make sure there are no errors. It is more than embarrassing to have your client point out the mistakes on your website. This happens more often than you can imagine.

- **Check that images reflect your intention to be inclusive.** Ensure that the images you use include a variety of people. Pay attention and include men, women, people with disabilities, and people from a variety of orientations and cultural backgrounds.

Learning Objectives in Review

 Why do we need to study intercultural communication and workplace diversity? *(pages 96–100)*

- **Understand the impact of culture and diversity on communication.** Culture describes learned and shared patterns in a society. People are shaped by the cultures they come from and they develop a set of assumptions about how to act based on those cultural influences.
- **Know that each individual is unique.** We work with individuals, not "members of groups." Each person, including yourself, has at least three "stories" that create identity. Keep this in mind when assessing your audience and reflecting on your response to different cultural expectations.
- **Develop a mindset of cultural intelligence.** Cultural intelligence combines awareness, flexibility, observation, and balance. Adaptability is a key skill to becoming culturally intelligent.

LO 4.2 What do you need to know to improve your cultural intelligence? *(pages 100–109)*

- **Understand how cultures differ.** Cultures do have different expectations and norms. Some have been identified and analyzed, as noted in this chapter. Understanding these specific areas will help you adapt to new situations with greater ease.
- **Integrate communication style and culture: The Lewis model of cultural types.** Examining the "national norms" of a variety of cultures has value in informing both your

understanding of communications styles and your cultural intelligence.

- **Be aware that common language does not equal common meaning or culture.** All languages evolve and change over time. In many cases, new dialects and meanings have regional variations. Be aware of areas where meaning can be misinterpreted, even when all parties speak a common language.
- **Develop strategies that help you communicate interculturally.** In addition to becoming more culturally intelligent, a variety of additional strategies can help you succeed in a cross-cultural environment.

 How can you make your communications inclusive? *(pages 109–121)*

- **Develop a mindset of inclusion.** For many Canadian businesses and organizations, inclusiveness is a key value. This means that many leading Canadian employers take the recognition of diversity very seriously. Developing a similar mindset will help you adapt to the Canadian employment environment.
- **Learn the art of respectful inquiry.** There are strategies you can employ to ask directly for sensitive information, should you need it.
- **Use ACE to navigate diverse and intercultural situations.** Remember that ACE applies. Analyze your audience and your assumptions. Compose your message using language that is appropriate to the audience. Evaluate carefully to improve your intercultural and diversity skills and to eliminate areas of possible friction or misunderstanding.

KEY TERMS

collectivist culture p. 101	ethnocentrism p. 96	Inuit p. 110	polychronic culture p. 104
context p. 100	First Nations p. 97	jargon p. 108	power distance p. 103
cultural intelligence p. 98	idiom p. 108	Métis p. 109	slang p. 108
culture p. 96	inclusiveness p. 109	monochronic culture p. 104	stereotype p. 96
diversity p. 109	individualistic culture p. 101	organizational culture p. 97	uncertainty avoidance p. 103

CASE STUDY

Working as a Cross-Cultural Team

This case study will help you review the chapter material by applying it to a specific scenario.

The first three weeks of Brendan's internship at Kramer & Kaplin Market Research in Calgary were great. He enjoyed brainstorming marketing ideas with his manager and designing a survey

for an important client. However, the weeks that followed were pure misery. Brendan's supervisor assigned him to join three other interns on a team to create a comprehensive online handbook for interns. Each summer the company hires seven interns at the Calgary location and seven more in the company's programming and data processing department in New Delhi, India. Brendan will work on this project with one other intern from the Calgary office and two interns from New Delhi.

Planning the first meeting was difficult. Brendan lost two days of work trying to set a meeting time because there is a 12 1/2-hour time difference between Calgary and New Delhi: at 9 a.m. Central Standard Time in Calgary it is 9:30 p.m. in New Delhi. Brendan suggested a 7 a.m. teleconference, but his Calgary teammate, Roberto, said he could not arrive in the office early for a meeting. Brendan suggested an 8:30 a.m. teleconference, which would be 9:00 p.m. in New Delhi. Both his New Delhi teammates, Maansi and Anant, were vague about whether they could stay late. Brendan begged Roberto to arrange to get to work early just one day so that the team could hold a kickoff meeting. Roberto admitted that he could easily get to the office early, but preferred to sleep later. "And anyway," he admitted, "I didn't sign up for human resources work when I accepted an internship in consumer research. How will this help me get a job?"

Finally, Brendan was able to convince Roberto to accommodate Maansi and Anant. The first meeting was scheduled for 7:30 a.m. Central Standard Time. The meeting seemed to begin well enough. Everyone arrived on time, the teleconferencing system worked, and the meeting started with friendly introductions. Within five minutes, though, Brendan knew the team was in trouble. When Anant introduced himself, he spoke so quickly that Brendan and Roberto missed everything he said. Brendan felt too embarrassed to ask him to repeat it, so Brendan remained quiet and pretended to understand. No one thought to make an agenda, so no one knew what the team was trying to accomplish. After a few moments of painful silence, Brendan said, "Well maybe we should just start sharing ideas about coming up with a plan for the online handbook."

Anant jumped right in. Brendan still did not understand much of what he said, but heard the words "user interface," "programming," "database," and "search functions." Brendan and Roberto looked at each other in amazement. Why was Anant talking about computer programming? And why was he continuing to talk without stopping for five minutes? Would it be rude to interrupt? Finally, Roberto said, "Anant, it sounds like you have some good ideas, but we don't understand. We thought our job was to plan an online handbook." Anant replied, "That's what I'm talking about." Throughout all of this, Maansi remained silent. After the first meeting, Brendan felt like it was going to be a long five weeks until the end of his summer internship.

QUESTION 1: *What interpersonal, intercultural, and teamwork communication issues are emerging in this scenario? How many can you clearly define?*

Managing Cultural Diversity

Brendan and Roberto ask for a meeting with their supervisor, Caitlin. They make a list of questions to be discussed:

- What does "a plan" mean? What would "a plan" include? What is the goal of the team?
- Is there some specific reason Brendan and Roberto were put on the team? Is there some specific reason Maansi and Anant are on the team?
- What should be the final deliverable this summer?

The meeting with Caitlin was very helpful. Through much questioning, clarifying, and paraphrasing, Brendan and Roberto identified four tasks for the summer:

- Evaluate the material in the current paper handbook
- Gather information from current interns in both locations
- Put together a content outline for the website
- Develop an easy-to-use structure for the website

By the second week of the project, the team was working efficiently, with all team members doing their tasks. Yet there was tension at every team meeting. Roberto appeared to be looking for the fastest way through the project, and he tended to be frustrated with Brendan's attention to detail. Brendan was losing patience with Roberto, seeing him as capable of great work but lacking any commitment to quality. Meanwhile, Maansi and Anant continued to focus on the programming aspects of the online handbook and were not interested in talking about content.

To streamline communications while working with Anant and Maansi, Brendan set weekly meeting times on Tuesdays and Thursdays at 8 a.m. Central Standard Time, which worked out well for both the Canadian and Indian team members. Every meeting had an agenda, and team members exchanged important information in writing before and after the meeting. This eased the problem of understanding foreign accents. (Brendan was surprised to learn that Anant had as much difficulty understanding his Western Canadian accent as Brendan had understanding Anant's Indian accent.)

Nonetheless, although some aspects improved, the team continued to have some difficulties working together. Anant and Maansi always seemed busy with several projects and did not treat this one with any urgency. They were indirect in presenting what they had accomplished, and Brendan was never confident about how far along they were. At one meeting, when Brendan asked Maansi to give them a virtual tour of their prototype website, she became silent. Brendan did not intend the question as a criticism but she seemed to have taken it that way. Anant, by contrast, was never silent, always trying to engage in an intellectual debate about various programming techniques and user interfaces. Trying to sort out intercultural communications had proved very challenging.

QUESTION 2: *Review section 4.2 of this chapter. What specific factors may explain the cultural differences between the Canadian and Indian team members? Do any of these cultural factors apply when looking at Brendan and Roberto's working relationship? What strategies can Brendan use to make the summer more pleasant and productive? List and describe as many as you can.*

QUESTION 3: *If Maansi and Anant were asked to describe the intercultural challenges of working with Brendan and Roberto, what do you think they might say? Would it be valuable or productive for Brendan and Roberto to understand those challenges from Maansi and Anant's perspective?*

Reaping the Benefits of Teamwork

At the end of the summer internship, despite the conflicts and communication challenges, Brendan is surprised at everything the team has accomplished. Working as a team, they have done all of the following tasks:

- Interviewed all the current interns and compiled the results into a report identifying the most important content for the handbook
- Developed a site map for the handbook
- Wrote content for two sections of the handbook
- Gathered inspirational quotations from senior management
- Programmed a prototype site
- Conducted a round of user testing
- Developed a list of necessary revisions

Brendan remembered two of Roberto's comments from earlier in the summer. At one point Roberto complained, "It doesn't sound like Maansi and Anant will be too helpful on this project. Maybe we should do it on our own." It would have been easier to create the content with just Brendan and Roberto, but so much less work would have been done: no site mapping, no programming, and no user testing. The team needed people with programming expertise to get that done. At another point Roberto asked, "How will this help me get a job?" The answer to that question is now obvious: Everyone learned some strategies for working collaboratively with others while completing a complicated project. Compared to other interns who learned only technical skills in market research, Brendan has developed a transferrable set of skills that will be crucial on the job no matter what field he enters.

QUESTION 4: *Ultimately, this team was successful. How did Brendan demonstrate and strengthen his skills in intercultural communications to support his team's success? Explain in detail.*

REVIEW QUESTIONS

1. What are the "three stories" that most people use to self-identify?
2. What is cultural intelligence?
3. What is a stereotype?
4. What is ethnocentrism?
5. Name one way that an individualistic culture differs from a collectivist culture.
6. What is organizational culture?
7. How would you know you were working in a high-context culture?
8. How would you know you were working in a low-context culture?
9. Give an example of uncertainty avoidance.
10. Give an example of an English phrase that has a different meaning depending on whether it is used in Canada or the United Kingdom.
11. What is the difference between the concept of "diversity" and the concept of "culture"?

CRITICAL THINKING

1. Imagine you have been hired by a global company that is holding a two-week orientation for all new employees at the head office in Montreal. You have never visited the province of Quebec, and you wonder if the business culture is the same there. You will be staying in a hotel for two weeks, and you have been assigned to share a room with a new employee from Zurich, Switzerland.

   - What can you do in advance to find out about the business culture in the province of Quebec? What can you do in advance to find out about the business culture in the city of Montreal? Do you think some knowledge in advance would be useful? Why?
   - What can you do in advance to find out a little bit about the culture in Zurich? Do you think some knowledge in advance would be useful? Why?
   - Once you have identified some characteristics of these cultures, what can you do to ensure that you do not make too many assumptions, either about your roommate or your regional location?

2. Some Canadian companies appear to have no international business dealings. Do such companies need to be concerned with intercultural communications? Explain your answer, referring to at least three points from Chapter 4 as evidence.

3. Do you feel you have "three stories" that create your cultural self-identity? If yes, can you describe each of them? If no, can you define your own identity in another way?

4. Give an example of a "single story" perception others have had about you. Explain why you feel these assumptions were incorrect.

5. Give an example of a "single story" perception you may have about another student, a professor, or a member of your community. Explain why you suspect your assumptions are either incorrect or incomplete.

6. (For Domestic Students) Imagine you decide to go to school for a year in a country that you have never visited. What would be the hardest part of such a choice? List at least five difficulties you think you would encounter. In what ways would such a choice make you a stronger candidate for employment after you graduate?

7. (For International Students) What are the hardest adjustments for you as you attend school in Canada? List at least five difficulties. In what ways will success in this endeavour make you a stronger candidate for employment after you graduate?

CHAPTER 4

DEVELOPING YOUR COMMUNICATION SKILLS

LO 4.1 **Why do we need to study intercultural communication and workplace diversity?** *(pages 96–100)*

EXERCISE 1 Understand the impact of culture and diversity [Related to the Culture feature on page 117]

Find a news article published in the last 12 months that reveals a communications misunderstanding between businesses or people related to culture or diversity. Bring it to class with your analysis of what occurred. How could the misunderstanding have been avoided? What could be done now, after the fact, to repair any damaged relationships?

EXERCISE 2 Know that each individual is unique [Related to the Culture feature on page 117]

Each student should answer these three questions individually:

1. What characteristics, beliefs, or values do I have that I believe everyone shares?

2. How do I define myself culturally or socially? (You can have more than one such definition.)

3. What are my most important unique characteristics? (These could be hobbies, sports, skills, interests, elements of personal history, or any other attribute.)

Form groups of four or five students. Try to create a table of characteristics. It might look like this:

Name	Items in Common	Cultural/Social	Unique
Brian	Wants a good job after graduation Family is central	Fifth-generation Canadian (British/Scottish/German)	Enjoys video games, lacrosse, and jazz/fusion music
Sami	Wants to travel Wants a good job after graduation	Third-generation Canadian (South Asian), gay	Enjoys hockey, Mexican food, and writing hip-hop music lyrics
Nik	Would like to be successful and rich	South Asian (international student)	Breeds tropical fish Enjoys tae kwon doe
Mai	Desires success as an entrepreneur and wants to be independent	Second-generation Canadian (Chinese), mobility impaired	Enjoys video games Collects samples of beach sand from places she has visited around the world

As a group, discuss the following:

- Are all your assumptions about "common" beliefs actually true?
- Are your assumptions about other cultures actually true?
- What did you learn about your classmates that surprised you?

Finally, describe how this deeper knowledge of this "audience" might influence your preparation for communicating in the future. Will you make more assumptions about the people receiving your business messages, or fewer? How might this have an impact on your choices as a communicator? Explain.

LO 4.2 **What do you need to know to improve your cultural intelligence?** *(pages 100–109)*

EXERCISE 3 Cultural norms versus stereotypes [Related to the Culture feature on page 100]

(This exercise can be assigned as an individual or group exercise. It can also form the foundation of a classroom debate.)

a. Begin by creating your own definition for each of these terms:
   - Cultural norm
   - Stereotype
   You may need to do some additional reading and research to inform your work.

b. Consider the following statements. Using your definitions from part (a), decide if the statement represents a verifiable cultural norm, a stereotype based on assumptions, or both. You may need to do some research for each statement. Be prepared to defend your answer in writing or in a presentation or debate.
   - Asians are terrible drivers.
   - The French will never be on time when they come for dinner.
   - Germans are so detail oriented. Everything must be written down and documented!
   - You can't trust people from India. They say "yes" when they really mean "no."
   - Americans are so loud and they never listen.
   - Arab businessmen won't work with businesswomen.
   - Canadians are so polite. They always say "I'm sorry."
   - Gay men want to be women.
   - Spaniards are so emotional!
   - Scottish people never spend money on anything.
   - Chinese women are so shy. They *never* make eye contact.
   - Canadians end every sentence with "eh."

c. Examine the statements that you decided represented both a stereotype and a cultural norm. How is this possible? Write one or two paragraphs to explain.

EXERCISE 4 Understand how cultures differ [Related to the Culture feature on page 117]

Step One: Select a country you have never visited. Research through published sources (not social media) the "business culture" of that country. Based on what you learn, write two paragraphs on how you would prepare for a business trip to that country.

Step Two: Find someone at your school or in your community who is from that country. Show them your written results. Ask them what you "got right" and what you "got wrong" in your research. Ask them what you left out. Ask them how they would recommend you prepare for a business trip to that country.

Step Three: Rewrite your paragraphs with the new knowledge gained from your associate. Be prepared to share your findings with the class.

EXERCISE 5 Planning a meeting [Related to the Culture feature on page 117]

Select a city in a country you have never visited. Assume you are planning your first face-to-face meeting in that city with a team of employees you have never met. The purpose of the meeting is to launch a new project that you will all be working on together.

You will need to research the best way to have this meeting to make it as successful as possible. You may research online and by interviewing people from this city or country. Consider the following questions within your research, and think about how each factor will affect your planning for the meeting:

- Have you selected a high-context or a low-context culture?
- Does this culture have an individualistic or a collectivist preference?
- Does this culture have a tendency to avoid uncertainty?
- Is this culture's attitude toward power and distance a factor?
- How does this culture regard time?
- Does this culture tend to practise holistic or specific thinking?
- Does this culture accept certain kinds of physical touch in a professional context, or does it prefer less touch?

Write your recommendations for preparation for this meeting down. Be prepared to share your findings with the class.

EXERCISE 6 Canadian expectations [Related to the Culture feature on page 117]

"Canadians tend to be somewhat individualistic, somewhat open to collectivism, relatively low context, and monochronic." Would you agree? How do these characteristics complement each other? How might they contradict each other? Explain your reasoning.

EXERCISE 7 Time zones and dominant religions [Related to the Culture feature on page 117]

You work for a company in Winnipeg, Manitoba, and the vice-president of purchasing is planning a series of teleconferences with suppliers in various parts of the world: China, Saudi Arabia, Israel, India, and Costa Rica. Each country is in a different time zone. The vice-president has asked you to help schedule these meetings. She would like each meeting to take place during the standard workweek for the country and she wants to avoid offending any participants by suggesting a meeting time that conflicts with any weekly or daily religious observances for the dominant religions in these countries: Buddhism, Islam, Judaism, Hinduism, and Christianity. Research the time zones, standard workweek, and days of religious observances in the various countries. Prepare a five-minute briefing for the vice-president, proposing a series of meeting times and supporting your proposal with your research.

EXERCISE 8 Nonverbal communication [Related to the Culture feature on page 117]

Nonverbal communication differs among cultures. For example, a degree of eye contact is important to establish credibility in Canada. However, people in Japan and other Asian cultures often show respect by avoiding direct eye contact. Research nonverbal communication in a country you have never visited. How does that country differ in their nonverbal communication from your cultural norms? Be prepared to share your findings with the class.

EXERCISE 9 English variations

The phrase "to table an idea" in a meeting has two completely different meanings, depending on whether you hear the phrase in the United Kingdom or in the United States. In the UK, this means to present something for discussion and debate. In the United States, it means to leave the idea for debate at another time. (In Canada, it is best to clarify with the speaker which meaning they are intending!) Find three other examples of words or phrases in English that have different meanings depending on the region in which they are spoken. Be prepared to share your findings with the class.

EXERCISE 10 Humour does not always travel well

Find an example of humour (a written joke, a story, a visual) that originates from a non-English-speaking source. For the purposes of this exercise, find an example that does not touch on religion, sexuality, or politics. Bring the example to class. Discuss in groups whether or not it is "funny." If there are people in the group who find it humorous, ask them to explain why. If there are people who do not find it humorous, ask them to explain why. Be prepared to share your findings with the class.

EXERCISE 11 Idiom [Related to the Culture feature on page 117]

Imagine you are talking to a group of international businesspeople, and in conversation you use one of the following idiomatic phrases (or another one of your choice):

- Drive me up the wall
- Out of sync
- Out of the box
- We will face off against our competitors
- Threw me for a loop
- That's cool
- Hit a home run
- Hit the ground running
- He hasn't got a leg to stand on

Your international visitors ask you to explain. How would you explain that phrase? What could you have said instead of that phrase to be more easily understood?

EXERCISE 12 Cultural variations [Related to the Culture feature on page 117]

You represent Vroom, an auto parts distributor in Canada. You are negotiating with Warrior Auto Parts, a manufacturer based in Kyoto, Japan. Before your first meeting, your supervisor instructed you to be very firm on two things:

- Vroom must approve all design specifications of parts before they are produced.
- Vroom must have final approval on quality assurance for raw materials used by Warrior to fabricate the parts.

With previous suppliers, Vroom has received inferior products, and your supervisor wants to make sure this does not happen again.

You are at your first meeting with the Warrior representative and it seems cordial and friendly. As directed by your supervisor, you are polite but firm in communicating Vroom's expectations about design and materials. However, you sense that something is going wrong. It seems that the clearer you are on these points, the more distant and noncommittal your Japanese counterpart is. The partnership between your two companies is financially lucrative to the Japanese company, so you are confused. Why isn't the Japanese representative showing more enthusiasm? You were instructed to "get a deal" at this meeting and you feel your opportunity slipping away. This causes you to put more energy and vigour into your negotiation. This does not seem to be working.

What is going wrong? What cultural variations may be having an impact on this negotiation? Be prepared to present your analysis to the class.

EXERCISE 13 The welcoming email [Related to the Culture feature on page 117]

Your CEO wants to write a friendly, welcoming email message to 12 employees recently transferred from Seoul, South Korea, to your location in Halifax, Nova Scotia. All the transferred employees speak English as an acquired language. Your CEO wants to get the tone and wording of this message exactly right. She asks you to review her first draft and provide her with feedback:

> Welcome to beautiful Halifax! I wanted to reach out to you ASAP to let you know that "mi casa es su casa." Whatever you need, don't hesitate to ask. We are all family here. When the nor'easters blow, we'll be here to lend a hand. We know you would feel the same if the shoe were on the other foot. Let's meet for a coffee on Day One, at SunDial Coffee, which is kitty-corner to our office building, at 9:30 a.m. We can have some face time and rub elbows with our newest family members!

What would your feedback be to your well-meaning CEO? Could you rewrite this message to be more appropriate to the audience?

 How can you make your communications inclusive?
(pages 109–121)

EXERCISE 14 Accommodations

Constance is a member of your team, and she has a hearing impairment. Occasionally she misses key items at meetings. Suggest at least three things that you and the rest of the team can do to make it easier for Constance to get more out of team meetings. Suggest at least three things Constance can do to help herself get all the information she needs during meetings.

EXERCISE 15 First Nations: Expanding your knowledge

Research First Nations bands (i.e., councils) in the province where you attend school. Try to find answers to the following questions:

- How many distinct First Nations communities can you find in your province? Of these, how many were you aware of before this research?

- Some of these communities have websites where they post mission and vision statements, policies, bylaws, and other information. Can you describe what is distinct about how these communities refer to themselves, the Canadian government, and the land they live on? What can you learn from this?

- If you were planning to hire a First Nations employee or to engage in a business relationship with an Indigenous-owned business, how would you find out about your audience and their communications preferences?

EXERCISE 16 First Nations: Communications styles

Research First Nations bands (i.e., councils) in the province where you attend school. Locate a First Nations council near your school that has an economic development officer. Invite the chief or the economic development officer to your class to speak with you about the communications styles they have experienced and that they prefer.

EXERCISE 17 Accessibility for people with disabilities

You are a customer service manager for a company with 100 employees located in Ottawa, Ontario. Your company's website administrator, Keith, seems distressed. Apparently your company must make major changes to its website to be deemed "accessible" to Ontarians with disabilities. You wonder what this means, so you type "Ontario," "website," "accessible," and "disabilities" into Google.

- What do you find?
- Which companies must make adjustments to their websites?
- Can you define the "target audience" for these revisions?
- Do other provinces in Canada have similar regulations about accessibility?

Be prepared to share your findings with the class.

EXERCISE 18 What's in a name?

In March 2015, the Ontario Undergraduate Student Alliance (OUSA) published a policy paper on LGBTQ+ students. The report is based on input from university students in five universities in Ontario and was produced by the students who are part of OUSA. Here is an excerpt from the executive summary of the report:

> Names and perceptions can have significant impacts on a student's sense of comfort in certain situations as well as a student's overall sense of self. For students undergoing a sex or gender transition, identity and identifying records assume both a practical and symbolic significance. However, some universities do not have reliable processes for students to choose a preferred name or gender in their class listings, student cards, etc. Universities must adopt policies along these lines that allow the change to be reflected throughout all the services and staff that students might interact with. (Murphy, Hobbs, Rose, Madden, & Irwin, 2015, p. 5)

What advantage would it be to a business to offer employees the opportunity to choose preferred name and gender preferences as part of their employment record or agreement?

EXERCISE 19 Gender neutral?

See the description of the policy paper on LGBTQ+ students in Exercise 18. Here is another excerpt from the executive summary of that report:

> Lastly, universities need to turn to infrastructure to help improve the student experience for LGBTQ+ students. . . . [G]ender-neutral bathrooms are essential for the safety and human rights of students who identify as trans and non-binary. (Murphy et al., 2015, p. 4)

What is a gender-neutral washroom? How would an organization effectively communicate the existence of a gender-neutral washroom to the entire organizational community? What challenges do you see in communicating this message? How would you overcome them?

EXERCISE 20 Honest reflection [Related to the Ethics feature on page 102]

Canada has a reputation for tolerance, courtesy, and respect. Nonetheless, many people face discriminatory and disrespectful behaviour. This can happen in the workplace, during hiring, or simply when out in public enjoying the freedoms that come with living in this country. Some believe that biased, hostile, or disrespectful behaviour toward visible minorities, women, senior citizens, gay and lesbian people, transgendered people, people with disabilities, and others cannot be changed.

Find a current, relevant news story about bias or discrimination in Canada against one of the identified groups here. Or use your own experience. Describe a time when there was a serious miscommunication or similar incident based on assumptions someone else had about you. Write a summary of the news story or of your experience. Using what you have learned in Chapter 4, provide at least three strategies for addressing the situation in a positive manner. Be prepared to share your findings with the class.

5

What Are the Tools and What Are the Rules? Communications Technologies in the Workplace

Robert Churchill/123RF.

LEARNING OBJECTIVES

LO 5.1 **Why is an understanding of communications technologies important?**
pages 130–135

Understand media richness theory (MRT)
Consider a few basics about using communications technologies
Ask important questions about technology tools

LO 5.2 **What are the main functions of communications technologies?** *pages 136–146*

Use distribution tools to share information

Use networking tools to discuss, build community, and expand connections
Use collaboration tools to work virtually with others

LO 5.3 **What are the "best practices" of experienced virtual communicators?**
pages 147–153

Email
Conference calls
Virtual meetings and videoconferences
Webinars
Social media

@ WORK

Wendy Kam Marcy
Cofounder and Lifestyle Blogger,
Hip + Urban Girl's Guide

Director of Marketing,
Adfluent Media

How can we keep it together when we are so far apart?

What started out as a hobby blog in 2010, Hip + Urban Girl's Guide (HUG), quickly grew to become a popular women's lifestyle website. We cover food, style, travel, and local events in Toronto. We also work with various public relations agencies and brands to promote their products and events through our site and social media.

Now in its fifth year, HUG is a successful small business with an international support team. My business partner and cofounder lives in Los Angeles, I live in Toronto, and our guest bloggers are scattered throughout the city. The agencies we work with and clients we represent are primarily in Canada. My accountant is in Edmonton and I have a business advisor/mentor in San Francisco.

Everything happens so fast in the digital world. Assignments often arrive on our desk with extremely tight turnaround times. How do we successfully juggle multiple campaigns, accommodate everyone's schedules (without inconveniencing one another), keep track of deliverables and deadlines, and manage all the different time zones?

Check the end of this chapter to find out how Wendy uses ACE to professionally manage all these important stakeholders, decisions, and action plans!

Introduction

In Chapter 3 we looked at individual communications styles and their impact on interpersonal communications. In Chapter 4 we looked at some key aspects of interpersonal communications in the context of cultural variables and diverse identities. In practice, how will you use this knowledge and these skills on a day-to-day basis?

Working relationships and business partnerships can now span great distances while being rooted in a strong local network. Virtual business relationships can cross borders or they can take the form of telecommuting within a province, region, or city. Although global business travel and face-to-face meetings remain important to initiate and solidify business relationships, many day-to-day operational aspects of long-distance relationships can be supported using current and emerging communications technologies. Similarly, some aspects of your work will likely remain local: interactions with colleagues, teammates, supervisors, and clients. Communications technologies can also enhance and support local communications efforts. In reality, the average business day may involve a mix of long-distance and local interactions using many modes, from face-to-face conversations to email to web conferencing. For example:

- 9:00 a.m.: Staff meeting with eight people in person, two connecting by teleconference, and one connecting by Skype
- 10:30 a.m.: Emails to connections within the local office, provincial head office, and across to Asian and European destinations
- 12:30 p.m.: Lunch event with clients and partners
- 2:30 p.m.: Videoconference with team in South America
- 4:30 p.m.: Final edit of presentation materials for use tomorrow in a videoconference with Asian team (simultaneous edit/review with Canadian contacts across three provinces using Google Docs)
- 5:30 p.m.: A quick blog entry to inform all subscribed clients of a change in product specifications

This chapter explores how you can

- understand the basics about communications technologies so you can manage both upsides and risks involved in their use,
- understand the functional application of communications technologies,
- assess the available tools and channels to select the right one for your purpose, and
- acquire "best practices" when employing virtual communication tools.

Why is an understanding of communications technologies important?

A comprehensive survey, spanning 102 different countries, was completed by RW[3] CultureWizard in 2012. Here are some of their key findings:

- 95% of respondents reported that they worked often or very often with people using the telephone, email, or an online tool.
- 33% of respondents indicated that at least half of their virtual teams were located outside the home country.
- 61% of respondents reported virtual work with individuals based both domestically and internationally (Solomon, 2012).

The same survey reported the following findings when respondents were asked about using virtual communications:

- 88% of respondents noted their greatest challenge as the inability to read nonverbal cues.
- 75% of respondents noted difficulty establishing rapport and trust.
- 70% of respondents felt that the absence of collegiality hampered their productivity (Solomon, 2012).

Productivity, collaboration, and communications technologies are inextricably linked. While virtual communications can produce efficiencies and enhance productivity, a poor understanding of your audience and their expectations can cause profound damage to working relationships and company reputation. This is true regardless of whether the interaction happens with someone at the next desk, a group of employees across the globe, or an entire population of people in a new market.

Learning more about the technologies that support virtual communications will help you select the best tools and channels for your messaging. Furthermore, if you consider that a key objective of business communication is to build and maintain your business relationships, then it is useful to know about some "best practices" that will help you make the most of your virtual presence.

Understand media richness theory (MRT)

What is the difference between communicating face to face and communicating virtually? Media richness theory (MRT) helps us understand the differences more clearly. The two original MRT researchers, Daft and Lengel, presented a media richness hierarchy, arranged from high to low **degrees of richness**. The criteria are

- the availability of instant feedback (as in synchronous communication),
- the capacity of the medium to transmit multiple cues, such as body language, voice tone, and inflection,
- the use of natural language, and
- the personal focus of the medium (University of Twente, n.d.).

FIGURE 5.1 illustrates this concept.

In the workplace, people want to avoid ambiguity in their communications. In a face-to-face conversation, each person has the full range of possible signals to build a sense of meaning in their conversation. Everything from body posture to eye contact to tone of voice to volume of speech adds a layer of nuance and meaning to the messages sent and received. In a videoconference, the distance between participants and the limitations of technology (screen resolution and size, camera framing, audio recording, etc.) subtracts some layers of signal and therefore some meaning can be lost. In a purely audio exchange, as in a telephone or VoIP exchange, while the conversation remains synchronous all other visual elements are lost. Owing partially to their asynchronous nature, written exchanges have even less media richness. Written messages communicate explicit, often detailed information without implicit cues such as body language,

Degree of richness (in MRT) Describes the amount of information transmitted in a particular medium, including nonverbal and subtextual information.

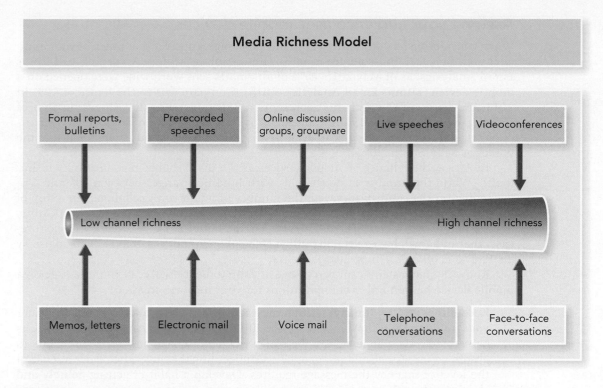

FIGURE 5.1   Low to High Richness Media Channels

Source: ROBBINS, STEPHEN P.; JUDGE, TIMOTHY A., ORGANIZATIONAL BEHAVIOR, 15th Ed., ©2013, p. 350. Reprinted and Electronically reproduced by permission of Pearson Education, Inc., New York, NY.

voice tone, and inflection. Written business messages tend to use more formal (less natural) language and often have a less personal focus.

It is not surprising that many business professionals prefer face-to-face interactions, even at great cost or time investment. For example, choosing to fly to another city to have an important meeting costs more, in terms of time and money, than attempting to have that meeting via videoconference. Therefore, to make that financial and time investment, the "richness" of such a face-to-face interaction must provide considerable value. Nonetheless, as communications technologies evolve to offer greater richness, and as business professionals become more skilled at simulating nonverbal communication, establishing rapport and trust, and creating collegiality online, virtual interactions are likely to become more common.

Consider a few basics about using communications technologies

One of the challenges of preparing a textbook that includes a discussion of communications technology is that new technology tools are launched and gain popularity with great speed. The options you are reading about in this book may or may not have the same level of usage now as when this book was written. Therefore, this section takes the approach of analyzing communications channels current to mid-2015 using criteria that can be applied to future technology options as they appear.

When you are considering which technologies to use for your communications purposes, there are a few general principles to consider.

- Assume your audience uses mobile devices.
- Consider bandwidth (wired and wireless).
- Look for **platform agnostic** tools.
- Understand **cloud computing** and **software as a service**.
- Never assume privacy or security is fully guaranteed.
- Watch for tools to evolve and change.

Platform agnostic A term that describes software and applications that are able to fully function across all operating systems and devices. Most web-based tools are platform agnostic since they can be accessed by most devices regardless of their operating system.

Cloud computing A general term for the storage of data and services in a central location, accessible via the Internet.

Software as a service (SaaS) Similar to cloud computing, companies can offer services (email, data processing, database management, word processing, collaboration tools, and thousands of others) by providing the processing and software at a central location and allowing users to sign in and access services via the Internet.

Assume your audience uses mobile devices

When considering how to distribute or send a message, consider that much of your audience will be receiving your information on a mobile device. According to Litmus Email Analytics, as of May 2015, 47% of all emails sent worldwide were opened on a mobile device (Litmus Email Analytics, 2015). Compare this to the figure of 10% in 2011 and you will see that this represents a 350% increase that shows no sign of slowing down (Jordan, 2013). In Canada, as of early 2015, 68% of adults own a smartphone (Catalyst, n.d.), which is an even larger percentage than our friends south of the border at 64% (Smith, 2015).

In Africa, the reliance on mobile devices as the main source of connectivity is dramatic. While the number of households with landlines ranges between 2% and 6%, depending on the country surveyed, the number of adults with cellphones in many of these same countries ranges from 65% to 89% (Pew Research Center, 2015). In China, 37% of adults own a smartphone (Pew Research Center, 2014). A study by Cisco forecasts that India will have over 650 million smartphones and 18 million tablets in use by 2019 (*The Economic Times*, 2015).

Knowing that a significant percentage of your audience will read your message on a mobile device has a number of implications for your message creation:

- **Keep direct (1:1 or 1:many) written messages short, clear, and on point.** Consider your audience and their mobile device. If your email, text, or instant message is being read on a mobile device, the reader is likely to have only a few moments to absorb your message and respond. Use a subject line that gives the reader a sense of the level of urgency the message requires. Develop a habit of getting politely and clearly to the point.

- **Keep file attachments in generally accepted formats.** You cannot always control or predict which operating system or software version your receiver is using on their mobile device. For most operating systems, **portable document format (PDF)** files open. If you need to send a document in its original format, double-check to ensure all recipients have the required software and version to open the file before sending.

- **Understand that graphics and layouts may not translate well to a smaller screen.** Complex documents that include many graphics and tables may not appear as originally designed when viewed on a smaller screen.

These observations are useful for you as a receiver as well as a sender. When someone sends you a document that does not look quite right on your mobile screen, you may wish to view it on a larger screen, such as a laptop or desktop, before providing feedback.

Consider bandwidth (wired and wireless)

Use of technology-mediated communications tools, by definition, requires access to either a wired or wireless network. Access to either type of network remains surprisingly inconsistent, even in regions that seem to be well developed. Sometimes access is restricted because of cost. Access can also be constricted by heavy use at certain times of the day. In some parts of the world, reliable network infrastructure simply has not yet been created. When choosing a technology tool, check to see what the implications are for connecting to that tool in each region where it will be needed.

Webinar and videoconferencing solutions put especially high demands on bandwidth and connectivity. If you are responsible for setting up such a meeting, go beyond considering whether your location has a stable and speedy Internet connection. If people are connecting from various parts of the world, the success of your communications effort will depend in large part on the stability of each participant's connection. The quality and value of your meeting time can be seriously compromised by weak or unreliable Internet connections.

Minimally, you should test the software and the connectivity prior to your meeting time. A best practice would be to test all the connections at the same time and day of the week. If you are planning a virtual team meeting for 10:00 a.m. EST on a Thursday, have someone from each location connect through the chosen medium at 10:00 a.m. EST on the Thursday prior to the meeting. This will give you the best gauge of how

1:1 One-to-one distribution, as in a conversation or exchange between two people.

1:many One-to-many distribution, as in posting an article online for many people to view or sending an email to a wide distribution list.

Portable document format (PDF) A file format that provides an image of a document that is usually readable across multiple platforms and can be saved in editable and noneditable formats.

Internet traffic on that day and time is likely to affect the quality of your connection. Furthermore, if many people are joining the web conference, this will ensure that any issues with individual security settings at each location (e.g., **firewalls** or other security settings) have been identified and can be addressed.

Look for platform agnostic tools

If you are collaborating with people outside your organization, you should choose a technology channel that will work across a wide variety of platforms or operating systems. Choosing, for example, a project management system that only works in a Windows environment will exclude or restrict participation by collaborators who use iOS or Android operating systems.

Understand cloud computing and software as a service

Cloud computing and SaaS solve some of the mobility and platform challenges that mobile devices have created. If data and information are stored in a centralized virtual space, then **credentials** (user ID and password) can control access, regardless of the physical location of the user. Similarly, software features that are delivered over the Internet through a browser or mobile application, such as Google Docs, most learning management systems, Facebook, Gmail, and thousands of others, overcome the need for any user to be tied to any particular platform or device.

The downside of using services "in the cloud" includes the storage of your data or your company's data on another organization's servers. Our easy access to online services creates an assumption of trust that an external partner will not share, distribute, mine, or expose the data you provide for their own purposes or gain. Even if a cloud-based service appears to have a solid privacy and security policy at the time you initially use their services, such policies are not under your control. As Facebook has demonstrated repeatedly during their evolution as a service provider, their privacy policies and data use policies will shift to accommodate their needs as an organization (Loomer, 2012).

In Canada there are legal restrictions and consequences when information is violated, stolen, or otherwise misused. These laws include the following:

- **The Personal Information Protection and Electronic Documents Act (PIPEDA),** which sets out rules for how private sector organizations may collect, use, and disclose personal information collected in the course of commercial activities (Office of the Privacy Commissioner of Canada, 2015).

- **The Access to Information Act,** which governs and provides access to information collected and stored by government agencies and institutions (Government of Canada, 1985a).

- **The Copyright Act,** which defines ownership, rights, and use of artistic and intellectual property (Government of Canada, 1985b).

While these laws function to protect Canadians and their personal information, most cloud-based servers that store uploaded data are located outside of Canada's borders and, therefore, are outside the protection and jurisdiction of these laws. Before committing your employer's data to an external organization, you need to check with your organization's information technology department for guidance.

Never assume privacy or security is fully guaranteed

For every problem solved, such as needing a global reach across many operating platforms, new issues arise. Many cloud-based services will speak confidently about the security of your data and information. Nonetheless, as years pass and privacy and security systems become more robust and sophisticated, so do the skills of unauthorized personnel (i.e., **hackers**) who target both individuals and organizations to access data or disrupt the services provided.

When you use a social network for personal purposes, the damage from security and privacy breaches are limited to your own individual account and data. Understandably, this is distressing when it occurs. However, consider the damage that could arise from

Firewall A network tool that examines network traffic and allows or disallows information to pass based on the rules provided by the network administrator.

Credentials A term that refers to the user ID and password combination that is usually required to access online services.

Hacker A person who uses computers to gain unauthorized access to systems and data.

trusting a cloud-based solution to share data or information that does not belong to you (e.g., company information and data). For example, if you are welcoming a new member to your team and decide to use a private messaging system embedded within a social media tool to exchange information, you may have exposed your company's systems and data to attack the next time that social media tool has a security issue.

When using any communications technology for business purposes, you must analyze and manage the risk involved. The level of risk is never "zero," even for internal enterprise systems, cellphone conversations, or email. However, risks are often tolerated in exchange for the speed, convenience, and geographic reach that many such tools offer. Deciding which option to use for workplace communications should always happen in consultation with your supervisors and in accordance with any security policies your company may have in place.

Watch for tools to evolve and change

The way in which users deploy online tools is closely monitored by the organizations that make them available. For example, Wordpress was originally designed and launched in May 2003 as a blogging tool (Colao, 2012). However, as its use evolved over time, many people were using the Wordpress platform to manage content for websites that were not **blogs**. As this "nonblog" usage increased, Wordpress responded by improving features that would appeal to the nonblog users of the platform. As of January 2015, Wordpress was the **content management system (CMS)** for 23.4% of all discoverable websites (WTechs, 2015). Therefore, as the primary purpose of online tools changes over time, so do the tools themselves.

For most users, the evolution of an online tool will result in additional useful features. On occasion, you may find that a key feature of an online tool, perhaps something that you depended on or found valuable, will disappear as part of a new version. If you or your organization is especially reliant on a particular online tool, pay attention to version releases and upgrades.

Ask important questions about technology tools

To examine the available technology tools in some detail, a series of questions has been constructed to help you understand how these tools operate and what their features and limitations are. Appendix B: Questions to Ask about Key Communications Technologies, summarizes much of the following discussion in table format, for reference. Most types of communications technology have been included: social media, software, web services, and mobile applications. This allows a comprehensive comparison of features and attributes. In all but a few cases, tools have been generically identified. This is not possible in the case of a few social media tools that have become so popular that they need to be identified specifically:

- Facebook
- Google
- LinkedIn
- Twitter
- YouTube

New technology tools and options are launched frequently. If you or your team wants to use a tool that does not appear on this list, it may serve you well to review these questions to see if that specific tool is going to give you the results you need in your particular situation. Here is a more detailed review of these questions:

- **What resources do I need?** This refers to any specific software, bandwidth, operating system, or platform that a tool might require. For most tools reviewed in this chapter, the user needs a reliable, moderate-speed Internet connection and an up-to-date browser.
- **Is shared information searchable?** Many people are surprised at how easy it is to search for information shared via social media and other high-traffic applications.

Blog (derived from the term "web log") A regularly updated webpage run by an individual or group, either independently or as part of a larger organization, that is usually written in a conversational style and often comments on topics current to the individual or organization.

Content management system (CMS) A web-based application for creating, managing, and updating the content of a website to allow the website content to be managed easily by nontechnical content experts.

This is an important consideration when making comments in a public forum, when running a Facebook page or Twitter account on behalf of your employer, or making job applications on your own behalf. Posts you have made anywhere on the Internet using an identity that can be connected to you are likely discoverable by your current and future employers.

Many companies use blogs, discussion forums, and web chat windows to provide service assistance to their customers. If you are responding to customer inquiries online as a representative of your company, everything you write "represents" your employer. This is an important responsibility. The considerations for posting as a professional are much different than if you are posting on behalf of your self alone. A simple, clear writing style, delivered with courtesy and empathy, are critical. When working in a synchronous chat window, attentive "listening" skills (i.e., reading carefully and clarifying meaning where needed) are very important. Chapters 2, 3, 7, 8, and 9 have deeper discussions on developing professional writing habits and listening skills.

- **Can I limit access?** In some cases you want the widest, most public audience possible. For example, if you are making a public announcement that you wish to have in wide distribution, you want it shared and distributed as much as possible. In other situations you want to carefully restrict readership and participation in collaboration and discussions. Consider carefully the amount of control you need over audience access when selecting a medium for distribution or collaboration.

- **Can shared information be easily reshared?** All digital information is shareable. If information within a specific tool can be reposted or shared with one or two clicks, then this information is "easily" reshared. The ease of sharing affects the size and scope of secondary distribution.

  One of the most powerful aspects of social media tools is their ability to distribute **URLs** quickly and easily to a wide audience. In some cases this is a desired outcome. In other cases it is not. Consider this carefully when selecting a medium for distribution or collaboration.

- **Is it synchronous or asynchronous?** In Chapter 2 we defined the terms "synchronous" and "asynchronous." In summary, an asynchronous tool allows users to collaborate or share without the need or expectation that the users are online at exactly the same time. A synchronous tool depends on participating users to be online and available at the same time.

  In some situations you will want a tool that will act as a repository for documents, graphics, or other digital assets that you are using as part of your teamwork. This is an asynchronous use since you can share materials with team members without regard to time zones or scheduling. Anyone with access can download or upload at any time. For other situations you will want to schedule a "real-time" meeting or conversation in which all contributors are online at the same time. This is a synchronous use. It is quite common for some virtual teams to select one tool for their repository and another tool for their meetings.

- **Is there a cost?** At first glance, "free" seems very appealing. However, tools that are offered for free should be carefully scrutinized. You may be choosing an option that is cluttered with advertising that will interrupt productivity. "Free" may also imply less-than-adequate (or no) privacy or security features, or limitations on storage space. When you choose a tool that comes at even a moderate cost, you can eliminate the advertising interventions and usually acquire additional features such as increased storage and enhanced security and privacy.

  Furthermore, tools that are "free" to use actually do come at a cost. Users "pay" with their data in the form of clicks, "likes," status updates, and other types of posts and uploads. When aggregated on a large scale, this pool of data creates valuable information that can be sold to third parties for a variety of purposes. Consider carefully that every online task and choice you make on behalf of an employer leaves a data trail. When you are making these choices for your employer, and not for yourself, it is important to do so in consultation with your employer's information technology department.

URL Uniform Resource Locator. Also called a "link," "hyperlink," or "web address."

What are the main functions of communications technologies?

For the purposes of analyzing specific communications technologies, the most common technology tools can be categorized into three broad functional types:

- Distribution tools, for sharing information, either 1:1 or 1:many
- Networking tools, for discussing issues or expanding your business connections
- Collaboration tools, for virtual team work and productivity

Technology tools can have more than one type of use. **FIGURE 5.2** gives an overview of commonly used technologies and the three types of uses examined here.

Use distribution tools to share information

Some key tools for the distribution of information include:

- Blogs
- Cloud storage tools
- Discussion forums
- Email
- Facebook
- LinkedIn
- Twitter
- Web chat
- Webinars
- YouTube

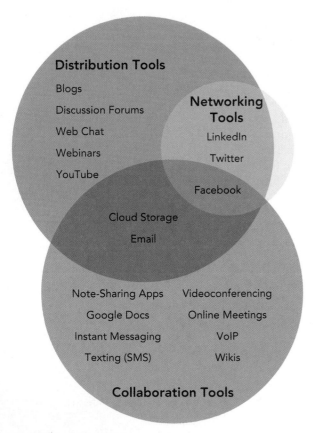

FIGURE 5.2   Key Technology Tools Grouped by Use

Blogs

Blog sites are a popular way for businesses, consultants, and individuals to get their expertise out to the masses. Most blogging platforms allow for ample space to explain, instruct, or expand on any topic. Businesses can use blogs for a variety of purposes, from providing updated product information to customers to showcasing their advanced expertise in their field. To be successful, a business blog's content must be up to date, relevant, and concise. To be credible, valid sources for data should be clearly shown and linked, if possible.

Power Feature for Distribution: One of the most powerful features of a blog is the ability for blog-post URLs to be reposted, shared, and distributed via social media tools such as Facebook and Twitter. This allows you to exploit the blog space to fully explain your ideas while also leveraging the ease with which social networks can popularize your posts.

Caution: For every opinion that is expressed, there exists somewhere an equal and opposite opinion. For bloggers, this means that the comment section below each post can become fractious and possibly offensive. On the one hand, increased activity in the comments section can cause the blog post to draw more traffic and thus more readership. On the other hand, if you are the author of the post, it can become difficult to respond professionally and courteously in this very public space. If you have chosen to participate online as a blogger, you have chosen to put your ideas forward for critique and discussion, be that positive or negative. If you are blogging on behalf of your employer, remember to always maintain your composure and professionalism, even in the face of the harshest criticism.

Cloud storage tools

Many businesses and individuals have become reliant on services that allow users to upload their files to "the cloud" and to selectively share either folders or files using URLs. Group sharing can allow many users to upload and download work from this type of service. This means you can access your work or your team's work from almost any location.

Power Feature for Distribution: The ability to post, text, or email a URL, as opposed to needing to send a full document, reduces bandwidth demand. For example, from your mobile device you can send a link to a document in the cloud rather than needing to use wireless bandwidth to attempt to send it via text or email, which could be unwieldy depending on the file size. Sending a link places very low demand on bandwidth.

Caution: The ease with which a link can be sent means it can equally as easily be mistakenly sent to the wrong recipient, thus compromising the privacy of the file. Take extra care when distributing your employer's information in this manner.

Discussion forums

Discussion forums arise around topics of interest, products, services, politics, sports, or any other area in which discussion and information sharing can occur. Some businesses, particularly those in the technology field, have chosen to host their own discussion boards to allow their customers to provide peer-to-peer troubleshooting and product support. Examples include Microsoft Community (http://answers.microsoft.com) and Apple Support Communities (https://discussions.apple.com/welcome).

Power Feature for Distribution: One of the strong advantages of discussion forums is that they are easily and often catalogued by search engines. Therefore, if you are looking for the answer to a technical issue or a customer service problem, it is likely that someone else has had the same problem at one time or another and has posted the answer in a discussion forum. From a business perspective, this means that technical or customer service information posted to a discussion forum can potentially solve problems and answer questions for literally thousands of users, thus reducing the workload of synchronous customer service representatives.

Caution: As with bloggers who post opinions and expertise, some discussion forum users express their opinions strongly and often. If you become a discussion forum administrator or a moderator for your employer, ask for very clear direction and authority to manage or remove disruptive and argumentative forum members and their contributions.

Email

As a distribution tool, email seems to be the default for electronic material. According to statistics gathered by The Radicati Group, there were over 108.7 billion business-related emails sent and received per day in 2014. This figure is expected to increase to 139.4 billion by 2018 (Radicati, 2014). The average business user will be sending 126 emails per day by 2019 (Radicati, 2015).

Power Feature for Distribution: Email remains popular and ubiquitous because, from the sender's perspective, the channel seems to offer a great deal of control. You select specific recipients, attach documents or include links, and assume receipt occurs seconds after you have hit "send." With the growing popularity of mobile devices that receive email, this channel has become even more "preferred" as senders assume that emails will be read anywhere, anytime.

Caution: In practice, email usage presents numerous problems:

- **A lack of privacy and security.** Unencrypted email is absolutely not secure nor is it private. Copies of your email will be left on every server it passes through on its way to its destination.

- **File size restrictions.** If you are using a proprietary email system from within a corporation, there may be a restriction on file sizes for incoming and outgoing emails. This means that you may think you have sent your file attachment, but the other person may not receive it if their email system has been programmed to remove it.

- **Attachment restrictions.** To maintain system integrity and security, some corporate email services forbid incoming file attachments. This means that some email recipients may not be able to receive your attachments at all.

- **Large margin of human error.** The most common error made with email would have to be the "reply all" error. This occurs when an original message was sent to numerous recipients (1:many). When one of the "many" recipients mistakenly hits "reply all" instead of "reply," their response will be sent to all original recipients. The ramifications of this mistake can range from simple embarrassment to legal action to job loss. To avoid an accidental "reply all" error, when you are sending an email to a large list of recipients, put all the recipients' email addresses in the **BCC** field. If a recipient does hit "reply all," the message reply will be sent only to the originator of the email.

Other common human errors with email include the following:

- Sending the message to the wrong recipient(s)
- Forgetting to add an attachment
- Adding the wrong attachment

Although email has become the de facto communications default in business exchanges, use it with care and attention to detail.

Facebook

With 1.4 billion users as of March 2015 (Statista, 2015a), Facebook has become an effective way to reach a large audience with links to articles, product launches, business videos, blog posts, and other types of business information. As of late 2014, 59% of Canadian adults had a Facebook account (Andrew-Gee, 2015). Typically, the audience will self-select which organizations they wish to receive information from via their newsfeed. Popular items will be shared and reach an even wider virtual audience. Posted articles and announcements tend to be **time sensitive**, meaning that they relate to current or immediate events and issues.

Power Feature for Distribution: As mentioned previously, the power of a social media tool is its ability to allow its network of users to easily share information. Smart business communicators have learned how to leverage this to get their articles, press releases, and other key items out to a mass audience.

Caution: Although Facebook newsfeeds are asynchronous, viewership is also time sensitive. Users who have particularly active newsfeeds may miss posts that have been made while they were not online. Thus, posting information to Facebook does not guarantee that all subscribed users have seen it.

LinkedIn

With 30% of online Canadians now using this site regularly, LinkedIn is showing a strong trend to being the preferred business information distribution site for connected Canadians. Its user base increased 15% per year in 2013 and 2014, and there is no indication that this growth will slow (Andrew-Gee, 2015).

LinkedIn users have a clearly defined business audience and, in addition to posting and updating their own professional profiles, have the option of posting updates, blog posts, articles, and commentary to showcase their expertise and value. Over time, LinkedIn has already become the primary source for recruiting and is well on its way to becoming the first stop for current business articles and thought leadership.

Power Feature for Distribution: The most valuable element LinkedIn offers is its audience. The active membership participates primarily to maintain business connections and **currency**. Profiles are posted there and may become, over time, the de facto "résumé" for job seekers. Human resource professionals scan profiles for targeted leads to fill positions. Almost all professionals are encouraged to keep their profiles and connections up to date.

Caution: If your profile and professional image on LinkedIn are well presented, there is little downside to using the site. However, if your photo is not professional or if your profile is substandard or unprofessional in some way, LinkedIn can do your career a great deal of damage. The fault would lie not with the service but with the quality of the content you share. Keep this in mind as you develop and hone your image on this important business networking site.

Twitter

As of the fourth quarter of 2014, Twitter boasts 288 million active users worldwide (Statista, 2015b). Of these users, 78% (225 million) are outside of the United States,

BCC An acronym that stands for blind courtesy copy or blind carbon copy. Email addresses entered into the BCC field will be hidden from all recipients, allowing a copy to be sent to additional recipients without the named recipient knowing it.

Time sensitive Information that is relevant to a particular, defined timeframe. The relevance expires after the timeframe has passed.

Currency Can either mean (1) a system of money/legal tender, usually within a defined geopolitical area, or (2) the quality of being up to date, current, in use, or generally accepted.

making Twitter an effective tool for reaching beyond the borders of the world's largest economy (Statista, 2015c). In 2014, Canadian Twitter users plateaued at about 25% of online users. However, the user satisfaction rate for Twitter dwindled from 33% to 24% between 2012 and 2014 (Andrew-Gee, 2015).

Power Feature for Distribution: If you have urgent, immediate information to provide to a mass audience, there may be no better channel than Twitter. The ability for your followers to retweet to audiences well beyond your original reach allows for powerful sharing and spreading of current events and public announcements.

Caution: During peak usage times, especially during times of compelling media or public events, the sheer volume of information tweeted can be overwhelming. Your message can get lost in the fast-paced feed of links and commentary. Furthermore, if your followers see you tweeting direct sales messages the majority of the time, they will quickly lose interest in your content. Be sure to restrict any sales, marketing, or self-promotional tweets to 20% or less of your overall Twitter activity. The remaining 80% should focus on interactive networking activity (see the next section).

Web chat

A web chat screen appears most often as a service offered within commercial or service-based websites. A web chat allows a customer service representative (CSR) to have a direct, one-to-one conversation with a customer online in a text window that is similar to an instant messaging window. The conversation can be initiated by either the CSR or the customer.

Power Feature for Distribution: The CSR has thousands of text-based answers to known customer problems at his or her disposal. Clear written responses, without regard for problems with accents or cultural issues, that are customized for each problem presented can be offered to the customer in "real time." Additional features can be sold or offered to the customer. The customer can copy and paste responses into a note program to be saved for future reference without worrying about misunderstanding crucial pieces of information.

Caution: Not all customers are comfortable with this form of service. Consider your audience carefully before you invest in providing this kind of service.

Webinar

A webinar is a seminar, workshop, or lecture delivered to a mass audience online. In terms of experience, it is similar to a videoconference except that the audience tends to be larger and interactivity between the presenter and the audience is usually limited. Many companies are delivering training or product information sessions using this format. The webinar itself will take place at a specific time and place (i.e., it is synchronous), but the recording of the event will often be posted for review by registered participants. As an archive or recording of an event, it is asynchronous.

Power Feature for Distribution: A well-run webinar offers a rich experience for the audience. Video, audio, presentation slides, and screen demonstrations can all be incorporated into the event. Therefore a large amount of complex information can be shared in a short period of time. Furthermore, the ability to review the information after the event is extremely valuable to participants.

Caution: From the audience member's point of view, a webinar is easy to ignore. Typically, participants are not asked to turn on their own web cams. Therefore it is possible to multitask one's time away and not gather any useful information. If you are offering a webinar and 100 people register for it, you can estimate that less than 50 will be giving their full attention to your presentation.

YouTube

This service has become the global cloud solution for distributing information by video. When uploading video, settings can be adjusted to control distribution:

- **Public:** Searchable by the public and viewable by anyone
- **Unlisted:** Hidden from searches and viewable by anyone with the link
- **Private:** Hidden from searches and viewable only by the users selected

Power Feature for Distribution: With the advent of YouTube, video became as easy to distribute as text by using a URL to link to the video source. Prior to the advent of YouTube, video distribution relied on actually transferring the video file. This put huge demands on bandwidth that made the process prohibitively expensive in terms of time and cost. Now, web-based training, webinars, advertisements, and other product and business information can be easily shared with public audiences and controlled groups.

Caution: The ease of sharing and **repurposing** material has created myriad opportunities for users to violate copyright, trademark, and originality of content. Always be certain that anything you upload on behalf of your employer is original and does not contain material that could cause legal action to be taken against your employer.

For example, imagine your marketing team decides to create a **flash mob** to promote the launch of a product, service, or event. A videographer has been hired to produce the YouTube version of the flash mob. Be aware that when such an event is held on behalf of an institution, the music selected for such a production will need to be cleared for commercial use and distribution. Carol Isherwood, a lawyer specializing in music rights, states that "Without obtaining the appropriate consents from the copyright holders of the music and recording that you are intending to use, you risk being on the receiving end of a copyright infringement claim and as well as potentially being liable for costs and damages" (*Voice Council Magazine*, 2014).

Use networking tools to discuss, build community, and expand connections

As previously noted, relationship building is a key aspect of business communication. Some key tools for building new relationships and expanding your professional network include the following:

- Facebook
- LinkedIn
- Twitter

In the early stages of career building, you will be especially interested in connecting with potential employers. Be aware that employers are making extensive use of social media tools to research future employees. For more on how you can use this to your benefit, please refer to Appendix A: Communicating Your Professional Brand: Social Media, Résumés, Cover Letters, and Interviews.

Facebook

Although it is known primarily as a social network, having a business presence on Facebook can result in huge benefits in terms of relationship building with a specific, self-selected, highly targeted market. Depending on the nature of the business, special offers, coupons, contests, and even customer service can be used to build this audience. Knowledge workers, thought leaders, writers, artists, and others who post digital content as part of their business can use Facebook to interact directly with subscribers who have chosen to be part of that network.

Power Feature for Networking: Facebook is uniquely designed to allow a sense of community to build around a movement, idea, fashion, current event and, yes, even a business, product, or service. For organizations that have a local focus, such as a restaurant, service provider, or charity, this can be invaluable. Peer-to-peer communication, even if not always positive, can help build a sense of credibility and online buzz. You always want your customers and contacts talking to each other about your business. If professionally managed, negative remarks on social media can be leveraged to show an organization's ability to adapt to the sensitivities and expectations of their audience. You can read more about this in the Technology box on page 142.

Repurpose To change something so that it can be used for a different purpose.

Flash mob A seemingly spontaneous public performance, usually a dance, that appears to begin out of nowhere and then quickly disperses. These are often organized through the use of social media and used to promote other events, charities, companies, ideas, or movements.

Caution: Many employers see Facebook as a useful window into a potential employee's personal habits and lifestyle. Before heading out to find that first career-focused job, take time to review your Facebook presence from the point of view of a potential employer. Are there pictures that show you in a less-than-positive light? Did you mention evidence of volunteer work on your résumé yet have no evidence of that commitment on your Facebook page? Take action before you begin your job search to audit your Facebook account to ensure it is a positive contribution to your personal brand image.

LinkedIn

If Facebook is seen as the "king" of social networks (Ackerman, 2015), then LinkedIn is certainly the "king" of business networks. LinkedIn is actually more popular than Twitter among its core demographic: career-oriented, educated people of all genders between the ages of 30 and 49 (Guimaraes, 2015). LinkedIn is the place for your professional online profile, your business-related updates, and your highly valued professional connections.

Power Feature for Networking: The users of LinkedIn are there for business purposes, the most important of which is networking. Therefore, you can assume that people who are there wish to be found and contacted by people with relevant and valuable reasons to connect. The likelihood that you will find someone relevant to your immediate professional interests and requirements is much higher than with any other online network.

Caution: Many first-time job seekers dramatically underestimate the importance of their LinkedIn profile. It is not uncommon to find a newly posted profile with spelling errors, typos, or inaccurate content. The message this sends to possible employers and business partners is that the owner of the profile is careless and lacks attention to detail. If you value your personal brand image, you will take the time and energy to ensure your profile is complete, accurate, and error free.

Twitter

When you select an effective hashtag to identify your content on Twitter, you are inviting others who are interested in that content to find you. Therefore, experienced Twitter users have naturally expanded their business networks, both virtually and face to face, simply by being active and professional tweeters and drawing in an audience of like-minded followers.

Power Feature for Networking: As noted in the previous section, to become an effective Twitter networker, you should make 80% or more of your Twitter activity interactive. This means replying to tweets, starting or joining Twitter conversations using hashtagged content, favouriting tweets made by others, and using Twitter handles to single out or mention specific people in your tweets. See **FIGURE 5.3** for an explanation of these Twitter usage terms. Being interactive makes your Twitter presence more dynamic and signals your openness to engage with your audience.

Caution: Of course, social media in all its forms empowers all your external stakeholders, including your customers. When things go wrong, it is now very easy for someone to take a video of poor customer service and tweet it to a worldwide audience or to lodge a complaint publicly and dramatically. For examples of how much impact customers can have online, please see the **TECHNOLOGY BOX**.

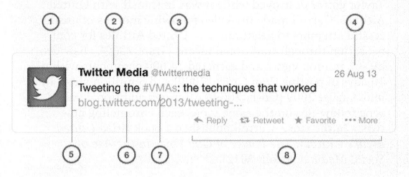

(1) **Profile picture**: The personal image uploaded to your Twitter profile in the Settings tab.

(2) **Twitter account name**: The name of your account. Think about whether you want to use your real name or some other identification.

(3) **Twitter @username**

: Your @username is your unique identity on Twitter. Think of it as your Twitter URL, as in:

twitter.com/username

. The @ sign is also used to mention people in Tweets, like this: Hello @Twitter! Your account name and username do not need to be the same.

(4) **Tweet timestamp/date**: This tells you when the Tweet was sent. Click the date or time to view the permalink page for a Tweet.

(5) **Tweet text**: Every Tweet fits into a space that's under 140 characters. Just the right size for a big idea, a headline or a timely observation.

(6) **Links**: You can link to other websites, articles, photos and videos within a Tweet.

(7) **Hashtags**: A hashtag is any word or phrase with the # symbol immediately in front of it. This symbol turns the word into a link that makes it easier to find and follow a conversation about that topic.

(8) **Tweet actions**: Here you can reply to, retweet and favorite a Tweet.

FIGURE 5.3 The Anatomy of a Tweet

Source: Twitter Inc. (2015). Anatomy of a tweet. Retrieved from https://media.twitter.com/best-practice/anatomy-of-a-tweet

TECHNOLOGY
WHEN COMPLAINTS GO VIRAL

What can happen when companies do not create professional and respectful responses to customers? Often, instead of generating valuable goodwill, the instantaneous nature of social media means that badly managed messages can create a great deal of public bad will. The "United Breaks Guitars" case is a great example:

In July 2009, Canadian musician Dave Carroll released a video of his song "United Breaks Guitars" on YouTube. The video details his experience of having his one-of-a-kind Taylor guitar destroyed while it was in transit with United Airlines. Carroll made the video following months of unsuccessful attempts to negotiate with United Airlines for compensation through traditional means (Tran, 2009). His video hit 3.2 million views and garnered 14,000 comments within 10 days of posting (Van Grove, 2009) and 5 million views by mid-August 2009 (Cosh, 2009). After two additional video/song follow-ups on the same topic, each chronicling new twists in the story, Carroll published a book titled *United Breaks Guitars: The Power of One Voice in the Age of Social Media* (Carroll, 2012).

Andrew Vaughan/The Canadian Press.

What does a smart social media or online content manager do when a negative public relations incident is unfolding? Here are two suggestions:

1. **Is it a real crisis or is it an opportunity?** In the first few moments you become aware that something may be going wrong online, it is natural to panic. It may be more important than ever to take the time to evaluate carefully what is going on. Not every online problem will result in negative publicity or damaged customer relations. For example, in August 2014 Greggs, a UK bakery chain, began to get notifications from thousands of their online Twitter followers that the Greggs's logo being presented by Google UK was, in fact, the incorrect logo. The problem originated with Google's search algorithm. Greggs's social media team could have countered with anger. Instead, they responded with humour, using Twitter to publicly offer Google's staff fudge donuts if they would kindly repair the mistake. This gentle and classy response drew even more loyalty and online discussion from Greggs's Twitter fan base (S. Harris, 2014).

2. **Take responsibility: fast!** In social media time, hours are like days. If after a few moments of careful consideration with your team you realize your company is at fault, then you must quickly and clearly speak up in an appropriate manner. This could be an apology or an acknowledgement of fault. On April 14, 2014, at about 3:22 p.m., US Airways inadvertently tweeted an offensive image out to all their Twitter followers. US Airways were alerted to this error and removed the image from their Twitterfeed. At 4:26 they tweeted this message: "We apologize for an inappropriate image shared as a link in one of our responses. We've removed the tweet and are investigating." Although the image was up and available for just over one hour, the *Business Insider* article on the incident describes the image being available for "a very long time" (Moss, 2014).

For TECHNOLOGY questions, see the Case Study, Review Questions, Critical Thinking Questions, and Exercises at the end of this chapter.

Use collaboration tools to work virtually with others

There are many online options for working collaboratively with teammates or business partners. Some of these include the following:

- Cloud storage tools (such as Dropbox, iCloud, OneDrive, Google Docs/Drive, and others)
- Email

- Facebook
- Instant messaging
- Note-sharing apps (such as Evernote, OneNote, and others)
- Texting (SMS)
- Videoconferencing/online meetings
- Voice over Internet protocol (VoIP)
- Wikis

Cloud storage tools

When people say their files are "in the cloud," what they mean is that they have uploaded their files to a centralized server that can be accessed from any connected device. This is of particular use when you are collaborating with others to produce written work, presentation materials, videos, or other digital content. Depending on the nature of your account, there may be storage limitations.

Power Feature for Collaboration: Most cloud solutions offer the ability for multiple editors and writers to work on a single document from anywhere in the world. This is a powerful and efficient way to produce team-generated documents without leaving your own office.

Caution: In the first section of this chapter there is a discussion of the possible security and privacy issues related to using online tools. Be aware that if you are sharing or storing your company's **digital assets** on your own personal cloud account, you are placing those assets at risk. You could be held financially responsible if those assets are stolen or corrupted. Inquire with your organization's information technology department to find out if there is an authorized cloud solution to help support your team's collaboration efforts.

Email

Email remains the "go to" tool for the majority of people in business to collaborate. It is a familiar interface that has no learning curve and near-immediate delivery to anyone with a mobile device.

Power Feature for Collaboration: Unlike most other online tools, email is a **push technology**. This means that its messages are actively delivered directly to the recipient rather than being posted somewhere passively, waiting for the intended team members to download the content and review. This lends a sense of immediacy to messages that still makes it the all-time **killer app**. Dave Pell, creator and editor of the email newsletter *NextDraft*, says "Email was the original killer app, and I think it still is. . . . [It] is personal, it doesn't stream by and disappear, it's universal, and it works" (Guppta, 2014).

Caution: Some of the same cautions apply when using email to collaborate as when using email to distribute (see the discussion earlier in this chapter).

- **A lack of privacy and security.** As noted earlier, unencrypted email is neither private nor secure. Internal team members may have a false sense of security when sending emails with valuable digital assets (e.g., company intellectual property) in an unencrypted format. Check with your information technology department to learn how you can use encrypted emails for sensitive communications.
- **File size restrictions.** If your file sizes are restricted, you can use a cloud-based storage solution and email a link to the file instead.
- **Document versions.** There is no easy way to track document versions, authors, and changes when you use email to share documents within a team. While this information can be embedded within a single document that is edited, once you have sent a document to four team members there are now four different versions of the document available. There are better technology options for collaborative writing, such as Google Docs.
- **Too much email.** Many business professionals find themselves overwhelmed with email. If this is the case, and if your team requires an immediate response, you may need to follow up via text or flag the email as "urgent" to receive a response in a timely manner.

Digital assets Electronic files containing data, information, or intellectual property that have monetary value to the legal owner.

Push technology Communications technology that delivers messages directly to an account or device.

Killer app A feature, function, or application that becomes highly valued or indispensable and thus becomes pervasive in use.

Facebook

With over a billion users worldwide, it is no wonder that some teams have turned to Facebook to support their team collaboration efforts. Creating a group page and controlling access to it provides direct team interaction in a common virtual space. For most team members, the learning curve would be minimal and access to the platform is usually easy.

Power Feature for Collaboration: Familiarity and comfort with the medium are the key attractions to using Facebook for team collaboration. Many team members will likely be using Facebook for personal networking and socializing already, so adding a work component seems natural and keeps the team's efforts close at hand, virtually speaking.

Caution: Privacy and security are the key cautions with any social networking platform. Facebook has undergone a number of policy shifts over the years with regard to their privacy settings (Loomer, 2012). As of January 1, 2015, a simplified policy called "Privacy Basics" was launched in an effort to help users feel more in control of their information (Kovach, 2014). Yet, as with any social networking platform that is not directly managed by you or your company, you have very little control over what actually happens to anything you may post there. Exercise extreme caution when sharing valuable digital assets via Facebook.

Instant messaging

The use of a synchronous instant messaging application can add a powerful relational dimension to long-distance team building. Colleagues who work together in the same location can have casual, non-task-related relationship-building interactions easily. Daily use of an instant messaging tool can create the same opportunities to build friendships and social connections between team members.

Power Feature for Collaboration: When all team members sign onto the same instant messaging application as a regular part of their work day, it becomes easy to exchange short messages, ask questions, check in, or simply chat in an unstructured, nondemanding way. The opportunity to build strong, supportive work relationships in this manner is extremely valuable. In her paper on this topic, Erika Darics noted that "non-task oriented talk is used as a means of doing relational work, and contributes to forming a collaborative working environment that enhances cooperation and efficient work" (Darics, 2010).

Caution: Instant messaging is a medium that can become very distracting. It is similar to text messaging in that a notification from a friend online can evoke a reactive response that feels like urgency. In other words, chatting online can waste a great deal of time. It is important to self-regulate and monitor the time you invest in instant messaging while working with your virtual teams.

Note-sharing applications

Note-sharing applications (such as Evernote, OneNote, and others) are an efficient and seamless way for teams to share working drafts of content, notes, photos, visuals, and even audio annotations. These programs are often cross-platform and cross-device, allowing users to modify content and receive updates on mobile devices as well as desktop computers. For collaborative and creative tasks such as storyboarding, outlining, and brainstorming, a note-sharing application is hard to beat. These programs usually put low demand on connectivity while keeping the latest editions and edits available to an entire team at any time.

Power Feature for Collaboration: The cross-platform nature of these tools is what makes them especially valuable. For example, a team member can update a team note on her desktop computer just before leaving the office to commute home by bus. While on the bus, that same team member can look at the same note via a mobile app on her phone or tablet, viewing any new input. Assuming the app is also available on her laptop at home, the team member can view the note again from that platform later in the evening, if necessary, to contribute or participate.

Caution: Note-sharing applications store the data in their cloud servers and allow users to sync their devices with the latest updates. Thus the same warning applies to note-sharing applications as applies to other cloud-based storage solutions: Exercise caution when sharing valuable digital assets through a cloud-based platform.

Texting (SMS)

Texting is similar to instant messaging in terms of creating relational ties. Also, while texting would not be the channel of choice to collaborate on the creation of an important document or presentation, if there is a time-sensitive piece of information that a colleague must have immediately then texting is a great choice.

Power Feature for Collaboration: The mobility of SMS texting, as well as the familiarity that most cellphone users have with texting, makes it an attractive way to contact team members anywhere, anytime. Like email, texts are a push technology, delivering a message directly to the user almost immediately. Text messages seem to imply a sense of urgency, and receivers find texts hard to ignore once the audible notification has been heard.

Caution: Regular SMS texting is not a secure method of communication. However, companies that view texting as a key platform for company communications are investing in their own integrated **enterprise social collaboration (ESC)** platforms that include encrypted texting.

Videoconferencing/online meetings

Collaboration is now possible with team members and colleagues spread across vast distances. One of the key technologies that makes this possible is the ability to meet virtually using platforms such as WebEx, GoToMeeting, Adobe Connect, and others. Other more robust enterprise systems are also available.

Power Feature for Collaboration: A well-run virtual meeting, in which all participants are present by video feed and all audio is clear, is the next best thing to a face-to-face meeting. Facial expression, tone, eye contact (of a sort), and other nonverbal signals are part of the overall messaging, and this type of relational contact is extremely valuable.

Caution: Online events like this take a fair amount of organization and preparation, from the traditional tasks like preparing an appropriate agenda to the technology-driven tasks like testing connections and bandwidth to the logistical tasks of confirming time zones and scheduling around local working customs and holidays. With so many more details involved, some may find the organization of such meetings too onerous and complex.

Voice over Internet protocol (VoIP)

With so many people working from networked desktop or laptop computers, it only makes sense to use the connection that is already present to share screens and conduct video as well as audio conversations. Typical consumer-grade platforms for **voice over Internet protocol (VoIP)** connections include Skype, ooVoo, and similar. Many of these platforms also feature instant messaging.

Power Feature for Collaboration: A VoIP connection makes it easy for a team member to connect, either in a preplanned manner or "on the fly" as part of the workday, with anyone, anywhere in the world. This means that detailed small group collaboration can take place whenever it is required without a significant planning investment.

Caution: The quality of connection through a VoIP platform can be unreliable and unpredictable. If you are relying on a VoIP interaction for a critical exchange of information, you should have a backup plan in case the VoIP connection is not as clear as you require.

Wikis

A **wiki** is a website that users can log onto and edit. Both the content and the structure of the site can be changed by any user. The most famous example of a collaborative wiki is Wikipedia, the online wiki/encyclopedia that is produced and edited by its own reader community, which anyone can join. On a smaller scale, any team can set up and use its own wiki for online collaboration among virtual team members using a site like PBworks, Wikispaces, and others.

Enterprise social collaboration (ESC) The use of social media and other communications technologies (integrated voice, mobile apps, video, instant messaging, SMS texting, and others) to foster increased teamwork and knowledge sharing for the purpose of improving business outcomes.

Voice over Internet protocol (VoIP) A connectivity platform that allows users to send voice data over Internet Protocol (IP). It is gradually replacing conventional telephone transmissions. VoIP tends to make moderately high bandwidth demands.

Wiki (derived from the Hawaiian word for "quick" as well as an acronym for "What I Know Is . . .") A type of online collaborative site that allows all contributors/team members to edit both content and structure.

CULTURE
ASSUMPTIONS AND ACCESS

Skylar is in her third semester and is required to take a course called Business, Technology, & Social Media. This course introduces the fundamental importance that technology plays in business communications both locally and globally.

Skylar is very interested in technology use across the globe and wonders what topic she should focus on for her major assignment. First, she takes a few minutes to do a little online research. She finds a map from Pew Research Center, a US firm, comparing the level of Internet access across selected developing or emerging economies with access in the United States.

Skylar notices that the level of Internet access is not at all strong in many of the countries shown. She wonders what impact this variability has on creating and maintaining cross-border business relationships.

Let's see how O-A-R can help Skylar:

- **Observe:** Skylar's current work placement is with Couture Ads. While there, Skylar observes carefully which digital channels seem to generate the best success with the company's global partners. There seem to be some locations that respond best to emails. Some international contacts prefer videoconferencing, but only at certain times of the day.

- **Ask:** Skylar interviews two online friends, Maria from El Salvador and Rosaline from Nigeria, about mobile and

Internet access in their countries. Skylar realizes, after speaking with Maria and Rosaline, that it could be offensive to make too many assumptions about bandwidth and access in some areas of the world. If you are planning a cross-border communication using technology, it may be appropriate and respectful to ask the person you are planning to communicate with about their preferences.

- **Research:** Skylar's preliminary discussions with Maria and Rosaline are so fruitful that she decides to prepare her own survey about Internet access, mobile technologies, and social media. She uses a popular online survey tool to distribute her questions among the international students in her business program. She asks particularly about the most popular social media platforms in other countries, type of connectivity, and relationship to cultural norms. Not only does Skylar use her own results to supply data and information for her major assignment, she shares the information with her supervisors at Couture Ads. Needless to say, the company finds her current and detailed results useful and is impressed with her initiative.

For CULTURE exercises, go to Exercises 5 and 14 on pages 157 and 158 respectively .

Power Feature for Collaboration: In addition to being very flexible in design, wikis are typically easy to access. As a mostly text-based medium, wikis put very low demands on bandwidth and would be an excellent choice if some team members had concerns about their connectivity.

Caution: As with any cloud-based solution, the standard cautions about security and privacy apply.

Fully grasping the complexities of technology-mediated communications in a globalized, intercultural world is a challenge. Check out the **CULTURE BOX** for an introduction to some of the issues that may be at play in your technology-mediated communications.

LO 5.3 What are the "best practices" of experienced virtual communicators?

Throughout your career you will use many different types of communications technologies. Below are some of the best practices that you should follow in the workplace.

Email

Many inexperienced business communicators make the mistake of thinking that emailing a business associate or a prospective employer is the same as texting or emailing a personal friend. It is not. There are new rules to follow to make your communications seem professional, intentional, and clear. If you send an email laden with emoticons, **textspeak**, and incomplete sentences, your business contact is going to assume you are an inexperienced amateur. In addition to the comments earlier in this chapter about keeping emails short and to the point, here are some other pointers to keep in mind:

- Start each new email with a suitable salutation. Do not simply start writing your message in the top line. Here are some examples:
  - Dear Dr. Jones
  - Hello, Prof. Milligan
  - Hi, Ramanjit

  If you are exchanging emails rapidly as a form of discussion, you can forgo the salutation in your reply emails.

- Keep paragraphs short and on point.

- Refrain from discussing personal matters in a business email.

- Use bullet points for lists.

- Stick to one topic per email. For example, imagine you had a meeting with your supervisor about three aspects of an assignment she has asked you to complete. These three aspects involve other departments: finance (regarding a budget matter), marketing (regarding use of the corporate logo), and human resources (regarding procedures for hiring an intern). You return to your desk to write a **confirmation email** to your supervisor. This would be quite a long email. Upon reflection, you decide to write three emails, one covering each topic. The advantage of doing this is that it allows your supervisor to forward each email, as required, to each respective department for attention without sharing extraneous information about the requests made to the other two departments.

- Use a suitable email signoff. Justin Bariso, a specialist in global communications, says that selecting the right signoff at the end of an email is like the "cherry on top" (Bariso, 2014). It is the last thing the reader sees and may set just the right tone for the reader's reply. Here are some examples of possible signoff choices:
  - Regards (simple, polite, and positive)
  - Best regards (more powerful and respectful)
  - Kind regards (simple, warm, and respectful)
  - Sincerely (simple, polite, possibly for someone not well known to the writer)
  - Best wishes (for someone you do not expect to see face to face in the near future)
  - Thanks (informal and appropriate if someone has done something for you that is discussed in the email)
  - Thank you, Sincere Thanks, Many thanks, Much appreciated (more formal and more appropriate if the gesture discussed was more significant)
  - Respectfully (often used when the email has content in disagreement with the recipient's known views)
  - Hope this helps, Hope to see you soon, Great hearing from you (variations on friendly signoffs)
  - Cheers (British in origin, can imply "thanks" but more commonly used now as a slightly informal, friendly, and upbeat email signoff) (Bariso, 2014)

- Create and use a suitable signature for all business emails. Most email software and web-based email systems allow you to create a **plain text** or **HTML** signature that is automatically attached to each outgoing email. Your employer may have certain expectations or guidelines for this that you should follow.

  In general, most signature files should contain the following:
  - Your name
  - Job title
  - Company name
  - Email address
  - Work phone number
  - Cellphone number (if applicable)

Textspeak Text-based word usage that has been shortened to accommodate communications that are limited to 140 characters. It often features the absence of vowels and lowercase "i" instead of uppercase "I," and it is regarded as extremely poor form in any context.

Confirmation email An email message sent shortly after a verbal exchange to verify the details discussed. The sender will expect a short reply of agreement or a longer reply to alter the details within the email.

Plain text Digital text that has no special formatting or code attached to it. It is often saved in a *.txt file.

HTML HyperText MarkUp Language. One of the foundational languages of the Internet that allows the user to insert formatting and images into text that will be viewed in a browser or email program.

- Company logo (optional and possible only in an HTML signature file)
- Company URL
- Proofread your email to ensure the following:
  - All textspeak has been removed. Pay particular attention to ensuring that your use of "I" is in uppercase.
  - All sentences begin with an uppercase letter.
  - You have not WRITTEN YOUR MESSAGE IN UPPERCASE. Such messages appear to the reader as shouting.
  - There are no emoticons, except when you are writing to a business associate that you know very well.
  - All information that can appear as a list has been converted to a bulleted list.
  - You have used a suitable email signoff.

FIGURE 5.4 demonstrates poor email form and excellent email form.

Conference calls

Conference calls are often used to conduct meetings when the participants are not physically in the same location. Here are some guidelines that are specific to this medium:

Consider what the other participants can hear

Be aware that ambient noise at any participant's location will become part of the conference call.

- **Use a land line.** A cellphone with a strong signal may be acceptable, but a land line is best. Avoid VoIP, speakerphones, and cordless handsets because these may all create interference noise.
- **Disable all features that beep, chirp, or sing.** Disable call waiting and any second lines that may beep to signal an incoming call. Do not use the hold button because most will either beep occasionally or, in many corporate situations, play music. All of these sounds will be audible to the other participants on the call.
- **Use the mute button.** Use a mute button to keep all background noise on your end to a minimum.
- **Pick a quiet spot.** Call from an environment where you will not be disturbed by colleagues, pets, children, or other noisy interruptions. Use a sign on your office to let people know you are on a call. Avoid shuffling papers, opening noisy packages, eating, or drinking while on a call. If you have not used your mute button, all of these sounds can be heard.

Observe common courtesies

Here are some behaviours that can help you communicate professionalism and confidence while participating in a conference call:

- **Call early.** If your call is set for 2:00 p.m. EST, then be on the call at 1:55 p.m. EST.
- **When asked, introduce yourself.** As with most regular meetings, most conference calls should have a moderator. This person may ask people to introduce themselves. Keep this short. Say your name slowly and clearly, include the name of your company or division, and the location you are calling from.
- **Give your full attention.** The most common and annoying behaviour that people exhibit on conference calls is multitasking. This makes the participant seem distracted and rude. Instead, take notes and ask questions. Respond quickly to questions when appropriate. Do not make other people on the call work to regain your attention.
- **Give your name and location.** If the call has many participants, and you wish to speak up or respond to a question, it is helpful to say your first name and your location before you make your contribution to the call. If someone is taking notes during the meeting, they will find this enormously helpful: for example, "This is Milt in Moose Jaw. Have we looked at all the possible outcomes of using this service provider in some of our more remote locations?"

FIGURE 5.4 Poor Email Form versus Excellent Email Form

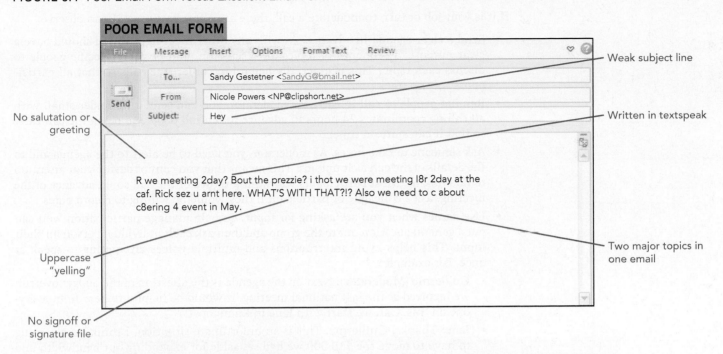

Moderate effectively

If it is your job or turn to moderate a call, there are a few best practices to observe:

- **Send a clear agenda in advance.** As with any other meeting, the call should have a clear purpose, a sequence of topics for discussion, and possibly specific people to discuss each topic. This is especially helpful in conference calls so that all participants stay on track.
- **Remind people to call in early.** As moderator, you can send a reminder email with all calling coordinates 24 hours in advance to remind people to be on the call early so that it can start on time.
- **Ask someone to take notes.** As moderator, you need to be alert to the agenda and to the details of the call as it unfolds. This means that you cannot devote your attention to note-taking. Most participants will want a record of the call so, in advance of the meeting, ask a colleague or participant if they would be willing to record notes.
- **Use names when you are asking for input.** To help manage participation, you can put a general question out to the group and then ask each individual person for their input. This helps avoid interruptions and multiple voices attempting to speak at once. For example:
  - **Guillermo (Moderator):** Next on the agenda is the question of the budget overrun we incurred at the last national meeting. It would be helpful to hear from everyone on this. Can we start with Jane in Kamloops?
  - **Jane:** Thanks, Guillermo. This is an unfortunate situation. I think we are going to have to move the $10,000 we had set aside for expanding our bandwidth and defer that upgrade to next fiscal year.
  - **Guillermo:** Thanks, Jane. Ravi in Red Deer, what do you think?
  - **Ravi:** I wondered if we had any contingency allowance in that budget that can be applied to the $10,000 overrun?
  - **Guillermo:** Good question. Tan, you prepared the final budget. Do you have that information?
  - **Tan:** Yes, the contingency total was $8,000 and we applied $4,000 to cover the extra hotel fees when the Ontario attendees had their flights delayed because of weather. So we can apply the other $4,000 to the other meeting overrun.
- **Ask for the common courtesies to be observed.** If there is a lot of extra noise or interference on the line, the moderator should ask for each person to check their line for noise, calm their environment, and use their mute buttons appropriately.

Virtual meetings and videoconferences

Virtual meetings and videoconferences are quite similar to conference calls, with the added enriched element of video. Be sure to review the previous section on conference calls since many of these same points apply, such as the use of an agenda, finding a quiet location, and managing interruptions. There are a few extra guidelines that are specific to this medium:

- **Check your camera angle and lighting.** You will be expected to use a web cam for a videoconference. Test it ahead of time to ensure the angle shows you in a natural way (not too high or too low) and that your face has enough light so it can be seen clearly.
- **Check the background.** What can the other participants see in the background behind you? If you are participating from your home office, which is in a corner of your kitchen, you may wish to consider relocating to another space. Whatever is behind you should be neutral, professional, and free of distraction.
- **Test the connection(s) before the meeting.** If you are the moderator, ask people to download, install, and connect with the videoconference software in advance. This will allow participants to identify and address any technical problems before the meeting.

- **Mute with care.** This is one guideline that deviates a bit from conference call behaviour. In a videoconference all the participants can be seen on camera. This means that your demeanour and behaviour should be similar to your behaviour in a real, face-to-face meeting. You can be seen multitasking, or getting up and walking away, or having an unrelated conversation with someone else. Use mute from time to time when you feel your environment is too noisy. In general, though, keep your connection, conversation, and behaviour as close to face-to-face communication as you can. Manage your distractions and noise without the aid of the mute button if you possibly can.

Webinars (mass audience)

Although the technology to support a webinar is similar to the technology used for virtual meetings, the actual dynamic of a webinar is different. (Please review the information for virtual meetings and videoconferences for technical tips.) In a webinar there are one or two presenters who offer information, usually to a much larger group who have registered for the privilege of receiving the information.

- **Be prepared.** If you are a presenter, it is especially important that you are entirely ready with your presentation. (See Chapter 12 for support on the preparation of presentations and materials.) If you appear to be less than professional and prepared, that poor performance will remain on record as a sharable, searchable webinar archive. On the other hand, if you are fully prepared and professional, this positive record of your work will serve you well as you build your career.

- **Practise.** If you are a presenter, try out the software, hardware, web cam, microphone, and headset before you are "live" in front of your audience. Not only will this increase your comfort level, it will reduce possible technical issues with your presentation. Rehearse the timing of your commentary with the slides or other presentation materials you may be offering.

- **Have a "host" or "moderator."** It is common practice now for webinars to be hosted by one person with presentation(s) by others. The role of the host or moderator is to respond to direct questions from the audience, compile questions for the presenter, and often to assist with technical issues that arise. The host would also be responsible for introducing the speaker(s) and making a few concluding remarks at the end. If you are a moderator for such an event, see the previous section for assistance on how to make a professional introduction.

Social media

Building a vibrant online community means keeping your content fresh. Most successful organizations post to their social media network between 38 and 100 times per month. This volume of social media engagement requires that a great deal of content be generated. Many companies encourage their employees to contribute to the conversation. Satisfied employees can be among the greatest ambassadors for a company or a brand (McAbee, 2010), but only if they communicate responsibly and use best practices in social media communication. Anyone communicating through social media in business would benefit from following the social media guidelines that Intel publishes for its employees (Intel, 2010). The guidelines encourage the following employee behaviours:

- **Be honest.** Always disclose that you are an employee of the company.
- **Be authentic.** Speak of your own experiences with a product rather than "advertising" the product.
- **Be natural.** Sound like yourself to add a human face to the business.
- **Be discreet.** Do not disclose company secrets.
- **Add value.** Provide content that your audience will appreciate.

FIGURE 5.5 ACE for Communications
Technologies

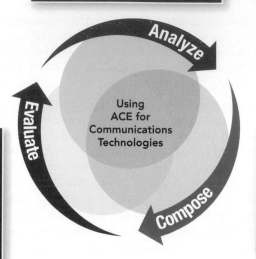

Analyze and identify your purpose for communicating when you are choosing communications channels (distributing, networking, or collaborating).

Analyze your audience location, culture, work style, and expectations.

Ask the right questions to manage both advantages and risks of the various tools you are using.

Evaluate the most successful instances of virtual communication to understand what works well.

Evaluate the least successful instances of virtual communication to define improvements.

Where possible, provide feedback to tool developers for improvements to technology offerings.

Ensure that your messaging fits the medium or channel you have chosen, especially in terms of length, formality, and format.

Ensure that your messaging shares only that which you are authorized to share.

Using ACE for Communications Technologies

Analyze

Compose

Evaluate

In summary, the workplace now spans great distances while often also being rooted in a strong local network. Virtual business relationships can cross borders or they can take the form of telecommuting within a province, region, or city. This chapter outlined the basics about communications technologies, providing analytical questions to help you manage both the upsides and the risks involved in their use. An understanding of currently available tools and tool categories will help you select the right one for your purpose. Finally, understanding the "best practices" when employing virtual communications tools will help you maintain your professionalism and image in this complex communications environment. Check out **FIGURE 5.5** for some ideas on how to apply ACE to the selection, use, and evaluation of communications technologies.

Photo courtesy of Wendy Kam Marcy and Geoff Marcy.

Wendy Kam Marcy

Cofounder and Lifestyle Blogger,
Hip + Urban Girl's Guide

Director of Marketing,
Adfluent Media

@ WORK

At the beginning of this chapter, Wendy described her complex working relationships with internal and external partners spread across a wide geographic area. How does Wendy use ACE to manage her choices?

Clear, thoughtful, and timely communication is the key to making everything flow seamlessly in the blogging business.

- **Analyze.** When a pitch arrives by email, my business partner and I analyze each request. Typically, we know right away if the campaign is a "fit" for our audience and if it is worth our time to pursue it. We look at immediate profitability, the potential for an ongoing business relationship, and any other opportunities a new campaign might open up.

  With this information we reply to each other via email with our thoughts. Usually we are in agreement, but there are times when one of us needs to persuade and sell the other person on the idea. When this happens, we discuss further by phone or Skype.

  Once we accept the campaign, we determine how we should proceed:

  - Should we continue correspondence by email?
  - Would it be better to schedule a teleconference with the agency/client?
  - Should we meet the agency/client in person?

  We make this decision knowing that some people communicate effectively electronically whereas others prefer face-to-face interaction. From experience, when it comes to the initial client briefing, it is best to do it in person when

possible. This is especially true for larger projects. Having the decision makers in one room (or in one real-time video-conference) allows for more fluent communication, proper introductions, and a stronger foundation of trust.

- **Compose.** Our typical order of operation is as follows:
  1. A briefing with the client to discuss objectives
  2. The creation of a marketing strategy and an execution plan
  3. Gaining approval and signoff from the client

  As one can see, the other cofounder and I would find emailing all this information back and forth very tedious and time consuming. We typically find it more productive to communicate in real time over the phone or via Skype, where we can share screens and prepare documents in real time.

  As cofounders, we also have to make decisions on who is going to write the post, which social channels to leverage, and how to prioritize other content.

  The entire team has to ensure we are all on the same page by constantly engaging with one another. Opportunities for our team to meet in person are rare, so we rely heavily on virtual tools to collaborate and check in with each other. Spontaneous communication needs to occur regularly.

- **Evaluate.** Our team stays organized and well prepared using cloud-based tools like Google Drive. We are able to share and evaluate draft work and make corrections in a single document. This is all accessible anytime, anywhere, with a single login using a Gmail account.

  When the team needs a status meeting to review or evaluate our work, we use Google Hangouts. Regardless of where my team members are located or what device they prefer to use, I can hold videoconferences and even livestream meetings. This tool allows me to keep a history of my Hangouts, so I can always reference past conversations.

The Google suite of products, Skype, FaceTime, and other tools are all very powerful collaborative communications tools that make it possible for long-distance teams such as ours to stay productive. It is pretty remarkable how we have managed to run a successful, creative business with minimal face-to-face interaction!

End of Chapter

Learning Objectives in Review

LO 5.1 **Why is an understanding of communications technologies important?** *pages 130–135*

Learning more about the technologies that support virtual communications will help you select the best tools and channels for your messaging.

- **Understand media richness theory (MRT).** MRT looks at various media or channels and their "degree of richness." Criteria include
  - the availability of instant feedback (as in synchronous communication),
  - the capacity of the medium to transmit multiple cues, such as body language, voice tone, and inflection,
  - the use of natural language, and
  - the personal focus of the medium.
- **Consider a few basics about using communications technologies.** Some basic points include the following:
  - Assume your audience uses mobile devices.
  - Consider bandwidth (wired and wireless).
  - Look for platform agnostic tools.
  - Understand cloud computing and software as a service.
  - Never assume privacy or security is fully guaranteed.
  - Watch for tools to evolve and change.
- **Ask important questions about technology tools.** Some of these questions could include the following:
  - What resources do I need?
  - Is shared information searchable?
  - Can I limit access?
  - Can shared information be easily reshared?
  - Is it synchronous or asynchronous?
  - Is there a cost?

LO 5.2 **What are the main functions of communications technologies?** *pages 136–146*

- Use distribution tools to share information.
- Use networking tools to discuss, build community, and expand connections.
- Use collaboration tools to work virtually with others.

LO 5.3 **What are the "best practices" of experienced virtual communicators?** *pages 147–153*

If you consider that a key objective of business communication is to build and maintain your business relationships, then it is useful to know about some "best practices" that will help you make the most of your virtual presence.

- **Email.** Develp professional habits with regard to formality, salutations, length, signoff, and signature file.
- **Conference calls.** Control ambient noise, observe common courtesies, and moderate effectively.
- **Virtual meetings and videoconferences.** Control for the best quality of the video and audio, and test all connections prior to meeting time.
- **Webinars.** Be fully prepared, rehearse your presentation, and select a host or moderator to assist with fielding questions.
- **Social media.** When posting on behalf of your employer, be honest, authentic, natural, discreet, and provide valuable content.

KEY TERMS

1:1 p. 132
1:many p. 132
BCC p. 138
blog p. 134
cloud computing p. 131
confirmation email p. 147
content management system (CMS) p. 134

credentials p. 133
currency p. 138
degree of richness (in MRT) p. 130
digital assets p. 143
enterprise social collaboration (ESC) p. 145
firewall p. 133
flash mob p. 140

hacker p. 133
killer app p. 143
plain text p. 148
platform agnostic p. 131
portable document format (PDF) p. 132
push technology p. 143
repurpose p. 140

software as a service (SaaS) p. 131
textspeak p. 147
time sensitive p. 138
URL p. 135
voice over Internet protocol (VoIP) p. 145
wiki p. 145
HTML p. 147

CASE STUDY

Selecting Tools and Channels

This case study will help you review the chapter material by applying it to a specific scenario. To achieve this, the case is related to the Chapter 4 Case Study on page 122.

Brendan's internship at Kramer & Kaplin Market Research in Calgary started out well. He enjoyed brainstorming ideas with his manager and designing a survey for an important client.

However, the past few weeks have been pure misery. Brendan's supervisor assigned him to join three other interns on a team to create a comprehensive online handbook for interns. Brendan will work on this project with one other intern from the Calgary office (Roberto) and two interns from New Delhi, India (Maansi and Anant).

Planning the first meeting was difficult. Brendan lost two days of work trying to set a meeting time because there is a $12\frac{1}{2}$-hour time difference between Calgary and New Delhi: at 9 a.m. Central Standard Time in Calgary it is 9:30 p.m. in New Delhi. Brendan suggested a 7 a.m. teleconference, but his Calgary teammate, Roberto, said he could not arrive in the office early for a meeting. Brendan suggested an 8:30 a.m. teleconference, which would be 9:00 p.m. in New Delhi. Both his New Delhi teammates, Maansi and Anant, were vague about whether they could stay late. Brendan begged Roberto to arrange to get to work early just one day so that the team could hold a kickoff meeting. Roberto admitted that he could easily get to the office early, but preferred to sleep later. After much difficulty, the first meeting is scheduled for 7:30 a.m. Central Standard Time on Wednesday.

QUESTION 1: *Are there any online scheduling tools that could have made this initial task easier? Identify at least three such tools and describe how they would have facilitated this task.*

QUESTION 2: *If the criteria for the selection of a tool for this meeting include low-cost or free, easy access, synchronous connectivity, and the ability to share screens, what would be the three best tools to use for this first virtual meeting? Which of the three would you recommend and why?*

QUESTION 3: *Can the tool you recommend help with Roberto's participation in future meetings? How?*

After the meeting, it is clear that all four interns seem to share at least one goal in common: to create an excellent handbook for interns. However, each intern has a different opinion about what is required to achieve that goal. While Brendan and Roberto are focused on providing useful content for a print or ebook version, Maansi and Anant are focused on the technical aspects of delivering an engaging, interactive website to deliver the content. They believe that programming is key. Existing content can simply be imported into the new site.

QUESTION 4: *Which asynchronous document management tool would you recommend to house the content for this project?*

QUESTION 5: *How would you rate the level of security needed for the digital assets related to this project: very high, high, medium, or low? Explain. Does the tool you recommend provide the appropriate level of security?*

As the summer and the project progress, the team begins to communicate informally through an instant messaging platform. Although their workdays are inverse because of time zone differences, the instant messaging platform allows them to keep in touch through their mobile devices. At the end of the project, all four team members credit this synchronous connectivity with their relationship building and the creation of a sense of trust and cohesion.

QUESTION 6: *Research and consider the following possible alternatives for the instant messaging platform used by this team:*

- WhatsApp
- Viber
- Voxer
- Slack
- Facebook Messenger
- Skype

Which platform do you think they used? Why?

REVIEW QUESTIONS

1. What is unique and useful about portable document format (PDF) files?

2. What does "platform agnostic" mean?

3. What communications technologies are best for storing collaborative work so that all team members can access and edit the same document?

4. Is information shared in blog comments searchable?

5. If you are writing a blog for your employer, are you sharing your personal opinion or are you representing your employer?

6. Which communications tool is the most used and most common?

7. What are some of the possible problems that email can present for senders and receivers?

8. Which online site is most often used for recruitment of new employees and business partners?

9. Are online web chats, such as those offered for customer service purposes, synchronous or asynchronous?

10. What is a digital asset?

11. What is meant by "push technology"?

12. What is a confirmation email?

13. What is an example of an email signoff?

14. What should be included in an email signature?

15. What is the difference between a videoconference and a webinar?

16. What is the role of a host or moderator during a webinar?

CRITICAL THINKING

1. Media richness theory examines the use of various communications technologies and ranks them according to the amount of communications cues or intakes. A "rich" medium has many cues to help communicate meaning: tone, body language, facial expression, and so on. A "poor" medium has fewer cues. When using text, email, or instant messaging, it becomes even

156 **Chapter 5** What Are the Tools and What Are the Rules? Communication Technologies in the Workplace

CHAPTER 5

more important that cues like tone accurately express the sender's intent. Face-to-face communication has the highest media richness and gives much information with regard to honesty, apprehension, or intention. (See pages 130–131.)

Meredith is a student in the second-last semester of her business co-op program and is currently at her co-op work placement. She notices the amount of time and money her field placement company spends on arranging smooth and flawless videoconferencing. Dates, times, and technology are thoughtfully organized to ensure the maximum number of people can either be present in the company boardroom or participate by video from their location. Every effort is made to ensure that the audio and video feeds are strong and clear. Times and dates are chosen in consultation with all participants. In other words, something about the richest forms of interaction has great value within her company.

Meredith considers MRT when she observes her own preferences and those of her classmates. When she spends social time with her two BFFs, she suddenly becomes aware of how much time they spend looking at their devices instead of talking to each other. In other words, the three friends naturally engage in low-media-rich activities, using text-based communications with people who are not present instead of indulging

in the richest of interactions, a face-to-face conversation, with the people who are present.

Explain why a company would invest heavily in ensuring the most media-rich experience of communication while Meredith's interpersonal experience suggests a strong personal preference for the least media-rich experiences.

2. In Chapter 4, the concept of high-context and low-context cultures was presented. Is there a relationship between this theory of cultural communications norms and media richness theory? In other words, do you think there is a preference in high-context cultures for high media richness? Do low-context cultures prefer low media richness? Can you find any sources to validate either assumption?

3. Some people argue that reliance on social media and mobile devices will prevent a person from developing interpersonal communication skills. Other people take the opposite point of view, arguing that the use of social media may help a person improve interpersonal communication skills. Take a stance on this issue and write a one-page paper arguing your position. Be sure to provide clear reasons and supporting evidence.

DEVELOPING YOUR COMMUNICATION SKILLS

 Why is an understanding of communications technologies important? *(pages 130–135)*

EXERCISE 1 Think like an employer

Trade a current copy of your résumé with another student. Using your best online searching skills, try to find out as much as you can about the other student. The other student will try to find out as much as possible about you. Report back to each other and to the class. Did the other person find out more or less about you than you expected? Do you feel your information is safe online? Would your results cause you to change your "online personal brand"?

EXERCISE 2 Screens and layouts

Find or create a one-page Microsoft Word document that has a heading, a subheading, some paragraphs of text, a table, and a graphic in it. Save it as a Word document and also as a PDF. Using email to share the files, view them on a smartphone screen, a tablet screen, and a laptop screen. Do the documents look the same at each viewing? Is one format more consistent and easier to view?

EXERCISE 3 Analyzing needs and choosing tools (1)

You are on a student team working on a project. The project is due in three weeks and involves researching a topic and creating a two-page summary as well as a five-minute presentation, with visuals. There are five members on your team. You have met face to face once. One of the team members, Saurabh, has to return to his home town in India for two weeks due to a family emergency. He wants to continue working on the project with the team and will be back in time to participate in the presentation.

a. Answer the following questions:
   - Should shared information be searchable?
     Yes/No/Not applicable
   - Does access need to be limited or controlled?
     Yes/No/Not applicable
   - Should shared information be easily reshared?
     Yes/No/Not applicable
   - Does this call for a synchronous or asynchronous tool?
     Synchronous/Asynchronous
   - What level of security is called for on this project?
     Very High/High/Medium/Low
   - Is cost a factor in choosing a tool? Yes/No/Not applicable

b. Based on your answers to part (a), write a proposal for a tool or suite of tools that your team could use. Be sure to justify your answer.

EXERCISE 4 Analyzing needs and choosing tools (2)

You are assisting a team of four senior managers at your company as they make a top-secret bid to buy a competing, smaller company. This opportunity has appeared quickly and there is no time to install an internal, highly secure system. It is your job to make sure everyone has secure access to all the relevant documents, proposals, budgets, and financial information, regardless of where they are in the world or which device they are using.

a. Answer the following questions:
   - Should shared information be searchable?
     Yes/No/Not applicable
   - Does access need to be limited or controlled?
     Yes/No/Not applicable
   - Should shared information be easily reshared?
     Yes/No/Not applicable

- Does this call for a synchronous or asynchronous tool?
  Synchronous/Asynchronous
- What level of security is called for on this project?
  Very High/High/Medium/Low
- Is cost a factor in choosing a tool? Yes/No/Not applicable

b. Based on your answers to part (a), write a proposal for a tool or suite of tools that your company could use. Be sure to justify your answer.

EXERCISE 5 Analyzing needs and choosing tools (3) [Related to the Culture feature on page 146]

You are on a team of five people who are in charge of organizing your company's annual general meeting. The annual general meeting is so large it is almost like a conference. The event will last three days and there will be at least 300 employees attending. Some may be coming with spouses. The location is São Paulo, Brazil. You are in Halifax, Nova Scotia. Your other four teammates are in Vancouver, São Paulo, Miami, and Chicago. As a team, you need to take care of all aspects of the event, including online registration, selecting a site, all meals, producing a printed and online schedule of events, booking hotels, arranging speakers and breakout sessions, arranging a spousal activity program, and booking evening entertainment. This will be the full-time focus for the entire team for the next eight months.

a. Answer the following questions:
- Should shared information be searchable?
  Yes/No/Not applicable
- Does access need to be limited or controlled?
  Yes/No/Not applicable
- Should shared information be easily reshared?
  Yes/No/Not applicable
- Does this call for a synchronous or asynchronous tool?
  Synchronous/Asynchronous
- What level of security is called for on this project?
  Very High/High/Medium/Low
- Is cost a factor in choosing a tool? Yes/No/Not applicable
- Are there any intercultural, regional, or geographic issues your team may need to address? Can you identify at least five?

b. Based on your answers to part (a), write a proposal for a tool or suite of tools that your team could use. Be sure to justify your answer.

EXERCISE 6 Representing your employer

Preston is a newly hired communications intern at Shady Spaces, a company that imports and assembles outdoor umbrellas for patios. He has been put in charge of writing a weekly blog post as part of his company's website. Here is his first draft:

> WOW!!!! DUDES!! I AM SO EXCITED to be making my first blog post as YOUR shady spaces expert and guru. what an honour!!!! i can't wait to read your comments.
>
> this week i'm so happy to report that our imported canvas/bamboo umbrellas have arrived from thailand just in time for this wknd's sunny weather report u know these bamboo creations can be purchased with the piece of mind that yur supporting renewable resources as well as bying a light-weight, attractively designed item that will bring be-u-tee to ur outdoor space for yonks. Hurry – don't be L8!!

When Preston shows you his first draft, you know that it will not be acceptable to his supervisor. Rewrite this blog entry as a more appropriate post for this company's website.

 What are the main functions of communications technologies? *(pages 136–146)*

EXERCISE 7 Facebook

Create a Facebook page for one of the following types of businesses. Include an appropriate cover and profile graphic as well as at least three content postings.

- A company you would like to start after you graduate
- A company that already exists (with permission)
- Shady Spaces, a company that imports and assembles outdoor umbrellas for patios

Answer the following questions, in writing:

a. What is the main purpose of this page? Distribution, networking, or collaboration?

b. Why do some businesses benefit from a Facebook page and others do not?

c. Do you want access to this page to be restricted only to certain users or to be open for anyone to find and "like"? Why?

d. When someone clicks on "like" for this page, what happens from their point of view?

e. What would cause someone to un-"like" a page? How can you guard against this?

f. How are your choices as page administrator for this business page different than your choices for a personal Facebook account? Explain at least three key differences.

EXERCISE 8 Twitter

Create a Twitter account for one of the following types of businesses. Include an appropriate profile graphic. Compose and send three tweets on behalf of the business you select.

- A company you would like to start after you graduate
- A company that already exists (with permission)
- Any imaginary company that could operate within the bounds of the laws of Canada
- Shady Spaces, a company that imports and manufactures outdoor umbrellas for patios

Answer the following questions, in writing:

a. What is the main purpose of this account? Distribution, networking, or collaboration?

b. Could you make an argument that all businesses, regardless of size, scope, or type of business, could benefit from having an active Twitter account? If so, write your rationale for this assertion in three paragraphs.

c. Do you want access to this Twitterfeed to be restricted only to certain users or to be open for anyone to find and follow? Why?

d. What kind of content would draw the most followers?

e. When someone follows this account, what happens from their point of view?

f. Create five hashtags that could be used to draw followers to this account. For each,

    i. Identify whether you are distributing or networking with this hashtag.

    ii. Explain why this hashtag would be effective at distributing or networking.

g. What would cause someone to un-follow an account? How can you guard against this?

h. How are your choices as Twitter administrator for this business account different than your choices for a personal Twitter account? Explain at least three key differences.

EXERCISE 9 Think like a recruiter

Working from the most recent copy of your résumé, create or update your LinkedIn account.

a. Find three to five LinkedIn profiles that you feel effectively represent the professional presence of their creators. What makes them effective? Can you use this knowledge to improve your profile?

b. Find a partner and link to each other's LinkedIn profiles. Provide at least three recommendations to improve each other's professional presence.

EXERCISE 10 Selecting collaboration tools

Assume your company is looking to invest in collaboration tools to support teamwork. Currently teams in your company share files via email. Your supervisor, Maury Phillips, thinks that web-based collaboration tools will help teams be more productive because of the geographic spread of the team members (Winnipeg, Manitoba, London, UK, and Mumbai, India). Research at least three tools and write a brief memo (no more than one page) identifying all three tools and then persuasively recommending one. Be sure to identify key features of the tool and why those features will help your teams.

EXERCISE 11 Using Google Docs for collaboration

Create a Google account if you do not already have one. Use this account to access Google Docs. Create a few sample files (a document, spreadsheet, and presentation) to become familiar with the file-creation process. Practise sharing files with others and publishing them as webpages. Email your sample documents to your instructor to document your Google Docs experience.

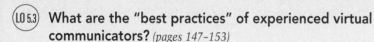 **What are the "best practices" of experienced virtual communicators?** *(pages 147–153)*

EXERCISE 12 Technology and collaboration

Form a team of five to six classmates. Your team's primary task is to do the following:

- Identify a Facebook page for a business that is local to your college's main campus. The page should be in need of some improvement or attention.

- Prepare a professionally worded email to the owner of the Facebook page with at least three well-worded recommendations for the page.

To complete this task, you must conduct all communications and collaboration virtually, even if you see each other every day. Therefore, your secondary set of tasks involves agreeing on which tools to use. You must include synchronous virtual meetings as part of your team process.

Once your primary task is complete, meet with your team face to face (or via virtual meeting if necessary). Review the following questions together and produce a one-page summary of answers for your instructor:

a. What worked especially well in this exercise? Why?

b. What did not work well? Why?

c. What surprised you about using the tools for online collaboration?

d. What would you do differently next time?

EXERCISE 13 Online customer service

Research shows that customers appreciate being able to communicate with a company to receive customer support through social media, for example, through chats, tweets, or Facebook. Employees who provide this customer support will be more effective if they have effective interpersonal communication skills. Review this chapter and identify three specific communication skills that you believe are important in communicating with customers through social media. Provide explanations and examples for your three choices.

EXERCISE 14 Testing for virtual meetings/webinars [Related to the Culture feature on page 146]

Form a team of four to five students. Select a common collaboration tool such as Skype, Adobe Connect, WebEx, GoToMeeting, or similar. Spread out to different parts of your campus. For example, one person could be in the library, one in the cafeteria, one in a hallway, one in an empty classroom, and so on. Test the ability of a synchronous meeting with audio and video. Try using a headset or earbuds, and also try without if your equipment allows it. Try using smartphones, tablets, and laptops, if possible. Try using Wi-Fi on some devices and a cellular data plan on others (if possible). If possible, try the exercise twice at different times of the day. Answer the following questions:

a. What was the best possible configuration for clarity of audio?

b. Did using the video feature have an impact on audio quality?

c. Was the outcome better with or without headsets or earbuds?

d. Did Wi-Fi versus a cellular data plan have an impact on quality?

e. Did the time of day have an impact on the quality of the outcome?

f. If your team were spread across the globe and not across a small regional area, do you think the outcomes would have been different? How?

g. What did you learn from this that you can use the next time you have a virtual meeting?

EXERCISE 15 Email

Review the last 10 business, work, or school-related emails you have received. For this exercise, it is important that you select emails you have received from people and organizations who are not your personal associates or friends. Assess these emails for "best practices," such as the following:

- An appropriate salutation
- Short paragraphs
- Bulleted lists (as required for lists)
- One topic per email
- A suitable, professional signoff

- A signature file
- No textspeak and emoticons
- No UPPERCASE writing
- No typos or spelling errors
- No grammar or sentence structure errors
- No use of "i" when "I" is correct

In general, do the business, work, or school-related emails you receive demonstrate "best practices"? Why or why not?

6

How Can We Be Better, Together? Collaboration and Productivity

mbbirdy/E+/Getty Images.

MyBCommLab®   **Improve Your Grade!**

Over 10 million students improved their results using the Pearson MyLabs. Visit **mybcommlab.com** for simulations, tutorials, media share assignments, interactive lesson presentations, and other helpful learning apps.

LEARNING OBJECTIVES

(LO 6.1) **How do you communicate effectively as part of a team?** *pages 162–169*

Create a team charter
Give the team time to develop
Plan for effective meetings
Be a valued team member

(LO 6.2) **How can working on a team help you develop leadership skills?** *pages 169–175*

Identify and practise key leadership fundamentals
Use conflict management to help develop
    leadership skills

(LO 6.3) **What are some key aspects of high-performance team collaboration?** *pages 175–183*

Enhance productivity with virtual best practices
Develop the "c factor" in your teams
Use a peer coaching model for feedback

Amy Elder
Director of Career Services,
Brock University

@ WORK

"What do you mean you're leaving?!?"

Courtesy of Amy Elder and Murray Hawrn.

At our career centre, we often organize events to create networking opportunities for students and employers. There are many details to arrange, contracts to put in place, and services to secure. Employer and student registration, facility

logistics, marketing and advertising, food services, parking vouchers, and more are arranged by our event coordinator. Other team members are usually required to assist on the day of the event. Typically, a large event takes several months of preliminary preparation with many more details being arranged in the weeks prior to the event.

Not long ago, six weeks prior to our largest event, our event coordinator unexpectedly resigned with short notice. The hiring process for a replacement usually takes weeks. As a team, my staff and I needed to find a way to make sure the event took place as planned without sacrificing our usual high level of detail and customer service. How were we going to get this team organized to tackle these tasks that were "above and beyond" their usual job responsibilities?

Check out the end of this chapter to find out how Amy used ACE to solve this team communications problem.

Introduction

Most organizations have come to rely on well-coordinated teams, with each person doing his or her part to complete critical projects and to achieve organizational goals. Individuals benefit from teamwork, too. When you work on a **team**, you improve your interpersonal skills, expand your personal network, and use your best individual strengths while learning new skills from others.

In Chapter 3 we learned that everyone has a personal communications style that affects his or her interpersonal skills. Chapter 4 introduced concepts of identity, cultural norms, and diversity and their impact on communication. In Chapter 5, communications technologies, some of which are designed to support collaboration, were reviewed.

How can you become a collaborative co-worker on teams with diverse communications styles? Is it possible to create pro-

ductive, innovative teams when team members feel separated by geography and culture? Can virtual teams, using technology to connect both asynchronously and synchronously, really be effective? This chapter addresses these questions, focusing on developing the skills you need to help you work collaboratively with others. Additionally, this chapter presents strategies to help you develop your leadership abilities and to advance your team's **productivity** into a peak performance zone.

Team Two or more people who recognize and share a commitment to a specific, common goal and who collaborate in their efforts to achieve that goal.

Productivity The rate, quality, or effectiveness of effort. A measure of the efficiency of a person, machine, factory, system, and so on in converting inputs into useful outputs (BusinessDictionary.com, 2015b).

LO 6.1 # How do you communicate effectively as part of a team?

Teams are included in this book because the most commonly noted key success factor for effective team performance is communication. The best performing teams communicate often, communicate fearlessly, and communicate complete information in a timely manner. Conversely, many people report that the single factor that causes team failure is a lack of ability to communicate effectively.

Another common barrier to effective team communications, and thus team performance, is unnecessary conflict. One of the objectives of this chapter is to help you develop team communication skills with a view to reducing or eliminating some of the common sources of unnecessary conflict that teams often report. When conflict does arise, the information in this chapter will help you develop the leadership skills to recognize productive conflict as opposed to nonproductive conflict, and to help you support your teams through these more challenging times.

Team communication skills must be consciously developed with intention and foresight. Many workplace teams are put at an immediate disadvantage when they are assembled without sufficient guidance and agreement on how the team members should communicate with each other. This section suggests four methods you and your teammates can use at the outset of team development to improve team communications and make teamwork an enjoyable and productive experience:

- Create a team charter
- Give the team time to develop
- Plan for effective meetings
- Be a valued team member

Create a team charter

For a team to be successful, all team members need to agree on key elements at the beginning of the project (LaFasto & Lasron, 2001). Newly formed teams should focus first on **process** issues. This means that in addition to your team deciding *what* they need to do, or *who* is going to do it, your team must come to an agreement on *how* you will work together. A great deal of unnecessary conflict can be avoided if specific elements of team performance have been agreed upon first. When your team has come to an agreement on these issues, create a **team charter** to document what you have decided. Most teams can create a rudimentary team charter in their first meeting together. The document does not need to be complex, nor does it need "legal" language. It should be clear, concise, and unambiguous. For maximum effectiveness, all team members should actively participate in the creation of the charter.

An effective team charter can be developed if a team can agree on the following items. It is possible that the nature of the tasks your team has undertaken may require additional areas to be explored. This list is intended as a guideline for getting started.

- Goals and **deliverables**
- Team performance expectations, including
  - Roles and responsibilities
  - Division of work
  - Feedback
  - Quality of work
  - Decision making
- Team function and communication, including
  - Primary and secondary modes of communication
  - Contact information
  - Meeting times and location
  - Technology requirements
  - Technology guidelines
  - Record keeping

Process An explicit or implicit set of operations or actions, usually aimed toward a specified outcome.

Team charter A document that describes a team's agreed-upon style of working together and their commitment to specific standards and expectations. It is most effective when it is created with the participation of each team member.

Deliverables The items or services you agree to deliver to your audience.

- Meetings
- Timelines
- Calendar review

Want to see some great examples of team charters? Check out our online resources at **MyBCommLab**!

Goals and deliverables

Effective teams are goal oriented. All members share a common understanding of their purpose as a team. They have a shared commitment to achieve a specific goal, and they share a common definition of success. A goal can also be a specific deliverable, like a report or a presentation. Write the team's agreed-upon goals and deliverables into your team charter.

Team performance expectations

One of the most common causes of conflict within teams tends to be a misunderstanding or misalignment of the team members' expectations of each other. A discussion of specific team expectations prior to beginning work together will dramatically reduce your team conflict. Some key areas for discussion include the following:

- **Roles and responsibilities.** All team members should have a clear role, defined responsibilities, and accountability for their contributions.
- **Division of work.** Work should be divided equitably. Some tasks may require more effort than others, so it is important to discuss the work to ensure that the team is aware of each member's responsibilities and no one is overburdened with too much work.
- **Feedback.** Team members should expect to both give and receive feedback on their performance from their team members. Remember to look for opportunities to give positive feedback for jobs well done.
- **Quality of work.** Some projects require only a minimum level of quality. Most projects demand a fairly high standard of input from each team member. For example, many work and school projects include a significant amount of writing. Clearly define expectations around the quality of work each team member should prepare. Are you expecting full sentences and paragraphs? Headers and bullet points? Citations? Failure to discuss and agree on this point can mean that some work appears in half-formed sentences and bullet points, and some work appears in full sentences but no paragraphs, and yet other work appears in full sentences, headers, paragraphs, and with citations. Clarify the team's expectations ahead of time to avoid this misalignment.
- **Decision making.** How will your team make decisions? Will you vote and go with the majority, or will you discuss issues until you have a full team consensus? Will you give one person the freedom to make decisions about their area of expertise? Is there a leader, and is that person empowered to make decisions on his or her own? Examine this crucial team function carefully to avoid misunderstandings in the future.

Team function and communication

These are the important "process" areas that your team needs to discuss and have recorded in the team charter. These areas usually include the following:

- **Primary and secondary modes of communication.** Decide what the primary mode of communication, aside from meetings, will be among the team. Many teams select email because it provides a written record of information and allows for attachments of files.
- **Contact information.** Be sure that all email addresses, phone numbers, and any other important contact information is shared. If your team has decided on titles for the roles assumed by team members (e.g., team leader, communications director, researcher), remember to include this information as well.
- **Meeting times and locations.** Survey your team members to ascertain the best possible times for meetings. Note the location for meetings or assign one team member

the task of booking space for meetings. Ask team members to schedule the agreed-upon common times for meetings.

- **Technology requirements.** If your team works virtually, be sure to note which virtual environment or software you plan to use. Have a primary virtual environment and a secondary option in case there are technical issues with the primary tool.
- **Technology guidelines.** These will depend on your team's working style and requirements. You may wish, for example, to create a rule that all team members check their primary mode of communication (e.g., email) every 12 to 24 hours and ask for a commitment for a response to emails sent within that same timeframe. You may wish to note that mobile devices, other than those needed for work purposes, are not welcome during team meetings (e.g., no texting or instant messaging during team meetings).
- **Recording minutes.** Decide who will take **minutes** or notes at team meetings. Usually this person is also responsible for distributing the minutes to the team. Guidelines for minute taking will follow later in this chapter.
- **Meetings.** Set rules and expectations about meetings. Consider how many meetings you may need to have, and how often you will need to meet. This will be different for every team, depending on deadlines, team availability, and the nature of the work being completed. Consider the need for an **agenda** to be prepared ahead of time, and decide who will be responsible for this. Guidelines for agenda creation will follow later in this chapter.
- **Milestones.** Be sure the team understands the deadline for completion of work and any **milestones** that occur along the way. For example, if a written report is due on December 15, your team may schedule all the team members' individual contributions to be due on November 15. This would be a milestone, allowing one month for work to be compiled, edited, proofread, and finalized. You may also agree that all research should be completed by October 15 to allow everyone time to prepare their work with ample access to research. This would be another milestone.
- **Calendar review.** One of the features of working in a diverse environment is the existence of many important calendar dates that need attention. Not everyone is aware of all the dates that are important within all cultural groups. Each team member should take a close look at your project's timeline and milestones to make sure that they do not conflict with personal or cultural calendar dates. Be ready to help each other work around these dates. Looking ahead to avoid these situations is extremely helpful in avoiding unnecessary delays and misunderstandings.

As noted earlier in this section, the function of the team charter is to establish expectations and to ensure everyone has the same understanding of their role and obligations. When team members are not clear about what is expected of them, it is easier for them to make poor or even unethical choices. Check out the **ETHICS BOX** for some examples.

Give the team time to develop

Although some teams quickly learn how to work well together, most teams need time to develop their collaborative working relationship. **FIGURE 6.1** illustrates a model for understanding team development first proposed by Bruce W. Tuckman. He identified four stages of development in teams that had no formal team training: **forming**, **storming**, **norming**, and **performing** (T. E. Harris & Sherblom, 2011; Tuckman, 1965). Here is what happens in each stage:

- **Forming.** When a team first begins to form, everyone is usually polite and considerate. You exchange information about your schedules, when and where you can meet, and how you can contact each other. Usually, expectations for the team and its success are high and conflicts are not evident.
- **Storming.** The team eventually begins to encounter problems that are not easily resolved. Members begin to feel tense and anxious about the success of the project. Some team members may begin to feel disillusioned and discouraged. As you experience conflict, try to identify the reasons for the conflict to help the group move to the next stage of development. Conflict management is detailed later in this chapter.

Minutes Notes that describe what was discussed at a meeting, what was decided, and what actions will follow.

Agenda A detailed plan or outline of the items to be discussed at a meeting.

Milestone A "mini-deadline" for completion of a small task that contributes to the overall completion of a larger project.

Forming A stage of team development in which members get to know each other.

Storming A stage of team development in which teams experience conflict and begin to confront differences.

Norming A stage of team development in which team members learn how to manage conflict and work with each other effectively.

Performing A stage of team development in which team members work collaboratively and achieve a high level of productivity.

ETHICS
TEAM DYNAMICS = TEAM ETHICS?

Ethical issues can arise in all aspects of your personal, professional, or school life. As a business student in college, Skylar is provided with learning environments that include group assignments. Some of these challenges are similar to what she will experience as a business professional, so even the simple act of being part of a team facing these issues is excellent preparation for the workplace.

In the first class of her human resources course, teams have been assigned in groups of five by the instructor. The groups are purposefully organized to allow learners to experience teams of different backgrounds, language groups, learning, and leadership styles. During the term, Skylar noticed that three students formed a friendship that often left Skylar and Marek, the other quieter student, out of their conversations. Furthermore, Skylar noticed that their team meetings were often filled with conversations focused on social life rather than the assignment. As the deadline approached, the group divided the assignment into two parts: The three friends would complete one part, and Skylar and Marek would complete the other. The night before the assignment was due, Marek agreed to compile the two halves of the work together to form the full assignment.

After the work was compiled and submitted to the online drop box for the course, Skylar overheard that one of the three students on her team had "borrowed" a copy of a similar assignment from another student who had taken the course previously. Skylar suspected, but could not be certain, that the work handed in by the three friends was not original. It was actually produced by a student who had already passed this course in a previous semester. Unsure how to handle this, Skylar asked for a one-on-one appointment with the professor to discuss the matter.

How can O-A-R help?

- **Observe:** Skylar observed and experienced wide variations in team expectations, work ethic, and standards of quality. These same wide variations are present in the workplace as well. Consider whether taking proactive action, like working first on a small team charter or agreement before beginning work on the assignment or project, would help solve these issues.

- **Ask:** One of the ethical challenges in this sample involves possible plagiarism. This is a serious offence, both in an academic as well as a legal context. You may wish to ask student team members if they are aware of this as a serious issue, or if they are aware of the negative long-term implications to the team, its members, and their academic careers. When dealing with issues of plagiarism at school, it is important that you speak to a professor right away to ensure your academic standing and transcript are not affected by any penalties or consequences. If you suspect that similar behaviour is being exhibited in the workplace, you should bring this to the attention of your supervisor.

- **Research:** In your course outlines or syllabi, there may be explicit areas that discuss the seriousness of plagiarism. Check out this website that explains plagiarism in more detail: www.plagiarism.org

When issues of work productivity and quality arise, the ethical issue has to do with managing expectations. Setting standards early about what is to be done and when is a fair way to be sure that everyone knows what is expected. When expectations about timeliness and quality are not clearly set out, team members are free to work to their own expectations rather than the team's expectations. Setting and communicating expectations at the outset is a key function of a team charter.

For an ETHICS exercise, go to Exercise 13 on page 189.

FORMING	STORMING	NORMING	PERFORMING
Exchange vital information	Experience conflict and tension	Discuss and resolve problems	Work collaboratively
Learn about each other	Feel disillusioned and discouraged	Create standards for communicating	Use individual differences as a source of strength
Have high expectations for success		Plan regular meetings	Put project above individual goals
Act politely and considerately	Identify reasons for conflict	Hold members accountable	Achieve high level of productivity

FIGURE 6.1 Stages of Team Development

- **Norming.** Norming begins when team members start to manage conflict and achieve positive outcomes. In the norming stage, teams can begin to be truly productive.
- **Performing.** At the performing stage of team development, team members have learned how to work collaboratively and are able to use their differences as a source of strength, not weakness. Although problems will continue to arise, a performing team feels comfortable confronting and resolving the problems that might jeopardize the success of the project. Members begin to enjoy working together and are glad they don't have to complete the project alone. They often get so involved and excited about what they are doing that they lose track of time, and the success of the project becomes more important than individual goals.

Almost all teams experience this sort of evolution, although many do not make it fully to the performing stage. If you know to expect politeness at the outset, some conflict along the way, and some normal performance after the conflict has resolved, then you will have a better chance of navigating all these stages with a positive outlook.

Plan for effective meetings

Team meetings are crucial for determining tasks, sharing ideas, and making decisions. To avoid falling into the trap of holding too many meetings where not enough gets done, plan your meetings in advance following these guidelines:

- Create an effective agenda
- Assign special roles to team members

Create an effective agenda

Base the agenda on input from each team member. At the top of the agenda, include the day, time, and place of the meeting. Also state the purpose of the meeting. This will help keep the discussion on track. List all the topics to be discussed, or all the decisions to be made, and estimate the amount of time each item will require. Although you may need to be flexible with time during the meeting, the time estimates will help the team get through all the topics efficiently. It is recommended practice that you assign each topic to a team member to ensure that all team members have some responsibility during the meeting. If team members are not responsible for anything on the agenda, reconsider whether they need to attend the meeting.

Always include a wrap-up as the last item on your agenda. This reminds you to end the meeting by reviewing the actions and deadlines that everyone agreed upon and scheduling the next meeting's time and place.

FIGURE 6.2 shows a sample agenda. Notice that the agenda provides the list of topics to be discussed, the names of the individuals responsible for each item, and the amount of time to be spent discussing each item.

Distributing the agenda before the meeting ensures that all the team members know what will be expected, who is responsible, and what their roles will be during the meeting.

Assign special roles to team members

One team member should agree to "chair" or "facilitate" each meeting. This role can be held by the same person for the duration of your time as a team, or you can share this duty with a new chair each meeting. The chair keeps track of how well the meeting follows the agenda. If the meeting becomes sidetracked on unrelated matters or if participants get stuck on unproductive tangents, the chair (or facilitator) can bring the conversation back to the necessary topic.

Another team member should take notes. Again, this role can be held by the same person each time, or the role can be shared throughout your time as a team. The note taker will produce meeting *minutes*, a written description of what was discussed, what was decided, and what actions will follow. Notice, in Figure 6.2, that the minutes focus on what the team decided and on action items for completion. Not everything that was said is recorded. The minutes also include assignments (who agreed to do what) and deadlines (when they agreed to submit deliverables).

FIGURE 6.2 Agenda and Minutes

AGENDA	MINUTES

AGENDA

Online Internship Handbook Team

Human Resources Conference Room
Tuesday, July 31, 20XX
4:00–5:00 p.m.

MEETING PURPOSE:
To kick off the internship handbook project and develop a six-week plan.

I.   Introductions   5–10 min.

    a. Jay Macintosh, Intern to Director for Human Resources, Team Leader
    b. Rachel Ferrera, Intern to Assistant to CEO
    c. Arnie Glover, Intern to Temp Pool Supervisor
    d. Roberto Washington, Intern, Web Development Department

II. Project Overview   – Jay Macintosh   10–15 min.

    a. Brainstorm Initial Ideas for Topic Content
    b. Assign Responsibilities

III. Web Development Support   – Roberto Washington   10–15 min.

    a. Discuss Format / Layout Options
    b. Determine Resource Needs (Materials)

IV. Six-Week Timeline   – Jay Macintosh   10–15 min.

    a. Meeting Times
    b. Progress Reports and Submission Schedule
    c. Interns Who Will Provide Feedback:
        1. Sarah Fernandez, Marketing Department
        2. Paul Mason, Research & Development
        3. Soren Afzabi, Research & Development
        4. Melanie Godfarb, Accounting

V.   Other?   5–10 min.

VI. Due Next Week: Content Reports

MINUTES

Online Internship Handbook Team

Human Resources Conference Room
July 31, 20XX

Present: Jay Macintosh, Intern to Director for Human Resources, Team Leader
Rachel Ferrera, Intern to Assistant to CEO
Arnie Glover, Intern to Temp Pool Supervisor
Roberto Washington, Intern, Web Development Department

I.   **Introductions:** Jay Macintosh called the meeting to order, introduced himself, and asked the others to state their department, experience, and skills.

II. **Project Overview:** Jay Macintosh explained the project goals. The team brainstormed ideas for topics and assigned content as follows:

    a. Welcome to the Company   – Rachel Ferrera
        1. History of the Organization
        2. Mission / Vision Statements
        3. Organizational Chart
        4. Your Role as an Intern

    b. Policies and Procedures   – Arnie Glover
        1. Maintaining Work Hours and Reporting Absences
        2. Sending and Responding to Email
        3. Logging Telephone Calls
        4. Using the Internet
        5. Using Social Media
        6. Submitting Reimbursement Requests

    c. Human Resources   – Jay Macintosh
        1. Salary and Payroll Procedures
        2. Health Benefits
        3. Educational Resources
        4. Applying for Permanent Employment

III. **Web Development Support:** Roberto Washington explained company policies about website format, layout, and design options. The team discussed where on the current company website the internship handbook should be located. Decision: Roberto will check with his supervisor about content and resource needs and report to the team by email before the end of the week.

IV. **Six-Week Timeline: Decisions:**
    1. We will meet on Tuesdays from 3 to 5 p.m. Between meetings we will update each other by email.
    2. Jay will send our weekly meeting minutes to his supervisor as our progress reports.
    3. We will send the completed version of our first draft to the other interns who volunteered for this project to get their feedback by Week 3.
    4. We will submit a draft to the Director of Human Resources by Week 4.
    5. Roberto will begin putting the material on the web in Week 5.

V.   **Next meeting:** The team will meet on August 7 to discuss the content reports.

Be a valued team member

Although a team works together to achieve a common goal, it is still made up of individuals. Each individual needs to take responsibility for his or her own tasks and also contribute to a productive working relationship with others. Being a valued team member includes the following behaviours:

- Making a commitment to the team and its goals
- Creating a collaborative working environment
- Supporting team decisions

Making a commitment to the team and its goals

At times, it may be tempting to do minimal work for the team and assume that others will pick up the slack. But a team will succeed only if everyone shares a similar intensity of commitment. Every member must be reliable and pull his or her own weight. In addition, every team member must be willing to do whatever it takes to make the team successful, including helping each other if the need arises.

Too often teams of students feel as though they have not chosen the team or the assignments within their courses. While it is true that such decisions may be out of your control, you can control your choice to commit to the team and its objectives. You can choose to prioritize the team and its objectives. Making this choice moves your perception of the team effort from "incidental" or "accidental" to "intentional." You have a huge influence on your team's success, simply by shifting your attitude toward the team and its work. It is worth considering that you will not have a great deal of control in the working world over the choice of teammates or projects. To get the best quality work from a team, employers look for people who can manage this attitudinal shift.

Creating a collaborative working environment

To work well together, team members need to trust each other and believe that everyone is working in the team's best interests. This means that, as a valued team member, you need to be worthy of that trust. Listen to your teammates without criticism or judgment and give everyone a chance to participate in decision making. Respond constructively to feedback from others, and address conflicts when they arise rather than letting them grow silently and weaken team cohesion.

One of the most powerful behaviours you can develop when working on a team is the art of asking questions that help others communicate their ideas. When a team is working through new ideas, you may notice one of your teammates contributing only part of an idea or an unfinished thought. They may need your encouragement and support to keep developing the idea or thought verbally. Learn simple, nonjudgmental prompts, questions, and phrases that encourage people to continue speaking once they have started. These can include the following:

- That sounds interesting. Can you say more?
- I'm not sure I understand this idea completely. Can you tell us more?
- Can you elaborate? This sounds really interesting.

Sometimes more direct questioning can sound harsh or judgmental. If you can learn how to prompt others into describing their ideas more fully, your team will benefit from higher-quality input from all members. Simultaneously, you will be contributing to maintaining a positive and collaborative working environment.

Supporting team decisions

It is critical that you support team decisions, even if the team has made a decision that differs from what you wanted. Once the decision is made, support that decision gracefully and work toward implementing it. Learn how to gracefully "agree to disagree." You may wish to develop your own version of the following example of "agreeing to disagree":

> I understand everyone's opinion. (Paraphrase all opinions to demonstrate your understanding. Include your own opinion last.) The team seems to prefer (describe preference). As discussed, I have a different preference. I am happy to support the team preference going forward. I know that you will have opportunities to support my ideas later in this project.

Being prepared with a professional-sounding, supportive message to deliver on those occasions when a decision does not go your way will enhance your value as a team member. Avoid the words "but" and "however" when "agreeing to disagree," as these words may make your full commitment seem less sincere.

If you have concerns about the decision or believe it may cause problems, voice your concerns to the team. Do not try to undermine the decision by complaining about it to others when your teammates are not around. Discussing team disagreements with peers who are not on the team can be extremely damaging to team cohesion and performance.

Before you can become a respected leader, you need to master the skills of being a valued team member. Leadership skills build on membership skills. Leadership cannot develop without the ability to make a full commitment to the team and its goals, to create a collaborative working environment, and to support and encourage teammates to bring their best to the team effort.

LO 6.2 How can working on a team help you develop leadership skills?

A team can establish leadership in a number of ways. One person can serve as leader, leadership can rotate during phases of the project, or different leaders can take responsibility for different aspects of the project. It is not crucial for the team to have one single leader. However, it is crucial for the team to have capable leadership that keeps the overall goal of the team and the project in mind. Remember that if you agree to be team leader, that role does not put you "in charge" of the team. Instead, it puts you at the service of the team.

Identify and practise key leadership fundamentals

An effective leader is a person who has the skills to bring out the best in others, manage work processes, and help the team succeed. Here are some ways that a leader can serve the team and help it succeed:

- Overcommunicate
- Reinforce team objectives
- Create a supportive climate

Overcommunicate

Teams can get nervous about someone assuming "leadership," even if they have explicitly asked that person to do so. You can help your team feel at ease with you if you are as transparent as possible. What does this mean? It means share all information you have, all decisions made, and all new incoming communications from outside the team with the team. You can do this by having regular and active meetings, through email if appropriate, or via any collaboration or discussion boards you are using to share information. The more you communicate with your team, the more they will trust your leadership (DeWitt, 2014).

Reinforce team objectives

One of the most valuable roles for any leader is to keep the team focused on the ultimate objective and remind the team why that goal is valuable. Teams can easily get bogged down in the details of the work and forget why the project is worthwhile. An effective leader will reenergize team members by refocusing them on the long-term goal.

For example, although individual members of the team may work on separate tasks, a leader creates opportunities for the team to communicate synchronously throughout the project. Team members need time together to discuss progress, share updates, and encourage feedback and input. Scheduling regular meetings keeps the project on track to meet established deadlines while also allowing for changes in the plan to be reviewed and discussed by the entire team. A leader can use this opportunity to connect all team activities to the overall goals and objectives.

Create a supportive climate

Teams work best when team members feel that they can take risks and will be listened to and respected. A team leader can set the tone for the team by encouraging creativity and being a positive and respectful role model.

For example, an experienced leader will model effective listening, questioning, and paraphrasing techniques to ensure that all members of the team are assured that their input has been heard. Leaders also encourage positive collaboration among team members while monitoring unconstructive feedback or personality conflicts. In the next section of this chapter, you will review conflict resolution techniques that all team members, especially those within leadership roles, can use to identify, diffuse, and resolve such situations.

Although teams can take many approaches, like majority vote, to decision making, important decisions should never be made by giving in to the team member who is the loudest and most assertive. A team leader can ensure that the team makes fact-based judgments and is able to support all its decisions with sound evidence and reasoning.

Use conflict management to help develop leadership skills

It is counterintuitive to imagine that the most successful teams encourage and manage conflict. Yet, as anyone who has had a successful workplace team experience will tell you, conflict plays an important and significant part in team development. Once conflict energy has been transformed into collaborative energy, teams can employ additional, proactive communications techniques to gain even higher performance and productivity. This section of the chapter looks at conflict, collaboration, and communications to help you optimize all that your team has to offer.

Recognizing that conflict is an essential part of team development (the "storming" phase), some organizations encourage active disagreement and clashes of opinion. For example, at Bridgewater Associates, one of the world's biggest hedge funds, founder Raymond Dalio encourages his employees to challenge one another's views. Dalio says, "I believe that the biggest problem humanity faces is ego sensitivity to finding out whether one is right or wrong and identifying what one's strengths and weaknesses are" (Cassidy, 2011). In an atmosphere where people know how to challenge others' ideas respectfully, people's sensitivity about their ego decreases and their productivity increases.

Even if you follow all of this chapter's advice about team dynamics, and previous chapters' advice about knowing your audience, listening effectively and allowing for variance in style and culture, conflict will inevitably arise when you work with others. Conflict can include differences in opinion, disagreements about how to handle issues, complaints about performance or fairness, criticism about the behaviour of others, and personality conflicts between people who just do not get along. When working virtually, unresolved conflict can be especially challenging. Researchers have noted that one of the most striking differences between virtual teams and nonvirtual teams is their difficulty managing conflict (Solomon, 2012).

Although people often use the term "conflict resolution" to discuss handling conflict, "conflict management" is a more helpful term. "Conflict resolution" implies that the conflict will go away. By contrast, "conflict management" recognizes that some conflicts cannot be resolved.

Conflict can be divided into two broad categories: **cognitive conflict**, which results from differences in understanding content or tasks, and **affective conflict**, which results from differences in personalities and relationships. All high-performing work teams experience disagreements (cognitive conflict) while collaborating. Working through these disagreements can have positive results for the quality of team decisions and the final work product (CPP, Inc., 2008). As teamwork expert Paul Glover points out, "If a team always agreed on everything, they'd be satisfied with the *first* answer to the problem instead of working, arguing, and debating to figure out the *best* answer" (Glover, 2012).

Problems arise when teams allow these cognitive conflicts to become affective conflicts. For example, two people working on a marketing plan may disagree about the best way to reach the company's target market. If they work through the cognitive conflict, listen carefully to each other's concerns, and achieve consensus, the result may be better than if they pursued only one idea without challenging it. If the two people cannot reach agreement and leave the meeting in anger, this emotional conflict may damage the working relationship. Problems also arise if conflicts remain unstated and unaddressed, leading to tension, stress, and dysfunctional work processes.

Cognitive conflict A conflict that results from differences in understanding content or tasks. Working through a cognitive conflict often leads to better decisions and work products.

Affective conflict A conflict that results from differences in personalities and relationships. If affective conflicts remain unstated and unaddressed, they can lead to tension, stress, and dysfunctional work processes.

Consider this situation in the context of a virtual team. The nature of virtual work and communication is that there is significantly more task-oriented communication (cognitive) than relationship-oriented communication (affective). This suggests that conflict is likely to begin as a task-related disagreement and develop into a relational one. Consider the speed with which a poorly worded email exchange about a work-related topic can create bad feeling between two co-workers. When this happens to people who are thousands of kilometres apart, how can the conflict be managed?

To be properly managed, conflict and disagreements need to be explicitly identified and discussed in a virtual environment. All team members need to be fully committed to working through their disagreements without the benefit of extra nonverbal signals that might soften words or mitigate tone. This can be especially challenging when working across cultures using technology. One common method employed to support this method of conflict management is the creation of a specific virtual space, accessible only by team members and set aside to discuss any issues or concerns that have arisen. If all team members are committed to the overall goals of the project, and if enough trust has been developed relationally, this strategy can be very successful (Ferrazzi, 2012).

Over the next few pages you will find a two-step process for managing conflict: Identify the cause of the conflict and then decide how to respond.

Identify the cause of the conflict

As **FIGURE 6.3** illustrates, cognitive and affective conflicts generally occur for a few well-defined reasons. Note in Figure 6.3 that the line between cognitive and affective conflicts can be unclear. In fact, it is sometimes difficult to know whether a conflict is cognitive or affective. For example, do you truly object to that person's idea (cognitive), or do you simply do not like that person (affective)? Analyzing the cause of a conflict is useful because different causes call for different conflict management strategies.

Competing goals

People who collaborate may not always be motivated to achieve the same goals. In fact, for a business to succeed it must work toward a number of goals that are sometimes in competition with each other. A business strives to make a profit while planning for future growth, keeping employees and customers satisfied, and meeting governmental requirements for employee and consumer safety. Employees have their own goals, such as increasing their income, enhancing their reputation, gaining new customers, getting a promotion, or spending more quality time with family and friends. Consider this scenario:

Marcus and Allison of Green Earth Landscapes are barely speaking to each other. This morning Marcus promised one of the company's best customers, a large museum, that Green Earth could complete a major landscape installation by the end of October. Marcus's supervisor told him that keeping this customer happy was a high priority because the museum was responsible for 30% of Green Earth's income last year. When Marcus approached Allison, who does the scheduling, Allison exploded: "We are 100% booked through the end of the

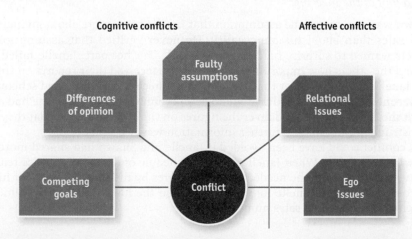

FIGURE 6.3 Causes of Conflict

year. We cannot take on any new projects, no matter who the client is. I received explicit instructions from the head of project management that we need to keep costs down. I'm not going to schedule any overtime. We'd lose money rather than make it. Why didn't you talk to me before you made a promise?"

Marcus's goal is to keep the customer happy. By contrast, Allison's goal is to keep costs in line by eliminating all overtime. This example illustrates how easily competing goals, a cognitive conflict, can disintegrate into an affective conflict. Allison thinks Marcus does what he wants without concern for the consequences. Marcus thinks Allison always argues with him and that she does not understand the big picture of how the company works. By recognizing that each person is trying to achieve different goals, they can discuss the issue with their supervisors to determine which goal has priority. At that point, they can agree to satisfy the most important goal or collaborate to find a solution that addresses both goals.

Differences of opinion

Even if people agree on a goal, they may have differences of opinion about how to achieve it. Consider this scenario:

Rotel Plumbing Supplies wants to become the premier plumbing distributor in the northwest. What is the best way to accomplish this goal? Valerie argues that investing in marketing and customer relations is the key because Rotel needs more and bigger customers. Corinne argues that investing in distribution is the key. To be the premier distributor, Rotel needs to guarantee next-day delivery, which will require creating more distribution centres.

Differences of opinion can also easily lead to affective conflicts, especially if the differences result in a contest of wills. Differences of opinion are best resolved by a rational decision-making process, which may involve some research to collect data to turn opinions into validated statements. Resolution will likely also involve compromise.

Faulty assumptions

People often draw conclusions or make decisions based on faulty assumptions. They do not have all the information they need and jump to conclusions. Consider this scenario:

Janelle gave her sales team a schedule of dates to submit quarterly sales data. She told them she expected them to meet these dates. On the due date for the fourth-quarter data, Shawn realized that he could include a very large sale worth hundreds of thousands of dollars if he waited just a few days to submit his figures. He knew that Janelle, his supervisor, was interested in increased sales figures, so he decided to wait and surprise her with unexpectedly positive results. The next morning, Shawn arrived at work at 9 a.m. to find an angry email from Janelle: "Where are your sales figures? I was up all night preparing a presentation for management at 8 a.m. and didn't realize until 4 a.m. that you hadn't submitted your numbers. You knew they were due yesterday. I looked like a fool at the meeting."

Shawn was working on the assumption that Janelle cared more about an increase in reported sales than about his punctuality. He never verified that assumption with Janelle. He wanted to surprise her with the big sale. For her part, Janelle failed to tell Shawn and the others how important it was that she received their reports on time this quarter. Janelle did not consider that her staff might need to know she had scheduled an 8 a.m. presentation that required up-to-date data. From her perspective, she had already told them she expected them to deliver the figures on time. She assumed that they would follow instructions and that no further information was necessary.

This conflict could have been avoided if Janelle and Shawn had shared more information with each other. When Janelle sent the schedule of dates to her sales team, she could have explained *why* she needed the sales figures by the specific date. For his part, Shawn could have asked Janelle for an extension on the fourth-quarter deadline so he could include the increased sales numbers.

Relational issues

Sometimes people just do not get along well and they do not make the effort to overcome their differences. We often prefer to work with people whose communication, personality, and work styles resemble our own. For example, if you are detail oriented, you most likely feel comfortable working with other detail-oriented people. If you like to make quick decisions, you enjoy working with other decisive people. Styles that differ from our own often create tension, and we may place a negative label on that behaviour. A more productive perspective is to realize that different styles may complement each other and help a team achieve balance.

The following example illustrates how relational conflicts can stand in the way of productive discussions about content and substance:

> At first, Derek was excited to work on a new project with his consulting company's biggest client because it would give him a chance to learn new skills and gain valuable exposure. However, from the first day of the project he has been in conflict with his new teammate Ed. Ed interrupts him, argues against his ideas, and then tries to take credit for his ideas when they work. Sometimes Ed has a great idea of his own, but Derek has difficulty acknowledging it because he is so angry at Ed most of the time. Derek thinks that Ed is egotistical and stubborn. He often finds himself arguing against an idea just because Ed brought it up.

Affective personality conflicts like this are costly. Researchers have found that

- 53% of workers lost time at work because they worried about confrontations with co-workers, and
- 37% of workers feel that arguments with colleagues caused them to reduce their commitment to the job (Zupeck, 2008).

Relational conflicts do not simply go away if you ignore them. When you have a personality clash with someone, explore ways to resolve it. Remember to argue only about things that make a real difference (cognitive conflict). Ask if you can meet to discuss the affective conflict itself, being sure to listen actively by focusing on the content rather than personalities. Use neutral rather than accusatory language. Ask for help from managers, if you need it. Mediation from supervisors may sometimes be necessary.

Ego issues

Ego conflicts threaten someone's sense of professional identity or self-image. In professional contexts, people typically see themselves as honest, reasonable, intelligent, and committed to the well-being of the organization. When someone accuses you of something negative or challenges your sense of identity, you may find it difficult to work productively with that person. Consider the following scenario:

> Nadia is the youngest customer relationship manager in the company, and she is proud of her quick rise through the ranks. In three years, she has progressed faster than any other employee and is responsible for 35% of the company's sales. Yet whenever she meets with Brian, the head of engineering, to discuss her customers' needs, she feels personally insulted. If Brian does not like what she proposes for a project, he often says, "We can't do that. You're not an engineer. You don't know what you're talking about." Or he might say, "How old are you? You've only been here for three years. I've been doing this kind of work for 20 years, and I know the best way to get it done." Things are so strained between Brian and Nadia that they avoid face-to-face encounters, resorting to email to discuss projects.

When a conflict becomes personal, as this one has, one wise approach is to shift the focus back to business. Nadia might say, "I know you have 20 years of experience. That's why I'm sure you can help me meet this customer's needs." This approach not only shifts the focus of the conversation, but it also offers Brian a subtle compliment and may make him more willing to take Nadia seriously.

Select an appropriate management technique

As the scenarios above suggest, not all conflicts are best managed the same way. If you are involved in affective conflict that focuses on relationships or ego, you will need to address the emotional issues before you can productively discuss the content of your work. If you are involved in a cognitive conflict, however, you can consider five different strategies to move toward an acceptable outcome. Each strategy has advantages and disadvantages, and different strategies work well in different situations.

1. Avoidance
2. Accommodation
3. Competition
4. Compromise
5. Collaboration (Kilmann, 2011)

Avoidance

Instead of addressing a conflict, you may choose to avoid a conflict: deny the problem exists, change the topic, screen your telephone calls, or even avoid the person completely, as Nadia and Brian did in the previous example. Avoiding confrontation is occasionally the right choice, especially when you believe you have no chance of resolving the conflict to your satisfaction and the conflict does not interfere with productivity.

More often, however, everyone loses when you avoid a conflict. If problems are not addressed, they tend to get worse. If Brian and Nadia continue to avoid each other and communicate only by email, they will have no opportunity to develop a sense of shared goals that will allow them to work in the best interests of the business. Ultimately, the customers will suffer. Instead of avoidance, Nadia and Brian need to adopt a different strategy.

Accommodation ("giving in")

Accommodating essentially means that one person gives in and allows the other person to have his or her way. Graciously accommodating is a wise choice if you decide that your position was wrong and you change your mind. Accommodating is also an excellent choice when the conflict is trivial or you do not care deeply about the result. That is why accommodation should be part of your negotiation strategy: You can give in about something less important to you so that you can get your way on something more important. Colloquially, this is known as "picking your battles."

Accommodating does pose a danger if you give in to the point of sacrificing your principles and beliefs. Such accommodation can lead to loss of self-esteem or ineffective results. A team that fears conflict and always accommodates the strongest person is engaging in **groupthink**. This is one of the most damaging behaviours a team can display. A groupthink approach to eliminating conflict can lead a group to ignore differing opinions that may be valuable or settle on a solution that may be wrong. Groupthink sacrifices valuable creativity and innovation (Rabe, 2006).

Competition

Sometimes a conflict becomes a contest, with participants competing to win, even at another person's expense. Like accommodating, competing results in an "I win, you lose" outcome. Competitive tactics can include finding fault or blaming others, rejecting the other party's point of view, and minimizing one's own responsibility for a mistake.

Competitive approaches to resolving conflicts may result in quick solutions, but they often lead to relational conflicts. For example, Marcus and Allison of Green Earth (first introduced on page 171) could bring their conflict to the president of the company to decide which goal to prioritize: keeping customers happy or keeping costs down. If the president decided to accommodate old customers, Marcus and Allison would have a clear resolution to their cognitive conflict. They would still need to work out the personal anger (i.e., the affective conflict) that had developed between them.

Groupthink A behaviour exhibited by a group that values conformity and avoids conflict. Team members will state they are in agreement when, in fact, they are not. It can result in one strong team member making most of the decisions while the creativity and individualism of other team members are suppressed.

Compromise

Compromising is a more cooperative approach than competing. In a compromise, all the parties involved get something they want or can accept, but everyone also needs to sacrifice something.

Compromising is often an appropriate way to achieve workable solutions under time pressure. Imagine that Valerie and Corinne of Rotel Plumbing (see page 172 for the earlier scenario) need to present a budget to the board of directors the next day, even though they continue to have differences of opinion about how best to achieve the goal of being the premier plumbing supplier in the northwest: Should they invest in marketing or distribution? They could reach a compromise and create budgets for two smaller projects: one for marketing and another for distribution. Neither will get everything she wants, but this solution offers several benefits:

- Each person will get some of what she wants.
- Valerie and Corinne will be able to project a united front at the board of directors meeting.
- They will gather data from the two projects that may help them resolve their difference of opinion.

By compromising, each person's goal is partially achieved.

Collaboration

Although collaboration is a time-consuming approach, it is often the best approach for managing complex conflicts. In collaboration, all the parties work together to determine the best possible solution. For example, Marcus and Allison could have realized they would not be able to easily resolve their conflict because their supervisors gave them conflicting requirements. Although they could individually talk to their supervisors, another approach would be to work together to find a solution in the best interests of the company. Perhaps the company could charge more for rush jobs, give clients the option of paying a retainer to save space on the Green Earth schedule, or develop a new procedure for calculating revenues versus overtime costs. Marcus and Allison could then present these collaborative solutions in a meeting with their two supervisors. Collaboration like this has the benefit not only of providing a solution but also ensuring buy-in from all parties and strengthening the relationships between people.

What are some key aspects of high-performance team collaboration?

One reason to study teamwork in a business communication course is so that you can move more quickly to the performing stage. A performing team may also evolve into a *high-performing team*: a team with members who are deeply committed to each other's growth and success (Katzenbach & Smith, 1993; L. L. Thompson, 2011). Achieving this level of performance requires time commitment and hard work. However, when you get there, you will find the team experience to be exhilarating and rewarding.

Enhance productivity with virtual best practices

Keith Ferrazzi is the founder and CEO of Ferrazzi Greenlight, a research institute studying human behaviour change. In 2013, his institute looked into identifying behaviours that must change, given our technology-mediated business practices, to unleash value and enhance productivity. His research group found that relational and collaborative behaviours were the behaviours that needed to change the most (Ferrazzi, 2013). Ferrazzi says that "just because we are in a technology-enabled world and we don't see each other doesn't necessarily mean that we're doing the right things to enable the technology" (Ferrazzi, 2013). In other words, just because we have all the tools available to us does not mean we are using them to become as effective and productive as we can be.

Scania is a Swedish truck manufacturer that delivers more vehicles to Brazil than to any other country. Flavio Liviero, the chief project coordinator at Scania, believes that technology has played a huge role in improving the performance of cross-border teams over that time: "We didn't even have fax machines at the start. At least now we have all the necessary tools for communication in place." Nevertheless, Mr. Liviero knows that cultural barriers need to be constantly managed. He notes that an effective way to overcome such obstacles is to meet in person at the project's outset: "What we noted quite early on was that face-to-face contact really helps interaction" (Bolchover, 2012, p. 13).

To make sure that your teams are as productive and collaborative as possible, be sure you understand and implement some virtual best practices:

- **Start face to face.** It may be counterintuitive to suggest this when discussing virtual teams, but as we learned in Chapter 5, face-to-face communication is still richer than virtual when it comes to building relationships and fostering trust, and these elements are essential for productive teamwork. Help team members get to know each other better, personally and professionally. You can also use the time to create a team charter. Schedule face-to-face reunions regularly, semiannually, or annually if possible, for long-term teams (Watkins, 2013).

- **Stay aware of possible cultural, diversity, and regional sensitivities.** All of the discussion regarding intercultural and diverse communication skills remains valid in virtual team communication. Working virtually adds other dimensions to these skills:
  - Being aware of time zone implications for "real-time" virtual meetings
  - Being aware of cultural and regional holidays and celebrations when scheduling online meetings and events
  - Remembering levels of directness, formality, context, and other variables when communicating across borders
  - Making it "safe" for team members to ask for items to be clarified
  - Being patient when team members need communication to be clarified
  - Being fearless about asking for clarification when you need it

When creating a team charter for a virtual team, adding agreements in advance about these points would be very valuable.

- **Be prepared and present during online meetings.** If you have received materials ahead of the meeting, be sure to read them and be ready to discuss the content. Ferrazzi suggests that not reading the materials ahead of time is unethical, and disrespectful of the other team members' time (Ferrazzi, 2015).

- **Avoid misuse of the online meeting time.** An online meeting is a poor choice for "reporting in" on the status of projects, budgets, or other initiatives. This type of information can be distributed in print in preparation for the meeting. Virtual meeting time is best used for collaborative problem solving, brainstorming, and idea generation (Ferrazzi, 2015). A meeting that is simply a series of voices and faces reading from progress reports is unengaging. A meeting that generates active input and fresh ideas can be engaging and fruitful.

- **Optimize the video interface.** The use of video to enhance online meetings brings the richest possible level of communication without actually having people in the room together face to face. Remember this when tempted to multitask or look away from the camera. Others can see your behaviour, including smiling when something on your phone (like a text or a tweet) amuses you, or when you are staring out the window in boredom. Conversely, if you put your full attention on the camera, the conversation, and the ideas being discussed, this will also be evident in your facial expressions, gestures, and posture.

- **Create a space online for informal communication.** In addition to selecting an online meeting interface, select a separate "water cooler" space for informal conversation, personal updates, and other types of relational interaction. It has long been observed that the "meeting after the meeting" is where the true communication and relationship building takes place. This can be true of virtual co-workers as well. For example, if the technology platform for scheduled meetings is Adobe Connect, your team could create a private Facebook page for personal updates, informal banter, and other non-work-related exchanges. If your home office acknowledges birthdays or other special events in the lives of employees, be sure to carry that type of acknowledgement over to your virtual colleagues as well, if culturally appropriate.

There is a strong argument for the use of synchronous platforms (such as instant messaging) to connect virtual team members during nonmeeting times. A skilled communicator can use this medium effectively to build and maintain relationships on a day-to-day, operational basis. Erika Darics, in her research on computer-mediated communication, confirmed that to give an "opportunity for the development of the team and the Community of Practice norms, and for impression formation and the maintenance of familiar relationships, communicators should be able to engage in talk that is not strictly task oriented; for virtual team members cannot discuss non-task-oriented issues during coffee breaks or in the copier room" (Darics, 2010).

Some larger companies are investing in their own internal "social collaboration" systems that behave similarly to social media sites, offering immediate and social-style updates and messaging while allowing companies to maintain control over privacy and security issues, as discussed in Chapter 5. To explore this further, check out the **TECHNOLOGY BOX**.

TECHNOLOGY
SOCIAL COLLABORATION: TAKING THE TEAM ONLINE

The term "social collaboration" refers to the use of social media style tools within an organization to facilitate communication and teamwork. Gartner predicts that "by 2016, 50% of large organizations will have internal Facebook-like social networks, and 30% of these will be considered as essential as email and telephones are today" (Gartner Newsroom, 2013). Social technologies like wikis, broadly accessible instant messaging, content searches, and user forums are particularly effective among so called "interactions workers." These people are general managers, consultative sales representatives, and engineers working with teams to figure out new products (Chui et al., 2012). Since they work with a lot of autonomy but also in consultation with others, interactions workers benefit the most from knowing such things as which employees have the deepest knowledge in certain subjects, who last contributed to a project, and how to get in touch with them quickly. "The industries with the highest percentage of interactions workers have the highest spread of profits per employee," says Michael Chui of McKinsey (Chui et al., 2012).

How do social media and collaboration tools facilitate communication within an organization?

- **File sharing and real-time collaborative writing.** When teammates need to work on the same document or spreadsheet, file-sharing tools like Google Docs ensure that everyone can access the most up-to-date version available. Team members who are working in different offices, or even in different parts of the world, can access a document and write or edit at the same time. Document collaboration appears to be more prevalent than any other type of internal social media (Central Desktop, 2011).

- **Brainstorming and getting feedback on ideas.** Companies that value innovation encourage employees to share ideas and engage in discussions that develop new ideas. Virtual whiteboards, such as those that are embedded in many meeting software apps, blogs, note-sharing apps like Evernote, and many other emerging tools, help people communicate and share and enhance their ideas collaboratively.

- **Sharing knowledge.** Wikis have proven to be a great collaboration tool for sales, information technology, and cross-functional teams. Sales representatives need the newest and best product information available at all times to understand and sell the goods and services their companies offer (Fiorella, 2011). Information technology teams need constant and current communication on development and deployment of project elements. Wikis ensure everyone has access to up-to-date information.

Employee collaboration and information sharing have tremendous value to customers. With the right collaborative technologies, employees are able to provide superior support and product intelligence by being able to quickly tap into internal experts, information, and resources. Consider the customer who has contacted a support representative with a product issue. If that representative cannot solve the customer's problem, he or she can have access to the entire organization to find the right information and share it with the customer (Morgan, 2013).

For exercises related to TECHNOLOGY, go to Review Question 13 on page 186 and Exercises 9c, 10e, and 11e on page 188.

Develop the "c factor" in your team

There is a growing sense that the Internet can destroy interpersonal skills, kill our emotional intelligence, and turn us into warm-blooded versions of the very robots that we fear will one day take our jobs. But these studies suggest that the rules of empathy hold both on- and offline. Emotionally sensitive people are gifted at reading between the lines, whether the literal lines are brow wrinkles or text messages. (D. Thompson, 2015)

Researchers at MIT's Center for Collective Intelligence have been working on defining a "c factor" in teams since 2006. The "c factor" could be described as the collective intelligence that explains a group's performance. Surprisingly, the sum of each group member's IQ has only a minor correlation to the group's ultimate success (Woolley & Malone, 2011). Researchers state that the "c factor is not strongly correlated with the average or maximum individual intelligence of group members, but it is correlated with the average social sensitivity of group members, the equality in distribution of conversational turn-taking, and the proportion of females in the group" (MIT Center for Collective Intelligence, n.d.). In other words, the "single most important element of smart groups was their 'average social sensitivity.' That is, the best groups were also the best at reading the non-verbal cues of their teammates" (Thompson, 2015). As noted by one of the principal researchers, Anita Woolley of Carnegie Mellon University, "Part of that finding can be explained by differences in social sensitivity, which we found is also important to group performance. Many studies have shown that women tend to score higher on tests of social sensitivity than men do. So what is really important is to have people who are high in social sensitivity, whether they are men or women" (Woolley & Malone, 2011).

How can you use this emerging knowledge to create a more successful team? There are two simple ways to approach this:

1. **Make sure your team has adequate social or "play" time.** Make sure you build in social time for your team to get to know each other well. The higher the level of interpersonal knowledge, the easier it is to build trust and to build a "literacy" of each other's nonverbal cues. Some successful teams participate in recreational sports together or have family meals together on the occasional weekend. DIALOG, a Canadian design company with locations in Vancouver, Calgary, Edmonton, and Toronto, actively promotes such social connections among its employees. Not surprisingly, DIALOG was named among Canada's Top 100 employers from 2012 to 2014 and, in 2013, was also listed as one of Canada's 50 Most Engaged Workplaces. The "most engaged" award recognizes employers that "display leadership and innovation in engaging employees and making their workplaces more productive" (DIALOG, 2014). According to DIALOG's managing principal, Tom Sutherland, "Success is highly dependent on our people engaging each other outside of their traditional professional silos. The more they do so, the greater the project success" (DIALOG, 2014).

   Some creativity and imagination may be required to create this type of collegiality in far-flung virtual teams. Internal contests, video game tournaments, or other social interactions may help your team members build a stronger sense of each other.

   The creation of high "c factor" teams is tied to the idea of creating organizational culture. For an example of how this might work, and how you might play a key role in creating an environment in which the "c factor" can thrive, check out the **CULTURE BOX**.

2. **Include equal turn-taking in your team charter.** When developing your team charter to guide how your team functions, suggest that equal "turn-taking" be included as a key collaborative principle. At the very least, agreeing on this as an operational guideline ensures that everyone will have a chance to participate. More important, this makes it difficult for a conversation to be controlled by one or two individuals. "Power," in the form of participation and ideas, is shared. Thus, a more equal

CULTURE
THE "SECOND HOUR": CREATING A "C FACTOR" TEAM CULTURE

Skylar walked into her organizational behaviour class with a sense of dread. She knew that this was the day that the instructor would be creating teams for the big research assignment due six weeks later in the term. Sure enough, by the end of the class she found herself seated with four other people she barely knew: Elliot, Avery, Valeeta, and Ester.

Looking back on her previous semesters, Skylar estimated that she had been on about 10 teams in the last 18 months. One team experience was truly excellent: fun, challenging, and memorable. About five of the teams were "OK." Four team experiences were disasters, with one of those projects resulting in complaints to the instructor and the dean of the school. Skylar wished deeply not to have a repeat of these negative experiences.

As she glanced around the table at Elliot, Avery, Valeeta, and Ester, Skylar wondered what she could do to push this team into "excellent" and away from "disaster." Perhaps O-A-R could help:

- **Observe:** Skylar reflected back on the excellent team experience, wondering what made that experience so positive. When she thought about it carefully, she realized that everyone knew what was expected of them and each team member actually completed those tasks on time. That seemed like a basic foundation of teamwork. There was something else, though, about that team. She remembered that student team scheduling longer meeting times and using the second half of their time to do something fun. Sometimes they would go to the student centre and have a darts tournament. Occasionally they borrowed some sports equipment from the gym and played some casual soccer or broomball. Once they all went to a board game café on a Sunday afternoon and had a raucous "extreme" board game tournament, fuelled by lattes and laughs. Skylar wondered if the social and physical activities had anything to do with improved communication and teamwork.

- **Ask:** At her work placement, Couture Ads, Skylar asked her supervisor for advice on creating a positive team culture. Her supervisor considered this question and then said, "Well, I know that we have one meeting a month outside of work, over dinner at a restaurant. It helps us get to know each other better. At the end of the year, we have a big dinner, with spouses and partners invited. Sometimes at a restaurant, sometimes a potluck at someone's house. This really helps us feel like we have many things, other than work, in common."

- **Research:** When Skylar did some research on positive team dynamics, she found a number of articles on emotional intelligence (EI), emotional quotient (EQ), and the "c factor." Clearly, current research was validating both her observations and her supervisor's experience. Team performance and cohesion seemed to be linked to being able to know and understand each others' nonverbal signals and emotional states.

Skylar asked her new teammates to add an hour onto their next team meeting. At that second team meeting, when the business portion was over, Skylar suggested that they all head to the mini-putt golf course next to the campus for a quick round of "golf." The team was still in its forming stage, and everyone was too polite to turn down the suggestion. By the end of the game, however, there had been a lot of laughs and enjoyment of the recreational time together. Ester suggested that they should brainstorm not only about their project but also about what they could do with their "second hour" next time. Soon, the "second hour" became an eagerly anticipated part of each team meeting. Thanks to Skylar's initiative, this team was well on its way to creating an excellent team experience on this assignment.

For a CULTURE exercise, go to Critical Thinking Question 3 on page 186 and Exercise 12 on page 188.

participation is emphasized, giving all team members an opportunity develop "c factor" skills and a "literacy" in each other's verbal and nonverbal cues.

Many Canadian First Nations can trace a long history of this kind of participatory communication style. Bob Joseph, founder of Indigenous Corporate Training Inc. and member of the Gwawaenuk Nation in British Columbia (Indigenous Corporate Training Inc., 2015), notes that the use of a **Talking Stick** "is an ancient and powerful communication tool that ensures a code of conduct of respect during meetings is followed. The person holding the stick, and only that person, is designated as having the right to speak and all others must listen quietly and respectfully" (Joseph, 2015).

Talking Stick In some First Nations cultures, a stick or other symbolic item is held in turn by each speaker in a gathering. Only the person with the Talking Stick is permitted to speak, and that person may continue to hold the item for as long as required to finish speaking.

Here are some suggestions regarding the use of a Talking Stick (as adapted from those provided by Bob Joseph for use in a First Nations Talking Circle):

- The most senior member speaks first.
- All in attendance are expected to listen with respect, quietness, and full attention (turn off your phone).
- Listen carefully. Do not repeat information that has already been shared.
- Do not rush or interrupt the person speaking.
- When the speaker is finished he or she will pass the stick to the next person.
- If the receiver does not wish to speak, he or she can pass the stick to the next person.
- If you are handed the Talking Stick and wish to speak, introduce yourself first.
- When everyone who wishes to speak has spoken, the Talking Stick is placed in the centre of the table. At the end of the meeting, a designated team member will be in charge of keeping it safe and bringing it to the next meeting (Joseph, 2015).

With some imagination, this process could be adapted to any type of team meeting to ensure equal turn-taking. For example, if your virtual team had a face-to-face launch meeting, part of the meeting could include some kind of gift exchange. Each team member could arrive with one item to exchange with another team member, such as a pen or a hat from the gift-giver's home region. When the team meets virtually by videoconference, turns can be taken and symbolized by each speaker taking his or her turn with the gift that was presented when the team was last together in the same space.

Use a peer coaching model for feedback

The ability for peers to coach each other is extremely powerful. No leader, manager, supervisor, or trainer can be with each team member each moment of the day. Colleagues and peers, however, will see you at your worst and at your best and are often in the best position to help you learn and improve.

You can discuss peer coaching as part of the development of your team charter. A key element of allowing peer coaching is exactly that: giving permission. All team members need to agree to allow all other team members to provide feedback and guidance on work performance. Without this open and explicit discussion, you may find yourself providing or receiving feedback that is misinterpreted as supervision or direction. Here are some other suggestions for implementing a peer coaching process:

- **Set up a coaching triangle.** Peer coaching will work best if you are not coaching the same person who is coaching you. Therefore, try to work in a group of three in which A coaches B, B coaches C, and C coaches A. See **FIGURE 6.4** for an illustration.

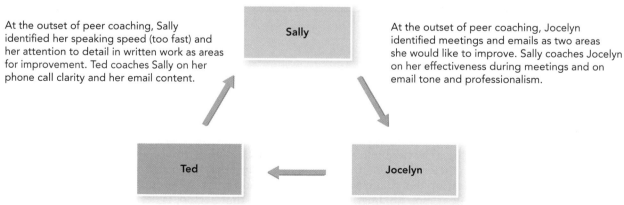

At the outset of peer coaching, Sally identified her speaking speed (too fast) and her attention to detail in written work as areas for improvement. Ted coaches Sally on her phone call clarity and her email content.

At the outset of peer coaching, Jocelyn identified meetings and emails as two areas she would like to improve. Sally coaches Jocelyn on her effectiveness during meetings and on email tone and professionalism.

At the outset of peer coaching, Ted identified emails and listening skills as areas for improvement. Jocelyn coaches Ted on his email clarity and his multitasking behaviour.

FIGURE 6.4 Peer Coaching Triangle

- **Discuss goals.** Both the coach and the person being coached should have goals. What are the particular areas that you are targeting for improvement? Is there some skill area in which you feel particularly weak and would like some feedback on? Perhaps the coach wants to learn how to deliver feedback in a more positive and helpful way.

When you are a coach:

- **Maintain focus on the other person.** Use stories about your own experience only as a way to help the other person feel accepted and comfortable. Do not become the focus of the coaching conversation.
- **Listen carefully and ask simple questions.** This will help the person being coached know that you are paying attention. The right questions also communicate empathy and support.
- **Avoid criticism.** Instead, offer alternatives. The coaching relationship is one of trust that develops over time. If you make judgmental statements about the other person's behaviour or responses, the coaching opportunity will be lost. Ask the other person if there were other alternatives he or she could have chosen. If the other person cannot think of any, you may be able to offer some suggestions.

When you are being coached:

- **Set aside a regular coaching time.** Agree to meet with your peer coach at a regular time and place. Short weekly or biweekly meetings could work well. The time can be informal and also may work well in a virtual setting.
- **Ask for feedback.** If your coach is shy or uncomfortable about giving you feedback, you can ask for it directly. Here are some ways to do this:
  - "Thanks for agreeing to do this. I am really interested in improving. Did you see anything this week that you feel I could have done better?"
  - "I thought my presentation on Monday was pretty good. What did you think? I'd really like your honest opinion so I can improve."
  - "Thanks for agreeing to do this. I'd love to know what you think the three best parts of my work have been this week and why. I'd also like to know what the three weakest parts of my work were and why. I am really hoping to improve."

People with strong coaching skills experience an unexpected benefit: increased **self-awareness**. The best peer coaches tend to reflect on their own behaviour to examine what they could be doing better themselves. A 2015 study examined 58 teams made up of over 300 executives competing in a business-simulation exercise. Many factors of team performance were measured. The one factor that most commonly predicted team success was self-awareness. The teams with the highest level of self-awareness consistently outperformed teams with a low level of self-awareness (Dierdorff & Rubin, 2015). See **FIGURE 6.5** to review the results of this aspect of the study.

Clearly, supportive peer coaching skills help both the coach and the team members being coached.

Self-awareness Understanding who we are and how we are similar to and different from others. How we see our various personality traits, values, attitudes, and behaviours. Understanding how consistent or inconsistent our self-view is compared with how other people see us.

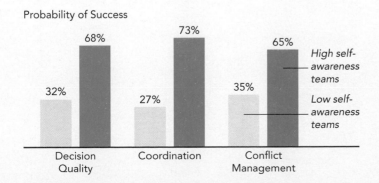

Probability of Success

FIGURE 6.5 High Self-Awareness Leads to Better Team Performance

Source: Dierdorff, E., & Rubin, R. S. (2015, March 12). Research: We're not very self-aware, especially at work. *Harvard Business Review.* Retrieved from https://hbr.org/2015/03/research-were-not-very-self-aware-especially-at-work

FIGURE 6.6 Applying ACE to Support
Positive Team Dynamics

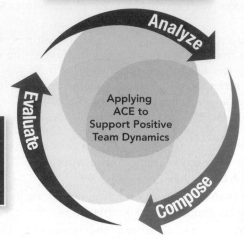

Discuss and review goals, deliverables, expectations, communications. Make sure all team members are involved.

Employ all available listening skills.

Observe carefully for possible conflicts related to communication style, culture, diversity, or other factors.

Ask for feedback on verbal exchanges to ensure understanding.

Use peer coaching model for detailed feedback.

Create a team charter that makes all process agreements explicit.

Use clear, unambiguous language.

Use positive language.

Use agendas and minutes for each meeting.

Ensure speaking time is shared equally during meetings.

Create opportunities for social team time.

Analyze

Compose

Evaluate

Applying
ACE to
Support Positive
Team Dynamics

In summary, a team that is prepared to work together by discussing and creating a team charter, and that is prepared to play together to build an effective "c factor," is a team that is ready to embrace high performance and successful outcomes. Check out **FIGURE 6.6** to see how ACE can be applied to productivity, collaboration, and positive team dynamics.

Amy Elder
Director of Career Services,
Brock University

@ **WORK**

Courtesy of Amy Elder and Murray Hawrn.

At the beginning of the chapter, Amy Elder explained how she and her events team were left with a large, important event to manage without their key organizer. How can the team pull this off in such a short time frame?

For a successful event, we needed to ensure that all communications were clear, precise, and thorough for all team members (internal) and stakeholders (external).

- **Analyze.** Together, we developed a plan that reassigned the coordinator's duties among the team. This included developing a communications strategy to keep us on track. We created a project chart listing all of the stakeholders: employers, students, faculty, security, parking services, facilities management, and food services. We determined what work needed to be done with each stakeholder group, as well as the nature and frequency of the communication required. Each member of the team assumed responsibility for at least one stakeholder group.

- **Compose.** Team members were responsible for drafting and sending all communications to their assigned stakeholder group(s). Communications could be electronic or in print. It was important to be compliant with university branding requirements. We instituted a buddy system to pair team members for proofreading and editing if needed. Director approval was required on campus-wide or publicly distributed communications. We scheduled weekly meetings to track progress. Minutes were taken, with action items identified per team member. Each week, meetings started with updates on action items.

- **Evaluate.** We evaluated our communications strategy before and after the event:

Pre-event:

- The project chart was posted on a shared folder in our computer system. Each staff member was responsible for updating progress on a daily basis.
- Weekly meetings were held to review progress and resolve issues or concerns.

Post-event:

- An evaluation survey that had been previously used at other events was modified and sent to external stakeholders to ask specific questions about their experience interacting with new contacts in the department.
- A debrief meeting with internal stakeholder departments was held a few days after the event.
- An online survey was sent to all student attendees.
- Feedback from all stakeholders was reviewed by the team at the next staff meeting. A summary was prepared by the director for review by the new event coordinator when hired.

This process allowed the team to effectively share the responsibilities, including communications, that were normally handled by a single event coordinator. Our analysis, creation of a project chart, and weekly meetings ensured timely, relevant, and appropriate communication with each stakeholder group. These meetings also ensured that team members were kept informed of progress, while providing a forum for collaborative resolution of issues and concerns. The use of minutes for our meetings ensured that a clear record of our process was kept for future evaluation or reference. This detailed evaluation process provided us with feedback and suggestions that could be used by the incoming event coordinator for planning future events.

End of Chapter

Learning Objectives in Review

(LO 6.1) How do you communicate effectively as part of a team? *pages 162–169*

- **Create a team charter.** Define goals and deliverables, and identify and agree on process issues and team expectations.
- **Give the team time to develop.** Be patient as the team progresses through the normal stages of development (forming, storming, norming, and performing).
- **Plan for effective meetings.** Create agendas and distribute minutes.
- **Be a valued team member.** Make a commitment to the team, create a collaborative working environment, and support team decisions.

(LO 6.2) How can working on a team help you develop leadership skills? *pages 169–175*

- **Identify and practise key leadership fundamentals:** Overcommunicate, reinforce team objectives, and create a supportive climate.

- **Use conflict management to help develop leadership skills.** Identify the types and causes of conflict and select the appropriate management response.

(LO 6.3) What are some key aspects of high-performance team collaboration? *pages 175–183*

- **Enhance productivity with virtual best practices.** Start with a face-to-face meeting and be fully prepared and present during online meetings.
- **Develop the "c factor" in your teams.** Make sure your team has social time with each other, and develop a strategy for sharing speaking time equally during meetings.
- **Use a peer coaching model for feedback.** Set up a coaching triangle, where goals are set, criticism is avoided, and feedback is sought.

KEY TERMS

affective conflict p. 170	groupthink p. 174	process p. 162	team p. 161
agenda p. 164	milestone p. 164	productivity p. 161	team charter p. 162
cognitive conflict p. 170	minutes p. 164	self-awareness p. 181	
deliverables p. 162	norming p. 164	storming p. 164	
forming p. 164	performing p. 164	Talking Stick p. 179	

CASE STUDY

Managing Conflict in a Virtual Cross-Cultural Team

This case study builds on the case provided at the end of Chapters 4 and 5.

Brendan's internship at Kramer & Kaplin Market Research in Calgary started out well. He enjoyed brainstorming ideas with his manager and designing a survey for an important client. However, the past few weeks have been pure misery. Brendan's supervisor assigned him to join three other interns on a team to create a comprehensive online handbook for interns. Brendan will work on this project with one other intern from the Calgary office (Roberto) and two interns from New Delhi, India (Maansi and Anant).

Planning the first meeting was difficult. Brendan lost two days of work trying to set a meeting time because there is a 12 $\frac{1}{2}$-hour time difference between Calgary and New Delhi. After much difficulty (see page 123), the first meeting is scheduled for 7:30 a.m. Central Standard Time on Wednesday.

Before the first meeting, Brendan becomes concerned about Roberto's attitude. Roberto simply cannot hide his contempt for this project. Just before the meeting begins, Roberto whispers to Brendan, "Let's just get this meeting over with. No one needs a handbook. This project is just more busywork for interns." Brendan finds it difficult to focus on the content of the meeting because he is fuming about Roberto's attitude. Originally, Brendan was looking forward to working with Roberto because he is very smart and creative. Now he is afraid that his attitude may stand in the way of completing the project.

After the meeting, Brendan gives this situation a lot of thought. He prepares two different ways to talk to Roberto about this:

- **Option 1.** "Roberto, you are so negative all the time. I know you really don't want to do this project, but that's our job. We both need good evaluations from this internship. If you don't change your mindset, you'll cause us both to fail."

- **Option 2.** "Roberto, I'm really looking forward to working with you. You always have such great ideas. But I'm worried that you don't think this project is important and won't give it your best effort. I want to get a strong evaluation from this internship. I know if we work together we can plan a great handbook, and I think we can have a good time working together."

QUESTION 1: *How would you describe the difference between the two approaches? Which approach would help Roberto accept the feedback well enough to change his behaviour?*

Understanding Conflict

When you ask Maansi to help you gather information about content needs from New Delhi interns she says, "I won't have time to do that. We can take content from the current handbook. To have an excellent handbook, what's really important is developing an interactive website." Brendan finds this insulting because he has been working hard to develop clear and appropriate content. Before bad feelings take over, Brendan decides to schedule a meeting with his supervisor, Caitlin, to talk about these conflicts.

QUESTION 2: *Caitlin asks Brendan, "What kind of conflicts are these? Are these personality conflicts? Or do the conflicts stem from differences of opinion about how to get the best handbook? Or do team members have competing goals?" How would you respond to these questions?*

All four interns seem to have at least one goal in common: to create an excellent handbook for interns. However, each intern has a different opinion about what is required to achieve that goal. While Brendan and Roberto are focused on providing rich content, Maansi and Anant are focused on the technical aspects of delivering an engaging, interactive website. They believe that programming is the key. Existing content can simply be imported into the new site.

Perhaps the best way to address this conflict is simply to accommodate Maansi and Anant and let them focus solely on programming. Brendan is concerned that the New Delhi interns may need different information from the handbook. If Maansi and Anant are not interested in interviewing their fellow local interns to gather information, Brendan and Roberto are wondering how they can uncover this information.

QUESTION 3: *Is accommodating the best choice? Why or why not?*

After the handbook is published (hard copy) and launched (online), the results are extremely well received by all stakeholders: the management at Kramer & Kaplin Market Research, the employees, the recruiters, and the interns. Brendan, Roberto, Maansi, and Anant are very proud of their efforts together. Although they all return to full-time studies in September, they decide to stay in touch via Facebook. In November, Roberto invites the other three interns to join him in a new online role-playing adventure game called Krystalline. They team up online to win quests and battles against other teams. They have appointed game nights or mornings (depending on the time zone) and enjoy the cooperative/competitive team play together.

QUESTION 4: *Imagine that this team of interns is hired again for a second summer at Kramer & Kaplin Market Research. Do you think this team is prepared to be more productive or less productive than in their first summer as interns? Why? Are there any peak performance strategies that they might be ready to adopt? Explain.*

REVIEW QUESTIONS

1. What is a team charter?

2. List three ways that a team charter can prevent future team conflict.

3. Name and describe the stages of team formation.

4. What is the purpose of an agenda?

5. When should meeting attendees receive the agenda?

6. What is the purpose of meeting minutes?

7. When should meeting attendees receive the minutes?

8. What is the role of the meeting chair?

9. Why should you avoid the words "however" and "but" when agreeing to disagree?

10. What does it mean to be "transparent"?

11. Is it possible for a team to avoid conflict?

12. Is team conflict always a negative occurrence?

13. Why is "conflict management" a better term than "conflict resolution"?

14. What is the "c" factor?

15. What is the purpose of a Talking Stick?

16. What is peer coaching?

186 **Chapter 6** How Can We Be Better, Together? Collaboration and Productivity

CHAPTER 6

CRITICAL THINKING

1. Imagine you have a teammate who wants to do all the project work himself because he does not trust anyone else on the team to produce high-quality results. How would you respond to that teammate?

2. Some organizations provide the services of mediators to help resolve workplace conflicts. What are the advantages of having a neutral third party assist in resolving a conflict? What are the advantages of having people involved in the conflict work it out on their own?

3. Research the topics of emotional intelligence (EI) and emotional quotient (EQ). Would you rather have teammates with high EI, EQ, or IQ? Does your answer change if you are working face to face rather than virtually? Explain.

DEVELOPING YOUR COMMUNICATION SKILLS

 LO 6.1 **How can you communicate effectively as part of a team?** *(pages 162–169)*

EXERCISE 1 Analyzing team effectiveness

Select a recent team experience in which you participated, whether for a sport, organization, or class project. In a few paragraphs, describe the team and identify the goal of the activity. Then outline the pros and cons of the experience. Was the team successful? Which benefits of effective teamwork did your group experience? Did conflict occur? What changes would have improved the team's effectiveness?

EXERCISE 2 Create a team charter

Search the web for "team charter." Find three examples that include as many of the following items as possible:

- Defined goals or deliverables
- Team performance expectations, such as
  - Roles and responsibilities
  - Division of work
  - Feedback
  - Quality of work/standards
  - Decision making
- Team function and communication, such as
  - Primary and secondary modes of communication
  - Contact information
  - Meeting times and locations
  - Technology requirements and guidelines
  - Record keeping
  - Meetings
  - Timelines
  - Calendar review

What content do the examples share? What differences exist? Consider a recent team experience that could have benefited from a team charter. What elements from the sample charters would you recommend? Create an outline of the topics you would include in a team charter for a similar group experience.

EXERCISE 3 Give the team time to develop

Some teams do not advance through all stages of the forming, storming, norming, and performing process. Some teams get stuck in the storming stage and never reach norming, which is the stage where team members work effectively with each other. Other teams work through their conflicts but run out of time before they can effectively perform. Summarize one of your recent team experiences, using some (but not necessarily all) of the following questions to help you describe the development of your team:

- What was the goal or purpose of the team?
- How was the team formed (e.g., assigned or selected)?
- What happened during the forming stage?
- Did the team experience any storming? If so, describe what happened.
- Did your team develop an approach to working together well? If so, what was it? If not, why not?
- Did the team end up accomplishing its goal?
- Would you want to work with that team again? Why or why not?

EXERCISE 4 Plan for effective meetings

Meetings are common, often daily, events for most business professionals. You may be asked to take minutes at a meeting, either as one of your team assignments or for someone who is not able to attend the meeting. To practise your note-taking skills, watch a half-hour news broadcast, either by a local news station or a national network, or attend a seminar or workshop offered by your school. Record the important information you hear and organize the content for easy reference. Because you won't have an agenda, you will need to listen (and watch) carefully for major ideas. Create a professional-looking document similar to the sample provided in the chapter. Proofread carefully before submitting your minutes to your instructor.

EXERCISE 5 Be a valued team member

For each step of the following scenario, identify the problem and describe how you would respond. Explain your reasoning.

a. You and four other students have just been assigned to work together on a presentation that will be delivered in three weeks. You are appointed as the team leader. After class, you meet briefly with your team to determine when you can schedule time in the next few days to meet in the library to plan your project. However, a single day and time does not seem to work well for the entire group. Ted, who is already late for his next class, gets impatient and says to go ahead and meet without him. He'll go along with whatever the group decides and walks away. When asked for his contact information, he says, "Don't bother. I'll catch up with you next class."

b. Your group meets later that evening without Ted and assigns tasks to all team members. At the next class session, you tell Ted that the rest of the team members will research the content and that he has been assigned to put the content together in a PowerPoint file and present the summary slide. Ted says, "That's nuts! I'd have to wait to work on the file until the rest of you guys have finished your work, which will probably be the night before the presentation. No way! That's not fair!" You disagree.

c. You agree to swap assignments with Ted, but he does not send his part of the content to you by the deadline. You call him to ask if you can help, and he says, "Don't worry. I'm working on it now, and I'll bring it to the presentation tomorrow." You tell him that you can't create a summary slide if you don't have his information. He says, "You can work it in tomorrow before class and fake your way through a summary. No problem." You disagree.

d. During your presentation, Ted's part takes less than one minute when you had expected it to take three minutes. You have to fill the extra time during the summary to ensure your team meets the 10-minute presentation requirement. You do not feel that your team did as well as it could have if Ted had provided his information on time. Back at your seats, Ted says to you, "Great job! We pulled it together. I think we had the best presentation in the class." You disagree.

e. At the next class session, your instructor asks your team to write a one-paragraph assessment of your team's effectiveness, both in terms of the team's collaborative process and the quality of the presentation. Each team member must sign the assessment. Ted thinks everything was great. You disagree.

 How can working on a team help you develop leadership skills? *(pages 169–175)*

EXERCISE 6 Develop leadership fundamentals

Some people are born leaders. Others have to work hard to develop leadership skills. Researchers have investigated leadership styles for decades. As early as 1939, Kurt Lewin identified three major leadership styles: authoritarian (autocratic), participative (democratic), and delegative (laissez-faire) (Lewin, Llippit, & White,

1939). Search the web to learn more about leadership styles and identify one that best represents a leadership style with which you would be comfortable. Document your source, describe the leadership style, and explain how it best fits your personality. Summarize your findings in a few paragraphs.

EXERCISE 7 Identify the cause of conflict

Identifying the cause of conflict is not always easy. Review the five different causes of conflict you learned in this chapter: competing goals, differences of opinion, faulty assumptions, relational issues, and ego issues. For each of the following scenarios, identify the cause or causes of the conflict and explain your reasoning.

a. Your company is planning to install a new air conditioning system for the administrative offices. The vice-president of operations has asked you and a co-worker to research air conditioning systems and to recommend one. You and your co-worker have narrowed your search to two systems, but you have reached an impasse. Your co-worker argues that you should propose the AirCo system because it is the most cost efficient to install. You, by contrast, want to propose CoolRite because it has the best long-term reliability record.

b. You and two classmates have decided to start a small business to help fund your college education. As part of your planning, you have asked an art student friend to design a logo for you. You have all decided that, above all else, the logo must look professional. Your friend gives you four options to choose from, but you and your business partners cannot agree on an option.

c. It is 9 a.m. on Tuesday morning, and it doesn't look as if your team paper will be finished and edited in time to hand in by the 10 a.m. deadline. When you received the parts from everyone on Monday at 8 p.m., you saw many grammatical and formatting errors that you needed to fix. You've been working on the paper all night. Your teammates say, "Just print it out and hand it in. It's good enough, and it's important that the paper be in on time." You say, "We'll get points off for grammar errors, and the paper will only be an hour or so late." Your teammates are getting angry and feel as though you are holding them hostage because the edited version of the paper is on your computer. One of your teammates says, "You are such a nitpicky perfectionist! That's what we get for having an English major on our team!"

EXERCISE 8 Select an appropriate management technique

You and a teammate are working on a presentation that will be given at a budget meeting on Monday. On Thursday night you think the project is far from complete. You'd like the presentation to be as polished as possible, so you suggest to your teammate that you get together over the weekend to finish it. He says that he wants to finish the presentation by Friday because he wants to relax over the weekend. You begin to argue. You know you won't be able to complete the presentation in one day. What is the cause of this conflict and how would you respond?

Explain in writing each of the following conflict management techniques:

- **Avoid.** How could you avoid dealing with the conflict? What would be the likely outcome? Do you recommend this choice?
- **Accommodate.** What would you do to accommodate your teammate? What would be the likely outcome? Do you recommend this choice?
- **Compete.** What would a competitive approach look like? What would be the likely outcome? Do you recommend this choice?
- **Compromise.** What would a compromise look like? What would be the likely outcome? Do you recommend this choice?
- **Collaborate.** What would you do to try to collaborate? What would be the likely outcome? Do you recommend this choice?

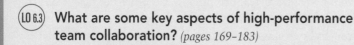 **What are some key aspects of high-performance team collaboration?** *(pages 169–183)*

EXERCISE 9 Creating an environment for the "c factor" to thrive

Make a list of six nontask activities that a student team at your college could regularly participate in. These might include physical or sporting activities, common interest activities, or social activities. Try to get one of your student teams to agree to include one of these nontask activities as part of your regular team work (i.e., replacing a meeting with something "fun"). Prepare to answer these questions in a form requested by your instructor.

a. What challenges did you face in introducing nontask activities in student teams?

b. Were you successful in getting your team to participate in a nontask activity? Was this a positive experience?

c. How would you include nontask activities in a virtual team situation?

EXERCISE 10 Equal Turn-Taking

Review the concept of the Talking Stick on pages 179–180. In your next team meeting for any student project, suggest the use of a Talking Stick for the first half of the meeting. Prepare to answer these questions in a form requested by your instructor:

a. What challenges did you face in introducing equal turn-taking in your student team?

b. Was the concept of equal turn-taking received positively or negatively by your team? Can you explain why?

c. If you were successful in getting your team to agree to a Talking Stick experiment, was it a positive experience? Explain.

d. Would you add this communications strategy to your next team charter? Why or why not?

e. What are some ways that a Talking Stick could be used in a virtual meeting?

EXERCISE 11 Peer Coaching

Review the concept of peer coaching on pages 180–181. In your next team meeting for any student project, suggest that you adopt a peer coaching circle or triangle, depending on the number of people on the team. To do this, each person needs to identify one or two key areas that they wish to improve on as a result of participating in the team. Each person should explain these areas to their "coach." Each "coach" will then observe his or her peer in the normal process of team interaction. Each coach/peer partnership should set aside 15 minutes weekly to talk about the identified key areas and to explore ways for the peer to improve.

Prepare to answer these questions in a form requested by your instructor:

a. What challenges did you face in introducing peer coaching on your student team?

b. Was the concept of peer coaching received positively or negatively by your team? Can you explain why?

c. If you were successful in getting your team to agree to a peer coaching experiment, was it a positive experience? Explain.

d. Would you add this communications strategy to your next team charter? Why or why not?

e. Can peer coaching be effective within a virtual team? What technologies could be used to facilitate the coaching meetings?

EXERCISE 12 Creating Team Cohesion [Related to the Culture feature on page 179]

A student team is created by a professor and assigned a team project with a written and a presentation component. When the team has its first meeting, they discover the following language proficiencies:

	First Language (100% proficiency)	**Acquired Language**
Student #1	Mandarin	English (35% proficiency)
Student #2	Mandarin	English (45% proficiency)
Student #3	Hindi	English (45% proficiency)
Student #4	Hindi	English (65% proficiency)
Student #5	English	French (25% proficiency)
Student #6	English	Spanish (50% proficiency)

Almost immediately during the first meeting, the three "pairs" of common language speakers began speaking to each other, almost exclusively. This creats three teams of two rather than one team of six. How can this team operate in a way that ensures that no one feels excluded from conversation and that work is completed in the most efficient manner possible? Name three strategies this team can actively employ to ensure the team is cohesive and inclusive. Be prepared to share your findings with the class.

EXERCISE 13 Ethics in teamwork [Related to the Ethics feature on page 165]

Review the full five-stage scenario in Exercise 5.

a. Does Ted's behaviour present any ethical challenges for the team? Explain.

b. Are the other four team members in any way responsible for Ted's behaviour? Explain.

c. What options does the team have to manage Ted's behaviour prior to the presentation? List and describe three.

7

Communicating Routine Messages and Building Goodwill

pixdeluxe/E+/Getty Images.

MyBCommLab® Improve Your Grade!

Over 10 million students improved their results using the Pearson MyLabs. Visit **mybcommlab.com** for simulations, tutorials, media share assignments, interactive lesson presentations, and other helpful learning apps.

LEARNING OBJECTIVES

(LO 7.1) How do you compose messages containing questions and requests? *pages 192–196*

Decide between a direct or an indirect message

Provide reasons for the request

Adopt the receiver's perspective and include audience benefits

Conclude with gratitude and a call for action

(LO 7.2) How do you compose informational messages? *pages 197–204*

Reply to questions with a direct answer

Respond to customer requests by creating goodwill

Highlight key points in confirmation messages

Organize routine announcements so they are easy to skim

Format instructions so readers can easily follow the steps

Use your own templates to save time and reduce errors

(LO 7.3) What kinds of messages build goodwill in business relationships? *pages 204–209*

Thank you messages

Congratulatory messages

Sympathy messages

"For-your-information" messages

(LO 7.4) How can you use social media to build goodwill in business? *pages 210–213*

Provide quick responses to questions and concerns

Build "real-time goodwill" by creating community with social media

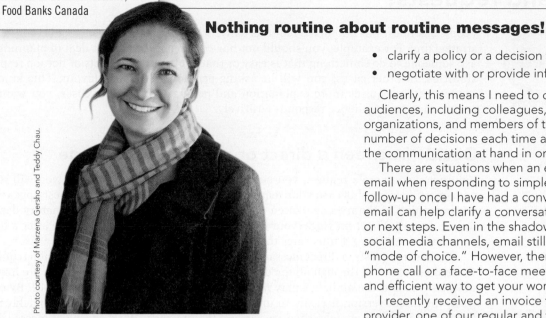
Marzena Gersho
Director of Communications,
Food Banks Canada

@ WORK

Nothing routine about routine messages!

As part of my day-to-day work, I need to address many routine business functions. I may be called upon to

- explain a new process to a colleague,
- respond to a question from a member of the public,
- clarify a policy or a decision to an external partner, or
- negotiate with or provide information to a vendor.

Clearly, this means I need to communicate with a variety of audiences, including colleagues, vendors, partner organizations, and members of the public. I need to make a number of decisions each time about the best way to handle the communication at hand in order to get the best outcome.

There are situations when an email will do. I prefer to use email when responding to simple questions or to use as a follow-up once I have had a conversation with someone. An email can help clarify a conversation or outline complex facts or next steps. Even in the shadow of the enormous growth of social media channels, email still dominates in business as the "mode of choice." However, there are many times when a phone call or a face-to-face meeting can be the most effective and efficient way to get your work done.

I recently received an invoice from a graphic design provider, one of our regular and trusted suppliers, and the invoice appeared to have an error in the amount charged for the work. I have so many different channels and options I can choose from to contact this supplier. How can I select the correct approach for this situation?

Find out at the end of this chapter how Marzena uses ACE to solve these communication dilemmas.

Introduction

Businesses produce millions of messages every day as a routine part of getting work done. In the workplace, you will communicate **routine business messages** through emails, telephone calls, face-to-face conversations, text messages, tweets, blogs, and social networking sites. Examples of routine business messages include the following:

- Emailing a colleague in the accounting department to explain a travel expense
- Calling a vendor to request a correction to a shipment that included the wrong merchandise
- Texting a colleague to indicate your meeting is running late

Routine messages are short, straightforward, and not sensitive. They do not require you to persuade your audience to accept your point, nor do they require you to worry about upsetting your audience. They simply require that you be clear, complete, and respectful. However, meeting these requirements can be challenging. You need to decide

- how to phrase your main point so that it is clear,
- how to organize the message so that it is easily understood,
- what information to include, and
- how to evaluate the message to ensure that it will be effective.

Because businesses generate so many routine messages each day, these types of messages present powerful opportunities to cement strong working relationships by demonstrating professional style, courtesy, and tone. This chapter offers guidelines for composing specific types of routine messages, including the following:

- Questions and requests
- Informational messages
- Social media interactions
- **Goodwill messages**

Throughout the chapter, you will see the ACE logo where the discussion offers new insight on how to use ACE to prepare routine and goodwill messages.

Routine business message A short, nonsensitive, straightforward communication that asks questions, answers questions, provides information, or confirms agreements.

Goodwill message Any message that gives you the opportunity to establish and sustain a positive relationship with your audience.

How do you compose messages containing questions and requests?

ACE

Compose

People ask questions and make requests daily. Some of these requests require very little strategizing. For example, you should not have to engage in a great deal of planning to ask someone to do something that is easy or that is clearly part of his or her job responsibilities. In other cases, you will be asking people to do you a favour. This kind of request often requires more explanation and persuasion. In both cases, you want to ensure that your audience responds positively.

Decide between a direct or an indirect message

Before you compose a request, you need to decide where in the message you will state your main idea, in this case your request. In a *direct message*, your request appears at the beginning of the message, often as early as the first sentence. Explanatory details follow. In an *indirect message*, your question appears later in the message after a brief explanation. **FIGURE 7.1** illustrates the difference between the two.

For most requests, a direct message is the better choice. The indirect version requires the audience to read through all the details before learning why those details are important. As a result, the audience may need to read the message more than once. By contrast, the direct version is easier to understand because it gets to the point quickly and lets the audience know why they are reading the message. With dozens of messages to navigate throughout the day, your audience will appreciate messages that are direct.

In some circumstances, you may find that it is better to use an indirect message. If the audience needs additional information to fully understand your request, a brief introduction can be helpful. For example, imagine that you work for a construction firm in Yarmouth, Nova Scotia. A client hires your company to build a retail plaza in Digby, Nova Scotia. Your business banker in Yarmouth, Jerry, used to work in Digby and may have some useful information for you. To ask Jerry for this information by email, an indirect request is appropriate because Jerry could be confused by your question without some introductory context. **FIGURE 7.2** illustrates the difference between a direct and indirect request.

Note that you will need to consider the wording of your subject line based on whether your message is direct or indirect. When you compose a direct message, you can state your request clearly in the subject line. However, an indirect message requires that the subject line be neutral, indicating only the general purpose of the email.

Always phrase your request so that your audience knows exactly what you are asking and will be able to answer easily. If you have a series of questions, list or number them so that the audience can respond to each question individually. For example, here is a variation of the message communicated in Figure 7.1:

> *The latest version I have of the third-quarter sales figures is dated three weeks ago. I know your report is not yet complete, but we will be discussing the data in tomorrow's budget meeting at 4 p.m. Could you please send me*

INDIRECT ORGANIZATION (Less effective for this message)

The latest version I have of the third-quarter sales figures is dated three weeks ago. I know your report is not yet complete, but we will be discussing the data in tomorrow's budget meeting at 4 p.m. Can your please send me the most up-to-date figures? Thanks! —— Request comes last, after the details.

DIRECT ORGANIZATION (More effective for this message)

Please send me the latest draft of the —— third-quarter sales figures. I know your report is not yet complete, but we will be discussing the data in tomorrow's budget meeting at 4 p.m., and the latest draft I have was dated three weeks ago. Thanks! —— Request comes first, before the details.

FIGURE 7.1 A Direct Organization Is Best for Most Requests

FIGURE 7.2 An Indirect Organization Is Useful for Confusing Questions

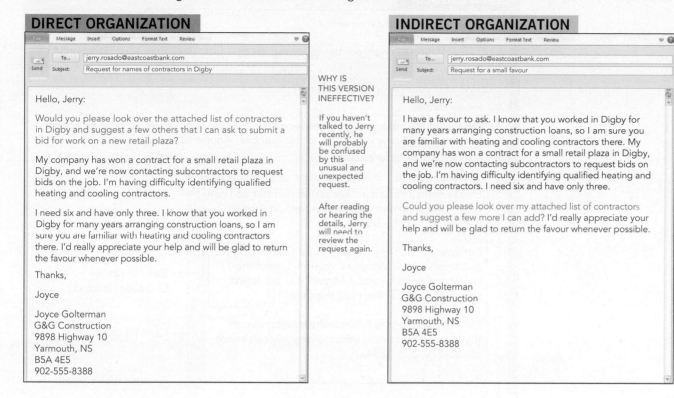

DIRECT ORGANIZATION

To... jerry.rosado@eastcoastbank.com
Subject: Request for names of contractors in Digby

Hello, Jerry:

Would you please look over the attached list of contractors in Digby and suggest a few others that I can ask to submit a bid for work on a new retail plaza?

My company has won a contract for a small retail plaza in Digby, and we're now contacting subcontractors to request bids on the job. I'm having difficulty identifying qualified heating and cooling contractors.

I need six and have only three. I know that you worked in Digby for many years arranging construction loans, so I am sure you are familiar with heating and cooling contractors there. I'd really appreciate your help and will be glad to return the favour whenever possible.

Thanks,

Joyce

Joyce Golterman
G&G Construction
9898 Highway 10
Yarmouth, NS
B5A 4E5
902-555-8388

WHY IS THIS VERSION INEFFECTIVE?

If you haven't talked to Jerry recently, he will probably be confused by this unusual and unexpected request.

After reading or hearing the details, Jerry will need to review the request again.

INDIRECT ORGANIZATION

To... jerry.rosado@eastcoastbank.com
Subject: Request for a small favour

Hello, Jerry:

I have a favour to ask. I know that you worked in Digby for many years arranging construction loans, so I am sure you are familiar with heating and cooling contractors there. My company has won a contract for a small retail plaza in Digby, and we're now contacting subcontractors to request bids on the job. I'm having difficulty identifying qualified heating and cooling contractors. I need six and have only three.

Could you please look over my attached list of contractors and suggest a few more I can add? I'd really appreciate your help and will be glad to return the favour whenever possible.

Thanks,

Joyce

Joyce Golterman
G&G Construction
9898 Highway 10
Yarmouth, NS
B5A 4E5
902-555-8388

WHY IS THIS VERSION MORE EFFECTIVE?

First sentence signals to Jerry that a request is coming.

Details prepare him for the request.

Following the details, the request will make sense to Jerry.

- *The most up-to-date figures for sales for the third quarter*
- *The top-performing product sales in the first, second, and (to date) third quarter*
- *The top-performing stores in the first, second, and (to date) third quarter*

Remember that when you use a list like this, there is an *implied* prioritization. The reader will assume that the first items listed are more important than the ones that appear later in the list. Use this to your advantage by making sure that the first item you list is actually the most important.

Provide reasons for the request

How much detail does your audience need to know? As the example in Figure 7.2 illustrates, if the reason for your request is not obvious you will need to explain it. Other messages will require much less detail. For example, most customer requests for refunds or merchandise exchanges, sometimes called *claim requests,* require minor explanation.

FIGURE 7.3 provides an example of a request a customer submitted to a company that shipped the wrong order. Many companies provide online customer service support, and this message was entered on the company's website. Notice that it begins with the direct request for a return authorization number, which is the first step in initiating a product return. Although it may seem abrupt to begin the message by stating what you want, the reader of this message (the "audience") will appreciate the direct approach. Companies deal with many claim messages each day, and readers need to find the main point quickly, followed by a short explanation of the reason. If a claim request requires more explanation or evidence, you would write a persuasive claim. Persuasive messages are described in Chapter 8.

Adopt the receiver's perspective and include audience benefits

Like other messages, routine requests will get the best reception from your audience if you compose the message from *their* perspective, not your own. Too often, writers and

FIGURE 7.3 Request Requiring Brief Explanation

CLAIM REQUEST

Required items indicated with *.

1. Please choose one from the following list that best describes your question: *

Return ▾

2. What is your name (first and last)? *

Henry Pinnix

3. We want to make sure you get service as quickly as possible. To help us access your account, please enter your order number, Adobe ID, or email address: *

h.pinnix@realventures.com

4. Please provide a brief description of your question: *

Please send a return authorization number so I can return the incorrect order I received on August 2 (Order No. 10345-22). — Specific request

I ordered a Mac version of Adobe Creative Suite, but received the Windows version. I need the replacement softwareby August 9 at the latest, so I would appreciate rush shipping. — Explanation and details / Call for action and date needed

My email address is h.pinnix@realventures.com. If you need additional information, you can reach me at (880) 555-1234. — Contact information

Thank you! — Appreciative signoff

speakers focus on what they themselves want to say, often organizing the communication to reflect their own thought process. This "I" perspective is likely to completely disengage the audience and reduce the impact of the message. By contrast, using the **receiver's perspective** helps you think primarily about what your audience takes into account. This includes:

- What your audience needs or wants to know
- What questions your audience might have
- What organization of content will make the most sense to your audience
- How your audience will benefit from your message

FIGURE 7.4 offers versions of messages from an "I" perspective and from the receiver's perspective.

You'll notice that the messages written from the receiver's perspective have a different focus than the "I" perspective versions. Instead of addressing why the writer ("I") needs to get the sales figures, it focuses on how the receiver will benefit from sending the figures. Focusing on **audience or receiver benefits**, the positive outcomes your audience will experience by responding favourably to your request, helps the audience feel more positive about taking the time to respond.

Creating a "receiver's perspective," can be challenging because it requires you to consider other people's viewpoints. Although you can never be certain what someone else will perceive as a benefit, brainstorming ideas can help. As you brainstorm, analyze two different categories of benefits. **Internal benefits** are advantages that your audience directly receives from complying with your request, for example, reduced workload, increased professional recognition, or financial gains. The first example in Figure 7.4 illustrates an internal benefit: By sending the sales figures, the audience will receive the budget information she needs to begin planning sales forecasts. **External benefits** are advantages that someone else, a third party, gains. Your message may have positive effects on people or things your audience cares about. The second example in Figure 7.4 describes an external benefit: The local workforce will benefit by having new opportunities for employment.

Receiver's perspective An approach to communication that presents the information from the audience's point of view. The receiver's perspective focuses on what the audience needs and wants. It also considers how the audience benefits from your message.

Audience or receiver benefits The positive outcomes your audience will experience by responding favourably to your request.

Internal benefits Advantages that your audience will directly receive from complying with your request. These may include reduced workload, increased professional recognition, or financial gains.

External benefits Advantages that someone else (i.e., a third party) gains when your audience complies with a request.

Analyze

"I" PERSPECTIVE	RECEIVER'S PERSPECTIVE
I really need the latest draft of the third-quarter sales figures. I will be presenting the data in tomorrow's budget meeting, and the latest draft I have was dated three weeks ago. I don't want to appear before the committee with old information.	Could you please send me your updated third-quarter sales figures today? If the budget committee has the figures to discuss at tomorrow's meeting, they can get you a preliminary budget by Thursday and you'll be able to start planning next year's sales forecasts.
If I don't get more contact information for heating and air conditioning specialists in Digby, I'm in big trouble. Can you help me?	Our new contract to build a retail plaza means that we are bringing new work to Digby. I'd like to involve as many qualified contractors as possible in the bidding process so that everyone in your area has a fair chance to get this work. Can you provide me with the contact information for qualified contractors who you feel would be suitable?
Can you fill in for me at the 2 p.m. division meeting today? I have a client meeting before that will likely run long and I don't want to rush this meeting because I might lose the sale. Then I need to stop for gas on the way back to the office. I don't want to get a speeding ticket.	Can you please fill in for me at the 2 p.m. division meeting? I might be back from my client in time, but there is a chance I could be late. You researched the data and know it as well as I do. This would be a great opportunity for you to impress the VP and become more well-known within the division.

FIGURE 7.4 "I" versus Receiver's Perspective

Notice that in all the examples the word "you" is associated with polite requests and with positive audience benefits. Avoid using "you" in negative statements. Using "you" when issuing orders, making corrections, or giving direction can be interpreted as being accusatory and arrogant. In those cases, rewrite to express your thoughts in an impersonal manner. For example:

Accusatory statement: You made errors on these forms. You must correct them and resubmit them.

Impersonal statement: Please correct the highlighted errors and resubmit the forms.

Conclude with gratitude and a call for action

Two elements are typical at the end of requests:

- An expression of gratitude
- A specific call for action

The "call to action" should make clear what you need and when you need it. In short requests, a simple "Thanks" may be all that is needed to show your gratitude for the audience's desired response. However, when you are requesting a favour or something that will be an inconvenience, your audience will appreciate a fuller expression of gratitude.

FIGURE 7.5 illustrates a short request that is spoken but could also be emailed. In this case, Stan's manager is asking him to give a presentation at a meeting on short

- Begins by stating the request. No introduction is needed.
- Provides concise explanation and rationale for request.
- Expresses gratitude and offers possible audience benefit.
- Concludes with call for action.

REQUEST

Hi, Stan. Can you cover for me at the 2 p.m. division meeting today? I have a client lunch that I'm sure will run long, and you know all the data we need to report since you researched everything and put it together. I'd appreciate your help, and this might be a great opportunity for you to impress the VP. Sound okay?

FIGURE 7.5 Spoken or Emailed Request for a Favour

notice. The manager chose a face-to-face conversation because doing so might encourage Stan to respond more positively. Stan will most likely find it more difficult to decline the request in a face-to-face conversation or over the phone than if he had received the same message by email.

FIGURE 7.6 illustrates a more complex request that requires a detailed call for action as well as expressions of gratitude.

LETTER

Reed Hall, Box 1054
Brandon University
Brandon, MB
R7A 6A9
January 14, 20XX

Mr. Paul Rashid, Advisor
Students in Free Enterprise
Western University
410 Bedden Hall
London, ON N6A 3K7

Dear Mr. Rashid:

My cousin, Marlina Robertson, is a member of the Students in Free Enterprise (SiFE) chapter you advise at Western University. She gave me your name and address. We are hoping to start our own SiFE club here at Brandon University and would greatly appreciate your answers to a few questions that I did not find answered on the SiFE website (www.sife.org).

1. How many student members are required for a club to be recognized by the governing international organization?

2. Does the governing organization provide any financial assistance for newly developed clubs to support on-campus promotions for membership drives, such as T-shirts and brochures?

3. Do you develop relationships with other SiFE clubs to collaborate on projects? Or are the projects competitive?

Since our first membership drive is scheduled in March, could you please get back to us before January 31? If you prefer to discuss my questions by phone, please call me at your convenience at (204) 555-1234.

If SiFE projects can be collaborative, rather than competitive, we would enjoy developing a collaborative relationship with your SiFE club to design a joint project that would benefit both our campuses and communities. I look forward to talking with you about that once our club is underway.

Thank you for sharing your knowledge with us.

Sincerely,

Dominique Robertson

Dominique Robertson
Brandon University

Annotations (left margin):

The letter begins with an introduction, and the first paragraph ends with the request, phrased politely.

Mentioning the website shows the reader that you have done research before writing and are not wasting his time.

Numbered questions help the audience respond to each item in the reply.

The letter indicates when a response is needed.

An alternate reply method (phone call) gives the reader flexibility.

The potential "collaborative relationship" may be perceived as a benefit.

A "thank you" at the end expresses gratitude.

FIGURE 7.6 Written Request for Information

How do you compose informational messages?

Not all routine messages involve requests or questions. You will sometimes be writing to convey information. For example, you may be replying to requests, responding to claims, confirming information, making announcements, or providing instructions. You can consider these messages routine if the information will not surprise, disappoint, or anger the audience. The following sections explain how to address each kind of informational message.

Compose

Reply to questions with a direct answer

Most answers to questions benefit from a direct response:

- Begin with the direct response and then provide explanatory details.
- For a message with multiple questions, follow the organization of the original message, answering each question in sequence.
- End with a friendly closing.

See **FIGURE 7.7** for a response to the letter in Figure 7.6. In the original request, a student wrote to an advisor at another university requesting information about a student club. As the advisor prepares to respond to the student's request for information, he uses ACE to analyze the purpose, audience, content, and medium. His purpose is not just to provide the requested information, but also to encourage the students to pursue their plans. Because his audience will probably respond favourably to the message, the writer can begin with a positive response and number his answers to mirror the student's original letter. The advisor decides that a letter is the best medium because he can mail sample brochures and flyers with the letter.

Analyze

When someone asks you a question verbally, whether face to face or by phone, you can organize your message exactly as you would when writing a response. If your response is not controversial or likely to disappoint the receiver, begin with a direct answer and then follow up with details. If you do not have the answer immediately available, then say that right away.

For example, imagine that Stan is responding to the question his manager asked him in Figure 7.5 on page 195. Stan's manager cannot attend a meeting and asks Stan to attend and present his department's report. Even if Stan decides he cannot provide a definitive answer at that moment, he can still provide a short and direct answer: "I would like to review the research for about 15 minutes to see if I can effectively present the information. Can I call you?" After determining that he feels comfortable with the task, Stan can either email his response to his supervisor or he can call.

Respond to customer requests by creating goodwill

When a customer requests a refund, exchange, or repair, the business has an opportunity to create goodwill. Assuming that the business decides to satisfy the claim, a well-written response can strengthen its relationship with the customer. Failing to build goodwill when responding to customers can result in negative social media comments (Holmes, 2013). In other words, failing to create goodwill in the world of social media can quickly result in **badwill**. Badwill can result in a company losing clients, market share, and revenues. Research indicates that customers are "far more likely to share information about a bad experience with a product or service than a good one" (CSM, 2011).

When composing positive responses to customer requests, use the same general format as for other routine replies:

- **Begin with the positive response.** Since you can grant the claim, state that immediately. Your subject line may be neutral ("Response to Your Request for Platinum Status") or positive ("Congratulations on Your New Elite Status"). The first paragraph should always be positive, simple, and clear. Avoid sounding as if you are doing the customer a favour.

Badwill Negative press or public relations that result from a poor business practice on the part of a company or organization. It can affect the behaviour of investors and shareholders and can result in decreased revenues, loss of investors and customers, and decreased market share. Once incurred, badwill can require a company to invest time and money in "damage control" and thus experience a reduction in productivity as resources previously assigned to operational work are now assigned to resolving the badwill issue.

FIGURE 7.7 Written Reply to a
Request for Information

LETTER

WESTERN UNIVERSITY

London, ON
N6A 3K7

January 18, 20XX

Ms. Dominique Robertson
Brandon University
Reed Hall, Box 1054
Brandon, MB
R7A 6A9

Dear Ms. Robertson:

Congratulations on your goal of beginning a SiFE club at Brandon University. Below are the answers to your questions.

1. Your campus club can be as small or large as you like. SiFE does not require a specific number of student members to recognize a campus club. However, based on our experience, you should have at least 15 active members (including your executive officers) to ensure your club's success. Of course, the more members you have the better.

2. Although SiFE does not provide financial assistance to help you promote your club, I am enclosing several sample documents that we have successfully used here. Your cousin, Marlina, has helped us design many of these materials. Her desktop publishing skills are exceptional. Perhaps she can share these files with you.

3. We look forward to developing a collaborative relationship with your SiFE club. Our current president is Colin Withers. His email address is cwithers@uwo.ca. Please contact him to discuss this possibility.

If you have any other questions, please feel free to call me at (519) 123-9874. I would be happy to serve as a mentor until you establish your own faculty advisor.

Best regards,

Paul Rashid

Paul Rashid, M.Ed.
SiFE Faculty Advisor

Enclosures

The opening builds goodwill by including a congratulatory statement. It quickly gets to the point by indicating that the requested answers are included.

The answers to the questions are numbered.

Each numbered item begins with a direct answer to the corresponding question.

The paragraphs provide additional related information, including suggestions, references to sample documents, and additional contact information.

The closing includes contact information and a friendly offer of additional assistance.

- **Bad example:** Although you have not reached the required number of frequent flyer miles to achieve platinum status, we will make an exception in your case because you are a valuable customer.
- **Good example:** Because we value your loyalty, we are pleased to offer you platinum status.
- **Follow up with any necessary information.** If a customer has reported a problem, provide a short explanation and detail your plans to prevent the problem from recurring. A credible explanation can inspire consumer confidence. An explanation that sounds like an excuse may result in a negative reaction. Although it is not necessary to apologize, it is also important not to blame the customer. You may wish to acknowledge any inconvenience they experienced as a result of the problem they

DRAFT

| File | Message | Insert | Options | Format Text | Review |

To... h.pinnix@realventuzres.com

Cc...

Subject: Corrected Order Will Ship Today

Dear Mr. Pinnix:

We are shipping your corrected order today. SpeedEx has guaranteed delivery by August 7. The tracking number is 532-23334-63421.

Attached is a return shipping label formatted as a PDF file that you can print. Simply tape the label to your return and drop it off at any SpeedEx office. We prepaid the postage.

Thank you for your continued business. Your satisfaction is important to us.

Sincerely,

Hiemey Hallam
Customer Relations
SoftWarehouse
hiemey.hallam@softwarehouse.com

FIGURE 7.8 Positive Response to a Claim Request

Subject line communicates the positive response.

First sentence restates the positive response. No introduction is needed.

Second paragraph explains how to return and offers an audience benefit: free shipping on the return.

Last paragraph expresses appreciation and desire for continued business.

Email ends with complimentary closing, signature, and contact information.

reported. You can win customer confidence and strengthen customer loyalty simply by expressing genuine concern.

- **End with a friendly closing and express appreciation.** Here's an example: "You are correct. Your cellphone account was incorrectly billed last month. We have credited your account for $32.60. If you have further questions, please call us at 1-800-555-1234 and we would be happy to help. Thank you for choosing EastCoastTel."

FIGURE 7.8 illustrates a positive response to the claim in Figure 7.3 on page 194. Notice that the sales representative does not apologize but does include a goodwill strategy at the end.

Highlight key points in confirmation messages

A **confirmation** is a message acknowledging that you have received information or checking that you have understood information correctly. When you make oral agreements with someone, it is a good practice to confirm those agreements in writing. For example, assume that while you are eating lunch in the break room you discuss with a colleague the need to change the scheduled day and time of a meeting. You might make mental notes of the possible scheduling options, but you also need to communicate confirmation with your co-worker to ensure you both have the same understanding of the change. This has the advantage of getting his or her response in writing. Compare the two versions of the confirmation email drafts in **FIGURE 7.9**. The effective version is clearer and more professional.

Email confirmation messages are one type of email message that you might find yourself copying to others so they are aware of what has been agreed to. When is it appropriate to **CC** (courtesy copy) or **BCC** (blind courtesy copy) a message? Read more about this in the **ETHICS BOX**.

Organize routine announcements so they are easy to skim

Announcements are messages that publicly notify people of information they need or want to know. For example, you might notify

- customers about a sale or a change in policy,
- employees about a new CEO or other significant hiring within the organization, or
- the public about job opportunities in your company.

Depending on your company's policies and general communications culture, you can announce information through any medium. You can publish announcements to the general public through newspapers, television, radio, and company websites. For

Confirmation An acknowledgement that you have received information or understood a message correctly.

CC An acronym that stands for courtesy copy. An email feature that allows a copy of a message to be sent to additional recipients.

BCC An acronym that stands for blind courtesy copy or blind carbon copy. Email addresses entered into the BCC field will be hidden from all recipients, allowing a copy to be sent to additional recipients without the named recipient knowing it.

Announcement A message that publicly notifies people of information they need or want to know.

ACE

Compose

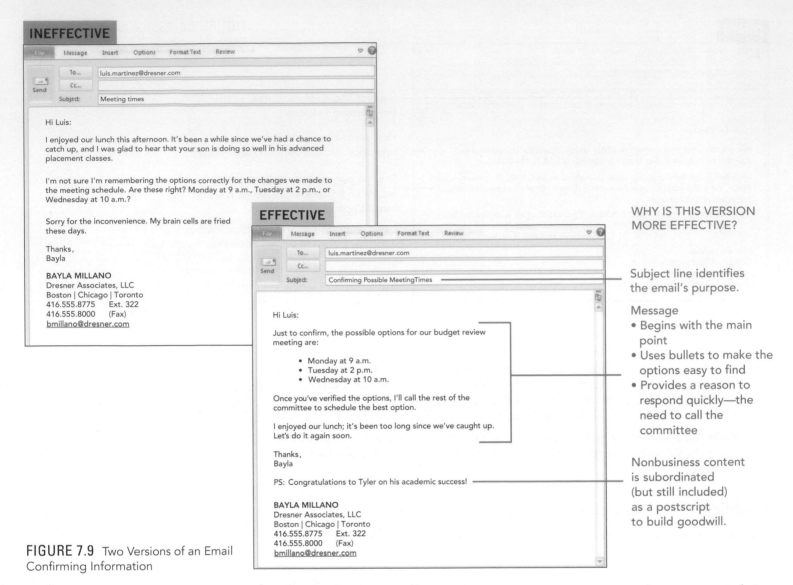

FIGURE 7.9 Two Versions of an Email Confirming Information

announcements to employees at your company, you can use the company website, email, or a flyer. Announcements to customers are typically sent by email or letter, but you may also post them on social networking sites like Facebook.

How does an announcement message differ from other messages you may write? One difference is that an announcement will go to a broad audience, not just one or two people. Another difference is that an announcement rarely requires a response. However, like any other routine message, an upbeat announcement will clearly state its purpose and be organized so that the audience can find important information.

FIGURE 7.10 on page 202 illustrates a routine announcement to bank customers. The bank is changing some of its policies and is required by law to notify customers. Rather than using legal language that may confuse readers, the announcement uses less formal language, active voice, and bullet points to entice the audience to read it.

Format instructions so readers can easily follow the steps

In addition to requests and replies, routine business messages may include procedural information or brief instructions about how to do things. Examples include:

- Directions to complete a new travel authorization form
- Instructions to process budget requests
- Procedures for submitting reimbursement documentation

ETHICS
IS BLIND COURTESY COPY (BCC) LIKE SPYING?

Flashback to Chapter 2: Ethics are a set of values or beliefs we use to govern ourselves. Our ethics are based on our beliefs of what is "right" and "wrong" and they influence the way we interpret, think, and act. A culture can follow a set of understood ethics. Therefore, living or working in a "multicultural" society means that we are also in a "multi-ethical" world.

In your email program, the *blind courtesy copy* feature (bcc) allows you to copy someone on an email without the recipient knowing it. Does sharing an email "secretly" with someone else raise any ethical issues? This is an instance where O Λ R can help:

- **Observe:** How do your colleagues at your workplace, whom you respect, handle bcc situations? What is the usage pattern in your company?
- **Ask:** What is your company's policy regarding the usage of bcc in work-related emails? Who can you ask? Even when you feel a bcc is harmless, there may be a business practice or other ethical expectation that you may not have considered.
- **Research:** When you search the Internet for opinions on the use of bcc, you will find a variety of examples and usages. Which seem to fit best with the ethical position of your company? Which "feels" right to you?

Consider two different scenarios for sending a bcc:

- **Using bcc to reduce long recipient lists.** You send an email to all employees who are late submitting their travel reimbursement requests and warn them that they will not be reimbursed unless they submit their requests today. The list of names is long. By using the bcc feature, you help ensure that your recipients focus on the message content rather than be distracted by an overly long header with many email addresses shown.

In this case, the use of bcc will likely be seen as more ethical than including everyone on the cc line. Recipients do not need to know the email addresses of all the others who have missed the deadline. Making this information invisible in the email may reduce the chance of embarrassing some people on the list.

- **Using bcc to share information with interested parties.** You write an email to negotiate the price of a product with a new supplier. Your best friend, who works in a position similar to yours but for another company, has asked to be bcc'd on your messages to this supplier because she wants access to "inside" pricing information. She feels this will help her negotiate a better price from this supplier.

This use of a bcc could be considered a form of corporate spying since your colleague intends to use the information to disadvantage the recipient. Furthermore, your company likely has a policy in place that restricts releasing pricing information for materials to outside parties.

As you compose emails, how do you decide if you should use a bcc and if it is ethical? After applying O-A-R to your scenario, also apply these three tests:

1. Are you trying to deceive the "to" recipient by hiding the fact that other people will also receive the email?
2. Can the recipient be disadvantaged or hurt if the content in the email is shared with the bcc readers and the recipient does not know it?
3. Can your company be damaged by the use of bcc to release information that it may deem to be "privileged"?

If you can say "yes" to any of these, then do not use bcc.

For an ETHICS exercise, go to Critical Thinking Question 2 on page 217.

Good instructions allow the audience to understand the task and complete it accurately. Make it easy for the audience to follow the instructions by using the guidelines below, as illustrated in **FIGURE 7.11**.

- **Begin with a brief overview** that helps your audience understand when and why they need to use the instructions.
- **Divide the instructions into numbered or bulleted steps**, including only *one* action per step. Numbers are more effective than bullets when you want to be able to refer to other steps in the procedure, or when the steps must be followed in a specific sequence.
- **Begin each step with a verb**, using **parallel phrasing**. There is one exception to this rule. If an instruction is **conditional**, begin the step by identifying the condition (see item 6 in Figure 7.11 as an example).
- **Place explanatory text after the action** rather than before it (see item 5 in Figure 7.11).

Parallel phrasing Using the same grammatical form for each item in a list.

Conditional Something that occurs only under certain conditions.

Explanatory text Written explanations that offer additional useful detail.

FIGURE 7.10 Routine Informational Announcement

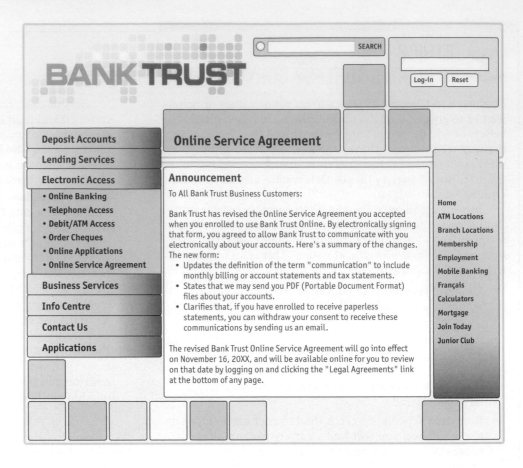

FIGURE 7.11 Email Providing Instructions

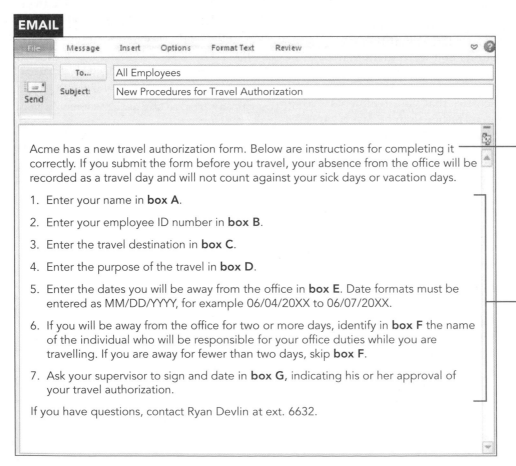

Use your own templates to save time and reduce errors

Consider the following examples already provided in this chapter:

- The written reply to a request for information (Figure 7.7)
- The positive response to a claim request (Figure 7.8)
- The routine informational announcement (Figure 7.10)
- The memo providing instructions (Figure 7.11)

The authors of these messages will likely have future opportunities to create these types of communications again. How can these message authors save themselves time while producing consistent and error-free communications? Many business professionals find it useful to create an **archive** of message **templates** to refer to when creating similar messages. Recycling good message phrasing and structure from past messages can reduce the amount of time and thought needed to produce a professional message. For example, **FIGURE 7.12** shows how the structure and format of Figure 7.11, the email providing instructions, can be recycled to produce a new set of instructions.

Recycle the message structures and formats that represent you in a professional and clear manner. Be sure not to reuse messages that have typos or other errors in them since this will project an image of you as someone who repeats the same mistakes. Check out the **TECHNOLOGY BOX** for some ideas on how to efficiently manage an archive of routinely recycled text samples.

Archive An organized collection of documents or materials that can be referenced or accessed when needed.

Template A prototype or example of how a document can be organized, structured, or formatted.

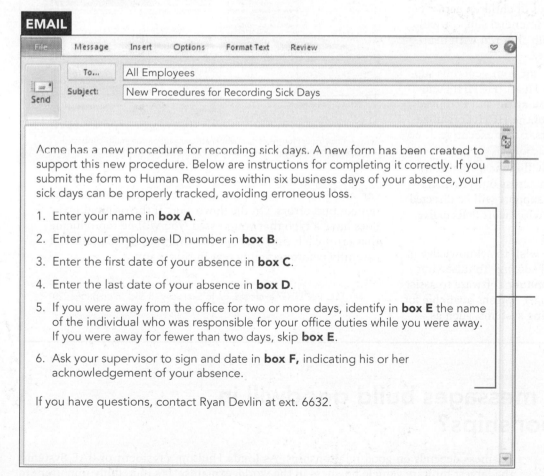

First paragraph still begins with an overview of the procedure, outlining its purpose and benefits to motivate the reader.

Actions are divided into numbered steps.

Steps 1–4 and Step 6 begin with an action verb, using parallel phrasing.

Step 5 begins with a conditional phrase because the step needs to be completed only under certain conditions.

FIGURE 7.12 Email Providing Different Instructions

TECHNOLOGY
RAISE EFFICIENCY AND ACCURACY WITH CLIPBOARD MANAGER SOFTWARE

One of the most common situations you will face is the need to write almost the same lines of text regularly. For example, if you are thanking key clients for attending an important fundraiser, you may write this generic response:

Generic Response: Thank you very much for your generous support of the Healthy Child Happy Heart (HCHH) Fundraiser. Your presence at the event will make a significant difference in the lives of children across our province. Please know that your financial support will be directed to finding ways to help children with heart defects live longer, stress-free lives.

While this captures the essence and the tone of what you want to say, you will want to customize this message for each recipient.

Client #1: Thank you very much for your generous support of the Healthy Child Happy Heart (HCHH) Fundraiser. It was a pleasure to see you again, and to meet your partner, Gilda McDonald, and to hear more about her personal experience with children who are challenged by congenital heart defects.

Your company's sponsorship of this event will make a significant difference in the lives of children across our province. Please know that your financial support will be directed to finding ways to help children with heart defects live longer, stress-free lives.

Client #2: Thank you very much for your generous support of the Healthy Child Happy Heart (HCHH) Fundraiser. It was a pleasure to see you again and I enjoyed our discussion about the future of the HCHH organization. I will forward your thoughts to our executive director in a separate email.

Your presence at this event will make a significant difference in the lives of children across our province. Please know that your financial support will be directed to finding ways to help children with heart defects live longer, stress-free lives.

If there are 10 major clients you wish to acknowledge in this way, that is a lot of retyping and editing. To raise your efficiency, you can use **clipboard manager** software to assist you. There are many clipboard manager options available for all major desktop and mobile operating systems, such as

PasteItIn, Clipboard Magic, ClipMate, QuickClip, Spartan, and a variety of others. Some versions of this software will allow you to store clips on a central cloud server and retrieve them from multiple devices and platforms.

Most clipboard managers function in essentially the same way. Every time you cut or copy text, a clipboard manager saves a history of your copied text in an easily accessed menu. You can click on a menu item or button in the onscreen menu to simply drop the clipped text back in. Clipboard managers can save hundreds of clips, and many will allow you to organize them by subject or usage type for easy retrieval later. So, for example, you could store several of the best "thank you" messages sent after this fundraiser for your use the next time you need to send "thank you" messages after an event.

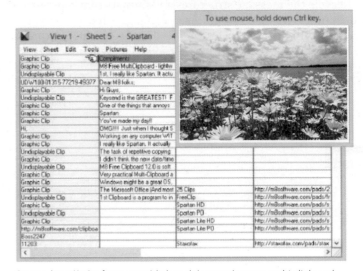

Source: http://m8software.com/clipboards/spartan/spartan-multi-clipboard-manager.htm. Used by permission; yanikap/Fotolia

Recycling messages in this way does save time and it can also reduce errors, provided that the original text does not contain errors. On the down side, if the original text does have a typo that you missed, you will be reproducing that error each time you use the clip. Be sure to proofread carefully before recycling text in this manner.

For TECHNOLOGY exercises, go to Exercises 15 and 16 on pages 220 and 221.

LO 7.3 What kinds of messages build goodwill in business relationships?

Clipboard manager Software that allows a user to copy, organize, edit, save, and quickly reuse text excerpts, graphics, and other digital assets.

Business depends on good relationships. As Linda Hudson, president of BAE Systems, the largest military vehicle business in the world, explains, "It's incredibly important to realize that relationships define everything that we do, and it's all about the quality of those relationships that makes an organization work" (Hudson, 2009). *Goodwill* is a term used to describe an attitude of friendliness and caring that is central to creating, solidifying, and maintaining relationships.

The routine, day-to-day operations of any organization offer multiple opportunities to create goodwill and positive relationships. Each organization has its own culture or way of approaching daily communications tasks in a way that strengthens and enhances business relationships. Read more about this in the **CULTURE BOX.**

Throughout this chapter, you have seen examples of goodwill techniques: expressing appreciation, offering help, using the receiver's perspective, and highlighting audience benefits. Although some of these techniques might appear to be superficial attempts

---

CULTURE
ROUTINE MESSAGES AND CORPORATE CULTURE: HOW CAN YOU GET IT RIGHT?

Skylar has been at the uptown marketing firm Couture Ads for a few weeks now and has been enjoying learning the everyday routines and work culture. Skylar's role, as a new intern, includes administrative work that requires regular communication on a daily and weekly basis with a wide range of clients. On Tuesday morning Skylar's boss, Michaela, asks her to connect with their long-standing client, Noble Global, to ask them to send their edits of a new ad campaign. On Tuesday afternoon, Skylar receives a text from Michaela asking her to connect with their newly acquired client, Itsy Jewels, to confirm their availability at a meeting that has been rescheduled for Thursday morning at 10 a.m.

Routine messages such as these are essential to building and keeping goodwill with new and existing clients. Yet Skylar is left wondering how to ensure her communications are professional and in line with the firm's culture.

- How should Skylar contact these clients in these two different instances? Which communications channel should she use?
- Who is the right person to connect with in each instance?

This is an instance where O-A-R can help:

- **Observe:** How do colleagues at your workplace whom you respect handle these types of communications? Is it normal to ask clients for their edited ad copy by email, or is a phone call better? Is it appropriate to text or email a meeting confirmation?
- **Ask:** A good supervisor will always appreciate a clarifying question. In both of these instances, it is appropriate for Skylar to ask Michaela about key contacts and appropriate communications channels.
- **Research:** What options does Skylar have in terms of communicating with these clients? Is there a previously agreed upon manner in which these clients wish to be contacted that could, for example, form part of their written agreement or contract? It would be important to find out before Skylar selects a communications approach.

Most business workplaces are very fast paced. It would be unrealistic to imagine that Skylar's supervisor is going to have time to train her on every last detail. Therefore, a newly hired intern like Skylar will need to learn to observe, ask questions, and do research to fill in the missing pieces of information. Most importantly, Skylar needs to know that she is missing key culture details so that she can ask the right questions!

IMPORTANT FACTORS TO CONSIDER

- **When in doubt, choose a more "formal" approach.** Goodwill and relationship building motivate Michaela to connect with her clients in both of these instances. Skylar is representing Michaela and does not have a familiar relationship with the clients herself. Business culture would dictate a more formal tone and approach for both clients.
- **Avoid gender and status assumptions.** Skylar may be instructed to contact assistants or interns at both Nobel Global and Itsy Jewels. It would be a mistake for Skylar to assume that the interns are female and that their supervisors are male. She should take care to ensure her communication content is gender neutral. Furthermore, Skylar should prepare her written content with the same care and indicating the same level of respect regardless of whether the receiver is of high status (a supervisor) or of a lower status (an assistant or intern).
- **Avoid overfamiliarity.** Skylar has seen Michaela behave in a quite relaxed and casual manner, in person, with both of these clients. Michaela's ability to do this does not transfer to her intern, Skylar. She should not assume that Michaela's clients know who Skylar is. Despite having a great rapport with Couture Ads and Michaela, these clients do not yet have a familiar relationship with Skylar.

For CULTURE exercises, go to Critical Thinking Question 8 on page 217 and Exercise 10 on page 220.

to make your message seem more polite, these audience-oriented expressions in fact serve two important communication goals:

1. They make your audience more receptive to your message.
2. They make your audience feel good about their business relationship with you.

With a good business relationship established, you will be able to work more easily and effectively with people, whether they are co-workers, managers, vendors, customers, or clients.

Because relationships are so important, you will want to look for opportunities to express appreciation and thoughtfulness, both in your routine messages and also in special messages designed primarily to communicate goodwill and keep the channels of communication open. These include thank you messages, congratulations, expressions of sympathy, and for-your-information messages.

Thank you messages

Thank you messages offer you the opportunity to express appreciation and make recipients feel good about something they have done for you. You might write a thank you message to someone who writes a recommendation or reference letter for you, to a client who hosts a business dinner, or to a colleague who has sent you a congratulatory gift to celebrate your promotion. Thank you messages also offer you the opportunity to display your professionalism. A well-written thank you note following a job interview communicates to an employer that you are motivated, thoughtful, and articulate.

The form your message takes will depend on the situation. Thank you messages range from formal letters to informal emails, handwritten notes, telephone calls, and even Facebook posts. Following a job interview, you would choose to write a formal letter and, if time allows, send it by mail. A letter like this should be written on a computer, examined and proofread for structure and errors, and then printed out. In more informal situations, an email can be appropriate. In many situations, a handwritten note can be a meaningful expression of gratitude because handwritten notes are so rare in today's digital age (Mueller, 2012). **FIGURE 7.13** illustrates a handwritten thank you note.

The main challenge in writing a good thank you note is to include specific content that relates to the reason why you are thanking someone. In Figure 7.13, Holt was easily able to write a customized note because he was thanking Tom for a specific act of hospitality. However, customized thank you messages may be more difficult to compose when you need to write many similar notes, such as in the scenario illustrated in **FIGURE 7.14**. Avoid the temptation to use the template approach for this task. As the first example in Figure 7.14 illustrates, a generic note loses much of its effectiveness because it could be used for any speaker by just changing the name of the person being addressed.

Thank you message An expression of appreciation when someone has done something for you.

Hi Tom:

Thank you for inviting me to your club while I was in Edmonton last week. I really enjoyed the spa, and the workout equipment was spectacular. If I had access to that kind of facility around here, I would be in great shape. —— Message begins with the thank you, followed by supporting comments.

I look forward to seeing you again next month for our regional conference in Montreal. —— Message concludes with a forward-looking statement.

Regards,
Holt

FIGURE 7.13 Handwritten Thank You Note

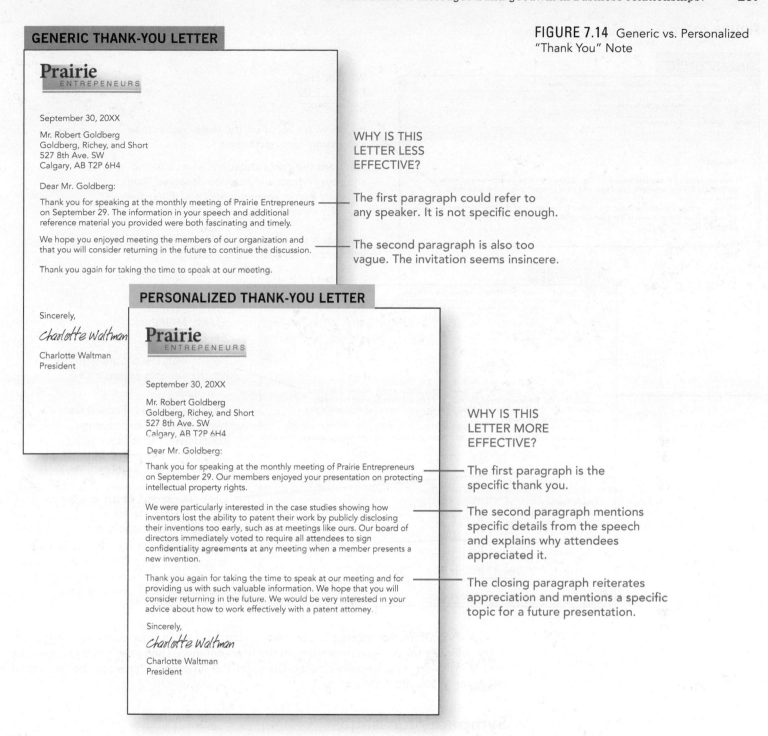

FIGURE 7.14 Generic vs. Personalized "Thank You" Note

The second example in Figure 7.14 is much more effective. By including details relating to the speech, the personalized version sounds more sincere and will make the recipient feel genuinely appreciated.

Congratulatory messages

Congratulatory messages build goodwill by recognizing important professional or personal events and achievements. For example, you can write a congratulatory message when your supervisor is promoted, your colleague has a baby, or your customer wins her city's entrepreneur-of-the-year award.

Congratulatory message Communication sent to recognize someone's achievements or important events.

FIGURE 7.15 Congratulatory Email Message

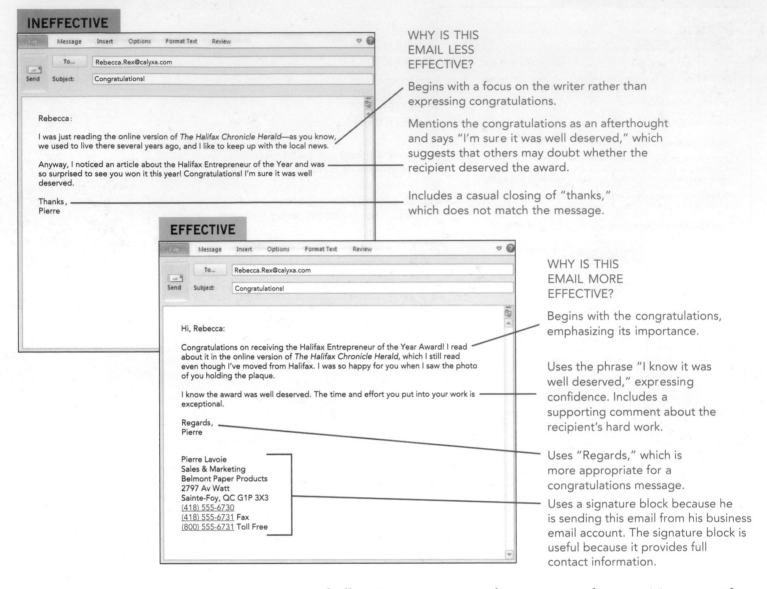

INEFFECTIVE

To... Rebecca.Rex@calyxa.com
Subject: Congratulations!

Rebecca:

I was just reading the online version of *The Halifax Chronicle Herald*—as you know, we used to live there several years ago, and I like to keep up with the local news.

Anyway, I noticed an article about the Halifax Entrepreneur of the Year and was so surprised to see you won it this year! Congratulations! I'm sure it was well deserved.

Thanks,
Pierre

WHY IS THIS EMAIL LESS EFFECTIVE?

Begins with a focus on the writer rather than expressing congratulations.

Mentions the congratulations as an afterthought and says "I'm sure it was well deserved," which suggests that others may doubt whether the recipient deserved the award.

Includes a casual closing of "thanks," which does not match the message.

EFFECTIVE

To... Rebecca.Rex@calyxa.com
Subject: Congratulations!

Hi, Rebecca:

Congratulations on receiving the Halifax Entrepreneur of the Year Award! I read about it in the online version of *The Halifax Chronicle Herald*, which I still read even though I've moved from Halifax. I was so happy for you when I saw the photo of you holding the plaque.

I know the award was well deserved. The time and effort you put into your work is exceptional.

Regards,
Pierre

Pierre Lavoie
Sales & Marketing
Belmont Paper Products
2797 Av Watt
Sainte-Foy, QC G1P 3X3
(418) 555-6730
(418) 555-6731 Fax
(800) 555-6731 Toll Free

WHY IS THIS EMAIL MORE EFFECTIVE?

Begins with the congratulations, emphasizing its importance.

Uses the phrase "I know it was well deserved," expressing confidence. Includes a supporting comment about the recipient's hard work.

Uses "Regards," which is more appropriate for a congratulations message.

Uses a signature block because he is sending this email from his business email account. The signature block is useful because it provides full contact information.

As with all routine messages, use a direct structure when organizing congratulatory notes. Identify the purpose for writing in the first sentence. Then provide any supporting details, followed by a friendly closing. Consider the differences between the two email messages in **FIGURE 7.15**.

Sympathy messages

Even if you do not have a close personal relationship with co-workers or business acquaintances, they will appreciate your expressions of sympathy when they have experienced a loss. Many people do not know what to say when a colleague becomes seriously ill or has experienced a death in the family. Although you can use purchased get-well cards and preprinted sympathy notes to deliver your message, be sure to also include a few lines that show your compassion and understanding. Just like thank you notes, **sympathy messages** (also called **condolences**) are more meaningful when handwritten and sent shortly after you hear about the situation. Read the example in **FIGURE 7.16**.

"For-your-information" messages

This final category of goodwill messages, illustrated in **FIGURE 7.17**, has no formal name, but you can think of them as **for-your-information (FYI) messages**: Messages sent to

Sympathy message (also called condolences) A message that expresses compassion and understanding when someone experiences a loss.

For-your-information (FYI) message A message written as an act of kindness to pass along information you think someone will appreciate knowing.

Dear George:

I was sorry to hear about the passing of your mother last — Begins with expression of sympathy.
week. I can only imagine how great your loss must be at this
difficult time. Please know that you have many friends here
at work who are keeping you in their thoughts. If I can do — Closes on a friendly note, with an offer of assistance.
anything to help you or your family, please do not hesitate to
call me.

With sympathy,
Camilla

FIGURE 7.16 Sympathy Message

pass along information or communicate something you believe your audience will appreciate. For example, when reading an article on the web about a new restaurant in Vancouver, you may remember that a customer is planning a vacation in Vancouver next month. Or, while talking to your tax accountant you may learn about a new tax rule that you think a colleague may appreciate knowing about.

Taking the opportunity to pass along information like this can lead to several benefits:

1. **Keep channels of communication open in a positive way.** This is an important part of networking. Every business relationship benefits from periodic communication to ensure that your audience continues to have you in mind.

2. **Solidify relationships.** You will get personal satisfaction from writing these messages, and your audience will be pleased to hear from you.

3. **Start a dialogue.** FYI messages may start a dialogue that can lead to possible business benefits.

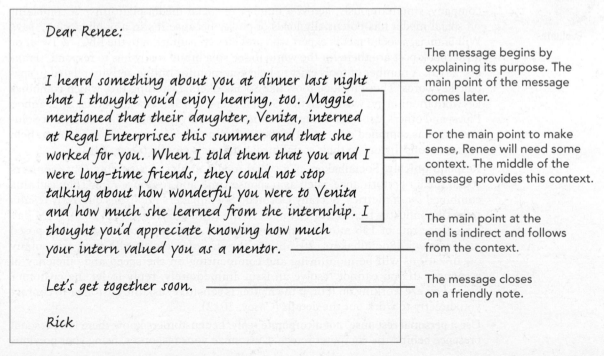

Dear Renee:

I heard something about you at dinner last night — The message begins by explaining its purpose. The main point of the message comes later.
that I thought you'd enjoy hearing, too. Maggie
mentioned that their daughter, Venita, interned
at Regal Enterprises this summer and that she — For the main point to make sense, Renee will need some context. The middle of the message provides this context.
worked for you. When I told them that you and I
were long-time friends, they could not stop
talking about how wonderful you were to Venita
and how much she learned from the internship. I — The main point at the end is indirect and follows from the context.
thought you'd appreciate knowing how much
your intern valued you as a mentor.

Let's get together soon. — The message closes on a friendly note.

Rick

FIGURE 7.17 For-Your-Information Message

LO 7.4 How can you use social media to build goodwill in business?

seewhatmitchsee/Alamy

You can use social media to attract potential customers, provide service to existing customers, and enhance long-term customer relationships. For example, you can use social networking sites to interact with customers, learn about their preferences, and increase their loyalty to your company. Companies are increasingly using social media in this way to manage relationships with their customers (Baird & Parasnis, 2011; Morgan, 2010).

Provide quick responses to questions and concerns

Social media networks create excellent opportunities for customers to note suggestions and complaints and for organizations to respond to them quickly. The faster you can respond to a customer issue, the more memorable the goodwill is to the customer. To do this, some companies hire social media specialists or create social media listening platforms to monitor reviews, blogs, or posts shared through various social media applications (Sapountzis, 2012).

For example, Whole Foods Market, the world's leading natural and organic grocer, is an active user of Twitter. The company's integrated media team monitors all tweets that mention Whole Foods Market and addresses complaints immediately. A customer in London, England, complained that the apples he purchased during his last trip to Whole Foods Market were not good and that his local store was "understaffed at the till" (the British word for cash register). The integrated media team at Whole Foods Market responded within a few hours and defused the situation. In fact, the initially irate customer felt much better about his Whole Foods Market experience at the end of the exchange. Each tweet from Whole Foods was clear and respectful, expressing a receiver's perspective in fewer than 140 characters.

Use the following techniques to effectively respond to customers' questions or concerns with social media:

ACE

Evaluate

- **Monitor online chatter.** Social media has put new meaning to the concept of "listening." In Chapter 1 we discussed the importance and complexity of listening in a traditional sense. Online, many people could be speaking good or ill of you or your company, simultaneously, across a number of social media platforms. "A complaint on social media has potentially loads of power because it's in a public forum," says Will Francis, a social media expert who provides consultation to the BBC. "A Tweet or a Facebook post are there for the world to see so a brand really has to respond" (Francis, 2013). A number of tools exist to help you monitor online activity related to specific keywords. These include tools like Socialbakers' Listening Pro, which combines keyword monitoring with analytics (Socialbakers, 2015a). Google Alerts, Zite, Yahoo Pipes, and others also offer online monitoring. Pam Dyer, marketing manager at SolutionsIQ, has compiled a list of 50 of the top online monitoring tools available to help organizations "listen" to their social media channels closely (Dyer, 2013).

- **Respond quickly.** Socialbakers is a social media analytics company that monitors social media performance, such as response time and response rate. They call this combined set of metrics "Socially Devoted." Socialbakers publishes quarterly results reflecting industry trends. For example, in the third quarter (Q3) of 2014, KLM had a response rate of 135 minutes and answered 98.76% of customer questions posed via Facebook (Socialbakers, 2015b). As the use of social media increases, many organizations will be monitoring and commenting on the speed and efficiency of responses. If you cannot resolve an issue immediately, reply to let the customer know you are working on it or, if the matter is sensitive, ask the customer to contact you directly to work out the details (Casey, 2012).

- **Use a personal response, not a corporate reply.** Let customers know there is a personal presence behind the computer screen. Customize your responses, using your previous remarks as a template. Refer to the customer by name occasionally during your exchange. If you use the customer's name too often, it will sound unnatural. If you use their name once or twice during your interaction, it will sound more conversational.

Build "real-time goodwill" by creating community with social media

You can also use your company's social media tools to build a positive online community that will enhance communication, solidify the company's reputation, and ultimately build business. Here are some strategies to build a positive social media community by engaging and interacting with consumers and potential customers:

- **Encourage input through surveys.** Use social media surveys to engage consumers in your company's decision making about its products and services. You can elicit consumers' input about ideas for new products, preferences for service options, or locations for new stores. For example, Dell Computer asks customers to visit its Idea Storm page to suggest and vote on new product ideas (Dell Computer, 2012).

- **Provide a platform for peer-to-peer support.** Although some negative interactions can occur on user-driven customer support forums, much can be gained if a company encourages customers to share with each other information about products and services. Hosting a platform for this kind of feedback, and responding quickly when appropriate, will only enhance a company's reputation as being transparent and approachable. On average, 40% of customers can resolve their issues within an online community, reducing demand on traditional customer service channels. All positive opportunities for a customer to interact with a company, even through interaction with other customers, help build brand reputation (Maoz, 2012).

- **Offer social media fans exclusive perks**, such as coupons or discounts (Kelly, 2012). Large companies like P. F. Chang's create mobile applications to interact with customers through games and rewards programs (see **FIGURE 7.18**). However, even small companies can create check-in specials through Facebook (Meyer, 2012) and other social media sites.

Note how P.F. Chang's builds a positive social media community through engagement and interaction with consumers . . .

Incentive programs, such as Warrior Rewards, entice consumers to frequently return to the restaurant.

Interactive games and tools, such as "Dish of Destiny," personalize products and enhance consumers' knowledge about menu items.

Creative features, such as the MadLib-style "Fortune Cookie," encourage consumers to share their interactive experience with friends through social media connections.

FIGURE 7.18 Screenshot from P. F. Chang's China Bistro, Inc. website.

Source: Screenshot from P. F. Chang's China Bistro, Inc. website.

In summary, routine and goodwill messages like those explained in this chapter are fundamental elements of business communication. They are the day-to-day messages you produce to get work done and to build and maintain healthy working relationships. To accomplish your goals with these messages, use the ACE process that you learned in Chapter 2. The ACE process will help ensure that you target the message to your purpose and audience, make it easy to understand, and avoid errors that will undermine your professionalism. **FIGURE 7.19** offers a graphic representation of ACE as applied to routine, positive, and goodwill messages.

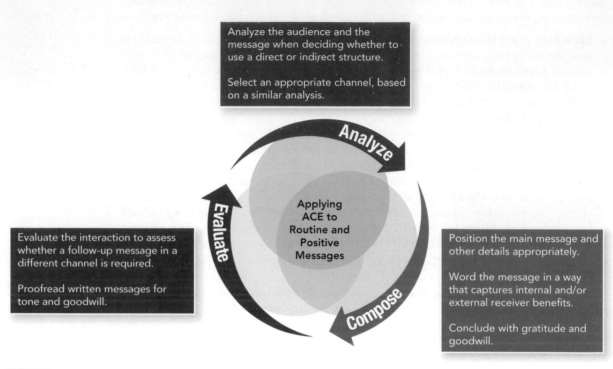

Analyze the audience and the message when deciding whether to use a direct or indirect structure.

Select an appropriate channel, based on a similar analysis.

Evaluate the interaction to assess whether a follow-up message in a different channel is required.

Proofread written messages for tone and goodwill.

Position the main message and other details appropriately.

Word the message in a way that captures internal and/or external receiver benefits.

Conclude with gratitude and goodwill.

Analyze

Evaluate

Compose

Applying ACE to Routine and Positive Messages

FIGURE 7.19 ACE Applied to Routine and Positive Messages.

@ WORK

Marzena Gersho
Director of Communications,
Food Banks Canada

Photo courtesy of Marzena Gersho and Teddy Chau.

At the beginning of the chapter, Marzena needed to select the right communications channel for a discussion with a service provider about an incorrect invoice. How does Marzena use ACE to help make this decision?

- **Analyze.** Consider a few key points before sending out any communications. What is my contact's most preferred communication method? What is the message that I'm sending? How might it be interpreted? How quickly do I need a response?

- In the case of the erroneous invoice, I regularly communicate with this supplier by email. However, a discussion about a billing error could be misinterpreted if my email tone is not just right. I decided to make a phone call to discuss the error and to follow up our discussion with an email summary.

- **Compose.** If I'm speaking to someone in person or on the phone, I like to write out a few notes for myself so I don't forget any important specific details. Detailed notes also allow me keep the conversation focused.

    In the case of the erroneous invoice, I made the phone call with the following details in writing in front of me:

    - A copy of the incorrect invoice
    - A copy of the corrections
    - The name of our staff member who processes payments
    - The details of the job being invoiced
    - My notes highlighting the key points I wanted to cover and the outcome I was hoping to achieve

    After we finished speaking and resolving the issue, I then wrote an email, copied to all relevant parties, to summarize this conversation with the supplier's billing department.

- **Evaluate.** When using email, it helps to write out the email first and then go back and review it for accuracy and clarity. Think about the tone, word choices, spelling, and even formatting. Imagine you are on the receiving end and consider how you might perceive the communication. Once you write something and hit "send" it is difficult to retract! Being a good communicator is like being a good carpenter. The carpenter's mantra is "Measure twice and cut once." A professional communicator's mantra could be "Review twice and send once." Don't put yourself in a position of having to retract or explain or apologize!

End of Chapter

Learning Objectives in Review

(LO 7.1) How do you compose messages containing questions and requests? *(pages 192–196)*

Most workplace communication involves routine business messages that are short and to the point. Use the ACE process to make positive decisions when analyzing, composing, and evaluating your messages.

- **Decide between a direct or an indirect message** when composing routine messages that ask questions or make requests. In most cases, state your request directly. However, if the audience needs information to understand or be convinced about your request, use an indirect message.
- **Provide reasons for the request** when necessary.
- **Adopt the receiver's perspective and include audience benefits** in all messages that ask questions or make requests. Internal benefits are advantages that your audience directly receives, and external benefits are advantages that someone else gains.
- **Conclude with gratitude and a call for action.**

(LO 7.2) How do you compose informational messages? *(pages 197–204)*

- **Reply to questions with a direct answer.** Begin with a positive response, follow the organization of the original message (using corresponding numbers when appropriate), and end with a friendly closing.
- **Respond to customer requests by creating goodwill.** This is especially important when customers are requesting refunds, exchanges, or repairs.
- **Highlight key points in confirmation messages.** A confirmation is a message acknowledging that you have received information or checking that you have understood information correctly.
- **Organize routine announcements so they are easy to skim.** Announcements are messages that publicly notify people of information they need or want to know.
- **Format instructions so readers can easily follow the steps.** Begin with an overview, divide instructions into numbered or bulleted lists, and begin each step with an action verb (or a conditional phrase, if the step is necessary only under certain conditions). Use parallel phrasing to ensure the same grammatical form is used for each item. Position any needed explanation after the action rather than before it.
- **Use your own templates to save time and reduce errors.** Save examples of your best work for future recycling. Organize these as simple text files in folders or by using a clipboard manager (see the Technology box on page 204).

(LO 7.3) What kinds of messages build goodwill in business relationships? *(pages 204–209)*

Goodwill is a term used to describe the attitude of friendliness and caring that is central to creating, solidifying, and maintaining relationships.

- **Thank-you messages** offer you the opportunity to express appreciation and make your recipients feel positive about something they have done for you. They also offer you the opportunity to express and display your professionalism. Thank-you messages range from formal letters to informal emails, handwritten notes, and telephone calls. The main challenge in writing a thank you note is to include specific content that relates to the act for which you are thanking someone. A generic note loses much of its effectiveness.
- **Congratulatory messages** build goodwill by recognizing someone else's achievements or important events. These events could be professional or personal.
- **Sympathy messages** are written to colleagues and business acquaintances to show your compassion and understanding. Although you can take advantage of get-well cards and sympathy notes to deliver your messages, also include a few handwritten lines to personalize the message and promote goodwill.
- **"For-your-information" messages** are sent to pass along information or communicate something you believe your audience will appreciate. These friendly messages keep channels of communication open, solidify relationships, and initiate dialogues that may lead to business benefits.

(LO 7.4) How can you use social media to build goodwill in business? *(pages 210–213)*

Social media builds goodwill by creating positive customer relationships.

- **Provide quick responses to questions and concerns.** Social media networks like Twitter provide expanded opportunities to receive customer suggestions and complaints while also allowing companies to respond quickly. Experts suggest researching mobile applications, creating content that fits social networking formats, integrating social media as a routine method of communicating, and enticing customer interaction.
- **Build "real-time goodwill" by creating community with social media.** Building a positive online community will solidify a company's reputation and, ultimately, will help build business. One way to do this is to provide a platform for peer-to-peer support. Much can be gained if a company encourages customers to share information about products and services with each other. Hosting a platform for this kind of feedback, and responding quickly when appropriate, will only enhance a company's reputation for being transparent and approachable.

KEY TERMS

announcement p. 199
archive p. 203
audience or receiver benefits
  p. 194
badwill p. 197
bcc (blind courtest copy) p. 199

cc (courtesy copy) p. 199
clipboard manager p. 204
conditional p. 201
condolences p. 208
confirmation p. 199
congratulatory message p. 207

explanatory text p. 201
external benefits p. 194
for-your-information (FYI)
  message p. 208
goodwill message p. 191
internal benefits p. 194

parallel phrasing p. 201
receiver's perspective p. 194
routine business messages p. 191
sympathy message p. 208
template p. 203
thank you message p. 206

CASE STUDY

A Day's Worth of Routine Messages

This case study will help you review the chapter material by applying it to a specific scenario.

For the past year, Miguel Ramirez has worked for his father's insurance agency, Ramirez & Associates Insurance. The small company has only five employees: Miguel and his father, Carlos; Melinda and Reggie, both senior associates; and Theresa, the office manager.

On a Friday morning, Miguel opens the office and checks the company's voice mail. The first message is from his father, saying he won't be in today because he decided to leave for vacation one day early. The second message is from Reggie, reminding everyone that he will be out calling on clients. The third message from Melinda says that the insurance supplier she planned to visit next week requested that she come today instead, so she will be out of the office all day. The last message is from Theresa, the office manager, who says she has the flu and will not be in today. This leaves Miguel in charge.

Miguel sits down at Theresa's computer and opens the central email for the office. He also glances at the stack of regular mail on Theresa's desk. Here is a summary of the 11 messages he found:

In the email:

1. A notice from one of the insurance companies whose products Ramirez & Associates sells. The company has adjusted auto insurance rates and coverage for all customers in the province based on claims and costs from the previous year. These changes will affect almost all customers.

2. A notice from another company that it will not renew the insurance for a customer who filed three claims during the past year.

3. Two requests for insurance quotes from new customers.

4. A request from a summer intern for a job recommendation.

5. A request from a corporate client asking that Ramirez & Associates confirm the details of an insurance policy covering its fleet of 1,000 cars.

6. A notice that a customer's claim for wind damage to her garage will be completely covered by the insuring company, minus the $250 deductible.

7. An email from Melinda asking someone in the office to place an order of office supplies with Office-To-Go. She left the list of supplies on her desk, and she needs them by Monday.

In the regular mail:

8. Three insurance policies that need to be mailed to customers. These policies are complex, and the customers will not understand the details without a clear summary.

9. An invitation addressed to Miguel's father, Carlos, asking him to speak at a college career night next month. The school requests a reply within 10 days, and Miguel's father is not going to be back in the office for two weeks.

10. A letter from the Insurance Brokers Association of Canada indicating that Carlos Ramirez has been nominated for a prestigious award.

11. A news release from Office-To-Go, one of the major office equipment suppliers in the area. The company has been purchased by a larger corporation, which may affect pricing and delivery policies. The news release offers no details, but raises many questions about whether Office-To-Go will remain competitive with other suppliers.

Analyzing Tasks and Choosing the Best Medium

Because Miguel is alone, he decides to spend the day following up on business leads, answering the phone, and responding to emails and letters. As a first step, Miguel uses the first phase of the ACE process to analyze his communication tasks using three criteria: Do others need the information quickly? Will the task be easy for me to do, or should someone else handle it later? Is it in the business's best interest for me to answer quickly?

TASK 1: *Review the 11 messages and prioritize each item by putting a **1** next to those that must be handled today, a **2** next to items that should be handled today if there is time, and a **3** next to items that can wait. Then, for each item, do a quick analysis. Identify the purpose of Miguel's communication, the audience, and the best medium option: letter, email, instant message, telephone, meeting, and so forth. Be prepared to explain your choices.*

Composing Good News in Response to a Claim

Miguel has good news to deliver to his client Kristina Ivanska. He received an email from her insurer saying that the company will pay 100% of the replacement/repair cost for her roof, which was severely damaged in a wind storm, minus the $250 deductible.

Ms. Ivanska will get her payment in two instalments. She will immediately receive a cheque for $7,242, which is the value of her seven-year-old roof. Then, when she has the roof repaired, the company will pay the difference between what it has already paid and the actual repair cost minus the $250 insurance deductible. She doesn't need to rush to have the roof repaired because she has up to 180 days to submit the bill for the repairs.

Miguel is eager to communicate this news to Ms. Ivanska, so he decides to call her. He begins the conversation with good news: "Ms. Ivanska, I wanted to let you know that Bill Baker, the insurance adjuster, will be stopping by your house next week with a cheque for $7,242 to cover your roof damage." Much to Miguel's surprise, Ms. Ivanska is very upset. She said: "But I just got an estimate from the roofing company for $9,850 to replace the roof. I thought my insurance covered "replacement value." There's a $2,500 difference! How can I pay for that?"

Miguel immediately realizes that he has organized his message the wrong way. He tries to calm Ms. Ivanska: "Don't worry. The insurance will cover the full cost except for your $250 deductible. I'm just explaining it wrong. Let me write you a letter, and I'll drop it by your house on my way home. It will make everything clear."

TASK 2: *Write the good news letter for Miguel. Be sure it does the following:*

- *Delivers the good news in a way that Ms. Ivanska will understand and that calms her concerns*
- *Explains what the insurance company will do and what she needs to do*
- *Re-establishes her confidence in Ramirez & Associates as an insurance broker*

Evaluating a Routine Message

After he handles the priority messages, Miguel turns his attention to the Office-To-Go announcement. Although it looks like a routine message, it is bad news to Miguel because he spent the past two months researching new office furniture and computer equipment from Office-To-Go. He made his choices and was about to prepare a proposal for his father. Now it is unclear whether the new vendor will carry the same brands, charge the same prices, or have the same service agreements.

Miguel decides to compose an email to the Office-To-Go manager requesting information that will help him decide whether to find a new vendor. Miguel composes the following message quickly and hopes to revise it by the end of the day.

TASK 3: *Evaluate this message and suggest revisions and corrections Miguel should make before sending it.*

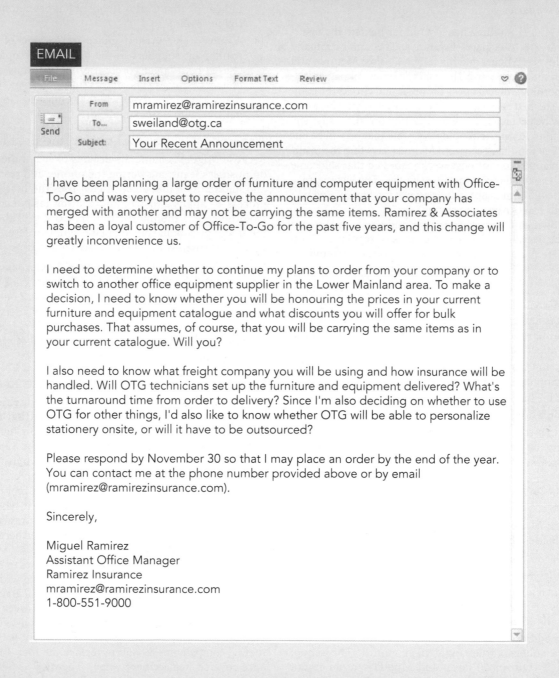

EMAIL

File	Message	Insert	Options	Format Text	Review

From: mramirez@ramirezinsurance.com
To...: sweiland@otg.ca
Subject: Your Recent Announcement

I have been planning a large order of furniture and computer equipment with Office-To-Go and was very upset to receive the announcement that your company has merged with another and may not be carrying the same items. Ramirez & Associates has been a loyal customer of Office-To-Go for the past five years, and this change will greatly inconvenience us.

I need to determine whether to continue my plans to order from your company or to switch to another office equipment supplier in the Lower Mainland area. To make a decision, I need to know whether you will be honouring the prices in your current furniture and equipment catalogue and what discounts you will offer for bulk purchases. That assumes, of course, that you will be carrying the same items as in your current catalogue. Will you?

I also need to know what freight company you will be using and how insurance will be handled. Will OTG technicians set up the furniture and equipment delivered? What's the turnaround time from order to delivery? Since I'm also deciding on whether to use OTG for other things, I'd also like to know whether OTG will be able to personalize stationery onsite, or will it have to be outsourced?

Please respond by November 30 so that I may place an order by the end of the year. You can contact me at the phone number provided above or by email (mramirez@ramirezinsurance.com).

Sincerely,

Miguel Ramirez
Assistant Office Manager
Ramirez Insurance
mramirez@ramirezinsurance.com
1-800-551-9000

Spending a Few Moments to Create Goodwill

It is 4:45 p.m. and Miguel has barely left his desk. He has been talking on the telephone, composing messages, and placing orders. As Miguel sits back in his chair, he recalls his father saying, "Miguel, every day before I leave work, I make sure I've given someone a 'gift,' such as a thank you, a word of congratulations, or even just a smile. Remember, the time you invest making someone else feel good will help you build goodwill."

Miguel has been so intent on his work today that he hasn't spent one moment thinking about how to give someone a "gift." He glances down at his list of messages, looking for an opportunity to build goodwill for Ramirez & Associates or for himself.

TASK 4: *Review the 11 messages at the beginning of this case study to identify ways to build goodwill. This is a great opportunity to think creatively.*

REVIEW QUESTIONS

1. Under what circumstances would you choose to use an indirect routine message rather than a direct one?

2. Why is the receiver's perspective suggested for routine requests?

3. Why is goodwill so important to business communication, especially when responding to customer requests?

4. How can you organize a routine announcement to make it easy to skim?

5. Explain three formatting techniques that make instructions easy for readers to follow.

6. Should thank you messages be handwritten or typed?

7. List three examples of "for-your-information" messages that build goodwill. Create examples that are not already listed in this chapter.

8. How can social media support effective customer relationships?

CRITICAL THINKING

1. Many of the routine messages in this chapter are just a few sentences long. Explain why using each phase of the ACE communication process (Analyzing, Composing, and Evaluating) is helpful even for short, routine messages.

2. As this chapter explains, in some instances it may be unethical to include a bcc in an email. Explain a situation, other than those described in the chapter, in which *forwarding* an email might be considered unethical. **[Related to the Ethics feature on page 201]**

3. Writing a message to request a refund, repair, or exchange provides one advantage over a telephone call: You have written documentation of your request and you are likely to receive a written response. However, sometimes you may prefer to call a customer service representative because an oral conversation allows better feedback and a quicker resolution. If you choose to communicate your claim request by telephone, what details about the conversation should you document? What method of documentation would you choose?

4. If you were granting a customer a refund for a faulty product, why might you also include a discount for a future purchase? The customer is getting what she asked for, so why do more?

5. Explain why a thank you note is an important follow-up to all your employment interviews, even with those companies you are no longer interested in pursuing.

6. Business culture is competitive. People compete for jobs, promotions, and raises. In this competitive culture, why should you concern yourself with building goodwill with your peers and colleagues?

7. If you were writing a goodwill message to someone from another culture, would you choose to follow your own cultural standards or those of your audience? Why? How could you find out what those cultural standards are?

8. Examine the following messages, related to the Culture feature on page 205. Is one more appropriate than the others? Why? What is wrong with the ones you did not pick?

   - Hey, we just wanted to find out if you knew that the firm's meeting was changed to Thursday at 10 a.m.
   - I am happy to make your acquaintance and to tell you that the firm's meeting was rescheduled for Thursday, at 10 a.m.
   - Good morning! Michaela emailed me to ask you if you will be able to submit your second draft suggestions to us. Thanks!
   - Meeting Rescheduled: Thursday, 10 a.m., at Couture Ads.
   - Good morning, my name is Skylar, and I am one of the new interns working at Couture Ads. I have been asked by Michaela to confirm with you the rescheduled meeting time between Itsy Bitsy and Couture Ads for the date of Thursday, October 17, 20XX, at 10 a.m. If you require any further assistance, please do not hesitate to contact me at skylar@CoutureAds.com or extension 0101.

DEVELOPING YOUR COMMUNICATION SKILLS

 (LO 7.1) **How do you compose messages containing questions and requests?** *(pages 192–196)*

EXERCISE 1 Decide between a direct or an indirect message

Most routine messages should be organized directly, with the main point positioned at the beginning of the message. Rewrite the following messages to use a direct approach and revise the wording to create a more effective message based on clarity, conciseness, style, and tone. Compare your direct revision to the indirect original. Which version would you choose to send? Explain why.

a. Email to Professor Tran: My sister is getting married this weekend, and I am in the wedding party. It's a five-hour drive, so to get to the wedding rehearsal Friday afternoon, I have to leave before noon on Friday, which means I won't be able to attend our 2 p.m. class. I know that missing your lecture will put me at a disadvantage for next week's exam, but you said you would take our term papers early if we got them done, which I did, so it's attached. Please confirm that you received the attachment. I'd be happy to bring by a hard copy if you would prefer. Thanks, [Your Name]

b. Voice mail message to a customer service department: Hi. This is Kent from Slocan Valley Automotive. Last week we placed an order from your recent promotional catalogue. We ordered 24 sets of your model #42 windshield wipers. We received the shipment today, but found 42 sets of your model #24 windshield wipers. Although we stock both models, our supply of model #42 is very low, and we now have twice as many model #24 sets. What can you do to help? Please call me at 250–555–1234. Thanks!

c. Letter to a prospective tenant: Dear Mr. Abrams: Thank you for your recent request for additional information about our summer rental facilities. I agree that we have several interesting options to choose from, and without specific pricing details it is difficult to make an informed decision. If you reserve your rental from the attached pricing list before April 1 I can offer you a 10% discount. Enclosed is the price list you requested. Thanks, [Your Name]

d. Face-to-face conversation: Hi, Hiro. You know that email about the new travel forms we're supposed to use? Well, I'm going to a conference next week in Las Vegas (nice, huh?). Although I've already asked Thad to cover for me while I'm gone, after reading the email I wasn't sure if we had to ask someone who is actually in our department to cover for us. I was hired to replace Thad when he moved up to management, so he knows my job better than anyone else, not that I think there will be much for him to do while I'm gone, but I didn't want my travel request to get hung up in the process if I had to ask someone else. Do you know?

EXERCISE 2 Provide reasons for the request

Your first job after college requires you to move to a new city, Regina, Saskatchewan, where you don't know anyone. You want to get involved with activities outside of work where you can meet people, so you attend a meeting of the Young Professionals Association of Regina. Because you enjoyed the meeting, you sign up to join and provide your credit card number for the membership fee. Two weeks later, as you review your online credit card statement information, you notice that your annual dues were charged at the $100 premium member fee rather than the $50 new member fee that was advertised during the meeting. To get your $50 back, you email the organization. You do not know the name of the president or the treasurer. However, you do have a general email address: YPAR@shaw.net. Draft your email requesting a refund.

EXERCISE 3 Adopt the receiver's perspective and include audience benefits

For each of the following claim responses, revise the message to use the receiver's perspective and include audience benefits.

a. Thank you for contacting us about the Internet outage in your area. We restored the connection.

b. We are sorry that one of the pizzas delivered to your office last week was cold. Enclosed is a refund.

c. We regret that one of the eight office chairs you ordered was damaged during delivery. We are shipping a replacement today.

d. The headset you returned could not be repaired. We're enclosing a new one for your convenience.

EXERCISE 4 Conclude with gratitude and a call for action

The following email exchange consists of five separate short messages. Revise the messages to conclude with an appropriate call for action. Where appropriate, include other techniques such as an expression of gratitude, the receiver perspective, and audience benefits.

a. Hi, Peter: Will you be able to take on the new Meggison marketing project? I'm simply overwhelmed with the Pagel campaign and don't know how I would handle both projects simultaneously. Thanks, Larry

b. Hi, Larry: Sure, I can work on the Meggison project. Peter

c. Peter: I am so glad you accepted my offer to lead the new Meggison marketing project. I have so much on my plate right now, you just can't imagine! I expect you will call me with any questions you have. I need your proposal as soon as possible. Larry

d. Larry: Attached is my rough draft for the Meggison proposal. Peter

e. Peter: Attached are my suggested revisions for the Meggison proposal. Larry

(LO 7.2) **How do you compose informational messages?**
(pages 197–204)

EXERCISE 5 Reply to questions with a direct answer

As the director of human resources at UrbanLife, you receive several requests each week from students for information about internship opportunities at your company. Although you respond to each request individually, you often reply with the same information. Rather than typing the same information each time, you decide to create a template of responses that you can cut, paste, and modify as necessary to personalize each message. The questions often include the following:

- Do you provide internships? *Answer:* Yes
- If so, in what areas? *Answer:* All departments
- What is the timeline for reviewing applications? *Answer:* Usually a four- to six-week response
- When during the academic year do you hire interns? *Answer:* Accepted throughout the year

Draft a sample email response that you could use to respond to any request for internship information. Include the suggested elements: Begin with the positive response, include all requested information, and end with a friendly closing. Remember the importance of creating goodwill with your response by striking an appropriate tone.

EXERCISE 6 Respond to customer requests by creating goodwill

Callan Reis wrote to her company's employee benefits director to appeal the director's decision not to reimburse certain healthcare expenses. The benefits director drafted the following message, responding positively to Callan's appeal. However, in evaluating this message before sending, the writer determined the message did not promote goodwill. What changes would you recommend to the writer?

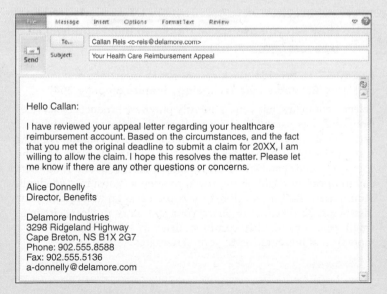

Accompanies Exercise 6

EXERCISE 7 Highlight key points in confirmation messages

As a new intern at a large marketing company, you provide assistance to a wide variety of project managers and their staff. The diverse experience is valuable but requires significant attention to detail to ensure you remember what you're supposed to do for whom and by when. You have been keeping detailed notes, but sometimes in the course of running an errand someone will ask you to do something when you don't have your notes with you. This happened today. As you were copying documents and collating materials into presentation packets for a client meeting, Lydia Homer, the team leader for the project presentation, looked in the copy room and said, "Don't forget to include the original RFP in the packets. When you're done with all that, take the packets to Brian for labelling. Use the 5164 size. Sally has the list of names. Thanks." Before you could respond, Lydia hurried down the hall to another meeting. You realize you don't know what an RFP is, you don't know Brian or Sally, and now you can't remember whether she said 5164 or 5614. Because your copy machine has another 500 pages to print, you decide to email Lydia confirming the information and asking for clarification. Draft the message.

EXERCISE 8 Organize routine announcements so they are easy to skim

You manage City Kids, a large daycare facility in the downtown area. You want to announce your expanded hours to your current clientele as well as employees of local businesses (potential customers) near your facility. Your old hours were 7:30 a.m. to 6:30 p.m. Beginning the first of next month, you will be open from 7:00 a.m. until 7:00 p.m. The daycare facility has a comprehensive website and an active listserv that includes each parent's email address. Create additional information to draft an announcement, and identify the medium options you could use to distribute this message. How would the draft change based on the medium?

EXERCISE 9 Format instructions so readers can easily follow the steps

Your company is planning to recruit new employees at several college-sponsored job fairs and has decided to staff the booths with current employees from throughout the company. You have a full schedule of volunteers for the fairs. You wrote the short set of instructions in the following paragraph, which you plan to distribute at an orientation session for volunteers. Before the session, though, you decide to revise the instructions to make them easier to follow. Reformat (and if necessary, revise) the following text to create a one-page instruction sheet for volunteers. As you revise, consider which steps are separate and which can be grouped together.

Protocol for Job Fair Booth Volunteers

Greet the student (that is, prospective employee). Shake hands and introduce yourself. Ask the student's name. Give the student the company brochure. Outline the nature of the jobs you are recruiting for, without going into too much detail. Focus on the benefits of working for our company. Ask if the student has any questions. Answer any questions you can and take notes about any question that you cannot answer. Thank the student for his or her interest in our company and wish the student good luck in his or her job search.

Accompanies Exercise 9

EXERCISE 10 Check Your Tone [Related to the Culture feature on page 205]

Review the Culture box on page 205. Prepare an email message to be sent to Nobel Global to check in on their edits for their ad campaign, keeping in mind a need to stay formal with unfamiliar or new business relationships, to avoid gender assumptions, and to avoid overfamiliarity. The message can be short, but it must be professional.

 What kinds of messages build goodwill in business relationships? *(pages 204–209)*

EXERCISE 11 Thank you messages

You work for a large tax accounting firm, and one of your satisfied customers, Rajmohan Siva, wrote a very complimentary email about you to the senior vice-president. The customer also referred a colleague (Andrea Kwan) to your company based on your work. The senior vice-president forwarded you a copy of this email. Send your customer a thank you message.

EXERCISE 12 Congratulatory messages

This is your fifth year as the head of new client development for a small consulting company. Your assistant, Madeline, has been extremely helpful since your first day. After 30 years of service to the company, Madeline is retiring. You have organized her retirement party and selected a beautifully inscribed silver plaque. However, you're not sure what to write in her farewell card. Although you will miss her knowledge and talents, you know she is looking forward to retirement and plans to begin with a two-week Caribbean cruise. Draft a congratulatory message to Madeline.

EXERCISE 13 Sympathy messages

You are a sales consultant for a regional distribution company. Your biggest client, Jana, has also become a good friend. Last year, Jana's son, Brian, was diagnosed with leukemia. Your client meetings have been less frequent lately since Jana has been working from home, but you've managed to stay in contact by email. This morning, the first email you open is from Jana. It's a message sent to dozens of people informing them that Brian died peacefully in his sleep a week ago. Jana's message thanks the group for their continued support during the past year, and indicates that donations can be made in Brian's name to the Children's Leukemia Centre. Although your instinct is to reply by email, you know a handwritten sympathy note is more appropriate. Draft your message.

EXERCISE 14 "For-your-information" messages

Jim O'Callahan is your company's vice-president of marketing. Last week you sat next to Jim at a business dinner. In conversation, Jim mentioned how much he admired Abraham Lincoln as a leader. The next day as you were browsing through your local bookstore, you saw a book by Eric Foner, *The Fiery Trial: Abraham Lincoln and American Slavery*. This made you think of Jim's comments, and you bought the book. You're only three chapters through it but you are really enjoying it. You wonder if Jim has read it. Write a message to Jim that lets him know about this new book.

 How can you use social media to build goodwill in business? *(pages 210–213)*

EXERCISE 15 Provide quick responses to questions and concerns [Related to the Technology feature on page 204]

Select a company that you frequently purchase products or services from that has established a social media presence. Analyze its social media interactions with customers. Provide examples of how it responds to consumer questions and concerns. Explain how the company builds goodwill in its responses or, if it does not, how its communication could be improved to support consumer goodwill. Summarize the information in a three-paragraph email to your instructor. Be prepared to share your summary in class, either in small groups to identify commonalities in your research or in a more formal presentation to your classmates.

EXERCISE 16 Build a positive social media community by engaging and interacting with your audience [Related to the Technology feature on page 204]

Select a company that has established a positive social media community and perhaps uses social media to engage consumers in the decision-making process about products or services. Analyze how it engages the audience among different social media outlets.

If possible, determine how it uses audience input, such as if it reports survey results or identifies consumer preferences, when the company posts its final decisions. Summarize the information in a three-paragraph email to your instructor. Be prepared to share your summary in class, either in small groups to identify commonalities in your research or in a more formal presentation to your classmates.

8

Communicating Persuasive Messages

kzenon/123RF.

LEARNING OBJECTIVES

(LO 8.1) How can the ACE process help you persuade your audience? *pages 224–229*

Analyzing helps you plan your message
Composing implements the persuasive plan
Evaluating helps you review the draft for effectiveness

(LO 8.2) What are the basic elements of persuasion? *pages 229–238*

Building credibility
Constructing a logical argument
Appealing to your audience's emotions

(LO 8.3) What types of business messages require persuasion? *pages 239–249*

Recommendations for action
Sales messages
Social media: Indirect persuasion
Persuasion helps you motivate others

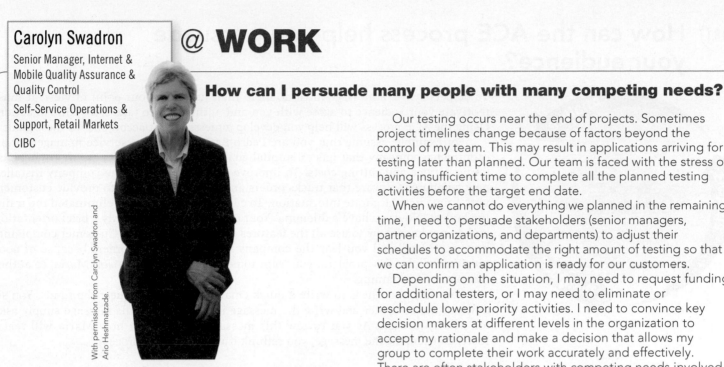

Carolyn Swadron

Senior Manager, Internet & Mobile Quality Assurance & Quality Control

Self-Service Operations & Support, Retail Markets

CIBC

With permission from Carolyn Swadron and Ario Heshmatzade.

@ WORK

How can I persuade many people with many competing needs?

My crackerjack Internet & Mobile Quality Assurance & Quality Control team is responsible for certifying that online and mobile banking applications work correctly before we make them available to our customers.

Our testing occurs near the end of projects. Sometimes project timelines change because of factors beyond the control of my team. This may result in applications arriving for testing later than planned. Our team is faced with the stress of having insufficient time to complete all the planned testing activities before the target end date.

When we cannot do everything we planned in the remaining time, I need to persuade stakeholders (senior managers, partner organizations, and departments) to adjust their schedules to accommodate the right amount of testing so that we can confirm an application is ready for our customers.

Depending on the situation, I may need to request funding for additional testers, or I may need to eliminate or reschedule lower priority activities. I need to convince key decision makers at different levels in the organization to accept my rationale and make a decision that allows my group to complete their work accurately and effectively. There are often stakeholders with competing needs involved in such a decision. How can I successfully persuade them to support my requests?

Find out at the end of this chapter how Carolyn uses ACE to write persuasive messages.

Introduction

Persuasion is the process of influencing your audience to agree with your point of view, recommendation, or request. In your daily life, you often need to communicate persuasively. As a student, you may need to persuade your advisor or dean to grant you credit for a course taken at another school. As a consumer, you may need to persuade a manufacturer to give you a refund for a faulty product. In the workplace, too, there are many situations that require persuasion:

- Sell a new service to a potential client who has not heard of your company
- Recommend a policy change to a supervisor

- Persuade your supervisor to provide funding for a project that you feel will benefit your company

Being persuasive requires that you know your audience and understand why they may resist your ideas. It also requires understanding persuasive techniques that will help you overcome resistance. The ACE process will help you achieve that understanding and choose effective persuasive strategies when communicating in typical business situations.

Persuasion The process of influencing your audience to agree with your point of view, recommendation, or request.

How can the ACE process help you persuade your audience?

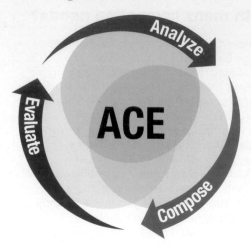

To be persuasive, a message must do more than just state your point of view: It must motivate your audience to agree with you and, ultimately, to take some kind of action. Using the ACE process will help you develop a message that accomplishes these goals.

For example, assume that you are Pedro Baca, a customer service manager for an ecommerce company that has an annual goal of increasing profits by improving customer service and cutting costs. To improve customer service, the company installed new computer software that tracks orders and allows employees to provide customers with immediate, accurate information. To cut costs, the company eliminated the training budget. Now you have a dilemma. Your employees received only a brief orientation and do not know how to use all the features of the new software. Customer complaints have increased, and you fear the company may alienate customers because of poor service. To solve this problem, you want to persuade your supervisor, Maria, to authorize money for training.

Your first thought is to write a quick email to Maria to request the funds. You sit down at the computer and write the message in **FIGURE 8.1**. This message simply asks for what you want. As you review this message, you wonder how Maria will react. Instead of sending the message, you rethink it using the ACE process.

Analyzing helps you plan your message

Analyze

In persuasive situations, you will increase your chances of getting a positive response by spending extra time on the analyzing phase of the ACE communication process. Recall that analyzing involves thinking strategically about your

- purpose, desired outcome, and business results,
- audiences' and stakeholders' needs,
- content needs, and
- medium choices.

EMAIL

| File | Message | Insert | Options | Format Text | Review |

To... Maria Cardoni <mcardoni@pilotproducts.com

Send Subject: Request for Funding

Maria:

I am requesting funding to support a computer training workshop to ensure my department's employees will be more productive and customer complaints will decrease. I will call your assistant to schedule an appointment to discuss this soon.

Thanks,
Pedro

Pedro Baca
Customer Service Manager
PILOT PRODUCTS, INC.
pbaca@pilotproducts.com

(519) 555-7764, Ext. 2110
(519) 555-3950, FAX

FIGURE 8.1 An Ineffective Request

Analyze your purpose, desired outcome, and business result

Before focusing on what you will say in your message, think about your goal. What is the *purpose* of the message (why are you communicating?) and what *outcome* would you like to achieve (how would you like your audience to respond)? If your audience agrees to your request or recommendation, what will the *business result* be? Understanding how your request will affect others and your business helps you anticipate audience response.

For example, your message to persuade Maria has the following purpose, outcome, and business result:

- The *purpose* is to request funding to support a training workshop.
- The *outcome* is that your audience (your supervisor) will provide the requested funds.
- The *business result* is that the employees will be more productive and provide improved customer service.

Analyze your audiences' and stakeholders' needs

After you have determined your purpose, desired outcome, and business result, consider how to persuade your audience. Because persuasion involves influencing your audience's thinking and behaviour, the more you know about your audience the more persuasive you can be. Audience analysis involves imagining yourself in your audience's position and interpreting your message from your audience's perspective.

Consider both the **primary audience**, the direct recipient of the message, as well as the **secondary audience**, other people who may read or hear your message. The secondary audience may receive a copy of your message either from you or from your primary audience. You may even want to consider stakeholders who may be affected by the message. In the computer training workshop example, your supervisor (Maria) is your primary audience. The secondary audience may include the vice-president of finance if Maria forwards your request to approve additional funds. Additional stakeholders include employees in the department and customers. Although employees and customers will not see your message, they will certainly be affected by the outcome.

To create a persuasive message for your audience, focus on information needs, motivation and benefits, and potential resistance.

- **Information needs: What does your audience know about the situation?** What do you need to tell your audience? Maria knows that budget cuts have eliminated all professional development activities throughout the organization. She also knows that the company is committed to improving customer service. However, she does not yet know that productivity and customer service have suffered in your department because employees have not been trained to use the new computer systems.

- **Motivation and benefits: What will motivate your audience to accept your idea or comply with your request? How will your audience benefit from your proposed idea?** Maria probably will be motivated to solve the problem once she is aware that it exists. She and the company will benefit from improved productivity and customer satisfaction, as long as it does not cost too much. The vice-president of finance may be motivated to solve the problem if he understands that his investment in the new computer system is not yielding the expected benefit and is, in fact, causing customer complaints to increase.

  When building a persuasive argument and defining benefits, you should understand that many business professionals are open to a discussion of **return on investment (ROI)**. Any effort you can make to reasonably calculate time savings or money savings as a result of an investment will be time well spent.

- **Potential resistance: What concerns and objections will the audience have?** Maria may have two concerns. She may argue that training is the wrong solution because employees received some training when the system was installed. She may also argue that the department simply cannot afford the training. She may be hesitant to bring a request for funds to the vice-president of finance because the company is committed to cutting costs.

Primary audience The person or people to whom your message is directly addressed.

Secondary audience People whom the primary audience may communicate with or influence, based on the content, format, or tone of your message. The secondary audience may receive a copy or hear about your message without you knowing.

Return on investment (ROI) the benefits to be experienced after investing a resource, such as time or money. It is most effectively expressed in terms of profitability, but can be expressed in terms of time saved or efficiencies gained.

Productivity and improved customer relations usually lead to increased revenues for most organizations.

Analyze content needs

Based on your audience analysis, you can determine what content you will need to provide.

- **Information.** You will need to inform Maria that a costly problem exists and that the problem is related to insufficient training. You may have to research the actual costs associated with this problem.
- **Motivation and benefits.** For Maria, the main benefits to emphasize are cost savings, improved productivity, and customer retention. For the vice-president of finance, you can emphasize an additional benefit: The training will increase the value of the investment already made in purchasing customer service software. The company will not see benefits from the software until the representatives are adequately trained. You may be able to do some research to calculate an approximate return on investment from the training.
- **Response to potential resistance.** Once you identify potential objections, you may either **refute** them or **concede** them. You refute points by arguing that they are wrong. Alternatively, you concede points by admitting that they have some merit but do not invalidate your argument. Whichever approach you use, be sure to state the opposing argument fairly and thoroughly and to let the audience know that you understand their concerns.

Because you anticipate Maria may object to your request for training funds, develop responses to her possible objections as part of your planning process. The more objections you anticipate and address, the more persuasive you will be. For example:

Possible objection: Employees already received sufficient training.

To Refute: "The training taught the employees only the minimum features necessary to operate the system. Employees do not know how to use several of the software functions necessary to deal effectively with customers' needs."

Possible objection: Training is costly, and one of our corporate goals is to cut costs.

To Concede: "Although training is costly, customer service problems caused by insufficient training will cost even more in lost revenue opportunities and a damaged company reputation."

Notice that these responses to potential objections are subtle. They do not explicitly say that the audience actually does object. Avoid stating your assumptions about audience objections prior to the audience stating their objections themselves. For example, avoid statements such as "You may believe that training is too costly. However, customer service problems caused by insufficient training will cost more." You will be more effective if you simply build your argument so that it accounts for potential objections. For example, "Although training can be costly, customer service problems caused by a lack of training can cost even more."

Analyze medium choices

Selecting the best medium for your persuasive message depends on many variables:

- The number of people in your audience and your ability to reach them all in a timely way
- The complexity of your content
- The amount of resistance you expect
- Your audience's communication preferences

If you need to persuade only one person, consider that person's communication preferences. For example, if you know your audience will be more open to discussing an issue in person, plan a face-to-face meeting or a phone call. However, if you think your audience would prefer to spend time considering a response to your message without being put "on the spot" in a face-to-face conversation, then communicate by email or

Refute A response intended to prove an objection is wrong.

Concede An admission that the opposing point of view has merit but does not invalidate your argument.

voice mail message instead. If you need to persuade many people, you may want to plan a meeting where you can make a persuasive presentation. Alternatively, you may want to email all the people involved. An email will also allow you to send a copy to a broader secondary audience of people who will be affected by your proposal or idea.

FIGURE 8.2 summarizes reasons why you might choose various medium options when you need to persuade an audience.

Because persuasion is a process that happens in stages, it often requires multiple communications that build to your persuasive goal. For example, if you know that Maria does not like surprise requests, you might consider sending an email message to mention your training idea and then scheduling an appointment to discuss the issue in more detail. The email must persuade Maria to meet with you, as a first step toward your ultimate objective of securing the funding for training.

Choose a medium option based on the criteria below that are important for your message:	One-to-One	Group Meeting	Telephone	Text/IM	Email	Memo	Letter	Newsletter	Website	Social Networking	Wikis, Blogs
Audience-Related Criteria											
Communicate a personal appeal to an individual	■		■	■	■		■				
Communicate with large audiences		■		■	■	■		■	■	■	■
Communicate with people already interested in your topic	■	■	■	■	■		■		■	■	■
Communicate with potential audiences you cannot yet identify									■	■	■
Content- and Response-Related Criteria											
Communicate a complex message	■	■	■		■	■	■	■	■		
Include additional documents or supporting material (images, charts, video, etc.) that may help persuade your audience	■	■			■	■	■	■	■	■	■
Receive immediate feedback so you can alter your appeal "on the fly" if necessary	■	■	■								■
Take time to think about any objections in the audience's reply, collect evidence if necessary, and compose a response				■	■	■	■				
Give the audience time to consider your appeal carefully before responding				■	■	■	■	■	■	■	■
Make it more uncomfortable for the audience to respond negatively (given the interpersonal interaction)	■	■	■								

FIGURE 8.2 Selecting the Best Medium for Persuasive Messages

Composing implements the persuasive plan

After you analyze your persuasive plan, the composing stage helps you put the plan into action and draft the message. As **FIGURE 8.3** illustrates, a well-planned message will be much more persuasive than a message composed without planning.

Evaluating helps you review the draft for effectiveness

Even when you have thoroughly analyzed all the elements that contribute to a message and carefully composed the content, take additional time to evaluate the message before delivering it. Ask yourself several questions to ensure you have implemented an

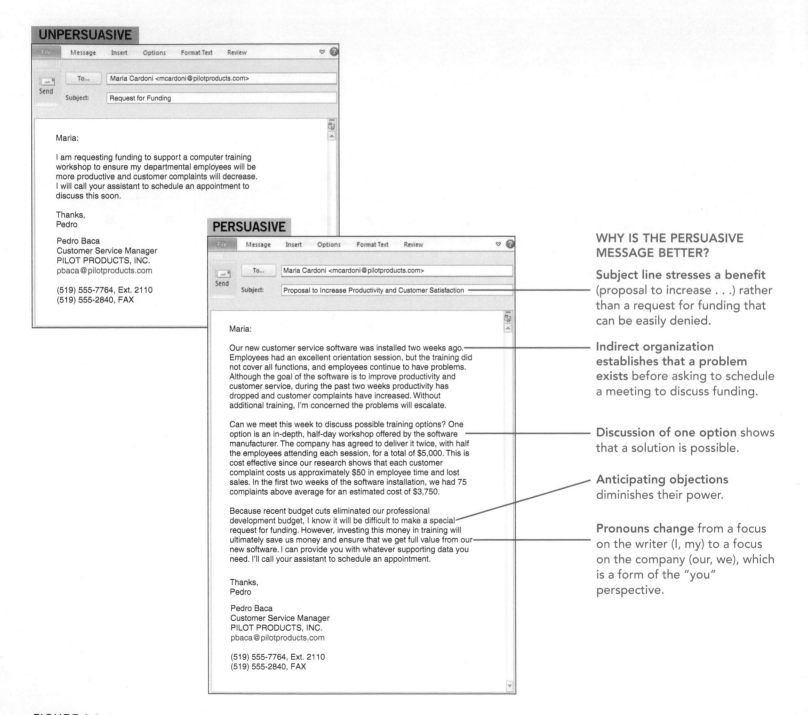

UNPERSUASIVE

File | Message | Insert | Options | Format Text | Review

To... Maria Cardoni <mcardoni@pilotproducts.com>

Subject: Request for Funding

Maria:

I am requesting funding to support a computer training workshop to ensure my departmental employees will be more productive and customer complaints will decrease. I will call your assistant to schedule an appointment to discuss this soon.

Thanks,
Pedro

Pedro Baca
Customer Service Manager
PILOT PRODUCTS, INC.
pbaca@pilotproducts.com

(519) 555-7764, Ext. 2110
(519) 555-2840, FAX

PERSUASIVE

File | Message | Insert | Options | Format Text | Review

To... Maria Cardoni <mcardoni@pilotproducts.com>

Subject: Proposal to Increase Productivity and Customer Satisfaction

Maria:

Our new customer service software was installed two weeks ago. Employees had an excellent orientation session, but the training did not cover all functions, and employees continue to have problems. Although the goal of the software is to improve productivity and customer service, during the past two weeks productivity has dropped and customer complaints have increased. Without additional training, I'm concerned the problems will escalate.

Can we meet this week to discuss possible training options? One option is an in-depth, half-day workshop offered by the software manufacturer. The company has agreed to deliver it twice, with half the employees attending each session, for a total of $5,000. This is cost effective since our research shows that each customer complaint costs us approximately $50 in employee time and lost sales. In the first two weeks of the software installation, we had 75 complaints above average for an estimated cost of $3,750.

Because recent budget cuts eliminated our professional development budget, I know it will be difficult to make a special request for funding. However, investing this money in training will ultimately save us money and ensure that we get full value from our new software. I can provide you with whatever supporting data you need. I'll call your assistant to schedule an appointment.

Thanks,
Pedro

Pedro Baca
Customer Service Manager
PILOT PRODUCTS, INC.
pbaca@pilotproducts.com

(519) 555-7764, Ext. 2110
(519) 555-2840, FAX

WHY IS THE PERSUASIVE MESSAGE BETTER?

Subject line stresses a benefit (proposal to increase . . .) rather than a request for funding that can be easily denied.

Indirect organization establishes that a problem exists before asking to schedule a meeting to discuss funding.

Discussion of one option shows that a solution is possible.

Anticipating objections diminishes their power.

Pronouns change from a focus on the writer (I, my) to a focus on the company (our, we), which is a form of the "you" perspective.

FIGURE 8.3 Composing an Effective Persuasive Message

effective persuasive strategy. Here is how you, as Pedro, might evaluate the persuasive message in Figure 8.3:

- **Have you convincingly shown that a problem or opportunity exists?** The email shows that productivity is dropping and customer complaints are rising. The email also shows that customer complaints are costly.

- **Is the proposed solution appropriate?** The email presents the training option as a realistic solution that is also cost effective.

- **Is the evidence and reasoning sound?** You provide documented evidence that each complaint costs $50. You provide sound reasoning that the cost of training is less than the cost of the problem.

- **Have you addressed all of the objections that you can anticipate?** The email addresses Maria's potential objections: initial training should have been sufficient, the company has no money, and it's difficult to secure special funding.

- **Have you stressed benefits?** Most of the benefits are implied. If you solve the problems, you likely will increase productivity, reduce complaints, and retain more customers. The last paragraph of the message addresses one additional benefit: getting full value from the customer service software.

- **Is the message easy to read?** The order of the content is logical (problem, request for meeting to discuss possible solutions, next steps), and the email uses effective paragraphing techniques.

- **Is the information complete, concise, clear, and correct?** The message includes all the necessary information and nothing else. The wording is clear, and the language and content are correct.

- **Is the message structured to be well received by your audience?** Evaluate the message from Maria's perspective. Will she believe a problem exists? Will she believe your solution is reasonable? Will she believe she will benefit from meeting with you? If so, then the message is ready to send. If not, then revise the message to accomplish your purpose.

Although Pedro's final email to Maria is much longer than his original draft, the revised message takes advantage of the ACE process and has a greater chance of helping Pedro gain funding because its content and structure are persuasive.

(LO 8.2) What are the basic elements of persuasion?

To develop the most persuasive content for your communication, you will need to understand the basics of persuasion. What kind of content will motivate your audience to trust you, believe your points, agree with your position, and do what you request? You learned about three elements of persuasion in the first section of this chapter, when Pedro prepared his email to Maria. His persuasive strategy included the following:

- Establishing a problem or need
- Focusing on benefits
- Anticipating potential resistance and objections

This section addresses three additional elements that have been recognized as important since Aristotle identified them as the core of effective persuasion (Aristotle & Kennedy, 2006; Dlugan, 2010):

- Building credibility *(ethos)*
- Constructing a logical argument *(logos)*
- Appealing to emotion *(pathos)*

Most persuasive business arguments combine all these elements, but you may decide to emphasize one element more than another (Cialdini, 2001; Conger, 1998; Kendrick, Goldstein, & Braver, 2012).

Building credibility

When trying to persuade an audience, you will be more effective if you have **credibility**, that is, if your audience believes you have expertise and are trustworthy based on your knowledge, character, reputation, and behaviour (Stiff & Mongeau, 2002, p. 107). You may already have credibility with your audience if they know and respect you or if you are an acknowledged expert (Conger, 1998; Wallace, 2009). In these cases, you will not need to focus on building credibility in your message. However, if you do not already have credibility with your audience, you will need to establish it to be persuasive. Use one or more of the following techniques:

- **Spend time getting to know your audience.** Have you ever noticed how skilled salespeople often spend a few minutes chatting with potential customers before trying to make a sale (Cialdini, 2009)? Talking with your audience before trying to persuade them helps you understand their concerns and allows you to build rapport and trust. It is easier to persuade an audience who likes you than one who does not know you.

In an increasingly diverse business world, "knowing your audience" can present many challenges. Check out the **CULTURE BOX** for a look at this challenge in a marketing capacity.

    Introduce yourself effectively. You can build credibility with your audience by mentioning key credentials, including education, experience, and expertise. You can also mention your relationship with someone the audience knows, respects, and believes to be credible. This *affinity*, or connection with a credible source, will help convince the audience that you are trustworthy.

    Present your ideas effectively. The quality of your communication also builds credibility. Audiences are more likely to believe you if you present an unbiased point of view, organize your ideas logically, and support those ideas with solid research and sound reasoning. Even if you are not an expert yourself, you can add weight to your ideas by citing authorities and experts.

Credibility is critical for capturing an audience's attention and persuading them to listen. However, although credibility is important, it has two important limitations as a persuasive technique:

- **Credibility is hard to earn and easy to lose.** A person with a reputation for honesty can quickly lose credibility by making false statements, failing to be accountable for mistakes, or making promises that are not fulfilled. For example, in 2013 Ed Burkhardt, president of Rail World, chose to blame others for a tragic rail accident in Lac-Mégantic, Quebec, that left 47 people dead and destroyed 30 buildings in the centre of the town. He lost almost all his credibility when he first blamed local volunteer firefighters and then suggested that a locomotive engineer did not set the brakes properly. John Baldoni of *Forbes* magazine stated that "Burkhardt . . . has proven one thing—that he is clueless as well as careless, not to mention disrespectful, in handling a crisis of this magnitude. . . . Such behavior shows callous disregard for the citizens whose town and livelihoods were destroyed in an oil-tanker fuel firestorm." Baldoni goes on to say that "When Burkhardt assigns blame without the facts, he looks callous as well as out of touch. He seems more interested in protecting his own skin than even the fate of his enterprise" (Baldoni, 2013). A few thoughtless, unplanned remarks on the part of this company president have caused so much public relations damage that he and his company may find it difficult to recover.

- **Credibility alone often is not strong enough** to change the mind of someone who is deeply interested in an issue, including people committed to an opposing point of view (Stiff & Mongeau, 2002). For example, Steve Jobs, the former CEO of Apple, had a great deal of credibility as a technology innovator and a producer of award-winning products. However, that credibility, even coupled with the quality and credibility of Apple products, has persuaded only 10.6% of computer buyers to purchase Apple computers (Gartner Newsroom, 2012). Credibility cannot overcome the resistance caused by higher costs and entrenched corporate commitment to Microsoft operating systems.

Credibility An audience's belief that you have expertise and are trustworthy based on your knowledge, character, reputation, and behaviour.

CULTURE
ADAPTING PERSUASIVE APPEALS

Of the five big marketing firms, Couture Ads has a reputation among its clients for having a sophisticated yet personable business approach. This reputation has contributed to the success of the firm in gaining the trust of international clients. Over the year of her internship, Skylar's position has expanded to include more communication with established clients, new clients, and potential clients. Skylar has become well known to Javier, a marketing director at the Spanish clothing producer Morena. Morena is interested in becoming a client of Couture Ads for assistance in marketing their clothing lines in the Canadian market.

The request: Javier mentioned in an email to Skylar that images used to promote their clothing must use "Spanish-looking" models with darker features and skin tone. This choice would be an effort to keep true to the name Morena which, in Spanish, means "beautiful dark-skinned girl."

The challenge: Skylar understands that the Canadian consumer market for this clothing is more diverse than the Spanish market and may need a different, more inclusive, approach. However, she notes that the key need for Javier is a connection to Spanish identity and culture. Therefore, perhaps if the line were promoted with authentic Spanish flare and attention to cultural detail, in conjunction with other lines from Morena, it could be a successful marketing launch. Skylar *must persuade* Javier to change his thinking about Morena's marketing strategy.

This is where O-A-R can assist:

- **Observe:** Observe interactions between other colleagues and clients from diverse cultural and ethnic backgrounds. What are some of the common and successful practices when a question of culture arises? Skylar respects her supervisor, Michaela, and needs to consider how she would handle this situation with sensitivity and clarity.
- **Ask:** Ask a mentor or experienced colleague about successful and respectful strategies that can be used to persuade and discuss cultural issues in marketing with international clients. If there is an established rapport between Skylar and Javier, it may be acceptable for

Skylar to ask Javier how he would feel about such a major alteration to his approach to the Canadian market. Before proceeding, Skylar should ask Michaela if this is the right approach.
- **Research:** In addition to researching what the approaches are to persuading clients, Skylar can also research specifics on acceptable negotiation strategies in Spanish business culture. Googling "Business negotiations in Spain" can bring up the latest in governmental and consultancy documents on this topic, such as this example: Meeting Etiquette in Spain (http://business-culture.org/southern-europe/business-culture-in-spain/meeting-etiquette-in-spain). This page has a section on negotiations, which suggests that more time is taken with these business activities and that the hierarchical nature of business structures suggests that the most senior managers make major decisions. Therefore, Skylar should expect to approach negotiating Morena's Canadian campaign gradually, over several meetings, and should expect Javier to present a proposal to a more senior manager within his company for final approval. Doing a little preliminary research of this nature can be invaluable in learning what kind of persuasive approaches are likely to be well received.

ANOTHER IMPORTANT FACTOR TO CONSIDER

Aim for Objectivity and Clarity. Choosing persuasive yet culturally sensitive language is not always obvious or easy. Be mindful not to be evasive, elusive, or confusing. Being clear and factual is rarely a mistake. For example, instead of expressing her concerns as an *opinion* about the Canadian market, Skylar could present the most recent *research* on Morena's target market and allow Javier to make his own assessments without her direct influence. Or Skylar may also want to take a consumer poll to bring findings that inform her or the client of the potential response and interest in such a clothing line.

Check out the CULTURE exercises in Critical Thinking questions 6 and 7 on page 252 and Exercise 12 on page 254.

Credibility may convince your audience to trust you, but successfully persuading an audience requires additional persuasive techniques, including a logical argument.

Constructing a logical argument

Logical arguments provide the foundation for most persuasive business messages. This means taking a position, supporting the position with reasons, and supporting those reasons with verifiable evidence.

Earlier in this chapter you considered how Pedro could persuade his supervisor, Maria, to support his request for funds to provide computer training to the customer

FIGURE 8.4 Structure of a Logical Argument

service department. Pedro emailed Maria a short version of his argument (see Figure 8.3 on page 228) to persuade her to meet with him. Assume that Maria responded to Pedro with the following email:

Pedro, your recommendation makes sense, and your timing is good. I am scheduled to meet with the vice-president of finance tomorrow morning and would like to present your recommendation so that we can schedule the training as soon as possible. Please write a one-page document outlining the reasons and evidence that I can bring to the meeting. Thanks, Maria.

FIGURE 8.4 offers one way to structure that argument logically by defining the position, identifying reasons, and outlining evidence.

In a logical argument like the one represented in Figure 8.4, the quality of your evidence is important. You can collect evidence by conducting your own original research (*primary research*) or by reading research that others have conducted (*secondary research*). Your evidence may take different forms, depending on the argument you are trying to support and the needs of your audience. Consider the types of evidence that Pedro can use to support his argument:

- **Numerical data.** Many business arguments are based on numbers. Some arguments require data about costs, time, or revenue and are typically expressed in terms of a return on investment. Other arguments require data about customer preferences or business trends. You may find some of the numbers you need in published sources. Others will come from company records or from surveys and questionnaires. You can present the data in tables, graphs, or paragraphs. Pedro's current argument requesting funds to support a computer training workshop relies primarily on numerical data about the number of customer complaints, the number of customers served, and the cost of customer complaints.

- **Facts.** A fact is documented information that someone can verify. If the fact is not already well known to the audience, you should cite the source. For example:

  Inc. *magazine cites research showing that getting new customers costs 5 to 10 times as much as keeping an existing one. In addition, repeat customers spend 67 percent more than new ones. (Fenn, 2010)*

- **Expert authority.** For additional support, you may cite the opinions of people with acknowledged expertise. For example:

  According to sales expert Jonathan Farrington, "the cost of an unhappy customer is much greater than the cost of any individual lost sale." It also includes the loss of that person's future business and the potential lost sales from people who have talked to the unhappy customer. (Farrington, 2008)

- **Personal experience.** Your experiences and observations may provide compelling support for a claim, although they are rarely conclusive on their own. For example:

  This software is too difficult to learn without training. I've spent 10 hours trying to learn all its functions, and I still can't figure out how to issue a refund.

- **Examples.** Although examples are not conclusive evidence, they can clarify your point and help your audience understand. For example:

  Customer complaints have increased 50%. We have received complaints about dropped calls, orders being lost, and refunds not being credited.

Pedro uses most of this evidence in his message for Maria and the vice-president of finance. The memo, illustrated in **FIGURE 8.5**, follows the logical structure outlined in

FIGURE 8.5 Logical Argument for Computer Training

MEMO

TO: Maria Cardoni
FROM: Pedro Baca
DATE: June 11, 20XX
SUBJECT: Proposed Solution for Costly Customer Service Problems

Subject line focuses on solving a cost problem, which will interest the audience.

Problem

Two weeks ago, the customer service department installed new software designed to improve productivity and customer service. Employees received the standard three-hour orientation that comes with the software package. However, the training did not cover the customized functions necessary to process returns, exchanges, and refunds.

In the two weeks that employees have been using the software, we have logged 75 complaints more than average. Customers have complained about dropped calls, exchanged orders being lost, and refunds not being credited. In addition, because representatives are addressing so many time-consuming complaints, they are handling fewer calls, and their productivity has decreased by 15 percent. Although we cannot prove that lack of training on the new software caused the customer service problems, the coincidence is too great to be ignored.

The first two paragraphs document the problem and anticipate the objection that employees have received sufficient training.

These problems are costly to our company. Last year we researched the cost of customer complaints and determined that each complaint costs us approximately $50 in employee time and lost sales. This means that in the past two weeks, handling the 75 additional complaints has cost us $3,750. If these problems continue, costs will conservatively exceed $10,000 in two months.

We also need to consider the long-term costs of unhappy customers. According to sales expert Jonathan Farrington, "the cost of an unhappy customer is much greater than the cost of any individual lost sale."* It includes the loss of that person's future business and the potential lost sales from people who have talked to the unhappy customer.

The next two paragraphs document the immediate and long-term costs of the problem. Pedro cites both research conducted by the department and a sales authority.

Proposed Solution

I have discussed this problem with the software developer, Mark Richey from Viking Systems, and he has agreed to provide an additional three-hour training session for all employees addressing the important customized functions in our system. To ensure that all employees are trained, he has also agreed to deliver the session twice, with half of the representatives attending each session.

The first paragraph of this section provides the details of the solution.

The cost for this customized training will be $5,000, the exact amount it would have cost us to add the training to our original purchase. Although the amount may seem expensive, it is actually cost effective, considering the losses we project if the customer service problems persist. I do not believe employees will be able to master the system without training. I've spent 10 hours trying to learn all the functions of the new system on my own, and I still cannot figure out how to issue a refund.

The second paragraph presents the cost and anticipates several objections: Viking Systems is charging too much, the training will not be cost effective, and employees can learn on their own.

Mark is prepared to deliver the session next week if we can approve the funding. The more quickly we provide the training, the more quickly we can realize the customer service benefits from the company's investment in the new system.

The final paragraph reminds the audience of the main benefit of funding training—it is the only way the department will receive the intended results from the new system.

* Farrington, J. (2008). Customer complaints: The income multiplier effect. CRM-Daily.com. Retrieved from www.crm-daily.com

Figure 8.4. It also anticipates objections and stresses benefits. Pedro's logical writing style and thorough analysis will give him a solid credibility with his audience.

Avoiding Logical Fallacies

When constructing an argument, you may be tempted to strengthen a weak position by overstating your case, diverting attention away from problems with your position, or even attacking an opponent. These violations of logical reasoning that lead to a flawed argument are called **fallacies**, and intentionally using them is dishonest, misleading, and unethical.

FIGURE 8.6 describes some logical fallacies that Pedro might have used to enhance his argument to Maria and the vice-president of finance. Fortunately, he did not. As you read each, identify what is misleading about the statements. Avoid using any of these fallacies in your own communications, and recognize fallacies when others use them so that you are not persuaded by unsound ideas.

The habitual use of misleading fallacies will not only make you an ineffective communicator whom, over time, no one will trust, it will also make you an unethical communicator. Check out the **ETHICS BOX** for further ideas on how to avoid ethical pitfalls while constructing your persuasive messages.

Appealing to your audience's emotions

Fallacy A violation of logical reasoning that leads to a flawed argument.

Although logic is critical for business decisions, logic alone may not always be enough to persuade an audience. You may also need to appeal to their emotions (Conger, 1998).

TYPE OF FALLACY	DESCRIPTION	EXAMPLE FALLACY FROM PEDRO TO MARIA
Appeal to Popular Opinion	Offering as evidence statements such as "everybody knows"	Everybody knows that without training new computer systems lead to productivity losses. It's obvious.
Hasty Generalization	Drawing a conclusion from a sample that is either too small or does not represent the larger population	Two of our most experienced sales reps say that they are having difficulty with the computer system. If they are having trouble, it's likely everyone is.
Ignoring the Burden of Proof	Stating a claim but providing no evidence to support it	Providing computer training will immediately reverse our losses.
False Cause	Assuming there is a cause and effect relationship between two things without proving the relationship	As soon as we got new computers, customer complaints increased. The new system is clearly the cause.
False Analogy	Supporting an idea by comparing it to something that is not comparable	We require everyone to receive sufficient instruction before operating a car. Similarly, we should require all customer service reps to get sufficient training before operating the new computer system.
False Dilemma	Asserting that only two choices exist while ignoring other options	Either we provide more training or we will continue to see losses in productivity.
Red Herring	Focusing on an irrelevant issue to draw attention away from a central issue	If management wants to cut budgets, then it would be much better to eliminate executive bonuses. The company spends millions on bonuses, and what benefit do we see from that?
Ad Hominem Attack	Attacking a person who disagrees with you rather than addressing the issues	The managers who instituted the budget cuts are just a bunch of corporate pencil pushers who don't have any idea what employees really need to do their jobs well.

FIGURE 8.6   Samples of Misleading Fallacies

ETHICS
IS BEING PERSUASIVE LIKE BEING DISHONEST?

The purpose of a persuasive message is to influence your audience to agree with your point of view. The purpose is NOT to get others to make decisions that would cause themselves or others harm. Some individuals do not examine their own motivations prior to engaging in persuasive communication. Therefore, there are many people who have become naturally suspicious of persuasion. This reality makes the process of ethical persuasion even more challenging. It is crucial to be more than just convincing. You must differentiate yourself as a credible communicator.

Here are three inappropriate shortcuts that people often take in an effort to be persuasive. These unethical choices may work in the short run but will cause long-term damage to a communicator's reputation and effectiveness. Here are some examples and some suggestions for better choices.

Unethical Shortcut	Long-Term Outcome	Better Choice	Result
Presenting an opinion and suggesting it is a fact	The receiver may decline to do future business with you upon realizing that you confuse opinion with fact.	When stating an opinion, be clear that it is an opinion. Feel free to justify your opinion with fact.	The receiver will appreciate your clarity and begin to build trust.
Fabricating and presenting false data or research	The receiver may decline to do future business with you upon learning of your deception.	Take the time to find accurate data that reflects a true picture of a situation.	The receiver may or may not be persuaded in each specific instance, but will develop an overall relationship of trust.
Omitting information crucial to a decision	The receiver may decline to do future business with you upon learning that he or she did not have all the information needed.	Be sure to provide all the information you have that the receiver needs.	The receiver may or may not be persuaded in each specific instance, but will develop an overall relationship of trust in your ability to provide complete and accurate information.

Consider Skylar and her challenge in persuading Javier to change his marketing approach to bring his company's new clothing line to Canada. (See the Culture box on page 231.)

Unethical Shortcut	Better Choice	Result
Skylar states that it is obvious that the Canadian market is different and that Javier needs to rethink his choice of images.	Skylar states that it is her opinion that the Canadian market needs a different approach. She follows this up with fresh market data.	Javier appreciates Skylar's attention to detail and remains open to being persuaded.
Skylar creates false market data, including pie charts and other graphics, which support her opinion 100%. She fails to offer her sources for this data.	Skylar forwards independent, validated market research for Javier's consideration.	Javier appreciates Skylar's thoroughness and remains open to being persuaded.
Skylar "forgets" to mention that the data suggest that at least two target market segments would be receptive to Javier's approach.	Skylar points out that two market segments would be receptive to Javier's approach. She balances this by pointing out that six profitable segments would be less receptive.	Javier respects Skylar's comprehensive analysis of his proposal and continues the negotiation.

Allowing the receiver to remain open to your ideas is a fundamental aspect of ethical persuasion. Sometimes using the right phrases to direct the conversation is all it takes. Here are some examples that you can borrow from Skylar:

- *You may wish to consider* this recent market research report on your target market segments.
- *To be diligent, could we discuss an alternative approach* for our unique Canadian market?

- *This recently published research shows us that* certain segments will be more successful and profitable than others.
- *It is in your best interests to have a full picture of the current situation. Therefore, please accept the attached market research report,* published just last week by the Independent Market Research Association, which gives you a full assessment of the current market.

For an ETHICS Exercise, go to Exercise 13 on page 254.

Psychologists and other researchers have identified several techniques for engaging your audience on an emotional level.

Appeal to your audience's emotional and psychological needs

You may wonder how you can address your audience's psychological needs, especially when communicating with an audience you do not know. However, psychologist Abraham Maslow argued that all people, even people of different cultures and different generations, share a common set of needs (Cialdini, 2009). At the basic level are physiological needs for food, clothing, and shelter. Once those needs are met, people will seek to meet increasingly higher levels of need. Advertisers routinely appeal to these needs as part of their persuasive strategy:

- **Safety.** Home security companies appeal to the audience's desire for safety. Banks and investment companies appeal to the audience's desire for financial security.

- **Love and belonging.** Cosmetics and beauty companies appeal to the audience's desire to be attractive and admired. Manufacturers of convenience foods appeal to the audience's desire for dinners that bring the family closer, even when you have no time to cook.

- **Self-esteem.** Charities often appeal to the increase in audience self-esteem that will result from the good works enabled by a donation: "Your donation of a dollar a day will prevent a child from starving." Educational institutions focus on the respect you earn and the self-respect you feel from completing your education.

- **Self-actualization.** The US Army's long-lived advertising slogan "Be all that you can be" appealed to people's desire to make the most of their abilities. Advertisements for luxury travel experiences often appeal to travellers who want to "find themselves" in exotic places.

You can use these types of appeals in your business communication. For example, assume you want to persuade someone to donate to a charity. You can appeal to your audience's self-esteem by praising them for past actions, focusing on how they will make a difference in the world, showing them that their actions are greatly needed, or even complimenting them for their character. **FIGURE 8.7** illustrates a fundraising message that uses all these emotional appeals to persuade a donor who has supported a charitable organization in the past.

In addition to appealing to self-esteem , the letter in Figure 8.7 uses additional persuasive techniques based on psychological principles that have been studied extensively by Robert Cialdini and have proven effective in engaging people's emotions (Cialdini, 2009). These principles are summarized in **FIGURE 8.8**.

Show your own emotional commitment

If you want your audience to commit to an idea, they need to know that you are committed to it also. In other words, you will be more persuasive if you speak, and write, from the heart (Gordon, 2006). One reason that Rio de Janeiro won the bid for the 2016 Summer Olympics may have been that Brazilian President Luiz Inácio Lula da Silva demonstrated extraordinary emotional commitment to hosting the Olympics. Not only did he spend two years personally lobbying the Olympic committee and other heads of state, he also spent the week before the final vote in Copenhagen visiting with members of the International Olympic Committee to make his case. The day before the vote, he gave a heartfelt speech explaining what it would mean to South America to host the Olympic Games for the first time in the competition's history. He described how athletes throughout South America would be affected by being part of this experience. He noted that the world would take notice if the International Olympic Committee awarded this honour to a continent that it had previously ignored. After the speech, Lula said, "It was extraordinary the emotion we put into our presentation . . . I almost cried two times during my speech" (*Telegraph* staff, 2009). One delegate of the International Olympic Committee commented, "I told the president

LETTER

2025 Chatham Drive • Calgary, AB T1X 1E1 • P: 403.555.1477 • F: 403.555.1478

November 18, 20XX

Ms. Julie Benjamin
106 W. Third Avenue
Calgary, AB
T1Y 1N3

Dear Ms. Benjamin:

Thank you for your past support of The Greenwald Centre. Your generosity has helped create opportunities and successes for people in our community who live with disabilities. As you make your year-ending giving decisions, please consider renewing your support with a gift of $100.

Each year at The Greenwald Centre, 5,000 people with disabilities strive to increase their independence step by step—finding accessible housing or steady employment, learning to read or cook, or managing household finances. The Greenwald Centre supports these efforts one person at a time, helping people achieve their individual goals. As our four-star rating from Charity Navigator indicates, every dollar that you contribute goes directly toward helping people.

Here are some of the successes your contribution supported this past year:

- 350 people found jobs, ranging from car porter to sales representative
- 93 people learned to read bus signs, make medical appointments, and conduct personal banking on their own
- 100 percent of families surveyed have learned ways to assist their children's development at home

In an era of shrinking government support, we increasingly rely on sustainable funding from friends like you, extraordinary people who see ability in everyone. Your gift can help train a literacy volunteer, facilitate a "mock" interview session, hire a guest cooking instructor or, in other ways, support the success of people living with disabilities.

Please use the enclosed self-addressed stamped envelope to return your pledge today or contribute on our website at www.greenwaldcentre.ca

Thank you for generously continuing to support The Greenwald Centre.

Sincerely,

Allan I. Bergman

Allan I. Bergman
President/CEO

P.S. As a token of our appreciation, we have enclosed a DVD, *Introduction to The Greenwald Centre,* so that you can see the good work you are supporting. We also have a limited number of tickets available for a December 15 holiday concert at City Orchestra. The tickets sell for $75 each, but we will give them free of charge to donors who request them, on a first-come, first-served basis.

HOW DOES THIS LETTER APPEAL TO SELF-ESTEEM?

Praises past action.

Provides quantitative data to illustrate that the donor's support makes a difference.

Shows that the support is greatly needed.

Compliments donors as exceptional people.

Concludes by assuming that this good person will, of course, continue to exhibit the same generosity.

FIGURE 8.7 Persuasive Fundraising Message Using Emotional Appeals

FIGURE 8.8 Techniques for Appealing to Emotion

PRINCIPLE	HOW IT IS USED IN FIGURE 8.7
Consistency People like to act consistently and make decisions that are similar to ones they have made in the past. Remind your audience they have made similar decisions in the past.	*Thank you for your past support of The Greenwald Centre. Your generosity has helped create opportunities and successes for people in our community who live with disabilities.*
Social Proof People follow the lead of others they respect. Include names and testimonials.	*As our four-star rating from Charity Navigator indicates, every dollar that you contribute goes directly toward helping people.*
Liking People respond more positively to those whom they like and who like them. Show that you appreciate your audience.	*In an era of shrinking government support, we increasingly rely on sustainable funding from friends like you, extraordinary people who see ability in everyone.*
Reciprocity People want to reciprocate if they receive a gift. The gift can be as small as a compliment or a recommendation of a book to read.	*P.S. As a token of our appreciation, we have enclosed a DVD, Introduction to The Greenwald Centre, so that you can see the good work you are supporting.*
Scarcity People want things more if those things are scarce. Highlight the exclusivity of your offer.	*We also have a limited number of tickets available for a December 15 holiday concert at City Orchestra. The tickets sell for $75 each, but we will give them free of charge to donors who request them, on a first-come, first-served basis.*

Source: Based on Cialdini, R. (2009). *Influence: Science and practice* (5th ed.). Upper Saddle River, NJ: Pearson Education.

(Lula), whom I know very well for a long time, that his speech went under my skin" (Grohmann, 2009).

Use compelling evidence and powerful language

Evidence is typically the "logic" part of an argument. However, compelling evidence is presented in clear and vivid language that can also touch an audience emotionally and motivate them to act (Conger, 1998). For example, the late Princess Diana spoke at a seminar sponsored by the Landmines Survivors Network and the Mines Advisory Board in London. Her goals were to highlight the issue of landmines and increase international efforts to remove landmines from those countries where mines continued to harm people long after a conflict had ended. In this speech, Princess Diana explicitly chose not to describe the injuries of children who are victims of these mines. Instead, she focused on alarming facts, such as a death roll of 800 people every month, including women and children. Princess Diana then noted that another 1,200 victims a month are handicapped for life. (Diana, Princess of Wales, 1997)

Powerful facts are powerful persuaders. A week after Diana gave this speech, British Prime Minister Tony Blair led the British government to reverse its former position against banning landmines. Six months later, 125 countries signed an international agreement to ban landmines. Although Diana's speech was not the sole cause of these changes, it played a role in changing hearts and minds.

What types of business messages require persuasion?

Chapter 11 and Appendix A cover other examples of communication that requires persuasion, such as proposals, cover letters, résumés, and interviews.

Persuasion is a required skill when:

- making recommendations for action
- preparing sales messages
- managing indirect persuasion through social media
- motivating others in a team or workplace situation

This section provides insight into each of these applications of persuasion.

Recommendations for action

When you make a **recommendation**, you need to:

1. establish that a problem or a need exists, and
2. show how your solution is effective.

The content of your recommendation can include a range of persuasive elements, such as the following:

- Focusing on benefits
- Anticipating objections
- Building credibility
- Constructing a logical argument
- Appealing to the audience's emotion

One challenge is to determine the order for this content. Should your recommendation be a **direct message**, starting with a description of your recommendation as the main point? Or should it be an **indirect message**, building up to the main point? **FIGURE 8.9** shows an outline for both direct and indirect recommendations. The left column provides specific criteria to help you determine which organization you should choose. For example, if the audience has requested your recommendation, be direct.

Recommendation A business message that suggests a solution to a business problem.

Direct message A message structure that states the main point first before providing additional details, such as the background or rationale for a recommendation.

Indirect message A message structure that builds up a case for a main point, providing details, background, and rationale, before stating the main point of the message.

Use **DIRECT ORGANIZATION** if . . .	**DIRECT ORGANIZATION** follows this pattern . . .
your audience • requests the recommendation, • prefers directness, or • is likely to react positively, **and the recommendation will not** • negatively affect stakeholders or • require additional effort from stakeholders.	**BEGIN WITH MAIN POINT** Propose a specific recommendation. **PROVIDE CONTEXT** • Identify the issue, problem, or opportunity. • Provide evidence that the problem or opportunity is significant. **SUPPORT YOUR PROPOSAL** For example: • Justify recommendations with persuasive rationale. • Describe alternative solutions and negative implications. • Address potential objections. • Stress benefits. **MOTIVATE ACTION** Conclude with a call to action.

Use **INDIRECT ORGANIZATION** if . . .	**INDIRECT ORGANIZATION** follows this pattern . . .
your audience • is not expecting the recommendation, • prefers indirectness, or • is likely to react negatively, **and the recommendation will** • negatively affect stakeholders, or • require additional effort from stakeholders.	**BEGIN WITH CONTEXT** • Identify the issue, problem, or opportunity. • Provide evidence that the problem or opportunity is significant. **OPTIONAL: ELIMINATE OTHER ALTERNATIVES** • Describe alternative solutions and negative implications. **STATE MAIN POINT** • Propose a specific recommendation. **SUPPORT YOUR PROPOSAL** For example: • Justify recommendations with persuasive rationale. • Address potential objections. • Stress benefits. **MOTIVATE ACTION** Conclude with a call to action.

FIGURE 8.9 Two Ways to Organize Recommendation Messages

However, if your recommendation will come as a surprise, you may want to organize it indirectly.

As an example, assume you manage a 20-person technology support department in a company of 500 employees. Your staff supports every department in the company, from the proprietary accounting software for payroll to the janitorial staff's online form to order supplies. Currently you assign technicians as problems arise. The next technician in the rotation handles the next problem, no matter which department requests support. However, staff members have developed specialized skills by working repeatedly with specific software applications. Therefore, you believe the company would benefit from decentralizing technical support and assigning technicians to specific units. This would shift the supervisory lines from your technical support department to the various departments throughout the company. You mention the plan to your staff. They like it because it would provide them with more specialized experience and streamline their duties.

You decide to prepare a persuasive recommendation for the vice-president (VP) of operations. Although the primary audience is the VP, you decide to copy your message to all the department heads (the secondary audience) because your proposed change would affect them.

In this situation, would it be better to organize the content directly or indirectly? Consider two scenarios:

- Assume that your audience did not request the information. However, you predict they will not be surprised by your recommendation. You think the primary audience, the VP of operations, prefers direct messages. You also think he will react positively to your recommendation because he personally requests the same tech support person when he needs assistance. Because other department heads have complained about slow response times when requesting technical support, you think the secondary audience will not need significant persuading either. You believe all stakeholders will benefit from the change even though it will require a significant effort to reorganize the department. Therefore, you draft the direct message in **FIGURE 8.10.**

- Now assume a different scenario. The VP of operations is newly appointed to the position. He has been on the job only a few weeks and he may be very surprised at a recommendation to reorganize your department. Because he is new, you cannot be sure whether he prefers directness or if he will react positively. Although the recommendation will not negatively affect stakeholders, the change will require significant effort to reassign supervisory roles. In fact, you predict several of the department heads may not appreciate having to manage and house your technical staff in their departments. Under these circumstances, you would draft a message like the indirect recommendation in Figure 8.10. The last two paragraphs of the messages are identical. Notice three main differences in the indirect version: the wording of the subject line, the position of the recommendation, and the extra background information.

You may be called upon to present your recommendation using presentation software. Depending on how the presentation is to be used, the resulting document will need to follow some specific guidelines to be effective. Check out the **TECHNOLOGY BOX** to become familiar with some best practices for using presentation software to construct a recommendation.

Sales messages

Persuasion is also an important element in most sales messages, where your goal is to motivate someone to buy a product or service. Sales and marketing people often use the acronym **AIDA**, which stands for **A**ttention, **I**nterest, **D**esire, and **A**ction, to create persuasive sales messages. **FIGURE 8.11** (on page 244) summarizes the four AIDA components.

AIDA relies on the basic components of persuasion that you learned in the second section of this chapter: build credibility, construct logical arguments, and appeal to emotion.

AIDA An acronym used in marketing to suggest the organization of sales communication: Attention, Interest, Desire, Action.

FIGURE 8.10 Persuasive Recommendation (Email Message)

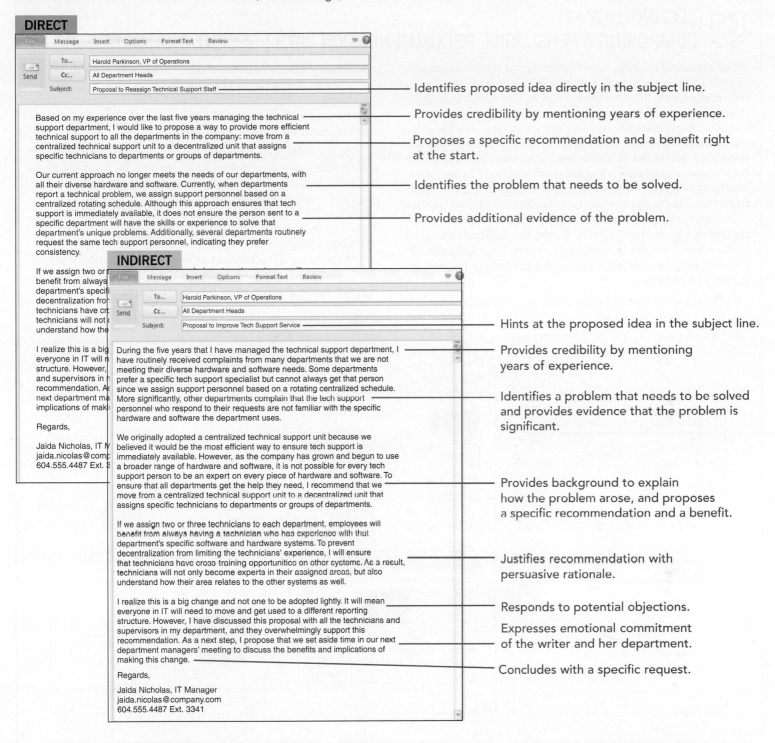

DIRECT

To... Harold Parkinson, VP of Operations
Cc... All Department Heads
Subject: Proposal to Reassign Technical Support Staff

Based on my experience over the last five years managing the technical support department, I would like to propose a way to provide more efficient technical support to all the departments in the company: move from a centralized technical support unit to a decentralized unit that assigns specific technicians to departments or groups of departments.

Our current approach no longer meets the needs of our departments, with all their diverse hardware and software. Currently, when departments report a technical problem, we assign support personnel based on a centralized rotating schedule. Although this approach ensures that tech support is immediately available, it does not ensure the person sent to a specific department will have the skills or experience to solve that department's unique problems. Additionally, several departments routinely request the same tech support personnel, indicating they prefer consistency.

- Identifies proposed idea directly in the subject line.
- Provides credibility by mentioning years of experience.
- Proposes a specific recommendation and a benefit right at the start.
- Identifies the problem that needs to be solved.
- Provides additional evidence of the problem.

INDIRECT

To... Harold Parkinson, VP of Operations
Cc... All Department Heads
Subject: Proposal to Improve Tech Support Service

During the five years that I have managed the technical support department, I have routinely received complaints from many departments that we are not meeting their diverse hardware and software needs. Some departments prefer a specific tech support specialist but cannot always get that person since we assign support personnel based on a rotating centralized schedule. More significantly, other departments complain that the tech support personnel who respond to their requests are not familiar with the specific hardware and software the department uses.

We originally adopted a centralized technical support unit because we believed it would be the most efficient way to ensure tech support is immediately available. However, as the company has grown and begun to use a broader range of hardware and software, it is not possible for every tech support person to be an expert on every piece of hardware and software. To ensure that all departments get the help they need, I recommend that we move from a centralized technical support unit to a decentralized unit that assigns specific technicians to departments or groups of departments.

If we assign two or three technicians to each department, employees will benefit from always having a technician who has experience with that department's specific software and hardware systems. To prevent decentralization from limiting the technicians' experience, I will ensure that technicians have cross training opportunities on other systems. As a result, technicians will not only become experts in their assigned areas, but also understand how their area relates to the other systems as well.

I realize this is a big change and not one to be adopted lightly. It will mean everyone in IT will need to move and get used to a different reporting structure. However, I have discussed this proposal with all the technicians and supervisors in my department, and they overwhelmingly support this recommendation. As a next step, I propose that we set aside time in our next department managers' meeting to discuss the benefits and implications of making this change.

Regards,

Jaida Nicholas, IT Manager
jaida.nicolas@company.com
604.555.4487 Ext. 3341

- Hints at the proposed idea in the subject line.
- Provides credibility by mentioning years of experience.
- Identifies a problem that needs to be solved and provides evidence that the problem is significant.
- Provides background to explain how the problem arose, and proposes a specific recommendation and a benefit.
- Justifies recommendation with persuasive rationale.
- Responds to potential objections.
- Expresses emotional commitment of the writer and her department.
- Concludes with a specific request.

TECHNOLOGY
COMPOSING A PERSUASIVE RECOMMENDATION WITH PRESENTATION SOFTWARE

When you need to make a recommendation to a small group or even to just one person, you may decide to present the information with slide software such as PowerPoint rather than create a word-processed document, such as a report or handout. Businesses are increasingly using presentation software as a composing tool for sharing information that needs to be read, presented, and discussed interactively. These *boardroom presentations* are designed to be read independently, in contrast to *ballroom presentations* that are designed to be visual support for a presenter (Gabrielle, 2010).

Boardroom presentations provide all their evidence and reasoning clearly on the slides so that the audience can refer to the slides later when making decisions. Four key principles will help you create a logical and persuasive recommendation presentation:

1. Organize your presentation into well-defined sections that indicate your logic.
2. Design every slide to support one main idea.

3. Write *message headlines*: short sentences or meaningful phrases at the top of the slide that represent your main ideas.
4. Present material in the body of the slide that supports the main idea in your headline.

To see these four principles in action, review the following recommendation presentation. Written by a not-for-profit organization, the slides are designed to be presented in meetings with individual state legislators to persuade them to introduce legislation requiring calorie labelling in Illinois restaurants. The presentation is divided into three sections: Problem, Causes, and Proposed Solution.

As you read the presentation, notice how it follows the four principles. The persuasive argument flows from slide to slide. You can follow the argument just by reading the slide headlines.

For a TECHNOLOGY exercise, go to Exercise 9 on page 254.

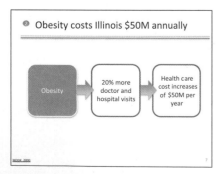

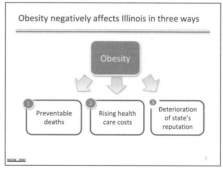

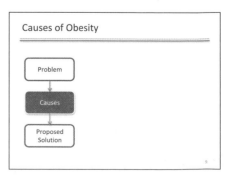

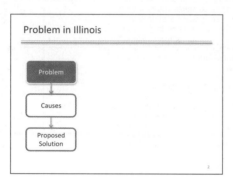

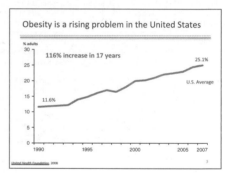

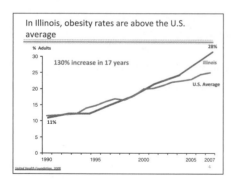

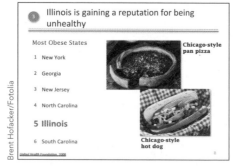

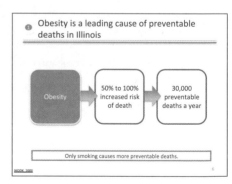

(continued)

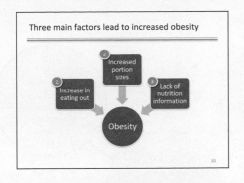

Three main factors lead to increased obesity

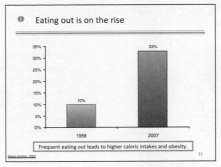

❶ Eating out is on the rise

Frequent eating out leads to higher caloric intakes and obesity.

Meals Matter, 2007

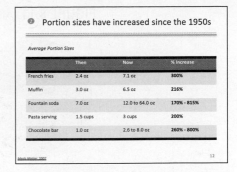

❷ Portion sizes have increased since the 1950s

Average Portion Sizes

	Then	Now	% Increase
French fries	2.4 oz	7.1 oz	**300%**
Muffin	3.0 oz	6.5 oz	**216%**
Fountain soda	7.0 oz	12.0 to 64.0 oz	**170% - 815%**
Pasta serving	1.5 cups	3 cups	**200%**
Chocolate bar	1.0 oz	2.6 to 8.0 oz	**260% - 800%**

Meals Matter, 2007

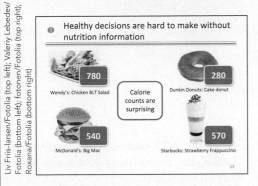

❸ Healthy decisions are hard to make without nutrition information

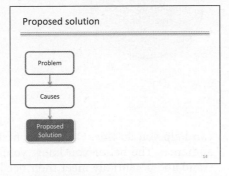

Proposed solution

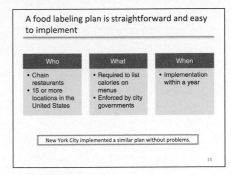

A food labeling plan is straightforward and easy to implement

Who	What	When
• Chain restaurants • 15 or more locations in the United States	• Required to list calories on menus • Enforced by city governments	• Implementation within a year

New York City implemented a similar plan without problems.

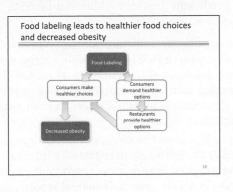

Food labeling leads to healthier food choices and decreased obesity

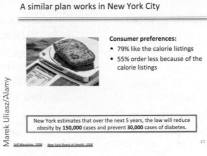

A similar plan works in New York City

Consumer preferences:
• 79% like the calorie listings
• 55% order less because of the calorie listings

New York estimates that over the next 5 years, the law will reduce obesity by **150,000** cases and prevent **30,000** cases of diabetes.

Self Magazine, 2008   New York Board of Health, 2008

Marek Uliasz/Alamy

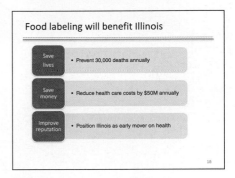

Food labeling will benefit Illinois

Save lives — • Prevent 30,000 deaths annually

Save money — • Reduce health care costs by $50M annually

Improve reputation — • Position Illinois as early mover on health

Liv Friis-larsen/Fotolia (top left); Valeriy Lebedev/Fotolia (bottom left); fotonen/Fotolia (top right); Roxana/Fotolia (bottom right)

- **Attention.** The first part of a sales message should grab the audience's attention. Your wording should make the audience want to read or hear more about your product or service by focusing their awareness. In business communication, you can grab the audience's attention in a professional way by sharing a startling fact, thought-provoking story, or motivating question. Consider these examples:

Startling Fact:	Did you know that 50% of all small businesses fail within the first five years?
Thought-Provoking Story:	Imagine yourself running your own business with no one to answer to except yourself! You're the boss. Your ideas are taken seriously, and everyone looks to you for guidance. Entrepreneurs who use our CustomerBase software suite have a good chance of achieving this rewarding dream.
Motivating Question:	Would you like to achieve your full financial potential rather than limiting your income to a monthly salary? Of course you would! Make your dream job come true with the CustomerBase software suite, designed to build your business and increase your financial success.

- **Interest.** After gaining the audience's attention, you need to build their interest in the product or service by describing how you can meet their needs. The ACE process

FIGURE 8.11 AIDA Structure for Organizing Sales Messages

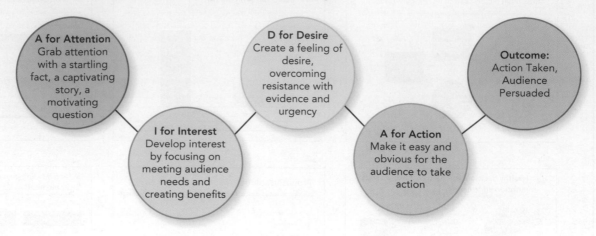

can help you do this. One of the first steps of the ACE process is to analyze your audience. The better you know your audience, the more likely you are to understand and potentially meet their needs. You can build interest by emphasizing how your product or service meets those needs and provides additional benefits. Consider these examples:

Meeting Needs: In addition to organizing and maintaining your customer information, CustomerBase also tracks your employees' sales by region, department, and individual person. This new feature makes identifying individual sales quotas a breeze. With CustomerBase, you'll never have to analyze complex spreadsheets again.

Audience Benefits: CustomerBase eliminates the stress of managing your customer relationships. With one user-friendly interface, you can easily keep track of information about your customers and their needs, generate custom-designed reports, and effortlessly maintain contact with your customers.

- **Desire.** Creating a sense of desire involves reducing the audience's resistance to the sales message, which is especially important when you create **unsolicited sales communications**, or *cold-call sales messages*. Reducing resistance is also important in **solicited sales communications**. Customers who request information are expressing interest in a product, but you may have to reduce their resistance if the price is more than they predicted or if the item does not fulfill all their needs. To create a sense of desire, consider using one of the principles of persuasion introduced in Figure 8.8 on page 238. Social proof and scarcity can be particularly useful approaches:

Social Proof: A survey of 2,500 CustomerBase users from across the country indicates that this software increases sales and enhances long-term business success. Over 85% of these businesses say they reached their target market sales goals within the first two years. Compare that to the national failure rate and it's easy to see how an investment in CustomerBase now is a sound investment in your future success.

Scarcity: For a limited time, we can offer you substantial savings on your CustomerBase contract. By placing your order today, you will receive free technical support for the first six months of your service contract. This offer is available only to first-time customers.

Unsolicited sales communication Sales messages you send to audiences who did not request the information. Also called "cold-call sales messages."

Solicited sales communication A response to a request for sales information.

- **Action.** The final step of the AIDA persuasive strategy is to motivate your customer to take action. Your task here is to ensure that you are making it easy for your customer to make this decision. If you want the customer to download your software package, the message could take the form of an email that includes a link to easily download the product. If your sales message is a phone call, you should be able to process the customer's order over the telephone. If you are mailing a letter or sales brochure, enclose a postage-paid return envelope in which the customer can easily place an order. Motivating action requires a professional approach. You do not want to assume the customer will purchase the product, but you do not want to use weak wording either. Motivate action by making the response easy and using strong, professional wording.

Easy Response:	Click here to download a free two-week trial copy of CustomerBase. After two weeks, you will be prompted to download the full version, which can easily be charged to your credit card account.
Strong, Professional Wording:	In the meantime, please call me at 1-800-555-1234 to discuss how CustomerBase can enhance your business success.

FIGURE 8.12 provides an example of a sales message that uses the AIDA strategy. Although AIDA is usually associated with sales messages to a general audience, you can use the AIDA approach even more effectively in situations when you know the audience. For those messages, you can apply your knowledge of audience needs to determine what specific information will effectively grab their attention, build interest, create desire, and motivate action.

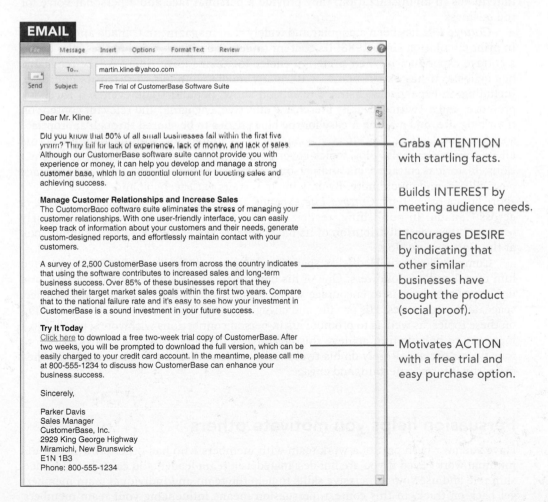

FIGURE 8.12 Unsolicited Sales Message

Social media: Indirect persuasion

Social media communication can be ideal for persuading people, especially consumers who have indicated some interest in your products and services by becoming part of your social media community. Surprisingly, one of the best ways of being persuasive in social media is by trying not to be persuasive. Businesses are increasingly recognizing the value of **content marketing**, a technique of providing information that audiences value without explicitly attempting to sell a product or service. This type of persuasion can be considered "indirect" because the purpose is not expressly stated. The Content Marketing Institute explains the concept this way: "Content marketing is the art of communicating with your customers and prospects without selling. It is non-interruption marketing. Instead of pitching your products or services, you are delivering information that makes your buyer more intelligent. The essence of this content strategy is the belief that if we, as businesses, deliver consistent, ongoing valuable information to buyers, they ultimately reward us with their business and loyalty" (Content Marketing Institute, 2013).

By delivering valuable content, you begin a relationship with the audience, who will consider you to be a trusted source when they make purchase decisions or pay for advice. What kind of content can you deliver to your audience, and what medium should you use? The content should be information your audience cares about or needs to hear, which will require research and audience analysis. This content can be delivered in any medium that will reach your audience, including videos, interactive websites, mobile apps, social networking sites, blogs, and microblogs.

Blogs are an effective tool for delivering content to customers and potential customers and for establishing you or your organization as subject matter experts or thought leaders in a field. In addition, because blog entries are typically written by individuals in an organization, they provide a personal face and a personal voice for the business.

Cottage Life has been a popular and widely read magazine in Canada and has been in print circulation since 1988. Its content targets individuals and families who desire a cottage experience as their preferred choice for their "down time." As the magazine has evolved, it has experimented with many media channels to reach its audience, including an expanded website, a television show, popular trade events, a Facebook presence, and a Twitter feed. By presenting effective, engaging, and relevant content on their blog site, and making it easy for the blog entries to be shared through appropriate social media, *Cottage Life* effectively enhances its connection with its audience across all its media channels. Blog topics cover cottage safety, spectacular wildlife interactions, historical cottage facts and personalities, real estate trends, food and beverage possibilities, and much more. By drawing in readers via Facebook and Twitter to these short bursts of content, *Cottage Life* expands and builds on its foundation of readers across Canada. In publishing, readership drives revenues, and *Cottage Life* clearly leverages the smart distribution of its blog content. See **FIGURE 8.13** for a sample look at the *Cottage Life* blog.

Commander Chris Hadfield's space-breaking use of Twitter in 2013 has garnered him over 1 million followers. One of his objectives, as an author, public speaker, and university professor, is to encourage young people to consider studying math, science, space, and aeronautics. His prolific and engaging use of Twitter to provide information on these topics, as well as to promote his in-person connections with young people, go a long way to helping him achieve this objective. Currently, Hadfield sends out two to four tweets per day. Rarely do his tweets ask for his audience to take any action. They primarily inform, entertain, and engage.

Persuasion helps you motivate others

Have you ever been part of a work team with members who had other priorities or did minimal work? Even if you are not designated as a team leader, you can adopt a leadership role and use your persuasive skills to help the team and individual team members get back on track. In this context, persuasion means influencing your team members' attitudes to bring about a change in behaviour.

Content marketing A technique for persuading customers by providing them with valuable information without trying to sell them anything.

Cottage Life

Search...

Blog   DIY + Design   Food + Entertaining   Real Estate   Outdoor L

FIGURE 8.13 Magazine Blog with Options for Social Media Sharing

Source: Screenshot http://cottagelife.com/news/whales-flaunt-their-mugs-for-photos-videos-on-b-c-coast from http://cottagelife.com/blog by Brenlee Coates. Used by permission.

Whales flaunt their mugs for photos, videos on B.C. Coast

By Brenlee Coates

NancyS/Shutterstock

Some of the first instances known as whale "muggings" have been reported in the Salish Sea on the B.C. coast.

Muggings, as they're labeled by the whale-watching industry, are interactions which whales initiate with vessels or its passengers.

In this case, the instances involved juvenile humpbacks, brought on by their sometimes social and curious demeanours.

Muggings have become more common as humpbacks become more populous and more accustomed to seeing vessels in these waters.

Click here to see the *Vancouver Sun*'s video.

Before the reported incidents, the executive director of the Pacific Whale Watch Association, Michael Harris, had been unaware of any instances of humpback whales befriending vessels since the 1980's.

No comments   Print   Email

 Share   Tweet   8+1   A A

RELATED STORIES

- World's most endangered whales spotted in B.C. waters »
- 'Friendly' deer

Effective team leaders use the following techniques to influence attitudes and motivate people to make a commitment to a team:

- **Remind the team why the work is important.** As you learned in Chapter 6, the best teams share a concrete goal and vision for success. Depending on the project, success may mean that the company will launch a new product or save time and money. Success may mean that the organization will better understand the competition or that each team member will receive a bonus. Success in student teams means an improved grade and more respect from classmates on future projects. If team members lose sight of the goal, remind them of their vision for success and why it is important.

- **Help others take pride in their work.** People lose motivation when they feel unappreciated and when they do not feel positive about their work. By showing appreciation and acknowledging team members' contributions, you can persuade team members to continue working at a high level.

- **Understand and acknowledge the emotions of team members.** Emotions can stand in the way of a team's success. If a team member is angry or frustrated or feels excluded from decision making, productivity will decline. Rather than try to convince someone to feel differently, actively listen to him or her, try to understand the feelings, and acknowledge the validity of those feelings. With that kind of support, many team members persuade themselves to make some changes and work harder (Managing People at Work, 2005).

- **Make it possible for a team member to succeed.** Sometimes external factors stand in the way of team success. For example, team members may have competing responsibilities at home and may not be able to commit to the team as fully as necessary.

If you help people resolve these conflicts, you may be able to persuade them to work harder on your project. Can you reschedule a meeting? Allow them to work from home? Redistribute tasks? Help them with another project that is taking too much of their time? Helping others makes it possible for them to participate in the team and, following Robert Cialdini's principle of reciprocity, may also lead them to reciprocate and do more for your project (Cialdini, 2009, p. 41).

In summary, being a persuasive business communicator requires that you adopt a "receiver" perspective and understand what will motivate your audience as well as what will prevent them from agreeing with you. The techniques you learned in this chapter are tools that you can use to address your audience's needs and concerns while helping your audience agree with and accept your ideas. If your content is sufficiently targeted to your audience, you may find that they will persuade themselves to agree with you. **FIGURE 8.14** summarizes how ACE can be employed in a persuasive message.

FIGURE 8.14 ACE in Persuasive Messaging

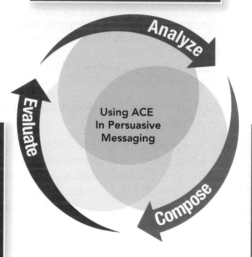

Focus on the purpose and your desired outcome.

Examine your primary and secondary audiences (stakeholders) carefully, identifying their needs. Use the receiver attitude to appeal to audience needs.

Identify possible objections.

Select the best channel for your message.

Analyze

Using ACE In Persuasive Messaging

Compose

Select a direct or indirect approach, depending on your audience.

Articulate audience needs to build confidence and rapport. Write with the receiver's perspective in mind.

Prepare responses for possible objections.

Evaluate

Check for a convincing argument that is written from the receiver's perspective and addresses possible objections.

Review for accuracy, clarity, and completeness.

Proofread for errors, paying special attention to numbers and dates.

Carolyn Swadron

Senior Manager, Internet & Mobile Quality Assurance & Quality Control

Self-Service Operations & Support, Retail Markets

CIBC

With permission from Carolyn Swadron and Ario Heshmatzade.

@ WORK

At the beginning of this chapter, Carolyn described the challenge of needing to persuade multiple stakeholders to adjust their timelines and budgets. How can she use ACE to help?

First, it is important to reinforce that stakeholders want the same result: the successful delivery of an application that our customers will love. When I express myself from the perspective that we all have the same goal, it becomes much easier to *analyze* options and key stakeholders, *compose* meaningful messages, and *evaluate* accurately how to communicate effectively with each decision maker.

- **Analyze.** Ethical persuasion means that each stakeholder must have all the relevant information, the pros and the cons, before arriving at a decision. Therefore, I must determine and evaluate the benefits and risks implied with each option I am proposing. I need to understand which risks are acceptable or unacceptable and recommend the best option for our internal departments, senior managers, and of course our customers.

  I confirm the amount of testing required, I prioritize the relative importance of test cases for assessing the application, and I estimate the number of days needed to complete testing with the available resources. I analyze my options: for example, acquiring more testers,

extending the testing schedule, eliminating less important test cases, and other options.

  Finally, I analyze my audience to determine what is important to each individual and to thoroughly understand how to prioritize that information most effectively.

- **Compose.** I write recommendations providing several levels of detail:

  1. **A high-level summary** of the challenge and my best recommendation for senior management.

  2. **Background information** explaining the situation, challenges, history supporting what is feasible, pros and cons of the options analyzed, and why my recommendation is the best option for decision makers who crave more information.

  3. **An appendix** with data and historical precedents for those who want even more details.

  This gives everyone in my audience access to the information that they want and need to accept my recommendation. I ensure that the recommendation is accurate and well written. It must be concise with no grammar, spelling, or accuracy errors that could impact its credibility.

- **Evaluate.** Before sending or presenting my recommendation, I carefully review it. Where necessary, I tighten language and content to eliminate unnecessary details. Then I consider the best way to present it:

  - Sending an email and requesting a response
  - Sending meeting invitations with my recommendation attached
  - Meeting individually with each stakeholder to present my recommendation and get agreement

  Depending on my audience, I may choose a combination of these approaches. I know from experience that certain stakeholders respond better if approached in a particular way. Over time, I make a point of remembering this information for future use.

By effectively analyzing, composing, and evaluating my communication, we agree on an approach and a schedule that are feasible and meet the needs of the project.

End of Chapter

Learning Objectives in Review

(LO 8.1) How can the ACE process help you persuade your audience? *(pages 224–229)*

- **Analyzing helps you plan your message** by focusing on your purpose, desired outcome, and business result. Analyzing your primary and secondary audiences' (and stakeholders') needs helps you determine the content of the message. If you anticipate specific objections, you can use refutation or concession to address them. Analyzing also helps you select the best medium based on audience-, content-, and response-related criteria.
- **Composing implements the persuasive plan** by putting words into action.
- **Evaluating helps you review the draft for effectiveness** by considering whether the message is convincing, proposes an appropriate solution, includes sound reasoning, anticipates possible objections, and stresses audience benefits. Evaluating also ensures a complete, concise, clear, and correct message.

(LO 8.2) What are the basic elements of persuasion? *(pages 229–238)*

- **Building credibility** enhances the audience's perception that you have expertise and are trustworthy. You can build credibility by getting to know the audience, introducing yourself effectively, and presenting your ideas persuasively.
- **Constructing a logical argument** involves making a claim that is supported by reasons and evidence, which can be in the form of numerical data, facts, expert opinion, personal experience, or examples. When constructing

arguments, avoid fallacies, which are violations of logic. They are dishonest and misleading.
- **Appealing to your audience's emotions** helps you sell your persuasive idea by appealing to your audience's emotional or psychological needs, such as safety, love and belonging, self-esteem, and self-actualization. Other psychological principles include consistency, social proof, liking, reciprocity, and scarcity. You can show your own emotional commitment by using compelling evidence and powerful language.

(LO 8.3) What types of business messages require persuasion? *(pages 239–249)*

- **Recommendations for action** require that you convince someone that a problem or opportunity exists and that your idea is the best way to address it.
- **Sales messages** often incorporate the components of AIDA, an acronym used in marketing to suggest the organization of sales communications: Attention, Interest, Desire, and Action. These components are useful in both solicited and unsolicited sales communications.
- **Social media: Indirect persuasion.** Identify the kind of information your audience wants and needs and provide that without trying to persuade. You can deliver this content by any medium, such as websites, videos, mobile apps, blogs, and social media sites.
- **Persuasion helps you motivate others.** Remind a team you are working with why the work is important, help others feel pride in their work, acknowledge team members' emotions, and make it possible for each team member to succeed.

KEY TERMS

AIDA p. 240
concede p. 226
content marketing p. 246
credibility p. 230
direct message p. 239

fallacy p. 234
indirect message p. 239
persuasion p. 223
primary audience p. 225
recommendation p. 239

refute p. 226
return on investment (ROI) p. 225
secondary audience p. 225

solicited sales communication p. 244
unsolicited sales communication p. 244

CASE STUDY

Starting a New Business

This case study will help you review the chapter material by applying it to a specific scenario.

Kelly Lee and Raj Khan meet in a marketing class and recognize they have two things in common. First, they enjoy working with

animals. Kelly's family breeds Irish Setters, and Raj works part time in a veterinary office. Second, they both want to be entrepreneurs. After some initial market analysis, they decide to collaborate on creating a pet daycare centre, Pet Haven, that will offer daily workouts for the animals, hourly playtime and attention from individual handlers, and clean and roomy cages or containment areas.

To get Pet Haven up and running, Kelly and Raj realize they must persuade either a bank or other investors to give them a small business loan. Then they must persuade potential customers to use their service.

Persuading Lenders to Fund a Loan

When Kelly and Raj go to the bank to discuss a loan for Pet Haven, the banker is interested in the idea but tells them their interest rate will be very high because they have an insufficient credit history and no collateral for the loan. To secure a more reasonable rate, he suggests they ask relatives to cosign the loan application. In other words, their parents would have to agree to repay the loan if Kelly and Raj could not.

Kelly and Raj decide they need to convince their parents that Pet Haven is a sound financial idea. To prepare for these meetings, they brainstorm a list of questions their parents could ask:

- Are you ready to run a business?
- What services will you provide? How do you know these are the right services? What will you need to deliver these services?
- Who is your customer base? Are there enough customers to support your business?
- What is the competition in our city? What will you offer to make you stand out?
- Have these kinds of pet daycare businesses been successful in other towns? What makes them successful? Have any such businesses failed? Why?
- How will you market your services to your customers? How will you communicate and what will you communicate?
- What kind of licensing and credentials do you need?
- Do you have a location yet? What kind of space do you need? What kinds of equipment do you need?
- What will the startup costs be for leases, employees, licences, advertising, and equipment?
- What size loan do you need? How will you repay this loan from cash flow?
- Why don't you get a job first and get some experience? You can open a business later.

QUESTION 1: *How can Kelly and Raj prepare for a successfully persuasive conversation with their parents?*

a. Which questions require a logical argument using claims, reasons, and evidence?

b. How should Kelly and Raj gather information to support these arguments?

c. How can Kelly and Raj establish credibility about their ability to run a business and repay a loan?

d. What kinds of emotional appeals might be effective as part of their argument to their parents to motivate action?

Identifying Benefits and Objections

Based on Kelly's and Raj's persuasive business plans, their parents agree to cosign the loan. However, they insist that Kelly and Raj

begin to market their business before graduation. As a next step, Kelly and Raj decide to learn more about what their potential customers (their audience) might already know about this kind of business:

- What do they know about pet daycare services?
- What benefits will they perceive from the service?
- What objections and concerns may prevent them from using the service?

QUESTION 2: *Raj and Kelly need to do some research. Alone or with a small group, search the Internet for animal or pet daycare centres. Select at least two companies and read their websites thoroughly. List the customer benefits that each company stresses. Which benefits seem most compelling? What benefits would you recommend Raj and Kelly stress? Can you think of other potential benefits that you did not read about in competitors' websites?*

Writing a Persuasive Sales Message

As a next step, Kelly and Raj compose two sales letters for Pet Haven. One is targeted at pet owners in the area. The other is more personalized and targeted at pet owners Kelly and Raj know.

QUESTION 3: *Raj and Kelly have brainstormed some claims that they would like to include in the sales letters. Evaluate each claim to determine if it can be supported or if it represents a logical fallacy. If it can be supported, what kinds of evidence would be effective for each claim? Where can Kelly and Raj find this evidence?*

- If you have a pet and work all day, you can either allow your pet to remain lonely or take advantage of high-quality daycare services.
- Pets that are stimulated during the day are happier and healthier than pets left alone.
- If you are willing to bring a child to daycare, then you should certainly be willing to do the same for your pet.
- Daycare is as good as medicine for a pet's health. For example, Mrs. Jones' dog was sickly before becoming a daycare client. Now the dog is healthy and energetic.
- Daycare clients receive a discount on routine grooming.

QUESTION 4: *Raj and Kelly have decided to use the AIDA form for both letters. Alone or working with a small group of classmates, draft either of the sales letters. Use your imagination to develop specific details for the pet owners Kelly and Raj know. End each letter by asking the audience to go to the Pet Haven website for more information.*

In class, compare and evaluate the various letters to see different implementations of AIDA.

Using Social Media to Persuade

Raj and Kelly understand that they can reach a broader audience and be more persuasive if they use social media in addition to a website, but they have not yet focused on how best to use social media.

QUESTION 5: *Working by yourself or with a small group of classmates, identify at least two ways that Raj and Kelly can use social media to persuade potential customers of their reliability and trustworthiness.*

REVIEW QUESTIONS

1. What elements do you need to analyze when planning your persuasive message?

2. What is the difference between your primary audience and your secondary audience?

3. What are the eight questions you should ask yourself when evaluating your persuasive messages?

4. What are the five ways you can be persuasive through a logical argument?

5. What does AIDA stand for?

6. Identify how any three of Robert Cialdini's techniques for appealing to emotion can be used by businesses in social media communication.

CRITICAL THINKING

1. This chapter defines persuasion as the "process of influencing your audience to agree with your point of view, recommendation, or request." In what way is persuasion a process?

2. When you identify potential audience objections to your ideas, as part of planning a persuasive conversation or written message, should you address those objections directly as part of your persuasive strategy, or should you ignore them? Describe a situation where it might be better to address possible objections. Then identify another situation where it might be better to ignore potential objections until your audience actually objects.

3. Suppose you are making a presentation to your boss that recommends a change that will eliminate budget overruns. Is it important to present details about the budget overruns, or is it better just to focus on your solution to this problem? How would you decide the best approach?

4. AIDA (attention, interest, desire, and action) is a long-established and widely used pattern for persuasive sales messages. Why do you think AIDA works so well?

5. In this chapter, you learned about how fallacious reasoning can be unethical if you intentionally use it to mislead your audience. What else could you do in an attempt to persuade that could be considered unethical?

6. You are working on a project with a team of people from Mexico and Canada and your primary mode of communication is email. One of your Mexican teammates often takes three to four days to respond to messages that you have marked urgent. So far, this has not been a problem. However, now you need a quick response from him. Your team is running late on a project deadline, and your ability to meet this deadline will have a great impact on your performance review.

You decide to conduct some research and find that, in Mexico, it is important to develop strong working relationships. A phone call could signal that you are making an effort to build a relationship. Your research suggests that showing respect for your teammate's work would indicate you value the individual as well as the work and would also signal that the relationship is important to you (Communicaid Group, Ltd., 2009).

You think carefully about this while planning your next communication to this teammate. How can you persuade your Mexican teammate to respond to you quickly and to help meet the deadline?

7. You are part of a team that is presenting a proposal to a client in the Netherlands. Your client has sent you a list of people who will be attending the meeting, along with background information on each. You notice that they represent a wide range of functions in the company. You also notice that no senior decision maker will be attending the meeting. Typically, when your company presents a persuasive proposal you target the senior decision maker and aim primarily to persuade that person. This approach has been successful throughout North America and in the United Kingdom and has led to quick sales.

You conduct some research and find, to your surprise, that although the Netherlands is a highly individualistic culture, important business decisions are made by consensus (UK Trade and Investment, 2010).

In this case, what should your team do? Can you explain why?

DEVELOPING YOUR COMMUNICATION SKILLS

(LO 8.1) **How can the ACE process help you persuade your audience?** *(pages 224–229)*

EXERCISE 1 Analyzing helps you plan your message

Assume that you have the opportunity to travel to China during the summer as part of a global business initiatives project at your school. The goal of the trip is to visit businesses in that country, learn more about the differences between Canadian and Chinese businesses, and make some international contacts. The school will provide the funding for your trip. Each student, however, is asked to request donations from local companies to support the project. You decide to approach Keith Dinsmore, the president of a shoe manufacturing company in your community, to request a donation. You selected this person because he graduated from your university and because many of his company's products are manufactured in China. Analyze the communication situation to plan your communication:

a. What should be the specific purpose of your communication? What specific outcome do you want?

b. What information will Mr. Dinsmore need to make his decision?

c. What benefits can you offer Mr. Dinsmore to support why he should donate?

d. What objections do you anticipate? How would you prepare for these?

e. What medium should you use to communicate with Mr. Dinsmore? Should you make your request by email? By phone? Should you ask for a meeting? What are the advantages and disadvantages of each option?

EXERCISE 2 Composing implements the persuasive plan

a. Refer to Exercise 1. Assume that you chose to write a persuasive email to Mr. Dinsmore. Based on your analysis from that exercise, compose a first draft of the message.

b. Refer to Exercise 1. Assume that you secured a meeting with Mr. Dinsmore. Create a set of seven PowerPoint slides that would support your presentation.

EXERCISE 3 Evaluating helps you review the draft for effectiveness

Refer to Exercises 1 and 2. Evaluate your first draft email OR your PowerPoint slides and explain how they meet the following criteria. If your message doesn't meet these criteria, identify how you could modify the message.

a. Have you convincingly shown that a problem or opportunity exists?

b. Is the proposed solution appropriate?

c. Are the evidence and reasoning sound? Are the data presented objective and unbiased?

d. Have you addressed potential objections and stressed benefits?

e. Is the message clear and easy to understand?

f. Is the information complete, concise, and correct?

 What are the basic elements of persuasion?
(pages 229–238)

EXERCISE 4 Building credibility

In your entrepreneurship class, you and three classmates developed an idea that you would like to turn into a business: a tutoring service for high school and middle school students in your community. Tutors would be students at your college or university who are majoring in the subject that they are tutoring and who have prior experience tutoring in the subject. The tutoring services would be advertised online. Prices would be $40/hour if the clients come to campus and $50/hour if tutors go to the clients' homes or other locations. For the business to succeed, you know that you will need to build credibility with the local school administration and with local families. Review the approaches to building credibility on pages 230–231 earlier in this chapter. How would you build credibility for yourself and your new company?

EXERCISE 5 Constructing a logical argument

You work for a development and construction company that specializes in commercial real estate. You need to make a persuasive presentation to your town council requesting that the town rezone a parcel of land (Parcel 5812) from residential to commercial in a fast-growing area so you can build a retail shopping area anchored by a grocery store. Based on your research, you are going to provide three reasons why the town should rezone the land for a new shopping area:

1. The residential population in the area is growing while nearby shopping options are not.

2. The nearest grocery store, which is 10 kilometres away in a different town, is accessible only by a two-lane highway, suggesting that without a nearby store traffic congestion may increase.

3. The retail space will stimulate growth and help increase the town's tax base.

What kind of evidence would you include to support each of these three reasons? For example, what kind of evidence would help you prove the residential population is growing?

EXERCISE 6 Appealing to your audience's emotions

Review Robert Cialdini's persuasive techniques: consistency, social proof, likeability, reciprocity, and scarcity. In small groups, identify and discuss a company that promotes its products or services using these techniques. If possible, find a company that demonstrates *all* five elements in its social media communications. Provide specific examples of each technique. You may be asked to summarize your findings in writing or to present them using screen grabs on presentation slides.

 What types of business messages require persuasion? *(pages 239–249)*

EXERCISE 7 Recommendations for action

A friend attends Northern Ontario University (NOU), where all students receive a laptop upon registration. Many of the classes at NOU use ebooks, which significantly reduces textbook costs. You believe the students at your campus would benefit from the savings as well as the technology. You want to persuade your school's administration to become a "laptop campus." However, you predict many objections. The costs of purchasing and maintaining the laptops are an obvious concern. Other potential problems include theft and misuse. Additionally, some faculty may not want students to be distracted by web browsing and social networking during class. To prepare a persuasive communication, first identify possible concessions or refutations for these and other objections. Then focus on audience benefits and other persuasive strategies you learned in this chapter. Compose a message requesting a meeting to discuss the program in more detail. Then draft a presentation to use during the meeting.

EXERCISE 8 Sales messages

You are the assistant sales director for a company that is a market leader in hand sanitizers. You have a new product, SaniPlus, that you plan to target to existing business customers through unsolicited sales messages. The product is a portable, touch-free dispenser of hand sanitizer. The dispenser stands on the floor, can be positioned in strategic locations, and can be moved to other locations.

The director of sales asks you to draft a message that incorporates the AIDA elements to persuade existing customers to purchase your new product. Create information about the product to support your persuasive message.

EXERCISE 9 Writing logical arguments with presentation software [Related to the Technology feature on page 242]

As a team, find a website that effectively uses the techniques and principles described in this chapter to persuade its audience. Develop a short slide presentation that identifies three ways in which the website is persuasive. Organize your slides this way:

Slide 1. Your title slide. Include the name of the website, a screen shot of the home page, and information that identifies your team and assignment.

Slide 2. Identify the purpose and audience of the website.

Slide 3. Identify and illustrate the first way in which the site is persuasive.

Slide 4. Identify and illustrate the second way in which the site is persuasive.

Slide 7. Identify and illustrate the third way in which the site is persuasive.

For slides 2–5, use a message headline that briefly states the main point of the slide. Then, on the body of the slide, present evidence to support the headline. Evidence may include screen shots, excerpts of text, and graphics from the website. Use the presentation on pages 242–243 earlier in this chapter as an example of how to write message headlines and support them on the slide.

EXERCISE 10 Build credibility by providing valuable content

Find an example of a business that uses social media to provide value-added content in addition to its primary products or services. (For example, a travel company that provides health-related information and updates in addition to travel services.) Determine the following:

- Does the company use more than one medium to deliver the content? Why?
- Why does the audience care about or need this information?
- From the audience perspective, what would be the best channel to receive this inforamtion? Why?
- How does the company's content marketing relate to its primary products or services?
- Does the value-added content help the company develop a relationship with the audience? How?

Summarize your findings in a one-page message to your instructor, or be prepared to present your findings in class.

EXERCISE 11 Persuasion helps you motivate others

In small groups, describe a recent situation when you had to use persuasion to motivate a co-worker or team member. If you were successful, explain the strategies or techniques from this chapter that you used to persuade your audience. If you were not successful, identify a strategy or technique that you could have used. Record comments from each person in the group and analyze your findings. What commonalities exist? Prepare a short report that summarizes your findings.

EXERCISE 12 Values and persuasion [Related to the Culture feature on page 231]

When people of similar cultural backgrounds settle in new areas, they often form business associations together to capitalize quickly on networking opportunities (e.g., the Toronto Chinese Business Association, www.tcbacanada.com). These types of business associations often ask guest speakers to attend their meetings to speak on their areas of expertise. Often such speaking opportunities are accepted on a volunteer (nonpaid) basis.

Interview three people of a cultural background other than your own. Ask each interviewee to imagine that it is their job to ask a professor from your school to speak at a business association meeting. Gather specific information about how they would approach this persuasive task. How exactly would they approach this task? Compare results relating to different cultures and write a brief message to your instructor describing your findings. Be sure to support each finding with evidence.

EXERCISE 13 Ethical Persuasion [Related to the Ethics feature on page 235]

You work at a sporting goods store. One day a customer arrives to purchase gear for a winter camping trip. Specifically, she wants a sleeping bag that is rated to –30°C and a parka that has an equally strong temperature rating. You find a parka that is rated to –28°C on the label, but you are certain she will be warm enough in this coat. The warmest sleeping bag that you have in stock does not have a specific rating, but other winter campers purchase this bag and report that it is very warm.

Write a "script" outlining how you would handle this customer's concerns about these products in an ethical way. Be prepared to defend your choices to your classmates.

EXERCISE 14 Impromptu presentations

Make a one- to two-minute presentation designed to persuade your classmates to do one of the following:

a. Change their major to yours.

b. Join a new student organization that has an expensive membership fee.

c. Spend a year doing public service before entering the workforce.

d. Begin contributing to individual retirement accounts as soon as they can.

In your presentation, include at least one statement designed to establish credibility, one logical argument with reasons and evidence, and one benefit designed to motivate.

EXERCISE 15 Impromptu speaking: Business role-plays

In a one- to two-minute presentation, explain how you would persuade your audience in each of the following business situations:

a. Assume you are the new director of fundraising for a nonprofit organization. In the past, your organization has created targeted fundraising events, such as galas and pledge drives, to increase donations and contributions. You think a monthly e-newsletter to regular donors could keep them informed of how their money is put to use and promote the events now promoted only through fundraising letters and web advertising. Although collecting email addresses and developing an email database would be time consuming, you believe the benefits would certainly outweigh the effort.

The board of directors supports your idea, but the membership director, who would be responsible for collecting the email addresses and distributing the monthly e-newsletter, is resistant because she is very busy and does not have the time. You see her at lunch and decide to discuss the matter with her individually. In one to two minutes, persuade her to agree to this idea.

b. You are on a sales team that is planning an important presentation for a prospective client. During the meeting, the team leader discusses the content to present and the [visual] aids and handouts to create. During the discus[sion you are] surprised that no one mentions analyzing the au[dience. You] believe that audience analysis is necessary to create a [presenta]tion that meets the client's need. In one to two minu[tes, per]suade your team to analyze the audience.

9 Communicating Bad News Messages

Andrey Popov/Fotolia.

LEARNING OBJECTIVES

LO 9.1 **How does the ACE process help you deliver bad news effectively?** *pages 258–270*

Analyzing and planning bad news messages
Using effective strategies to compose bad news messages
Evaluating bad news messages
Checking cultural assumptions about delivering bad news

LO 9.2 **What types of bad news messages are common in business?** *pages 271–274*

Denying customer claims
Acknowledging mistakes or problems
Communicating negative change

LO 9.3 **How can you control the spread of bad news through social media?** *pages 275–278*

Having a plan in place

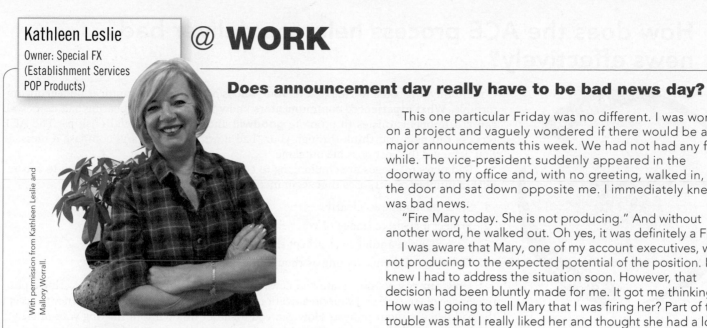

Kathleen Leslie
Owner: Special FX
(Establishment Services
POP Products)

@ WORK

Does announcement day really have to be bad news day?

At one of my major corporate employers, Friday was always "announcement day." This was the day that any new programs, plans, or announcements were made. This meant that our key employees had the entire weekend to worry about new directives.

This one particular Friday was no different. I was working on a project and vaguely wondered if there would be any major announcements this week. We had not had any for a while. The vice-president suddenly appeared in the doorway to my office and, with no greeting, walked in, shut the door and sat down opposite me. I immediately knew it was bad news.

"Fire Mary today. She is not producing." And without another word, he walked out. Oh yes, it was definitely a Friday.

I was aware that Mary, one of my account executives, was not producing to the expected potential of the position. I knew I had to address the situation soon. However, that decision had been bluntly made for me. It got me thinking. How was I going to tell Mary that I was firing her? Part of the trouble was that I really liked her and thought she had a lot to offer. This job was just not playing to her strengths. One thing was for sure: I was not going to use the same method as the vice-president. How do I turn this negative into a positive?

Find out at the end of this chapter how Kathleen used ACE to help her deliver this bad news message.

Introduction

During your working career, you will have to deliver messages that disappoint, inconvenience, or even anger your audience. For example, you might need to

- tell a co-worker you cannot help with a project,
- explain an unexpected problem,
- deny a customer's request for a refund,
- reject an employee's request for a promotion, raise, or time off, or
- turn down someone who applied for a job.

If you communicate bad news poorly, you risk not only angering people but also hurting your own business by potentially losing customers, clients, or valued employees. Will a customer continue to do business with you if you deny a refund? Will an employee's productivity decline after you reject that employee's request for a

raise? In complex situations legal liabilities may also be an issue. For example, if you cannot fulfill a contract you previously agreed to, you have to communicate the bad news as well as deal with the consequences of breaking (or modifying) the contract.

The rise of social media puts additional pressure on businesses to handle bad news messages professionally. Dissatisfied customers can easily take their complaints to the court of public opinion, posting negative comments on TripAdvisor, Yelp, Amazon, Twitter, Facebook, or other similar sites. As a business communicator, you will want to do everything possible to use social media effectively to respond to bad publicity when it arises.

This chapter outlines several techniques that you can use to communicate bad news and respond to bad news while still maintaining the audience's goodwill. The chapter also shows you how you can adapt the ACE process to achieve these goals.

LO 9.1 How does the ACE process help you deliver bad news effectively?

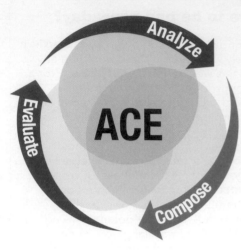

Communicating bad news makes everyone who is part of the communication feel uncomfortable. What experienced communicators know is that communicating bad news well can create opportunities to promote **goodwill** and strengthen relationships. The ACE process can help you think through your "bad news" situation and compose a message that achieves the best possible outcome.

Bad news messages are challenging to compose because they require you to accomplish a number of purposes that seem incompatible at first glance:

1. State the bad news clearly.
2. Project a positive image of yourself and your organization.
3. Convince the audience to accept the bad news without protest.
4. Leave the audience feeling as though they have been treated fairly.

How can you possibly state bad news clearly while simultaneously projecting a positive image of yourself and your organization? How can you convince the audience to accept the bad news without protest? How can you do all of this without making your audience feel as if they have been treated unfairly and perhaps have grounds for a lawsuit?

Being successful in all these purposes requires thoughtful planning, organization, and careful wording. **FIGURE 9.1** is an example of a bad news message that achieves all of these outcomes.

Despite the many challenges of writing bad news messages, you can achieve a positive outcome by practising and applying the ACE process. **FIGURE 9.2** provides a helpful set of questions for adapting ACE to bad news messages. As you work through a specific communication challenge, you may identify additional helpful questions.

Analyze

Analyzing and planning bad news messages

Before composing a bad news message, analyze the situation by asking yourself several questions to help you develop content and choose the best medium.

Ask questions that help you develop content

Assume you run a one-person web development business. Yesterday you made a proposal to a new client, Great Expectations Books, a small local business, to add an ecommerce function to its website. After meeting with the manager, you proposed installing an inventory database and online ordering function within a month.

However, today you receive a request from a long-time client, South Shore Community Television (SSCT), which needs your immediate help with a time-sensitive request. SSCT is one week away from a major fundraising pledge drive and needs their online pledge function repaired. Currently, it is generating an error message when accessed by potential donors.

You feel obligated to help SSCT for several reasons:

- You originally programmed the SSCT website and your original work may be causing the problem.
- You may be the only person who can fix this problem quickly.
- SSCT is a long-time client that gives you a lot of business each year.

Although you made a commitment to Great Expectations and do not want to disappoint this new client, you decide to inform the manager at Great Expectations that you cannot meet the original deadline and need a two-week extension.

How will you deliver this bad news? Analyzing is crucial to developing a message that supports your business goals and positively affects audience reaction. Consider the analyzing questions outlined in Figure 9.2.

- **What is the bad news?** The bad news is that you cannot meet the original deadline, but you can get the job done with an additional two weeks.

Goodwill The positive relationship between you (or your company) and your audience.

LETTER

FIGURE 9.1 Example of a Bad News Message

‖Paradigm
DESIGN GROUP

217 Commercial Drive
Vancouver, BC V5L 4X1

www.Paradigm.Design.com
800.555.6674 | Fax: 604.555.6675

HOW DOES THE LETTER EFFECTIVELY COMMUNICATE BAD NEWS?

March 15, 20XX

Mr. Harsha Patel
925 Rosedale Street
Burnaby, BC V5H 4A2

Dear Harsha:

Thank you for taking the time to meet with our hiring committee and sharing information about your background and qualifications. We enjoyed meeting you and discussing your career goals.

Following the interviews, the hiring committee further reviewed the needs of our marketing department. After much consideration, we have offered the position to another candidate.

We wish you every personal and professional success with your job search and future career. Thank you for your interest in our organization.

Sincerely,

Meredith Baldwin

Meredith Baldwin
Human Resources Manager
Paradigm Design Group

Projects a positive image of the organization by thanking the candidate, showing appreciation for his effort, and expressing interest in his background.

Conveys the bad news clearly but sensitively by using positive phrasing.

Convinces the audience to accept the bad news by making clear that the decision is final: another candidate has been offered the job.

Avoids legal complications by saying nothing that can be interpreted as age, gender, or racial discrimination.

- **What outcome would you like to achieve in communicating the bad news?** You would like Great Expectations to grant you an extension rather than withdraw its agreement and hire a new web developer.
- **How is the audience likely to react to this news?** Although you cannot exactly predict the audience's reaction, you can think about the situation from Great Expectations' perspective. It currently does not use an ecommerce function and has an informational website that works. You also know it plans to launch an "order online" advertising campaign at the end of the month. You think Great Expectations will be disappointed with the extended deadline but will not be upset enough to find a different website developer. You would like the company to accept your request and postpone its ad campaign for two weeks.
- **What justification and explanation should you include?** To be effective, a bad news message should explain the reasons behind the bad news. Of all the features in your message, this explanation has the most power to influence the audience to accept your bad news (Creelman, 2012; Jansen & Janssen, 2010). Consider the questions the audience may have: "Why can't you deliver your services as agreed?" If you want an ongoing relationship with Great Expectations, you will need to provide a reason for the delay. You can explain, for example, that another client has had an

FIGURE 9.2 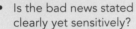 Using ACE for Bad News Messages

- What is the bad news?
- What business result do you want to achieve?
- How will the audience react to this news?
- What justification and explanation should you include? Is there anything you can say to soften the bad news?
- Should you include an apology?
- Can you do anything else to project a positive image and maintain goodwill?
- What is the best medium for this message?

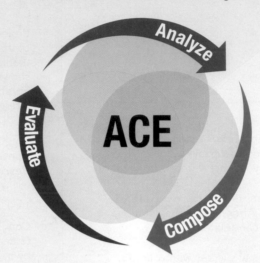

- Is the bad news stated clearly yet sensitively?
- Will the message convince the audience to accept the bad news?
- Does the message project a good image of you and maintain goodwill with the audience?
- Will the message achieve a good business result?
- Have you avoided legal complications?

- Should you begin with the bad news or build up to it?
- How can you clearly phrase the bad news?
- What content and techniques should you use to soften the impact of the message?
- How can you close the message appropriately?

emergency that only you can handle. You do not need to name the client or explain the nature of the emergency.

- **Is there anything you can say to soften the bad news? For example, is there any good news to include? Will the audience benefit in any way? Does this cloud have a silver lining?** To soften the bad news, you can communicate to Great Expectations how much you value its business. You can let the company know why the other client's request took priority, taking care to ensure that the Great Expectations project has not been made less important. If there are no direct audience benefits to be had, you can subtly suggest that this situation demonstrates your commitment to your long-term customers. Finally, you might find a *silver lining*, or a hidden benefit, in this delay. For example, with more time before programming the ecommerce site, Great Expectations can survey customers to learn more about how they would like the site organized.

- **Should you include an apology?** You are responsible for needing to change the agreed-on deadline, and perhaps delaying Great Expectations' advertising campaign. You decide that you owe this new client a sincere apology that acknowledges that you understand the implications of this delay.

- **Can you do anything else to project a positive image and maintain goodwill and the relationship?** Your professionalism and apology will project a positive image. In addition, you can offer your client an alternative, rather than simply agreeing to your request. For example, Great Expectations might allow you to complete the most critical parts of the project by the original deadline, with the rest coming later. By giving the company options, you can manage the relationship.

Select the best medium to achieve your goal

The final analyzing question in Figure 9.2 focuses on choosing a medium. When you communicate bad news, select a medium that best fits the purpose of the message, the audience, and the situation. **FIGURE 9.3** outlines the advantages and disadvantages of various medium options for communicating bad news messages.

	One-to-One	Group Meeting	Telephone	Web/Video Chat	Text/IM	Email	Memo	Letter	Website	Social Networking	Wikis, Blogs
Audience-Related Criteria											
Share bad news with a single person	■		■	■	■	■	■	■			
Communicate to many employees and shareholders simultaneously		■		■	■	■	■	■	■	■	
Provide instantaneous news to people at geographically diverse locations				■	■	■			■	■	■
Share bad news with the public				■					■	■	■
Content- and Response-Related Criteria											
Share insignificant bad news quickly, such as letting your lunch appointment know you're running a few minutes late			■		■	■					
Share important bad news in a way that does not seem impersonal or evasive	■	■	■			■	■				
Hear your audience's tone of voice and silences, which convey meaning and feedback	■	■	■	■							
See facial expressions and body language, and hear tone of voice, which convey meaning and feedback	■	■		■							
Encourage immediate discussion of the news	■	■	■	■	■					■	■
Prevent immediate discussion or give the audience (and you) time to carefully consider a response						■	■	■	■	■	■
Ensure that you have written documentation of the communication						■	■	■	■	■	■

FIGURE 9.3 Selecting the Best Medium for Bad News Messages

What medium should you use to communicate the bad news to your client, Great Expectations Books? Only three options in Figure 9.3 are usually appropriate choices: a face-to-face meeting, telephone conversation, or email message. The remaining options will not be effective: Letters take too long to arrive, and text messages are too informal. Websites, social networking, wikis, and blogs are clearly not appropriate choices for individual communication.

Of the three acceptable choices, which is best? A face-to-face meeting would be appropriate, but may take some time to arrange. Both email and telephone have advantages and disadvantages. A telephone call allows you to make a personal contact and to hear your audience's tone of voice. You will be able to gauge whether or not the Great

Expectations manager is upset, and you can adjust what you say accordingly. However, the manager may not answer the phone immediately. Never leave bad news in a voice mail. If the manager does answer the telephone, your call may be misinterpreted as being overly urgent, suggesting that he needs to renegotiate your deadlines immediately. An email may allow the manager more time to review the original contract and to think about whether this delay will have a serious impact.

When you face a dilemma like this, often the best solution is to select a "first and follow-up" strategy. This means selecting the best way to first expose the bad news to the recipient and an immediate follow-up. For example, you could reach the Great Expectations manager by phone for a discussion on your need to renegotiate deadlines with a commitment to follow up within hours with a detailed confirmation email.

As business communication moves more and more into a digital mode, you will be faced with decisions relating to the communication of bad news via some quite new channels. For a review of the impact of transmitting bad news via email, text, and Twitter, check out the **TECHNOLOGY BOX**.

TECHNOLOGY
CAN YOU EMAIL, TEXT, OR TWEET BAD NEWS?

Communicators often wonder whether they should avoid email or text messages for delivering bad news and instead talk to their audience in person or over the telephone. Most experts agree that, when possible, a face-to-face conversation is usually the best choice: "Just like getting dumped from a romantic relationship, no one wants to hear bad news from a boss via email" (Donnelly, 2011).

When companies choose email or texts to deliver bad news, they often suffer serious public relations consequences. In one highly publicized incident, Radio Shack sent emails to 400 workers at its headquarters, notifying them that they were being let go. Infuriated workers who felt the company was treating them disrespectfully immediately leaked this action to the press. Robert Bies, a professor of management at Georgetown University's McDonough School of Business, notes in his First Commandment for Delivering Bad News (Ries, 2012) that "Thou shalt always treat people with respect and dignity." He goes on to say that actions such as firing people by email "send a clear message that people do not matter. On the other hand, positive interactions can increase workplace morale. A study has found that layoff victims who felt they were treated with dignity when hearing the news, with sincere explanation and caring conveyed in announcing it, actually worked harder than before they received the news" (Ries, 2012).

Even worse is the practice of firing someone by text message, which some companies have justified because their workforce is young and comfortable with that medium. Jodie Hernandez received the following text messages after confusion with her work schedule at a restaurant: "Ok I've text u and mike has called u, I hate to do a termination by text but I can't get a hold of u. Ur off the schedule as of today, pick up ur cheque" (Zuber, 2012). This disrespectful method of communicating may justifiably anger employees and lead them to seek legal counsel, talk to the media, or post negative comments on social media sites. A face-to-face conversation may be more uncomfortable, but it will be more effective.

Is email or social media ever the right choice for communicating bad news? It may be in the following circumstances:

- **If you want to give your audience time to think carefully before having to reply.** In the Great Expectations scenario, you may choose to communicate the bad news by email to give your audience time to think about the implications of the news and to consider the best way to respond to your request.

- **If it is crucial that you avoid miscommunication and misinformation.** Researchers have found that people who are uncomfortable communicating bad news face to face are more likely to sugarcoat the bad news when talking in person to reduce their own and their audience's discomfort. This distortion can lead to misunderstandings. By contrast, communicators are more likely to be accurate, complete, and honest in email because they do not worry about being confronted by an angry audience (Donnelly, 2011; Sussman & Sproull, 1999). Another alternative would be to follow the "first and follow-up" method: Deliver the news respectfully in person, then follow up with a detailed written communication to ensure that no misunderstandings have occurred.

- **If you need to communicate bad news to many people in different locations at exactly the same time.** When it is critical to communicate bad news to a broad audience, companies sometimes use multiple media to ensure the audience receives the message. For example, data breach security specialists now include multiple mainstream (TV, radio, print media) and digital media (social media, websites, text, and email) in their stakeholder reporting strategies (Experian, 2013). When the public at large needs to be made aware of a negative situation, social media may be the fastest way to spread the word and advise your audience of actions they need to take to protect themselves.

For a TECHNOLOGY exercise, go to Exercise 17 and Exercise 19 on page 285.

Using effective strategies to compose bad news messages

The analyzing questions in Figure 9.2 on page 260 help you develop *what to say* in a bad news message. The composing questions in this section will help you focus on *how to say it*.

- Should you begin with the bad news or build up to it?
- How should you phrase the bad news?
- Is it possible to soften the impact of the message while still being clear and firm?

Decide where to state the bad news

As you learned in Chapters 2 and 7, most routine business communications benefit from a *direct organization*, stating the purpose and main idea of the message before the supporting details. Audiences who are inundated with too much information and have too little time may not have the patience to sit through several minutes of introductory details to learn the main idea. The decision of where to introduce unwelcome news is more complex and depends on the context (Creelman, 2012):

- Will the news come as a surprise?
- Will the recipient be able to understand the news without a preliminary explanation?
- How much patience will they have to read through an entire message before getting to the main point?

In bad news situations, the direct approach may be appropriate if the news will not come as a big surprise (Halperin, 2012). In other bad news situations, you can help your audience understand and accept the news by using an *indirect organization*, providing explanation before the main idea. An indirect organization allows you to prepare the audience and explain your position before delivering the bad news.

FIGURE 9.4 outlines the differences between the direct and indirect approaches for communicating bad news and identifies when each is likely to be more effective. Note that the content communicated in each version is similar. The difference between the two methods is the placement of the bad news and the use of a **buffer**, an introductory sentence or paragraph that leads up to the bad news and softens it.

Buffer An introductory sentence or paragraph that leads up to and softens a bad news message.

Use **DIRECT ORGANIZATION** if . . .	**DIRECT ORGANIZATION** follows this pattern:
your audience • is unlikely to be upset or angry, or • expects the news and will not be surprised, **and the news** • is easy to explain and understand, • is important for the audience to see immediately, or • is relevant to health and safety.	1. STATE THE BAD NEWS DIRECTLY. (main idea) 2. Provide supporting explanation. 3. Conclude with goodwill.

Use **INDIRECT ORGANIZATION** if . . .	**INDIRECT ORGANIZATION** follows this pattern:
your audience • is likely to be upset or angry, or • does not expect the news, **or the news** • is difficult to understand without introductory explanation.	1. Begin with a buffer. 2. Provide supporting explanation. 3. STATE THE BAD NEWS CLEARLY. 4. Conclude with goodwill.

FIGURE 9.4 Two Ways to Organize Bad News Messages

FIGURE 9.5 Example of Bad News Requiring a Direct Organization

INDIRECT

Dear Richards Electronics Customer:

Thank you for your recent purchase of our LS520 microwave oven.

Although all of our products are rigorously tested before they are put on the market, we have found some minor abnormalities with the model LS520 under certain conditions. Recent customer experience revealed risk of overheating and fire when the microwave operates at the highest level for more than one hour. Therefore, we are recalling the LS520 and will either refund your full purchase price or exchange your microwave for another product.

Please contact the retail store where you purchased your LS520 microwave to arrange to return it, or call our toll-free number to request free express shipping pickup. We regret the inconvenience this recall will cause you but assure you that your health and safety are our primary concern.

Regards,

WHAT'S WRONG WITH THE INDIRECT VERSION?

The indirect version is misleading. It begins by thanking customers for their purchase. Although this is a neutral buffer, the audience may assume this message is a routine thank you letter and not read the rest of the message, putting them at risk for a kitchen fire.

No important ideas stand out. Someone reading quickly may miss the main point.

DIRECT

IMPORTANT PRODUCT SAFETY RECALL NOTICE
RICHARDS LS520 MICROWAVE OVEN FIRE HAZARD

Dear Richards Electronics Customer:

Richards Electronics is voluntarily recalling the LS520 microwave oven because we have received 11 reports worldwide of overheating and fires when the oven operates for longer than one hour at full power.

Our records indicate you have purchased this model. To protect your health and safety, Richards advises you to take the following steps:

• Stop using the microwave oven immediately.
• Return the product to the retail store where you purchased it, or call us toll free at 1-888-123-4567 to request free express shipping pickup. You can either receive a full refund or exchange your microwave for another model.

We apologize for the inconvenience this recall will cause you. We are modifying our research protocols to ensure future products exceed all industry specifications. Your safety and satisfaction with our products are our primary goals.

Regards,

WHY IS THE DIRECT VERSION BETTER?

The direct version gets to the point directly by announcing the product recall in a headline and then repeating the bad news in the first sentence. Although the audience will be surprised and potentially upset about this information, their safety is too important not to grab their attention.

The bulleted content highlights the necessary actions so they stand out.

The message concludes with goodwill by assuring readers that the company is taking action to prevent similar problems in the future.

FIGURE 9.5 is an announcement warning customers about a health and safety problem. The figure illustrates content that needs to be communicated directly. If the problem is buried, as it is in the indirect version, the audience may mistake the message for a routine communication and decide not to read it. The direct version solves that problem by stating the main idea in the first sentence.

By contrast, **FIGURE 9.6** illustrates a bad news message that needs to be organized indirectly. Assume you work for RemCo, a company that developed Vi-Spy, a virus

FIGURE 9.6 Example of Bad News Requiring an Indirect Organization

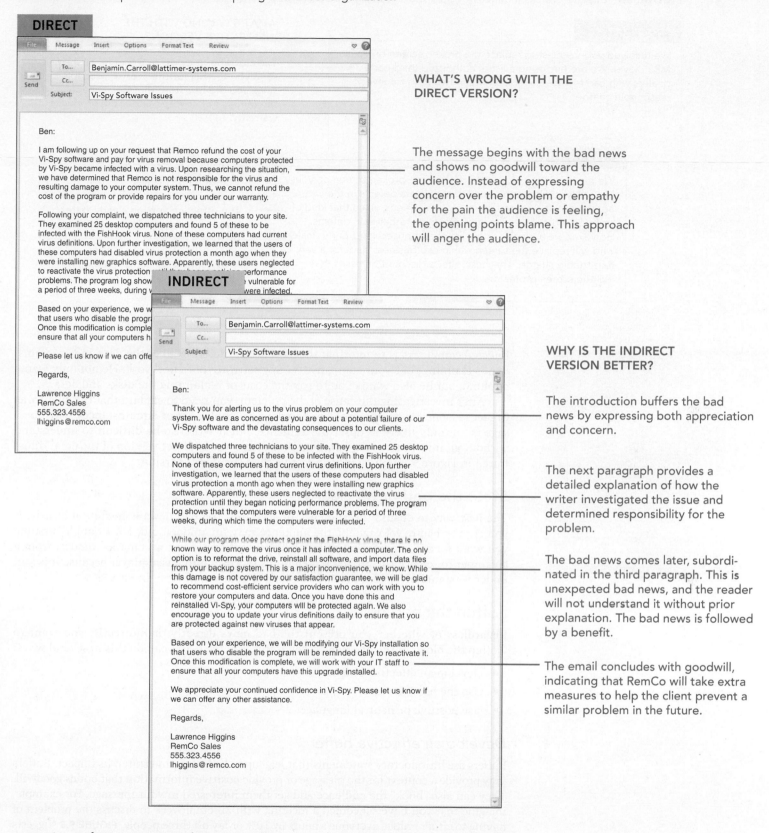

WHAT'S WRONG WITH THE DIRECT VERSION?

The message begins with the bad news and shows no goodwill toward the audience. Instead of expressing concern over the problem or empathy for the pain the audience is feeling, the opening points blame. This approach will anger the audience.

WHY IS THE INDIRECT VERSION BETTER?

The introduction buffers the bad news by expressing both appreciation and concern.

The next paragraph provides a detailed explanation of how the writer investigated the issue and determined responsibility for the problem.

The bad news comes later, subordinated in the third paragraph. This is unexpected bad news, and the reader will not understand it without prior explanation. The bad news is followed by a benefit.

The email concludes with goodwill, indicating that RemCo will take extra measures to help the client prevent a similar problem in the future.

protection and spyware removal program. The program continually protects against the latest viruses as long as the users routinely download new virus definitions. One of your corporate clients, Ben Carroll, calls you in a panic. Ben relied on your product to protect his company's computers, but many of the computers in the system are now infected with a virus that cannot be removed. The only way to eliminate the virus from the

FIGURE 9.7 Effective versus Ineffective Versions of Phrasing the Bad News

INEFFECTIVE

We received your request to replace the broken screen on your MP3 player. We are enclosing a list of authorized third-party dealers who can replace the screen within two days for a very reasonable charge.

WHAT'S WRONG WITH THE INEFFECTIVE VERSION?

The customer may assume that he or she can send you the bill for the "very reasonable charge" since you did not state that the damage to the MP3 is not covered under the product's warranty.

EFFECTIVE

We received your request to replace the broken screen on your MP3 player. Although our warranty covers defects in the equipment, it does not cover broken screens, since that kind of damage typically results from accidents rather than defects. However, we are enclosing a list of authorized third-party dealers who will replace the screen within two business days for a very reasonable charge. They also offer a discount on cases that include screen protectors.

WHY IS THE EFFECTIVE VERSION BETTER?

The effective version clearly states that the warranty does not cover broken screens.

It also offers advice about how to prevent broken screens in the future.

infected computers is to reformat the hard drives, deleting all of the data and programs. Ben is claiming that your company's Vi-Spy software does not work. He not only wants a refund, but he also wants you to pay the costs of reclaiming the disks and data.

After investigating the cause of the problem, you need to explain that the client was in fact responsible for the problem based on a complex set of circumstances. This message is not only likely to upset the audience, but it will also be difficult to understand without an introductory explanation. As a result, the indirect version of the email illustrated in Figure 9.6 will be more effective than the direct version.

State the bad news clearly

The best way to ensure the audience understands the bad news is to state it clearly. If you convey bad news vaguely, the audience may misunderstand. For example, assume you work for a company that sells MP3 players. You receive an emailed request from a customer to replace the broken screen of his recently purchased player because it is still under warranty. Consider the two versions of your email reply in **FIGURE 9.7**.

Soften the bad news

Regardless of whether you present the bad news directly or indirectly, you want to "soften the blow" of the bad news, even if it is expected. You can do this in several ways:

- Develop an effective buffer.
- Use the passive voice.
- Use positive or neutral language.

Develop an effective buffer

Buffers are introductory statements that lead up to bad news and soften its impact. Buffers may provide a context for the message or provide positive information that builds goodwill. They can also "hook" the audience and get them interested in your message. For example, imagine that you have scheduled a meeting with 30 employees to discuss the problem of having to either reduce everyone's hours by 10% or lay off three people. **FIGURE 9.8** suggests several buffer statements you could use at the beginning of the meeting to encourage your audience to listen to the rest of your message with a positive attitude.

Notice that all the buffer statements in Figure 9.8 indicate that bad news may be coming later in the message. A buffer statement that does not provide this signal may mislead and ultimately anger the audience.

FIGURE 9.8 Types of Buffer Statements

TYPE OF BUFFER	EXAMPLE
Background Information	Over the past six months, the economy has slowed, and our sales have dropped significantly.
Facts That Signal a Problem	In order to stay in business, our store needs to meet its payroll obligations.
Good News	Despite the soft economy and slowing sales, we have identified a way to keep the store open and meet our payroll obligations.
Thanks or Compliments	Thank you for your efforts this past year to improve sales at our store. Your knowledge of the merchandise and concern for customers have resulted in our highest-ever customer satisfaction rating, even in these difficult economic times.
Generally Accepted Truths	In these lean times, we need to watch our budget and eliminate all unnecessary spending. These cuts will require sacrifices from us all.
Empathy with Audience	I know how hard you have worked to keep costs down, so I understand how you might think we're unfair coming back to you this year with yet another request.

Use the passive voice

Although you need to state bad news clearly, you can ease its impact by using a subtle technique called the *passive voice*. (See Chapter 2 for more information about active and passive voice.) The term "voice" refers to the relationship between the subject and verb in a sentence. In *active voice* sentences, the subject performs the action of the verb. In *passive voice* sentences, the subject does not perform the action of the verb. In the following examples, the passive version avoids placing blame on the audience.

        subject verb   **verb**

Active: You damaged your MP3 player and invalidated the warranty.

              subject   **verb**

Passive: Your MP3 player was damaged by an accident or misuse, invalidating the warranty.

Use positive or neutral language

The words you choose to use in bad news messages will influence the audience's response as much as the organization of the message itself. The tone and style of the message should help the audience feel as positive as possible about you, the situation, and themselves.

The key circumstance you are trying to avoid is blaming your audience. Your audience will be more open to accepting the bad news if you treat them politely and respectfully. Show that you understand their needs and concerns. If you use the word "you" too much in a bad news message, the audience might feel blamed rather than respected.

Accusing tone: *Your* warranty does not cover breakages that *you* caused.

More neutral: The warranty does not cover accidental breakage.

Accusing tone: Because *you* did not purchase an extended warranty, *you* forfeited *your* right to free repairs.

More neutral: The repair would have been covered free of charge under our extended warranty.

Close the message positively

Several strategies help create a sense of goodwill when communicating bad news messages, including using an effective buffer, explaining audience benefits, and expressing the bad news in the passive voice. The positive conclusion provides an additional opportunity to instill confidence and promote goodwill. A positive closing should be forward-looking and optimistic. Depending on the situation, any of the following approaches may be appropriate:

- **Propose a solution.** If your bad news focuses on a problem, you may want to conclude by proposing a solution: "To increase your investment return next year, I suggest we rebalance your portfolio to include less risky investments."

- **Propose an alternative.** If you are refusing a request, consider whether you can grant a portion of the request or offer an alternative: "We encourage you to contact our affiliates to see if they have any internship openings for the coming summer. Enclosed is a brochure listing all our affiliates and their locations."
- **Create options for future business.** If you are turning down a vendor's proposal because of technical requirements, you could close your response by inviting the vendor to submit a proposal for a different project. "Our next round of requests for proposals will begin in six months. We hope you will consider submitting a proposal that meets the enclosed technical requirements."
- **Focus on a benefit.** When communicating negative situations, try to focus on the "silver lining," if one exists. For example, assume you learn that a new product designed by your company has flaws. When communicating this bad news to management, conclude by stressing good news: "Fortunately, the flaw appeared before the design went into production."

Evaluating bad news messages

Evaluate

Evaluation is important to ensure that your message is effective. For sensitive communication like bad news messages, evaluation is particularly important because, if handled poorly, this type of communication can have significant negative business results.

As you evaluate your message, look at it objectively and consider whether it is clear, easy to understand, and honest. Also consider whether you are communicating a sense of goodwill toward your audience. Then, step back and put yourself in your audience's position to evaluate how they are likely to respond and whether the message will achieve the business result that you intend.

Evaluate the message's clarity, honesty, and sense of goodwill

Consider the Great Expectations scenario on page 258 earlier in this chapter. You had decided on a "first and follow-up" strategy, beginning with a phone call and followed up by an email. You plan the message before calling. Here is your first version, which takes a direct approach:

> *Hello, Bill. I have some bad news. Due to circumstances beyond my control, I cannot begin working on your website for two weeks. As a result, it will take me an additional two weeks to complete the project. I hope that you will understand and be willing to reschedule your promotional campaign accordingly.*

Before you make the phone call, evaluate this message. It seems concise, clear, and easy to understand. However, is it honest? You say circumstances are beyond your control, but that is not true. You can choose to work with Great Expectations rather than your other client. The choice is within your control.

Also consider how effective this message will be for maintaining the client relationship. It does not communicate a sense of goodwill or make the client feel valued. It does not express appreciation or apologize. It offers no good news or any alternatives. It does not give the client any reason to work with you rather than hire someone else to do the job. This message clearly needs revising.

For your second draft, you make a few changes. You use an indirect organization to build up to the bad news, eliminate dishonesty, provide some reasons for the news, and express appreciation:

> *Hello, Bill. I'd like to talk with you about the completion date I promised for your project. One of my other clients has a time-sensitive web emergency that has to be addressed by next week. Because that organization's website is uniquely programmed, I am the only person who can solve this problem. As a result, I will not be able to begin your project for two weeks. I appreciate your understanding and your willingness to reschedule your promotional campaign.*

Is the second draft better? It softens the unexpected bad news by moving it later in the message. In addition, this version provides an honest explanation without giving too much information about the other client, and it does express some appreciation.

However, it still does not apologize, offer alternatives, communicate goodwill, or indicate that Great Expectations is a valuable customer. In fact, the tone may be slightly presumptuous, assuming that Bill will accept the bad news graciously and reschedule his promotional campaign.

Evaluate the business result

Review the message from your audience's point of view and think carefully about the business result. Your goal is to get your client to extend the deadline. However, the first two drafts of the message gave your client no reason to comply with your request. If you want this new client to accept your news, you will need to take a different approach. So you try a third version: one that offers alternatives and provides a better possible business result. You also rethink the purpose of this message. Do you want to impose bad news on your new client? Or would it be better to make a request and allow your client to determine if he can afford to wait for you? Is your overall purpose to maintain a long-term, positive relationship with this client?

> *Hello, Bill. I have a favour to ask. Would it be possible to extend the due date for your project for two weeks? As I mentioned yesterday, I'm committed to doing the best possible job for all my clients, and I plan to do an outstanding job for you. However, one of my other clients, a not-for-profit agency, has an emergency and requires a last-minute reprogramming of its website so that it will work with a new server. The work must be done before the launch of its annual pledge drive next week. Because I did the original programming, I'm the only person who can reprogram the system quickly. I realize that I made a commitment to you, and I apologize for any inconvenience a delay will cause. I would very much appreciate your extending the deadline. If that is not possible, could we identify the most crucial elements of the project that need to be done by the original deadline, with the remainder coming later?*

The evaluation process led to a very different message than the first draft. The most important change is that you are giving your client the opportunity to do you a favour or to say "no, you may not extend the deadline" and to negotiate a mutually acceptable solution. This message is much more likely to achieve a positive business result than the two previous versions.

Checking cultural assumptions about delivering bad news

Many Western business cultures are comfortable with the explicit, direct communication of bad news. Bad news might get softened by using a buffer or the passive voice, but at some point in the message the bad news will be clearly and explicitly articulated. For example, if you ask a Canadian whether she has finished analyzing data for a meeting, a bad news answer might sound like this:

- The analysis is not complete but we have enough for the meeting.
- The analysis was more difficult than I anticipated, so I'm not quite ready.

By contrast, in many non-Western cultures, people say "no" very differently. They may ignore the question, change the subject, respond with another question, or make a statement from which you will infer the negative news. In *Speaking of India*, intercultural expert Craig Storti illustrates a range of possible ways someone from India might say no without actually saying it (Storti, 2007):

- Who exactly is going to be at the meeting?
- Do you mean all the data?
- Is tomorrow good for you?
- Let me ask my team.
- We'll try our best.
- We have been working late every night.

Within the Indian culture, these answers would not be considered evasive. The audience would understand that all these answers equally mean that the analysis is not ready and the speaker is uncomfortable saying "no." However, to a Western audience these answers seem evasive.

When you communicate with people from different cultures, start by understanding your own communication style. Others will deal with bad news differently. For a deeper review on managing cultural assumptions, check out the **CULTURE BOX.**

CULTURE
GAINING INTERCULTURAL PERSPECTIVE ON BAD NEWS

Skylar has been excelling as an intern at Couture Ads. Not surprisingly, her supervisor has been giving her more important roles and responsibilities. One of those responsibilities is to deliver particularly bad news to a long-standing client. BigWigs is an international wig manufacturing company from India. Couture Ads also provides a local (Canadian) lead/referral service and, through this service, Skylar has been in discussion with Beauty By Bates, a national retail chain, regarding BigWigs' products. Mr. Jahari, the owner of BigWigs, will be flying in this week and wants to set up a meeting to follow up on the latest developments with this possible retail client for his wigs.

Issue: Skylar has been asked to meet with Mr. Jahari to convey the news that the latest marketing ads were not received well by Beauty By Bates. This potential client is not interested in buying wigs from BigWigs at this time.

Challenge: Skylar is not familiar with Mr. Jahari, nor with doing business in India. What should she consider?

- How should she prepare to deliver a bad news message to any client?
- When does culture matter in conveying bad news messages?

Assume the role of Skylar for a moment. This is where O-A-R can guide you:

- **Observe:** If possible and where appropriate, observe interactions between other colleagues and clients from diverse cultural and ethnic backgrounds. What are some of the practices when a question of culture arises? Are there protocols of practice that Couture Ads commonly follows?
- **Ask:** Ask a mentor or experienced colleague about strategies used to communicate bad news to international clients and partners. Specifically, ask your mentor or experienced colleague about his or her knowledge of this client or clients from India in general. Some questions to ask include the following:
  - Is it good business practice to call or email Mr. Jahari first to prepare him?
  - Would it be better to use a direct or an indirect approach?
  - Which communications "channel" is he likely to be most receptive to?

- **Research:** While researching this issue, you find out that business relationships in India are far more "relationship based" than "transaction based" (Hume, 2012). This leads you to assume that an indirect approach during a face-to-face meeting would be best. You confirm this assumption with your mentor. In addition to researching what the approaches are in communicating bad news messages, you can seek out a company "file" on BigWigs to see if you can understand the long-standing business relationship in more depth.

IMPORTANT FACTORS TO CONSIDER

- **Strengthen long-distance connections with trust and clarity.** It is a challenge to be respectful and culturally sensitive in situations that are tense or negative. Be mindful not to be evasive or elusive. It can negatively affect goodwill, trust, and rapport. Remember that the client relationship is especially important when business is transacted over great distances, both literally and culturally. Your client must return to his home country trusting in the strength of your long-standing relationship, regardless of this particular situation.
- **Be prepared.** Skylar needs to ensure that the latest marketing numbers are up to date and brought to the meeting, with a copy to share with Mr. Jahari. These may provide unbiased context regarding the potential client's decision not to proceed with BigWigs. Additionally, have alternatives or solutions ready to offer Mr. Jahari. This establishes a forward-thinking approach and conveys to Mr. Jahari that Couture Ads has BigWigs' best interests at heart.
- **Understand your role.** If hierarchy is an important factor in the client's business culture, then Skylar's position as an intern may pose some cultural and ethical challenges. There may be some international clients who believe that bad news should be delivered by more senior administrative personnel. This is a consideration that needs discussion with your supervisor.

For CULTURE exercises, go to Critical Thinking Question 2 on page 282 and Exercise 16 on page 285.

(LO 9.2) What types of bad news messages are common in business?

Many common business situations require a skilled approach to delivering bad news. This section provides examples of denying consumer claims, identifying issues or problems, and communicating negative change.

Denying customer claims

When you are denying customer claim requests, maintaining goodwill is important because you want to retain your customers' future business as well as win the business of their colleagues and acquaintances. Bad news about customer service travels fast and far. Research shows that customers tell nearly twice as many people about their bad experiences as they tell about their positive experiences (Buttle, 2011).

What communication techniques help customers feel good about continuing their relationship with a company? When you have to communicate bad news, customers need to know that you value them and have acceptable reasons for denying their request. Most important, customers need to know the company has corrected all errors and is willing to apologize if it is at fault. If customers are happy with the resolution, they are likely to remain customers (Hocutt, Bowers, & Donavan, 2008).

FIGURE 9.9 offers an example of a denial message that follows these guidelines. John Stevens, an unhappy customer, emailed Tuttle Office Supply, asking the company to replace 10 printers visibly damaged during shipping. He also requested onsite service to ensure that the remaining 15 printers sent in the shipment were undamaged. Maggie

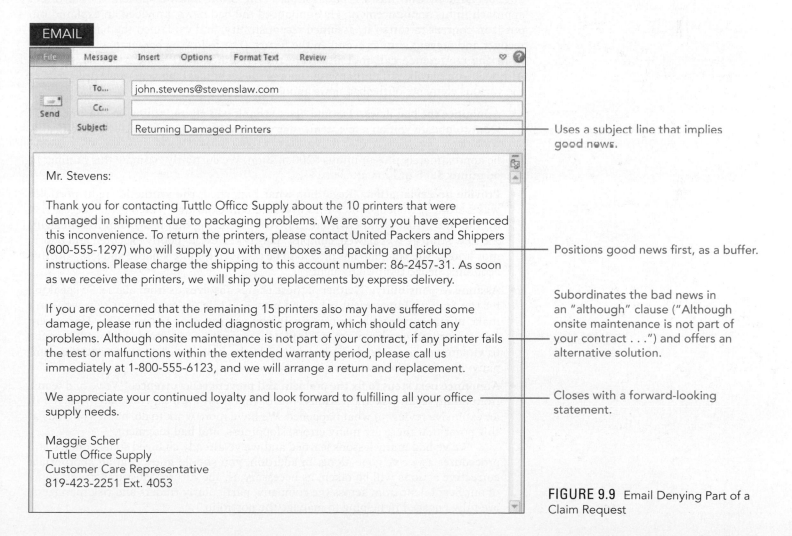

EMAIL

| Message | Insert | Options | Format Text | Review |

To... john.stevens@stevenslaw.com
Cc...
Subject: Returning Damaged Printers — Uses a subject line that implies good news.

Mr. Stevens:

Thank you for contacting Tuttle Office Supply about the 10 printers that were damaged in shipment due to packaging problems. We are sorry you have experienced this inconvenience. To return the printers, please contact United Packers and Shippers (800-555-1297) who will supply you with new boxes and packing and pickup instructions. Please charge the shipping to this account number: 86-2457-31. As soon as we receive the printers, we will ship you replacements by express delivery. — Positions good news first, as a buffer.

If you are concerned that the remaining 15 printers also may have suffered some damage, please run the included diagnostic program, which should catch any problems. Although onsite maintenance is not part of your contract, if any printer fails the test or malfunctions within the extended warranty period, please call us immediately at 1-800-555-6123, and we will arrange a return and replacement. — Subordinates the bad news in an "although" clause ("Although onsite maintenance is not part of your contract . . .") and offers an alternative solution.

We appreciate your continued loyalty and look forward to fulfilling all your office supply needs. — Closes with a forward-looking statement.

Maggie Scher
Tuttle Office Supply
Customer Care Representative
819-423-2251 Ext. 4053

FIGURE 9.9 Email Denying Part of a Claim Request

Scher, the customer care representative at Tuttle Office Supply, is able to replace the broken printers. However, she also has to communicate the bad news that the company cannot provide onsite service.

Note how the email reply in Figure 9.9 softens the bad news in four ways:

- Positioning the good news before the bad news as a buffer
- Subordinating the bad news in an "although" clause
- Offering an alternative solution to the request for onsite service
- Expressing empathy

Notice that the tone of the email is both factual and polite. This approach is designed to convince the customer that Tuttle Office Supplies values him.

Acknowledging mistakes or problems

People are usually uncomfortable when they need to acknowledge mistakes they have made or problems they have caused. Yet in business, taking responsibility for mistakes and bad decisions is critical for maintaining both credibility and goodwill.

When JPMorgan Chase lost billions of dollars in risky stock trades, CEO Jamie Dimon had to share the news with employees, shareholders, customers, and the media (Clarke & Henry, 2012; Langley, 2012). Given the severity of the situation, the significance of the bad news, and the large audience with which he had to share the news, Dimon could not avoid a large-scale public announcement of the bad news. Instead, he chose to acknowledge the mistakes via the medium that companies often use to communicate with shareholders and the media: a *shareholder conference call* via webcast, which allowed shareholders to log in, listen, and ask questions (JPMorgan Chase, 2012b). Dimon, who has a reputation as being blunt and outspoken, took a direct approach in his announcement. He announced the bad news, provided an explanation, put it in context to soften it, assumed responsibility, and explained the bank's plan to recover and prevent similar events in the future. The following paragraphs are excerpts from the conference call that illustrate these elements (JPMorgan Chase, 2012a). Although you may be unfamiliar with some of the technical language, you can recognize the various elements of the bad news announcement:

- **Announce the bad news.** "I would like to thank you all for joining on short notice. I want to update you on a few items that we have in our just-filed 10-Q. Specifically, we had given prior guidance that . . . net income in the Corporate segment . . . would be approximately plus or minus $200 million. We currently estimate this number to be minus $800 million after-tax."

- **Provide an explanation.** "Regarding what happened, the synthetic credit portfolio was a strategy to hedge the Firm's overall credit exposure, which is our largest risk overall in its trust credit environment. We're reducing that hedge. But in hindsight, the new strategy was flawed, complex, poorly reviewed, poorly executed and poorly monitored. The portfolio has proven to be [a] riskier, more volatile and less effective economic hedge than we thought."

- **Assume responsibility.** "Neither of these things absolves us from blame. So speaking for the Senior Management team and myself, while we can't assure you we won't make mistakes, we will—we can assure you we are going to try not to. These were grievous mistakes, they were self inflicted, we were accountable and we happened to violate our own standards and principles by how we want to operate the company. This is not how we want to run a business."

- **Announce next steps to fix the problem and prevent reoccurrence.** "We've had teams from audit, legal, risk and various control functions all from corporate involved in an extensive review of what happened. We have more work to do, but it's obvious at this point that there are many errors, sloppiness, and bad judgment.

    "We've had many lessons learned and we've already changed some policies and procedures as we've gone along. In addition, you should know that all appropriate corrective actions will be taken, as necessary, in the future. Most important, some of our best talent from across the company, particularly traders and risk managers, are fully engaged in helping to manage the portfolio."

ETHICS
TO APOLOGIZE . . . OR NOT TO APOLOGIZE

You may have noticed that, among all the elements in his bad news message, Jamie Dimon did not apologize to shareholders for the risky investments that led to JPMorgan Chase stock losing almost 30% of its value. Communication experts debate the wisdom of apologizing as part of a bad news message. Some people believe that apologies are dangerous because they put a business in a defensive position that could imply legal liability. However, others argue that apologies can have a positive effect (Agnes, 2012c; Patel & Reinsch, 2003). In fact, research shows that medical malpractice suits decrease when doctors admit their mistakes and sincerely apologize (Goodwin, 2010). Taking a "receiver perspective" in the face of a mistake is not only ethical, but also a practical business decision. A well-worded and sincere apology can improve a company's public image, facilitate forgiveness, and even decrease damages if a case goes to court.

However, if the apology is perceived by the public audience as insincere, the results can be quite damaging. In 2013, the Royal Bank of Canada bungled its communications as it attempted to manage public information about its participation in the temporary foreign worker program (Beltram & Paddon, 2013). There was a week-long delay between the revelation that RBC was bringing in foreign IT workers and training them to replace fully trained Canadian IT workers and RBC's response. Many felt this delay was too long. The apology itself was not fully accepted by many readers, and they made their responses known via Twitter and other social media channels (Beltram & Paddon, 2013).

One of the most famous and successful apologies in Canadian business history took place in 2008. Maple Leaf Foods had an outbreak of listeria bacteria in its packaged deli products. Immediately upon discovering that their products were the cause of several deaths and countless

infections and hospitalizations, CEO Michael McCain used both mainstream media (T. Wilson, 2011) and YouTube (Rosenblatt, 2011) to respond to the crisis. "It's so rare to see a white-collar executive descend from the ivory tower, apologize and reach out to the public in such plain language" said Ruth Davenport, a commentator with CJNI Radio in Halifax (Canadian Press, 2009). According to Tony Wilson, the author of the book *Manage Your Online Reputation*, McCain managed to do four things right with his public apology:

1. He took responsibility, on behalf of the company, for the mistake.
2. He actually apologized, in his own words, with sincerity.
3. He delivered the apology himself as opposed to hiring a professional PR representative.
4. He delivered on his promises to take action. The company acted quickly, decisively, and transparently. Tens of thousands of packages were recalled and destroyed (T. Wilson, 2011).

David Dunne, professor and director of MBA programs at the Peter V. Gustavson School of Business at the University of Victoria, noted that "McCain's response showed more than just sincerity. It also showed a business savvy that recognized the danger of waiting too long to respond to the crisis" (Canadian Press, 2009).

Maple Leaf Foods' listeria outbreak occurred in August of 2008. By the end of that year, McCain was voted the business newsmaker of the year by the Canadian Press, based on his handling of the issue (Canadian Press, 2009).

For ETHICS exercises, go to Exercise 14 and Exercise 18 on **pages 284** and 285.

Not all mistakes are as severe as the one Dimon had to admit to, but the elements of his bad news message provide a useful guide. You may have noticed that, among all the elements in his bad news message, Jamie Dimon did not apologize to shareholders for the risky investments that led to JPMorgan Chase stock losing almost 30% of its value. Should an apology be part of a message like this? Check out the **ETHICS BOX** for a deeper look at apologies within bad news messages.

Communicating negative change

There is a saying that "nothing is constant in business except change." Change is so pervasive in business and industry that "change management" has emerged as a discipline to help organizations and individuals implement and adapt to change. Communication is typically a key element in change management plans, especially when change negatively affects an audience, as is the case with layoffs and reductions in benefits.

For example, assume Jason Easterling, CEO of Reliant Textiles, needs to communicate to all employees in the Winnipeg, Manitoba, plant that the facility will be closing and all operations will be moving to Surrey, British Columbia. Only half the employees will be offered transfers. Although this is a final decision, he needs to help employees accept the decision and secure their assistance with the plant closing.

Easterling wants all plant employees to learn this news at the same time, so he holds a large meeting. However, because some employees work a night shift and cannot attend the meeting, he sends the follow-up email in **FIGURE 9.10** immediately after the meeting so that he can communicate simultaneously with everyone in the facility. For workers who do not have email access, he creates a written notice to be distributed at the plant the next day. Notice that he uses the direct approach because he knows that the employees would have heard about the plant closure from their co-workers or the media and thus will be expecting this news before receiving the email or written notice.

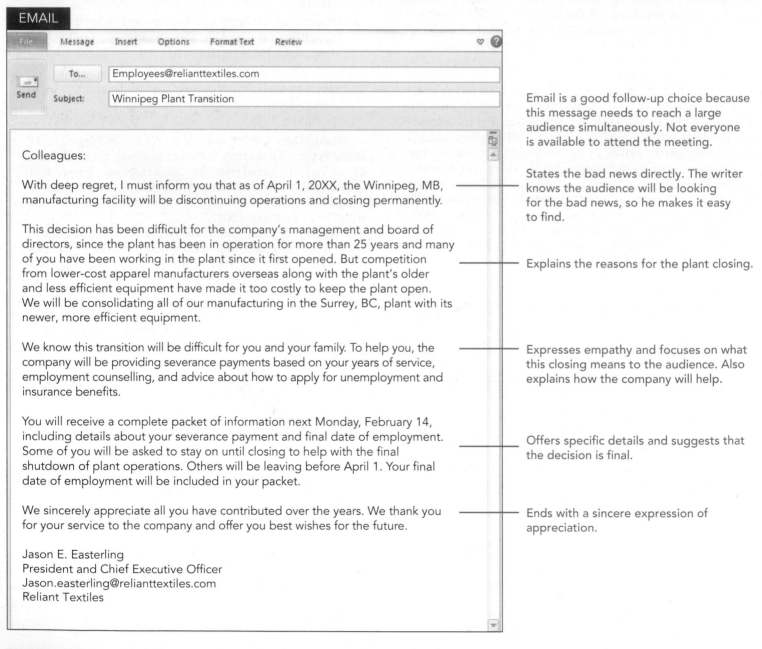

EMAIL

File | Message | Insert | Options | Format Text | Review

Send

To... Employees@relianttextiles.com

Subject: Winnipeg Plant Transition

Colleagues:

With deep regret, I must inform you that as of April 1, 20XX, the Winnipeg, MB, manufacturing facility will be discontinuing operations and closing permanently.

This decision has been difficult for the company's management and board of directors, since the plant has been in operation for more than 25 years and many of you have been working in the plant since it first opened. But competition from lower-cost apparel manufacturers overseas along with the plant's older and less efficient equipment have made it too costly to keep the plant open. We will be consolidating all of our manufacturing in the Surrey, BC, plant with its newer, more efficient equipment.

We know this transition will be difficult for you and your family. To help you, the company will be providing severance payments based on your years of service, employment counselling, and advice about how to apply for unemployment and insurance benefits.

You will receive a complete packet of information next Monday, February 14, including details about your severance payment and final date of employment. Some of you will be asked to stay on until closing to help with the final shutdown of plant operations. Others will be leaving before April 1. Your final date of employment will be included in your packet.

We sincerely appreciate all you have contributed over the years. We thank you for your service to the company and offer you best wishes for the future.

Jason E. Easterling
President and Chief Executive Officer
Jason.easterling@relianttextiles.com
Reliant Textiles

Email is a good follow-up choice because this message needs to reach a large audience simultaneously. Not everyone is available to attend the meeting.

States the bad news directly. The writer knows the audience will be looking for the bad news, so he makes it easy to find.

Explains the reasons for the plant closing.

Expresses empathy and focuses on what this closing means to the audience. Also explains how the company will help.

Offers specific details and suggests that the decision is final.

Ends with a sincere expression of appreciation.

FIGURE 9.10 Communicating Negative Change

LO 9.3 How can you control the spread of bad news through social media?

Communicating bad news in business requires more than just delivering the news effectively. You also need to control bad publicity that could result from the delivery of bad news to employees, customers, or other stakeholders. This role was traditionally handled by public relations or corporate communications professionals. However, with the rise of social media all employees must play a role in monitoring and controlling the spread of bad news through this emerging media channel.

Social media provides nearly everyone the opportunity to post comments about everything, including your business. Those posts can have serious consequences. Research suggests that consumers trust online commentary as much as they trust recommendations from friends (Neilsen, 2012), and when they read negative information about a company or product online, 80% will choose not to purchase that product (Faville & List, 2011). The bad news may originate as critical reviews on the company's ecommerce website, negative comments on reservation sites such as TripAdvisor or Yelp, damaging posts on social media sites such as Facebook, complaints on blogs and microblogs such as Twitter, and videos of product disasters on YouTube. No matter where the bad news originates, it travels fast on social media. News can be reposted and shared worldwide, escalating what could have been a minor crisis into a widespread public relations disaster. Check out the **TECHNOLOGY BOX** for a closer look at what can happen when the general public has the opportunity to use social media as a platform for negative publicity.

Having a plan in place

Research by Altimeter Group, a technology advisory firm, suggests that 78% of social media crises could have been avoided if the company had been prepared to respond by

---

TECHNOLOGY
FROM HASHTAG TO BASHTAG

Sometimes even the best attempts to appear accessible and transparent can go very wrong. Here are a few examples:

- **January 2012:** McDonald's tried to use #McDStories to generate positive buzz among customers about their Happy Meals. Instead, a brand-bashing stream of negative stories about their products hit the Twittersphere (Hill, 2012).

- **October 2013:** On the same day that British Gas raised its home heating fuel prices, customer services director Bert Pijls took an open Q&A (question and answer) session via Twitter, using #AskBG. Instead of fielding thoughtful questions about energy prices, Pijls found himself confronted with questions like "Have you considered converting the seething mass of human misery you generate into a renewable energy source?" (British Gas Twitter, 2013; Stockdale, 2014).

- **April 2014:** The New York Police Department invited people to tweet pictures of their dealings with "New York's finest" to #myNYPD. The results were primarily negative, with images of inappropriate police behaviour, including an image of a dog being frisked and names of people who had been shot by police. Tweets appeared at a rate of 10,000 per hour at the height of the activity (Tran, 2014).

In each of these cases, an organization made a sincere attempt to engage the public in a positive public relations exercise, only to have this effort go terribly wrong. Furthermore, these "bad news" stories would not have existed if each organization had not made the effort to attempt to create positive connections with their stakeholders.

What these types of stories demonstrate is the amount of care that must be taken to view your organization, honestly and clearly, from an external point of view. In Chapter 7 the idea of the "receiver's perspective" was introduced. Although Twitter and other forms of social media are relatively new forms of communication, the same principle exists. If you invite others to comment on your performance as an organization via any public forum, how will such an invitation be received? If the answer includes the possibility of the public leveraging social media to air personal or specific grievances, consider whether your organization has the capability and resources to convert a wave of negative publicity into a positive story.

For TECHNOLOGY exercises, go to Exercise 17 and Exercise 19 on page 285.

having a social media crisis management plan in place (Kirchner, 2011). This plan includes assessing your business risk, strengthening relationships with fans and customers, and understanding how to prevent minor crises from escalating (Agnes, 2012a). The following guidelines may form useful suggestions you can make to future employers who may not have taken the time to create such a plan. Do not wait for negative comments and then plan a response. Instead, be proactive.

Perform a thorough stakeholder/environmental scan

Assess your risk for negative comments. Although this question is often asked ironically, it is important to actually examine it: What could possibly go wrong with this social media initiative? Who might post such comments? Unhappy customers? Competitors? Activists and special interest groups? Disgruntled former employees? Sometimes businesses overlook the opportunity that social media provides to some interest groups to publicly denounce corporate decisions. The Dutch grocery chain Albert Heijn planned the launch of its Facebook page for months, but it did not plan well enough. During the first several days after the debut, conversations on the store's Facebook wall were dominated by an activist group that protested the sale of chicken grown quickly with hormones (Kerkhof, 2012). The Italian clothing giant Dolce & Gabbana was barraged by Facebook postings from an activist group called The Clean Clothes Campaign, demanding that the company stop sandblasting jeans to give them a worn look, claiming that the production method was dangerous to workers (Slater, 2011). Do a thorough environmental scan of the areas of vulnerability your company may expose to the public.

Monitor social media for early warnings

Ensure that you catch problems quickly by monitoring all mentions of your brand and company on all social media outlets, even on the weekends (Collier, 2011). You cannot respond if you are unaware of what is being said. Finally, empower trusted employees who monitor social media to respond. The bad news may go viral if employees need to wait for an official response.

Respond quickly

Do not ignore bad news or negative trends about your company in social media. If you use social media to respond quickly, your response will be distributed as quickly as the original posts. If you anticipate questions and concerns and incorporate them into your response, you can create a positive impression that enhances your business image (Kerpen, 2011).

Begin by responding in the social media channel where the bad news originated. Consider the video of a FedEx driver throwing a computer monitor delivery over a security gate. The delivery was recorded by a customer's security camera, and the customer posted the video to YouTube. Within five days, the video had over 5 million views (Dietrich, 2012). Just a few days later, FedEx responded with a video apology that was posted both to YouTube and FedEx's corporate blog. Customers and employees commented, most with positive responses about the company.

After the initial response, continue to comment in all your social media outlets to ensure that your response reaches as large an audience as possible and to promote the perception that your company is not being evasive. Link your tweets to your company's Facebook page and post more detailed information to your company website and blog. Video responses from senior administrators are very effective.

Respond authentically

Do not use a template or a generic message to respond to negative posts or even complaint emails. Research shows that social media audiences respond much better to personal-sounding responses than to impersonal ones (Kerkhof, Schultz, & Utz, 2011). Frédéric Gonzalo, vice-president of marketing for Le Massif, a ski resort in Canada, regrets his use of a generic message in the midst of a social media crisis (Agnes, 2012b). During a poor skiing season, the staff at Le Massif were delighted that a snowstorm was predicted for the Saturday of a late winter weekend and took the opportunity to generate excitement on the company's Facebook wall. By Sunday morning, however, all the chairlifts were frozen and Le Massif needed to turn away hundreds of disappointed customers, many of whom posted negative messages on the resort's Facebook wall. Gonzalo exacerbated the problem by posting this message (translated from French): "Thank you for your comments. Can you please send directly to our customer service at sac!!!!!!!!!!lemassif.com. We thank you for your understanding in advance, the Management Team." This response only made customers more angry. It took until Monday for Gonzalo to realize he needed to post a genuine apology with a genuine explanation. This response received very positive and understanding replies.

In summary, although bad news may disappoint your audience, you still want them to understand your rationale, to believe you are reasonable, and to feel confident and positive about you. Ottawa-based customer service consultant Shaun Belding says that, "While it seems like a paradox, sometimes by recovering from a failure you can create stronger word-of-mouth than by just providing good customer service" (Dwyer, 2010). This chapter provides techniques that will help you state bad news clearly and also soften its negative effect. It also provides techniques for countering bad news that others may spread about your business. Using these techniques will help you achieve your overall business goal: to maintain positive relations and project a positive image of your business. "Before, you're just another place they're doing business with," says Jeff Mowatt, a customer service strategist based in Calgary. "But now they're saying, 'You're unique, you're remarkable.' And they'll talk about it. You've actually created a more loyal situation" (Dwyer, 2010). Check out **FIGURE 9.11** for a summary of how ACE can help with the delivery of negative messages.

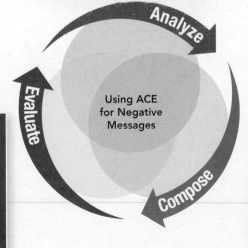

Define the negative message precisely. Ask yourself how the audience is likely to react.

Consider and prioritize the details you need to provide.

Weigh the advantages of including an apology.

Select the appropriate medium.

Analyze

Using ACE for Negative Messages

Evaluate

Assess the message's clarity, honesty, and sense of goodwill, as viewed from the receiver's perspective.

Evaluate the business result/outcome: Was it effective?

Double check for any cultural assumption you may have about the delivery of this bad news message. Could it be misinterpreted?

Compose

Select a direct or indirect approach, depending on your audience.

Articulate the message clearly and unambiguously.

If appropriate, use a buffer statement or passive voice statements to soften the impact of the news.

Construct a positive closing.

FIGURE 9.11 ACE for Negative Messages

Kathleen Leslie
Finding the Good
in the Bad

@ **WORK**

With permission from Kathleen Leslie and
Mallory Worrall.

At the beginning of this chapter, Kathleen was struggling with a directive to dismiss an employee who was not performing to corporate expectations. How can ACE help?

I knew that the most effective way to deliver bad news was to use the ACE formula: analyze, compose, and evaluate. By using this method, one is able to look clearly at a situation and formulate a supportive strategy.

- **Analyze.** I analyzed my audience's (Mary's) situation. First, I anticipated that financial security would be her immediate concern. Second, she was a very capable person, but she was not able to produce to the company's expectations. I had to ask myself why? Could it be that this was just not the right business for her? Third, she had made very solid connections with several vendors. Perhaps there was a possibility of networking with them for potential new opportunities. Finally, she was a composed individual and I did not anticipate a volatile reaction. Still, I prepared myself for a possible, but unexpected, emotional outburst.

- **Compose.** Next I composed a delivery of exactly what I was going to say to Mary. I wrote down the precise words I was going to use, included positive affirmations regarding her potential, and suggestions of possible opportunities outside of our organization.

- **Evaluate.** My final step before meeting with Mary was to evaluate my message. Had I covered all the issues of why she was being terminated? Was I sure that I was delivering a negative message in an affirming way? Was there anything I was missing to make this message easier for her to receive? I wanted Mary to leave with a positive opinion of both the company and myself. Once I was sure I was ready, I invited a representative from the HR department to attend the meeting to offset any potential legal ramifications, and then we went to meet with Mary.

Surprisingly, she took the news quite well and clearly understood everything I presented to her. As I had suspected, Mary confided that she had not felt competent in her position and hoped she would do better in a different organization. I assured her she would. I thanked her for her professionalism in the acceptance of the bad news. We closed the meeting on an optimistic note, as Mary left the company with a list of potential opportunities for her future.

Two months later I ran into Mary. She told me she had secured a great job and was very happy. She thanked me for firing her as this had opened up an opportunity for her to truly thrive. This was a win/win for all parties: the best possible outcome of delivering "bad" news.

Learning Objectives in Review

LO 9.1 How does the ACE process help you deliver bad news effectively? *(pages 258–270)*

- **Analyzing and planning bad news messages** requires that you ask and answer a number of questions: What is the bad news? What business result would you like to achieve in communicating the news? How will the audience react to this news? What justification and explanation should you include? Is there anything you can say to soften the bad news? Is there any good news to include? Will the audience benefit in any way? Does this cloud have a silver lining? Should you include an apology? Can you do anything else to project a positive image and maintain goodwill?
- **Using effective strategies to compose bad news messages** includes deciding where to state the bad news (direct or indirect organization), phrasing the bad news appropriately, softening the message, and closing positively.
- **Evaluating bad news messages** includes looking objectively for clarity and honesty. Consider whether the message will maintain a positive relationship with your audience. Examine the message from your audience's point of view and consider how the audience is likely to respond. Will the message achieve your intended outcome? Will it hurt or help your business?
- **Always checking cultural assumptions about delivering bad news** helps you ensure you do not cause an unintended impact or a misunderstanding.

LO 9.2 What types of bad news messages are common in business? *(pages 271–274)*

- **Denying customer claims** professionally means ensuring that customers know you value them and have acceptable reasons for denying their request. Customers need to know the company has corrected all errors and is willing to apologize if it is at fault.
- **Acknowledging mistakes or problems** quickly by providing an explanation and assuming responsibility is important. Be sure to articulate the next steps to be taken to fix the problem or prevent a recurrence. Construct a professional apology if appropriate.
- **Communicating negative change** is especially challenging. When the message is intended for a large audience, ensure that all members of the audience receive the same information at the same time. Be clear, thorough, and prepared to answer any questions that may arise.

LO 9.3 How can you control the spread of bad news through social media? *(pages 275–278)*

Have a plan in place. Assess your risk for negative comments and think about who might post them. Catch problems quickly by monitoring social media outlets, even on weekends. Ensure employees who monitor social media are empowered to respond.

KEY TERMS

buffer p. 263   goodwill p. 258

CASE STUDY

Making the Best of Bad News

This case study will help you review the chapter material by applying it to a specific scenario.

Henry Lai is having a bad week. On Monday, Henry's bus was delayed because of construction on a main road, making him late for his business communication class. Today he was almost late again. As Henry left his apartment, his neighbour stopped him in the hallway to ask if he had read the landlord's email announcing an increase in rent. Henry does not know how he'll handle his extra expenses. On top of a rent increase, he also needs to contribute money for an anniversary party he and his brothers are throwing for their parents in May. To add even more financial stress, Henry's home printer needs to be serviced and the store manager is not willing to honour the purchase agreement, which included two free maintenance or cleaning visits.

Henry slips into class just in time to get Professor Boychuk's assignment sheet. As Henry reads it, he begins to smile. This is an assignment he can definitely handle. Professor Boychuk is

requiring students to pick two types of writing (routine, persuasive, good news, or bad news). Over the next five weeks, students are to collect samples to analyze as part of an assignment. The goal is to evaluate these pieces according to the guidelines in the textbook and suggest revisions. A lot is going on in Henry's life, and many people are communicating with him. In fact, he could begin the assignment right after class by reading his landlord's email about the rent increase.

Softening the Impact of Bad News

After class, Henry checks his email. Will his landlord raise the rent to more than he can afford? He is not looking forward to reading the bad news. See the landlord's email message on page 280.

As Henry finishes reading, he thinks, "I'd like to stay. This must be a pretty good email." Would you agree?

QUESTION 1: *Evaluate this email. Would you recommend any revisions?*

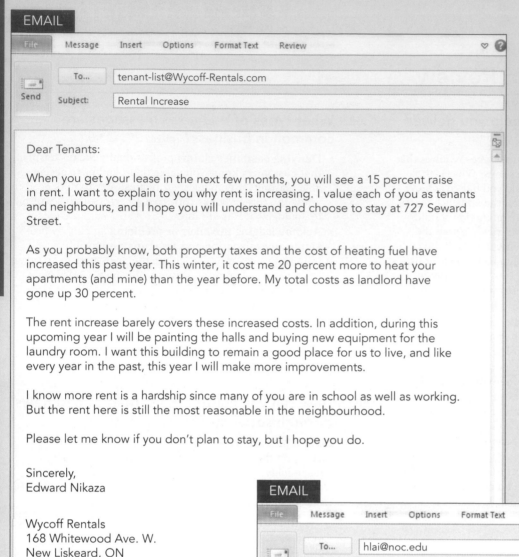

EMAIL

| File | Message | Insert | Options | Format Text | Review |

Send

To... | tenant-list@Wycoff-Rentals.com

Subject: | Rental Increase

Dear Tenants:

When you get your lease in the next few months, you will see a 15 percent raise in rent. I want to explain to you why rent is increasing. I value each of you as tenants and neighbours, and I hope you will understand and choose to stay at 727 Seward Street.

As you probably know, both property taxes and the cost of heating fuel have increased this past year. This winter, it cost me 20 percent more to heat your apartments (and mine) than the year before. My total costs as landlord have gone up 30 percent.

The rent increase barely covers these increased costs. In addition, during this upcoming year I will be painting the halls and buying new equipment for the laundry room. I want this building to remain a good place for us to live, and like every year in the past, this year I will make more improvements.

I know more rent is a hardship since many of you are in school as well as working. But the rent here is still the most reasonable in the neighbourhood.

Please let me know if you don't plan to stay, but I hope you do.

Sincerely,
Edward Nikaza

Wycoff Rentals
168 Whitewood Ave. W.
New Liskeard, ON
P0J 1P0
(705) 555-1926

Accompanies Question 1

Bad News from the Professor

After arriving late for his business communication class a third time, Henry is not surprised to see an email from Professor Boychuk in his inbox. Professor Boychuk has a strict attendance policy for her course. Henry is clearly finding this policy difficult to follow. If this is a bad news email, Henry hopes it is well written. He does not want to be in the position of critiquing his instructor in his final project.

Henry reads the email, reproduced here, and wonders: "If I can't pass the course, maybe I should drop it. Is that really the goal of this email?"

QUESTION 2: *Is this an effective bad news email? Would you recommend that Professor Boychuk make any revisions?*

EMAIL

| File | Message | Insert | Options | Format Text | Review |

Send

To... | hlai@noc.edu

Subject: | Class Tardiness in Bcomm 371

Dear Henry:

This week you arrived late to class for the third time. As you know, you can have no more than two unexcused absences or four late arrivals and still pass the class. I cannot stress enough how serious this is. Business Communication 371 is a requirement for graduation in your major. You must receive at least a C in this course. With one more absence or late arrival, you will need to repeat the course in order to graduate.

Professor Boychuk

Patricia V. Boychuk, Ph.D.
Professor of Business Communication
Department of Business Administration
Northern Ontario College, ON
P0J 2P0
pboychuk@noc.edu
(705) 555-2002

Accompanies Question 2

Bad News from the Electronics Store

Henry notices that there is an email from the electronics store regarding his printer issues.

Henry reads this last email, reproduced here. He is feeling angry and misled by the electronics store as he was not informed that there was a time limit to his service visits. He wonders how he will get anything printed for his school projects, and he feels frustrated at the option offered by the store of doing his printer repairs for a price.

QUESTION 3: *Is this an effective bad news email? Why or why not? Would you recommend any revisions to John McAvoy?*

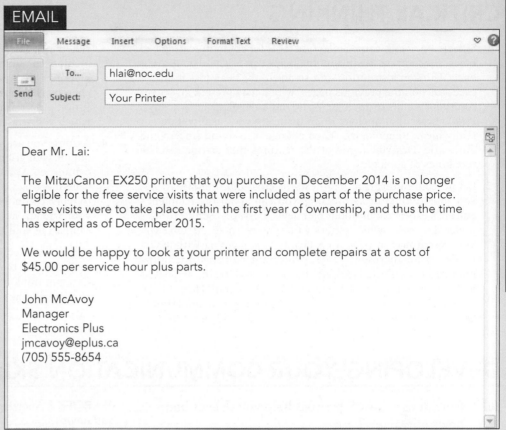

EMAIL

File   Message   Insert   Options   Format Text   Review

To...   hlai@noc.edu

Send   Subject: Your Printer

Dear Mr. Lai:

The MitzuCanon EX250 printer that you purchase in December 2014 is no longer eligible for the free service visits that were included as part of the purchase price. These visits were to take place within the first year of ownership, and thus the time has expired as of December 2015.

We would be happy to look at your printer and complete repairs at a cost of $45.00 per service hour plus parts.

John McAvoy
Manager
Electronics Plus
jmcavoy@eplus.ca
(705) 555-8654

Accompanies Question 3

How Would You Feel?

As Henry prepares to write his final business communication report by analyzing messages he has received during the term, he thinks about how important it is for a business to communicate effectively with its customers. Henry asks himself, "As a customer, how do I feel about the people who have been communicating with me? How do I feel about my landlord, Electronics Plus, and Professor Boychuk? Would I choose to have a continuing relationship with them or do business with them again? Will I spread goodwill or positive remarks about them?" These questions remain on Henry's mind as he analyzes his last business message: a voice mail from the River Inn where he planned his parents' anniversary party.

QUESTION 4: *Based on the four bad news communications noted here, which people or organizations would you do business with in the future? Why?*

VOICE MAIL

Mr. Lai. This is Darryl at the River Inn. We need to make some changes in the arrangements for your party in May. The room you reserved is undergoing extensive repairs for water damage caused by the storm and will not be ready by the 15th of next month. All of our other rooms are taken for that evening. Is it possible for you to change the date of your event to Sunday the 29th? If not, we will be glad to completely refund your deposit. Please return my call at your earliest convenience. I'm at 705-957-1344.

Accompanies Question 4

REVIEW QUESTIONS

1. Name four purposes that bad news messages must simultaneously accomplish.

2. How does the ACE process help you achieve the four purposes?

3. What questions should you ask yourself to help you develop content for bad news messages?

4. Under what circumstances should you state the bad news directly?

5. What techniques can you use to soften the bad news in an indirect message?

6. What are some options for closing a bad news message on a positive note?

7. Explain what you are looking for when evaluating a bad news message.

8. After you have delivered a bad news message, how can you evaluate the business outcome?

9. Identify the best strategies for communicating change.

CRITICAL THINKING

1. Sincere apologies can be effective tools for communicating bad news. By contrast, insincere apologies can alienate your audience. Think of a situation, or use one of the examples from the case study on the previous pages, which may present an opportunity for a sincere apology. Write out an apology in two ways. First, phrase that apology in an insincere way, as if you do not really mean to apologize. Then change it to sound sincere and authentic. Describe some of the features that distinguish the two kinds of apologies.

2. Before communicating bad news in cross-cultural situations, you should find out as much as you can about the recipient's culture's expectations about bad news messages. Some cultures prefer directness while others value indirectness. Assume you are presenting bad news in a face-to-face meeting with stakeholders who represent several different cultures, including high-context cultures (Arabic and Latin American) as well as low-context cultures (German and Scandinavian). How do you balance their differing perspectives about how bad news should be presented? [**Related to the Culture feature on page 270**]

3. When possible, face-to-face meetings are usually the best medium for sharing bad news, even if they need to be supplemented with an email for documentation. Many people are apprehensive about communicating bad news in person. What can you do to prepare yourself for a face-to-face meeting in which you will be delivering bad news?

4. Assume you are on the executive board of an organization, and one of your friends is chair of the organization's fundraising committee. Your friend has been doing a bad job and has not been meeting targets for over a year. The board has asked you to replace him. How would you communicate this bad news to your friend? Write out your step-by-step process and include samples of your communications.

5. One goal of communicating bad news is to convince your audience that the bad news should be accepted and not resisted. Can you think of any situations in which you might not want to convince the audience the news is final?

DEVELOPING YOUR COMMUNICATION SKILLS

 LO 9.1 **How does the ACE process help you deliver bad news effectively?** *(pages 258–270)*

EXERCISE 1 Analyze and plan: Ask questions that help you develop content

Assume you manage a video processing lab where customers bring in old home movies and have them transferred to DVDs. Yesterday a long-time client brought in a VHS videotape of her daughter's wedding and plans to pick up the DVD in two weeks after she returns from vacation. Today, one of your employees accidentally damaged the videotape and all your efforts to retrieve the data have failed. Answer these questions:

a. What is the bad news?

b. What business result do you want to achieve in communicating it?

c. How will the audience react to this information?

d. How do you want the audience to respond?

e. What justification and explanation should you include?

f. Is there anything you can say to soften the bad news? For example, is there any good news to include (audience benefits)?

g. Should you include an apology?

Be sure to explain and justify your answers.

EXERCISE 2 Analyze and plan: Select the best medium to achieve your goal

Assume you manage a local clothing store. One of your part-time employees, who frequently misses work or arrives late, emails to ask you to recommend her for a supervisory position. How will you communicate the bad news that you do not feel comfortable recommending her for a promotion? What is the best medium for communication: Would you write an email or choose face-to-face communication? Would you state the bad news directly or indirectly? Explain your reasoning.

EXERCISE 3 Analyze and plan: Decide where to state the bad news

For each of the following scenarios, explain whether you would organize the content directly or indirectly when communicating the bad news and justify your decision:

a. You are a marketing representative for a textbook publishing company. You told a customer that a new edition of a book would be available by July 1, in plenty of time to prepare for use in the fall semester. Today you learn that the book's publication has been delayed and that it won't be available until August 15, just days before the semester begins. How would you organize the message communicating this information to the customer?

b. Part of your job as the assistant manager of a large department store is to evaluate trainees as they transition from probationary status to regular full-time employees. Most of the time you are able to begin your face-to-face conversations with positive feedback before subordinating any constructive criticism. However, today you have to tell Phillip that if he wants to continue to work for the store he will remain on probation for two more weeks. He has not yet demonstrated that he can process returns on his own, and he struggles with the computer when processing any transaction. In fact, none of his supervisors could provide any positive feedback. How would you begin your face-to-face conversation with Phillip?

EXERCISE 4 Compose effectively: Soften the bad news

Rewrite each of the following badly written messages to soften the impact of the bad news:

a. Thank you for your recent order. I'm sorry you think your shipment was not complete. According to our records, all the items you ordered were delivered. Please refer to the attached copies of your order form and packing slip to confirm your complete shipment.

b. Although I hate to do it, we cannot offer bonuses this year due to declining sales. I'm sorry to disappoint you, especially during the holiday season. Better luck next year!

c. As we indicated last month, travel budgets have been frozen until next quarter. Why did you submit a request when you knew I'd have to deny it?

d. Thank you for your email indicating concern about the monthly premiums for family health insurance coverage. I agree that the difference between employee-only coverage ($10) and family coverage ($345) is unreasonable. Your proposal to split the difference makes sense. I wish I could support it, but the premiums are set by the insurance company.

e. Sorry to hear your iPod broke after only a week. We sell them, but we don't fix them. You'll have to contact the manufacturer who offered the warranty.

EXERCISE 5 Compose effectively: Close the message positively

For each of the badly written messages outlined in Exercise 4, create a concluding statement or paragraph that closes the message positively. Use one or more of the following techniques: propose a solution, propose an alternative, create options for future business, and focus on a benefit.

EXERCISE 6 Evaluate the message's clarity, honesty, and sense of goodwill

Two months ago Marla requested a week of vacation in early June to participate in her children's end-of-year school activities. However, yesterday she found out her husband's family reunion would be held over the Canada Day holiday. She decides to email her supervisor, Paul, to see if she can request a change in her vacation schedule. Unfortunately, Paul is not able to grant her request. Evaluate Paul's email message above right. Is it clear and easy to understand? Is it honest? Does it project a sense of goodwill toward the audience? What changes would you recommend?

EXERCISE 7 Evaluate the business result

You are an event planning consultant at Renew Retreat Centre. Several months ago Rena Murphy at Smith-Morrison and Associates (SMA) called you to coordinate the company's annual volunteer training seminar to be held at the retreat centre May 1–2. Rena booked the centre from 1 p.m. on Friday, May 1, through 8 p.m. on Saturday, May 2. Today is April 1, and Rena emails you to begin working on the logistics of the

EMAIL

To... Mmichaels@renthroproducts.com

Subject: Vacation Request

Marla:

I received your recent request to change your vacation week from the first week of June to the first week of July. Unfortunately, that's just not possible this year because of the end-of-year reports due by July 3. Also, as I am sure you are aware, company policy clearly states that vacations cannot be taken adjacent to scheduled holidays. Let me know if you'd like to select a different vacation week or keep your current first week of June.

Regards,
Paul

Paul O'Brien
Manager, Accounts Payable
Renthro Products
www.renthroproducts.com
Pobrien@renthroproducts.com
800.555.1660, Ext. 812

Accompanies Exercise 6

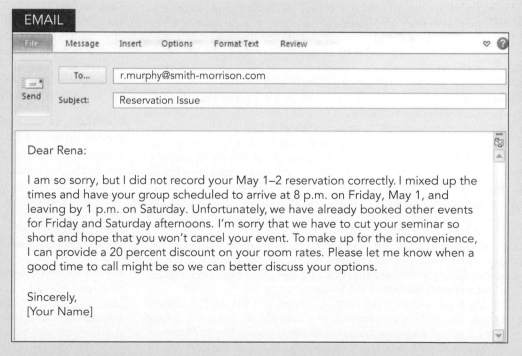

EMAIL

To... r.murphy@smith-morrison.com

Subject: Reservation Issue

Dear Rena:

I am so sorry, but I did not record your May 1–2 reservation correctly. I mixed up the times and have your group scheduled to arrive at 8 p.m. on Friday, May 1, and leaving by 1 p.m. on Saturday. Unfortunately, we have already booked other events for Friday and Saturday afternoons. I'm sorry that we have to cut your seminar so short and hope that you won't cancel your event. To make up for the inconvenience, I can provide a 20 percent discount on your room rates. Please let me know when a good time to call might be so we can better discuss your options.

Sincerely,
[Your Name]

Accompanies Exercise 7

seminar. As you retrieve the reservation from the system, you realize you accidentally mixed up the times. You have SMA coming in at 8 p.m. on Friday and leaving by 1 p.m. on Saturday. Other events have already been booked before and after these times, and it would be difficult to make changes. Saturday afternoon's event is a wedding, and you're quite sure the invitations have already been sent. How do you communicate this bad news to Rena without losing the event? Evaluate the email message to Rena on page 283. Assume you would like to retain this customer's business. Do you think that message will help you achieve the result? If so, why? If not, how would you recommend changing it?

 ## What types of bad news messages are common in business? *(pages 271–274)*

EXERCISE 8 Denying customer claims

You are the shipping manager for a toy company that does most of its sales through catalogue and online ordering. However, you also sell products to select local retailers across the country, including Toys R Us. Martha Hagler of Winnipeg, Manitoba, ordered a train set for her grandson's fifth birthday. The large set came in a unique tin container, which was damaged during shipping. Martha emailed your company to complain about the damage and request that a replacement be shipped to her overnight. Her grandson's birthday is in three days, and she wants another train set before the party. However, because the tin containers are made by another manufacturer and you are currently out of stock, you cannot replace her order before the party. Reply to Ms. Hagler with the bad news and an alternative solution.

EXERCISE 9 Acknowledging mistakes or problems

You run an online business selling unique gifts from a wide variety of manufacturers. A new customer placed an order for a product that was backordered by the manufacturer. Two weeks later, when you checked on the status of the shipment, you discovered that the manufacturer had discontinued the product. You spent several hours researching similar products from other manufacturers but have not yet found a viable replacement. You know you need to contact your customer to indicate that the product is no longer available. Decide on at least one strategy to buffer the bad news (see Figure 9.8 on page 267). Determine the best medium, and draft an effective message.

EXERCISE 10 Communicating negative change

You work for Plimpton Financial Services, a company that offers an extremely generous tuition plan for employees. The company pays 100% of postsecondary tuition for the children of all employees who have worked at the company for more than five years. This benefit can be worth hundreds of thousands of dollars for employees with multiple children. The CEO of Plimpton explains why the company has been so generous: "If we can take away the worry of paying for postsecondary education, employees will concentrate more and be more productive. We value our employees, and this is a great way to keep them."

Because of difficulties in the financial market, Plimpton has decided to phase out this benefit over a period of five years. This news will disappoint and anger many people who have been staying at the company to receive the benefit.

Your job is to plan the announcement. Use the ACE process to analyze the audience and compose a message. Because you do not have an actual audience available, imagine yourself as an employee of Plimpton who has three children to put through college or university.

 ## How can you control the spread of bad news through social media? *(pages 275–278)*

EXERCISE 11 Have a plan in place

Imagine two small businesses in your community: a bakery and a bank. Assume these businesses want to plan for negative comments on social media.

- Who might post negative comments and what might they comment about?
- Provide one or two ideas for each business about how they might minimize the chance of negative comments.

Now imagine a company that manufacturers a baby seat that the Canadian Standards Association has judged unsafe. The company has voluntarily recalled the seat. Assume this company wants to plan for negative comments on social media.

- What types of negative postings should the company anticipate? Where would people post these messages?
- What can the company do to minimize the chance of negative messages?

EXERCISE 12 Respond quickly

Find examples of negative comments posted by customers to third-party review sites, such as TripAdvisor or Yelp, or a company's Facebook wall. Did representatives from the business reply? If so, did they reply quickly? Do the responses suggest that they anticipated the audience's questions and concerns? Was the response positive? Were responses posted to all the business's social media outlets to reach as large an audience as possible? Explain how the business did or did not follow the strategies outlined in this chapter and, where applicable, offer suggested content that would have improved the company's response. Summarize your findings in a message to your professor or be prepared to present your findings to the class.

EXERCISE 13 Respond sincerely and authentically

Find examples of negative comments posted by customers to third-party review sites, such as TripAdvisor or Yelp, or a company's Facebook wall. Choose posts that include replies from the businesses. Then select two examples: one that responds sincerely and another that does not. Copy or print each negative comment and its response. Evaluate how each response is or is not polite, personal, and authentic. Summarize your findings and include the examples.

EXERCISE 14 Apologizing for a mistake [Related to the Ethics feature on page 273]

Select either Exercise 7 (SMA and the wrong booking date) or Exercise 8 (the damaged toy container). Create an apology strategy that would be appropriate to the situation. Which media would you use? What would you say? What written communications would you prepare? In the case of the written elements of this strategy, compose the written parts for evaluation. Use the guidelines outlined in the Ethics feature in this chapter to guide you in creating your strategy.

EXERCISE 15 Responding to a customer's complaint

You are a manager at Home Goods, which sells a wide variety of bath, kitchen, and other household items. Several months ago you offered a special sale on a specific FreshAir humidifier, Model 2850. A customer who purchased one of these humidifiers returned to your store last week to purchase more filters for the humidifier. However, your store no longer carries the FreshAir brand. Although the store offers several replacement filters for other brands, you do not carry the specific model the customer requires. He wrote a letter to "The Manager" complaining about the problem and indicating that he plans to tell everyone he knows not to bother buying products from your store because you don't stock the items needed to maintain them. Although you don't have the filters in your store, you can special-order them. How do you respond to the letter? What medium would you use? Draft a message.

EXERCISE 16 Analyze your audience: Prepare to communicate bad news in other countries [Related to the Culture feature on page 270]

You are working with an international team of research and design specialists that includes engineers from subsidiary offices in several countries. Last week you tried to tell Bhavna Asnani from the Mumbai office that there were serious problems with her report. Although Bhavna speaks fluent English, you had difficulty ensuring that she understood the problems. She readily agreed with your comments rather than asking questions for clarification or making suggestions to create a solution to the problems. This morning you shared the scenario with your supervisor, who explained how Indian cultures react to and communicate bad news. Now the conversation makes more sense to you, and you wish you had not been so direct with the bad news. To ensure you do not make the same mistake again, you decide to begin to research how to communicate effectively with international audiences. Use credible sources, such as http://geert-hofstede.com, and summarize your findings in a five-minute presentation including at least one visual aid.

EXERCISE 17 Damage control in social media [Related to the Technology features on pages 262 and 275]

Find a recent example of a company's social media strategy backfiring and causing a bad situation for that organization. Create a timeline to show how the events unfolded. Using the information in the Technology features, suggest how the company could have responded differently to create a more positive outcome.

EXERCISE 18 Apologies in social media [Related to the Ethics feature on page 273]

Find an example of a company that posted an apology about a problem on its website as well as on at least one social media outlet, such as Twitter, Facebook, or YouTube. Compare the apologies in these different social media outlets. Identify the timing of the problem and when the apology was posted to each medium. For each message, determine how (or if) the company acknowledged the mistake, expressed sympathy and concern, explained how the mistake occurred, and showed how it would prevent the problem from recurring. If the company did not do these things, suggest how it could have improved its communication. Summarize your findings in a one-page message to your instructor or be prepared to present your findings in class.

EXERCISE 19 Using digital media to distribute notice of bad news [Related to the Technology features on pages 262 and 275]

Find a recent (less than six months old) example of a company using digital media to let their stakeholders (employees, shareholders, partners, or others) know about some urgent bad news. This could include a food contamination, client data breach, a safety recall of a product, or some other similar situation. Create a timeline of events from the information you can gather. Analyze the events and evaluate. What did the company do well? What could it have done better? What recommendations would you make to this company for future situations like this? When you have finalized this evaluation, tackle one final question. Is this situation finished or are there more events to come? Justify your response.

10 Finding and Evaluating Business Information

Jasminko Ibrakovic/Shutterstock.

LEARNING OBJECTIVES

LO 10.1 How do you determine what information you need? *pages 288–295*

Analyze the research question and topic
Identify audience concerns and needs
Establish the scope of the research
Define research activities
Develop a work plan

LO 10.2 How do you conduct and evaluate research in print and online sources? *pages 295–300*

Gather relevant print and electronic files
Search the web strategically
Use an online index or database to find articles and business data
Use a library or bookseller to find relevant books
Follow leads in reliable sources
Evaluate your sources for credibility

LO 10.3 How do you conduct and evaluate primary research? *pages 300–310*

Conduct survey research to gather information that is easy to compare
Conduct interview research to gather in-depth information
Conduct observational research to understand how people act

LO 10.4 How can you use social media in your research? *pages 310–312*

Search for experts
Post questions to your network and beyond
Share information
Gather anecdotal evidence

LO 10.5 How can you effectively organize the results of your research? *pages 312–318*

Build your reference list as you research
Organize documents and notes on your computer and "in the cloud"
Organize your findings by research questions

Mark Federman, Ph.D.

Consultant & Educator,
Transformative Contemporary
Leadership: Facilitating
strategic insight,
innovation, and the
transformation of
contemporary leadership

@ WORK

"So what . . . ?"

Photo courtesy of Mark
Federman and Jennifer
Gilbert.

It was my first big presentation to the vice-president. I was understandably nervous, even though I had meticulously prepared for the event. My data analysis was, in my opinion, impeccable. I had a dozen charts prepared with the data broken out by market segment, geography, product breakdown, and profitability, among others. You name it, and I had probably thought of a way to slice and dice the data accordingly. After my allotted 20 minutes, during which I raced through what I had highlighted as the important data points, the vice-president looked me squarely in the eyes and said only two words: "So what?" If I could have disappeared from view by shrinking into my highly polished Oxford shoes, I certainly would have.

Decision making is essential to business. Decisions require information. Whether the decision involves acquiring equipment or software systems, launching a new product or service, or understanding how to increase sales or profitability, research provides the basis for reaching a desired outcome. Research begins with clear questions that relate to specific, intended business results. Valuable research questions carry with them a "so what?" element. How is *this* piece of information relevant to a decision that will enable the business

to take some action? Too often, for example, analysts compile lists of features and benefits for an acquisition, presuming that the decision will be self-evident. The "so what?" must consider how the listed benefits actually benefit the business's objectives. A market research study may result in multiple pages of charts, data tables, and quotations that are perfectly clear to the analyst. In many cases, the analyst may insist that the numerical details are essential to understanding the issue at hand. The numbers may indeed yield that understanding. However, the "so what?" for the decision maker in this case might be "What do these tables of numbers actually mean in business terms?" A "meta-study" of secondary sources may show a consensus of opinions about a particular market segment or an opportunity for innovation. If, however, the research report is little more than a laundry list of what each study concluded, the "so what?" that would identify how those conclusions apply to the specific business question at hand is missing.

In each of these instances, it is not the direct results of research such as the features, the data tables, or a list of conclusions that matter. Rather, it is how these results can be applied to solving the real questions of the business, how they can move the company to action, that makes the research valuable. Consider a hardware store. Despite the fact that the store may sell a lot of ¼-inch drill bits, no one is actually interested in ¼-inch drill bits. Rather, they are interested in ¼-inch holes. Similarly, few businesses are interested in research results for their own sake. Rather, they are interested in how those results inform actionable decisions that lead to achieving business success.

At the end of this chapter, Mark explains how he uses the ACE framework to provide research-based recommendations that are relevant and useful.

Introduction

In the workplace you may be assigned projects that require you to conduct research. For example, you may be asked to

- determine which product features are most important to your customers,
- compare the benefits packages offered by your company and its competitors,
- analyze how new provincial tax credits will affect your company, or
- decide where to locate a new warehouse.

Employers will not expect you to know how to answer these questions right away. Instead, the expectation will be that you enter *research mode* to collect relevant and pertinent data, and then share the results of your research, perhaps in a written report or in an official presentation.

As a student, you have been developing your research skills for many years. These skills will be useful to you in the workplace. Both academic and workplace research ask you to do the following:

1. Identify research questions
2. Find appropriate sources
3. Extract the correct information
4. Combine this information with what you have collected from other sources
5. Present findings in a useful format

You will find that academic and workplace research differ in two key ways: their starting points and their goals. Academic research typically starts with a topic. You need to focus on that topic, identify a research question, and then conduct the research. The goal of most academic research is for you (the researcher) to learn. Workplace research, by contrast, typically starts with a specific question or problem. The goal

FIGURE 10.1 Academic and Workplace Research

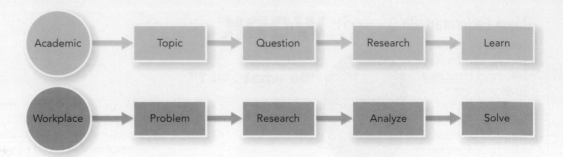

of the research is to find, analyze, and organize information that will help answer the question or solve the problem (see **FIGURE 10.1**).

This chapter discusses a process for finding and evaluating the business information necessary to prepare well-researched and well-documented proposals, reports, and presentations. You will learn

- how to develop a research plan,
- how to search different types of sources,
- how to conduct your own original research, and
- how to organize the results.

Chapters 11 and 12 will build on this chapter and show how to incorporate research into proposals, reports, and presentations.

 # How do you determine what information you need?

Business research usually starts with a specific question or problem. This gives you a distinct advantage over someone writing an academic paper, who starts with only a general research topic. However, it is still helpful to follow a structured process that outlines exactly what you are looking for and where to look for it.

As you read this chapter, keep the following research scenario in mind: Assume that you are Sarah Nguyen, learning and development manager for Marcato Brands, a large consumer product company with offices around the globe. You report to James Vandermeer, chief learning officer. Your department is responsible for orienting new employees and providing training and professional development opportunities for employees in all the company's offices. Specific tasks include designing instructional materials, organizing training sessions, training new trainers, maintaining employee training records, and providing data for supervisors to use during performance reviews.

Currently, the company's system for managing these tasks is expensive, inefficient, and out of date. All training is conducted face to face, with trainers travelling to specific offices or employees travelling to a central location. In addition, all training schedules and records exist only on one central computer at the company's headquarters. To reduce costs and improve efficiency, you suggest that the company invest in a learning management system (LMS) that will allow the company to provide some training online as well as manage all the content and record keeping for the system. Vandermeer thinks it is a great idea and asks you to research and recommend an LMS. He gives you four weeks to complete this project.

You have a lot of research ahead of you before you can determine which system to recommend. Here are some of the specific questions you will need to answer:

- What are the major differences between the types of learning management systems: products primarily used in academia (such as Blackboard or Desire2Learn), products specifically designed for business use (such as Saba and SuccessFactors), and open source products that can be customized (such as Sakai, Moodle, and ATutor)?
- What criteria should you use to evaluate LMS platforms?
- What are the experiences of other companies with specific LMS platforms?
- What are the costs of different options?

As you research, you will think of additional questions. To proceed you must consider the *where* and *how* of conducting your research: *Where* will you find the data you need to answer these questions? Once you find the data, *how* will you evaluate whether the information is useful?

Research Question 1:	**Would a learning management system (LMS) be an effective tool for our company?**	
	• What specific training and content management needs does our company have?	
	• What current problems are we facing?	
	• What are options for solving these problems?	
	• Is an LMS the best option?	
Research Question 2:	**If an LMS would be effective, which one is the best option to meet our specific training needs?**	
	• What are the various options for LMS programs?	
	• What criteria will we use to judge the options?	
	• Which option best meets the criteria?	
Research Question 3:	**What will be the costs of the recommended option, in money and time?**	
	• What is the initial purchase and installation cost?	
	• What are the ongoing costs, such as customer support?	
	• How much time will it take to get the new system up and ready to use?	

FIGURE 10.2 Questions to Guide LMS Research

Analyze the research question and topic

Be sure you have a firm understanding of your major research question or problem as well as the assumptions it is based upon. For example, in the Marcato Brands scenario, James Vandermeer asked you to research which LMS is best for the company. This question *assumes* that an LMS in general is the best solution to the problems of excess training expenses, inefficient content management and record keeping, and a dated system. You may need to broaden the research questions to find the information you need: Perhaps there is a better solution you have not considered yet. Based on this analysis, you might include the questions illustrated in **FIGURE 10.2**. Notice that each research question also includes subquestions that you will need to explore to answer your main question.

Before doing in-depth research to explore these specific questions, you need to understand your general topic. You can conduct background research to help you understand your topic's history, context, structure, and categories (Booth, Colomb, & Williams, 2008). **FIGURE 10.3** illustrates a set of background questions and then adapts those

CATEGORY	GENERIC QUESTION	SAMPLE QUESTIONS FOR THE LMS RESEARCH PROJECT
History	When and why did X first develop?	When and why did learning management systems first develop?
	How has X developed over time?	How have learning management systems changed and why? What have been the biggest influences on these systems?
Context and Structure	How does X function as part of a larger context or system?	How does a learning management system fit into a larger system of workplace training and development? What role does it play in relationship to the other elements in the system?
	What else exists that serves similar purposes?	Instead of a learning management system, what else could help solve our problem?
	What are the parts of X and how do the parts fit and work together?	What are the various elements of a learning management system? How do all the parts work together?
Categories	What types or categories of X exist?	What kinds of learning management systems are there? How are they grouped, and why are they grouped that way?
	How do different types of X compare and contrast with each other?	How do typical academic learning management systems, like Blackboard and Desire2Learn, compare and contrast with those primarily used in the workplace, like SuccessFactors and Saba?

FIGURE 10.3 Background Research Questions

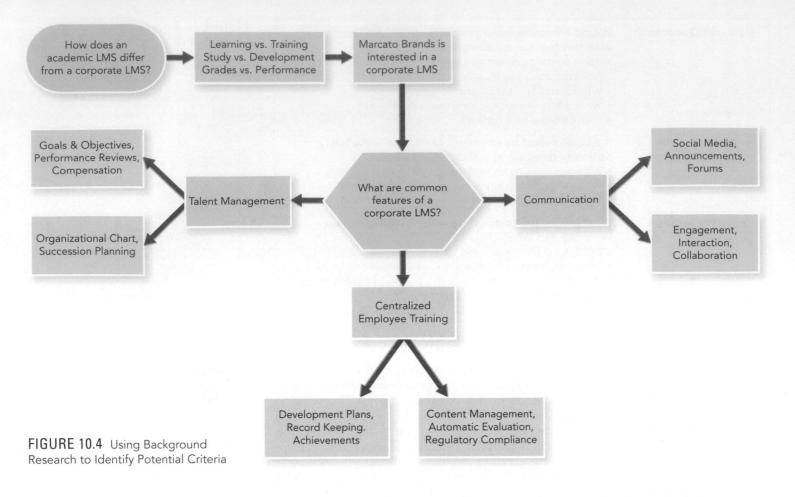

FIGURE 10.4 Using Background
Research to Identify Potential Criteria

questions to apply to learning management systems. For your specific topic, you will
need to decide which questions listed in the figure are most important.

The results of this background research are not meant for inclusion in your final
presentation or report. However, you will find that by broadening your understanding of
the topic it will be easier to structure your research. **FIGURE 10.4** illustrates how background information can help focus your research and identify required criteria.

Identify audience concerns and needs

As you search and collect research, keep in mind the interests of your potential
audience(s):

• What questions will your audience expect you to answer?
• What does the audience already know? What does the audience need to know?
• What sources will your audience expect you to consult?

That final question ("What sources will your audience expect you to consult?")
is important to establish your credibility. If you perform a quick Google search or rely
on a general and nonvalidated source like Wikipedia, even for background information, your audience may not respect your findings. A professional audience is more
likely to value your information if you use professional and highly credible sources.
These sources include journals and websites published by professional associations in
the industry, research published in academic journals, and books by reputable authors
and publishers.

Taking the time to analyze the members of your audience and other stakeholders
enables you to consider the problem from their point of view and identify concerns that
you will need to address.

Using the LMS research as an example, analyze your audience and stakeholders by considering these questions:

1. Who is the primary audience?
   - Your supervisor, James Vandermeer
2. Who is the secondary audience?
   - Marcato's senior-level decision makers, who will finance an LMS purchase
3. Who else may be affected by this problem or decision?
   - Marcato employees, who will be affected by the integration of an LMS
4. What sources might your audience expect you to consult?
   - Publications from the Institute of Performance and Learning
   - *Canadian Journal of Learning and Technology*, a journal published by the Canadian Network for Innovation in Education (CNIE)
   - Learning Circuits, a website devoted to e-learning belonging to the Association for Training and Development (ATD)
   - Books like *E-Learning and the Science of Instruction: Proven Guidelines for Consumers and Designers of Multimedia Learning* by Clark and Mayer (2008)
   - The websites and marketing departments of each LMS you are considering

Your audience may even expect you to conduct your own original research, such as interviewing people who have experience with your topic or surveying potential stakeholders.

Establish the scope of the research

The **scope** of a research study refers to the range of your research. Establishing the scope is like looking through binoculars. You can choose to view the landscape of a large area (broad scope) or to focus on the details of a small object (narrow scope). In your LMS research, you may look broadly at the information about many LMS platforms to determine if online content management and training would be an effective format for your company. However, to determine which system is the best option, you might have to narrow your focus to collect a lot of information about the final two or three platforms you believe are the best fit.

Establishing the scope of your research also allows you to define the limitations of your research. **Limitations** are the characteristics of the research that prevent you from generalizing your findings more broadly. For example, if you choose to narrow the scope of your research to established LMS platforms that have been widely used and reviewed rather than investigating new options, then you cannot generalize and suggest you have selected the best of all possible learning management systems. Rather, you have selected the best widely reviewed system.

How you decide on the scope of the research depends on the needs of the project, the amount of time available, and what you learn in your initial research. For example, if you have only a week to research LMS options, you may limit your research to include only material that is available from companies and product reviews in professional journals. With more time available, you may choose to interview people who use the programs and to collect anecdotal evidence from social media. If you learn in your initial background research that only two programs seem appropriate for your company, then you may decide to narrow your research to focus more deeply on those two programs.

Define research activities

Research activities are fuelled by your research questions. They are the *steps* you will take to find the information needed to answer the research questions. Here are some examples:

- To answer the question "What specific training and content management needs does our company have?" you might interview department heads at Marcato Brands
- To answer the question "What is the initial purchase and installation cost?" you might speak to the sales department of the selected LMS

Scope The range of your research. A broad scope includes a wide range of content, whereas a narrow scope focuses on specific aspects of the topic.

Limitations The characteristics of the research that prevent you from generalizing your findings more broadly.

The list of research activities helps you identify sources for the information. Typically, sources fall into one of three categories: primary, secondary, and tertiary sources.

Primary sources provide raw data. You can collect primary data by surveying, interviewing, or observing people. If you survey people who use different learning management systems, you are conducting *primary research*. Another form of primary research involves reading primary texts, such as the websites and marketing materials of various LMS providers. Primary research may be quantitative or qualitative. **Quantitative research** gathers numerical data, such as structured survey responses to which you can assign numbers. Quantitative research allows you to classify, count, and compare data, allowing you to identify patterns. By contrast, **qualitative research** uses open-ended questions and observations to gather data that provide insights into the attitudes, values, and concerns of the research subjects.

Secondary sources are the results of other people's research. The research may be published in articles, books, or research reports and is usually written by the researchers themselves. A journal article comparing three learning management systems is a secondary source.

One of the challenges of using secondary sources is the ease with which one can infringe on intellectual property ownership by plagiarizing someone else's work. Interestingly, different countries have different attitudes and approaches to the use of other people's intellectual property. For more information on this topic, check out the **CULTURE BOX**.

Primary sources Sources from which you collect your own raw data.

Quantitative research Research that relies on numerical data, such as that gathered from structured survey responses to which you can assign numbers.

Qualitative research Research that provides insight into the attitudes, values, and concerns of research subjects through interviews and observation.

Secondary sources The results of other people's research that you consult as part of your research.

CULTURE
BLURRED LINES?

In March 2015, the estate of the late Marvin Gaye won a $7.4 million award when a US court found that the mega hit "Blurred Lines," written by Robin Thicke and Pharrel Williams, was plagiarized, having borrowed eight distinct elements from a 1977 Marvin Gaye song (Associated Press, 2015). Skylar was listening to this news story on her way to campus from her internship placement. Working in the professional world enriches Skylar's student experience by adding real-life experience, professional perspectives, and cultural considerations. Many of Skylar's classmates are like her: part-time, mature, or international students who often work while going to school. This dynamic, while interesting and flexible, can pose challenges to group work. Scheduling meeting times can be difficult. Time pressures, as students attempt to balance work and school, can lead to academic "shortcuts." Also, Skylar is discovering that students have varying understandings of academic integrity and quality of work.

Skylar and two other students were given a group assignment on a topic they knew very little about: big data and its impact on business. There is a research component to the assignment, which is worth 25% of their final grade.

Issue: As the assignment due date approaches, Skylar realizes that two parts submitted by her group members were "copied and pasted" directly from the research they had found online. Additionally, one member who was responsible for providing a reflective analysis of the topic said that he just copied it from a blog. When Skylar raised the issue, the group members said that plagiarism was considered differently in their culture of origin. Also, one group member felt strongly that she just didn't have time to be more thorough or thoughtful. Skylar's teammates did not feel they had done anything wrong.

Perspectives on plagiarism do vary across the globe (see map). Different cultures have different values, which may influence the way they learn, teach, and view intellectual property (Yusof, 2009). "In many Asian, Middle Eastern, African, and First Nation cultures . . . knowledge is believed to belong to society as a whole, rather than an individual" (Hu, 2001). In fact, in China and Italy, students learning science and history "are only required by their teachers to find the source answers and copy them" (Hu, 2001). Similarly, in a 2014 article in *Fast Company*, Tina Amirtha writes that "one in 16 authors were found to have copied long phrases and sentences from their own previously published work, and about one out of every 1,000 authors copied about a paragraph's worth of text from other people's papers without citing them" (Amirtha, 2014).

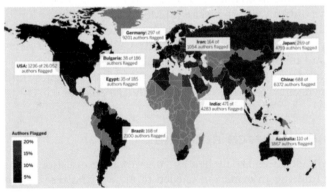

Challenge: The instructor made the students aware of plagiarism through their course syllabus as well as a brief discussion in the first class. In particular, the instructor emphasized clear and severe consequences for plagiarism. Skylar is deeply concerned that her grade and even her participation in the course may be in jeopardy if the work submitted by her group is viewed as being plagiarized. The song title "Blurred Lines" and the story about the costly plagiarism case involving this song continue to echo through Skylar's thoughts. She wonders how costly this assignment could be to her.

This is where O-A-R can help:

- **Observe:** Observing by "surveying" the cultural diversity within the class, group, or team can inform Skylar of potential challenges when dealing with plagiarism in her work groups. When it comes to plagiarism and differing cultural interpretations, she may want to discuss this issue explicitly with her teammates at the outset of the assignment. This would help uncover any discrepancies in views on plagiarism and allow all team members to move forward with a common perspective.
- **Ask:** Considering the varied perspectives on plagiarism above, mitigating potential challenges can be addressed by asking a few key questions:
  - What are the research components of the assignment?
  - What are our group's expectations with regard to validating and citing sources?

  Ask group members to review the course syllabus on plagiarism. Can they avoid producing work that would contravene this course's definition of plagiarism?
- **Research:** Considering the access to information now available through technology, it is important to understand how complex plagiarism is. According to the

plagiarism detection specialists Turnitin, instructors in US and Canadian schools have identified at least 10 different types of plagiarism:

Source: The plagiarism spectrum: Instructor insights into the 10 types of plagiarism. TurnItIn.com. 2012. http://go.turnitin.com/paper/plagiarism-spectrum?Product=Turnitin&Notification_Language=English&Lead_Origin=Website&source=Website%20-%20Download

Knowing this, it may be important to research each of these types of "blurred lines" that define plagiarism so that you can recognize them in your own work and in the work of others.

For CULTURE exercises, go to Critical Thinking Question 6 and Exercises 23 and 24d on pages 321 and 325.

Tertiary sources are books and articles that synthesize material from secondary sources, framing them for general readers. Tertiary sources include encyclopedias, textbooks, online tools like Wikipedia, and the results of most standard web searches. Sources like these are often excellent for background research. However, they may oversimplify the research they present. You will have more credibility with your audience if you try to find the original material that these sources summarize.

For the Marcato Brands LMS project, you will need to do a lot of primary research. For example, you could read websites and marketing materials of several learning management systems, speak to sales representatives, interview users of these systems, and interview people within your organization to identify criteria for judging the options. Reliable secondary sources will also make your job easier. If you can find reviews of different systems or case studies describing how people have used learning management systems, you will be able to save time. Although you should not rely on the material from a tertiary source such as a Wikipedia article on learning management systems, quickly reading that article or a summary article on the Institute for Performance and Learning website may be an excellent way to get background information or a list of other resources to consult.

Develop a work plan

The last step before beginning your research is to develop a work plan like that illustrated in **FIGURE 10.5** to help you track your progress over time and ensure you meet

Tertiary sources Books and articles that synthesize material from secondary sources.

FIGURE 10.5 Developing a Work Plan

RESEARCH QUESTIONS	RESEARCH ACTIVITIES	TARGET DATE	KEY FINDINGS	IMPLICATIONS/ CONCLUSIONS	RECOMMEN- DATIONS

RESEARCH QUESTIONS	RESEARCH ACTIVITIES	TARGET DATE
Background Research • What are the various types of learning management and course management systems? • How do the types compare? • What are the various elements of a system and how do they work?	Research training and education journals, books, and websites.	Weeks 1–2
	Find and interview an LMS expert.	Week 1
1. Would an LMS be an effective training tool for our company? • What specific training and content management needs does our company have? • What current problems are we facing? • What are alternatives/options for solving these problems? • Is an LMS the best option?	Interview the company's chief learning officer and department heads.	Week 2
	Survey or interview other companies.	Week 2
	Research training and education journals, books, and websites.	Weeks 1–2
	Compare options against the company's training needs.	Week 2
2. If an LMS would be effective, which one is the best option to meet our specific training needs? • What are the various options for LMS programs? • What criteria will we use to judge the options? • Which option best meets the criteria?	Review training and education journals, books, and websites.	Week 1
	Conduct a web search for LMS programs.	Week 1
	Speak to other companies in the industry.	Week 2
	Interview a chief learning officer and department heads.	Week 1
	Conduct a detailed comparative analysis.	Week 3
	Compare alternatives against selection criteria.	Week 3
3. What is the cost of the selected option? • What are the initial purchase and installation costs? • What are the ongoing costs, such as customer support?	Speak to the sales department of the selected company.	Week 3
	Interview other companies using the system.	Week 3

deadlines. Although you may need to modify your work plan as you discover new information and find alternative solutions to your problem, an initial plan gives focus to the project by dividing the tasks into manageable steps. The work plan in Figure 10.5 spreads the research over three weeks, leaving you one week to prepare your presentation. The plan begins with the *research questions*, which form the basis for the *research activities*. From there, you can chart your goals for determining key findings, implications, conclusions, and recommendations.

Figure 10.5 provides a close-up view of the first three columns of the work plan. Notice that the figure lists the tasks by question, not by sequential due date, because you may conduct several research tasks concurrently during the same week. In addition, if you are already interviewing people in other companies to find out how they handle training and record keeping (Research Question 1), you may also want to find out what specific LMS they use (Research Question 2) and what the costs are (Research Question 3).

The work plan also creates space for recording results, which will help you organize your final report or presentation. By taking the time to organize your data as you analyze it, you will be better prepared to translate it into meaningful information that effectively answers your research questions. You may need to create a modified version of the table to fit your notes. The next sections describe how you can use different sources of information to fill in the work plan.

(LO 10.2) How do you conduct and evaluate research in print and online sources?

Many students use only Google to find information. This is a shortsighted approach. Google is like a vending machine. The results are fast and perhaps "tasty," but speed does not guarantee quality. If students conduct research using only Google then their work will have the same academic value as the nutritional value of the vending machine snack.

You will not be able to find all the information you need through a web search, and many sources you do find will not be relevant or useful. Finding the best information requires you to use a variety of research tools and methods. To be an efficient researcher, you need to learn how to do the following:

- Gather relevant print and electronic files
- Search the web strategically
- Use an online index or database to find articles from print publications
- Use a library or bookseller to find relevant books
- Follow leads in appropriate sources
- Evaluate your sources for credibility

This section presents many different types of search tools. **FIGURE 10.6** summarizes these different tools and identifies what you can find with each one.

Gather relevant print and electronic files

For some research projects, you may already have relevant hardcopy materials, files on your computer, or access to files on your company's network. The challenge is to find these documents and organize them in one central location. Before you begin looking for them, create the system you will use to organize your research results as you progress through your project.

Whether you keep paper documents in a file folder or a binder, or scan the material to create electronic files, be sure to record the information you will need to cite the documents and include them in a reference list.

To find relevant electronic files such as meeting minutes, budgets, proposals, or previous research, consider using a **desktop search tool**, which is a search engine designed to search for files on your computer or file server that contain specific words or that were produced within a specific time period. Many search tools are available for download or purchase. However, before investing in new software, try the search functions built into your computer's operating system.

Apps like Genius Scan allow you to scan and email paper documents with your smart phone.

Search the web strategically

Basic search engines such as Google, Yahoo, and Bing index sites throughout the web. When you enter keywords, the search engine provides links to sites that use those terms. The sites that appear at the top or near the side of the list are usually those whose organizations have paid a fee to be featured in the search results. The main body of the results page begins with sites that are frequently accessed or that most closely match your search terms. As you scroll down the list or click on subsequent pages of the list, the results are likely to be less relevant.

Desktop search tool A search engine designed to search for files on your computer or file server that contain specific words or that were produced within a specific time period.

FIGURE 10.6 Tools for Finding Research Sources

TOOL...	SUCH AS...	SEARCHES...	TO FIND...
General Search Engine	Google, Yahoo, Bing	Web	Publicly available content
Deep Web Search Engine	Biznar.com	Web	Specialized content on the web, often not accessible through a general search engine
Desktop Search Tool	Windows Search, Apple Spotlight, Everything, Alfred	Your computer or your organization's server	Company or personal unpublished content
Online Publication Site Map	*Globe and Mail* Site Map	One publication, such as the *Globe and Mail*	Articles in that publication
Online Article Database	Canadian Business & Current Affairs (CBCA) Lexis/Nexis Sociological Abstracts	Abstracts and full texts of thousands of publications, gathered together in the database	Articles originally published in print journals, magazines, and newspapers
Online Business Research Tools	IBIS World Hoover's Standard and Poor's GlobeInvestorGold Financial Post Industry Canada	Corporate and industry research reports from various sources	Company, industry, and market data
Library Online Catalogue	Queen's University QCAT University of Alberta NEOS College of the North Atlantic iLINK Library & Archives Canada AMICUS	The library's paper and electronic holdings	Books and other publications available through that library
Online Bookstore	Amazon.ca, Chapters.Indigo.ca	Books available through that online bookstore and other used booksellers	Books available for sale

Although searching the web seems easy, finding useful information is challenging. A Google search for the words *learning management system* returns almost 160 million results. Which ones will be relevant to you? The following search tips will help narrow your search:

- **Use quotation marks around your phrase.** If you need an exact match, use quotation marks around your search terms. For example, searching for *"learning management system"* will result in a list of resources that include the exact phrase rather than sites that include those three words anywhere on the page. This reduces the results from 160 million to 5 million.

- **Add more words to the search.** Think of words that you believe must be included on a website that is relevant to your research, and add that word to your search terms. Typing *"learning management system"* and *"corporate"* will give you only sites that include both phrases (438,000). This will get you closer to your goal. If you would like only corporate systems that offer "assessment" features, add that term to your search. If you want to find articles that compare *"learning management systems"* and *"course management systems,"* perform a search using both phrases, each in its own set of quotation marks. If you would like to see if a specific company uses an LMS, then search for that *company's name* along with *"learning management system."*

- **Exclude words from the search.** Using the minus symbol (–) before a search term tells a search engine to exclude pages that mention that term. If you want to find information about learning management systems that do not use open source software, try this search string: *"learning management system" –"open source."*

- **Use wildcards.** When you play a card game, a designated wildcard can represent any other card in the deck. When you conduct a search in most web search engines, you can use an asterisk (*) as a wildcard symbol within a phrase to represent an unknown word. For example, if you would like to find websites about companies that have selected one specific LMS such as SuccessFactors, try constructing a search using a short sentence like this: "*selects SuccessFactors." This search will yield websites that include this short sentence, no matter what the first word is. For example "The Timken Company Selects SuccessFactors" or "Industrial Equipment Manufacturer, Edwards, Selects SuccessFactors." Vary the wording and word order of that sentence to provide even more results. Using the search string "*chooses SuccessFactors" yields different results, for example, "Gordon and Betty Moore Foundation chooses SuccessFactors."

- **Use Boolean operators.** In many search engines, you can use the words AND, OR, and NOT (spelled in ALL CAPS and called *Boolean operators* after mathematician George Boole) along with keywords to expand or reduce your search results. For example, results from a search on *"learning management" AND "system"* would include only pages that contained both "learning management" and "system." However, searching for *"learning management" AND (system OR software)* would result in pages that contained the phrase "learning management" with either the word "system" or the word "software," which would provide a much longer list of results.

- **Use synonyms or alternative wording.** As you search the web, pay attention to terms that are frequently used to discuss your subject, and conduct a web search for those terms. For example, discussions of "learning management systems" often use the term "e-learning." You can conduct a search using that term itself.

- **Search for specific file types.** In addition to websites, you can also search for documents that are on the web, such as PDF (Portable Document Format) files using the advanced search functions of most search engines. On Google, for example, you can search *"learning management system" filetype:pdf.* Similarly, to find Word documents, search *"learning management system" filetype:doc.* Using specific file types in your search may help you find additional articles, documents, or case studies published by reputable organizations.

The **TECHNOLOGY BOX** provides an overview of deep web portals and discusses the value of this type of search engine.

TECHNOLOGY
GOING BENEATH THE SURFACE OF THE WEB

An enormous amount of information is available to researchers through the web, but not all of that information is easy to find. Most people rely on search engines such as Google and Bing to find web-based information. However, those search engines gather information from the surface of the web, which is just a small percentage of what is available. As a researcher, you will want to go more deeply into the web, finding not just free information aimed at the public and consumers, but also information aimed at professionals and information in publications that require a subscription. To find that information, familiarize yourself with deep web portals (O'Leary, 2008; Zillman, 2012).

Deep web portals perform federated searches. These search engines select several useful databases available on the web and conduct your search on those databases. By doing this, they provide high-quality research knowledge designed for professionals.

For business research, you will find these deep web portals particularly useful:

- **Biznar.com** is designed for professional business researchers. Although it does include information from

sources like Wikipedia and blogs, it also searches databases of professional industry reports, academic articles, and articles in the business press.
- **Beaucoup.com** has a useful geographic drill-down feature.
- **DeeperWeb.com** allows you to search within specific time frames.
- **ipl2.org** is a merger of two portals, the Librarian's Internet Index and the Internet Public Library, and provides access to trustworthy websites on a number of topics, including business.
- **WorldWideScience.org** is a database that provides access to science news from around the globe.

Even when using material found through the reliable deep web portals, you need to verify the credibility and objectivity of the source. For example, you can go to the science website so that you are knowledgeable about a particular journal and the types of articles it publishes.

For TECHNOLOGY exercises, go to Exercise 7 and Exercise 24c on pages 322 and 325.

Use an online index or database to find articles and business data

Almost every academic and public library purchases subscriptions to specific publications such as the *Globe and Mail* and the *Journal of International Business Studies*. They also purchase subscriptions to online databases, like LexisNexis, that collect articles from thousands of publications, including newspapers like the *National Post*, magazines such as *Canadian Business*, professional publications (also called trade journals) like *the Canadian Business Journal*, and academic journals such as *Alt-J: Research in Learning Technology*. Articles from these publications are generally not available through a Google search because these publications require a paid subscription.

These articles are regarded as more reliable than websites because editors carefully review them. Articles in academic journals offer another advantage: They are both written and peer reviewed by professionals in the field. The *peer-review* process is designed to ensure that articles are accurate and honest.

You can check with local postsecondary institutions or public libraries to learn what online databases are available. Searching for articles in these databases resembles searching the web. You must use relevant search terms to get appropriate results. In addition, database searches allow you to limit results even further by identifying important characteristics of the articles. For example, you can specify that you want only articles that are peer reviewed, published within a certain date range, and available in full text online. **FIGURE 10.7** illustrates search results from one widely available database, *CBCA Complete*.

You can also use online databases and other research tools to find business data and analyses. For example, research organizations, such as Standard & Poor's, Hoover's, and GlobeInvestorGold, publish in-depth financial data about companies, markets, and industries. You can access some of this data on the web through publicly available tools, including the *Financial Post*. Other data will be available only through a library subscription. If your library subscribes to LexisNexis Academic, then you will have access to the data and analyses published by Standard & Poor's and Hoover's.

Google Scholar is a citation index that offers a free and accessible search engine of scholarly literature, including peer-reviewed papers, theses, books, abstracts, articles,

FIGURE 10.7 Searching an Online Database

and technical reports. Search results include a link to related articles and a link to different versions of the same article. As will be discussed later in this chapter, Google Scholar also offers a link listing the number of times (and where) an article has been cited elsewhere, as well as an option to create a bibliographic citation for the article in question.

Use a library or bookseller to find relevant books

Students often neglect to search for books because the web contains so much information. However, books (like print articles) can be more valuable than online resources because books are often professionally reviewed, edited, and produced by reputable authors and publishing companies with established credibility. By contrast, anyone can post resources online about nearly anything. The drawback with books is that they become outdated more quickly than online content, which can be updated regularly.

To find books that remain relevant and timely, your first stop may be your local library's online catalogue. The catalogue will allow you to do a keyword search using many of the same techniques you use for a web search. If you find one book that seems relevant to your research, check the online record to see what broader subject categories are associated with that book, and then search for other books in the same category. Remember to look for the most recent publications. You may find it equally useful to browse through the library bookshelves. If you find one book that looks useful, go to its location in the library and look at other books in the same section.

The advantage of looking at books in a school library is that the librarians and faculty have determined that those books are worthy of being in the library's collection. The disadvantage is that libraries rarely have the newest books since it often takes a long time for a library to acquire a book. For more recent books, try searching the websites of online booksellers like Amazon.ca or Chapters.Indigo.ca. For example, a quick search for "LMS selection" at Amazon.ca yields the title *The LMS Selection Checklist* by Katrina Baker, published in December 2014. However you must also consider the *nature* of your subject matter. In this case, learning management systems are continually evolving to adapt to and integrate new forms of technology. Published materials will be less current and better suited to background research.

Follow leads in reliable sources

If you find a book or article applicable to your subject, check the bibliography or reference list to find additional resources for your research. For example, if you read an interesting article in the journal *Chief Learning Officer* about transitioning an organization from traditional to online learning, look at the article's references. If the article is valuable to your research, then the references used to write the article might also be useful. As you browse through the library, check the bibliographies of the books you find. You may see references to other books and articles you should read.

Evaluate your sources for credibility

Even after narrowing your search results, you are often left with thousands of options. Another method of elimination is to examine the source and make a decision about its relevance, impact, and validity. No matter what kind of source you find (print or electronic) you must evaluate it. Is the information timely? Is it factual or opinion based? Is any research well documented? Are the author and publisher respected by others in the industry or your eventual audience? To determine the reliability and relevance of a source, use the "3 A's" approach: Authorship, Accuracy, and Age.

Authorship: Can you trust the author and publisher?

- If your source is a website, does it identify the author?
- Whether on the web, in an article, or in a book, is the author qualified or an expert in this content? Check the author's biography, or research the author on the web. If the author is a blogger, do not assume the material lacks credibility. Some

experts disseminate ideas through blogs as well as published works. To verify credibility, determine where the author works and what other books or articles the author has published.

- Is the source published by a reputable press, or is the website sponsored by a reputable organization? On the web, you can generally feel confident about information that is published by the government and universities. If you are unfamiliar with an organization that publishes information you would like to use, read more about that organization to determine whether it is respected by others and considered reputable.

- Does the author provide support for claims, or is the text mostly unsupported opinions? Unsupported opinions are less credible than arguments supported by evidence.

Accuracy: Can you trust the information?

- Was the book or article peer reviewed? If a text has been reviewed by other experts before publication, the result is likely to be more accurate.

- Do others frequently cite the source? You can find out by using a citation index such as Social Sciences Citation Index, ISI Science Citation Index, or Google Scholar (scholar.google.ca).

- Do other sources agree with this information?

- Does the author acknowledge and respond to opposing points of view?

- Does the author cite sources for numbers, facts, or research findings? Or does the author expect you to trust that the information is reliable?

Age: Is the information current or still relevant?

- How current is this information? If you are researching a technology topic the material needs to be very current. By contrast, if you are researching an issue in business ethics, the source may offer useful perspectives even if decades old.

- Does the source provide a last-updated date or copyright?

- Are any web links broken (often indicating an outdated page)?

Evaluating sources using these criteria of authorship, accuracy, and age helps you decide whether a source is useful and what to use it for. **FIGURE 10.8** illustrates an evaluation of four articles on learning management systems. Article 1 is a **white paper**. White papers are potentially biased because they may promote the organization's own products. In addition, this white paper is too old to cite as factual. Article 2 is more credible because it is both relatively recent and published by a highly respected, unbiased organization. Article 3 may be worth citing because it is more recent and the opinion of a well-respected industry journal. Article 4 may be worth citing because it is the most recent opinion of an acknowledged expert.

How do you conduct and evaluate primary research?

Some research questions or problems require that you conduct your own original, or primary, research. Imagine that you want to know which learning management systems are used most widely in your industry. If no one else has already done this research, you may decide to pursue some of the following options:

- Compose a *survey* or standardized questionnaire to distribute to the head of training of each company in your industry.

- *Interview* content experts to get their in-depth thoughts about various systems.

If you want to know whether it will be difficult for new managers to learn how to use a specific LMS for performance evaluations,

- Conduct *observational research*: Get a trial version of the software, input trial data, ask specific managers to do a task with the data, and observe them as they do this task, noting any problems that need to be addressed.

White paper A report produced by a company or organization to educate readers about a complex business issue, product, or technology.

FIGURE 10.8 Evaluation of Four Articles

SOURCE	EVALUATION	DECISION
Article 1: White Paper Element K. (2003). *Learning management systems in the work environment: Practical considerations for the selection and implementation of an e-learning platform.* [White paper]. Rochester, NY: Element K.	**AUTHORSHIP** Element K—a training and development organization that implements learning solutions for its clients **ACCURACY** • Includes citations • Is cited in several peer-reviewed articles • May be biased because Element K sells learning management systems **AGE** Not a recent source	This article is too old to cite as factual on this topic, since learning management systems change quickly. In addition, the article is probably biased toward certain LMS systems. However, it may provide useful background information.
Article 2: Research Report Tagoras, Inc. (2013). *Association learning management systems.* [Research report]. Carborro, NC: Tagoras, Inc.	**AUTHORSHIP** Tagoras is an independent research company that focuses on the online learning industry. Tagoras sells this research report for $299. All research and writing for this report were done by Tagoras principals Jeff Cobb and Celisa Steele, both with years of e-learning experience. **ACCURACY** • Includes primary research • Includes citations • Has a reputation for unbiased research **AGE** Published more recently than Article 1	This research report is fairly recent and probably unbiased. Tagoras, Inc. is well respected. This is a good study for understanding the criteria for selecting a system and for comparing multiple systems. However, it may not be 100% on target because it focuses on learning management systems for associations that provide professional development to members rather than businesses that provide training to employees.
Article 3: Article in an Industry Journal Little, B. (2014, September). Perspective on the e-learning industry. *Training Journal,* 19–22.	**AUTHORSHIP** *Training Journal* is a well-respected industry journal. Bob Little is an e-learning and technology specialist focused on the corporate learning sector. **ACCURACY** • Was reviewed by journal editors who are experts in the field • Cites various other experts and points of view • May not reflect needs of a Canadian company as it is written from a UK perspective **AGE** Published more recently than Article 2	This is a very recent article in a well-known journal. Little's other publications are well received in the industry. The information, though Eurocentric, is worth including.
Article 4: Blog Post from Industry Expert Weiss, C. (2015, February 24). Latest on LMS insight—before you buy. [Blog post]. Retrieved from http://elearninfo247.com/2015/02/24/latest-on-lms-insight-before-you-buy	**AUTHORSHIP** Craig Weiss is consistently named as one of the most influential e-learning experts in North America. He is the CEO of E-Learning 24/7. **ACCURACY** • Not peer reviewed or fact checked: It is the subjective opinion of one person • Includes pros and cons for LMS features, presenting balanced points of view • May be biased because the author is a consultant in the field **AGE** Published most recently	Because Weiss is an expert in the field, his opinions about learning management systems are valuable. It is important to acknowledge that they are just his opinions.

Each of the three types of research (survey, interview, and observation) is widely used in business. The sections that follow introduce you to all three methods. However, if you are working on an extensive project that requires you to become very skilled at any of these approaches, you may need to take a course or read a text devoted to research methods.

Conduct survey research to gather information that is easy to compare

Analyze

Survey research uses a predetermined list of questions, also known as a *survey instrument*, to collect a structured set of information from a selected audience. Surveys allow you to compare participants who respond in specific ways.

To analyze whether survey research will be useful, you first need to determine what data you need to gather and from whom. As you will recall from Figure 10.2, these are the three main research questions about learning management systems:

> **Research Question 1:** Would an LMS be an effective tool for our company?
>
> **Research Question 2:** If an LMS would be effective, which one is the best option to meet our specific training needs?
>
> **Research Question 3:** What will be the costs of the recommended option?

A survey asking employees and managers their opinions about Questions 1 and 2 will not be useful. The responses would simply give you a set of vague and general opinions without any detailed explanation to help you analyze them. However, as you consider how to answer Question 2, you may decide to survey employees to learn about their prior work experiences with specific learning management systems. Such a survey can provide information about what systems are used in other companies, how they are used, and how employees respond to the systems.

To administer a survey like this, you will need to do the following:

- Decide which people to survey
- Select a delivery method
- Compose effective questions
- Analyze the results

Choose which people to survey

The audience from whom you want to collect survey responses is your **survey population**. Oftentimes, you cannot survey the entire population because there are simply too many people to contact. In these cases, you can identify a **sample** or a representative portion of your population. Different kinds of samples can be used for different purposes. For example, if you determine that it would be easier or that you would get a better response rate by surveying the employees in your building rather than all the branches across the country, you would be using a **convenience sample**: a sample selected because you have easy access to that population. However, if you do most of your training with new hires, you could survey employees who were hired within the last year, which would be a **targeted sample** restricted to that specific group.

Keep in mind that your ability to generalize your findings to the larger population may be limited by using a convenience or targeted sample. If you need to generalize to everyone, the best alternative is to use a **random sample** selected broadly from all available members of the population you want to study. A sample is random when every member of the population has an equal chance of being selected. For example, if you want to survey all 500 employees in a company, you could generate an alphabetical list and distribute a survey to every second person on the list. A random sample increases the likelihood that the responses will be statistically valid and accurately represent the larger population.

Decide on a survey medium

To select a medium for delivering your survey questions to your participants, consider the advantages and disadvantages of the various options in **FIGURE 10.9**.

Survey A predetermined list of questions used to collect a structured set of information from a selected audience.

Survey population The audience from whom you want to collect survey responses.

Sample A representative portion of your population.

Convenience sample A survey population selected because you have easy access to that group.

Targeted sample A sample that consists of only specific people from the group you are studying.

Random sample A population selected broadly from all available members of the population you want to study.

FIGURE 10.9 Selecting the Best Medium for Survey Questions

ADVANTAGES	DISADVANTAGES
FACE-TO-FACE SURVEYS	
• Increase likelihood that participants will respond because you contact them personally • Allow participants to ask clarifying questions	• Are time consuming to conduct • Require researcher and respondent to be in the same place at the same time • Require researcher to enter results into a spreadsheet or tabulate them manually
TELEPHONE SURVEYS	
• Increase likelihood that participants will respond because you contact them personally • Allow participants to ask clarifying questions	• Are time consuming to conduct • Require researcher to enter results into a spreadsheet or tabulate them manually
MAIL SURVEYS	
• Project a professional image and as a result may encourage participants to respond	• Require researcher to find participants' mailing addresses and prepare mass mailing • Incur postage costs for mailing and for return mail • May be ignored by participants • Require participants to mail responses back to researcher • Require researcher to enter results into a spreadsheet or tabulate them manually
EMAIL SURVEYS	
• Are easy to disseminate and to access • Allow participants to contact researcher with questions through a link in the email • Cost little or nothing to distribute	• Require researcher to find participants' email addresses • May be ignored by participants • Require participants to email back
ONLINE SURVEYS	
• Are easy to disseminate and access through emailed link • Allow participants to contact researcher with questions through a link on the website • Cost little or nothing to distribute • Do not require researchers to enter data manually • May automatically tabulate results, analyze data, and provide easy-to-read data graphics	• Require researcher to find participants' email addresses to send link to web survey • May require researcher to pay for survey tool • May be ignored by participants

Compose effective survey questions

To determine the content of your survey questions, use your broader research questions as a guide. For example, if you want to determine which LMS would be most effective, you might ask your survey population how satisfied they were with systems they used in the past. Once you know what you want to ask, the next step is to determine how to write questions so that you get the information you need. Avoid ambiguous questions that can be interpreted in multiple ways. For instance, do not ask *"How would you rate the learning management system?"* because you will have no way of knowing what criteria the respondent is using for the rating. To fix this problem, identify the criteria for their response, such as, "how would you rate the effectiveness of the online training you have taken compared to traditional face-to-face training?" To ensure your survey questions are effective, you can pilot test them with a focus group before distributing the survey.

FIGURE 10.10 shows examples of several survey question formats. Examples include questions that require respondents to select a specific response (yes or no), rate or rank the listed options, or assign a value to a statement. Your survey may include a variety of

FIGURE 10.10 Five Types of Survey Questions

YES/NO

Have you used a learning management system (LMS) for training in any of your prior work experiences?
○ Yes   ○ No

MULTIPLE CHOICE

If yes, how would you rate your satisfaction with the effectiveness of the online training you have taken compared to traditional face-to-face training?

○ = More satisfied with LMS for ALL learning experiences
○ = More satisfied with LMS for MOST learning experiences
○ = Neither more satisfied nor more dissatisfied with LMS
○ = Less satisfied with LMS for MOST learning experiences
○ = Less satisfied with LMS for ALL learning experiences

LIKERT (AGREEMENT) SCALE

For each statement, indicate to what extent you agree with the statement:

If the company adopts an online LMS option . . .	Strongly Disagree	Disagree	Neutral	Agree	Strongly Agree
it would improve our company's overall training experience.	○	○	○	○	○
I might sign up for more elective training sessions.	○	○	○	○	○
I would miss the social interaction of meeting employees from other branches.	○	○	○	○	○

RATING SCALE

If you have experience with any of the following LMS systems, please rate how strongly you recommend that Marcato Brands adopt it, on a scale of 1 to 10. A score of 1 indicates you do not recommend the product, and a score of 10 indicates that you strongly recommend the product.

If the company adopts an online LMS option . . .	Do Not Recommend				Neutral				Strongly Recommend	
A2Z	1	2	3	4	5	6	7	8	9	10
Eclipse	1	2	3	4	5	6	7	8	9	10
Teach2Me	1	2	3	4	5	6	7	8	9	10

OPEN ENDED

If you recommend an LMS based on your experience, please provide the name of the LMS: _____

question formats, or you might find that one format, such as multiple choice, works well to gather data that answers your research questions.

If you choose an *online survey* format, you have the option of constructing some of these questions as *branching questions* (questions that lead respondents to different topics depending on how they answer) (CreateSurvey, 2012). For example, the yes/no question "Have you used a learning management system (LMS) for training in any of your prior work experiences?" might branch into two paths. Respondents who answer "yes" can be directed to questions that evaluate the systems they have used. Respondents who answer "no" can be directed to questions about traditional, face-to-face training.

Many surveys also request demographic information that allows you to categorize respondents' answers in relevant ways. For example, in some surveys you may find it relevant to ask participants about their age or where they live. For this LMS survey, however, age and location are not relevant. Instead, you might ask a question about when the participants joined the company and how many training courses they have taken.

Analyze, interpret, and evaluate results

After the survey is completed, you need to count, summarize, and analyze the responses. For each question, you will need to decide which measures to use to report responses: percentage, range, mean, median, mode, or the total count, called "n" for "number."

For some questions, percentage and total count are the most logical data to report. Consider, for example, the yes/no question in Figure 10.10:

Analyze   Evaluate

Have you used a learning management system (LMS) for training in any of your prior work experiences? OYes O No

You would report the percentage of people who have used a system in the past. This percentage lets you know whether most people or very few people in the population have LMS experience. You also want to know exactly how many people this percentage represents. If only 20% of the 130 people surveyed have LMS experience, you will have data from only 26 people. You will need this total count information to analyze the results of later questions, like the multiple-choice question in Figure 10.10 that asks

If yes, how would you rate your satisfaction with the effectiveness of the online training you have taken compared to traditional face-to-face training?

When you analyze the answers, you will need to know that only 26 people are qualified to answer this question. If you report the multiple-choice results of this question as percentages, you will need to acknowledge that these are percentages of 26, a very small number.

Other questions require data relating to averages: range, mean, medium, and mode. For example, consider the rating scale question in Figure 10.10:

If you have experience with any of the following LMS systems, please rate how strongly you recommend that Marcato Brands adopt it, on a scale of 1 to 10. A score of 1 indicates you do not recommend the product, and a score of 10 indicates that you strongly recommend the product.

Assume you received responses from 26 employees, summarized in **FIGURE 10.11**. The different measures provide different information about the data.

According to Figure 10.11, 11 employees, or 42% of the total number of people who responded, indicated experience with A2Z Systems. The **range** is the span between the

Range The span between the highest and lowest values.

	A2Z SYSTEMS	ECLIPSE SOFTWARE	TEACH2ME
Employee Ratings	1, 1, 1, 3, 6, 6, 7, 7, 8, 8, 9	5, 5, 5, 6, 6, 6, 7, 7, 7, 7	8, 9, 9, 9, 10
Number of Responses*	n = 11 (42%)	n = 10 (38%)	n = 5 (19%)
Range	1–9	5–7	8–10
Mean	5	6	9
Median	6	6	9
Mode	1	7	9

*Total does not add to 100% because of rounding.

FIGURE 10.11 Responses to Rating Scale Question in Figure 10.10

highest and lowest values and demonstrates that their responses varied greatly. Some people ranked A2Z poorly, but other people ranked it fairly well. The ranges for the other two products indicate a narrow distribution, indicating more consistent perceptions among the employees.

The **mean** is the average and is determined by adding all the responses and dividing the sum by the number of responses. Although Teach2Me has the highest mean, only five people (19%) had experience with that system. The high mean would inspire more confidence if it represented the opinion of more people. The **median** is the number that represents the middle of the responses or the most central number. Although the median and mean are the same for two of the products, the median is slightly higher for A2Z Systems, which indicates that more people responded above the average than below. The **mode** is the number that most frequently appears in the distribution. Although the mode is not typically calculated for survey data, you may find the mode useful to help you differentiate between items that have similar means or similar medians. For example, in Figure 10.11, the median rating for both A2Z and Eclipse is 6. However, the two programs have very different modes. For A2Z, the mode is 1, meaning that the program received more 1s or "do not recommend" than any other rating. By contrast, the mode for Eclipse is much higher, 7, reflecting a stronger recommendation for the product.

In addition to analyzing the survey results, you also need to evaluate them to determine how to best represent them. You may not feel confident about using your survey results if you did not get enough responses or you did not get responses from the right people. Even if you feel confident about your responses, you need to evaluate what you can say about them. Assume that your company has 130 employees and you received 80 responses, with 26 responses from employees who indicated experience with the three learning management systems you are considering. Can you say 20% of employees (26 out of 130) have experience with one of the three systems? Or is it more accurate to say of the 62% of employees who responded, 33% (26 out of 80) have experience with one of the three systems?

Conduct interview research to gather in-depth information

An **interview** is a discussion between two or more people, usually in a question-and-answer format. The interviewer asks questions and records the interviewee's responses. You can also conduct an interview by email, especially if you have only a few questions to ask.

Interviews have at least one significant benefit compared to surveys. Although survey research gives you numbers to analyze, it does not give you the opportunity to delve deeply into the answers. By contrast, interview research allows you to get richer, more detailed information because interviewees are not limited to predefined responses. In fact, your preplanned questions are often just a starting point that can lead to discussions you might not predict. However, interviews are more time consuming than surveys. For example, it would take you a lot longer to interview each of the 80 people who responded to the LMS survey than it would to distribute the survey questions.

Depending on the research questions you need to answer, consider interviewing *subject matter experts*, employees, customers, or product users. Experts can include authors of the books or articles you read, columnists who publish related blogs, and people who post comments to community message boards. In many cases, authors provide their contact information or at least their email addresses. You may choose to conduct your interview by email, posing specific questions. However, a conversation typically allows more in-depth discussion and may lead to valuable information that you had not originally planned to discuss.

For the learning management systems research, interviews are a key element of the work plan illustrated in Figure 10.5. The plan calls for you to find appropriate people in other companies and interview them about their experiences with learning management systems. If you secure an interview with someone, you will have only one chance to ask all the questions you need. Therefore, you need to plan carefully. Use the following advice for planning the interview, conducting the interview, and evaluating the results.

Mean The average derived by adding all responses and dividing the sum by the number of responses.

Median The number that represents the middle number in a distribution or the most central number.

Mode The number that most frequently appears in a distribution.

Interview A research method involving a structured discussion between two or more people, usually in a question-and-answer format.

Planning an interview

- **Generate a list of questions.** Brainstorm to generate as many questions as possible and record each one. Then evaluate your list to eliminate redundant or extraneous questions.

- **Organize related questions into categories.** Evaluate your long list of questions and organize them into categories. For the LMS research, these categories may include questions about how the company selected its LMS, how the system is used at that company, how the employees perceive the system, and where additional sources of information can be found.

- **Identify sources to answer questions.** You may need to consult a variety of sources or people to answer your questions. Identify the sources for each question and create a second list of the same questions organized by source.

- **Determine how you will record responses.** Even if you record the interview, take notes in case a mechanical problem occurs with your recording. Also, be sure to get the interviewee's permission to make a recording.

- **Write an interview guide.** An interview guide is a plan of action for the interview that outlines the questions you will ask. Writing down the questions ensures that you will not forget something important. You may want to construct the interview guide so that you have room for taking notes. You may also want to provide the interviewees with the list of questions before the interview. Doing so allows them to organize their thoughts and possibly collect examples or additional information that they would not have readily available at your scheduled interview.

Compose

Although your interview questions will depend on the nature of your problem or decision, the sample interview guide in **FIGURE 10.12** provides some generic questions you can adapt to meet the needs of your research.

INTERVIEW GUIDE

1. Introduce yourself and the purpose of the interview. Thank the interviewee for spending time with you.

2. Questions about the interviewee:
   a. What does your organization do?
   b. Who does your organization serve?
   c. What is your position in the organization?

3. Questions about the problem:
   a. How many LMS options did you consider before selecting one?
   b. What criteria did you use to select your learning management system?

4. Questions about users and stakeholders:
   a. What do your employees think about your learning management system?
   b. How often do your employees use your learning management system?
   c. How do you update your training modules?

5. Questions about features:
   a. What are the strengths of your learning management system?
   b. What are the weaknesses of your learning management system?

6. Questions about the research:
   a. Can you suggest experts or other people?
   b. Can you suggest relevant secondary sources (books, articles, websites)?
   c. What advice can you give me as we determine the best learning management system for our company?

7. End the interview on a positive note by thanking the interviewee again.

FIGURE 10.12 Sample Interview Guide

Conducting an interview

- **Arrive early.** You may need to set up recording equipment or review your notes.
- **Provide a foundation.** Introduce yourself, describe your research, state your purpose, and confirm the length of the interview. Even if you mentioned these things in your initial email or telephone conversation, providing this information again will set the context for the discussion and clarify expectations.
- **Be professional.** Speak clearly and be sure the interviewee understands your questions.
- **Listen carefully.** If you do not understand an answer, do not be afraid to ask for clarification. You may have to ask questions like "Why is that?" or "Can you explain that again?" to get the information you need.
- **Keep returning to the interview guide.** Responses to questions can lead to tangents that can provide useful information but also distract you from your list of questions. Watch the clock to ensure you do not run out of time before you have asked all the questions on your list. If the answers start to wander, bring the conversation back to its purpose.
- **Be flexible.** If an answer triggers a question not on the guide, ask it. For example, if the people you are interviewing comment about slow response from the technical support department of the software developer, ask if that was a pattern and how the slow response time affected the company.
- **Do not argue.** Your interviewees may make incorrect statements or state opinions as facts. Instead of correcting them or arguing the point, probe more deeply to understand why they hold that opinion. Putting your interviewee on the defensive may make him or her less willing to share knowledge with you. For example, if an interviewee says her company decided against a specific LMS because it was too expensive, do not argue that the LMS actually costs less than comparable products. Instead, ask if there were any other reasons why the company rejected that program or why it believed the program it chose was a better value.
- **Follow up with a thank you.** Expressing appreciation at the end of an interview is important. In addition, following up with a phone call or email is an effective professional practice and may prompt your interviewee to provide additional feedback.

Evaluating interview results

Evaluate

After the interview, draft a concise, well-organized summary of the conversation. In some situations you may decide to share your summary with your interviewee to confirm the information that you gathered is correct. Organize your findings so that related information is grouped together. Despite having an organized list of interview questions, you may find that the interviewee's responses included tangents that were informative but not systematically organized. This means you will need to organize your notes into logical categories instead of the order in which you recorded them. These categories may or may not be different from the ones you used to organize your questions in the original interview guide. Determine what, if any, additional information you now need. The interviewee might not have been able to answer all your questions, may have suggested new questions, or may have been able to give only part of an answer. Finally, determine how you will attain any remaining information.

Conduct observational research to understand how people act

For many topics, the process of observation is an important supplement to survey and interview research. **Observational research** involves watching people perform relevant activities and then recording details about what you have observed. For example, when gathering information about learning management systems, you could ask an LMS provider if you can observe (and even participate in) an online training session it is conducting for another customer.

Observation offers advantages over self-reported data from surveys and interviews. When people describe and evaluate their past experiences in a survey or interview, their

Observational research A research method that involves watching people perform relevant activities and recording details about what you observe.

reports may be inaccurate. They may not completely remember what happened, or they may want to give you the answer they believe you want to hear. Direct observation of actual behaviour can give you much more accurate results.

When you observe, do not trust your memory. Carefully record important information about what you saw and heard as the observation proceeds, and take time *immediately* after you conclude the observation to make additional notes.

To get the most information from your observational research, follow these steps:

- **Decide what kinds of observations will be most helpful.** In other words, do not observe for the sake of observing. Ideally, observe people performing the actual activities with the actual products in the actual settings where they are normally used.

- After scheduling the observation, **plan for time before the observation to set up recording equipment**, if you are using it, as well as time after the observation to make notes or follow up with participants.

- **Write an observation plan** that includes the day, time, and length of the observation as well as questions about features or actions and other issues relevant to your research.

- After completing your observations, **summarize the results** in writing.

In your working life and your student life you will have opportunities to gather and use both secondary and primary research. Both activities involve ethical choices and behaviours. See the **ETHICS BOX** for some important guidance on the ethical use of information.

ETHICS
HOW TO BE AN ETHICAL RESEARCHER

When presenting information to diverse groups, teams, or clientele, ethics remains an important consideration. Self-reflection and cultural biases are not often explored in the context of ethical business research. Nonetheless, when you present research in a business report or proposal, your audience has the right to expect that the information is reliable, accurate, and complete. To meet those expectations, as a researcher you have ethical responsibilities. The following six guidelines address both how to gather information and how to report it.

1. **Use reputable sources.** If you use secondary sources, take responsibility for ensuring that those sources are credible using the criteria of authorship, accuracy, and age. Also ensure that their information can be verified. For example, imagine you are conducting research to help your company decide whether to use direct mail advertising sent through Canada Post. You want to be able to report on the environmental impact of mail that people discard. What would be the best source to cite:
   - Wikipedia?
   - A company that is marketing software for electronic direct mail?
   - A study published by Environment Canada?

   If you originally found useful information in Wikipedia, look at the reference list at the end of the article and see if you can verify the information in a more credible source. Then cite the more credible source.

2. **Cite all sources.** In business research, just as in academic research, you are responsible for citing all sources for ideas, opinions, and facts that you learned from other sources. Citing sources gives credit to the original source of the idea, gives your work more credibility, and helps your audience evaluate the accuracy of your information. Imagine, for example, that you wanted to provide information about the unemployment rate in your province. The data may differ depending on whether you got the information from a political blog or from Employment and Social Development Canada, the federal government ministry that tracks this information.

3. **Ensure that all interview and survey sources provide informed consent.** When you interview or survey people, you have a legal and ethical obligation to let participants know how you plan to use the information and if they may experience any negative consequences from the way you use the data.

4. **Report research accurately.** Be sure that you understand the intention of a source before reporting it. Do not take quotations out of context, report data in a misleading way, or make claims that your research cannot support. For example, if your research consisted of interviewing 10 customers about to enter a coffee store, you cannot say "According to our interviews, consumers prefer coffee over tea." You have data from only 10 people. You do not have enough data to support the larger conclusion. In addition, your sample may be biased since you are

(*continued*)

interviewing people who are likely to be coffee drinkers. Similarly, if your data about economic growth came from a reputable source published in 2002, you cannot say, "According to the International Economics Statistics Database, Equatorial Guinea has the fastest-growing economy in the world." That was true in 2002, but is it true now? It would be more accurate and ethical to say, "In 2002, Equatorial Guinea had the fastest-growing economy in the world."

5. **Include all relevant information.** You may find it tempting to report only research that supports the position you want to argue. However, if you find information that contradicts your position, you have an ethical responsibility to address it in your report. For example, suppose you plan to argue that your company should not advertise through direct mail but instead use email advertising. You would like to be able to show that direct mail is not environmentally friendly because it contributes significantly to the municipal solid waste stream. In researching, however, you discover that the contribution to solid waste is not as significant as you originally believed. Ethically, instead of ignoring this information and maintaining your original position, choose one of these options:

    a. **Provide the contradictory data and explain why it does not undermine your position:**

        i.   Although direct mail advertising represents only a small percentage of our solid waste stream, every bit of extra solid waste costs money for disposal and takes up valuable space in landfills.

    b. **Eliminate the environmental argument** from your report and stress other arguments against direct mail advertising, such as a low return on investment.

    c. **Modify your position.** You may not often find information that convinces you to change your point of view, but this routinely happens when people conduct thorough research.

6. **Respect intellectual property and "fair dealing."** Under Canadian copyright law and the concept of fair dealing, there are some circumstances in which you may include brief quotations from others' work in your reports and presentations. However, this is not always the case. If you plan to draw heavily from someone else's text, it is safest to receive written permission from the copyright owner.

In your business research, consider and apply O-A-R to ensure ethical practices:

*   **Observe:** Simply put, observe the six principles above in all circumstances in which you need to use research or material produced by someone else in your own work.

*   **Ask:**

    *   About cultural expectations. Ask whether any colleagues have dealt with business partners or clients from specific regions, cultures, or countries that may have differing perspectives on ethical research and intellectual property.

    *   About your own organization's confidentiality and consent practices when asking for, receiving, and quoting business documents from a client.

    *   About ethical information sharing. Does your organization or your client allow you to share verbal or written documentation you receive from a client with internal colleagues in the normal course of conducting business?

    *   A colleague whether your work meets the six guidelines presented above. Sometimes a neutral third-party viewpoint is extremely useful in spotting possible ethical missteps.

*   **Research:** There are many online resources that use nonlegal language to explain legal terms related to intellectual property rights in Canada. Stay current on this topic. Useful search terms include:

    *   "Intellectual property rights" + Canada
    *   "Fair dealing" + copyright + Canada
    *   Plagiarism + business + Canada

For ETHICS exercises, go to Exercises 21 and 22 on page 324.

LO 10.4 # How can you use social media in your research?

Social media sources can extend your reach in gathering information. Consider the following possible ways that blogs, tweets, online videos, and slide-sharing sites can contribute to your research:

*   Help you find experts and other useful sources not published through books or articles

*   Allow you to request information through surveys and question-answer sites

*   Give you a platform for conducting primary research by collecting **anecdotal evidence** (evidence from people's experiences) that may not be scientifically valid or representative but may still provide insight into your topic.

Anecdotal evidence Information you can get from a subjective report that may not be scientifically valid or representative but that may provide insight into your topic.

This section discusses strategies for taking advantage of social media in your research process. Remember that when you conduct research through social media, you are responsible for documenting your sources just as you are when using more traditional media.

Search for experts

Many experts write and publish blogs on their topics of expertise. Reading those blogs is similar to interviewing experts. In addition, many companies sponsor blogs to promote discussions about their products or industry. To find relevant blogs, search for the name of your subject plus the word "blog." Be sure to evaluate the blog for authorship, accuracy, and age, as seen in Article 4 of Figure 10.8. Many blogs provide biographical profiles outlining the authors' professional credentials and expertise. Experts often post comments on other people's blogs (as well as their own), so you may identify experts by reading through comments.

Post questions to your network and beyond

Social media encourages two-way communication by offering many opportunities to ask questions and get quick responses. For example, you can use LinkedIn Groups to connect with people in the same industry or with shared interests. LinkedIn Groups encourages users to post questions, take part in discussions, and connect with industry experts. For example, you could conduct a search for a LinkedIn Group dedicated to learning management systems. With over 200 search results, joining a group might facilitate finding industry experts to interview or survey.

Posting a question on a social media site has many benefits. It creates an opportunity to receive an expert's consultation at no cost. It encourages networking between contacts previously unknown to each other. It extends the reach and influence of the experience of others. As well, it remains online and archived to assist others in background research or in furthering the discussion.

A second and different approach to gathering information is conducting surveys through social networks, either by posting a survey on your company's Facebook wall or by using Facebook, blogs, or microblogs to post links to surveys. You can also use social media to *crowdsource* the answer to a problem. For example, in 2008 the Canadian Broadcasting Corporation (CBC) crowdsourced new theme music to the popular program *Hockey Night in Canada* after a dispute erupted over the rights to the original theme music (NewsWire, 2008). CBC ran a nationwide contest online and invited Canadians to upload their song entry to the contest website. Over 14,000 entries were received, and the Canadian public rated and voted for their favourites, eventually selecting the semi-finalists (*CBC Sports*, 2008). CBC offered $100,000 and 50% royalties to the winner. This deal was presumably much less costly than renewing the rights to the original music (Bannerman, 2013). Similarly, the Government of Canada crowdsourced a logo design to celebrate Canada's 150th birthday. The contest challenged Canadian postsecondary students to design and upload a logo to be used in 2017 to celebrate the anniversary of Confederation. The prize was $5,000 and professional exposure in a Canadian institution (Government of Canada, 2015).

Share information

Slide-sharing sites such as LinkedIn's SlideShare (see **FIGURE 10.13**) allow users to benefit from the research done by other professionals on similar topics. For example, searching for "LMS" on SlideShare yields over 40,000 presentations (in various mediums, including slide shows, videos, documents, and infographics) that have been uploaded from around the world. SlideShares can be downloaded to your personal device and may be shared publicly or privately. These sites also provide another option for networking and finding new and possibly expert sources on your topic. Interestingly, the SlideShare search illustrated in Figure 10.13 includes a presentation authored by Katrina Baker, the author of a book discussed earlier in the chapter.

FIGURE 10.13 LinkedIn SlideShare

Gather anecdotal evidence

Anecdotal evidence comes from subjective reports or stories that people tell. While they are not scientific or verifiable evidence, you may find accounts of other people's experiences useful in your research. In social media sources, *social reviews,* such as consumer-generated product reviews on sites like Amazon, RedFlagDeals, MacRumors, and CNET Forums, provide a wealth of anecdotal information about products you may be researching. In fact, research by NM Incite shows that 60% of all social media users review products and services online, and other consumers value these reviews as a source of information (NM Incite, 2011). Additionally, research by AC Nielson shows that information shared on social media about a company's or product's reputation is an integral decision-making tool for consumers (Nielsen Insights, 2015). You can also find anecdotal evidence on blogs, microblogs, and videos, all of which can be excellent sources of testimonials or complaints about a product (CorpU TV, 2008). The search engine Social-Searcher.com allows you to search multiple social media platforms for sources related to the topic you are researching. It also provides you with search analytics such as sentiment, type of users, URLs, and keywords.

How can you effectively organize the results of your research?

If your research is successful, you may be overwhelmed with sources by the time you finish. Use the following steps to ensure that your information will be easy to access as you begin to prepare your report or presentation.

Build your reference list as you research

As you collect sources, record all the information you need to prepare a reference list, such as authors' names, date of publication, the publication's name, the complete web address if online, volume and issue numbers, and all page numbers (not just the starting page). This information will save you time as you prepare your final report and presentation. It will also ensure that you can find the information again when you need it.

To organize your research from online databases or indices (such as CBCA or Google Scholar), consider a citation manager such as RefWorks, EndNote, or Mendeley. These applications enable users to collect an unlimited number of records and to create instantly formatted bibliographies (see **FIGURE 10.14**). Google Scholar will also generate a bibliographic citation and then prompt you to store it using your citation manager of choice.

Smartphones and tablets can also be used to organize reference information. The application RefME lets you scan a book or journal barcode and instantly record its bibliographic information.

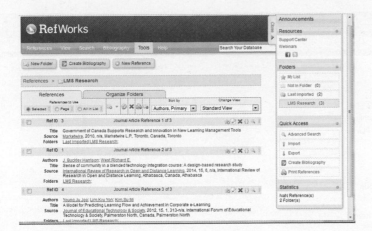

FIGURE 10.14 Citation Manager (RefWorks)

Source: Copyright © 2015 by RefWorks. All rights reserved.

These programs prompt you for information and then format your references in any one of several citation styles, including American Psychological Association (APA) style, Modern Language Association (MLA) style, and Chicago style, based on the *Chicago Manual of Style*. If you use the same sources for multiple research projects or courses, you can save the sources and reformat the references in any of the output formats.

The citation style you use will depend on the industry in which you work, the organization that is publishing your work, or your instructors' preferences. Both APA style and Chicago style are widely used in business. Although businesses rarely use MLA style, it may be required by your instructor. **FIGURE 10.15** illustrates how a citation from the same source would be formatted in APA, Chicago, and MLA style. Appendix D at the back of this book includes additional information about documentation in APA and MLA styles.

Organize documents and notes on your computer and "in the cloud"

As you research, you can organize your files just on your computer or you can take advantage of **cloud computing** to store your files on the Internet so that they are available to share with collaborators and to use on all your devices, including computers, tablets, and smartphones.

To organize your research on your computer, use a logical filing system that helps you find and retrieve documents when you need them, such as that illustrated in **FIGURE 10.16**.

Cloud computing A general term for the storage of data and services in a central location, accessible via the Internet.

APA STYLE (6th ed.)	CHICAGO STYLE (16th ed.)	MLA STYLE (9th ed.)
In-text citation:	*In-text citation:*	*In-text citation:*
. . . Moodle was used in a landmark case study analysis to demonstrate how course management systems can generate effective results (Romero, Ventura, & Garcia, 2008). This study effectively . . .	. . . Moodle was used in a landmark case study analysis to demonstrate how course management systems can generate effective results (Romero, Ventura, and Garcia 2008, 368). This study effectively . . .	. . . Moodle was used in a landmark case study analysis to demonstrate how course management systems can generate effective results (Romero, Ventura, and Garcia 368). This study effectively . . .
Reference page citation:	*Reference page citation:*	*Works Cited page citation:*
Romero, C., Ventura, S., & Garcia, E. (2008). Data mining in course management systems: Moodle case study and tutorial. *Computers & Education, 51*(1), 368–384.	Romero, Cristobal, Sebastian Ventura, and Enrique Garcia. 2008. "Data Mining in Course Management Systems: Moodle Case Study and Tutorial."Computers & *Education* 51 (1): 368–84.	Romero, Cristobal, Sebastian Ventura, and Enrique Garcia. "Data Mining in Course Management Systems: Moodle Case Study and Tutorial." *Computers & Education* 51.1 (2008): 368–84. Print.

FIGURE 10.15 Examples of Reference Citation Styles

FIGURE 10.16 File Folder Organization

Source: Used with permission from Microsoft.

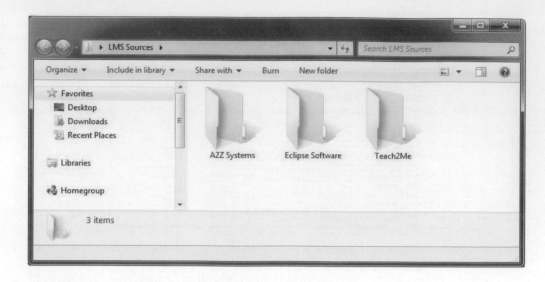

The following guidelines will help you organize your information for easy reference. Also be sure to back up your files so you do not lose valuable resources.

- **Create identifiable file names.** When you download a file from the web, such as a PDF, the file name may not adequately identify the file's contents. For example, you would have to open a file labelled "DEC1202.pdf" to determine what it was. If a file has a vague name, rename it so that you will be able to quickly identify it when you skim your file list later. You may decide to save the DEC1202.pdf file with the article's title, "Overview of Open Source Learning Management Systems," or by topic and publisher, "Open Source LMS–EDUCAUSE."

- **Group similar content for easy synthesis.** On your computer, create a folder for each research project. Within that folder, create subfolders that allow you to organize the information. You can organize folders by topic, as illustrated in Figure 10.16. Alternatively, you can organize them by type of information (e.g., survey results and software reviews) or by the research questions from your work plan.

To organize your research in one place and to facilitate the sharing of documents, consider using applications such as Dropbox or Google Drive. Dropbox enables file sharing between colleagues and provides cloud storage so that users can access their files from any device connected to the Internet. When you add a file to the Dropbox desktop client, it automatically uploads to your other DropBox-enabled computers, tablets, and smartphones, and even to the DropBox website. Users may also upload files manually through the Dropbox web application as seen in **FIGURE 10.17**. Shared folders enable collective access to documents and can be helpful when collarborating on a team project. All members of a shared folder can edit a document and upload the new version, replacing the previous one. Alternatively, links to specific files (or folders) can be sent to share documents in a read-only fashion.

FIGURE 10.17 Web Version of Dropbox

Source: "Desktop Version of Dropbox" and "Web Version of Dropbox" from Dropbox, Inc. Copyright © 2015 by Dropbox, Inc. Reprinted with permission.

Organize your findings by research questions

In addition to organizing your documents throughout your research process, you also need to organize what you extract from the documents and the rest of your notes. Inexperienced researchers often make the mistake of organizing their research by the source of information. Although you might first record information in that way, you will find it more useful to *synthesize*, or combine, information from various sources as you work through the research process.

The work plan outlined in Figure 10.5 on page 294 is a useful guide for organizing your findings within the original research questions. You may need to expand the format of the table to fit your data. **FIGURE 10.18** provides an example of findings organized for the first LMS research question: "Would a learning management system be an effective training tool for our company?" Note how the information in the figure is not organized by source. Instead, the information is integrated into the work plan by research activity. If you listed the information about A2Z Systems separately, you would find it difficult to compare it to the other options. By organizing the information by question, you will be able to make comparisons more easily.

RESEARCH QUESTIONS	RESEARCH ACTIVITIES	TARGET DATE	KEY FINDINGS	IMPLICATIONS/ CONCLUSIONS	RECOMMEN- DATIONS
1. Would an LMS be an effective training tool for our company?					

		Key Findings — LMS Options		
Research Activities	**Target Date**	A2Z Systems (A2Z.com)	Eclipse Software (Eclipse.com)	Teach2Me (Teach2Me.com)
Research training and education journals, books, and websites.	Weeks 1–2	• Supports multiple platforms • Online demo only; no onsite rep support	• Requires a single platform • Online demo and onsite rep support	• Supports multiple platforms • Online demo and onsite rep support
Compare options against company's training needs.	Week 2	• Customizable modules may provide flexible training; no online support provided • Supports both stand-alone and instructor-led training	• All modules are completely customizable; online support provided • All support included	• Customizable modules must be purchased separately • Online support billed separately
Survey or interview people in other companies	Week 2	**Agrulo Interview:** • Initial learning curve was difficult; required extensive startup training • Lack of online support frustrating • Phone support not enough • Bottom line: It's better than nothing	**Millersby Interview:** • Learning curve difficult, but manageable • Online support helpful • Bottom line: It's okay; we're still learning	**Takata Interview:** • Easy setup; user-friendly interface • No need yet for online support • Bottom line: We love it!

FIGURE 10.18 Adding Findings to the Work Plan

As you continue your research, you can use the same work plan to organize your conclusions and recommendations. Simply add extra columns to the right.

In summary, the process of doing research and organizing your findings begins during the analyzing phase of the ACE process (see **FIGURE 10.19**) and may continue until your document or project is completed. At any stage in the process, you may develop new questions that uncover new research needs. Your ability to research efficiently and effectively is dependent on having a clear research plan: knowing what you want to learn and what sources and research activities will provide the information. Organizing your research materials and findings puts you in a better position to use your research to write proposals, reports, and presentations.

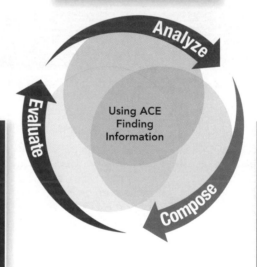

Analyze the research question. Create multiple questions and subquestions if appropriate.

Identify audience's concerns and needs.

Define the scope of the research and create a work plan.

Define research requirements: primary, secondary, or tertiary?

Build your reference list as you research.

Keep track of material that requires citations.

Consider creating visuals that represent your ideas more clearly than words.

Create new research questions as new information arises.

Review to ensure the research meets the audience's needs and expectations.

Proofread for material that should be cited from an external source. Be sure you have included all citations.

Be sure that citations are accurate.

Using ACE Finding Information

Analyze · Compose · Evaluate

FIGURE 10.19 Using ACE When Finding Information

Photo courtesy of Mark Federman and Jennifer Gilbert

Mark Federman, Ph.D.
Consultant & Educator, Transformative Contemporary Leadership: Facilitating strategic insight, innovation, and the transformation of contemporary leadership

@ **WORK**

At the opening of this chapter, Mark found himself presenting his analysis but not making the impact he wished. How can ACE help improve his outcome?

The ACE framework is a near-perfect model for reporting on research in a way that is most relevant and useful for decision makers.

- **Analyze.** A large part of the analysis begins by framing research questions that can directly translate into relevant business decisions and action. For each research question, consider the following:
  - Who is going to care about the answer to this question (i.e., who is the audience)?
  - How will the answer to this question help us to do what we cannot do today?

- Which specific business objectives will this answer support?

The amount of audience engagement in your research is directly related to selecting the most relevant question for that audience. For example, reporting that customer satisfaction went up might be *interesting*. Analyzing whether increased satisfaction resulted in a corresponding increase in sales or profitability is *useful*. Even more useful would be to identify the means through which satisfaction translates into sales.

Once the data are collected, whether from research sources like surveys, interviews, or focus groups or from sources like sales summaries, websites, or testimonials or through comparative analyses done by others, the analysis work begins. Tying the gathered information to both decision criteria and the larger business context is what makes data useful.

- **Compose.** Composing the message that conveys research results tells a story that is pertinent to the decision-makers' concerns. A chart of numbers does not tell a story. Nor do randomly selected quotations. Rather, composing the message uses specific numbers or quotations to build a logical argument that takes the decision maker from the starting point of the problem

RESEARCH QUESTION	WHO IS GOING TO CARE?	HOW WILL THIS HELP US?	WHICH BUSINESS OBJECTIVES WILL THIS SUPPORT?	USEFULNESS INDEX	
Has customer satisfaction increased? (closed question)	Key performance indicator analyst	Unclear: Have we done anything that created this change?	Unclear: This may indirectly lead to other results	Low	*Ho hum . . . So what?*
Has increased customer satisfaction resulted in increased sales? (closed question)	Sales manager	Unclear: Unless we know there is a strong correlation between satisfaction and increases in sales (there may be a correlation between dissatisfaction and *decreased* sales).	Achieving sales targets	Medium	*We are doing something right!*
How has increased customer satisfaction resulted in increased sales? (open-ended question)	Sales manager, operations manager, product manager	Once identified, we can duplicate these positive behaviours across the organization to have a larger impact.	Increased market share Loyalty and repeat sales Achieving sales targets	High	*Let's do more of what we are doing right!*

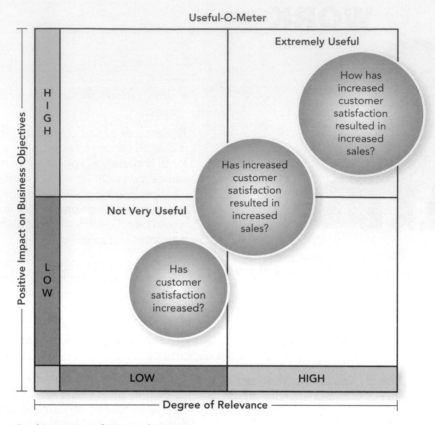

Sophistication of Research Question

or question to the endpoint of an action-oriented business recommendation.

- **Evaluate.** Finally, the message must be evaluated to determine whether it will in fact make sense to the target audience. Are the data sources dependable? Do the results actually answer the questions that were formed in the analysis phase? Are there underlying assumptions that affect our interpretation of the research? Perhaps most important, does the story created from the research results enable a decision maker to take action in ways that benefit the business?

Nearly a year to the day after that first fateful presentation to the vice-president, I once again found myself called upon to convey the results of a detailed research analysis. This time I chose to keep the 20 charts of analysis as an appendix, available for backup if required. The presentation itself framed the research question in terms that clearly linked it to an important business decision. The presentation's story followed three identified target buyers, each one created from the data as a composite person. Vividly illustrating the problem we were solving for each, how we could best convey our message to them individually, and what our expected market penetration trajectory would be was infinitely more effective than the prior year's data charts. This time, when the vice-president looked me squarely in the eyes, he had a very different message: "How soon can we start?"

Learning Objectives in Review

 LO 10.1 **How do you determine what information you need?** *(pages 288–295)*

- **Analyze the research question and topic** to understand the information you need to gather. You may find it useful to divide your research question into several subquestions. In addition, conduct background research to understand your topic's history, context and structure, and categories.
- **Identify audience concerns and needs** by determining what the primary and secondary audiences already know and what they need to know.
- **Establish the scope of the research** (how broad or specific your focus will be) by considering the needs of the project and the time available to do the work.
- **Define research activities** to gather information from primary, secondary, or tertiary sources.
- **Develop a work plan** that organizes your research process and ensures that you gather information to answer all your research questions.

 LO 10.2 **How do you conduct and evaluate research in print and online sources?** *(pages 295–300)*

- **Gather relevant print and electronic files.**
- **Search the web strategically.** Focus your search by using quotation marks, wildcards, and alternative wordings. You can also search for specific file types.
- **Use an online index or database to find articles and business data** such as in newspapers, magazines, trade journals, and academic journals. Peer-reviewed articles have more credibility than nonvalidated web articles.
- **Use a library or bookseller to find relevant books.** Much excellent information is published only in books. However, in some fields books can quickly become outdated.
- **Follow leads in reliable sources** to identify additional sources.
- **Evaluate your sources for credibility** using the "3 A's" approach: Authorship, Accuracy, and Age.

 LO 10.3 **How do you conduct and evaluate primary research?** *(pages 300–310)*

Three useful research techniques to collect original data are surveys, interviews, and observations.

- **Conduct survey research to gather information that is easy to compare,** such as quantitative data that can be reported as counts, percentages, ranges, means, medians,

and modes. Before conducting survey research, choose which people to survey by identifying the population and determining what kind of sample you will use (convenience, targeted, or random). Write effective survey questions, and decide on a survey medium. Following the survey, analyze, interpret, and evaluate the data.

- **Conduct interview research to gather in-depth information.** Effective researchers know how to plan the interview, what to do during the interview, and how to evaluate the interview results.
- **Conduct observational research to understand how people act.** A person's actions are often more revealing than his or her words.

 LO 10.4 **How can you use social media in your research?** *(pages 310–312)*

- **Search for experts.** Experts often write blogs as well as published books and articles. In addition, companies often sponsor blogs about their products and their industries.
- **Post questions to your network and beyond.** Social media platforms are perfect for posting research questions to people in your network as well as people outside your network through sites like LinkedIn Groups.
- **Share information.** Slide-sharing sites can expand your research, be helpful in finding sources and experts, and take you in directions you had not considered.
- **Gather anecdotal evidence.** Although anecdotal evidence may not be scientific, it can be useful in making business decisions. You can find anecdotal evidence in blogs, on Facebook, and in customer-generated product reviews.

 LO 10.5 **How can you effectively organize the results of your research?** *(pages 312–318)*

- **Build your reference list as you research** to save time as you prepare your final report and presentation and to ensure you can find the information again.
- **Organize documents and notes on the computer and "in the cloud."** On your computer, create identifiable file names and a useful filing system. Also organize your files online in the cloud with applications like Dropbox or Google Drive so that you can access your files from any computer and also share them with collaborators.
- **Organize your findings by research questions.** This will help you synthesize the material when it is time to compose.

KEY TERMS

anecdotal evidence p. 310
cloud computing p. 313
convenience sample p. 302
desktop search tool p. 295
interview p. 306
limitations p. 291

mean p. 306
median p. 306
mode p. 306
observational research p. 308
primary sources p. 292
qualitative research p. 292

quantitative research p. 292
random sample p. 302
range p. 305
sample p. 302
scope p. 291
secondary sources p. 292

survey p. 302
survey population p. 302
targeted sample p. 302
tertiary sources p. 293
white paper p. 300

CASE STUDY

Researching to Answer Business Questions

This case study will help you review the chapter material by applying it to a specific business situation.

Receiving a Research Assignment

Shuang Yu is a recent graduate of Trent University. She has started working in new business development at Affordable World Energy (AWE), a company that designs affordable products that generate electricity. The primary market for these products is countries with large rural populations that do not have access to electricity. As its next project, AWE is designing small-scale wind turbines to generate power for individual homes. The company needs to decide on the first market for this product and has narrowed the scope of its search to three countries that all have large populations without electricity: India, Kenya, and Panama. Shuang's assignment is to research which country has the best consumer base, the most suitable wind conditions, and best manufacturing infrastructure to manufacture the wind turbines locally.

Question 1: *Shuang will be presenting her findings to the company president and board of directors in a month. She needs to start structuring this research project immediately. If you were in Shuang's position, how would you proceed? Where would you look for information, what would you look for, and how would you organize this information?*

Developing a Work Plan

As a first step in planning her research, Shuang develops a purpose statement:

> **Purpose:** To determine whether India, Kenya, or Panama is the best country in which to produce and sell small-scale wind turbines to provide power to rural homes.

She also begins to develop a set of research questions:

1. What criteria should I use to evaluate these countries? How should I weight the criteria?
2. Which country has the best market for small wind turbines?
3. What are the necessary wind conditions for wind turbines?
4. Which countries have the necessary wind conditions?
5. What government regulations may affect the production and sale of wind turbines?
6. How much can the rural population afford to spend on a wind turbine?

Question 2: *Are there additional questions that Shuang should add to her work plan? For all the questions, what research activities would you plan to answer the questions?*

Researching Online Sources

Shuang begins her research by trying to identify which country has the best market for small-scale wind turbines. She hopes to find this information on the web. But what should she search for?

- **Search 1:** For her first Google search, she uses the terms *"rural wind turbine market."* This search yields some interesting results, including a market study by the World Wind Energy Association (2014) titled "Small Wind World Report 2014." Although the research report focuses primarily on the growth of the small wind market, it does include a section on global markets and, more importantly, a discussion of the driving factors of the small wind industry, including costs, government policies, standards, and certifications. This helps answer one of her research questions.

- **Search 2:** Shuang then decides to try a second set of terms to approach the search from a different angle. She decides that one way to identify the biggest market is to identify what country has the largest population without electricity. So she uses the search term *people "without electricity."* Much to her surprise, she finds a spreadsheet published by the International Energy Agency (2014) that lists the number of people (in millions) without electricity for countries around the world. Shuang finds that Panama has fewer than half a million people without electricity. By contrast, Kenya has about 35 million, and India has about 304 million. By reading the source citations in this report, Shuang also learns about several other agencies that study global energy needs and methods for financing energy development, including the Alliance for Rural Electrification, the International Finance Corporation, and the World Bank. She also identifies a book to read: *The Hidden Energy Crisis: How Policies Are Failing the World's Poor* by Teodoro Sanchez (2010).

Question 3: *Identify another research question that Shuang needs to answer and develop some alternative search terms to research this question using a general search engine, a deep web search engine, or an online article database. Which search terms offer the most useful results?*

Conducting Primary Research

Shuang has already identified at least one primary source she needs for research: her boss, the head of marketing at Affordable World Energy. As part of her research, Shuang needs to understand what criteria she should be using to evaluate the market opportunity in the three selected countries and how she should rank those criteria. Is it more important that the market is big? Or is it more important that the country has an industry that can manufacture the wind turbines? Her boss will know what criteria the company believes is most important.

She wonders, though, if she should be talking with anyone else or conducting any surveys. She has only a few weeks left to complete her research.

Question 4: *Is there any information that Shuang could get more easily by interview than by researching secondary sources? If so, what is this information and who would you recommend she contact?*

Organizing Research Results

Shuang's research project is such a major undertaking that she needs to develop a systematic plan to keep track of her sources and her results. Here is what she does:

1. She starts a Word file titled "Reference list," and she includes an entry for every item she reads. She formats these according to APA style and keeps the list in alphabetical order. She keeps a separate list of everyone she talks to, with the person's name, title, contact information, and date of interview.

2. She either prints out or downloads a PDF of her web-based sources. This ensures the material will remain available to her even if the website changes. She saves the files in folders organized by research question.

3. She creates a Word file for each of her research questions and types notes from her research right in those files, being sure to provide citations to all her sources.

Question 5: *Do you have any additional tips and tricks you use to organize research results? If so, explain how they would be useful for this project.*

REVIEW QUESTIONS

1. What is the difference between primary, secondary, and tertiary sources? Give an example of each.

2. What are the key elements of a research work plan?

3. What is a desktop search tool and how can it help you?

4. What is the effect of using quotation marks around search terms in web or database searches? What happens if you do not use quotation marks?

5. Explain the three criteria for evaluating whether a source is credible.

6. Name two advantages of conducting survey research and two advantages of conducting interview research.

7. Range, mean, median, and mode are four ways of reporting the quantitative data from a survey. Explain how they differ.

8. Identify at least two ways to find experts you can interview on a topic.

9. What is anecdotal evidence and how may it be useful in your research?

10. What are two benefits of organizing and storing research materials in the cloud rather than just on your computer?

CRITICAL THINKING

1. Of the following two options, which is the most efficient approach to research? Can you provide three reasons why?

   a. Identifying and articulating the research problem, analyzing the audience, determining the purpose, establishing the scope, and developing a work plan

   b. Finding a lot of information and then organizing it

2. Some people argue that libraries are becoming obsolete because so much research material is now available on the web. Compare the kinds of resources that are freely available on the web versus the kinds of resources that you can only access via a library. Based on that comparison, what value do you believe libraries offer? As a researcher, what would you use a library for?

3. Assume you are interested in getting a master's degree in accounting. Design a search string for Google that will help you identify available programs. How would using quotation marks and minus signs help you in this research?

4. Assume that you have distributed a survey to determine what frustrates employees most about the company's current approach to training, and you received only 25 responses from a population of 200 employees. How would you proceed? How could you use the information from your survey in your report? How could you get additional information?

5. Assume that you work for a company that manufactures luggage. The company would like to design a new line of luggage that meets the needs of business travellers who fly frequently. You have been assigned to conduct research to identify business travellers' needs. Where could you conduct observational research? What would you be able to learn from observational research that you could not learn from survey research or interviews? Is there any way social media can help you in your observational research?

6. Consider the Culture box on pages 292–293 and Skylar's dilemma.

   a. How can Skylar approach this problem with her current teammates without compromising the assignment, her team members' grades, or her cordial working relationship with her team members? Can you create a communication strategy for Skylar?

   b. Consider that different countries and cultures across the globe have different views on plagiarism. Is there a "right" view? Explain your answer.

   c. How can you avoid being in a situation similar to the one Skylar finds herself in? Devise a communication/action plan that you can follow for the remainder of your academic experience.

DEVELOPING YOUR COMMUNICATION SKILLS

 How do you determine what information you need?
(pages 288–295)

EXERCISE 1 Analyze the research question and topic

a. Identify a problem at your campus, such as a problem concerning parking, meal plans, or course registration. Imagine that you are beginning a research project to identify a solution to the problem. Develop a set of research questions to guide your research.

b. What background research will help you understand your topic? Use the table in Figure 10.3 on page 289 to list a set of relevant background research questions.

EXERCISE 2 Identify audience concerns and needs

In Exercise 1 you identified a campus problem and a set of research questions. Assume you plan to conduct the research and propose a solution to the appropriate audience(s) on your campus. Answer the following questions related to this problem:

a. Who is the primary audience?

b. Who is the secondary audience?

c. Who else may be affected by this problem or decision?

d. What does the audience already know? What do they need to know?

e. What questions will your audience expect you to answer when you present the research?

f. What sources will your audience expect you to consult?

EXERCISE 3 Establish the scope of the research

Use the problem identified in Exercise 1 and the audience analysis outlined in Exercise 2 to determine a purpose statement (or statements) and research questions. Refer to the examples in Figure 10.2 and Figure 10.3 on page 289.

EXERCISE 4 Define research activities

Use the problem identified in Exercise 1, the audience analysis outlined in Exercise 2, and the scope determined in Exercise 3 to define at least two research activities for each research question.

EXERCISE 5 Develop a work plan

How would you sequence the research activities identified in Exercise 4? Create a work plan like that in Figure 10.5 on page 294 and justify the order of events.

 How do you conduct and evaluate research in print and online sources? *(pages 295–300)*

EXERCISE 6 Gather relevant print and electronic files

Use your computer's file search feature to search for all files on your computer containing a key phrase such as the name of your college or university, the name of your city, or another phrase you believe you will find on your computer. Try searching for the phrase within quotation marks and without quotation marks. Is there a difference in the files you find?

EXERCISE 7 Search the web strategically [Related to the Technology feature on page 297]

a. **Select a topic of your choice.** Use the same keywords to search using two different online search engines, including one deep web search engine such as Biznar or WorldWideScience.org. Compare the first page of each list of results. Do differences exist between the two lists? Summarize the differences and similarities between the two lists and explain why the results were not identical.

b. Conduct a Google search for PDF documents using the search string *campus parking problem filetype:pdf*. Conduct a second search, this time for PowerPoint documents, using the search string *campus parking problem filetype:ppt*. From each of these searches, identify at least one document you might use in researching a proposal to improve parking on your campus. (If you use a different search engine, then use the advanced search feature to narrow your search to .pdf or .ppt files.)

EXERCISE 8 Use an online index or database to find articles and business data

a. Use an online database available through your school's library to find at least three articles or books related to the research topic you chose in Exercise 7a or a topic of your choice. Of the three sources, find at least one article from a magazine or trade journal, and find at least one article from an academic journal. Compare the information in the three sources. How does the information differ? How is it similar? If you found a book also, compare the information in the articles to that in the book. What are some key differences?

b. Use the online site map for your school newspaper, a local newspaper (e.g., *Montreal Gazette, Toronto Star, Ottawa Citizen, Edmonton Journal*), or a national newspaper (*Globe and Mail* or *National Post*) to search for at least one newspaper article related to the topic you chose in Exercise 7a or 8a. Identify all the search terms you tried. If your search was successful, summarize the information you found in the article. If your search was unsuccessful, explain why you believe you could find no newspaper articles on your topic.

EXERCISE 9 Use a library or bookseller to find relevant books

a. Assume you would like to propose that your college or university expand its experiential learning opportunities. You plan a research project to propose a new experiential learning model. One of your research questions is this: "How have other colleges and universities implemented experiential learning?" Using your campus or community library online catalogue, find two sources that you think would be relevant and do the following:

- Read through all the information in the online catalogue entry. Identify any information that helps you decide whether this book will be useful to your research.

- Go to the Amazon website and search for the books you found in the library. If Amazon has a listing for the books, read through the product descriptions and reviews on the page to learn more about the books.

- Using the information you found in your library catalogue and on Amazon, explain whether each book would be helpful to your research and, if it would be helpful, how. Be sure to provide a reference list using the documentation style that your instructor prefers.

b. Assume you would like to expand your search for information about experiential learning to identify appropriate books on the subject that your library does not own. Go to Amazon's website and search for "experiential learning" in the book department. Identify any books that you believe would be useful but are not in your library. Be sure to provide a reference list using the documentation style that your instructor prefers.

EXERCISE 10 Follow leads in reliable sources

a. Assume that in your research on learning management systems you found the following reference in one of the articles you read: Perry, B. (2009). Customized content at your fingertips. *T+D*, *63*(6), 29–31. How would you go about finding that source?

b. Assume that in your research on learning management systems you read a white paper by the consulting company Element K titled "*Learning Management Systems in the Work Environment.*" This document cites a report by the Hudson Institute stating that "By 2020, 60 percent of jobs will require skills that only 20 percent of the workforce now possesses." Unfortunately, the white paper does not provide complete documentation for the Hudson Institute report. How would you go about finding that report?

EXERCISE 11 Evaluate your sources for credibility

a. Consider the example of Sarah Nguyen working for Marcato Brands. Assume you have been asked to assist with the research to find the right learning management system. You have been tasked with choosing credible sources from a list Sarah has compiled of three books. Your preliminary research indicates the following:

  i. *Choosing the Right Learning Management System* is written by Benjamin A. Perez and Timothy J. Perez. It was published in 2011. A thorough Google search finds that the two authors are information technology specialists who also work as professors at several American universities. In addition, Benjamin A. Perez is a consultant for learning management systems. Their book was self-published using the Amazon company CreateSpace. The book has mixed reviews on Amazon, but you note that one comment indicates the book is written more as a narrative and does not include references, criterion metrics, or comparison tools.

  ii. *The LMS Selection Checklist* is written by Katrina Baker. It was published in 2014. A quick Google search will turn up her LinkedIn profile, where you discover that she is a member of the ATD Speakers Bureau and was a featured speaker at TechKnowledge 2015, confirmed by visiting the conference's website. Katrina Baker is an LMS consultant, and the book is self-published under her company's name. It does not have any reviews on Amazon.

  iii. *E-learning Tools and Technologies* is written by William Horton and Katherine Horton. It was published in 2003. The Hortons have a consulting business and they specialize in e-learning and online training. Their book lists potential vendors, describes product limitations, and includes a list of questions to ask vendors about their product. It is published by John Wiley & Sons. The book receives excellent reviews on Amazon.

  Using the "3 A's" approach, write a brief comparison of the three books, explaining which you would use and why.

b. Find three additional books on learning management systems. Using the "3 A's" approach evaluate the sources and rank them in order of usefulness for the Marcato Brands project.

c. Conduct a web search to find at least one blog on taxes and economics and write a brief explanation of whether you consider this source to be credible.

 How do you conduct and evaluate primary research? (pages 300–310)

EXERCISE 12 Conduct survey research to gather information that is easy to compare

a. You and a few classmates would like to launch your own entrepreneurial business. You want to provide a product or service that will meet a need in your community. As part of your initial research, you would like to conduct a survey to get ideas about products or services people in the community need. Write five survey questions that you believe will give you useful information. Be prepared to explain why you think these are appropriate questions. Also, select what you believe to be the best medium for this survey. Be prepared to explain why you think this is the best medium.

b. How would you select a sample of the population for your survey in Exercise 12a? Would you choose a convenience, targeted, or random sample? Explain why.

c. Calculate the mean, median, and mode for the following data and report your answers on a table adapted from the one in Figure 10.11 on page 305. Below your table, write a brief summary that highlights the differences among the three results.

  1. Have you used a learning management system for training purposes in any of your prior work experiences?

    Yes = 25 responses

    No = 32 responses

  2. If yes, how would you rate the use of a learning management system (LMS) compared to traditional face-to-face training?

Rating	Meaning	Number of Responses
5	More satisfied with LMS for all learning experiences	8
4	More satisfied with LMS for most learning experiences	6
3	Neither more nor less satisfied with LMS	9
2	Less satisfied with LMS for most learning experiences	1
1	Less satisfied with LMS for all learning experiences	1

EXERCISE 13 Conduct interview research to gather in-depth information

As part of your research for launching an entrepreneurial business (see Exercise 12a), you would like to interview successful small business owners in your community to get their advice about how to be successful and avoid mistakes. Identify at least one person to interview and write an interview guide you can use.

EXERCISE 14 Conduct observational research to understand how people act

A large consumer products company is interested in understanding how consumers make choices about which breakfast cereal to buy. In addition to surveying and interviewing consumers, the company would like to observe people's purchasing behaviour. Plan an observation session in a local supermarket. Assume that you will be standing near the cereal aisle for approximately 30 minutes, watching people make cereal decisions. What specific types of behaviour will you be looking for, and why do you think that information will be useful? (For example, you might gather information about how many different cereal boxes a consumer looks at before selecting one.)

 How can you use social media in your research?
(pages 310–312)

EXERCISE 15 Search for experts

Refer to Exercise 9. Assume you would like to propose that your university adopt or expand its experiential learning opportunities. You want to identify some experts on experiential learning to interview. Conduct a web search for blogs about experiential learning. Start by using the term *experiential learning blog.* Read at least three of the blog entries that appear in the search results. Write a brief message to your instructor evaluating the three blog entries using the "3 A's" approach, and explain whether you would contact any of the bloggers for more information.

EXERCISE 16 Post questions to your network and beyond

Referring to Exercises 9 and 15, assume that for your proposal on experiential learning you would like to identify people in your network who have had experience with experiential learning or who know others with experience. What approach would you take to identify these individuals? Be prepared to discuss your plan in class.

EXERCISE 17 Gather anecdotal evidence

Referring to Exercises 9, 15, and 16, assume that for your proposal on experiential learning you would like to include evidence of students' positive experiences with experiential learning. You would like to use social media to gather this information. Experiment with approaches to finding anecdotes and stories about experiential learning on the web. Can you find stories in blogs, on Facebook, in YouTube videos? Be prepared to present in class at least two items of anecdotal evidence you find in your search.

 How can you effectively organize the results of your research? *(pages 312–318)*

EXERCISE 18 Build your reference list as you research

a. In the case study at the end of the chapter (pages 320–321), Shuang found a number of sources that she will cite in her research to identify an initial market for Affordable World Energy's small-scale wind turbines. Build a reference list for these sources using the documentation style that your instructor prefers. You can find information for building reference lists in Appendix D at the back of this book.

b. Assume that Shuang also conducted telephone interviews with two or three experts whom she will cite in her paper. What is the correct method for documenting these sources in the documentation style you are using (APA, MLA, or Chicago style)?

EXERCISE 19 Organize documents and notes on your computer and "in the cloud"

You are an assistant to Madelyn Dupré, the director of training at a large company. She has been asked to make an hour-long presentation to new account representatives about business etiquette issues in the four countries where your company does most of its international business: Brazil, Russia, China, and India. Madelyn asks you to help find information by gathering relevant sources. Use the search tools outlined in the chapter to find at least 10 electronic sources. Ensure the files include complete citation information, save the sources with file names that are easily identifiable, and group them in a logical manner on a flash drive or CD to submit to your instructor. Alternatively, if your instructor requests, upload copies of the sources to an online tool like Dropbox or RefWorks and share the files with your instructor.

EXERCISE 20 Organize your findings by research questions

Assume that you are researching how to minimize your income tax. Brainstorm some research questions or categories you can use to organize your findings. For example, one category might be findings relating to tax credits. What other categories may be useful to your research?

EXERCISE 21 Evaluating conflicting information [Related to the Ethics feature on pages 309–310]

Assume during your search for information about learning management systems that you find a lot of support for Teach2Me software. Although only five of your employees indicated prior experience with this product, all of their responses were very positive. The cost of the product, including initial startup costs and ongoing maintenance and technical support, is less than your current travel budget for training. Your interviews with other companies who use Teach2Me have been positive. The online demo you went through impressed you more than the other two options. Therefore, you decide that you will recommend that your company choose Teach2Me as its LMS in your report to your supervisor.

However, as you review the information you gathered, you find a product review in a trade journal that suggests Teach2Me is not as robust as either A2Z Systems or Eclipse Software. The review indicates that Teach2Me does not offer as many features, the interface is more complicated to learn, and the tech support, though affordable, often requires long wait times.

This article is the only negative information you can find about Teach2Me, so you consider not including it in your report to your supervisor. You are concerned that because the information does not support your recommendation, your supervisor will question your decision. However, you know that excluding the information would not be ethical. Write a message to your instructor explaining how you would include the information while supporting your recommendation for Teach2Me.

EXERCISE 22 Making an ethical choice [Related to the Ethics feature on pages 309–310]

Suppose you are searching for secondary information to support a paper for your economics class. You find an article in a trade journal that nearly matches your assignment requirements. The headings are similar to the outline you have prepared for your paper, and you have found and evaluated many of the cited sources listed at the end of the article. However because your economics professor has listed this trade journal (although not this article) as a resource on the class website, you are concerned that she may assume you plagiarized the article. Even if you do not use any of the same wording as the article, the similarities to the outline of your paper may be interpreted as copying the author's content. How do you proceed?

a. Do you ignore the source, hoping not to draw your professor's attention to the article in case she is not familiar with it? If your wording is different enough from the article, you assume you can claim you never read the article.

b. Do you write the paper as you planned and simply cite the source?

c. Do you try to explain the problem to your professor and ask for guidance? If so, how can you document that you did not read the article prior to developing your outline?

d. Is there another step you could take?

Write a message to your instructor explaining what you would do and outline the specific pros, cons, and ethical issues related to your decision.

EXERCISE 23 Finding secondary information sources [Related to the Culture feature on page 292–293]

Your consulting company provides public relations services to a wide variety of manufacturing companies. Your headquarters are in Vancouver, British Columbia, but branch offices are located throughout the country. Your CEO is considering opening a new office in Guangdong Province, China, where many Canadian-based firms have outsourced their manufacturing contracts. Your manager asks you to provide information about the logistics of opening a branch in the province. He also wants to know how doing business in China may differ from doing business in Canada. Where would you find this information?

Outline a purpose statement and research questions. Then determine where you could find sources of secondary information. Create a work plan similar to the ones presented in the chapter that outlines your sources. List the possible sources for each research activity using the documentation style requested by your instructor. You do not need to summarize the findings of the sources.

EXERCISE 24 Presenting information

Conduct research to prepare for a three- to five-minute presentation on one of the following topics. Prepare a visual aid to support your presentation. The visual should cite your source(s) using complete reference citations (see Appendix D for examples).

a. Find two websites that provide information about a topic of your choice. One website should be a credible site based on the "3 A's" approach of Authorship, Accuracy, and Age. The second website's credibility should be questionable based on the same criteria. Present the two sources to the class, and identify how you used the "3 A's" to assess their credibility. Demonstrate how the questionable source lacks credibility.

b. Create a five-question survey on a topic of your choice. Use a variety of question types. Create one version of the survey that includes weak or vague wording that could possibly be misinterpreted. Create a second version of the survey that ensures measurable responses and elicits the information needed. Present the two versions of the survey to the class, explaining why the second set of questions will achieve better results.

c. Identify a specific research question you would like to answer. Search for sources using a general search engine, a deep web search engine, and an online database. Prepare a brief presentation comparing the results using the three different search tools. Identify which source gave you the most valuable results for your research and explain why. **[Related to the Technology feature on page 297]**

d. Assume that you work for Affordable World Energy (see the Case Study on pages 320–321 at the end of the chapter), and your managers have decided that India is a good market for the company's new windmill. To acquire government or private buyers, your company will need to present research findings in a culturally appropriate way. The managers ask you to prepare a five-minute presentation summarizing how research is presented ethically in Indian culture. **[Related to the Culture feature on pages 292–293]**

e. Wikipedia is a convenient source for research. However, many people argue it is not a credible source and should not be cited in high-quality research reports. Find and read at least two articles in the academic or popular press about Wikipedia and develop a five-minute presentation supporting an opinion about whether a researcher should or should not cite Wikipedia. Be sure to cite your sources in your presentation. For advice on how to cite sources in a presentation, see Appendix D: Documentation and Reference Styles.

11 Preparing Business Reports and Proposals

Syda Productions/Fotolia.

LEARNING OBJECTIVES

(LO11.1) How can ACE help you write a business report? *pages 328–331*

Analyze to understand the purpose and report type
Analyze to understand the audience's needs
Analyze to choose the best medium
Compose your report to meet audience expectations
Compose using an objective and easy-to-read style
Evaluate by reviewing on your own and getting feedback from others

(LO11.2) How should you structure typical business reports? *pages 332–350*

Progress reports
Travel reports
Formal reports

(LO11.3) How do you prepare an effective proposal? *pages 350–354*

Understand the problem and propose a well-balanced solution
Identify the appropriate type of proposal

(LO11.4) How do you properly respond to a request for proposal? *pages 354–359*

Structure an RFP proposal like a formal report
Follow specified guidelines when responding to RFPs
Use proposal-writing software to increase efficiency

(LO11.5) How do you integrate visuals into reports? *pages 360–367*

Choose the best form of display: table or graph
Choose the best type of graph
Design graphs and tables to communicate
Integrate data displays within the text

(LO11.6) How should you document your research? *pages 368–371*

Determine what needs to be documented
Prepare the documentation

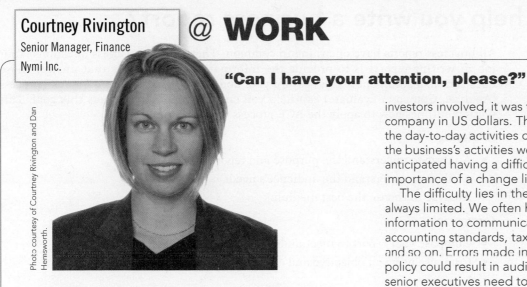

Courtney Rivington

Senior Manager, Finance

Nymi Inc.

Photo courtesy of Courtney Rivington and Dan Hemsworth.

@ WORK

"Can I have your attention, please?"

Nymi Inc., a Toronto-based tech startup, is developing a wristband that seamlessly unlocks devices, remembers passwords, and more through continuous proximity-based access control and your heart's unique signature. Think access to your office with a wristband that knows you by your heartbeat.

When I started working for Nymi Inc., the company had just raised its second round of funding, US$14 million, from venture capitalists in Toronto and San Francisco. With US investors involved, it was time to start accounting for the company in US dollars. This change had nothing to do with the day-to-day activities of the business but rather with how the business's activities were accounted for. The finance team anticipated having a difficult time communicating the importance of a change like this to the executive team.

The difficulty lies in the fact that the executives' time is always limited. We often have a lot of important and complex information to communicate in a very short amount of time: accounting standards, tax legislation, investor considerations, and so on. Errors made in the selection of this accounting policy could result in audits, penalties, or even lawsuits. The senior executives need to understand and approve this important change. However, to be honest, decision makers generally have more exciting things to be doing than reading a business report!

How can I capture and keep the executive team's attention to discuss an important change in business policy when they would rather be out looking for the next big technology breakthrough?

Check out the end of this chapter to see how Courtney uses ACE to solve this problem.

Introduction

Businesses run on information, and reports are designed to share that information with people who need to make decisions and solve problems. The term "report" refers to a wide range of documents and functions. Reports can take the form of emails, letters, manuscripts, slide decks, or interactive webpages. Report lengths can vary from a two-paragraph email message that documents your progress on a project to a several-hundred-page in-depth analysis of a complex business problem.

This chapter introduces you to a variety of report types and formats, along with some key writing techniques that will help you produce reports that are useful, clear, concise, readable, and accurate.

LO 11.1 How can ACE help you write a business report?

All business reports have one thing in common: They answer business questions. Your job in writing reports is to provide the information and analysis that answer those questions in a document that is easy for your audience to read and use. The ACE process (Analyze, Compose, Evaluate) can help you create a report that meets this goal. This section outlines how to apply the ACE process when writing reports.

Analyzing

- Analyze to understand the purpose and report type
- Analyze to understand the audience's needs
- Analyze to choose the best medium

Composing

- Compose your report to meet audience expectations
- Compose using an objective and easy-to-read style

Evaluating

- Evaluate by reviewing on your own and getting feedback from others

Informational report A report that provides readers with facts that they can easily understand and refer to when necessary. Progress reports, travel reports, and summary reports are types of informational reports.

Analytical report A report that analyzes information to solve a problem or support a business decision. Recommendation reports and evaluation reports are types of analytical reports. Proposals are a type of persuasive analytical report.

Analyze

Analyze to understand the purpose and report type

Typically, a report is either informational or analytical, depending on its purpose and the key question it answers. A report summarizing what happened in a meeting or on a trip would be an **informational report**. Its main goal is to provide readers with facts that they can easily understand and refer to when necessary. By contrast, an **analytical report** helps readers draw conclusions to solve problems or support business decisions. For example, a report that analyzes what you learned on a business trip and then makes a recommendation would be an analytical report. Similarly, the learning management software report example from Chapter 10 would be an analytical report.

The first step in writing a report is to identify the question you are answering and the type of report you are writing. **FIGURE 11.1** lists common business questions and the types of reports that answer them.

Analyze

Analyze to understand the audience's needs

When the process of researching a report is long and involved, you may be tempted to include everything you find. This approach will lead to a report that is overly long and unfocused. It is important to determine what information your audience needs to make

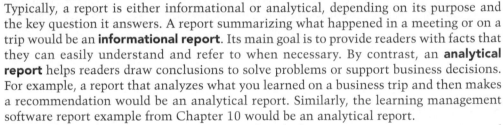

QUESTION	INFORMATIONAL REPORTS	ANALYTICAL REPORTS
What have you accomplished so far?	Progress Report	
What were the benefits of the trip?	Travel Report	
Are we complying with policies and regulations?	Compliance Report	
What is the better choice? Have our actions been successful?		Evaluation Report
What should we do?		Recommendation Report
Am I trying to persuade a decision maker?		Proposal

FIGURE 11.1 Common Report Questions and Types of Reports

ADVANTAGES	DISADVANTAGES
EMAIL REPORT	
• Can be distributed and received quickly	• May not be a private or secure medium for reporting sensitive content
LETTER REPORT	
• Can require recipient's signature to ensure report was received	• Takes at least a day to deliver
FORMAL REPORT (manuscript style)	
• Provides table of contents to help audience find information	• Can be time consuming to organize and format effectively
ONLINE REPORT (published as a web page or created with electronic tools such as online forms, wikis, and blogs)	
• Creates living documents that are never actually finished but continue to develop and grow over time	• Does not ensure immediate receipt because audience must check the website

FIGURE 11.2 Selecting the Best Medium for Reports

a business decision. Including more information than the audience needs reduces the efficacy of your report. Questions you need to consider include

1. **What is the audience's expectation?**
   - Does the audience expect information only?
   - Or does the audience expect analysis and recommendations?
2. **How much credibility do you have with your audience?**
   - What will you need to do in the report to ensure the audience has confidence in the information and analysis you provide?

Analyze to choose the best medium

A report may take the form of an email, letter, formal report, or an online report. When choosing the best medium for your report, consider the length, audience, and formality. In addition, consider the way you will deliver the report and how others will use it. **FIGURE 11.2** lists both an advantage and a disadvantage for each of the most common report options.

Analyze

Compose

Compose your report to meet audience expectations

When audiences read reports, they expect to find three or four kinds of information: identifying information, preview, detailed discussion, and (optionally) additional documentation.

Identifying information

Business reports clearly identify the author, the date, and the topic or title. Some reports also indicate the intended audience.

Where you find it:

Email. This information is included as part of the heading (To:, From:, Date:, Subject:, Distribution:, cc:)

Letter. Information about the author is in both the letterhead or return address and the signature block. Identifying information about the audience is in the *inside address* and salutation. Letter reports also include a subject line that identifies the type of report and the topic.

More formal reports. These reports usually have a title page that includes all the identifying information.

Web-based document. The identifying information is either toward the top of the webpage for a one-page report or on the first screen for a multipage report.

Preview

Almost all business reports are written with a direct organization, beginning with one or more preview elements that provide readers with a quick understanding of the purpose, structure, content, and main ideas of the report.

Where you find it:

Email and letters. The first paragraph provides the preview.

More formal reports. These reports include a combination of preview elements, including an abstract or executive summary, a table of contents, and an introduction.

Informational reports may include an **abstract**: one or two paragraphs that summarize the purpose and main points of the report so that a reader can determine whether the report includes information the reader needs. By contrast, analytical reports often include an **executive summary**, which is a separate, stand-alone mini-report inserted at the beginning of a formal report that completely summarizes the report's main ideas and recommendations. An executive summary is designed for decision makers who may not have time to read the detailed discussion.

Detailed discussion

Following the introduction, the body of the report provides the detailed discussion. As the longest part of the report, the discussion is typically divided into sections that provide background information, methods, analysis of the data (including any visuals such as graphs or tables that reveal insights), conclusions, and recommendations. Although some writers use these generic terms as headings, the audience will better understand the report if the headings are content focused and specific to that report. For example, "Risks and Benefits of Using Groupon as a Marketing Tool." This heading pinpoints exactly what information the reader will find in this section.

Supporting information

At the end of the report, you have the opportunity to add extra documentation to support your main points.

Where you find it:

Letter. In letter reports, any additional documentation takes the form of an **attachment** (a supplemental document that is included with the letter).

Attachments might provide details that not all readers would need and that would clutter the report if included. For example, imagine you were writing a report recommending that your company hold a corporate event at a local hotel. The body of the report would include complete costs, details of what you would get for those costs, and a discussion of how this choice best meets the company's needs. Everyone who reads the report will need this information. However, in an attachment you might include complete menus for the event, the hotel site map that provides the layout of the rooms, and detailed instructions about how to reserve parking for your guests.

More formal reports. In formal reports this additional information is included in an **appendix** or in multiple appendices. Reports that include information from secondary sources also include a **reference list** or *bibliography*.

Abstract One or two paragraphs often included at the beginning of a formal informational report that either (1) describe the content of the report so that a reader can decide whether to read the report or (2) briefly summarize the report, including the main points, conclusions, and recommendations.

Executive summary A separate, stand-alone mini-report included at the beginning of a formal analytical report that completely summarizes the main ideas and recommendations of the report and may be read instead of the main report.

Attachment A document that is included with a letter or email report to provide supplementary information.

Appendix A section (or multiple sections, called appendices) included at the end of a formal report or proposal that provides supplementary information.

Reference list A list of secondary research sources used in a research report.

Compose using an objective and easy-to-read style

The writing style of a report lends credibility to your results, which is important because reports are often used to support problem solving and decision making. To adopt a reliable report-writing style, follow this advice:

Compose

- **Avoid narrative.** Do not waste your reader's time providing a detailed account of what you did. Instead, focus on the findings, conclusions, and recommendations that result from your work. Even in a progress report, focus on accomplishments rather than activities.

- **Be objective.** For every claim you make, provide reasoning and supporting evidence. Also, be fair. Show that you have examined all sides of an issue and that you have evaluated the issue using reasonable and objective criteria.
- **Use an appropriate tone.** Although some informal internal reports may use informal language (including contractions such as *isn't, won't,* or *we'll*), reports for external audiences are typically more formal in style and avoid the use of contractions.
- **Use a straightforward sentence style.** All reports benefit from a writing style that uses concise sentences and active voice. This style makes the report easier to read and easier to translate for international audiences.

Evaluate by reviewing on your own and getting feedback from others

Evaluating involves both reviewing your own work and also responding to feedback from others. As you evaluate your report, ask yourself the following questions to improve your document:

Evaluate

- What question is the report answering?
- Is the answer to the question easy to find?
- Is the title (or subject line) of the report focused and informative?
- Does the report provide a useful preview in the introduction? When appropriate, does the report include an executive summary or abstract and a table of contents?
- Does the body of the report provide all the information and analysis the audience needs?
- Are the headings logical? Will someone who reads all the headings sequentially understand how the report is organized?
- Is each section well organized? Is the main point of the section easy to find?
- Are the paragraphs relatively short (four to eight sentences)? Does each paragraph begin with a strong topic sentence that states the main point of the paragraph?
- Are tables, graphs, and other visuals effective? Are they labelled and introduced within the document?
- Are the sentences relatively short and, when possible, written in the active voice?
- Are the appendices relevant and useful to the audience?
- Has the report been proofread carefully?

When a report is particularly important, be sure to have multiple people read it and provide feedback before you finalize the content. In fact, the most experienced workplace writers ask for feedback continually throughout the writing process instead of waiting until a draft is complete (Wolfe, 2010).

The evaluating process does not end when you have delivered the report. Your audience's response provides valuable feedback that can help you make better decisions the next time you write. If your report achieves your intended results, review it carefully to identify its strengths. If it does not achieve the results you intended (e.g., if your analysis confused the audience or your recommendation was not approved), try to determine the cause of the problem:

Refer to Chapter 2 for more information about reviewing your writing and requesting feedback from others.

- Did you include too much detail?
- Did you not provide enough support for your recommendations?
- Was the report so badly organized that readers had difficulty finding the information?
- Or was the failure caused by some external factor you could not control (e.g., the budget was cut and the organization did not have the funds to implement the recommendation)?

Whatever you learn from this evaluation will improve your future writing.

LO 11.2 # How should you structure typical business reports?

Most day-to-day business reports are short (less than five pages) and written in email or memo format. These reports are designed to inform your audience quickly about the work you have done and to provide documentation for future use.

Progress reports

If you are working on a long-term project, your supervisor may ask for a **progress report** that updates your status and indicates any potential problems or issues. **FIGURE 11.3** illustrates a progress report written by a team of designers who work for Adaptive Living, a company that designs and sells products to help people with disabilities function independently. The team is designing a swimsuit for women with conditions such as rheumatoid arthritis that severely limit their range of motion. The team has been working on this project for several months and needs to answer two questions: How is the project progressing, and when will a tested prototype be complete? The figure's annotations provide advice about how to organize a progress report.

Travel reports

When you return from a business trip, your manager may ask you to write a **travel report** to document your activities and to share what you accomplished or learned. Keep in mind that your employer will have most likely paid for the business trip and therefore will want to see a correlation between your experience and how it benefits the company. The biggest mistake writers make in preparing travel reports is to organize them chronologically in narrative style. Instead, identify the most useful way to categorize the information from the audience's perspective, for example, by the results you achieved, what you learned, or the customers you visited.

In **FIGURE 11.4**, Ned Walsh reports on his trip to Ottawa to meet with current and potential clients. The figure's annotations provide advice about how to write a report in email form and about how to organize a travel report. Notice that Ned organized the report by the clients he visited. He identified the people he met, what they talked about, and his plans for the next steps. The report serves a number of communication purposes. First, it gives Ned's boss, Sahar Nazari, vice-president of sales, a clear picture of potential new business. This information gives Sahar an opportunity to allocate resources. Second, it provides Sahar with an opportunity to review and evaluate the follow-up plans Ned has made and to offer suggestions. Finally, the report serves as a checklist so that Ned and Sahar can measure progress with the two accounts.

Formal reports

When you report on a major project or substantial research, you will most likely need to produce a formal report, such as a **recommendation report**, which examines options and recommends a course of action. A formal report is often analytical and may be as short as 8 to 10 pages or as long as several hundred pages.

A formal report is illustrated in **FIGURE 11.5** on pages 336–348. This report was prepared by Cordelia Burrows as part of her marketing internship at a small startup company: Cali's Low-Fat Frozen Yogourt. The owners of Cali's are considering using online discount vouchers, such as Groupons, as a marketing tool in conjunction with their store opening. Cordelia was assigned to conduct research on the effectiveness of Groupons and prepare a recommendation report addressing whether Cali's should offer Groupons to attract new customers and, if so, how to implement the Groupons.

Organize the report in distinct sections

To help your reader understand the organization of your report, separate the content into distinct sections. Most formal reports include a title page, preliminary sections, details, and

Progress report A report that updates supervisors on the status of a long-term project.

Travel report A report that documents activities on a business trip and presents accomplishments and issues.

Recommendation report A report that analyzes options and recommends a course of action.

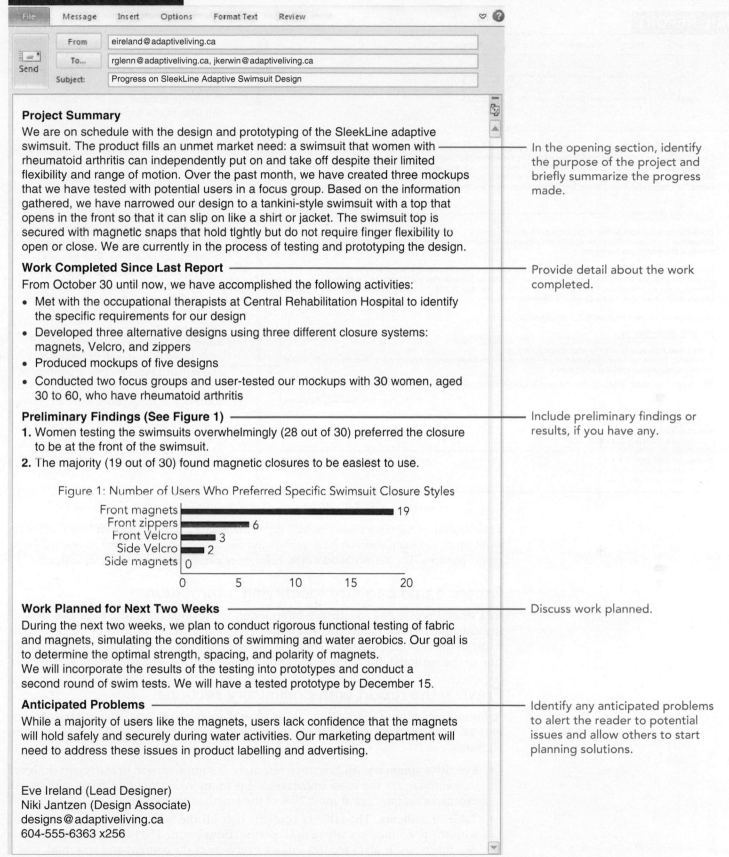

MEMO-STYLE REPORT

File Message Insert Options Format Text Review

From: eireland@adaptiveliving.ca
To...: rglenn@adaptiveliving.ca, jkerwin@adaptiveliving.ca
Subject: Progress on SleekLine Adaptive Swimsuit Design

Project Summary

We are on schedule with the design and prototyping of the SleekLine adaptive swimsuit. The product fills an unmet market need: a swimsuit that women with rheumatoid arthritis can independently put on and take off despite their limited flexibility and range of motion. Over the past month, we have created three mockups that we have tested with potential users in a focus group. Based on the information gathered, we have narrowed our design to a tankini-style swimsuit with a top that opens in the front so that it can slip on like a shirt or jacket. The swimsuit top is secured with magnetic snaps that hold tightly but do not require finger flexibility to open or close. We are currently in the process of testing and prototyping the design.

In the opening section, identify the purpose of the project and briefly summarize the progress made.

Work Completed Since Last Report

From October 30 until now, we have accomplished the following activities:

- Met with the occupational therapists at Central Rehabilitation Hospital to identify the specific requirements for our design
- Developed three alternative designs using three different closure systems: magnets, Velcro, and zippers
- Produced mockups of five designs
- Conducted two focus groups and user-tested our mockups with 30 women, aged 30 to 60, who have rheumatoid arthritis

Provide detail about the work completed.

Preliminary Findings (See Figure 1)

1. Women testing the swimsuits overwhelmingly (28 out of 30) preferred the closure to be at the front of the swimsuit.
2. The majority (19 out of 30) found magnetic closures to be easiest to use.

Include preliminary findings or results, if you have any.

Figure 1: Number of Users Who Preferred Specific Swimsuit Closure Styles

Front magnets — 19
Front zippers — 6
Front Velcro — 3
Side Velcro — 2
Side magnets — 0

(scale: 0 5 10 15 20)

Work Planned for Next Two Weeks

During the next two weeks, we plan to conduct rigorous functional testing of fabric and magnets, simulating the conditions of swimming and water aerobics. Our goal is to determine the optimal strength, spacing, and polarity of magnets.
We will incorporate the results of the testing into prototypes and conduct a second round of swim tests. We will have a tested prototype by December 15.

Discuss work planned.

Anticipated Problems

While a majority of users like the magnets, users lack confidence that the magnets will hold safely and securely during water activities. Our marketing department will need to address these issues in product labelling and advertising.

Identify any anticipated problems to alert the reader to potential issues and allow others to start planning solutions.

Eve Ireland (Lead Designer)
Niki Jantzen (Design Associate)
designs@adaptiveliving.ca
604-555-6363 x256

FIGURE 11.3 Memo-Style Progress Report

FIGURE 11.4 Email-Style Trip Report

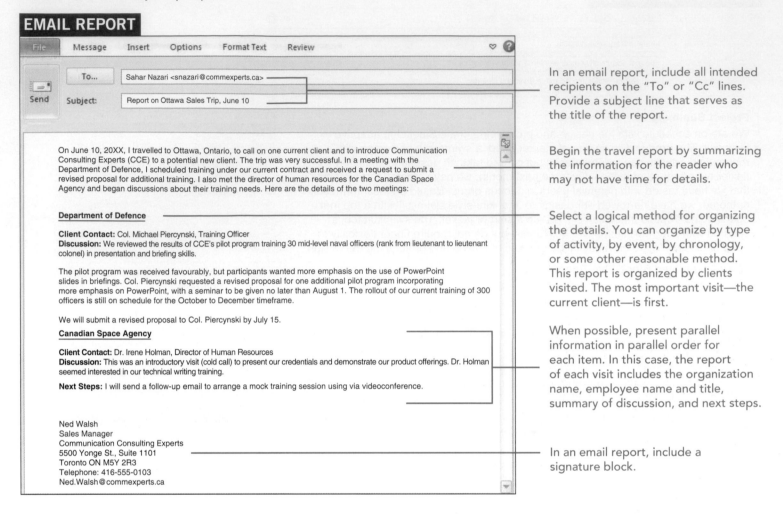

In an email report, include all intended recipients on the "To" or "Cc" lines. Provide a subject line that serves as the title of the report.

Begin the travel report by summarizing the information for the reader who may not have time for details.

Select a logical method for organizing the details. You can organize by type of activity, by event, by chronology, or some other reasonable method. This report is organized by clients visited. The most important visit—the current client—is first.

When possible, present parallel information in parallel order for each item. In this case, the report of each visit includes the organization name, employee name and title, summary of discussion, and next steps.

In an email report, include a signature block.

---

a conclusion. Some reports also include supplementary sections. Microsoft Word and other word processing applications have automated the development of some of the following report features. The **TECHNOLOGY BOX** looks more closely at these powerful features.

Create a title page for identifying information

In a formal report, the identifying information is provided on a title page like the one illustrated in **FIGURE 11.5A**. The **title page** of a report includes the title of the report, the name of the person or organization for whom the report was written, the name and position of the author(s), the name of the author's organization, and the date of submission.

Preview the report with preliminary sections

A formal report provides a reader with several ways to preview the report contents. **FIGURE 11.5B** illustrates how the Groupon report incorporates several of these preview elements.

- **Executive summary.** An executive summary is a mini-version of the report designed to communicate the most important ideas to an audience of decision makers. An executive summary is at most 10% of the length of the report.
- **Table of contents.** The table of contents lists all the headings in the report, along with the page numbers where the report sections begin. The table of contents serves two functions: It gives readers a quick overview of the content and structure, and it also helps readers find specific sections of the report.

  To make the table of contents easy to read, many writers connect the headings to the page numbers with spaced dots called "dot leaders." To ensure proper alignment

Title page The first page of a formal report, which includes identifying information such as the report's title, the name of the person or organization for whom the report was written, the author's name, position, and organization, and the date of submission.

TECHNOLOGY
USING SOFTWARE FEATURES TO HELP FORMAT FORMAL REPORTS

The following standard word processing features will save you time and improve the professional look of your work. To learn about other features, use your program's help files.

- **Automated styles.** Word has a number of different text styles that you can use in your report. A style consists of a font, size, colour, and placement on the page. You can use one style for normal paragraphs, another for headings, a third for quotations, and a fourth for captions. Using styles rather than manually formatting paragraphs offers an important advantage: If you mark text as a specific style and then decide to change that style, the change occurs to all the marked text throughout the document.

- **Automated headings.** Word offers a set of styles called *Heading 1, Heading 2,* and *Heading 3.* You can customize those styles with any font and size. If you use these heading styles in your report, you can take advantage of Word's automated table of contents feature.

- **Automated table of contents.** Many word processing applications offer an easy process to design and insert a table of contents. When you select "Insert Table of Contents" in Word, the program finds all of the headings that you have created using the automated heading styles and copies them into a preformatted table of contents along with their associated page numbers. As you modify your report, you can continue to update your table of contents to reflect changes in headings and page numbers.

- **Formatted tab styles, including dot leaders.** Many tables of contents include dots, called "dot leaders," connecting the section title and the page number. Word allows you

to insert those dot leaders automatically by formatting your tab style, regardless of whether you use an automated table of contents.

- **Automated page numbering using both Roman and Arabic numerals.** You can control the placement of page numbers in your document by inserting headers or footers. You can further control page numbers by using Word's "insert section break" feature and formatting the page numbers differently for each section. For example, you can create a title page with no page number. Then insert a section break and use small Roman numerals (i, ii, iii, etc.) for the page numbering on the table of contents page and executive summary. Insert another section break and begin the numbering again with Arabic numerals (1, 2, 3, etc.), with the introduction counting as page 1, even though sequentially it is not the first page of the file.

- **Automated footnotes, endnotes, citations, bibliographies.** Most word processing applications allow you to insert and number footnotes, endnotes, and citations automatically. As you add, remove, or cut and paste text in your draft, your note numbers automatically change to reflect their new position.

- **Automated labelling of figures and tables.** You can automatically number and label figures and tables using Word's "Insert Caption" command. As you move the figures and tables in your draft, you can instruct Word to update the figure and table numbers.

For a TECHNOLOGY exercise, go to Exercise 8 on page 376.

of the dot leaders and page numbers, do not create the leaders by inserting periods. Instead, create a right-aligned tab for placement of page numbers and format that tab to insert dot leaders automatically.

- **List of figures and list of tables.** When a report contains many figures and tables, you can help readers find specific items by including a list of figure titles and a list of table titles, along with their page numbers. These lists follow immediately after the table of contents.

- **Introduction.** Even though a report begins with an executive summary, the introduction is written as if the reader did not read the executive summary at all. The introduction typically explains the problem or issue that motivated the report. It also summarizes key points or main conclusions and previews how the rest of the report is structured.

Develop the details within sections

The detailed discussion (sometimes called the "body") of a formal report is always organized with headings. The headings are typically content specific. For example, if you are writing a recommendation report, then the major headings may be the key recommendations. As **FIGURE 11.5C** illustrates (pages 340–346), the Groupon report has three major sections following the introduction. Two of these sections are divided into subsections.

**Initiating a Groupon Marketing Campaign for
Cali's Low-Cal Frozen Yogourt**

The title page includes identifying information: title, business name, author and position, and date.

Prepared for
Cali's Low-Fat Frozen Yogourt

Prepared by
Cordelia Burrows
Marketing Intern

April 10, 2016

FIGURE 11.5A Title Page of a Formal Report

Executive Summary

Cali's Low-Cal Frozen Yogourt will benefit from offering a Groupon promotion to support the store's June grand opening in Vancouver. Both academic and business research suggest that Groupons provide effective low-cost advertising, especially for businesses that are new and need exposure.

How Groupons Work

Groupons are "group coupons": discount vouchers that are available for purchase on various city-specific Groupon websites. Groupon subscribers receive daily emails from Groupon featuring a deep discount on one or more "daily deals." The deals are advertised for a short period of time to encourage customers to purchase the discount quickly and share details of the Groupon with others, exponentially increasing the number of people who receive the advertising. When a deal is activated, Groupon keeps 50% of the revenue, and the business receives the other 50%, minus credit card processing fees.

Benefits and Risks of Offering Groupons

Research shows that Groupons will benefit Cali's in several ways:

- Guaranteed customers during the first month the store is open
- Broad exposure to all Groupon subscribers in Vancouver
- Additional social networking and word-of-mouth advertising beyond Groupon subscribers
- Minimal impact on cash flow

However, Groupons do pose several potential risks:

- Loss of profit on customers using Groupons
- Risk of attracting one-time-only customers
- Potential devaluation of Cali's product
- Risk of being unable to handle the influx of customers and thus alienating customers through bad service

Recommendation

Despite the risks, offering a Groupon is a good marketing decision for Cali's as a new and unknown business. However, to minimize the risks, Cali's should do the following:

1. Offer a limited number of Groupons.

2. Offer a short redemption period.

3. Limit the number of Groupons per person.

4. Offer a deal that is low risk to purchase.

5. Ensure a sufficient number of trained staff are available during the promotion.

6. Conduct in-store research on the impact of the Groupon.

ii

The executive summary is a miniature version of the report. The summary comes directly after the title page.

The executive summary includes all important findings, conclusions, and recommendations. This summary uses subheadings to guide the reader.

All page numbers before the introduction are in lowercase Roman numerals. The title page counts as page number i, even though it is not numbered.

FIGURE 11.5B Preview Elements in a Formal Report

(*continued*)

Table of Contents

Introduction 1

Why Offering a Groupon Is Preferable to Traditional Advertising 2

      How Does Groupon Work? 2

      How Does Groupon Differ from Other Advertising Options? 2

      How Does Groupon Compare with Other Online Deal Sites? 3

Benefits and Risks of Offering a Groupon 4

      Benefits of Offering a Groupon 4

      Risks of Offering a Groupon 5

Recommendation: Cali's Low-Cal Frozen Yogourt Should Offer a Groupon 7

References 9

Appendix: Contact Information for Business Owners Interviewed 10

The table of contents includes all the headings in the report and their page numbers.

Right-aligned tabs are formatted with dot leaders connecting the headings and page numbers.

This report does not need a list of figures and a list of tables because the report is relatively short and contains only one figure and one table.

FIGURE 11.5B (*continued*)

Introduction

Since 2008, Groupon has offered businesses a venue to advertise products and services at substantially discounted rates. Every day, Groupon subscribers receive a cleverly worded email announcing a "daily deal" from a local business. The email encourages customers to visit Groupon's highly trafficked website to learn more about the offer and purchase the deal quickly. The consumer saves money, and the business owner gets increased traffic in the store, including new customers.

Despite the popularity of Groupons, researchers and business owners have mixed opinions about the value of offering Groupons and other online vouchers to advertise and market a business. While some people argue that Groupons are an effective tool to attract new customers and gain exposure, others argue that Groupons are unprofitable and that Groupon buyers are unlikely to become loyal, repeat customers.

To determine whether to offer a Groupon in conjunction with its grand opening, Cali's Low-Fat Frozen Yogourt requested this study, which reviews the current research and opinions about Groupons (for contact information for business owners interviewed, see the Appendix). Although offering a Groupon daily deal does involve some risk, this report concludes that Cali's will benefit from a Groupon promotion. The research suggests that Groupons are ideal for small, startup businesses like Cali's, that need exposure to new customers. However, for a Groupon promotion to be successful, Cali's must implement it strategically.

This report does the following:
- Explains how Groupons work
- Compares Groupon promotions to other advertising methods
- Identifies the benefits and potential risks to Cali's
- Offers concrete suggestions for making a Groupon campaign a success

The introduction provides a complete preview of the report. In this introduction:

- The first paragraph provides context.
- The second paragraph discusses the reason for the research and the question the report is addressing.
- The third paragraph summarizes the report's most important findings and the recommendation.
- The final paragraph previews the organization of the content.

Paragraph 3 also refers to the report appendix. The reference explicitly states what the reader will find in that appendix.

1

FIGURE 11.5B *(continued)*

Why Offering a Groupon Is Preferable to Traditional Advertising

When allocating resources to promote the store, Cali's must decide whether offering a Groupon is a good substitute for traditional advertising. Cali's must also decide whether Groupon is the best partner for selling discount vouchers. This section of the report describes how Groupon works, how it differs from traditional advertising, and how it compares to its competitors.

How Does Groupon Work?

Groupon is a company that offers businesses in more than 500 markets around the world a venue to promote their products or services ("Groupon Works FAQ," 2015). Groupon has an estimated 260 million subscribers worldwide, with over 24 million active customers in North America (Groupon Investor Relations, 2015).

A participating business works with Groupon representatives to develop a promotion, which Groupon sends to its subscribers as a "daily deal" ("Groupon Works," 2015). This deal offers a deep discount on the business's products or services (e.g., $5 for $10 worth of frozen yogourt). Groupon takes 50% of the revenue, plus a surcharge of 2.5% for credit card fees, and sends the participating business a cheque for the remaining 47.5% (J. Lurie, personal communication, March 15, 2015).

Each Groupon has a discount expiration date. Purchasers who do not use the Groupon by that date are no longer entitled to the deep discount but can still redeem the Groupon for the amount originally paid. For example, if a customer pays $5 for $10 worth of yogourt and does not use the Groupon before the expiration date, the Groupon is worth the $5 originally paid. The Groupon itself does not expire.

How Does Groupon Differ from Other Advertising Options?

From a consumer standpoint, Groupons differ from standard coupons in three ways: Groupons are purchased in advance, offer a deeper discount, and are conditional. The deal is cancelled if a minimum number of people do not purchase it. This incentive to reach the minimum number of purchases motivates interested consumers to encourage family and friends to buy the Groupon before the offer ends ("Groupon Anxiety," 2011). Groupon advertises this "collective buying power" as something mutually beneficial for consumers, who save money, and for businesses, which benefit from the certainty of exposure and a guaranteed minimum number of responses ("Groupon Works FAQ," 2015).

The guaranteed exposure is part of Groupon's appeal, as financial journalist Felix Salmon (2011) explained:

> With traditional advertising or even with old-fashioned coupons, a merchant never has any guarantee that they will be noticed or make any difference. But with a Groupon, you know that hundreds of people will be so enticed by your offer that they're willing to pay real money to access it. That kind of guaranteed engagement is hugely valuable, and more or less unprecedented in the world of marketing and advertising. (para. 3)

2

Annotations (right margin):

The detailed discussion in this report is divided into three sections. Each section begins with a centred heading.

The first section is divided into three subsections, each starting with a heading at the left margin. All the headings in a subsection should be a similar style. In this case, they are all questions.

In APA documentation style, personal communications are cited within the text only. They are not included in the reference list.

To cite an article or webpage with no author, begin the citation with the name of the article placed in quotation marks.

In APA style, quotations of 40 or more words stand alone as *block* quotations, with no quotation marks. They start on a new line and are indented approximately ½ inch from the left margin of the text. The source citation, with page or paragraph number, follows the final punctuation mark.

FIGURE 11.5C Detailed Discussion Elements in a Report

How Does Groupon Compare with Other Online Deal Sites?

Groupon is the market leader in the online voucher space, attracting more customers and bringing in more revenue than its closest competitor, LivingSocial. The research firm ForeSee (2012) analyzed survey responses from 10,000 online shoppers during the 2011 holiday season and found that in a 90-day period, twice as many daily deal subscribers purchased a voucher from Groupon (50%) than from LivingSocial (25%). (See Figure 1.)

This paragraph introduces Figure 1 and directs the reader to look for specific information in the figure.

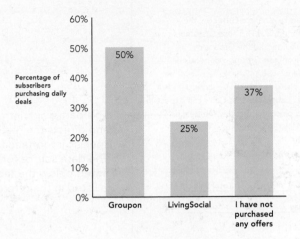

Figure 1: Percentage of Surveyed Subscribers Purchasing Deals from Special-Offer Websites during a 90-day Period in the 2011 Holiday Season. Data source: ForeSee, 2012.

Figure 1 graphs data from a source that is listed in the reference list. The caption of the figure provides a citation of that source. The label "data source" indicates that the original source provided the data but not the graph. The writer used the data to create an original graph.

Research by Synovate (acquired by Ipsos in 2011) looked specifically at Canadian consumers' awareness of online daily deal sites. Of the more than 1,000 Canadians surveyed, the study found that 50% of Canadians were familiar with Groupon versus 25% of Canadians who had heard of WagJag. When it came to generating revenue, Groupon attracted the most purchasers (18% of Canadians who were aware of such deal sites) and usage of Groupon was highest in British Columbia and the Prairies (Synovate, 2011).

These two studies suggest that if Cali's does offer a discount voucher deal, Groupon is a good business partner to choose.

3

FIGURE 11.5C *(continued)*

Benefits and Risks of Offering a Groupon

New sections of the report begin at the top of a new page.

Researchers and businesses offering Groupons have identified benefits and risks of using Groupon as a marketing tool. Below is a summary of those benefits and risks as they apply to Cali's.

Benefits of Offering a Groupon

Groupons will offer Cali's several benefits:

• **Guaranteed customers during the opening month.** When customers purchase a Groupon, they make a commitment to visit the business that is offering the deal (Salmon, 2011). These customers have an incentive to redeem the Groupon quickly because the discount provided by the Groupon ultimately expires. Therefore, the number of customers Cali will see from the Groupon depends on how many Groupons are sold and how quickly customers redeem them.

An analysis of Groupon sales for six frozen yogourt stores in June 2011 suggests that Cali's can expect to sell between 150 and 700 Groupons, with most of the sales taking place the first day the deal is offered (see Table 1).

This paragraph introduces Table 1 and directs the reader to look for specific information in the table. The data source for the table is noted below the table. The source is listed in the reference list.

Table 1: Sales of Groupons by Six Frozen Yogourt Businesses in June 2011

Businesses' Groupon Daily Deal	Sales per Day of Deal			Total Sales
	Day 1	Day 2	Day 3	
$5 for $10 — Yo-Way Yogourt and Crepes	480	117	78	675
$5 for $10 — Frozen Treats at Sno Biz	515	105	51	671
$10 for $20 — Maggie Moo's Ice Cream & Treatery	358	74	N/A	432
$10 for $20 — Fruit Shack Smoothies & Yogourt	328	87	N/A	415
$5 for $10 — The Cordial Cherry	208	88	N/A	296
$4 for $8 — Project: Yogourt	126	25	13	164

Data source: "Groupon Analytics," 2011.

Cali's can expect its customers to begin redeeming their Groupons immediately. Dholakia and Tsabar's (2011) research on Groupon redemption patterns suggests that approximately 30% of Cali's Groupons (between 45 and 210) will be redeemed within the first few weeks. Another, larger spike of Groupons will be redeemed near the discount expiration date. Assuming that Cali's sets a short expiration period of four weeks, the Groupon will guarantee customers during the opening month.

4

FIGURE 11.5C *(continued)*

- **Guaranteed exposure, even to customers who do not purchase the deal.** People who read the daily deal email and click on the link will learn a good deal about Cali's, even if they choose not to purchase the deal. A business's daily deal webpage on Groupon includes a map of the business's location, the business's contact information, a link to its website, and an explanation of its products or services. As Salmon (2011) indicated, this kind of information would be difficult and expensive to broadcast via traditional advertising methods.

- **Additional social network and word-of-mouth advertising.** A promotion through Groupon leads to additional, free social network and word-of-mouth advertising. Purchasers are motivated to tweet about the deals they purchase and to promote them on Facebook, both to inform their friends and to ensure that the deal is not cancelled ("Groupon Anxiety," 2011). In addition, as Salmon (2011) explained, when customers purchase Groupons, the business remains "in the back of their minds" all the time (para. 9). As a result, when a friend asks for a recommendation, Groupon purchasers are likely to mention the business, even if they have not yet redeemed the coupon. Businesses benefit from this word-of-mouth advertising.

- **Minimal negative impact on cash flow.** Rice University marketing professor Utpal M. Dholakia and his co-author Gur Tsabar (2011) argued that, compared to traditional advertising, Groupon daily deals are "more cost-effective and cash-flow friendly for businesses" (p. 2). Moreover, Groupon deals do not require "any financial investment when running the promotion except for maintaining inventory to fill orders" (p. 14). As a small business, Cali's does not have a large budget for marketing and advertising. Advertising in a newspaper or on the radio will cost hundreds or even thousands of dollars, without any certainty of motivating customers. By contrast, Groupon guarantees customers and requires no initial investment that will negatively impact cash flow.

Risks of Offering a Groupon

Although Groupons offer many potential benefits, any business that offers a Groupon must be prepared to face potential risks.

- **The likely loss of profit, at least initially.** Edith Lavallee owner of Sweet Goodness in Fredericton, New Brunswick, and Will Merryweather owner of Great Shakes'n'Smoothies in Moncton, New Brunswick, both confirmed an initial loss of revenue on their businesses' Groupon promotions. Merryweather stated that "Groupon doesn't necessarily increase your revenue; in fact, it gives you a big revenue dip because you have to make a drastic loss-leader discount offer in order to make your daily deal attractive. And then on top of that, you have to split the money with Groupon" (personal communication, March 15, 2012). Lavallee claimed that "not only did we lose profit on individual sales, but we lost money on the fact that some of those customers would have bought yogurt at full price." However, Lavallee acknowledged that losing money "would have happened with any coupon or any advertisement that I had sent out or special I did. I would have had full-price paying customers who found the coupons and used them" (personal communication, March 14, 2012).

5

This discussion of benefits and risks is divided into bulleted paragraphs. Bullets are appropriate when your discussion is organized as a list. Starting each bullet item with a bolded sentence that highlights the main point helps your audience quickly skim the content to get the main points.

FIGURE 11.5C *(continued)*

- **The risk of attracting one-time-only customers.** Groupon analysts Dholakia and Tsabar (2011) warn that Groupons may bring in "price-sensitive deal-seekers" who do not intend to make any future purchases from the business at full cost (p. 3). Sweta Patel (2011), the CEO/marketing strategist of Social Media Eatery, a group that focuses on helping businesses reach their objectives through social media venues, agrees:

  > Groupon is great to bring in new people to your business. However, it seems like they just use the coupon at your venue then run to the next best deal. This is really not a great deal for businesses because they do not gain loyal customers, they just gain the votes of people who like great deals. (para. 1)

  As retail expert Bob Phibbs (2011) explained, because Groupon is the one directly offering customers the discount voucher, the customer's loyalty is to Groupon rather than the business itself.

- **Potential devaluation of the product.** In his book *Groupon: You Can't Afford It—Why Deep Discounts Are Bad for Business and What to Do Instead*, Phibbs (2011) argued that Groupon is bad for business because the deep discounts devalue the product or service in the eyes of the customer. Once the deal is over, customers will try to find that same discount again and hesitate before buying it at the full undiscounted price. Therefore, perpetual discounts are necessary to ensure those same customers return. Ultimately, "you either lose the customer because they don't want to pay more than their discounted price, or you lose the customer because they don't value the product you're selling them anymore" (Phibbs, 2011, "Economics 101," para. 10).

- **The risk of alienating customers through bad service.** For a Groupon promotion to succeed, a business must be prepared to offer excellent service (Dholakia, 2011b). Phibbs (2011) highlighted the example of a restaurant in Tokyo that offered a Groupon and unexpectedly had over 500 customers attempt to redeem the voucher on New Year's Eve. The restaurant was understaffed and undersupplied, and the disappointed customers were unlikely to return.

6

Citations for direct quotations require sufficient information to allow the audience to find the quotation in the original source, as illustrated below.

This citation for an article in PDF form includes a page number.

This citation for a web-based article includes the paragraph number.

This citation for an ebook with no page numbers includes the chapter name and paragraph number.

FIGURE 11.5C *(continued)*

Recommendation: Cali's Low-Cal Frozen Yogourt Should Offer a Groupon

Despite the risks, offering a Groupon is a good marketing decision for Cali's Low-Cal Frozen Yogourt. As a new and unknown business, Cali's stands to benefit more from a Groupon than an established business would. In fact, according to the analysis of economists Edelman, Jaffe, and Kominers (2011), "vouchers are always profitable for 'sufficiently unknown' firms" (p. 7). In addition, owners of other frozen yogourt businesses confirm the exposure value of a Groupon. Jon Lurie of Fruit Shack Smoothies & Yogourt found that Groupon is certainly "a way to get the word out quickly about your business" (personal communication, March 15, 2012). Similarly, Audrianne Doucet of Project: Yogourt asserted that it "is one of the cheapest and easiest ways to send a widespread message" (personal communication, March 14, 2012).

To take advantage of Groupon's benefits while minimizing the risks, Cali's must implement the Groupon promotion strategically, following these recommended steps:

1. **Offer a limited number of Groupons.** Research shows that businesses offering a limited number of Groupons tend to sell more deals overall (Dholakia, 2011a). This limit magnifies the incentive for buyers to act quickly before the deal sells out.

2. **Offer a short redemption period.** No benefit is gained from offering a long redemption period. According to research, long redemption periods do not increase the number of Groupons sold (Dholakia, 2011a). Moreover, distant expiration dates encourage customers to wait to use their Groupons (Dholakia, 2011a). By contrast, a shorter redemption period will motivate customers to come in sooner, increasing the likelihood that they will become repeat customers early in the summer season.

3. **Limit the number of Groupons per person.** The mathematical analysis of Edelman et al. (2011) suggests that allowing one Groupon per customer is profitable, and allowing multiple Groupons is not. However, because Cali's goal is to introduce the store to as many new customers as possible, Cali's should consider following the common Groupon practice of allowing customers to purchase additional Groupons as gifts.

4. **Offer a deal that is low risk to purchase.** An analysis by Paul Butler (2011) in the *Harvard Business Review* shows that low-priced deals generate the most revenue on Groupon. The deal should be enticing enough that customers will purchase it yet moderate enough that customers will spend more than the value of the Groupon at the store (Salmon, 2011). As Table 1 showed, yogourt stores typically offer Groupons in two denominations: $4 for $8 worth of frozen yogourt and $5 for $10 worth of frozen yogourt. Cali's should adopt one of these pricing schemes.

5. **Be sure a sufficient number of trained staff are available during the promotion to make a good first impression.** Dholakia (2011b) argued that well-trained employees with a positive attitude are critical to the success of a Groupon. Chait (2010) recommended that restaurants double the number of staff during a Groupon promotion, station a greeter near the entrance, and distribute appetizers

7

Recommendations are numbered for easy reference. If someone refers to "recommendation 3" in a discussion about the report, the specific recommendation will be easy to find.

FIGURE 11.5C *(continued)*

if the wait is long. Following the spirit of this advice, Cali's should ensure that employees are trained and prepared for a potentially large influx of customers during the Groupon promotion. A greeter can welcome customers at the door and explain how the store works. If the line grows long, the greeter may offer samples to waiting customers.

6. **Conduct in-store research on the impact of the Groupon.** As Edelman et al. (2011) suggest, Cali's should conduct its own in-store research to determine the effectiveness of the Groupon. Staff stationed behind the counter can be directed to note whether Groupon customers (1) put money in the general employee tip jar, (2) spend over the value of the Groupon, and (3) agree to join Cali's email list. In addition, staff can quickly ask customers at checkout whether they have previously visited the store. To simplify this data gathering, employees can mark responses on a printed checklist next to the register or on the printed Groupon that customers present at checkout.

A Groupon promotion is ideal to support the opening of a new business like Cali's, which has an excellent product, no current customers, and very little money to spend on advertising. Although the store may lose money during the promotion, the widespread exposure and the opportunity to win loyal customers should ultimately make the Groupon promotion a success.

8

FIGURE 11.5C *(continued)*

Conclude the report with supporting information

Formal reports may conclude with two types of supporting information: reference lists and appendices. As **FIGURE 11.5D** illustrates, the Groupon report contains both types of supporting information.

References

If a report uses secondary research sources, create a reference section to list the sources. The reference section begins on its own page, immediately after the detailed discussion

---

References ———————————————

Butler, P. (2011). Deconstructing the Groupon phenomenon. *Harvard Business Review, 89*(7/8), 32–33.

Chait, E. (2010, October 6). 5 Tactics to make an unprofitable Groupon campaign successful [Blog post]. *Copilot*. Retrieved from http://blog.launchcopilot.com/2010/10/06/5-tips-to-make-groupon-work/

Dholakia, U. M. (2011a). What makes Groupon promotions profitable for businesses? Retrieved from http://ssrn.com/abstract=1790414

Dholakia, U. M. (2011b). Why employees can wreck promotional offers. *Harvard Business Review, 89*(1/2), 28.

Dholakia, U. M., & Tsabar, G. (2011). A startup's experience with running a Groupon promotion. Retrieved from http://papers.ssrn.com/sol3/papers.cfm?abstract_id=1828003

Edelman, B., Jaffe, S., & Kominers, S. D. (2011, June 16). To Groupon or not to Groupon: The profitability of deep discounts. *Harvard Business School Working Papers*. Retrieved from http://www.hbs.edu/research/pdf/11-063.pdf

ForeSee. (2012, March 12). *Daily deal websites and emails bring in new and existing customers for retailers.* [White paper]. Retrieved from http://www.foreseeresults.com/research-white-papers/_downloads/daily-deal-commentary-2012-foresee.pdf

Groupon analytics. (2011). Retrieved from http://www.grouponanalytics.com/deal/project-yogurt-1

Groupon anxiety. (2011, March 17). *The Economist*. Retrieved from http://www.economist.com/node/18388904

Groupon Investor Relations. (2015). Retrieved from http://investor.groupon.com/

Groupon works FAQ. (2015). Retrieved from https://www.grouponworks.com/merchant-resources/FAQs

Groupon works. (2015). Retrieved from http://www.grouponworks.com/

Patel, S. (2011, May 8). Re: Grouponomics [Blog post in response to article "Grouponomics" by F. Salmon]. Retrieved from http://blogs.reuters.com/felix-salmon/2011/05/04/grouponomics/

Phibbs, B. (2011, April 25). *Groupon: You can't afford it—Why deep discounts are bad for business and what to do instead* [Kindle Edition]. Beyond the Page Publishing. Retrieved from http://amazon.com

Salmon, F. (2011, May 4). Grouponomics. *Reuters*. Retrieved from http://blogs.reuters.com/felix-salmon/2011/05/04/grouponomics/

Synovate. (2011, April 18–22). 7 in 10 Canadian adults aware of online daily group deal sites; Groupon most popular [survey report]. Retrieved from http://www.ipsos-na.com/news-polls/pressrelease.aspx?id=5476

9

The reference list is prepared in APA style:

- Sources are listed alphabetically by last name (or title when there is no author).
- The publication date immediately follows the author (or title when there is no author).
- In source titles, only the first words and proper nouns are capitalized.
- In journal titles, each word in the title is capitalized.
- Note that periods are not used at the end of web addresses.

FIGURE 11.5D Supporting Information Sections of a Report

(continued)

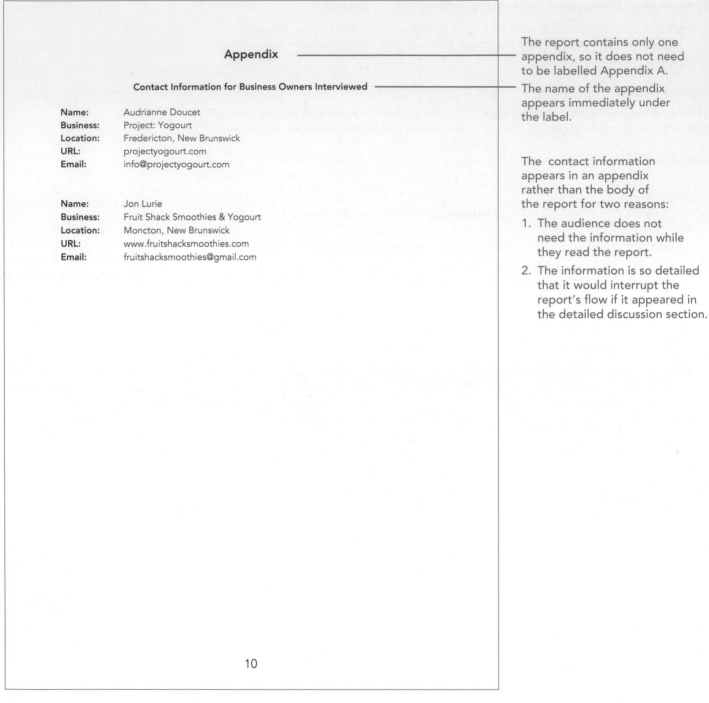

Appendix — The report contains only one appendix, so it does not need to be labelled Appendix A.

Contact Information for Business Owners Interviewed — The name of the appendix appears immediately under the label.

Name:	Audrianne Doucet
Business:	Project: Yogourt
Location:	Fredericton, New Brunswick
URL:	projectyogourt.com
Email:	info@projectyogourt.com

Name:	Jon Lurie
Business:	Fruit Shack Smoothies & Yogourt
Location:	Moncton, New Brunswick
URL:	www.fruitshacksmoothies.com
Email:	fruitshacksmoothies@gmail.com

The contact information appears in an appendix rather than the body of the report for two reasons:

1. The audience does not need the information while they read the report.
2. The information is so detailed that it would interrupt the report's flow if it appeared in the detailed discussion section.

10

FIGURE 11.5D *(continued)*

(or body) of the report. Use an appropriate documentation method, such as APA (American Psychological Association), CMS (Chicago Manual of Style), or MLA (Modern Language Association). You can find details about these documentation styles in Appendix D: Documentation and Reference Styles, at the back of this book.

Appendices

Following the reference list, a report may include additional supporting information in an appendix or multiple appendices. Appendices contain information that would interrupt the flow of the report but that readers may find useful. For example, raw data, calculations, large tables, or other graphics that you do not want to include in the body of the report. If the report includes more than one appendix, the series is labelled Appendix A, Appendix B, and so forth. Appendices are also given content-specific names, for example, "Appendix A: Map of Conference Centres within 10 Kilometres of Acme's Home Office." Typically, the body of the report will refer to each appendix in the order of its placement in the report. Appendix A is the first appendix the report refers to, Appendix B is the second, and so forth. This means you may need to rearrange the appendices as you revise the report.

Design the report for your audience and purpose

The report illustrated in Figure 11.5 is formatted in a traditional *manuscript style*. Although it incorporates some design features, such as headings and bullet points, it does not use more elaborate elements such as borders, multiple columns, call-out boxes, or contrasting fonts.

Manuscript-style reports are common in conservative fields, such as banking and accounting. You will also see manuscript style used for internal company reports, like the one illustrated in Figure 11.5. Although internal reports must be easy to read with effective headings and paragraphing, they do not have to be as eye-catching as external reports. The audience of internal reports typically needs the content and is motivated to read the information.

By contrast, reports that are written for a broader external audience tend to use more design features to motivate the audience to read the report. For example, many organizations produce reports called **white papers**, which serve as marketing or sales tools. A white paper is a report intended to educate the audience (often potential customers) on a topic that is central to a company's business. Companies publish white papers to build credibility, establish themselves as experts on a topic, and often to interest the audience in the company's products or services. Because no one is required to read a white paper, the document must entice the audience with the quality of both the content and the visual design.

Choose the best electronic format for online distribution

Internal reports are typically emailed to recipients. You may distribute the report as a *native file* (a file in its original program), such as Word, or as a PDF (Portable Document Format).

Deciding on the best electronic format for external reports is more complicated. PDF is by far the most common format for distributing reports electronically for three important reasons:

1. Documents are often easier to design than webpages.
2. Documents can be printed and stored on the audience's computer. They are durable and do not disappear when a web address changes.
3. Audiences can be required to submit contact information before downloading a PDF document, allowing the company to track people interested in the information and to market additional content and services to them.

By contrast, web-based reports offer different advantages:

1. Readers can browse through sections of a report without taking time to download it.
2. Web-based reports can be more interactive, with links to multimedia content and animated data displays.
3. Reports can be updated frequently, without republishing the PDF.

Many companies publish their annual reports in both PDF and web format. As **FIGURE 11.6** illustrates, a well-designed web-based report will include all its navigation features on the first screen, so audiences will know the report's contents and will be able to go to any section within a few clicks.

White paper A report produced by a company or organization to educate readers about a complex business issue, product, or technology.

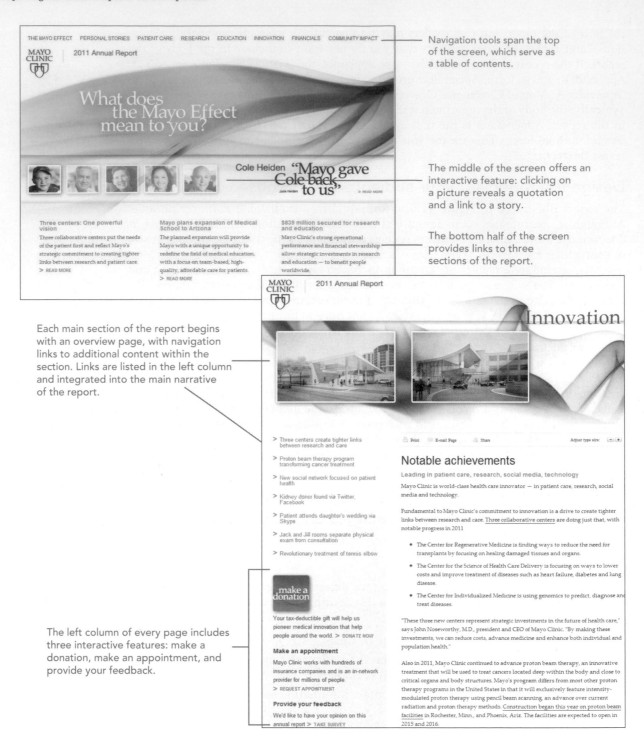

Navigation tools span the top of the screen, which serve as a table of contents.

The middle of the screen offers an interactive feature: clicking on a picture reveals a quotation and a link to a story.

The bottom half of the screen provides links to three sections of the report.

Each main section of the report begins with an overview page, with navigation links to additional content within the section. Links are listed in the left column and integrated into the main narrative of the report.

The left column of every page includes three interactive features: make a donation, make an appointment, and provide your feedback.

FIGURE 11.6 Two Pages of Mayo Clinic Interactive Annual Report
Source: mayoclinic.org. Copyright © 2011–2012. Reprinted with permission.

(LO 11.3) How do you prepare an effective proposal?

In the workplace, if you have a promising idea and want to implement it, or if you want a client to hire you to perform services, you will need to do more than make a request. You will need to sell your idea or service in a persuasive proposal.

A **proposal** is a communication, often in report form, designed to persuade a business decision maker to adopt a plan, approve a project, choose a product or service, or supply funding. To be effective, a proposal needs to convince your audience that your idea or solution is feasible and will meet their needs. Depending on the proposal, you

Proposal A communication, often in report form, designed to persuade a business decision maker to adopt a plan, approve a project, choose a product or service, or supply funding.

may also need to convince your audience that you are the right person (or yours is the right company) to implement the solution.

Understand the problem and propose a well-balanced solution

Preparing a proposal is complicated. It requires that you propose an idea that meets your audience's needs, develop a persuasive appeal, provide details about how to implement the proposal, and explain costs.

Like any other persuasive communication, a proposal benefits from in-depth analysis. You will be able to persuade your audience only if you understand the need your proposal meets (purpose), the type of proposal that is appropriate (context), and the arguments and information that will influence your audience (content).

The first step in preparing a proposal is to develop a clear idea of your purpose: What need are you addressing and how do you propose to meet that need? When readers get a proposal they are looking for specific types of information: statement of the problem or opportunity, your specific proposal, reasons for supporting it, implementation plans, **deliverables** (the items you are agreeing to provide to the audience) and costs.

Because a proposal is a persuasive document, it must not only provide information but also motivate your audience to act. Here is a list of things the proposal must do:

1. **Articulate the problem, need, or opportunity.** Build your credibility by giving the audience confidence that you have listened to them carefully, truly understood their needs, and are able to present an appropriate solution.
2. **Identify the outcomes, benefits, and potential objections.** Help the audience understand why this problem deserves attention and how the benefits of fixing it will outweigh the proposed cost. Explain why your unique solution will have the best outcome.
3. **Present a compelling recommendation.** Clearly demonstrate how your proposal meets the audience's needs and requirements.
4. **Provide persuasive supporting details that emphasize feasibility and credibility.** Present a realistic implementation plan, and in doing so establish that you have the qualifications, facilities, time, staff, and expertise to complete the project.

Chapter 8 discusses additional persuasive techniques that may strengthen your proposal.

Identify the appropriate type of proposal

During your career you may need to write different types of proposals. You will need to differentiate between different scenarios to write an appropriate proprosal.

Is it an internal or external proposal?

An *external proposal* is addressed to people outside your organization, such as a potential client or an agency that will provide funding. External proposals usually take the form of a letter, a report-style document, or a presentation. An *internal proposal* is addressed to people within your organization. Internal proposals can be less formal and, in most cases, may be written as an email.

Is it a competitive or noncompetitive proposal?

In a **noncompetitive proposal** situation, your audience will not be considering any offers other than yours. In a **competitive proposal** situation, others will be competing with you for the sale, the funding, or the opportunity.

Is it a solicited or unsolicited proposal?

A **solicited proposal** is one your audience has asked you to submit. A solicited sales proposal serves as a sales contract. It identifies exactly what you will deliver, at what cost, in what timeframe, and under what circumstances. When your client signs the proposal, both parties have made a commitment. **FIGURE 11.7** is a sales proposal from Cronin Environmental Services (CES) to a new client, Davis College. Because this is an

Deliverables The items or services you agree to deliver to your audience.

Noncompetitive proposal A proposal that has no competition because your audience will not be considering any offers other than yours.

Competitive proposal A proposal that will compete with other proposals for the same sale, funding, or opportunity.

Solicited proposal A proposal that your audience has requested.

LETTER

CRONIN
ENVIRONMENTAL Services, Inc.

1442 Industrial Parkway West
Kelowna, BC V1Y 6H0

250.555.5555
Fax: 250.555.6666
www.cronin.com

October 24, 20XX

Mr. Paul Phillips
Director of Physical Plant
Okanagan College
285 S. Kings Way
Kelowna, BC V1Y 6H2

Subject: Proposal to Update Okanagan College's Waste Reduction Plan ——— *Use a subject line that identifies the subject of the proposal.*

Dear Mr. Phillips:

Cronin Environmental Services, Inc. (CES) is pleased to submit this proposal to assist Okanagan College (OC) in preparing an updated Waste Reduction Plan as required by the Regional District of Central Okanagan (RDCO). CES has extensive experience producing RDCO waste reduction plans. Based on that experience, this letter identifies ——— CES's recommended scope of work, timeframe, and budget. It also provides background about CES's expertise.

Begin the proposal by (1) identifying the subject of the proposal and the reason for writing, (2) stressing your company's qualifications, and (3) previewing the organization of the proposal.

SCOPE OF WORK
To evaluate the waste composition at Okanagan College and prepare the required analyses and report, CES proposes to do the following: ———

Identify exactly what you will do or provide. If your work depends on your client providing information or timely responses, identify what your client must provide.

- Review waste hauling and recycling records for the past 12 months.

- Coordinate with the facilities management staff to schedule a representative sampling of the waste generated at the OC main campus. CES will work with the facilities management staff to identify a location for sorting to minimize inconvenience and, if needed, for temporarily storing the material being sorted (for less than one day).

- Conduct a sort-and-weigh audit using one day's worth of waste from the campus. The sort will address all the waste components required by RDCO, including glass, aluminum containers, plastic (high-density and low-density polyethylene, and polyethylene terepthalate), and landscape waste. In addition, the sort will identify weight components of newsprint, cardboard, printer paper, magazines, and a mixed paper category.

- Conduct a brief walkthrough of the college to evaluate the recycling and waste ——— reduction activities at the campus.

Use headings and bullets that make the proposal easy to skim.

- Meet with facilities management staff as necessary to discuss questions pertinent to the report.

- Prepare a draft report for OC to review and approve.

- Pr epare four copies of the Waste Reduction Plan Update, which OC can submit to RDCO, and two copies for the college's records.

FIGURE 11.7 Solicited Sales Proposal

Mr. Paul Phillips
October 24, 20XX
Page 2

The scope of work assumes that OC will provide the following information necessary to prepare the report:

- Data on procurement of recycled materials, such as paper
- Waste hauling and recycling records
- Data on numbers of students and employees

CES will supply the required forms to obtain this information.

PROPOSED TIME SCHEDULE

CES is able to begin the fieldwork within two weeks of the notification to proceed. The fieldwork will take three days.We can have the analysis complete within four weeks from the completion of the fieldwork, depending on how quickly OC provides the other required data for the report.

Identify the amount of time the project will take and when the project can begin.

BUDGET

CES proposes a not-to-exceed budget of $9,200 to complete this scope of work. The budget is based on the time estimated to complete the work. You will be billed for only the actual time and expenses related to the project. If our time and expenses are lower, the fee will be lower.

State the price of the project and whether this price is a flat fee or is conditional on the time and materials actually required.

CES EXPERIENCE

CES is an engineering consulting firm with offices throughout the province, including one in South Kelowna (located three blocks from the RDCO office). CES offers your company:

- **Extensive experience** conducting waste audits, performing analyses of recycling programs, and developing waste reduction plans for a diverse range of facilities, including commercial offices, elementary schools, postsecondary educational institutions, hospitals, and other institutions. CES was recently selected by Nanaimo County to provide waste reduction services for businesses and multifamily complexes throughout the county.

Add credibility by outlining your experience. You can also provide testimonials and publications to support your claims.

- **A track record of success.** In the past year, CES has produced waste reduction plans for 11 organizations. All of the plans were approved by the RDCO. In addition, CES has been extremely successful in helping its clients secure more than $2 million in grant funds.

An extensive client list is attached to this proposal. I have also attached a short article on CES, published in the *Engineering News Record*.

CONTRACT

Enclosed are two copies of our Standard Agreement for Professional Services. If you agree to this proposal, please sign both agreements, return one, and keep one for your records.

Attach an agreement sheet to make it easy for your client to accept your proposal.

Mr. Phillips, we look forward to working with you on this project. With our experience in producing RDCO reports, we are confident we can produce the documentation you need with minimal disruption to campus life. If you have any questions before signing the contract, please contact me at 250-555-5555 or kim.colgate@cronin.com.

Sincerely,

Kim Colgate

Kim Colgate
Project Manager

Enclosures

FIGURE 11.7 (*continued*)

external sales proposal to a new client, the tone is formal. Notice that the proposal is formatted with headings and bullets that make it easy to read. Also notice that the proposal devotes substantial space to identifying the scope and cost of what CES will deliver to ensure that there is no misunderstanding about the details.

An **unsolicited proposal** is one that you initiate, such as a targeted marketing letter directed to someone who you believe may benefit from your products or services. When you prepare an unsolicited proposal, you need to do more than just convince your audience that you have a good idea. You first need to grab your audience's attention by convincing them that they have an unmet need or can benefit from a new opportunity. This proposal does not discuss any contractual arrangements as a solicited sales proposal would.

If a proposal is solicited, your audience has already identified a problem or need and has requested a solution. You may be responding to an official **request for proposal (RFP)**, which identifies the need and is published widely so that the organization gets multiple competitive proposals. Solicited proposals usually take the form of a report-style document or a formal, detailed letter that uses a direct organization because your audience is expecting to hear your main idea.

Proposals that respond to RFPs are always competitive. The RFP will outline the important criteria on which you will compete. In some situations price will be the most important criterion. In other situations your ability to deliver your product or service quickly may be most important. In still others your proposal will be judged based on your ability to meet very specific requirements. When submitting a competitive proposal, you need to think carefully about what your audience is really looking for and what criteria they will use for judging.

(LO 11.4) How do you properly respond to a request for proposal?

In business, proposals are strongest when they make a **business case**: when they argue that a specific course of action will benefit an organization and also makes business sense. When writing a business case, you need to discuss benefits, costs, risks, and implementation plans (Gambles, 2009).

It is also important to consider what word choices will be most effective. In a proposal, use active voice rather than passive voice to describe the services you will provide and the activities your audience must complete. Active voice is both stronger and clearer, and it eliminates ambiguity about who must do what.

> **Passive:** After the internship program is approved, the internship coordinator will be contacted.
>
> **Active:** After **you** approve the internship program, **I** will contact the internship coordinator.

Different sections of a proposal require different verb tenses. When you write about what you propose, use future tense. When you write about your capabilities, use present tense. When you write about your past experience, use a verb form that refers to the past. For example,

> Cochran University's internship program **is** highly regarded in the local community. For the past 10 years the program **has placed** more than 200 students per year with local businesses. To ensure an appropriate match, the university **prequalifies** all applicants. We **will** see only candidates who meet our qualifications.

Structure an RFP proposal like a formal report

An RFP proposal looks much like a formal report with the addition of a cover message. In addition to the body of the proposal itself, formal proposals include these elements:

Unsolicited proposal A proposal that your audience is not expecting.

Request for proposal (RFP) An invitation for suppliers to competitively submit proposals to provide a product or service.

Business case A justification for a proposal showing that the recommended course of action benefits an organization and makes business sense.

cover message (letter or email), title page, executive summary, table of contents, references or works cited, and appendices if applicable.

A **cover message** introduces the audience to the proposal. This message can take the form of a cover letter for an external proposal, a cover memo for an internal proposal, or an email to which the proposal is attached. The cover message provides the reader with an overview of the content and is itself a persuasive document that convinces your audience to read the proposal carefully and positively. The cover message tells the reader

- what you are writing about (the subject of this proposal),
- what features and benefits the proposal offers, and
- what you plan to do next as a follow-up.

As in your formal report, the executive summary for your RFP proposal should briefly summarize the most important information from the rest of your proposal. Executive decision makers may read only the executive summary and, based on how persuasive it is, decide whether to read the entire document. An executive summary for a proposal typically includes the following information:

- The problem necessitating the proposal
- Suggested solutions
- Benefits that will result when the proposed suggestions are implemented
- Important implementation details
- The qualifications that indicate you can resolve the issue

Depending on the situation, the summary may also include the following:

- A project management plan and timetable
- A total project budget

Follow specified guidelines when responding to RFPs

Requests for proposals typically include a very specific set of requirements that the proposer must meet. In some industries RFPs can generate proposals that are more than 100 pages long. In most cases, though, responses are much shorter.

The key to writing an effective proposal in response to an RFP is to create a checklist of requirements and to ensure that your proposal addresses all these requirements. **FIGURE 11.8** is the cover letter that accompanied a 15-page RFP sent to the Revson Communication Group. When the Revson Group received this RFP, a manager read through the entire document, noting the proposal requirements in the margins. Figure 11.8 shows the Revson Group's annotations on the cover letter.

The formal RFP introduced in the Figure 11.8 cover letter required Revson to prepare a formal response that includes elements of both information and persuasion. To be successful, the proposal must do the following:

- Provide a quick overview at the beginning, either in an executive summary or an introduction
- Make the information easy to find, using a table of contents or other contents list
- Show an understanding of the client's needs
- Propose a solution that meets the needs as listed in the RFP
- Provide evidence that the course designers and instructors are qualified
- Propose a competitive fee
- Provide the required documentation

FIGURE 11.9 (page 358) shows a thumbnail view of Revson Communication Group's response. Notice how the proposal includes all the formal elements. Also notice how the section headings are designed to respond specifically to the content in the RFP.

Cover message A letter, memo, or email accompanying a formal report or proposal designed to explain the document and persuade the audience to read it.

LETTER

Industries

1000 Brandywine Blvd., Hamilton, ON L8E 0G2

November 7, 20XX

Revson Communication Group
5500 Kirkwood Highway
Ancaster, ON L9K 1J9

Subject: RFP for Strategic Communications Course

I am contacting you on behalf of Linus Industries (Linus). We are requesting a proposal to assist us with a one-day Strategic Communications course for senior-level managers who communicate with all levels of the organization.

Context

Linus is a broad-based health care company that discovers, develops, manufactures, and markets products and services that span the continuum of care—from prevention and diagnosis to treatment and cure. The Strategic Communications course will be one of the final pieces in a 16-course, in-depth communications cluster as part of our Business Skills curriculum. This advanced course will help Linus do a better job of communicating strategic messages with employees and leaders within the company as well as communicating externally. An initial description of the course is included on page 3 of the RFP.

Project Purpose

This project is to establish an instructor-led course that will help senior managers create appropriate strategic messages and communicate effectively with peers and employees. Our three broad areas of interest are:

- communicating strategic messages downward within the organization,
- creating an environment where dialogue is encouraged: one on one or within a larger group setting, and
- creating a strategic communications plan for major initiatives, such as oganizational changes.

Scope

The solution proposed may be an entirely new creation or customization of a current course offered by the supplier. Linus does not have a method of forecasting how many people might use this tool during a year. However, 48 to 108 users per year is a reasonable estimate.

Key Requirements:

Must be a one-day course.

Must focus on communicating strategic messages internally and externally.

Must address three key areas:.
- communicating downward
- creating an environment that encourages dialogue
- creating a strategic communications plan

FIGURE 11.8 Request for a Proposal with Added Checklist in the Margin

Revson Communication Group
November 7, 20XX
Page 2

This RFP is for development of course materials. However, please include the proposed audience size per session and the total costs of facilitating the course for a given session (excluding travel costs, which are reimbursed afterwards—see Travel & Living Expenses elsewhere in this document). Linus must approve the primary instructor, but such approval is not part of this RFP. Please include data describing potential instructors.

Critical Success Factors

The course must do the following:

- Emphasize skill building, rather than "learning about" the topic of strategic communications
- Offer opportunities for practice
- Be appropriate for senior-level managers who expect a high-level course and have little tolerance for basic information
- Be appropriate for audiences not just within Canada but throughout the world
- Account for cross-cultural nuances regarding either the speaker or audience
- Be able to be customized to fit Linus branding standards

Material Included in This RFP

On the following pages, please find:

1. Project Charter
2. Project Milestones
3. Response Terms and Conditions
4. Response Content and Evaluation
5. Proposal Submission Guidelines
6. Supplier Evaluation Criteria
7. Confidentiality Agreement

Linus expects the utmost in professional associations with its suppliers. We strive to work together in a harmonious relationship that is beneficial for both Linus and our chosen supplier(s). This RFP is an instrument designed to enable Linus to make the best possible decision in creating a business relationship with the selected supplier(s).

For more information, please contact me at 800.555.3978 or r.sklar@linusind.com. I look forward to your proposal.

Sincerely,

Richard Sklar

Richard Sklar, Manager
Professional Development

Proposal must include:
- proposed class size
- costs of developing materials
- costs for facilitating the course
- data describing potential instructors

Description of the course must emphasize:
- skill building
- opportunities for practice
- high-level content
- cross-cultural elements
- method of customizing to branding standards

Check proposal submission guidelines and evaluation criteria.

FIGURE 11.8 *(continued)*

FIGURE 11.9 Response to RFP

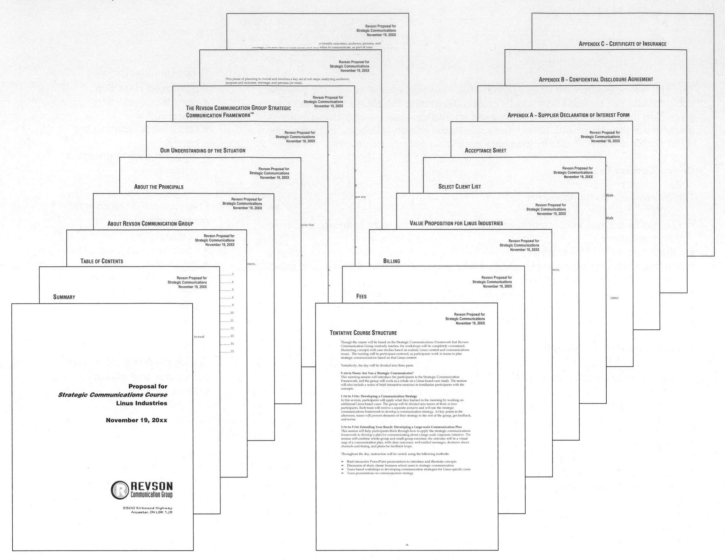

The guidance in this chapter is particularly relevant for business proposals intended for audiences within Canada. What if you need to make a proposal to a business associate or potential business partner in another country? Is it realistic to believe that you can simply write a proposal, including persuasive elements and the terms of an agreement, and expect your audience to respond positively? This challenge is reviewed in more detail in the **CULTURE BOX**.

Use proposal-writing software to increase efficiency

Businesses that routinely write formal proposals often invest in *proposal-writing software* that makes the writing process more efficient. This software allows a business to create a customized template for a proposal (including all the sections that are important to the business), write multiple versions of text for each section and store the text along with pricing information in an online catalogue, select text from the catalogue for each proposal, and deliver the completed proposal as a web document. There are many benefits to using proposal-writing software, including the efficiency of the process. Businesses can produce more proposals more quickly, leading to increased business.

CULTURE
PROPOSALS FOR A NON-CANADIAN AUDIENCE: EXTRA RESEARCH IS REQUIRED

Skylar is in her last semester in her business program. One of her major assignments is to develop a complex and detailed business proposal for a fictional international client. The instructor has suggested that there are three areas of possible discord between the development and presentation of a proposal for a Canadian audience and one for an audience of another culture:

- Differences in the proposal process itself
- Differences in persuasive content
- Differences in attitude toward signed and verbal agreements

The fictional international client and its culture of origin has not yet been assigned, but Skylar wants to get ahead on this challenging assignment. Where can she start? What does Skylar need to be aware of to ensure she creates a culturally appropriate proposal?

O-A-R CAN HELP

- **Observe:** While at her internship placement with Couture Ads, Skylar has noted that company representatives approach a negotiation with a China-based client completely differently than with Canadian, US, or some European clients. The proposal process itself takes much longer, often months rather than weeks. Several face-to-face visits seem to be normal with a China-based client. Indeed, according to ChinaTrade.com, "Chinese business people will seldom make a snap decision and prefer to give a business proposal careful and measured consideration" ("Business meeting etiquette," 2008). Because relationships are so important to Chinese businesspeople, the process of negotiating an agreement can take a long time. Business agreements in China begin with conversations and discussions where both parties can socialize and learn more about what the other party values and needs (Gong, 2011). The approach is to negotiate proposals verbally, and then finalize them with a written contract (Schuster, 2004).

   Skylar remembers what she learned about high-context cultures (see Chapter 4) and, suddenly, this in-depth relationship-building behaviour makes sense to her. Clearly, if her client is based in China or any other high-context culture, the proposal process will take more time and more social contact than with other cultures.

- **Ask:** A few months ago, Skylar helped one of the most experienced Couture Ads representatives, Isaac, prepare a proposal for a client in Brazil. She noticed that Isaac emphasized that the campaign would be the "most dynamic and interactive campaign of its type." Isaac particularly emphasized that the demographic "reach" of the campaign, the number of people across targeted buying sectors, would be larger than any other campaign attempted by Couture Ads. Isaac concluded the proposal

by assuring the Brazilian client that this campaign would vault this company's image into the stratosphere. In other proposals she had seen, the emphasis had always been on profit margin, cost per click, and other financial factors. Skylar asked why this proposal was different. Isaac responded that in Canada and many other Western countries, businesspeople are conditioned to think that profit and return on investment (ROI) are the biggest benefits to stress in a business proposal. In some countries, however, other benefits are more important. In Brazil, many consider gains in status and power to be more important than gains in profit (Katz, 2011). Therefore, in his proposal to a Brazilian company, Isaac knew that he needed to identify the social and status benefits as well as the financial benefits.

Skylar remembers this in the context of her proposal assignment for school. She needs to identify the cultural expectations for persuasive content in the company and culture she will be assigned. Specifically, she will need to find out what are the most important benefits that the company will be seeking, and she needs to recognize that these may not be the same as she would expect a Canadian company to be looking for.

- **Research:** Skylar decides that the third point that the instructor provided, the possible differences in attitude toward written and verbal agreements, needs some independent research. She finds out that for most Canadians and Americans, a signed proposal or contract means a final agreement that must be honoured. In fact, for most Canadians and Americans, an agreement is not finalized until it is put in writing. However, in other cultures a signed contract simply signals an interest in doing business rather than a commitment. For example, in China contracts are always open to renegotiation. This is the accepted business norm (Hupert, 2009). In still other cultures, for example Italy, it is expected that oral commitments will be honoured. Signing a contract is a mere formality, reflecting the commitment between business partners (Katz, 2008).

Skylar needs to find out more about this assignment. Specifically, she needs to know whether the instructor is expecting a written formal proposal or a presentation with a slide deck. It occurs to her that she may decide to produce both, especially if she is assigned a culture that puts more emphasis on oral agreements than on written agreements. Assuming that the instructor will be impressed if she produces an oral proposal framework for a culture that responds well to such an approach, Skylar expects this bit of research and knowledge to help her get a great grade on this assignment.

For CULTURE exercises, go to Critical Thinking Question 1 and Exercise 5 on pages 374 and 376.

How do you integrate visuals into reports?

Business reports often rely on numbers, and **data graphics** (tables and graphs) are the best tools for communicating these numbers. Have you ever read a complicated description of information and then looked at a table or graph and thought, "Now I understand"? Well-designed tables and graphs provide a picture of data and allow you to see relationships and trends much more clearly than with text alone. However, creating effective data graphics and integrating them into your text is not always easy. It involves a multistep process. This section provides a quick glimpse of that process so that you can begin using graphics effectively in your own documents.

Choose the best form of display: table or graph

Tables and graphs represent data in different ways. **Tables** arrange data in columns and rows, allowing you to read down or across to see different relationships. **Graphs** illustrate the relationship among variables or sets of data as an image or shape drawn in relationship to two axes.

Because they represent data in different ways, tables and graphs have different uses. **FIGURE 11.10** illustrates the same data presented in text, graph, and table form. As you can see, it is difficult to understand the significance of the numbers when they are embedded in the paragraph. The table makes it easy to find exact values. However, the table does not help you see specific patterns and trends. Although the graph does not provide exact values, it highlights trends and relationships by showing the data as a shape. You should choose the form of data graphic that helps your audience most clearly see the important points you want to make about the data.

Choose the best type of graph

Data graphics Visual representations of data in tables and graphs that allow you to see relationships and trends much more clearly than in text alone.

Table A graphic that arranges data in columns and rows, allowing you to read down or across to see different relationships.

Graph A visual representation of data that illustrates the relationship among variables, usually in relationship to x- and y-axes.

If a graph is the best way to display your data, make sure to choose the type of graph that most effectively communicates your message. Most business documents use the core set of nine graph types illustrated in **FIGURE 11.11**, along with some variations (Wong, 2010). You can create all of these graphs with commonly available spreadsheet and graphing software. For each type of graph, Figure 11.11 provides a statement of the purpose, an illustration, and best practices for designing that type of graph. These best practices, which are explained in more detail in the next section, will help you communicate meaningful information about your data.

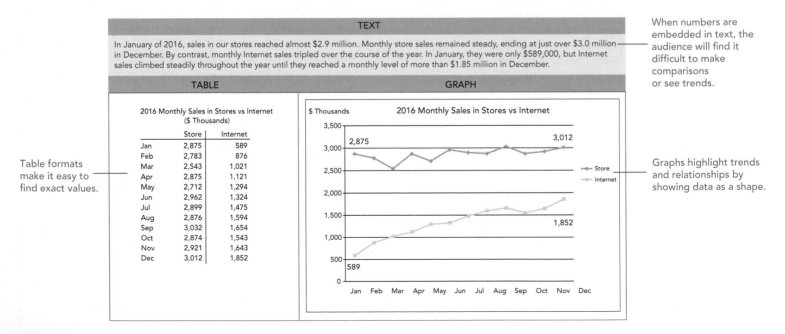

FIGURE 11.10 Comparing Text, Tables, and Graphs

PURPOSE	BEST GRAPH TO USE	BEST PRACTICES
Show how one item (100%) divides into multiple parts	**Pie chart** **Competitor A has smallest market share** 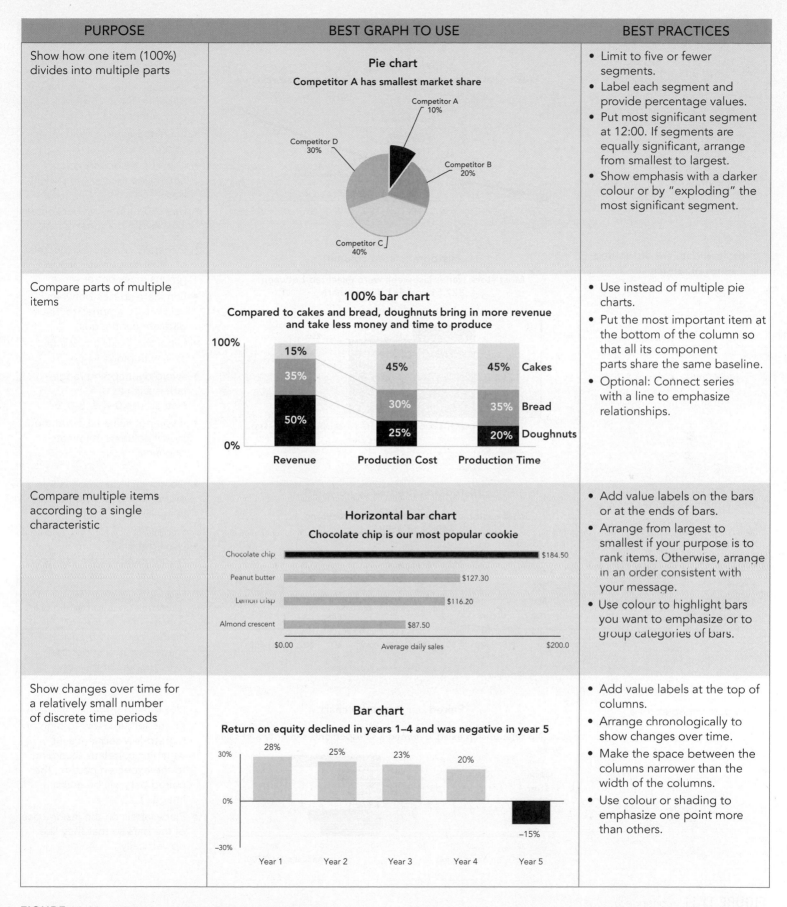	• Limit to five or fewer segments. • Label each segment and provide percentage values. • Put most significant segment at 12:00. If segments are equally significant, arrange from smallest to largest. • Show emphasis with a darker colour or by "exploding" the most significant segment.
Compare parts of multiple items	**100% bar chart** **Compared to cakes and bread, doughnuts bring in more revenue and take less money and time to produce**	• Use instead of multiple pie charts. • Put the most important item at the bottom of the column so that all its component parts share the same baseline. • Optional: Connect series with a line to emphasize relationships.
Compare multiple items according to a single characteristic	**Horizontal bar chart** **Chocolate chip is our most popular cookie**	• Add value labels on the bars or at the ends of bars. • Arrange from largest to smallest if your purpose is to rank items. Otherwise, arrange in an order consistent with your message. • Use colour to highlight bars you want to emphasize or to group categories of bars.
Show changes over time for a relatively small number of discrete time periods	**Bar chart** **Return on equity declined in years 1–4 and was negative in year 5**	• Add value labels at the top of columns. • Arrange chronologically to show changes over time. • Make the space between the columns narrower than the width of the columns. • Use colour or shading to emphasize one point more than others.

FIGURE 11.11 Guidelines for Selecting the Best Graph

(continued)

PURPOSE	BEST GRAPH TO USE	BEST PRACTICES
Show changes over time to emphasize a trend		• Limit the number of lines if the graph is difficult to read. • Provide value labels wherever possible. If too cluttered, label only select data points. • Label the lines instead of using a legend. • Use a bright or dark colour to emphasize the most important line. • Use short labels on horizontal axis. Avoid diagonal labels.
Show how data are distributed in a series of ranges		• Generally, use groups (buckets) of equal size, unless unequal groups make better sense. • Eliminate spaces between columns to emphasize that data are continuous. • Label the x-axis (horizontal axis) with range values. • Avoid overlapping range labels such as 0–5, 5–10, instead use 0–4.9, 5–9.9. • If you put value labels at the top of columns, eliminate gridlines.
Show the pattern of distribution for a continuous series of data		• Do not include range labels on the x-axis (horizontal axis). Instead, use discrete measurement points. • Use light gridlines to help a reader interpret the values on the y-axis (vertical axis). • Use light grey vertical reference lines to highlight a specific area of the distribution. Alternatively, shade the area under the relevant part of the curve.
Compare variables for a small data set		• Plot the independent variable on the left, in a low-to-high or high-to-low sequence. (If variables correlate according to the expected pattern, the paired bars will be mirror images.) • Place labels on the inside base of the bars so that they line up vertically.

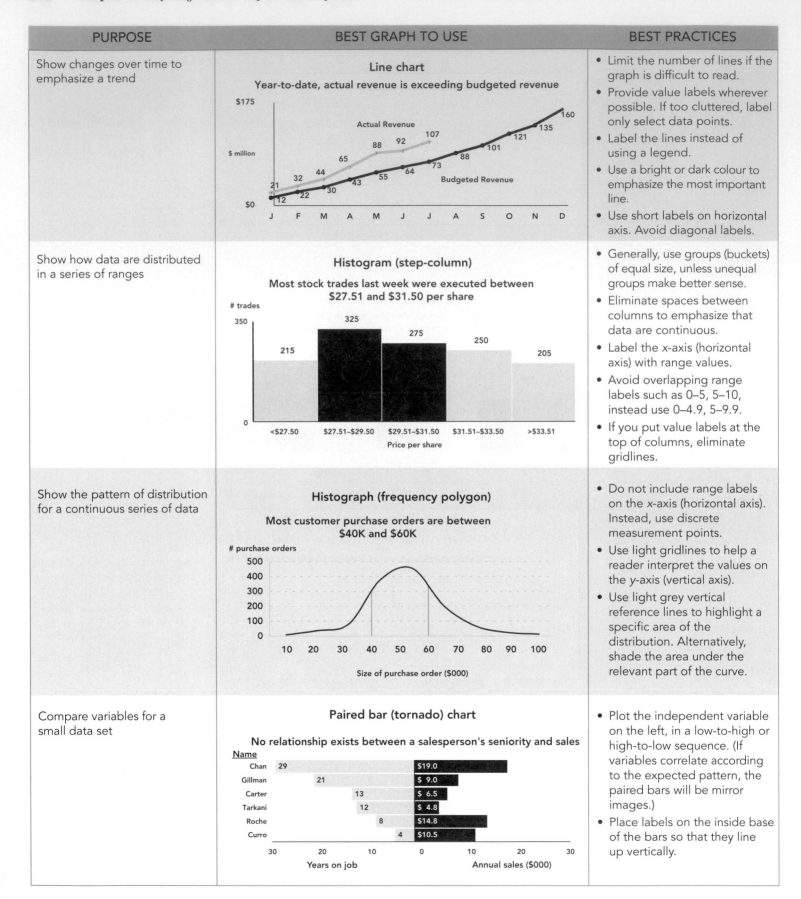

FIGURE 11.11 *(continued)*

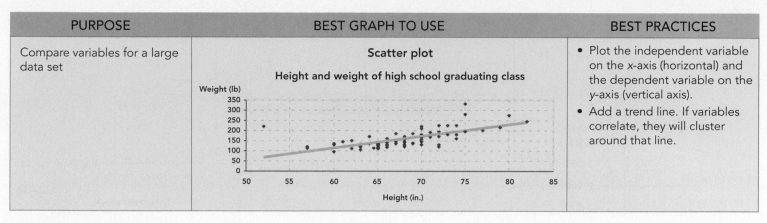

PURPOSE	BEST GRAPH TO USE	BEST PRACTICES
Compare variables for a large data set	**Scatter plot** **Height and weight of high school graduating class**	• Plot the independent variable on the x-axis (horizontal) and the dependent variable on the y-axis (vertical axis). • Add a trend line. If variables correlate, they will cluster around that line.

FIGURE 11.11 *(continued)*

Design graphs and tables to communicate

Whether you are designing graphs or tables, follow the core principle of Edward Tufte, one of the most famous information designers in the world. Tufte recommends eliminating all distractions that do not help the audience understand the data (Tufte, 1983). For tables, this means eliminating or minimizing all unnecessary gridlines and borders. For graphs, it means eliminating anything that exists only for decoration. All the graphs illustrated in Figure 11.11 follow current best practices in designing graphs.

Checklist for effective graph design

Use **FIGURE 11.12** and the following checklist for advice about designing graphs. The numbers on the checklist correspond to the numbered elements on the figure.

1. **Title.** Give every graph a title, or headline, that summarizes its data, purpose, or message. A concise yet specific headline means that people who skim a document will know exactly what the graph is about, even without reading the surrounding text. If the graph is plotting data from a specific timeframe, indicate the time period in the title (or in a footnote). Remember that in a formal report, all of the graph titles will appear in the list of figures that follows the table of contents.

2. **Data objects.** Design lines, bars, and points very simply. Keep lines thin. Avoid contrasting borders around data objects. Avoid 3D effects, which make the data less precise by distorting the scale and adding extra ink.

3. **Axis title.** Title all axes, and position the titles horizontally. Many software programs default to the vertical position with y-axis titles, which requires readers to tilt their heads or the document to read. Reorient those labels so they are positioned horizontally like normal text on the page.

4. **Axis labels.** Unless the title of the graph makes it obvious what each axis represents, label all axes to indicate what is being measured and the units of measurement (e.g., $ Thousands, Months, Widgets Sold). If possible, avoid orienting x-axis labels at an angle. Instead, try to establish abbreviations that allow you to use short, horizontal labels.

5. **Scales.** Begin numerical scales at zero. Starting the scale at a higher number distorts the information.

6. **Tick marks.** Use tick marks only when helpful. These small dashes on the x- and y-axes are sometimes helpful to align the axis labels with data points. However, in many instances, you can eliminate them.

7. **Value labels.** Place value labels on data points rather than relying only on the y-axis scale. Value labels communicate precise, not estimated, values. If your graph contains too many labels, delete some to avoid clutter. Use only enough labels to allow readers to interpret the data. If you use value labels on data points, you can also delete many of the numerical labels on the y-axis. Minimum and maximum values are often sufficient.

FIGURE 11.12 Graph
Terminology

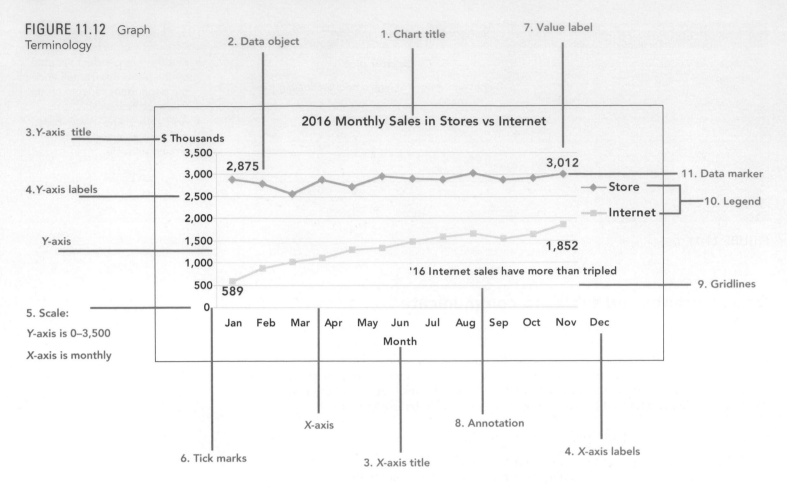

8. **Annotations.** Include descriptive text to highlight key data changes or to focus on specific data points.

9. **Gridlines.** Use minimal gridlines. If you must use gridlines, use light grey instead of black.

10. **Legends.** Avoid legends when possible. Consider using labels instead, placing them as closely as possible to the lines or bars. Legends require eye movement back and forth, which requires the audience to exert additional effort to match legend colours to the data on the graph. If you do need to use a legend, be sure distinctions are visible when viewed both in colour and in grayscale, and eliminate borders around legend boxes.

11. **Data markers.** Use subtle data markers to identify specific data points. In a line graph, data markers identify the specific data points you are connecting. For example, Figure 11.12 shows a graph that covers one year, but the lines are drawn from only 12 data points (one for each month). To avoid distracting readers, keep the data markers small, no more than two points larger than your smallest font.

Checklist for effective table design

Like graphs, tables should be designed so the audience can easily see the data without any distracting content or format. Follow these guidelines, which are illustrated in the table in **FIGURE 11.13**.

- **Title each table.** Identify the table's content and mention key elements you would like the reader to notice.
- **Arrange the columns and rows in a meaningful order.** In Figure 11.13, the table is ordered from shortest CD length to longest.
- **Label columns and rows effectively.** Review your table to ensure that readers will know exactly what is in each cell.
- **Eliminate heavy gridlines.** These are the horizontal and vertical lines that separate cells in a table. Do not imprison your data in a grid of black lines. You can separate columns and rows using light grey lines or white space, as Figure 11.13 illustrates.

FIGURE 11.13 Effective Table Design

FUNDS INVESTED IN CERTIFICATES OF DEPOSIT				
CD Length	Date Opened	Renewable	Interest Rate %	Value of Investment
Six Month	06/01/20XX	Y	1.15	$ 870.27
One Year	08/13/20XX	Y	2.00	2,250.50
Three Year	11/01/20XX	N	3.25	10,311.73
Five Year	03/03/20XX	N	4.25	15,215.50
Total				$ 28,648.00

- **Use shading strategically.** You can use light shading to highlight data or distinguish alternate rows. Notice how the last column is highlighted in the figure to emphasize the current value and total.
- **Remove unnecessary repetition from cells.** You do not need to include a $ or % in all cells in a column. Put signs in the appropriate column or row header (as shown in the "Interest Rate" column in Figure 11.13) or with the first value (as shown in the "Value of Investment" column in Figure 11.13).
- **Align numbers to the right.** Keep decimal points aligned. Use a consistent number of decimal places in all values in a column. For example, see the "Value of Investment" column in Figure 11.13.
- **Align text to the left.** Text is easier to read when it is left aligned (rather than centred). For example, see the "CD Length" column in Figure 11.13.
- **Do not centre content** unless every row in that column contains the same number of characters. In the "Renewable" column in Figure 11.13, Y and N are centred because each entry is one character long. In the "Date Opened" column, the dates are centred because they are written in identical format and have the identical number of characters. You can also centre the text in the "Interest Rate" column because the character lengths are identical. However, if one interest rate were 10% or larger, you would need to right align the numbers to make the decimal points line up.

Integrate data displays within the text

In a report or other document, text and data displays need to work together to communicate the full message. The graph or table presents the data, and the text contextualizes and interprets the data. Use text to explain what the audience is looking at and highlight the key point they should understand from the data. In **FIGURE 11.14**, the text in Version A simply repeats data that can be seen in the graph itself. Version B is better because it generalizes from the data and identifies significant patterns. The text also uses the data to support an argument.

Follow these guidelines to integrate the verbal and visual elements of your documents:

- **Label and number figures and tables sequentially throughout the report.** You may either number figures and tables in their individual sequences (Figure 1, Figure 2, Table 1, Table 2), or you may combine tables and figures into one list, calling them Exhibit 1, Exhibit 2, Exhibit 3.
- **Refer the audience to the graphic within the text** using the figure or table number, as illustrated in the Version A and Version B paragraphs in Figure 11.14, and as illustrated throughout this book.
- **Place the graphic as close as possible after the first reference.** Do not place graphics before the text mentions them because this will confuse readers.
- **Tell the audience what to notice in the graphic.** In a data graphic, what are the important findings or trends? In a picture or illustration, where should the audience focus their attention? In a diagram, how should the audience read the illustrated relationships? Answer these questions in the text that accompanies the graphic.

FIGURE 11.14 Using Text to Explain
Graphics
Source: "Smoking, 2012" from Statistics Canada.
Reprinted with permission.

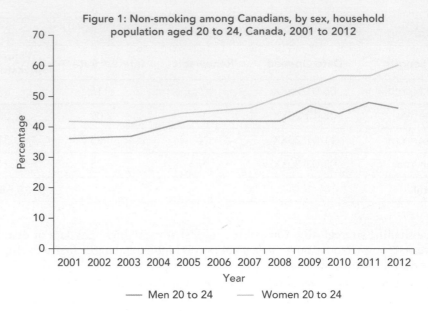

Figure 1: Non-smoking among Canadians, by sex, household population aged 20 to 24, Canada, 2001 to 2012

— Men 20 to 24   — Women 20 to 24

Version A: As Figure 1 illustrates, between 2001 and 2002, women were more likely to have never smoked than men. During this timeframe the increase of non-smokers has been less dramatic for men.

Version B: In Canada today, cigarette smoking is still the leading preventable cause of death. The Canadian Cancer Society estimates that each year about 37,000 people die as a result of smoking tobacco. People typically begin smoking during their teenage years, so the percentage of Canadians who have not started smoking by age 20 is an indicator of future smoking rates.

Attempts to decrease teenage smoking in the last decade have been largely successful. As Figure 1 shows, between 2001 and 2012, rates of cigarette non-smoking male and female Canadians aged 20 to 24 increased significantly. In 2012, 60.4% of female Canadians aged 20 to 24 had never smoked, and 46.1% of male Canadians aged 20 to 24 had never smoked. Both rates are significant increases from 2001 when the rate was 41.9% for females and 36.2% for males.

- **Design the graph to be self-explanatory, even though you have provided explanatory text.** Provide enough labelling on the graphic and enough description in the figure name and caption so that readers can understand what they are seeing without reading the accompanying text. This allows readers to scan the document and derive a lot of information by looking solely at the graphics.

  There are also some ethical considerations with regard to how data is presented in visual format. Check out the **ETHICS BOX** for a deeper look into this issue.

ETHICS
REPRESENTING DATA ETHICALLY

Skylar will need to include research data in her proposal assignment. (See the Culture box on page 359.) Choosing what to include is part of being ethical. As for any other report or proposal, Skylar needs data that are relevant, current, complete, and accurate. However, there are more ethical choices to be made.

Businesses rely on data to make informed decisions. Graphs that display data must do so in a way that does not mislead the audience. Graphs can mislead in many ways. For example, charts and graphs can

- manipulate scale,
- distort perspective, or
- show data out of context.

Because ethical representation of data is so important, many organizations have developed guides to data ethics (National Forum on Education Statistics, 2010). The following guidelines are among the most important to follow when representing data in a visual format:

1. **Always begin axis scales at zero.** When you alter the scale by starting at a number other than zero, the results may appear distorted and "not to scale." See Example 1.

2. **Avoid pictograms and 3D graphs.** These can distort size. Choose instead a format that makes differences in the size of data objects proportional to differences in the data. See Example 2.

3. **Show your data in context.** When you show only some of the data, rather than all the data points in a series, you are misrepresenting the research. See Example 3.

4. **Provide the absolute number "n" when you graph percentages.** Showing percentages is often very effective. However, it is misleading if the sample size is too small to accurately extrapolate a true result for a larger population. See Example 4.

In the visuals provided here, the graphs on the left are potentially misleading. The versions on the right correct the errors.

For ETHICS exercises, go to Exercise 13 on pages 378–379.

1. Begin axis scales at zero.

Misleading graph: Because the y-axis (vertical) begins at $1.50, the distance between the Year 3 value and Year 4 value looks disproportionately large. At first glance, the audience may assume that earnings per share in Year 4 almost doubled compared to earnings per share in Year 3.

More accurate graph: By starting the y-axis at $0.00, the graph more accurately displays the actual difference between Year 3 and Year 4 earnings per share: 22%.

2. Avoid pictograms and 3D graphs, which distort size. Make differences in the size of data objects proportional to differences in the data.

Misleading graph: The pictogram representing 2009 is twice as tall as the one representing 1950—and is also twice as wide. That means, in square inches, it is four times larger than the 1950 woman. The size difference between the two objects is not proportional to the difference in data. At first glance, the audience may assume the women in the workforce quadrupled.

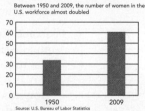

More accurate graph: The 2009 bar is almost twice the height of the 1950 bar and is the same width. It is nearly twice the size of the 1950 bar. The size difference between the two bars is proportional to the difference in the data.

3. Show your data in context.

Misleading graph: Presenting just two years of data gives the impression that increasing the price of the product was a bad business decision.

More accurate graph: When the data are placed in a larger context, you can see that the drop in revenue was temporary.

4. Provide the absolute number ("n") when you graph percentages.

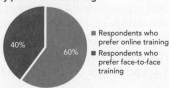

Misleading graph: The percentages give the impression that most employees prefer online training. However, the graph does not say how many employees responded to the survey, so it is unclear whether most employees prefer online or just a small subset.

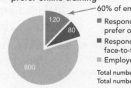

More accurate graph: This graph puts the data in a larger context and it provides absolute numbers. It tells the reader that very few employees responded to the survey, but those who did respond favoured online training.

LO 11.6 How should you document your research?

As discussed in Chapter 10, documenting or citing your sources is a key part of all writing in academia and most professional writing. Appropriate documentation serves many functions:

- **It adds credibility to your writing.** Many writers assume that they will seem smarter if they make their ideas appear original. In fact, the opposite is true. Your writing will be more impressive if it shows that you are well informed by having read relevant texts or talked to key people.

- **It strengthens your argument.** Most report writing relies on up-to-date and accurate data. By providing appropriate citations, you can give your audience confidence in the strength of your data.

- **It helps your audience locate information mentioned in your report.** Your audience may want to read more deeply in your topic. They will rely on your reference list to give them direction.

- **It helps demonstrate that you are ethical.** If you acknowledge all your sources, no one will accuse you of **plagiarism**, which is presenting others' ideas as your own.

To ensure proper documentation, use the advice that follows.

Determine what needs to be documented

You need to document (give credit for) any information or opinion that you originally found in another source. Specifically, you need to document the following:

- **Exact quotations. Quotations** are any phrases, sentences, paragraphs (even single, distinctive words) that you take from any of your sources. When you include a source's exact wording in your text, you need to enclose it in quotation marks. If it is a long quotation, indent and single space the block of text without quotation marks. With both formats, you need to document the original source. Depending on the documentation style you choose, you can use footnotes, endnotes, or parenthetical citations (inserting in parentheses the author's last name, year of publication, and page number where the quotation can be found in the original source).

  If you find that more than 10% of your content consists of quotations, then you are relying too heavily on your sources and not adding enough analysis, critique, or explanation of your own. Most business reports contain very few direct quotations. More often, writers choose to paraphrase or summarize the content. Reserve quotations for the following situations:

  - When you want to present someone else's point of view in that person's own words
  - When you are citing an authority whose exact words are well phrased and powerful
  - When you want to comment on what someone else has said
  - When you need to be very precise and the exact wording allows you to do so

- **Paraphrase. A paraphrase** is a version of someone else's original content but in your own words. The best paraphrase will have a completely different sentence structure than the original, not just a few replaced words. Cite paraphrased content with the author's name and year of publication. Including a page number is required in some documentation styles and just recommended in others.

- **Summary. A summary** is a brief version of another person's point of view. When you summarize, you still need to acknowledge the source of those ideas by using some form of citation.

- **Specific facts and data.** You also need to cite every piece of information that is not common knowledge or the result of your own primary research. This includes opinions, arguments, and speculations as well as facts, details, figures, and statistics. Writers are often confused about what is common knowledge. Simply put, common knowledge includes things that most people know. For example, most

Plagiarism Intentionally or unintentionally failing to acknowledge others' ideas in your work by presenting other people's work as your own.

Quotations Any phrases, sentences, paragraphs (even single, distinctive words) that you take from any of your sources.

Paraphrase A version of what someone else says, but in your own words and with your own emphasis.

Summary A brief version of someone else's text using your own words.

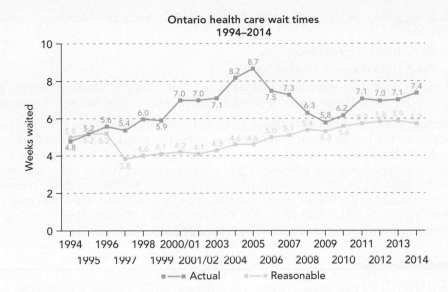

FIGURE 11.15 Adding an APA Source Citation to Graphics

Source: "Waiting your turn: Wait times for health care in Canada, 2014 Report." Reprinted with permission.

people know that Paris is the capital of France. You would not need to cite a source for that. By contrast, most people do not know that the population of Paris is approximately 2.2 million people. For that data, you would need to cite the French National Institute of Statistics and Economic Studies (INSEE, 2015). This citation adds credibility to your statement and helps readers identify where to look for more information.

- **Tables, graphs, photographs, and other graphics.** If you copy a visual from another source and place it in your document, you need to cite the source for that visual. You do this by including the citation in your caption or directly under the visual, as illustrated in **FIGURE 11.15**, which uses the APA format for citing graphics.

Prepare the documentation

In a formal report, you must acknowledge sources in three ways: in-text citations, textual references, and entries in a reference list or bibliography.

- **Citations.** Every time you use material from another source in your text, add a citation. Your citation may be in the form of a footnote, endnote, or parenthetical citation inserted directly after your reference. The form you use will depend on the requirements of your organization or school. The three most common formats or styles of documentation are as follows:
  - APA (American Psychological Association), frequently used in social sciences and business
  - MLA (Modern Language Association), commonly used in the humanities
  - CMS (Chicago Manual of Style), frequently used in business, history, and some social sciences.

  For details about these styles, see Appendix D: Documentation and Reference Styles at the back of this book.

- **Text references.** Do not rely exclusively on citations to orient readers to your sources. Instead, introduce cited material by explicitly referring to the source within your text:

  According to the INSEE (2015), the population of Paris is 2.2 million.

  or

  The French National Institute of Statistics and Economic Studies reports that the population of Paris is 2.2 million (INSEE, 2015).

- **Reference list or bibliography.** Provide a list of sources at the end of every research report. Each item in the list must include enough information for readers to find that document on their own. APA, MLA, and CMS each have different names for this list:

- APA titles the page *References*.
- MLA titles the page *Works Cited*.
- CMS offers two options. If you are using footnotes or endnotes, title the page *Bibliography*. If you are using parenthetical citations, title the page *References*.

In addition, each documentation style follows different rules about the kind of material to include in the list and how to format that material. For details and examples, see Appendix D: Documentation and Reference Styles, at the back of this book.

Write the citations, text references, and reference list entries as you work on your report. Do not wait to add them until after you've written your entire draft. Waiting to add citations and to document information leads to two problems. First, you may omit required information that will be hard to find later (and will waste time). Second, you may forget what you've quoted and unintentionally plagiarize material.

In summary,
no matter what company you work for you are likely to write reports. The term "report" refers to a wide range of documents that provide information or analysis to answer business questions. Reports may be written in many forms: as emails, memos, letters, formal report format, or webpages. Regardless of the medium, all reports use an objective style and a format that makes information easy to find. Many reports also include tables, graphs, diagrams, and documentation of research. The guidelines in this chapter help you manage all this material and present it in ways that will be clear to your audience, whether they read the report now or in the future. **FIGURE 11.16** offers a summary of how ACE is used when preparing business reports and proposals.

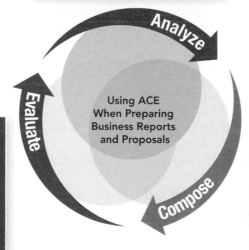

Understand the purpose and type of report.

Understand your audience's needs and expectations.

Decide on the best medium for delivery of the report. Design your information to fit that medium.

Analyze

Using ACE When Preparing Business Reports and Proposals

Evaluate

Review for accuracy, relevance, and length.

Get feedback from others.

Ensure you have met your audience's needs and expectations.

Double check all numeric data and graphic data for accuracy.

Compose

Prioritize your audience's needs and expectations when composing. Make choices that fit those needs and expectations.

Use an objective and easy-to-read, factual style.

Provide information that is relevant to the type of report (i.e., progress, travel, formal, other?).

Exclude information that is NOT relevant.

FIGURE 11.16 Using ACE When Preparing Business Reports and Proposals

@ **WORK**

Courtney Rivington
Senior Manager, Finance
Nymi Inc.

Photo courtesy of Courtney Rivington and Dan Hemsworth.

At the opening of this chapter, Courtney Rivington was discussing the need to make a business report about an important accounting change interesting and readable for her company's executives. Let's see how she uses ACE to help her.

The ultimate goal in writing a successful business report is giving the reader everything he or she needs, and *only* what he or she needs, in the most clear and concise manner possible. A logical flow of information allows readers to follow your train of thought through the options to land on the best possible solution. The ACE framework helps to specifically identify critical pieces of information and to present them in a way that leaves no questions in the mind of the reader.

- **Analyze: Put yourself in your readers' shoes.** I have to think carefully about the knowledge and experience the primary audience for this report already has. How much does each reader need to know to make an informed decision? In writing my report to the CFO, I might include specific accounting or tax guidance supporting each alternative accounting policy. I would detail the impacts the change might have on our annual financial statement audit and tax filings. In writing a report to the CEO, I might focus more on the impact a change in functional currency might have on the company's foreign exchange transactions and, ultimately, on the company's earnings.
- **Compose: Use a consistent, familiar structure.** I always structure my business reports in the same logical way:
  - **Purpose.** Tell them in one or two sentences why you are writing the report: "The purpose of this report is to document the decision-making process in determining Nymi Inc.'s functional currency. This section outlines all

key considerations, evaluates alternatives, and recommends a course of action based on Nymi Inc.'s current circumstances."
  - **Background.** What context must you provide to get all readers up to speed on the issue?
  - **Supporting materials.** Cite any resources you used to support your conclusions. For me, this usually means citing relevant international financial reporting standards, sections of the relevant tax legislation, or research from relevant industry or academic experts. This tells the reader that I have done the research and also lets them know where to look for more details.
  - **Analysis.** Describe alternatives and detail the advantages and disadvantages of each. This section should clearly state the impact on the business that can be expected for each alternative. In other words, I am answering questions like "so what?", "who cares?", and "why?"
  - **Conclusion.** Your recommendation should be evident at this point. The conclusion summarizes the solution and provides any additional information the reader might find useful, such as an implementation plan or next steps.
- **Evaluate: Take a break and then review.** I always set my reports aside for a few hours. Then I review the work with a fresh eye.
  - Have I tailored the report to the needs of my readers?
  - Have I provided all the information, and *only* the relevant information, that my reader needs to make an informed decision?
  - Is the report as concisely written as possible?
  - Is the report written in a tone that will be well received by the reader?

The report was a hit! Not only did the executive team agree with our recommendation, the draft was approved in hours and they were back out perfecting the Nymi Band to best meet our prospective clients' needs.

The ACE framework helps me think through what should be included in my reports, write them in a clear and concise manner, and review what I have written with a critical eye. By following these three steps when writing your reports, you have given yourself the best possible chance that you will successfully gain the reader's full attention as well as his or her confidence in your recommendations.

End of Chapter

Learning Objectives in Review

LO 11.1 **How can ACE help you write a business report?** *(pages 328–331)*

- **Analyze to understand the purpose and report type.** Some reports are informational, while others are analytic.
- **Analyze to understand the audience's needs** and determine what content to include.
- **Analyze to choose the best medium.** Email, memo, and letter reports are usually short. Formal reports are often longer.
- **Compose your report to meet audience expectations.** Include identifying information, a preview, detailed discussion, and supporting information. Most reports are organized directly.
- **Compose using an objective and easy-to-read style** by focusing on facts, analysis, and well-supported recommendations.
- **Evaluate by reviewing on your own and getting feedback from others** to ensure you are meeting audience and stakeholder needs. Use an evaluation checklist to review your report (see page 331).

LO 11.2 **How should you structure typical business reports?** *(pages 332–350)*

- **Progress reports** provide information about the status of a long-term project.
- **Travel reports** document activities during business trips and outline accomplishments and benefits.
- **Formal reports** are often analytical and may be as short as 8 to 10 pages or as long as several hundred pages.

LO 11.3 **How do you prepare an effective proposal?** *(pages 350–354)*

- **Understand the problem and propose a well-balanced solution:**
  - Develop a clear idea of your purpose
  - Articulate the problem, need, or opportunity
  - Identify the outcomes, benefits, and potential objections
  - Present a compelling recommendation
  - Provide persuasive supporting details that emphasize feasibility and credibility
  - Request action.

- **Identify the appropriate type of proposal.** Internal or external? Competitive or noncompetitive? Solicited or unsolicited?

LO 11.4 **How do you properly respond to a request for proposal?** *(pages 354–359)*

- **Structure an RFP proposal like a formal report.** Provide a quick overview at the beginning (either in an executive summary or an introduction), make the information easy to find using a table of contents or other contents list, show an understanding of the client's needs, propose a solution that meets the needs listed in the RFP, and provide evidence that the team you are proposing do the work is qualified.
- **Follow specified guidelines when responding to RFPs.** Write a checklist of requirements, propose a competitive fee, and provide the required documentation.
- **Use proposal-writing software to increase efficiency.**

LO 11.5 **How do you integrate visuals into reports?** *(pages 360–367)*

- **Choose the best form of display: table or graph.** Tables arrange data in columns and rows to demonstrate relationships. Graphs use images or shapes to illustrate relationships among variables or data.
- **Choose the best type of graph** by considering the purpose and relationship of the data.
- **Design graphs and tables to communicate.** Use titles, axis labels, thin lines, visible data markers, and annotations. Avoid 3D effects, contrasting borders, gridlines, tick marks, and legends.
- **Integrate data displays within the text.** Help readers focus on the display and understanding its information.

LO 11.6 **How should you document your research?** *(pages 368–371)*

- **Determine what needs to be documented.** Document all content taken from other sources.
- **Prepare the documentation** by introducing sources in the narrative, providing citations in the text, and preparing a reference list as you compose.

KEY TERMS

abstract p. 330
analytical report p. 328
appendix p. 330
attachment p. 330
business case p. 354
competitive proposal p. 351
cover message p. 355

data graphics p. 360
deliverables p. 351
executive summary p. 330
graph p. 360
informational report p. 328
noncompetitive proposal p. 351
paraphrase p. 368

plagiarism p. 368
progress report p. 332
proposal p. 350
quotations p. 368
recommendation report p. 332
reference list p. 330
request for proposal (RFP) p. 354

solicited proposal p. 351
summary p. 368
table p. 360
title page p. 334
travel report p. 332
unsolicited proposal p. 354
white paper p. 349

CASE STUDY

Reporting Results to a Client

This case study will help you review the chapter material by applying it to a specific scenario.

When Jeff Ellis graduated with a degree in civil engineering, he pictured himself designing buildings and bridges and managing construction teams. He never imagined himself behind a computer writing reports.

However, that is exactly where Jeff finds himself today. He has just finished his first major project at Schuyler Engineering: an environmental assessment of a plot of land on which a client wants to build an office park. Emily, the senior engineer on the project, has asked Jeff to write the client report. When Jeff asked Emily if she could give him a model to follow, Emily pointed to the file cabinet and said, "Sure, you'll find lots of reports in there."

Jeff did find a lot of reports: long ones, short ones, letter reports, and very formal reports. The diversity confused him and left him asking "What is the best approach to take?" Jeff is glad he saved his business communications text from university. That may give him some better ideas on how to structure a professional report.

Writing a Report Introduction

Jeff begins writing his report with the first step of the ACE process: analyzing to determine the purpose, audience, and medium. His audience, the CEO of Halvorson Properties, wants to know whether it is safe to build an office park on the property he owns. Because this decision has significant financial and environmental effects, Jeff decides to write a formal letter report that clearly communicates the message that the property is safe. His research indicated that it has not been affected by hazardous waste or contaminated groundwater. He will provide enough details about his methodology and findings to give Mr. Halvorson confidence in this assessment.

With those decisions in mind, Jeff sits down to write the report's introduction. After writing his first paragraph he emails it to Emily, who revises it.

Question 1: *Compare Jeff's draft of the introduction below with Emily's revision on the upper right. What key differences do you notice between the two openings? Which opening would you choose?*

JEFF'S FIRST DRAFT

Dear Mr. Halvorson:

At your request, we have conducted an investigation of the site defined by the attached survey map for the purposes of rendering an opinion as to whether the site contains hazardous waste or is being impacted by contaminated groundwater. Our investigations consisted of making soil borings and visual observations of the ground surface, vegetation, and drainage patterns and laboratory testing of soil samples. The testing included physical properties testing and chemical testing of the water extracted from the soil. In addition, we have examined various maps and aerial photos, contacted various government agencies, and contacted the power company in our efforts to determine whether hazardous waste is known to have impacted the site. Our findings are as follows.

EMILY'S REVISION

Dear Mr. Halvorson:

At your request, we have investigated the site defined by the attached survey map to determine (1) how the site was used, (2) whether the site contains hazardous waste, and (3) whether it is affected by contaminated groundwater. Our investigation is complete except for the results of governmental and power company records searches.

Assuming that these searches support our findings, it is our professional assessment that the site has not been impacted by hazardous waste or groundwater contamination that would render it unsuitable for development as an office park.

This letter describes our methodology and reports our findings.

Structuring the Report's Findings

As Jeff develops his investigation report, he decides that the detailed discussion of the report will include the specific findings of his investigation. Here is the first draft he produced.

JEFF'S FIRST DRAFT

Our investigations indicate that nearly all of Parcel 1 has been idle for at least 10 to 15 years. An old house foundation exists near the south central portion of Parcel 1. Parcel 2 appears to have been idle for many years. However, recent dumping of construction debris and fill is apparent, primarily along the eastern property line. Parcel 3 is vegetated with an old orchard near the centre of the property, and remnants of abandoned residences are apparent. Parcel 3 also has been impacted with piles of construction debris dumped along its easternmost side. Parcel 4 is primarily a protected wetlands area identified by Environment Canada. Some filling has occurred along the eastern and southern border of Parcel 4.

On the basis of soil borings, laboratory test results, and our observations of the previously referenced site, in our opinion it is unlikely that any storage, disposal, or release of oil, fuels, gases, chemicals, trash, garbage, or other solid or hazardous materials has taken place on this property. Only trace amounts of these materials are present, as associated with the residential occupancy and the relatively recent illegal dumping of debris. We have requested a letter from People's Electric certifying that the site is not presently served by transformers containing PCBs nor is the site known to have been impacted by spills of PCBs. Except for the possibility of old heating oil tanks or septic tanks associated with the previous homes, there are no buried tanks on the site. Considering the soil types encountered in the borings, it is extremely unlikely that fuel oils, even if they were present, could migrate more than a few inches. Therefore, we do not consider this site to have been affected by an oil spill or buried tanks or pesticides other than those associated with residential occupation and farming operations.

As Jeff reviews his draft, he realizes that the main ideas are not easy to find. This time, instead of giving his draft to Emily to review, he writes a new outline of the findings section on his own. His goal is to design the page so that the main ideas stand out, using both headings and strong topic sentences for the paragraphs.

Here is his outline:

Findings about land use

1. Parcel 1:
2. Parcel 2:
3. Parcel 3:
4. Parcel 4:

Findings about contamination

1. Our investigations indicate it is unlikely that this property has been contaminated by any storage, disposal, or release of oil, fuels, gases, chemicals, trash, garbage, or other solid or hazardous materials.

2. It is also unlikely that the groundwater or soil on the site has been contaminated by activities on the adjacent sites.

Question 2: *Using these headings, subheadings, and topic sentences, how would you complete the findings section of the report? Where would you place the supporting details from his draft?*

Phrasing a Conclusion Accurately

As Jeff completes his report, he wonders how he should phrase the conclusions he reaches. Here are two statements he is considering:

Option 1: It is our professional opinion that the site has not been impacted by hazardous waste or groundwater contamination that would render it unsuitable for development as an office park.

Option 2: It is our professional opinion that the site has not been impacted by hazardous waste or groundwater contamination and thus the site is safe for an office park.

Question 3: *Which statement do you think is better? Why?*

REVIEW QUESTIONS

1. What is the difference between an informational and an analytical report? Give an example of each kind.

2. What is the purpose of a report abstract? What kind of information does it include?

3. What is the purpose of an executive summary? What kind of information does it include?

4. What is the difference between an attachment and an appendix?

5. Why is it important to use an objective, easy-to-read style in a report?

6. What design features can you use in a report to enhance its visual appeal?

7. Name three reasons why businesses distribute electronic reports as PDFs.

8. Where should you place figures and tables within a report?

9. What is the difference between a paraphrase and a summary?

CRITICAL THINKING

1. The Culture feature on page 359 earlier in this chapter offers three suggestions for writing reports for international audiences who will read the report in English. Imagine that your report will be translated into another language, for example Spanish or Japanese. Would this same advice make the document easier to translate? In what ways? Based on your knowledge of other languages, what other advice would you give writers who are preparing reports that will be translated? **[Related to the Culture feature on page 359]**

2. Imagine that a classmate or co-worker argues that it is redundant to include both an executive summary and an introduction in a report. How would you explain the different functions of an executive summary and introduction, and the reason for including both?

3. According to the old saying, "A picture is worth 1,000 words." If that is the case, then why is it important to explain all graphics within the text of your report, rather than assuming the graphics will speak for themselves?

4. Imagine that your manager asks you to write a type of report not illustrated in this chapter, for example, a compliance report. How would you go about learning the key features of a compliance report and the type of content that is required?

5. Some organizations ask employees to post information in wikis rather than write traditional reports. What would be the advantages and disadvantages of reporting information on an internal corporate wiki?

DEVELOPING YOUR COMMUNICATION SKILLS

 LO 11.1 **How can ACE help you write a business report?**
(pages 328–331)

EXERCISE 1 Analyze to understand the audience's needs

For each of the following questions, consider the report that would provide the answer. Assume that your audience is a high-level manager or executive who has not been involved with your project.

a. Has our new marketing plan met our sales objectives?

b. Why are so many of our widgets being returned as defective?

c. Are we on track with our project?

d. Can our client, Rose's Bakery, afford to open a new store next year?

e. Who is responsible for the property damage in our client's building? The construction crew? The painters? The tenants? The maintenance staff?

f. What new sales leads did you develop at the trade show?

For each of these questions, determine what information the audience would need.

EXERCISE 2 Analyze to choose the best medium

For each of the questions listed in Exercise 1, decide what medium you would use to write the report. Pick a medium and explain why it is an appropriate choice.

- Memo report
- Letter report
- Email report
- Formal report

EXERCISE 3 Compose using an objective and easy-to-read style

Anya James works for AquaSafe Product Design, a company that designs and installs aquariums in homes and offices. Anya has been assigned to the new product development team. The team's job is to research and develop new product ideas. Currently the team is exploring the idea of an interactive aquarium that allows users to engage more with the fish. At the end of the first three weeks on the project, Anya's manager asks for a progress report.

Review Anya's first draft and evaluate this progress report:

a. Is the style objective, focusing on the project? Or does it focus on the team's activities?

b. Is the report sufficiently factual and detailed?

c. Should the report contain any additional information?

d. Based on your analysis, recommend at least two changes to the report.

REPORT

TO: Ryan Leffler, Project Manager

FROM: Anya James, New Product Development Team

DATE: March 16, 20XX

SUBJECT: Progress Report

For the past three weeks, we have been researching the interactive aquarium concept and have developed five concepts we plan to test. The interactive aquarium presents a unique problem to the design team. We began with a completely blank slate, since this project is based on an innovative idea and has very few comparable existing products. We had to consider a delicate group of users (fish) when making decisions about the requirements of our design concepts. It was important for us to balance the goals of our company with the needs of the animals and the desires of the users.

Research

We began by researching fish behaviour and learned interesting facts that will influence our design. We then had a productive brainstorming session in which we were able to generate design ideas. From there, we have identified five major design areas we would like to test.

Design Requirements

Based on our research and discussions with users, we developed a set of design requirements numbered and listed in Table 1. We rated these requirements by importance (5 is most important and 1 is least important).

Table 1: Design Requirements

REQUIREMENT #	REQUIREMENT	IMPORTANCE RATING
1	Child safe	5
2	Child friendly	3
3	Interesting	3
4	Animal safe	5
5	Animal friendly	5
6	Can be used in/around water	5
7	Environmentally sound	4
8	Durable	4
9	Easily cleaned	2
10	Easily accessible	3
11	Not too complicated to operate	1
12	Not too heavy	1
13	No complicated assembly	1

Plan

In the next two weeks, we plan to evaluate our five ideas according to these requirements.

EXERCISE 4 Evaluate by reviewing on your own and getting feedback from others

Using the questions on page 331 presented earlier in the chapter, evaluate the formal report in Figure 11.5 A, B, C, and D. Write an email to your instructor identifying what you believe is valuable about the report and what improvements, if any, you would recommend.

EXERCISE 5 Making reports reader friendly for international audiences [Related to the Culture feature on page 359]

The following well-written paragraphs come from the executive summary of a report titled "The State of the Paper Industry: Monitoring the Indicators of Environmental Performance." Imagine that this report was being read by someone from another country who speaks English as a second or third language. What words, phrases, or sentences do you think would be challenging for that reader to understand? What revisions would you suggest?

> Despite predictions that the digital revolution would make paper as obsolete as the typewriter, paper remains central to our lives. Yet most of us, most of the time, give little thought to how much we depend on paper products. Think of the hundreds of times a day we touch paper—newspapers, cereal boxes, toilet paper, water bottle labels, parking tickets, streams of catalogs and junk mail, money, tissues, books, shopping bags, receipts, napkins, printer and copier paper at home and work, magazines, to-go food packaging. The list could fill a paperback.
>
> What's more, few people pay much heed to the ways in which our use of paper affects the environment. Yet the paper industry's activities—and our individual use and disposal of paper in our daily lives—have enormous impacts. These include loss and degradation of forests that moderate climate change, destruction of habitat for countless plant and animal species, pollution of air and water with toxic chemicals such as mercury and dioxin, and production of methane, a potent greenhouse gas, as paper decomposes in landfills, to name just a few (Environmental Paper Network, 2007).

 How should you structure typical business reports?
(pages 332–350)

EXERCISE 6 Progress reports, meeting minutes, and trip reports

Use a web search engine or business portal like Biznar to find an example of one of the following types of reports:

- Progress report
- Meeting minutes
- Trip report

Evaluate the report in relation to the guidelines presented in this chapter. Write an email to your instructor identifying what you believe is useful about the report you found and what improvements you recommend.

EXERCISE 7 Choose the best electronic format for online distribution

The Pew Research Center distributes its reports in three electronic formats: standard web, mobile app, and PDF. Go to the Pew Research Center website, select a report to review, and compare the three versions of the report.

a. Which do you find easiest to read?

b. Which do you find easiest to navigate (i.e., go to a specific section)?

c. Which do you think will provide the easiest-to-read printout?

Based on your analysis, if you were to come back to the Pew website to read a different report, which format would you choose?

EXERCISE 8 Using software features to help format formal reports [Related to the Technology feature on page 335]

Your instructor will provide you with a "sample report" file for this exercise. This file includes unformatted text for a formal report. The following elements are obvious based on their content: title page, location for the table of contents, executive summary, introduction, body of the report (including headings), conclusions, recommendations, references, and appendices. Use your word processor's features to make the following formatting changes:

- Apply appropriate heading styles to section titles and headings.
- Create section breaks so the title page is not numbered and the table of contents and executive summary are numbered with small Roman numerals (ii and iii). Starting with the introduction, number the pages using Arabic numerals (1).
- Create a footer to add page numbers to the entire document, except the title page as noted above.
- Generate an automated table of contents to appear after the title page.
- Add automated captions for figures and tables throughout the report.

Save the file, adding your name to the end of the file name. Submit the file electronically to your instructor.

 How do you integrate visuals into reports?
(pages 360–367)

EXERCISE 9 Choose the best form of display: table or graph

Create a table based on the following paragraph. Then create a graph. Explain the differences and justify which would better represent the data. Submit both visuals and your justification in a one-page memo report to your instructor.

> Jamison Lumber Company has four regional branches: North, South, East, and West. Last year the branch sales were as follows: North = $1.23 million, South = $1.57 million, East = $2.26 million, and West = $2.10 million. This year, the North and South branches recorded a 2.5% and 3.4% increase, respectively. However, the East and West branches experienced decreases of 1.3% and 0.7%, respectively.

EXERCISE 10 Choose the best type of graph

For each of the following business messages, what type of graph will be most effective? Sketch a version of that graph and explain why your choice is the best option.

a. Gadget sales have tripled since 1995.

b. Of the four companies in the industry (Acme, Apex, Giant, and Excel), Acme has the smallest share of industry sales.

c. Sales of Product A exceed sales of Product B and Product C.

d. Earnings per share have decreased every year since 2003.

e. There is a strong relationship between the number of training courses a salesperson has completed and the amount of that person's annual sales.

EXERCISE 11 Design graphs and tables to communicate

What changes would you make to the table below to follow the table design guidelines presented in this chapter?

YTD International Revenue							
Product	Jan	Feb	Mar	Apr	May	Jun	Total
Disk Drives	$93,993.00	$84,773.00	$88,833.00	$95,838.00	$93,874.00	$83,994.00	$541,305.00
Monitors	$87,413.00	$78,838.00	$82,614.00	$89,129.00	$873,020.00	$78,114.00	$1,289,128.00
Printers	$90,035.00	$2,120,400.00	$85,093.00	$91,803.00	$899,210.00	$80,457.00	$3,366,998.00
Computers	$92,736.00	$83,640.00	$87,645.00	$94,557.00	$92,619.00	$82,871.00	$534,068.00
Memory Sticks	$3,624,500.00	$77,785.00	$81,510.00	$87,938.00	$86,136.00	$77,070.00	$4,034,939.00
Sound Cards	$88,832.00	$80,118.00	$83,956.00	$90,576.00	$88,720.00	$79,382.00	$511,584.00
Video Cards	$82,614.00	$74,510.00	$78,079.00	$84,236.00	$82,509.00	$73,825.00	$475,773.00
RAM	$85,092.00	$76,745.00	$80,421.00	$86,763.00	$84,985.00	$76,040.00	$490,046.00
Scanners	$87,645.00	$79,048.00	$82,834.00	$89,366.00	$87,534.00	$78,321.00	$504,748.00
Input Devices	$90,275.00	$81,419.00	$85,319.00	$920,470.00	$90,160.00	$80,671.00	$1,348,314.00
Total	$4,423,135.00	$2,837,276.00	$836,304.00	$1,730,676.00	$2,478,767.00	$790,745.00	$13,096,903.00

Accompanies Exercise 11

EXERCISE 12 Integrate data displays with the text

As a member of the Acme Electric Safety Committee, you have been asked to write a committee report to the CEO answering the question "Does our electrical equipment comply with safety standards?" You write the introduction to the report and decide to summarize the detailed findings in a table. However, you are unsure how to structure that table. Analyze the following introduction and three options for structuring the table on page 379. What are the advantages and disadvantages of each option? Which table design would you choose?

TO: George DiLeonardo, CEO
FROM: Acme Safety Review Committee
          (Devon Rasheed, Kevin Carroll, Risa Policaro,
          and Eric West)
DATE: February 12, 20XX
SUBJECT: Acme's Compliance with Safety Standards

Purpose of the Study
Over the past month, the Acme Safety Committee has conducted a thorough review of all the safety codes and standards that apply to Acme Electric's Moosejaw facility. These include two sets of mandatory standards that Acme must comply with and one set of voluntary standards.

Mandatory
- WorkSafe Saskatchewan standards
- CEC (Canadian Electrical Code) standards

Voluntary
- UL-1950 standards for information technology equipment, including electrical business equipment.

We have also reviewed all the wiring schematics and the equipment in the facility to identify all gaps in compliance.

Results of the Study
Although Acme's equipment is properly designed for electrical load/capacity, several design details do not comply with the codes and widely used standards. Some standards apply only to building wiring and other parts include equipment. These gaps compromise the safety of our employees and will put us at risk during regulatory inspections.

Table 1 summarizes the places where our equipment and wiring do not comply with applicable standards and offers recommendations for addressing the problems.

Accompanies Exercise 12

Option 1

Regulator	Rule	Affected Area	Violation	Recommendation
WorkSafe	Rule A Rule B Rule C			
CEC	Rule 1 Rule 2 Rule 3			

Option 2

Equipment	Rule	Violation	Recommendation
Generator 1	WorkSafe Rule A CEC Rule 1 Local Rule A		
Junction Box 65	WorkSafe Rule B CEC Rule 2 Local Rule B		

Option 3

Priority	Affected Area	Violation	Rule	Recommendation
High	Generator 1 Junction Box 65 Conduit 64-65			
Medium	Main Bus B Riser Pipe 37 Conduit 33-34			

Accompanies Exercise 12

EXERCISE 13 Represent data ethically [Related to the Ethics feature on pages 366–367]

On April 20, 2010, a BP oil drilling platform in the Gulf of Mexico exploded, resulting in the world's largest accidental oil spill (Robertson & Krauss, 2010). Nearly 5 million barrels of oil gushed from the wellhead into the Gulf before BP capped the well in July. During that time, BP worked diligently to contain the spill, capture oil, and develop a strategy to cap the wellhead. Approximately a month after the explosion, BP Senior Vice-President Karl Wells gave a technical presentation to update the public on BP's containment efforts (Wells, 2010). During this briefing, he presented a graph similar to Graph A below and discussed the amount of oil collected from the wellhead in the seven days between May 16 and May 23.

Here is what he said:

> There's been a lot of questions around how much oil is being collected. What I am showing you here is a graph. We originally inserted the riser insertion tool into the riser on May 16. Since that period our operations and engineer-

ing group have been focused on how do we maximize the amount of oil we collect from the end of the riser. . . . Here you can see how we've continued to ramp up. [He points at increasingly long bars.] Today, we've collected a total of 13,500 barrels, which is averaging a little less than 2,000 barrels a day. The team is continuing to focus on what we can do to capture more of that oil.

At first glance, this graph certainly looks as if BP is ramping up its oil collection and is in fact collecting an increasing amount each day. However, this graph shows the cumulative amount of oil collected, with each day's oil collection added to the previous days'.

Graph B is a different, alternative graph, produced by data analyst Stephen Few, which graphs the oil collected each day (Few, 2010).

a. Compare the two graphs and the two different representations of the data. Does the second graph support Wells' claim that oil collection has "continued to ramp up"?

b. Which graph represents the data more ethically?

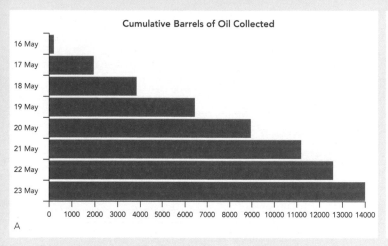

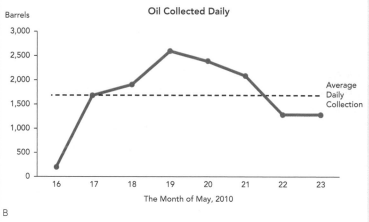

Accompanies Exercise 13

(LO 11.6) How should you document your research?
(pages 368–371)

EXERCISE 14 Determine what needs to be documented

For each of the following situations, imagine that you are writing a report and need to decide whether you must provide documentation to give credit to a source. If you decide to document the source, how would you document it? Would you refer to the source in the text itself, use a parenthetical citation (or footnotes), use quotation marks, or include an entry in a reference list? Indicate as many options as apply. If you decide not to document the source, explain why not.

a. In your report, you are arguing against an opinion column in the local newspaper.

b. You are providing evidence from your own experience.

c. You are including a story that one of your co-workers told you.

d. In your research, you find a phrase that you really like and decide to use it.

e. You want to quote something from a source but the quotation is too long so you change it a bit and leave out a few words.

f. You are writing a report analyzing the environmental issues relating to the newspaper industry, and in your research you come across some facts about how many trees are cut down each year for paper manufacture. You want to use these facts.

g. You mention that the majority of students on your campus did not vote in the last federal election.

h. You want to prove that your company has been complying with a certain regulation, so your reader will need to know what the regulation says.

i. You are presenting the results of a survey you conducted.

j. You are summarizing information that you learned from an interview with an expert.

EXERCISE 15 Prepare the documentation

For each of the following questions, find an appropriate source that you could use in a research report and prepare a reference list entry for that source. Use APA style, unless your instructor asks you to use a different style. (For a review of how to find reliable, credible sources, see Chapter 10.)

a. What is the current unemployment rate in Canada? How has the unemployment rate changed over the past 10 years?

b. What is the employment outlook for the career or profession you plan to enter?

c. What are some interesting facts about the history of your college or university?

d. What are some key facts about second-generation immigrants in Canada?

EXERCISE 16 Developing a mobile phone app

On-the-Go Software, a startup company in your community, would like to develop a new mobile phone app that will be profitable. As part of the company's preliminary planning, the CEO, Etta Hawkins, has hired you to research the most popular apps for iPhones and other mobile devices and to analyze why you believe these apps are successful. As you research, identify who is buying these apps and hypothesize why. Also identify features that have received positive comments and hypothesize why these features are important.

Write a three- to five-page letter report to present the results of your research. In addition, include a list of references as an attachment. You may include other attachments if you believe they will be helpful.

Address your report to Etta Hawkins, On-the-Go Software, 111 Main Street, Mytown, MyProvince, MyPostalCode.

EXERCISE 17 Reporting on consumer attitudes

Consumer Research, Inc. has hired your team to conduct a survey to learn how young adults respond to direct mail advertising sent by email. Research by the Direct Marketing Association indicates that, overall, advertising through postal mail results in more sales than advertising through email (Direct Marketing Association, 2012). However, the research did not focus on specific age groups. Consumer Research, Inc. wants to know whether young adults (ages 18–25) purchase more as a result of email or postal mail advertising. Identify a group of people your team can survey and develop a set of questions to ask. For example, you could ask

- How often do they open advertising they receive through email?
- What influences their decision to open the email? Is it the subject line, the sender, or something else?
- How often do they click through to a website?
- How often do they purchase something as a result of the email advertising?

Conduct your survey and then write a short report to Consumer Research presenting your results. If possible, draw conclusions about the effectiveness of email marketing to young adults.

EXERCISE 18 Evaluating fast-food restaurants

Your team works for a fast-food restaurant company that is planning to open a restaurant in your area. The district regional manager wants to know more about the competition. What are the strengths and weaknesses of the competitive restaurants? Is there opportunity for a new restaurant in the neighbourhood?

As a team, choose three fast-food restaurants in the area and observe each restaurant for an hour at least three times within the next two weeks. Vary the day of the week and the time of day for each visit. During each visit, observe and collect data on the appearance of the restaurant, how many customers entered during that time period, the length of wait to place an order, the length of wait to receive an order, the quality of service, and the quality of food. During each visit, make a qualitative judgment about how happy the customers seem to be, and support your judgment with specific observations.

At the end of the two-week observation period, write a report to your district manager evaluating the competition and making recommendations about how your new restaurant can provide better service than the competitive restaurants you have studied.

EXERCISE 19 Evaluating infographics on the web

Infographics are single-page reports that rely primarily on graphics to enhance the understanding and interpretation of data. Social media has fuelled the growth of infographics on the web. Search the social media site Pinterest or another source of your choice to find an infographic that interests you. Evaluate that infographic as a brief report. Is it informative? Is it clear and easy to follow? Do you know the source of the data? In your opinion, does the graphical representation of the data provide advantages over a written report? Be prepared to present your analysis in class or write a one-page evaluation report to your instructor.

EXERCISE 20 Evaluating social media reports

With the growth of social media, the number of reports *about* social media has also grown. Using the search engine of your choice, conduct a search using the terms "report" and either "social media" or "LinkedIn," "Facebook," or "Twitter." Select one report to evaluate. (Be sure to select an actual report, not a news story or article about a report.) Read the document and write a one-page evaluation report to your instructor answering these questions:

- Who is the author and publisher of the report?
- What is the purpose of the report, and who is its intended audience?
- How was the information in the report researched or gathered?
- What are the report's key findings and recommendations, if any?
- What is your assessment of the report? Is it credible? Do you believe it offers valuable information or not? Would you recommend it?

Pick an appropriate format for your report: email, memo, letter, or formal report. Do not construct the report as a series of bullet points answering the listed questions. Instead, follow the advice in this chapter: Write an effective introduction that previews your main ideas, develop headings that help organize your material, document your sources, and include a copy of the report you are evaluating as an attachment or appendix.

12 Preparing and Delivering Business Presentations

Monkey Business Images/Shutterstock.

LEARNING OBJECTIVES

(LO12.1) **What do you analyze when planning a business presentation?** *pages 384–387*

Analyze your purpose and outcome: Why?
Analyze your audience: Who?
Analyze your message: What?
Analyze your setting: Where?
Analyze your medium options: How?

(LO12.2) **How do you compose the presentation?** *pages 388–407*

Identify the type of presentation
Organize the content
Create a storyboard
Develop a template
Design individual slides
Evaluate your slides in a practice session
Create effective handouts

(LO12.3) **How do you deliver and evaluate the presentation?** *pages 407–413*

Set the stage
Control your body
Use your voice effectively
Present your visuals effectively
Coordinate with your team
Evaluate the audience's response

(LO12.4) **How do you handle questions and answers?** *pages 413–415*

Plan for a question-and-answer (Q&A) session
Answer questions skillfully

(LO12.5) **How do you adapt your approach for online presentations?** *pages 416–420*

In a live online presentation, manage the audience experience
In a podcast, provide content that offers lasting value

Jeff Plotnikoff
Corporate Training & Development

@ WORK

What could possibly go wrong?

Because I am a corporate trainer, both the subject matter I deal with and the audience can change constantly. Our company's clients expect that by the end of each session all of their employees will walk away from the training with stronger skills than they had when they arrived. Our mandate is to ensure that training sessions are right on target, well understood, and well received by each member of the group.

Our sessions are usually two-day experiences where we walk our clients through the materials and subject matter in depth. These sessions often take place at the client's chosen location. In most cases, we have not seen the room in advance and have not met our audience.

Lots of things can go wrong when you are working face to face with an unfamiliar audience in an unfamiliar room. Some members of the session may be exhausted, or bored, or unmotivated. Some could be hostile to the idea of a new way of thinking. There may be a supervisor in the same room as a mail clerk. There may be distractions: the physical space itself, social media and mobile devices, unanticipated questions or concerns from the audience, and so on. So many variables!

Everyone needs to leave each session feeling that they have had a positive and valuable experience. How can we possibly be confident that all the stakeholders, including the client, the audience, our company, and we, the trainers, will *all* reach our objectives?

Check out the end of this chapter to find out how Jeff uses ACE to prepare for and manage complex presentation situations!

Introduction

Employers consider oral communication to be a critical skill. Yet, according to human resource directors, only a small percentage (24%) of the graduates entering the workforce actually excel in oral communication (The Conference Board, 2008). Employers continue to express concern that new workers need additional on-the-job oral communication training (Brock, 2012). This chapter will help you develop skills so that you exceed employers' expectations in one of the most important and challenging forms of oral communication in the workplace: business presentations.

The ability to present information effectively is so critical that some companies assess applicants' presentation skills as part of the hiring process. Chris Cunningham, CEO of Appsavvy, explains that in his company all job candidates "must present to five to seven people as the final step before we hire them. We will give them a real-life example from our company and ask them to make a presentation. That is [how we] find out if they're an all-star or [if we have] just avoided making a bad hire. If some-one can come up with a great idea for the proposal, present it without becoming nervous or uncomfortable, and hold their own in the Q&A," then that is the person to hire (Bryant, 2011).

You can prepare yourself for this type of "on the spot" presentation, as well as other types of business presentations, by practising a systematic approach that you will learn in this chapter. The approach includes:

- Analyzing your purpose, audience, setting, and medium options
- Selecting and prioritizing your key points
- Composing visual support materials, including slides and handouts
- Evaluating your presentation by practising
- Delivering the presentation effectively
- Evaluating the audience's response

(LO 12.1) What do you analyze when planning a business presentation?

Analyze

In school, an instructor may give you a topic to research, such as business trends in China or the pros and cons of business outsourcing to India, and ask you to develop a presentation on that topic. Similarly, in business your manager may ask you to give a presentation on a specific topic. For example, you may need to present background information about a new client company and its industry or update your managers about new technologies that can benefit your company.

More often, however, a business presentation is based on a specific business question. This chapter uses a business scenario that poses such a question to describe the best practices of preparing and delivering a presentation. As you read the chapter, you will follow the ACE process (Analyze, Compose, Evaluate) to develop a presentation for a company called Rowland-Grey, a large company that owns six department store brands located across Canada.

Assume that you work for the human resources department of Rowland-Grey. Your job is to study the work environment in individual stores and to recommend changes that will improve worker satisfaction and productivity. One day your supervisor asks you to analyze the personnel problems in the company's computer call centres. The call centres handle both online orders and customer feedback. The manager of the Saskatchewan call centre has been complaining that his unit is experiencing high rates of staff turnover and absenteeism as well as low rates of productivity. Your supervisor gave you **exit interviews** from 10 online sales clerks, all of whom quit because of headaches and eyestrain. Based on the exit interviews and additional research, you learn the following information:

- The annual turnover rate for employees who work in the call centre is 55%, whereas the turnover rate for employees on the sales floor is 40%.
- The excess turnover in the call centres costs the company $660,000 a year in new employee training.
- Exit interviews show that people working in the call centre routinely complain about headaches.
- The type of computer monitors combined with the lighting in the call centres lead to glare, which may be contributing to the headaches.

In a meeting with your supervisor, you report your findings and suggest that Rowland-Grey conduct a pilot program to determine if purchasing new computer monitors will reduce turnover and increase productivity. Your supervisor likes the idea and asks you to make a presentation to Carolyn Reese, senior vice-president of planning and development, to get funding for this pilot program. The business question you will address is this: What is the cause of high turnover and low productivity, and what can be done about it?

Preparing this presentation begins long before the day you deliver it. In fact, it begins long before the day you start to write it. Using the ACE process, you can plan your presentation by analyzing the following:

- Purpose and outcome: Why?
- Audience: Who?
- Message: What?
- Setting: Where?
- Medium options: How?

This analysis will help you make important decisions and determine a plan of action. Based on the analysis, you may decide you need to do additional research to gather more information, talk with your audience in advance to learn more about their attitudes and concerns, or even visit the room where you will present so that you can design visuals that work well in that space. Begin to compose slides only after you have carefully analyzed the why, who, what, where, and how of your presentation.

Exit interview A survey or interview conducted with an individual who is leaving an organization or business relationship.

FIGURE 12.1 Four Possible General Outcomes for a Presentation

DO I WANT MY AUDIENCE TO ...	THEN MY PRESENTATION WILL BE ...	FOR EXAMPLE, AS A RESULT OF MY PRESENTATION, MY AUDIENCE WILL ...
know something?	informational.	know why the call centre turnover is so high and understand how glare leads to headaches.
believe something or do something?	persuasive.	implement a pilot program and purchase new monitors for the call centre.
know how to do something?	instructional.	know how to install new monitors.
work together with me to reach an answer?	collaborative.	discuss the pros and cons of purchasing new monitors or lighting sources.

Analyze your purpose and outcome: Why?

As leadership expert Steven Covey suggested, "Begin with the end in mind" (Covey, n.d.). Every professional business presentation has a specific objective or intended outcome. Ask yourself, "Why am I delivering this presentation, and what do I want to have happen as a result?" Visualize that outcome and then ensure that everything in the presentation contributes to achieving it.

Typically, presentations fall into one of four categories, each with its own specific type of intended outcome. You may want your audience to

- understand or learn something,
- believe or do something,
- know how to do something, or
- collaborate with you to achieve an objective.

FIGURE 12.1 lists those four general outcomes, along with specific examples of each outcome applied to the Rowland-Grey scenario. Although you may start with a general purpose like those in the left column, always move to a more specific outcome, like those in the right column. The more specific your outcome statement, the easier it is to create an effective presentation. In the Rowland-Grey scenario, you would choose just one of these outcomes.

For this scenario, the Rowland-Grey presentation clearly needs to be persuasive. The objective is to convince Carolyn Reese, the senior vice-president, to approve the plan and fund a pilot program to purchase 100 new computer monitors that will reduce glare. With this specific objective in mind you can analyze the audience: What will Ms. Reese need to know and believe to be convinced?

Analyze your audience: Who?

Analyzing your audience helps you develop content. If you know the people who will be in your audience, especially the decision makers, you can anticipate their needs, interests, attitudes, and possible biases. If you do not know your audience, imagine how they might respond. **FIGURE 12.2** lists questions that will help you understand your audience. By answering these questions, you'll be able to tailor the presentation to your audience, making it easier to achieve your goal.

In the Rowland-Grey scenario, the key decision maker is Carolyn Reese, who originally developed the call centre eight years ago. She wants it to succeed. Ms. Reese is very interested in cost savings and will not be motivated by arguments based solely on employee happiness or unhappiness. She is skeptical about big promises, and she values proposals that are supported by logic and research.

FIGURE 12.2 Audience Analysis
Questions

1. **Who are the key players?**

   Who are the key decision makers and important stakeholders whose response will affect your success?

2. **What do the key players care about?**

   What are their key questions and concerns? Attitudes and values? Personal agendas and hot buttons?

3. **How will the key players benefit?**

   How will the outcome or ideas you are presenting connect to what they care about? For example, will your ideas save money or time, resolve a pressing issue, or achieve a strategic objective?

4. **What does the audience already know about the situation or topic?**

   How much context do they need?

5. **How do they feel about you and your topic?**

   How much credibility do you have? What is their attitude toward your topic?

6. **What does the audience need or expect from you in this presentation?**

   Do their expectations match your intentions, or will you need to reset their expectations?

7. **How far do you need to move your audience before they act? Where do they fall on this continuum:**

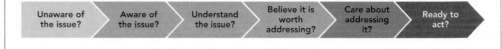

Analyze your message: What?

Imagine the audience of your presentation asking you "What is the one thing you want me to remember from this presentation?" That one thing is your main message. The best messages are short, clear, and structured to answer a key question for the audience. Sometimes your audience will come to the presentation with that question in mind. At other times you will need to raise the question for them in the first few minutes of your presentation.

For most business presentations, the main message should do the following:

1. Take the audience's point of view (often using the words *you*, *we*, and *us*) and include other key players, such as the board of directors, employees, investors, customers, or partners, if they are involved.

2. Address a problem, concern, or need that your audience cares about, for example, growing the business, saving money, increasing return on investment, or enhancing employee satisfaction.

3. Present your solution and highlight what the audience will gain from that solution.

4. Explicitly or implicitly lead your audience to the outcome you intend.

Here are some examples of main messages for other business scenarios that highlight the value of what is being presented:

- Your employees can complete more training more quickly by using our new online learning programs.
- Adding a customer information system will give us the tracking capabilities we need to exceed our sales goals in the next year.

- The time is right to expand into new markets because the demand for our products is rising sharply, and we are well positioned to enter with minimum investment.

In the Rowland-Grey scenario, the main message might be that "Investing in new computer monitors may help reduce costs associated with high employee turnover, currently estimated to be $660,000."

Analyze your setting: Where?

The setting of your presentation will affect the material you prepare and your presentation style. For some presentations, you may be standing in front of a screen with an audience arranged in rows or tables throughout the room. For other presentations, you may be sitting at a conference table with a few key decision makers. In other situations, you may be delivering the presentation to a remote audience by videoconference, webinar, or teleconference.

Analyze your medium options: How?

As you plan your presentation, consider what tools you want to use and what materials you can provide to help your audience understand your message. Do not restrict yourself to using only slides. You can take advantage of a range of options and combine them in effective ways. For example, many people choose to project slides and also provide the audience with a hardcopy handout. You can embed video or audio files within your slides, or use a document camera to project a paper document while making notes about it on a flipchart. The best options depend on your purpose, audience, content, and setting. The criteria in **FIGURE 12.3** can help you make smart choices about the best medium and presentation tools.

IF YOU WANT TO ...	FLIPCHARTS, WHITEBOARDS	SLIDES	VIDEO, AUDIO, PODCASTS	DOCUMENT CAMERAS	PROPS	HANDOUTS
Purpose- and content-related criteria						
Encourage the audience to collaborate, interact, and create content	■				■	■
Encourage the audience to listen and look carefully		■	■	■		■
Communicate complex material that people need to look at carefully		■				■
Share content that is not in electronic form				■	■	■
Present lengthy content that could not easily be seen in slide form						■
Provide a demonstration					■	■
Have an electronic record of the material		■	■			■
Audience- and setting-related criteria						
Present to a large audience in a large room		■		■		■
Present to a small audience in a small room	■	■			■	■
Present to one or two people in an office or conference room	■	■			■	■
Present to a distant audience accessible by computer technology		■	■			■
Have the presentation available to people at a later time		■	■			■

FIGURE 12.3 Selecting the Best Medium and Tools for Presentations

How do you compose the presentation?

ACE

Compose

What does it mean to *compose* a presentation? For some people, the first thing that comes to mind may be writing a speech. Other people may imagine writing a slide deck or putting together a set of visual aids. Still others may imagine a presentation that has no written component at all. In fact, some of the most powerful business presentations are based on a single visual image or a single prop that prompts and organizes the discussion.

Whether you envision your presentation as a speech or as a conversation with the audience supported by slides, props, and flipcharts, you will need to develop content that engages the audience and meets their needs. If you are developing a slide presentation, you will need to design a **slide deck** that supports the presentation without boring, distracting, or confusing the audience. This section explains the seven-step process illustrated in **FIGURE 12.4** for developing effective slide presentations.

Identify the type of presentation

Before you begin to develop your slides, you need to identify how you plan to use them. Typically, you will choose between two different types of presentations with two different uses: stand-alone presentations or visual aid presentations.

Stand-alone presentations

Many business presentations require that your slide decks serve as reference documents after the presentation and communicate the content effectively to people who did not attend the presentation. These slide decks need to make what managerial communication expert Mary Munter calls "stand-alone sense" (Munter, 2012). This does not mean that they need to be comprehensive or include every word you plan to say. Instead, it means the presentation material needs to make sense to anyone who views it without the benefit of the presenter to explain the information. In addition, each slide needs to make sense to someone who enters the room during the presentation.

A **stand-alone presentation** is distinguished by three key features:

- An agenda slide that communicates the main ideas and logic of the presentation
- Sentence-style **message headlines** that summarize the key point or message of each slide
- Support material in the body of the slide that develops and explains the headline

FIGURE 12.5 illustrates a slide from a stand-alone presentation.

Visual aid presentations

Presentations in which the speaker's words carry the main story of the presentation are called **visual aid presentations**. The slides primarily provide illustration and backup. Visual aid presentations ideally devote much more space to various forms of illustrations, photos, and graphics that focus discussion and demonstrate points. The slide in **FIGURE 12.6** is from a presentation promoting Community Foundations of Canada and its 150 Alliance Campaign. The slide is visually appealing, but a presenter needs to provide additional details orally.

Organize the content

Assuming you have done sufficient research and you understand your audience, intended outcome, and main message, you are ready to begin developing content. Think of your presentation as a three-act play with an opening, a middle, and an end.

Slide deck A common term used to refer to a set of projected slides that support or guide a presentation.

Stand-alone presentation A slide deck that makes sense without the benefit of a presenter.

Message headlines Slide headlines that summarize the key point or message of each slide.

Visual aid presentation A presentation in which the speaker's words carry the main story of the presentation and the slides provide illustration and backup.

| Identify the type of presentation | Organize the content | Create a storyboard | Develop a template | Design individual slides | Evaluate in a practice session | Create effective handouts |

FIGURE 12.4 Process for Designing Slide Presentations

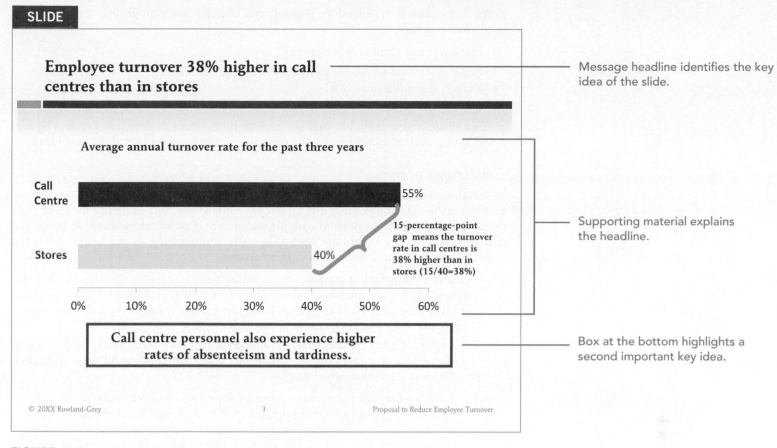

FIGURE 12.5 A Stand-Alone Slide with a Message Headline

Compose an opening that engages the audience

The opening of a presentation has four main goals:

- Establish rapport with your audience
- Capture the audience's attention
- Motivate your audience to care about your presentation and your goal
- Provide a map or framework for the rest of the presentation

Establish rapport

At the beginning of a presentation, your audience wants to connect with you. They want to feel confident that you have designed the presentation with their needs in mind. To

FIGURE 12.6 A Visually Appealing Slide That Does Not Stand Alone

Source: Community Foundations Canada: www. slideshare.net/CommFdnsCanada/pe-150-alliancecfc 2015may92015?qid=f828106f-ab95-4bf1-9c83-c5ce3e96747d&v=default&b=&from_search=3

make that connection, introduce yourself and identify common ground that you share with your audience:

- Have you had similar experiences?
- Are you worried about the same problems?
- Do you share the same goals?

Start with something familiar that your audience already knows. This technique communicates to the audience that you can see things from their point of view. The goal is to capture their attention and build their interest before you introduce new ideas.

Capture attention

Research shows that information relevant to the audience's goals and intentions is especially attention getting (Young, 2011, pp. 138–139), so get your audience involved right from the start of the presentation with information that is directly relevant to them. You can supplement this technique with other attention-getting devices. The following examples relate to the Rowland-Grey presentation:

- **Cite a surprising fact or statistic.** A surprising fact can capture the audience's attention quickly. Even a mundane fact can be effective if it gets people to nod in agreement. For example, "Next to payroll, annual employee training represents the single largest cost in Rowland-Grey's computer call centres."

- **Tell a relevant story or anecdote.** An **anecdote** is a very short story, usually a true one, that brings a subject to life. This is one of the most powerful ways to begin a presentation. Consider this example:

  A few weeks ago I was driving from Edmonton to Calgary and made the mistake of forgetting to bring sunglasses. Not only was it a beautiful, sunny day, the freshly fallen snow was reflecting that sunlight in all directions. Within about 10 minutes, the glare on the windshield was blinding, my eyes were squinting, and I started to get a headache. Fortunately, I was able to get off the road and buy some sunglasses at a service station. But the experience gave me a new perspective on the exit interviews I have been reading from employees who left our computer call centre. Many said they left because the computer glare caused headaches. I think I have begun to understand how they feel.

- **Quote someone or something significant and relevant: an expert, someone well known, a familiar saying, or even someone from your audience.** If you can find a quotation or saying that relates to your point, you can use it or a variation of it. Here is an example:

  As the old saying goes, you need to spend money to make money. It's also true that you sometimes need to spend money to save money. Today I'm presenting a proposal to spend money to update equipment, an expenditure that has the potential of saving us hundreds of thousands of dollars in costs related to employee turnover.

- **Ask a question.** Questions immediately involve your audience and get them thinking about your presentation. Your question can be a genuine one that you would actually like members of your audience to answer, either in words or by a show of hands. Or, your question can be a rhetorical question that you plan to answer yourself. For example, you could begin your Rowland-Grey presentation to Carolyn Reese with one of these questions:

  Would you be surprised to learn that employee turnover for call centre representatives costs Rowland-Grey $660,000 a year?

  Why do Rowland-Grey call centre representatives leave their jobs more quickly than any other employee category in the company?

Starting with a question may be risky, because your audience may consider it an invitation to provide an answer that takes the presentation off track. The key is finding the right question to engage your audience and to set up the remainder of your introduction.

Anecdote A short, usually true, story that serves as an example or metaphor.

Motivate your audience to care

An audience will care about your presentation if they believe it is valuable to them. Does your audience have a problem that you will solve? Is there a need for change? Are you identifying an opportunity that they can take advantage of? Is there a specific way that your audience will benefit?

For example, the proposal to replace computer monitors at Rowland-Grey offers employees the benefit of a more comfortable working environment and better health, and it offers managers the benefit of improved employee productivity. However, neither of these benefits is of primary importance to your audience, Carolyn Reese. She is probably more concerned with cost savings. As a result, the opening that you choose needs to focus on that benefit. You might say that your plan will save the company money. However, it would be be more effective to be specific. State that Rowland-Grey's computer call centres are suffering from excessive turnover, which results in approximately $660,000 in associated training and hiring costs per year. You will be proposing a solution that will reduce these costs by over 50% in year one and 75% in each subsequent year. When working with quantifiable problems and solutions, actual numbers are very effective in motivating your audience to continue to pay attention.

Provide a framework or map

Audiences easily get lost and bored if they cannot anticipate the twists and turns the presentation may take. Providing specific directions about the content at the beginning of the presentation helps them stay on course and follow your logic. This "roadmap" then becomes your agenda. You can return to it throughout the presentation to make transitions between different sections.

Organize the middle of the presentation to be easy to understand

A presentation is easiest to follow when it has a clear and simple organization. Within that organization, you can provide as much data as you need to accomplish your goal, as long as you prioritize points that are meaningful to the audience, limit the number of main points you include, and make the relationship between points clear by using recognizable patterns. A visual map can help you clarify the relationship between ideas.

Prioritize points that are meaningful to the audience

Presenters sometimes let their research dictate the content and organization of a presentation. After all, when you have secured enough information to make a two-hour presentation of interesting and seemingly pertinent facts, why should you take pains to select only specific points? In fact, it is critical that you think carefully about what is meaningful to the audience. Present only the points that are relevant to the audience, no matter how interesting or intriguing some of your other points may be. Instead of focusing on the features of a product, focus on how those features benefit the audience. Instead of explaining how a system works, highlight what problems the system solves. To identify the points most meaningful to the audience, return to the audience analysis questions you answered during the planning phase and identify what the audience wants to know during the presentation. Let that analysis be your guide.

Limit the number of main points

Your audience will remember your content better if you do not overload them with information. Presentation experts recommend that you limit your number of main points in a presentation to four or five. Your audience can only maintain four or five unrelated chunks of information in their short-term memory before forgetting important information (Baddeley, 2010; Cowan, 2001). If you keep your presentation to a small number of points, your audience will be able to remember them better when the presentation is over.

If you do have more than four or five points, group related items into meaningful categories. For example, if you have seven recommendations to present, your audience will process the information and remember the recommendations better if you present

ORGANIZATIONAL PATTERN . . .	EXPLANATION . . .
Categorization	Group the content under key categories, such as four reasons, five steps, or three options.
Component parts	If you are discussing the problems in the company, you may divide the discussion into the component regions—for example, Maritimes, Central, Prairies, and West Coast. Similarly, if you are talking about proposed changes to an automobile, you may present changes to the body, the engine and mechanical components, the chassis, and the interior.
Chronological order	Chronology works well if you are presenting the timeline for a project or phases to implement a new computer system—any topic in which time is particularly important and meaningful.
Conceptual order	For some presentations, you might find it useful to develop a model or diagram that illustrates the relationship between the ideas you plan to present, and then use that visual to organize your presentation. For example, if you were delivering an informative presentation about the ACE process, you might organize it by the three elements represented in the ACE diagram: Analyze, Compose, and Evaluate. In fact, you might even use this diagram as an agenda for the presentation. SLIDE. Analyze – Compose – Evaluate. Managing the Communication Process. Barbara Shwom, Lisa Gueldenzoph Snyder, and Liz Clarke
Problem/Solution	Because business presentations often aim to solve problems, organizing the content by problem/solution can be very useful. The main challenge is to determine how to weigh the two parts. Some business presentations fail to achieve their goal because they spend so much time on the problem that they never get to the solution. In a business presentation, the solution usually deserves the most weight.
Opportunity/Action	In this organizational style, rather than focusing on the problem, you emphasize an opportunity that will be valuable to your audience and then show how you can help them take advantage of this opportunity.
Questions/Answers	If you have done a good job of analyzing your audience, you may be able to imagine the questions that will be on their minds when they attend the presentation. These questions can help you organize the presentation. For example, if you are delivering an informational presentation about a new dental insurance option available to employees, you might organize the presentation around questions such as these: • Why did Acme add a new dental plan option? • What are the key features of each available option? • How can I choose between them? • How do I sign up for my preferred plan? • Can I change plans during the year? If you choose a question/answer structure, then the questions themselves become the agenda for your presentation.

FIGURE 12.7 Organizational Patterns for Presentations

it in two "chunks." For example, you can present three recommendations for saving costs and four recommendations for saving time.

Present your information using a recognizable pattern

Your audience will also find it easier to follow your information if they can recognize the pattern of your thinking. Consider the common patterns represented in **FIGURE 12.7**.

Which of these patterns will work best for the Rowland-Grey presentation? Although several approaches are feasible, the best one is the problem/solution pattern because this is likely the one that will best motivate the audience. Whether you choose one of these organizational patterns or a different one, be sure it fits your objective and the material you need to present. Remember to use key words that make the pattern obvious to your audience so that they understand your approach. In other words, if you are using a problem/solution pattern, use those words in your presentation.

Compose a memorable conclusion

The end of a presentation is as important as the beginning. Because the conclusion is the last thing the audience hears, it may be the first thing the audience remembers days or weeks after your presentation. This is called the *recency effect* (Sousa, 2011). Compose a powerful conclusion to your presentation by using at least one of the following strategies. The best endings typically use all four.

- **Summarize your main message.** All presentation guidelines recommend summarizing at the end. In other words, "Tell them what you told them." However, an effective summary does more than just say "I've talked about our turnover problem and a proposed solution." Remind the audience why you talked about those topics.
  - What makes your points important to you and to the audience?
  - What impact will the points and recommendations have?
  - What are the benefits to the audience?
  - How should the audience use the information or respond to it?
- **Ask for what you want.** What do you want the audience to do?
  - Send you information?
  - Schedule a meeting with a decision maker?
  - Approve your proposal?
  - Act on your recommendations?

  You'll need to create a call to action with specific, clear, and tangible tasks. As salespeople say, "Make the ask!"
- **Visualize the outcome for the audience.** Paint a picture of the audience's world when your plans, product, or recommendations are in place. What will be
  - more efficient?
  - less costly?
  - more comfortable?
  - more competitive or profitable?

  What kind of satisfaction will they experience? Describe it, in detail, to share that vision with your audience.
- **Make next steps clear.** If your presentation leads to future action, outline the next steps and identify who is responsible for what. A simple checklist or timeline can effectively display the content and provide a visual reference.

Create a storyboard

Once you know the organization of your content, you can begin outlining it as a series of slides by creating a storyboard. The concept of a storyboard comes from the film industry. Traditionally, a filmmaker will plan the film, scene by scene, sketching the vision for each scene and including notes for direction and filming. Applied to a presentation, a **storyboard** is a slide-by-slide sketch that helps create a story flow based on the

Storyboard A slide-by-slide sketch of the presentation that is used as a tool for organizing the flow of the presentation.

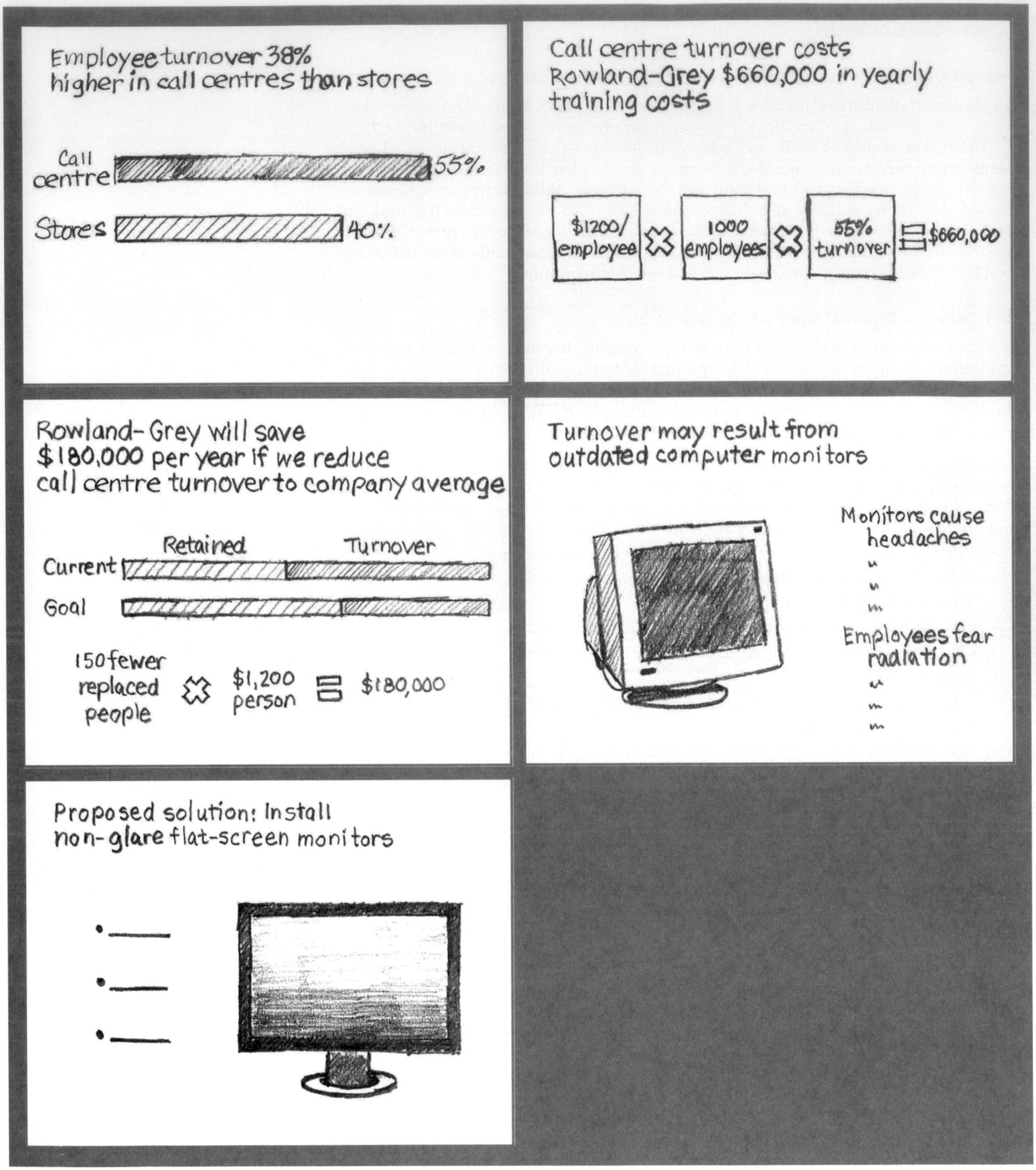

FIGURE 12.8 Presentation Storyboard

organization you developed. The storyboard also helps you see the big picture of the presentation before you get too involved in creating individual slides.

To create a storyboard, sketch boxes for your slides (or use note cards or Post-it notes) and write a headline in each box. Then sketch your vision for the body of each slide. How will you support that headline and illustrate that key idea? **FIGURE 12.8** illustrates a storyboard for the Rowland-Grey presentation.

Develop a template

In business communication, a presentation's slide design should always be secondary to your message. You do not want your audience to focus more on the template's images, colours, and borders than on the message itself. The best approach is to keep your slide design simple so your audience can concentrate on the content. Fortunately, slide programs like PowerPoint and Keynote allow you to create your own slide templates (PowerPoint templates are saved in the Microsoft template folder as .pot files).

The following fundamental design guidelines will help you develop a template that supports effective visual communication:

- **Use a slide master to design your template.** A **slide master** is a presentation editing tool that allows you to apply design features to all of your slides in that file. This tool will enforce consistency in your visual elements: Colours, fonts and font sizes, bullets, headers, footers, and margins will be consistent from slide to slide. Using this tool also saves you time because you will not need to make these changes on every slide you add. **FIGURE 12.9** illustrates how you might set up elements on a slide master for a report-like stand-alone presentation.

- **Use a simple look.** Avoid frequently used templates that immediately communicate a lack of originality. Also avoid templates with decorative, nonfunctional graphics. These graphics often take up a lot of space that you can better use for content relevant to your message. Slides work best when they have sufficient space for message content and when all graphics support that content. If you want to include a thematic graphic that relates to your presentation content, put it on the title slide. If you would like a logo or other corporate identity item on each slide, reduce the size and put it in the footer or in a corner of the slide master where it will be visible but will not detract from the message.

- **Use basic, solid backgrounds.** Avoid dramatic colour gradations on backgrounds. These will often conflict with the colour of the font you choose, at least on part of the screen. Light backgrounds work best for presentations intended to be read on a computer, projected in a small or well-lit room, or printed for your audience. Dark backgrounds usually work better in dark or large rooms. If you choose a dark background, be sure to check whether your presentation prints well in black and white.

- **Use contrasting colour for text.** Colour contrast is often sharper on your own computer screen than on a projected display. If you are planning to project slides, test your colour combinations in the room where you will present to make sure that the headlines and text contrast sufficiently with the background.

- **Use a consistent colour palette.** Choose an effective set of colours to use for graphs, tables, and emphasis in text. Most presentation software offers a range of themes that can be effective choices.

- **Use simple bullets.** Opt for bullets like this ■, and avoid overly ornate dingbats and arrows such as → that detract from your content and may not project or print correctly.

- **Use a coherent set of fonts.** Fonts can be categorized into two types: *serif* and *sans serif*. As illustrated in **FIGURE 12.10**, serif fonts such as Book Antiqua and Georgia have extra "tails" at the end of each character. Sans serif fonts such as Verdana and Arial do not have extra tails. Sans serif fonts are often easier to read, especially when projected. However, serif fonts are acceptable if they are clear and legible. Presentations typically use a single font along with variations in its style such as italic and bold, which you can see in the variations in Gill Sans font illustrated in **FIGURE 12.11**. You can also combine fonts within one family such as the Franklin Gothic font family illustrated in Figure 12.11.

Slide master A tool within presentation software that allows you to select design features that will apply to all slides.

FIGURE 12.9 Slide Master for a Title Slide and Body Slides

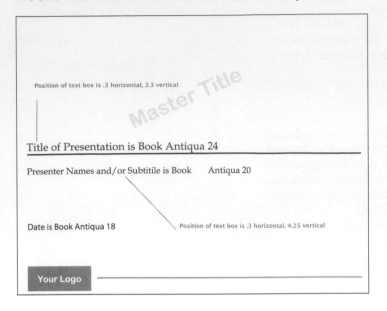
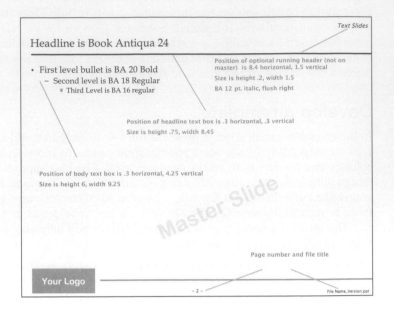

If you use fonts that are not part of the standard set included in Microsoft Windows, be sure to save your file with the fonts embedded. This will allow you to project your file on any other Windows-based computer.

- **Keep your font sizes consistent on all slides.** Do not shrink the font size on some slides to fit more text. Depending on how you will deliver the presentation and whether you are creating a stand-alone or visual aid presentation, font sizes for headlines should range from 24 to 48 points. Font sizes for text may be legible as small as 18 points if your audience will be sitting at close range. Use larger font sizes for presentations given in large rooms so people seated in the back will be able to read your slides.

- **Position headlines appropriately.** If you are using very short headlines, centre them at the top of the slide. However, if you are using message headlines, begin them at the left margin.

- **Include slide numbers.** Slide numbers can be as important in presentations as page numbers are in a traditional report. If you have provided handouts that replicate the slides, slide numbers allow your audience to refer easily to a specific slide during a question-and-answer session or in a follow-up telephone call or email message. Slide numbers also help you direct your audience to the right slide if they are navigating through your slide deck during an online presentation.

FIGURE 12.10 Serif versus Sans Serif Fonts

EXAMPLES OF SERIF FONTS	EXAMPLES OF SANS SERIF FONTS
Garamond	Avant Garde
Times New Roman	Gill Sans
Palatino	Franklin Gothic

FIGURE 12.11 Variations on the Same Font

EXAMPLE OF STYLES OF A SINGLE FONT: GILL SANS	EXAMPLE OF A FONT FAMILY: FRANKLIN GOTHIC
Gill Sans	Franklin Gothic Book
Gill Sans italics	**Franklin Gothic Heavy**
Gill Sans bold	Franklin Gothic Medium
	Franklin Gothic Medium Condensed

Design individual slides

After you finalize your template, you can begin designing and composing individual slides. Use the guiding principle of "less is more." Too many people use slides as their speaking script, crowding out all blank space with detailed text. With so much content on the slide, your audience will not be able to focus on either the speaker or the visuals. Ironically, if the slide contains less information, your audience will absorb more of the content. This "less is more" principle applies both to text slides and data slides.

Text slides

The bullet point layout is the default layout for new slides in most presentation software, including PowerPoint. This may be one reason why writers overuse bullet points rather than using other means of formatting text. Bullets work best for lists: items that can be labelled as members of one category, such as reasons, examples, results, solutions, steps, implications, or conclusions. To make the bullets easy to read, be sure they are both logically and grammatically parallel. In other words, all the items should begin with the same part of speech and be phrased the same way. **FIGURE 12.12** illustrates a before and after version of a slide that has been revised for *parallelism*.

As a general guideline, limit the number of bullets on a slide to three to five. For stand-alone presentations, you may need a few more words.

However, bullets are not always appropriate. For text that is not a list, eliminate the bullets and present the content in text boxes, shapes, or diagrams. If you choose to present text in the form of a diagram, be sure to choose a shape that reinforces the content. Avoid diagrams that are chosen only for visual appeal and that do not help your audience better understand the information. As **FIGURE 12.13** illustrates, a representative diagram will help your audience quickly see the relationships among ideas.

INEFFECTIVE: No Parallelism

Four potential coatings for the new lenses

- Polylight two-stage CC coating (the newest Polylight)
- Polylight two-stage BB coating (which we use on our current lenses)
- Two single-stage coating systems from different manufacturers
  - Kefvue
  - Reflezene
- Single-lot data has been collected for the BB and CC coatings and multiple-lot data has been collected for the single-stage systems.

At first glance, the four bullets on the "ineffective" slide appear to represent four coating systems. However, the final bullet does not present a coating system at all. Instead, it discusses data collected about those systems.

EFFECTIVE: Better Grouping and Parallelism

Four potential coating systems for the new lenses

- One-stage coating systems
  - Kefvue
  - Reflezene
- Two-stage coating systems
  - Polylight BB coating (used on our current lenses)
  - Polylight CC coating (the newest Polylight coating)

We have collected multiple-lot data for the one-stage systems and single-lot data for the two-stage systems.

In the revised slide, the four coatings are divided into two categories and phrased in similar ways. The point about data collection remains on the slide but has been moved to a box at the bottom of the slide.

FIGURE 12.12 Bullet Slide Revised for Parallelism

FIGURE 12.13 Diagram Slide Revised to Show Relationships

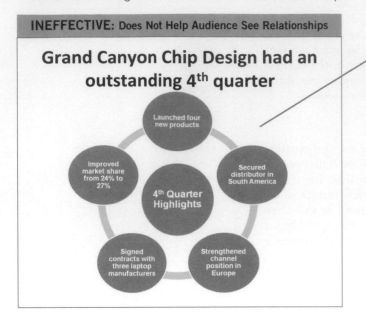

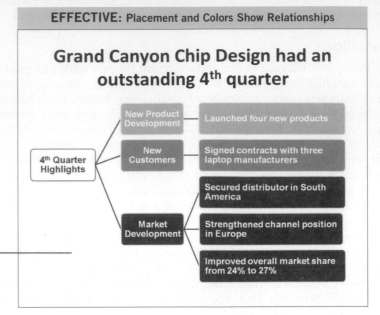

Although this circular diagram would be effective for content that is evenly distributed, in this case it implies the fourth-quarter highlights are separate and unrelated.

This diagram helps the audience see at a glance that fourth-quarter highlights fell into three groups: new product development, new customers, and market development. Market development is the biggest category.

Data slides

In business presentations, you will often need to represent numerical data on slides. As **FIGURE 12.14** illustrates, graphs typically do a better job than tables of showing the relationships between numbers and the meaning of the data.

Evaluate

Evaluate your slides in a practice session

As you design your slides, you may focus more on how a slide looks than on how you will present the slide. That is why it is important to practise presenting each slide and

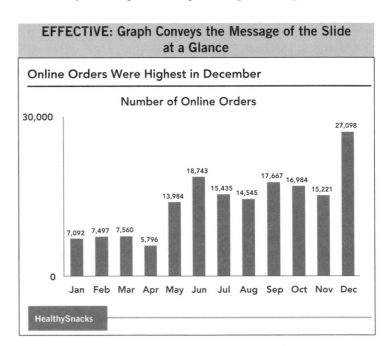

FIGURE 12.14 Quantitative Data Represented as a Table and a Graph

FIGURE 12.15 Slide Revised to Be Easier to Present

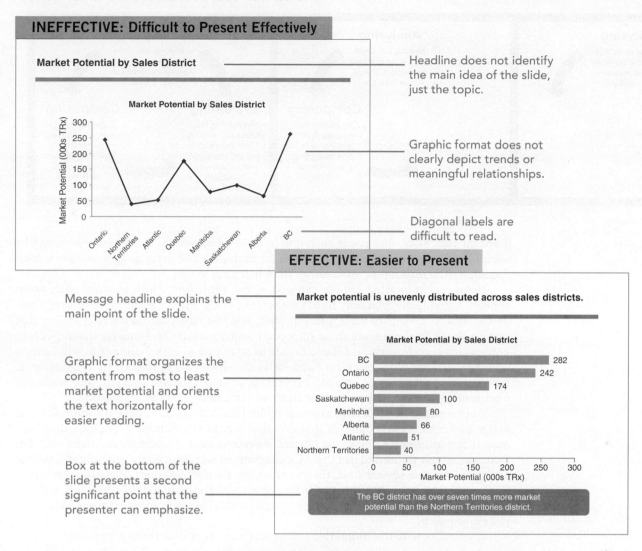

then to revise each slide to make it easier to present. As you evaluate your slides, consider both the arrangement of content and the animations.

Are the slides easy to present?

Consider the ineffective slide in **FIGURE 12.15**, which presents data about the potential number of total prescriptions for a medication (TRxs) organized by region. The slide is clean, clear, and easy to read. However, it would be difficult to present. What message do you see in the slide? What would you want to say about market potential? Because the regions are in no particular order, no clear message is obvious.

By contrast, the effective slide in Figure 12.15 is much easier to present. A presenter could look at the slide and say, "While there is substantial sales potential for our product throughout the country, that potential is not divided evenly across the sales districts. The graph on this slide is organized by size of potential. As you can see, the BC district has over seven times more market potential than the Northern Territories district."

Are animations effective?

Practising your presentation not only allows you to evaluate individual slides, but it also helps you make decisions about the value your **animations** add. As a general guideline, use animation only if it helps you present a slide effectively and if you believe it will help your audience better understand your points.

Some presenters like to animate all bullet point lists, making the points appear on the slide one by one. Animating bullet points lets you move sequentially through every

Animations Visual effects that control when and how elements appear on your slide when you present.

FIGURE 12.16 Using Animation to Present Parts of a Diagram

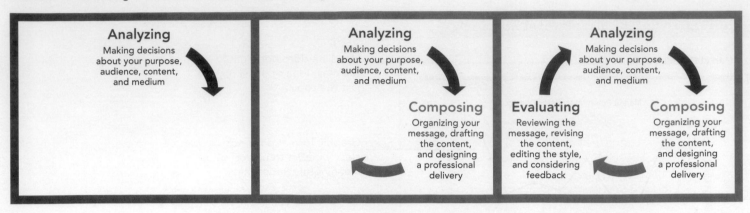

point on your slide, discussing each one in order of appearance. This technique can be useful to focus your audience's attention on each idea and prevent your audience from spending time reading the slide rather than listening to you.

However, animating bullets can also cause problems. First, because each point appears individually, you may find it awkward to skip a point if you need to save time. By contrast, if the entire list appears at once, you can easily introduce it by saying that certain items in the list are most important and you want to focus on those. Second, animations become awkward if you decide to return to an earlier slide. You will have to repeat every click going backward and forward, which can be tedious for the audience. Finally, this technique of gradually revealing your points will prevent your audience from seeing the "big picture" of your slide, which can hinder comprehension.

To prevent these problems, animate bullet lists only if you believe the audience will better understand each bullet if it is revealed separately. Similarly, animate diagrams only if the animation helps you present a process or a concept more effectively. For example, if you wanted to use the ACE diagram in a presentation, you might have the analyzing portion appear first, then composing, then evaluating, discussing each part in turn, as shown in **FIGURE 12.16**. By the end, the circle would be visible, and you would discuss why ACE is a circular process. In this case, the animation would support your discussion.

If you choose to use animations in a presentation, follow these guidelines:

- **Be consistent within the presentation.** Use only one technique (e.g., appear, dissolve, fade in) anywhere you use animations within the presentation.

- **Be conservative.** You may think it is entertaining to have images or words fly in from the left and right. However, this movement will not enhance your content. It will simply distract your audience. Most professional presenters use a limited amount of text movement within their slides.

- **When possible, show the whole picture or list first, then fade that picture and begin the animation.** Audiences often understand individual points better when they have first seen the big picture.

- **Practise.** Presenting an animated slide is more difficult than presenting one without animation. Practise delivering the slide so that you know how to take advantage of the animation. If you find the animation difficult to present, remove it from the slide.

The slide presentation in **FIGURE 12.17** incorporates all the best practices from this section. This is the final presentation prepared for Carolyn Reese, senior vice-president of planning and development at Rowland-Grey. A slide presentation is a reasonable medium choice for this scenario because you will be meeting with Ms. Reese and your supervisor in a small conference room that has a projector. Although you considered preparing just a handout with no slides, you decided it would be easier to present the problem and solution if you had a visual aid to focus your audience's attention. The paper copy of the slides will serve as a handout and will help Ms. Reese justify her decision to support the pilot program.

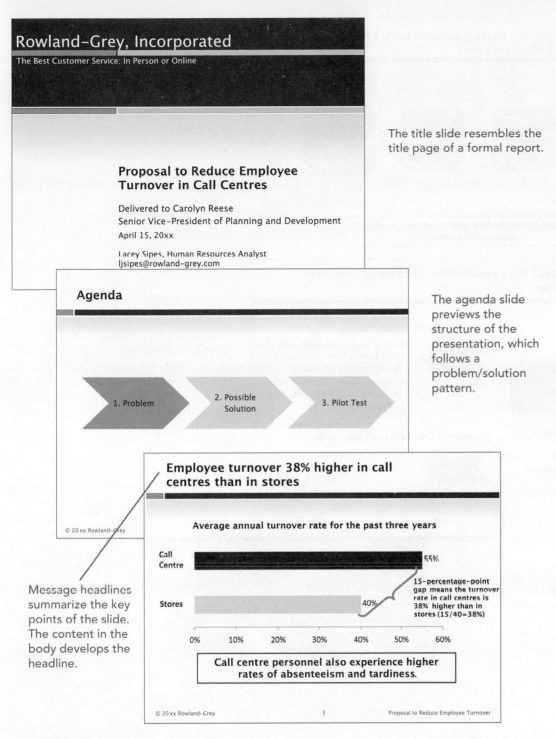

The title slide resembles the title page of a formal report.

The agenda slide previews the structure of the presentation, which follows a problem/solution pattern.

Message headlines summarize the key points of the slide. The content in the body develops the headline.

FIGURE 12.17 Rowland-Grey Slide Presentation

(continued)

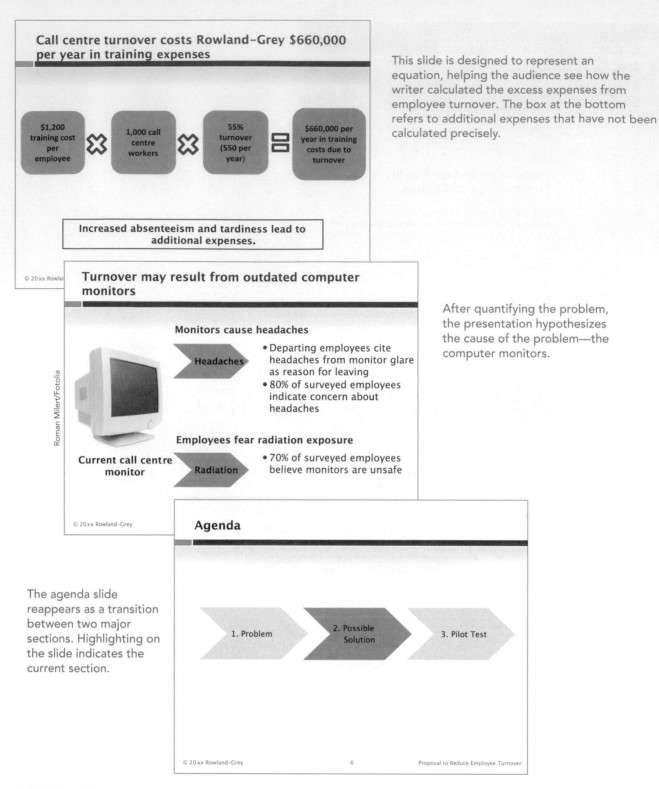

Call centre turnover costs Rowland–Grey $660,000 per year in training expenses

$1,200 training cost per employee ✕ 1,000 call centre workers ✕ 55% turnover (550 per year) ＝ $660,000 per year in training costs due to turnover

Increased absenteeism and tardiness lead to additional expenses.

© 20xx Rowland–Grey

This slide is designed to represent an equation, helping the audience see how the writer calculated the excess expenses from employee turnover. The box at the bottom refers to additional expenses that have not been calculated precisely.

Turnover may result from outdated computer monitors

Roman Milert/Fotolia

Monitors cause headaches

Headaches
• Departing employees cite headaches from monitor glare as reason for leaving
• 80% of surveyed employees indicate concern about headaches

Current call centre monitor

Employees fear radiation exposure

Radiation
• 70% of surveyed employees believe monitors are unsafe

© 20xx Rowland–Grey

After quantifying the problem, the presentation hypothesizes the cause of the problem—the computer monitors.

The agenda slide reappears as a transition between two major sections. Highlighting on the slide indicates the current section.

Agenda

1. Problem   2. Possible Solution   3. Pilot Test

© 20xx Rowland–Grey   6   Proposal to Reduce Employee Turnover

FIGURE 12.17 (continued)

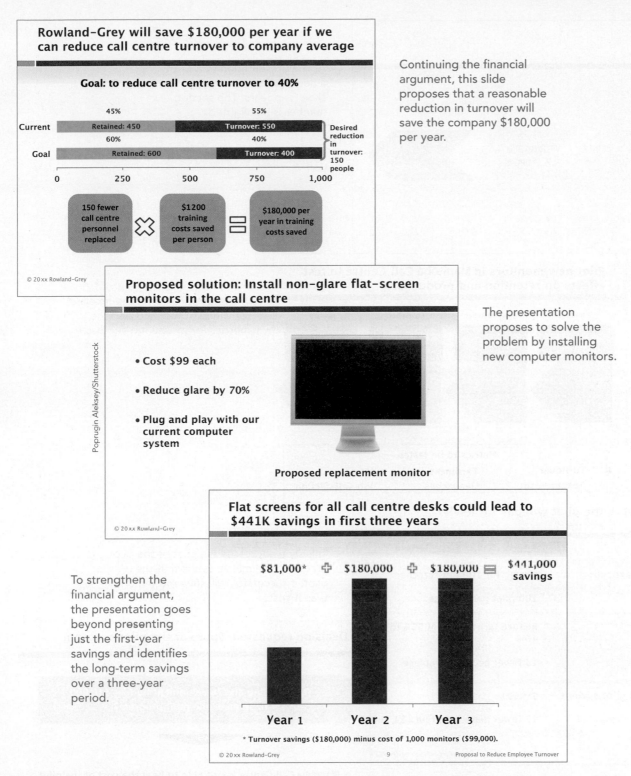

Continuing the financial argument, this slide proposes that a reasonable reduction in turnover will save the company $180,000 per year.

The presentation proposes to solve the problem by installing new computer monitors.

To strengthen the financial argument, the presentation goes beyond presenting just the first-year savings and identifies the long-term savings over a three-year period.

FIGURE 12.17 (continued)

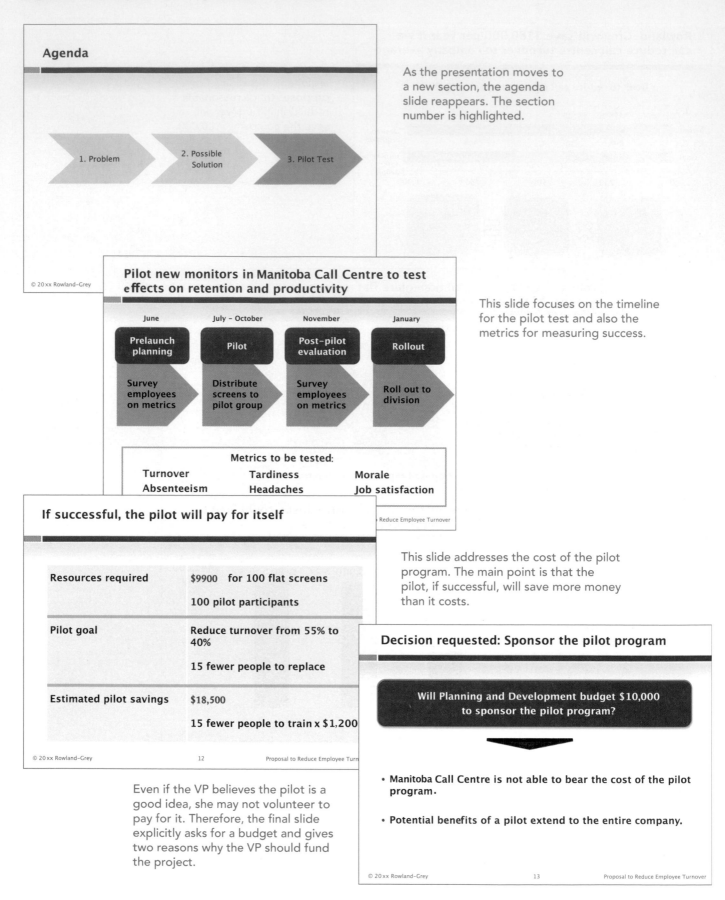

Agenda

1. Problem   2. Possible Solution   3. Pilot Test

© 20xx Rowland-Grey

As the presentation moves to a new section, the agenda slide reappears. The section number is highlighted.

Pilot new monitors in Manitoba Call Centre to test effects on retention and productivity

June	July – October	November	January
Prelaunch planning	Pilot	Post-pilot evaluation	Rollout
Survey employees on metrics	Distribute screens to pilot group	Survey employees on metrics	Roll out to division

Metrics to be tested:

Turnover	Tardiness	Morale
Absenteeism	Headaches	Job satisfaction

...Reduce Employee Turnover

This slide focuses on the timeline for the pilot test and also the metrics for measuring success.

If successful, the pilot will pay for itself

Resources required	$9900 for 100 flat screens
	100 pilot participants
Pilot goal	Reduce turnover from 55% to 40%
	15 fewer people to replace
Estimated pilot savings	$18,500
	15 fewer people to train x $1,200

© 20xx Rowland-Grey   12   Proposal to Reduce Employee Turn...

This slide addresses the cost of the pilot program. The main point is that the pilot, if successful, will save more money than it costs.

Decision requested: Sponsor the pilot program

Will Planning and Development budget $10,000 to sponsor the pilot program?

- Manitoba Call Centre is not able to bear the cost of the pilot program.

- Potential benefits of a pilot extend to the entire company.

© 20xx Rowland-Grey   13   Proposal to Reduce Employee Turnover

Even if the VP believes the pilot is a good idea, she may not volunteer to pay for it. Therefore, the final slide explicitly asks for a budget and gives two reasons why the VP should fund the project.

FIGURE 12.17 *(continued)*

TECHNOLOGY
POWERPOINT TIP: USE HYPERLINKS TO CUSTOMIZE PRESENTATIONS

PowerPoint is a powerful program that allows you to create highly visual presentations. Taking full advantage of the program effectively requires that you become familiar with its more sophisticated features. One of those features is the ability to hyperlink to other resources.

Hyperlinks help you create interactive presentations and give you the ability to navigate through your presentation in any way you like. Through hyperlinks, you can present slides out of order, link to other presentations, launch other programs, and even open a website.

Here are some examples of how to use hyperlinks:

- **Link to appendices.** You can create a detailed appendix slide containing a complex table or spreadsheet that you don't intend to present unless someone asks. During the presentation, if someone asks about this information, you can navigate to the appendix through a hyperlink and go into more detail.
- **Create navigation.** A "home" link at the bottom corner of every slide allows you to return to a navigation or index page that contains links to the various sections of your presentation. This approach gives you the option of presenting slides in the order that most interests your audience.
- **Connect to a website.** If you will have access to the Internet during your presentation, you can create links to live websites.

- **Launch other files.** You can create links to Word documents, spreadsheets, or slides in other presentations.
- **Support interaction.** To encourage participation, you can create multiple-choice or yes/no options for your audience. If you click the "Yes" link, the presentation displays a different slide than if you had clicked the "No" link.

To insert a hyperlink in PowerPoint, use the following instructions. If you use different presentation software, explore the help files to find similar instructions.

1. Use your cursor to select the text, autoshape, or image that you want to click on to create the link. (Note: you cannot insert a hyperlink on a blank slide.)
2. Go to *Insert* on the menu bar.
3. Select *Hyperlink*. The Insert Hyperlink menu will be displayed.
4. Select the object you want to "*Link to.*"
5. Click *OK*, and the hyperlink will be created.

Note that the hyperlink is active only in the Slide Show mode of PowerPoint. Also, when you click on a hyperlink that moves you to another slide in the presentation, you can return to the previous slide by right clicking on the slide and selecting *Last Viewed*.

For a TECHNOLOGY exercise, go to Exercise 12 on page 428.

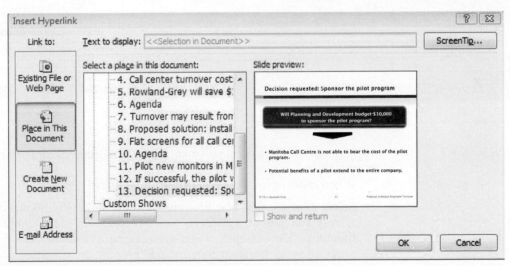

Source: Used with permission from Microsoft.

Check out the **TECHNOLOGY BOX** for an impactful PowerPoint tip you can use to add dynamism to your presentation.

Create effective handouts

You can create *handouts*, documents distributed to the audience during or after a presentation, in many forms. Standard formats for handouts include slide miniatures, slides

FIGURE 12.18 Sample Handout Formats

Slide Miniature Handouts
• Replicate the slides in reduced form
• Are used for stand-alone and report deck presentations
• May not be legible if font sizes are small

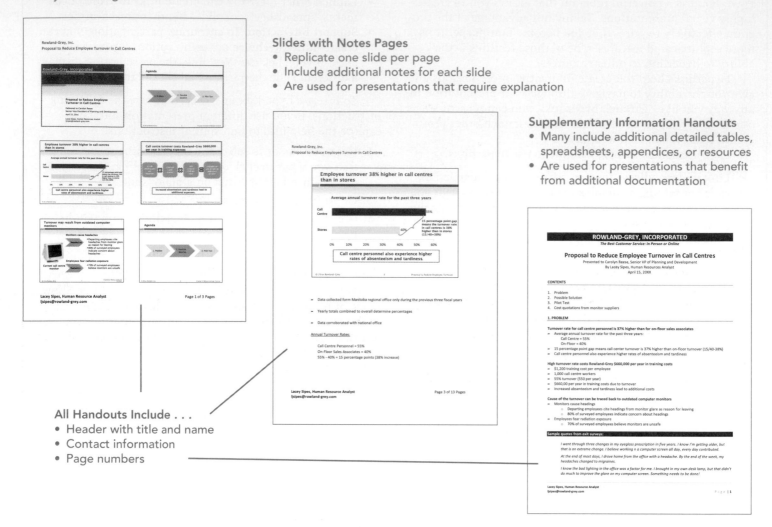

Slides with Notes Pages
• Replicate one slide per page
• Include additional notes for each slide
• Are used for presentations that require explanation

Supplementary Information Handouts
• Many include additional detailed tables, spreadsheets, appendices, or resources
• Are used for presentations that benefit from additional documentation

All Handouts Include . . .
• Header with title and name
• Contact information
• Page numbers

with "notes" pages, and supplementary information. Sample handouts are shown in **FIGURE 12.18**.

When creating handouts, use these guidelines:

• **Select a format that best fits your content.** Making handouts of presentation slides is very convenient. However, your presentation may benefit from other types of handouts. For example, if you are making a detailed sales presentation or client proposal, your handout may include product specification sheets or spreadsheets that would be too detailed to read on a screen. Providing that material in a handout is more effective. If you have several resources to share, such as forms, sample designs, or documentation, you can use folders, report covers, or binders to organize your handout materials.

• **Choose an effective format for note-taking.** Consider the needs of your audience. Will they want to make notes on your handouts? If so, be sure to leave ample margins or provide other blank space.

• **Consider the impact of colour.** Your audience may perceive handouts printed in colour as more impactful than black-and-white documents. However, colour handouts are considerably more expensive to produce. Printing handouts in greyscale provides contrast without additional expense.

- **Proofread carefully before copying.** You can easily make changes to your electronic files before your presentation. However, if you find an error after you copy your handouts, reprinting them will require extra time and money.

- **Make extra copies.** Make 10% more handouts than you think you need. Extra people may attend, or someone may want to share copies with colleagues.

- **Decide when to distribute your handouts**. Consider the three options for distributing your handouts:

  - **Before.** You may want to distribute your handouts as your audience enters the room or just as you begin speaking. The audience can preview the topic and begin to think about your information ahead of time. Having handouts during the presentation allows the audience to make notes and identify question areas as they follow along.

  - **During.** Your handouts may be designed to emphasize a specific point or highlight the "reveal" of a specific concept. Saving distribution to that moment in your presentation can be impactful.

  - **After.** If you do not want your audience to be distracted by reading a handout while you are presenting, you may decide to provide handouts only at the end of the presentation as a takeaway.

(LO 12.3) How do you deliver and evaluate the presentation?

Many people get nervous when making presentations. Minds go blank. Hands shake. Words come out too quickly or too softly. Even if you do not suffer from these specific problems, almost everyone can improve their comfort and professionalism when presenting. Mastering this skill is a sure way to be seen as outstanding among your peers.

The only way to become a memorable and professional presenter is to practise often and to practise well. Practising well means repeating and perfecting specific techniques that enhance your presentations. This section offers you proven tips for presenting effectively. Pick one or two specific items to work on each time you practise your presentation. In time, you can incorporate all of them into your presenting technique.

Making presentations can have some variance from culture to culture. This is explored further in the **CULTURE BOX**.

Set the stage

Use the following techniques to ensure a professional presentation:

- **Practise (out loud).** It is easy to feel nervous when you are not well prepared. Presenting is like an athletic performance. A presenter needs to get ready, just as an athlete would practise regularly and then stretch to warm up. Practise means saying the words out loud to create a "sound memory" to recall during your actual presentation.

- **Dress for the part.** For formal presentations, wear business-formal clothing, similar to what you would wear to a job interview. Even in less formal presentations, dress with care. Wear clothing that looks neat and allows you to move comfortably. You want people to pay attention to you, not your clothing. Empty your pockets of keys or loose change that can jingle when you move. Avoid distracting jewellery and, of course, turn off your cellphone.

- **Arrive early and warm up.** Warming up can take several forms. Greet your audience, introduce yourself, and get used to talking with them. Use relaxation techniques to focus your mind and relieve stress. Breathe deeply from your diaphragm to control the adrenaline and relax the neck and jaw muscles. This will help you project your voice. Take a quick look at your notes, and review your opening and closing remarks to refresh your memory. Double check handouts and equipment to ensure everything is ready.

- **Set up all equipment and props.** If you plan to use presentation slides, turn on the projector or electronic data display and have the title slide in place when the presentation begins. If you prefer to begin with a dark screen and display the title slide later, you can strike the letter "B" in PowerPoint to blacken the screen. Striking "B" again will make your slide appear. If you're using flipcharts, a whiteboard, or props, make sure they are positioned to be easy to reach during your presentation.

CULTURE
MEETING AUDIENCE EXPECTATIONS

In Chapter 11, Skylar developed a culturally and ethically conscious business proposal for her business program. It was her first opportunity to put into practice much of her college program learning. Skylar's instructor was very impressed with her broad perspective on culturally sensitive considerations and the integrity of her work. Since Skylar prepared so well, she has been given an opportunity to present her proposal at BizBrief, a global competition for business students in which they present their work before a panel of experienced international business professionals and judges.

Skylar is concerned. Although her proposal got a good grade, she has not presented to such a diverse audience. How can she prepare to present her work in a professional manner?

O-A-R can help!

- **Observe:** It is important to observe presentations in various settings and diverse audiences. Being an audience member can give rich feedback on how to present and how ideas, gestures, and tone are received. Here are some possibilities for Skylar to broaden her ideas on how presentations should be made:
  - TED Talks take place in a variety of locations across the globe. Using the TED.com site as a resource, compare the presenter and audience dynamic in a variety of locations:

    - Polychronic versus monochronic cultures
    - High- versus low-context locations
    - Hierarchical versus egalitarian cultures

- YouTube offers a wealth of business presentations across settings, cultures, and at varying levels of formality. Use search terms like "business presentation" + the name of the country or culture being researched. Some examples are more useful than others. However, various patterns of similarity between cultures, as well as differences between cultures, will begin to emerge.

- **Ask:** At her work placement, Skylar needs to ask to attend as many professional presentations as possible to gain experience and understanding. She can also ask colleagues and supervisors if they have any experience, guidance, hints, or tips to guide presentations to international audiences.

- **Research:** Skylar must find out more about her specific audience for this competition and research their expectations. Here is a chart with some preliminary ideas. However, Skylar will need much more specific information about her audience members to help her prepare for her proposal presentation.

For a CULTURE exercise, see Exercise 19 on page 429.

Meeting Audience Expectations

COMPONENT OF PRESENTATION	CANADIAN BUSINESS EXPECTATION/ETIQUETTE	A GLOBAL PERSPECTIVE
Preparation	Be prepared to start on time, including having materials and technology ready to go at the appointed time. Keep "small talk" to a minimum.	Punctuality has less meaning in polychronic cultures than in monochronic cultures. (See Chapter 4 for more information on cultural time perspectives.) When presenting to a more polychronic audience, use some of your preparation time in the room to chat informally, introduce yourself one-on-one to the early arrivers, and create a relaxed atmosphere.
Introductions	It is customary to introduce yourself to the participants before a presentation as well as to give credit or introduction to any other presenters or contributors.	In more formal and more hierarchical cultures, politeness dictates that presenters acknowledge and thank the senior members of their audience for attending before beginning the presentation. For example, meetings in Estonia are formal. It is proper etiquette for the most senior figure of the audience to open proceedings with a short speech and introductions. Similarly the most senior member of the presenting team should give a short speech thanking the hosts and introducing him- or herself. Small talk, if it occurs, is short and simple (Kwintessential, 2014).
Speed	In Canada, audiences respond well to a reasonably fast-paced presentation style with ample audience interaction.	In Europe and Asia, audiences often prefer presentations that are slower and offer them an opportunity to think carefully and process information.

(continued)

COMPONENT OF PRESENTATION	CANADIAN BUSINESS EXPECTATION/ETIQUETTE	A GLOBAL PERSPECTIVE
Body Language/ Eye Contact	Eye contact is very important when presenting to Canadian audiences. It signifies a connection with the audience as well as a level of confidence with the content. Expressive and mobile body language can be effective with a Canadian audience.	In more hierarchical cultures, presenters are more reserved and calm. To determine the appropriate use of hand gestures and expression, pay attention to other presenters from that culture. You can often find examples on YouTube and other media sites. In some Asian cultures, people are uncomfortable with direct eye contact and may look down or away rather than directly at the presenter. In these cultures, lack of eye contact may be a sign of respect (Zhou & Zhang, 2008).
Dress Code	Formal business attire is the safest and most expected dress code. In most cases, a presenter wearing jeans, a casual hat, or running shoes would be showing disrespect to the audience and to the material being presented.	Some cultures prefer a more casual approach to business presentations. For example, Finns are egalitarians and do not appreciate shows of ostentation. Overdressing for a presentation would be seen as a sign of arrogance (Kwintessential, 2014).
Language/Tone	Ensure that the language you use is easy to understand and references are relevant to the audience. The tone of a word can mean a lot as well. In Canada, it is easy for a slightly dismissive tone to be seen as sarcastic. This can be interpreted either as humorous or as disrespectful. Take care to maintain a professional and positive tone at all times.	Though many people in other cultures do speak English, there are many different forms and dialects of English. You can help an intercultural audience understand your meaning by speaking slowly and clearly. Use more common words instead of more academic words. For example, instead of "ubiquitous" use "widespread." Remember, too, that some English words have different meanings in different cultures. For example, in the United States, the word "billion" means a thousand million. In the United Kingdom, it means a million million. That is a huge difference. Some cultures do not respond well to a high degree of passion in a presentation. For example, in Singapore, presenters must maintain a moderate, gentle tone and remain calm even when under great pressure. This will gain you much more respect than becoming animated and "passionate" (Kwintessential, 2014).
Reading the Audience	In Canada, if audience members are nodding that usually means they agree with the presenter. Presenters also look for smiles as signs of agreement.	In some cultures, such as Japan, head nodding means only that the audience understands what the presenter is saying, not that they agree (Huang, 2010). In some Eastern European cultures, smiling is reserved for friends and relatives, people you know well (Krakovsky, 2009). Stony stares from an Eastern European audience may mean that they are paying attention, not that they are angry.

- **Decide where you will stand.** Whenever possible, avoid standing behind lecterns and large desks or tables because they create a barrier between you and the audience. If you are using a projector, position yourself on one side of the screen so that you do not have to walk between the screen and the projector's light. Clear space around the projector and other equipment so that you have plenty of room to move around comfortably and approach the audience. Using a remote control to change slides can help you navigate your presentation space.

- **Keep the lights up and attention on you.** If you choose a technology that requires low light, plan to begin speaking with the lights on. This guarantees that attention will be where you want it: on you and your message. It can be very effective to begin speaking before projecting any visuals. Connect with the audience and then move to the slides.

- **Have water available.** If you are speaking for a long time, you will need to drink water to prevent your mouth from drying out and your vocal cords from being constricted.

Control your body

The following presentation techniques will help you look confident and professional during your presentation:

- **Start from a "ready" position to control body movements.** Before you begin to speak, get your body into position, just as you would get into position to take a slapshot in hockey or make a jump shot in basketball. Try this stance:
  - Hands loose at your side
  - Knees and elbows relaxed
  - Weight balanced on both feet
  - Feet shoulder-width apart

  Once you are in a comfortable and confident position, your gestures and movements will feel more natural.

- **Maintain consistent eye contact with your audience.** Using eye contact appropriately is critical for success. If you are presenting with slides or a whiteboard, you may be tempted to move away from the audience and turn toward your visuals. Avoid doing this. The only way to keep your audience involved is to face them and look them in the eye. Hold eye contact with one person for two or three seconds, and then look at someone else. Engage everyone in your audience, not just the decision makers or those who are sitting front and centre.

- **Smile.** Like eye contact, smiling is a must. A smile projects energy and makes you appear happy to be presenting. It also relaxes facial muscles to help you get the most from your speaking voice. Finally, it encourages your audience to smile in return, which will make them more receptive to your presentation.

- **Animate with body language.** Rather than standing in one position, let your body move. Move away from the projector and screen, lean forward, and walk toward your audience. Use natural hand gestures to punctuate your points, just as you would in conversation. Do not overthink your gestures. Take your hands out of your pockets, unclasp them, and let them work naturally.

Use your voice effectively

Use the following techniques to improve your vocalization:

- **Speak to the back of the room.** Speaking to the back of the room will help you adjust your volume so that you project your voice effectively. When you make eye contact with people in the front of the room, maintain the same level of volume so that people throughout the room can hear you. Too often, speakers lower their voices when they answer questions from people in the front of the room. Even in a small room, the person who cannot hear you will feel left out.

- **Speak slowly, especially at the beginning of the presentation.** Your audience may need a few minutes to get used to your style of speaking. You can help them by speaking slowly and enunciating clearly, especially at the beginning of your presentation.

- **Modulate your voice.** Nothing destroys audience attention more than a monotone presenter. One technique for animating your voice is to emphasize important words and phrases. If you are using slides, take your cue from the words you emphasized on the slides with colour contrast or boldface.

- **Avoid note cards or a script.** You may want to have notes available as a backup. However, reading from notes or a script does not build rapport with your audience. In addition, holding on to cards or paper prevents natural gestures and makes you look like a student in a speech class rather than a professional in a business setting. If you need more memory cues than your visuals provide, try glancing discreetly at notes placed on a nearby table.

- **Minimize verbal tics.** Many people unconsciously use certain words as fillers. These include:
  - like
  - okay

- you know
- I mean
- basically

These are but a few examples of verbal tics. Be aware of your own speaking habits, and practise eliminating tics from your speech. One way to assess your verbal speech is to record yourself making a presentation and then listen to the playback, paying special attention to the words spoken. List and keep track of the filler words you use and then make an effort to remove them from your speech.

- **Pause.** Pausing intentionally is one of the best ways to prevent *"ers"* and *"ums"* because you give yourself permission to be silent. Silence can be a powerful tool. A quiet moment gives the audience time to process your information and indicates that something new is coming.

Present your visuals effectively

When presenting with visual aids, be sure to introduce each visual by explaining your intended point. One picture may be worth a thousand words, but without an introduction people will interpret the picture in their own way, which may be different from yours. To be sure that the audience sees what *you* intended, introduce the slide as soon as it appears. For text slides, do not read the slide word for word. Instead, explain the purpose or main point of the slide, then give the audience a few moments to look at the content before you launch into your discussion. For tables, identify how the information is organized and what appears in the columns and rows. For graphs, identify what the graph is depicting, what each axis is measuring, and the key point.

For example, if you were presenting the slide shown in **FIGURE 12.19** from the Rowland-Grey presentation, you might say something similar to the quoted text in the annotation.

Take care in how you source and use the visual images in your presentation slide decks. To learn more about the ethical issues involved in choosing images and other content, check out the **ETHICS BOX**.

Coordinate with your team

If you are presenting as a team, follow these guidelines:

- **Take advantage of everyone's strengths.** In a class, your instructor may require that everyone on your team participate equally in the presentation. However, in business the only reason to plan a team presentation is to take advantage of each

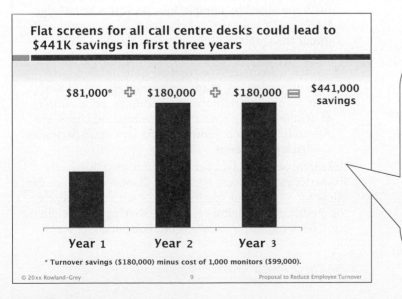

Flat screens for all call centre desks could lead to $441K savings in first three years

$81,000* ✛ $180,000 ✛ $180,000 ▭ $441,000 savings

Year 1   Year 2   Year 3

* Turnover savings ($180,000) minus cost of 1,000 monitors ($99,000).

© 20xx Rowland-Grey   9   Proposal to Reduce Employee Turnover

"If our pilot study shows that new monitors reduce turnover, we can save a substantial amount of money by implementing the screens throughout our call centres. Let's look at the anticipated savings over three years. As you can see from this graph, the monitors will more than pay for themselves in the first year. Although we will spend $99,000 on the monitors, we anticipate saving $180,000 in turnover costs, leaving a benefit of $81,000 in the first year. In the following two years, we can save the full turnover cost, leading to a three-year savings of $441,000."

FIGURE 12.19 Introduce Visuals

ETHICS
PLAGIARISM OR "REPURPOSING"?

Skylar is looking forward to presenting her proposal at Biz-Brief, a global competition for business students in which they present their work before a panel of experienced international business professionals and judges (see the Culture box on page 408). Skylar has prepared some slides to showcase her proposal, but when they were reviewed by a colleague, a classmate, and her instructor, she was advised to make it more visually appealing.

Visual images ensure that presenters connect with visual learners in the audience while providing variety and appeal. Before integrating "found" visuals into a presentation, reflect on the ethical considerations. Just because you have found the perfect image does not mean you have an automatic right to use it.

O-A-R can help:

- **Observe:** How are other respected professionals using visuals in their presentations? Under what circumstances are they giving credit or source information?

- **Ask:** Here are some fundamental questions to ask about copyright and intellectual property (IP) rights:

  1. **Does your workplace have an IP policy for visual images?** Ask whether your organization has intellectual property (IP) and copyright guidelines that can help you filter through usage issues. If a company has a marketing department, the right to use some photo and visual collections may already be in place.

  2. **Can I show pictures I have taken?** If you have taken pictures for research or choose to show pictures of people that you have taken, you must ask for permission in writing from everyone pictured to ensure that permission has been granted for the use of their image. Stay away from showing pictures of minors to negate any legal, human rights, or ethical issues. If you must show a photo of a child, you must get permission from their legal guardian or parent.

  3. **Is it acceptable for your presentation to include a photo found on the Internet? Do you need to acknowledge the source?** This is acceptable if you acknowledge the source in your presentation. You can include a source citation directly below the photo. However, if you are using your presentation for any commercial purposes, or if you are distributing it widely, just acknowledging the source is not enough. You must get permission from the original owner of the photo to use it. For example, if you create a presentation to persuade firms to invest in India and want to use a photo of new skyscrapers in India to communicate economic growth, you must acquire the rights to use that photo by contacting the photographer or other copyright holder.

  4. **If you purchase a licence to use a presentation photo from a digital media source such as Getty Images or Corbis Images, do you need to acknowledge the source?** You do not need to acknowledge the source and you may use the photo in your presentations in any way allowed by the terms of the licence. Some photos are "royalty free." This means you can use them multiple times for a single fee. Other photos come with more restrictions.

  5. **If other people in your company or organization have created effective slides, is it acceptable to use those slides in your business presentation? Do you need to acknowledge the source?** Within an organization, it is usually acceptable to share slides to use in presentations made on behalf of the organization. In fact, some companies create slide libraries to encourage employees to use slides that have been preapproved, especially for customer and other public presentations. Because your company "owns" the slide you are borrowing, you do not have to acknowledge the source.

  6. **If you find a slide template that you like on the web, is it acceptable to copy that slide template if you do not copy any of the content?** It is not acceptable to copy someone else's slide template because graphic designs can be copyrighted in the same way content is copyrighted. If someone is selling a slide template design through the Internet, you may purchase and use it. If a company is explicitly giving away a free template, you may download and use that. However, if you simply download a presentation file from the Internet and decide to use that design for your presentation, you may be violating copyright.

  7. **If you include other people's work in your presentation, for example, data from another source that has been converted to a graph, how do you acknowledge it?** Typically, you will acknowledge a data source under the graph or table that uses the data. Similarly, if you "borrow" concepts or ideas from another author, acknowledge it right on that slide. In business presentations, many slides contain "footnotes" that acknowledge information sources. For examples of acknowledging sources on presentation slides, see Appendix D: Documentation and Reference Styles, at the back of this book.

- **Research:** Some images can be used reasonably freely. Research your choices. A Creative Commons licence can allow for legal use of specific images with permissions for modification, digital creativity, sharing, and originality. Check out http://creativecommons.org.

For an ETHICS exercise, go to Exercise 17 on page 429.

person's strengths and knowledge. Ensure that everyone who is presenting has a defined role in the presentation and that the team projects a unified and confident image. The whole should be greater than the sum of the parts.

- **Decide how you will handle introductions.** Will the first presenter introduce everyone at the beginning? Or will people introduce themselves? This may seem like a minor point, but unless you have planned this, the team members may start talking over each other.

- **Practise transitions from person to person.** During team presentations, each speaker needs to make a connection between his or her content and the next speaker's. As you finish speaking, introduce the next speaker and topic, making that connection. For example, "Now that I've outlined the budget issues, Marla Whitt from IT will discuss implementation plans." These transitions help the audience follow the flow of your presentation.

- **Let your teammates speak.** If your teammate forgets to mention a point or presents material differently from the way you would like it explained, *do not interrupt to expand on the answer*. Doing that will damage the image of your team and undermine your teammate. Allow your teammate to finish. You can come back to the point later.

- **Correct a teammate only when necessary.** If your teammate fumbles or says something wrong, *do not immediately correct the error*, especially if the point is not very important. If it is an important point that must be clarified, make the correction very politely and considerately.

- **Be prepared to present other teammates' slides.** Emergencies arise and teammates may be late to a presentation or they may not come at all. Be sure that you are able to present every slide in the presentation in case you need to step in at the last moment.

Evaluate the audience's response

During the presentation, "listen" to the audience's feedback. Are they nodding in agreement with you or nodding off from boredom? Do they look interested in your content or confused by it? Listening while you present can be challenging because you are also trying to think about what to say, navigate your slides, and maintain eye contact with your audience. However, if you can gauge audience response as you are speaking, you have the opportunity to adjust your delivery style, if needed. Consider the following strategies to "listen" while you present:

Evaluate

- **Pause between sections.** Scan the audience during transitions between slides or between major ideas. Do they seem attentive and interested?

- **Ask questions.** Unless you want to open the floor to a Q&A session, limit questions during your presentation to close-ended inquiries that assess the audience's participation. For example, if you see someone looking confused, you could say, "I know this process is complicated. Does anyone need additional explanation?"

  After the presentation, consider your audience's overall response:

  - When did the audience nod in agreement? Why?
  - Which parts confused or amused the audience? Why?
  - Did you get the kinds of questions you expected?
  - Were there any surprises?
  - Could you have prevented confusion or disagreement by presenting something differently?

By answering these questions, you can evaluate your approach and your performance, using this information to plan future presentations.

How do you handle questions and answers?

During a presentation, a question-and-answer (Q&A) session offers many benefits:

- **Interaction.** The most effective presentations are interactive. You can make your presentation interactive by asking for questions.

- **Immediate feedback.** As a presenter, you are likely to learn something important from questions, especially how well your audience understands your points.
- **Increased emphasis.** Questions also give you a chance to emphasize and expand important points.
- **Enhanced credibility.** A thoughtful exchange with the audience helps build your credibility by demonstrating your expertise and openness. Skillful replies also help you diffuse criticism and objections.

Answering questions during a presentation is a form of **impromptu speaking**, speaking without advance knowledge of the topic or question. People often get nervous when required to speak spontaneously. This section offers advice about how to plan in advance for a Q&A session and how to structure appropriate answers to questions.

Plan for a question-and-answer (Q&A) session

Your presentation will be most effective if you give your audience the opportunity to ask questions. Here are some guidelines for running a smooth Q&A session.

Anticipate questions

Take some time, on your own or with your team, to brainstorm possible questions that your audience might have. Develop as long as list as you can, thinking critically about your material. Your audience will sense any inconsistencies or gaps in logic within your material. Find these yourself and be prepared to address them.

Plan short, clear answers

The main problem people face in impromptu speaking is the temptation to ramble. In other words, people talk aimlessly until they discover the point they want to make. The following advice will help you avoid that problem:

- **Map out an answer in advance.** Once you have pinpointed the questions that an audience may ask, organize your responses, writing down a few key points you want to cover to keep on track. Speak only on these points. Do not embellish in the moment.
- **Keep your answers concise.** Begin with the shortest possible version of the answer and then stop. If people require additional information, they will ask follow-up questions.

Decide how your team will handle questions

In a team presentation, you will want to avoid having team members look at each other blankly, waiting for someone else to answer. You will also want to avoid having multiple members trying to answer a question at the same time. Consider one of the following options for handling questions as a team. Both options depend on the team making a plan in advance about who will answer what kind of question. Once you have decided which approach to take, be sure to practise this as a team to ensure your delivery and transitions are smooth and professional.

- **Assign one team member to facilitate the Q&A session.** That team member will ask for questions and "assign" them to the team member designated to answer that kind of question. The facilitator may also answer questions, but must be careful not to answer too many. Otherwise, he or she will appear to be claiming the spotlight.
- **Allow team members to decide whether a question falls under their designated area.** For this option to work well, the team member should not just launch into the answer. Instead, identify that you plan to answer it by saying something like, "I'll take that question." This signals to the rest of the team that the question is covered, and it prevents two people from beginning to answer at the same time.

As with other phases of your presentation, there is no substitute for careful practice here.

Set up the Q&A session in your introduction

Tell the audience what to expect. Should they ask questions as you go? Or save them for the end? Even if you ask your audience to hold questions until the end, you will need to

Impromptu speaking Speaking without advance knowledge of the topic or question.

be prepared for the audience member who wants to ask questions during your presentation. In that situation, the best way to stay on track is to provide a brief answer and to promise to provide more detail at the end of the presentation. When you're ready for questions, do not ask, "Are there any questions?" Encourage participation by asking, "What questions do you have?"

Answer questions skillfully

Answering questions can be difficult, but with proper preparation you can handle any questions that are asked with skill and ease.

Give a three-part answer

A professional response has three parts:

1. **Restate or summarize the question to be sure everyone heard it and that you understand it correctly.** Repeating also gives you time to think of an answer.
2. **Respond in headlines.** Give the main point of your response at the beginning and then follow up with details. Otherwise, you may appear to be disorganized or evasive. As you answer, look at the entire audience, not just the person who asked the question. Get the entire room involved in caring about and understanding your point.
3. **Verify with the questioner**. Return to the original questioner to ensure you have provided a sufficient answer.

Break long and complex questions into parts

If you get a complex question that is difficult to answer, try breaking it into parts by listing the segments on a flipchart or whiteboard. Then answer each part separately, referring back to your list.

Be honest

If someone asks a question you cannot answer, you can say, "I don't know." Credibility disappears when a speaker gets caught making up an answer. Offer to find the answer and then follow up with the questioner as soon as possible.

Avoid being defensive or dismissive

Some types of questions tempt presenters to defend themselves or dismiss the audience's concerns. These types of questions require especially skillful answers:

- **A hostile question.** If a questioner seems antagonistic, be careful not to become defensive. First, reframe the question, stating it in a way that seems less hostile and more objective. Then acknowledge the other person's position and try to identify the source of the objection. Work on creating a mutual understanding of the issue rather than trying to be "right."
- **A question you plan to answer later.** If you plan to answer the question later, do not dismiss the question by saying "I'll get to that later." Instead, give the questioner a short answer immediately and then mention that more detail will follow. That should satisfy that person's need to know and keep him or her paying attention.
- **An idea that you have already rejected.** If someone raises an alternative you have already rejected, do not be too quick to dismiss the idea. The person could get defensive. Acknowledge the possible value of the alternative, and then explain objectively the reasoning that led you to reject it.
- **A question that takes the presentation off track.** If someone uses a question to try to take over the meeting, look for an opportunity to regain control of the discussion. Do not dismiss or insult the questioner by indicating that the question is irrelevant or off point. Instead, refer to the meeting agenda or the map of the presentation to get back on track.

How do you adapt your approach for online presentations?

Not all presentations are delivered face to face. Several different online modes offer the ability to present to people who are not in the room with you:

- **Virtual presentation at an online meeting.** Given the expense of travelling and the ease of connecting with others on the Internet, you may be asked to present your material to distant audiences online using one of the many available online presentation tools, such as WebEx, GoToMeeting, ooVoo, Adobe Connect, Slack, or Skype. Or you may choose to email a copy of your presentation deck to your audience or upload it to SlideShare so that your audiences can access it during a telephone meeting.
- **Webinar or webcast.** A **webinar** is a web-based seminar that is broadcast over the Internet. Webinars have a live audience and are intended to be interactive. A **webcast**, like a webinar, is broadcast over the Internet to an audience who logs in or registers for that event, but a webcast is typically not interactive. This is a one-way or unilateral communication. Although webinars and webcasts are originally delivered to a live audience over the Internet, they may be recorded and archived for future audiences. At that point, they resemble a podcast.
- **An audio or video podcast.** In contrast to a webcast, which has a live (although distant) audience, a **podcast** is recorded without an audience, posted on a website or a social media site such as YouTube or Vimeo, and distributed through website or social media links. Podcasts can be played online through streaming media or can be downloaded and played from your own computer or mobile device.

Chapter 5 has some foundational guidance on both the technology and etiquette best practices for using remote delivery channels. Delivering presentations in these online modes presents a different set of challenges than presenting face to face in a small meeting or larger group setting. You need to address each of these challenges to be a successful online presenter to a live audience or through a podcast.

In a live online presentation, manage the audience experience

When you present your material at an online meeting, you need to ensure your audience is engaged and understands. You cannot rely on visual or verbal feedback, so you need to be proactive in managing the audience's needs.

- **Ensure your audience has connectivity.** When you make a presentation face to face, you are the only one who has to worry about technology. Does your computer work? Can it connect to the projector? In contrast, when you deliver a presentation online, you need to confirm with your audience that they are connected and can see the presentation. Did they get the link you sent them? Can they log on to any special software you are using? Wait for them to confirm they can see your presentation slides on their own screen before you begin.
- **Make a plan for controlling what your audience sees on their screens.** Some online presentation software allows you to "share your screen," which means the audience sees on their screen exactly what's on your screen. As the presenter, you can control what they see and move forward from slide to slide at the pace you want. In this case, the online presentation resembles an in-person meeting. Other presentation technologies require the audience to have a copy of the presentation on their screens, which they control independently (equivalent to having sent them an email attachment that they can open on their own machine). When your audience can move through the slides independently, you need to provide cues about where you are in the presentation. For example, you can say, "Here on slide 3, you can see . . . On the next slide, slide 4 . . ." For this reason, it is important to remember to number your slides. If you direct the audience to the specific slide number, they will more likely focus on what you want them to see when you want them to see it rather than click ahead (or lag behind) in the presentation.

Webinar An interactive web-based seminar that is broadcast over the Internet to a live audience.

Webcast A web-based presentation that is broadcast over the Internet but is typically not very interactive.

Podcast An audio or video presentation or program that can be recorded with or without an audience, and posted on a website or a social media site such as YouTube or Vimeo, and distributed through links.

- **Open the meeting early and put a welcome slide on your computer screen,** confirming meeting details if you are using a screen-sharing program such as WebEx. This early start will allow those new to the technology to become familiar with the interface while they wait.

- **Use a webcam or provide a picture to help establish rapport with attendees.** If you are using a webcam, look frequently at the camera (rather than at the screen) so that remote people feel that you are making eye contact with them. If you are not using a webcam, you can display a picture of yourself on the welcome slide to help the audience visualize you.

- **Use professional telephone etiquette.** Online presentations are like phone calls, so professional phone etiquette applies. You need a reliable connection so your audience can hear you. Speakerphones can work if you want to be hands free, but you may hear occasional static. Headsets can also work, but test them first. Whether you use a traditional landline service or Internet-based telephony such as Skype or Google Talk, establish your voice connection before you have your audience look at the presentation slides.

- **Engage the audience with voice and screen movement.** With an online presentation, you cannot use body language, but you can engage the audience with excellent vocal delivery. To further engage the audience, plan for motion on the screen. Provide annotations on slides or use pointers to draw your audience's attention.

- **Invite questions frequently during interactive online presentations.** When you make an online presentation, you do not get visual feedback from your audience. As a result, it's important to hear from them frequently. If the audience remains silent, you may not know if they are confused or if they have fallen asleep. Ask for specific questions after each major point to ensure understanding. For webinars, build in additional opportunities for audience interaction, such as polls, if your software supports that function.

- **Keep the pace lively.** Do not dwell too long on one slide, especially in a webinar or webcast. The medium changes the audience's expectation of the pace. To facilitate a lively pace, divide your slide material into smaller chunks and change slides frequently. For example, as **FIGURE 12.20** illustrates, if you want to discuss a long quotation, do not put the full quotation on one slide and expect your audience to read it. Instead, break it into several slides and read it to your audience, modulating your voice to emphasize keywords and pausing just a bit before reading the last slide, to stress the final point (Courville, 2009).

In a podcast, provide content that offers lasting value

If you develop impressive, professional presenting skills, you may have the opportunity to create podcasts for your company. Both big and small organizations take advantage of podcasting as a way to reach audiences at the audience's own convenience. Listeners can download audio podcasts to MP3 players to enjoy while driving or jogging. Viewers can download video podcasts to watch on tablets or smartphones. Because podcasts are so versatile, the audience for them is growing (Edison Research, 2012).

Businesses and other organizations use podcasts to substitute for newsletters or marketing materials directed at external audiences. Organizations also use podcasting for internal communication to update and engage employees on company or industry news. For example, Roger Safian, a senior data security analyst at Northwestern University, hosts a weekly 10-minute podcast called "Information Security News," designed to provide the community with "timely information about security issues and tips for a more secure computing experience" (Northwestern University Information Technology, 2012). The podcast provides updates about local information security issues, but focuses most of its content on interesting computer-related stories from the news. It also provides links to these stories on an associated webpage. By providing an engaging podcast experience, Safian achieves the goal of improving computer security at the university and beyond. By providing an archive of that information on a webpage, Safian has also become an information **curator**: someone who selectively organizes material on a specific topic using a social media tool such as a podcast or blog and then shares this collection of material with

Curator Someone who selectively organizes material on a specific topic using a social media tool such as a blog, podcast, Pinterest, or Scoop.it, and then shares this collection of material with interested parties using social media tools such as Twitter, Facebook, or Google+.

FIGURE 12.20 Breaking Slide Content into Small Chunks for Online Delivery

Source: "Fourteen thought provoking social media quotes and resources," by M. Field, 2012. Retrieved from http://socialmediachimps.com/2012/14-thought-provoking-social-media-quotes-resources/

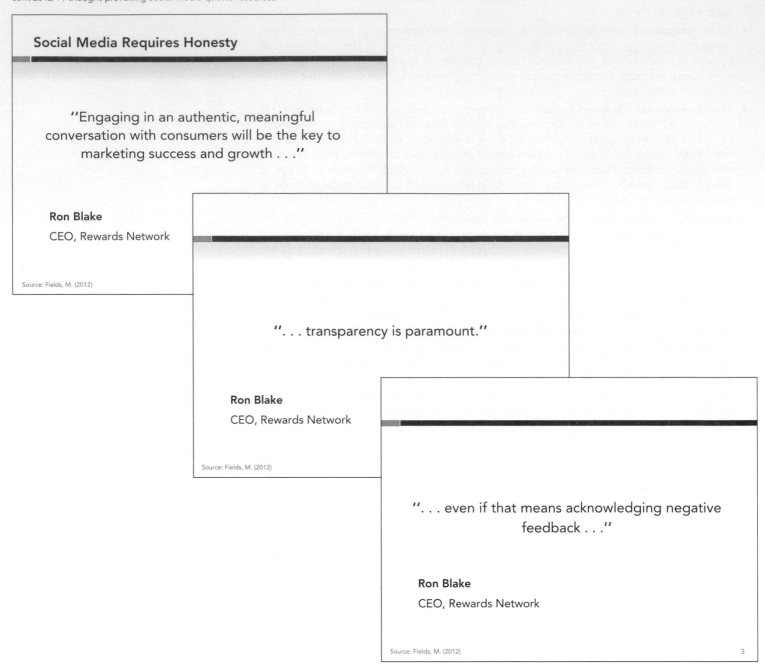

interested parties. By selectively providing only the most important or interesting information, curators play an important role in reducing information overload.

Podcasts can take many forms: some are interviews, some are panel discussions, and many sound like radio shows. However, many resemble presentations with one person offering engaging and relevant material for 10 to 20 minutes. If you become involved in podcasting, here are some guidelines to follow:

- **Choose the best medium for your audience, content, and purpose.** If you are podcasting about something with a strong visual component, choose a video podcast. Otherwise, an audio podcast may be more versatile and less expensive to produce.
- **Commit to a regular schedule so listeners will know when to expect your content.** Unlike a webinar or webcast, a podcast is not a one-time event. Gain a following by producing them weekly or monthly.

- **Choose content that will be relevant for a long time.** The audio and video files will be available on the web long after you first release them. Provide content that users will find useful at least for the near future.

- **Make your podcasts easy to find.** Provide links to your podcasts through email, social media, and websites.

- **Write a script and practise.** A podcast is not an opportunity to improvise. Rather, this is an opportunity to compose content that will provide value to your audience and make them return for more.

In summary, business presentations offer you the opportunity to address a business issue and to impress your audience with your analytic, persuasive, and speaking skills. Using the ACE communication process (see **FIGURE 12.21**) helps you develop well-organized content that is targeted to your audience and appropriate for the medium you choose, whether it is face to face or online. To communicate that content well, design effective slides, and practise both your presentation skills and the specific presentation so that you know how to make each point and present each slide. Building a confident and professional presentation style offers benefits beyond just improving your business presentations. Being a confident presenter will also help you sell your strengths during job interviews and increase your chances for promotion to leadership positions.

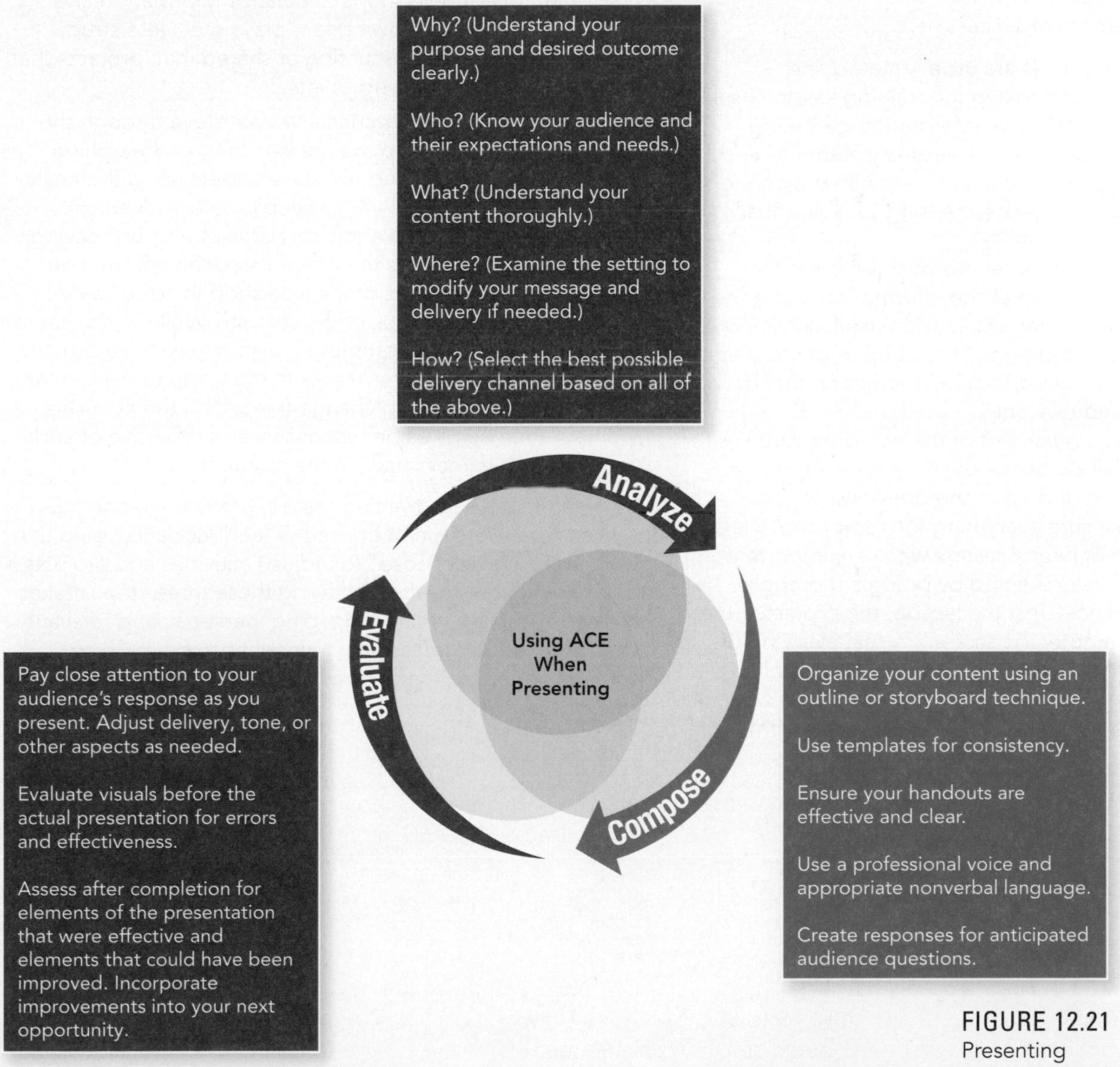

Why? (Understand your purpose and desired outcome clearly.)

Who? (Know your audience and their expectations and needs.)

What? (Understand your content thoroughly.)

Where? (Examine the setting to modify your message and delivery if needed.)

How? (Select the best possible delivery channel based on all of the above.)

Analyze

Using ACE When Presenting

Evaluate

Pay close attention to your audience's response as you present. Adjust delivery, tone, or other aspects as needed.

Evaluate visuals before the actual presentation for errors and effectiveness.

Assess after completion for elements of the presentation that were effective and elements that could have been improved. Incorporate improvements into your next opportunity.

Compose

Organize your content using an outline or storyboard technique.

Use templates for consistency.

Ensure your handouts are effective and clear.

Use a professional voice and appropriate nonverbal language.

Create responses for anticipated audience questions.

FIGURE 12.21 Using ACE When Presenting

Jeff Plotnikoff
Corporate Training &
Development

Photo courtesy of Jeff Plotnikoff and Patrick Lowney.

@ WORK

How to ACE every training!

In the opening of this chapter, Jeff listed many variables that need to be considered when preparing to deliver a training session. How can ACE help manage these variables?

In order to ensure that each stakeholder walks away from each training session knowing they have received solid value for their time and money, we need to know what they are expecting. ACE is the key element to success here.

- **Analyze.** The client's goals are usually stated and explored in advance of booking the training session itself. We send out a comprehensive information-gathering document used to clarify a number of key elements and variables in advance, following it up with either a phone/Skype session or a face-to-face meeting to review it all before we go live.

    However, it would be a serious mistake for us to proceed assuming we have *all* the information about the audience. Before beginning the session itself, it is important to always do a one-on-one "check-in" with the client stakeholders to uncover additional information that is more immediate and relevant.

    In addition, do a quick test of the equipment you will be using! Murphy's Law demands that whatever can go wrong, will go wrong. It is up to the presenter to take extra steps to make sure everything runs smoothly. We have had a couple of near disasters with very important clients that were only prevented by doing a thorough assessment in advance! Test the laptop, the projector, the microphone, the remote, the screen . . . test everything!

    It is the audience that can be a bit unpredictable. The responsibility is on us to find out exactly what they want. Before a session starts, walk around the room, informally chatting with people to get a sense of what they are like, what their attitude is toward the session, and what they expect to gain. We look for people who seem shy or reserved as well as noting the more extroverted or engaged people. Knowing this level of detail helps us anticipate their response to the materials and activities we have prepared.

- **Compose.** Our analysis identifies our goals and our clients' goals so we can now incorporate relevant elements into both the live presentation and the training materials that will make the training more meaningful to each unique audience.

    Our presentations always use concise, direct language that is reflected in the spoken elements and the printed materials. This ensures that audience members of varying language skills can benefit. We design each segment of our workshops to balance information and learning activities, allowing for "play time": less structured, peer-to-peer discussion or shared mini-projects that reinforce our key training points.

- **Evaluate:** This stage is critical. As we move through the presentation workshop, we are watching and weighing both the presenters and the stakeholders using the analysis as the foundation. Are we keeping the audience engaged? Are key stakeholders participating and having "Eureka" moments? Is the group using the information/tools from earlier parts of the workshop to solve/realize goals in the later stages of the session? While it may seem as though we are "impromptu" onstage, we have actually considered several alternatives in the Compose segment of ACE that allow us to change things "on the fly." This preparation helps us be responsive and reflective of audience needs immediately, in the moment.

Therefore, as each training session unfolds, we continuously "analyze" verbal and nonverbal feedback and, using this new knowledge, "compose" (or adjust) activities and projects, and "evaluate" our results. Following these three steps makes each session more exciting, engaging, personal, and relevant to the audience. A professional trainer has to be ready to change and adapt to the circumstances without losing sight of shared goals. You can be sure that you will succeed with ACE as part of your toolkit!

Learning Objectives in Review

LO 12.1 What do you analyze when planning a business presentation? *(pages 384–387)*

- **Analyze your purpose and outcome: Why?** What do you want to have happen as the outcome of the presentation? Do you want your audience to know something (informational presentation), believe or do something (persuasive presentation), know how to do something (instructional presentation), or work with you during the presentation (collaborative presentation)?
- **Analyze your audience: Who?** Understand who they are and what they need to know so you can achieve your outcome.
- **Analyze your message: What?** What is the main idea you would like your audience to remember from your presentation? That is your message. Be sure to phrase it in a way that will be meaningful to the audience.
- **Analyze your setting: Where?** Consider any constraints or opportunities your setting offers.
- **Analyze your medium options: How?** Identify the medium choices that best fit your needs (and your audience's). Possibilities include slides, handouts, video, audio, podcasts, flipcharts, posters, whiteboards, and props.

LO 12.2 How do you compose the presentation?
(pages 388–407)

- **Identify the type of presentation.** Slide presentations may be designed to stand alone without a speaker or to serve as a visual aid that requires a speaker to explain. Stand-alone presentations typically use message headlines and more complete content support than visual aid presentations.
- **Organize the content.** Think of the content as having three acts. Compose an opening that engages the audience, organize the middle of the presentation to be easy to understand, and compose a memorable conclusion.
- **Create a storyboard** before writing detailed slides. A storyboard helps you take the organization you developed and create a story flow.
- **Develop a template.** Choose a simple slide design that will not compete with your content, and create a master slide that uses a consistent set of fonts and design features.
- **Design individual slides** to be easy to understand at a glance. Slides will be more effective if they are not crowded with content. Text can be presented in grammatically parallel bullet points, in text boxes, or in shapes. Diagrams should effectively show relationships. Data slides should make their point clearly. Animations should facilitate the presentation rather than make it more cumbersome.

- **Evaluate your slides in a practice session.** If a slide is not easy to present, redesign it. Determine whether animations will help or hinder your presentation.
- **Create effective handouts.** Select a format that best fits your purpose and your audience's needs.

LO 12.3 How do you deliver and evaluate the presentation? *(pages 407–413)*

- **Set the stage** for a great presentation by warming up before the presentation and by dressing for the part. Arrive early to ensure that all equipment is functioning and to begin establishing rapport with your audience as they arrive.
- **Control your body.** Stand comfortably and confidently, use engaging body language, maintain eye contact with your audience, and smile.
- **Use your voice effectively.** Control your volume by speaking to the back of the room. Speak clearly, enunciate your words, use your voice to emphasize key ideas, and pause (or keep silent) as you are thinking, rather than filling the air with "ers" and "ums."
- **Present your visuals effectively.** Introduce each visual by explaining your point, direct attention to visuals with gestures and words, and use visuals as cues rather than referring to note cards or scripts.
- **Coordinate with your team.** Plan speaking roles, transitions, and responsibilities for answering questions.
- **Evaluate the audience's response** by "listening" to the audience's nonverbal feedback.

LO 12.4 How do you handle questions and answers?
(pages 413–415)

- **Plan for a question-and-answer (Q&A) session.** Anticipate questions, plan short answers, and begin the presentation by telling the audience when you would like to address questions.
- **Answer questions skillfully** using a three-part structure: repeat the question, give a short direct answer, and confirm the answer with the original questioner. Be prepared for challenging questions and plan strategies in advance.

LO 12.5 How do you adapt your approach for online presentations? *(pages 413–420)*

- **In a live online presentation, manage the audience experience.** Ensure your audience has connectivity, control what the audience sees, open the meeting early, use professional telephone etiquette, engage the audience, and invite questions frequently.
- **In a podcast, provide content that offers lasting value** and will keep the audience returning for more.

KEY TERMS

anecdote p. 390
animations p. 399
curator p. 417
exit interview p. 384

impromptu speaking p. 414
message headlines p. 388
podcast p. 416
slide deck p. 388

slide master p. 395
stand-alone presentation p. 388
storyboard p. 393
visual aid presentation p. 388

webcast p. 416
webinar p. 416

CASE STUDY

Culinary Adventure Tour Presentation

This case study will help you review the chapter material by applying it to a specific scenario.

Planning a Presentation

Stephanie Lo graduated from college with a major in French and a minor in communication. She was very happy to get a job with JourneyFree, LLC, a company that specializes in organizing educational tours for students, professionals, and other groups. Ultimately, Stephanie would like to become a tour leader, but for now she is the assistant to the vice-president of tour operations, Rachel Jones. Stephanie's role is to work on marketing communications.

Stephanie's first project requires that she use all her strengths. She will be developing communications to market JourneyFree's newest product, a culinary tour of France specifically designed for culinary arts and nutrition teachers in high schools and trade schools. In addition to advertising online and sending brochures to high schools, Stephanie's supervisor, Rachel, plans to visit school districts in major cities and present the program to superintendents, principals, department chairs, and teachers. She will give a brief and colourful slide presentation and offer samplings of the French food that culinary arts teachers will experience on the tour.

Thirty culinary arts teachers have invited Rachel to give a presentation next week, so she needs a slide presentation fast. She asks Stephanie to design and develop a draft of the presentation. Together they work out the following outline:

- The Educational Experience
- Trip Overview
- Trip Logistics and Costs
- About JourneyFree, LLC
- Q&A

Rachel and Stephanie also discuss the audience and key selling points to make in the presentation. The next day, Stephanie puts together a draft of presentation slides. She is planning to meet Rachel to review the slides and to discuss the talking points that will go with the slides.

Stephanie would like your help in analyzing the audience, evaluating the presentation, and composing the content for the presentation. After the slides, you will find questions designed to help you think systematically about the presentation using the ACE approach. Answer the questions to review the key concepts in the chapter.

France: A 7-Day Culinary Adventure Tour

①

RACHEL JONES,
VP OF TOUR OPERATIONS
JOURNEYFREE, LLC

felix/Fotolia

Why this tour will help culinary teachers

②

- Explore range of French culinary arts over a fun-filled seven-day journey through France
- Diversify and expand knowledge of culinary teachers in your vocational high schools
- Foster a stronger connection between teachers and French gastronomic culture

Visionsi/Fotolia

Slide 3

③

Today's Itinerary

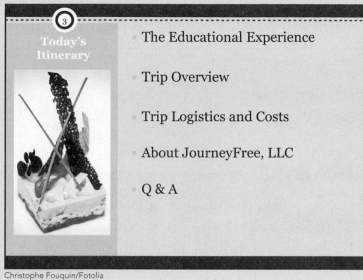

- The Educational Experience
- Trip Overview
- Trip Logistics and Costs
- About JourneyFree, LLC
- Q & A

Christophe Fouquin/Fotolia

Slide 4

The Educational Experience
Why do teachers need this trip?

④

- Expand teachers' cultural knowledge base
- Spark creativity
- Inspire new courses
- Refresh aging culinary school curriculum

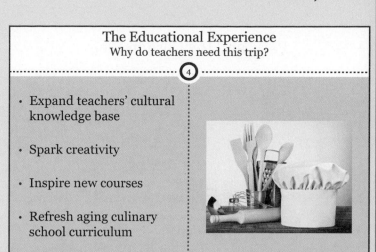

BillionPhotos.com/Fotolia

Slide 5

The "Educational Vacation" Experience

⑤

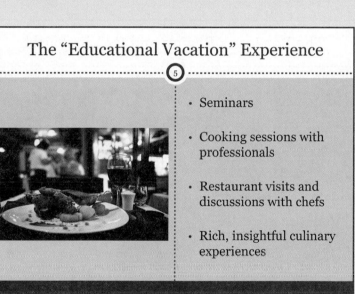

- Seminars
- Cooking sessions with professionals
- Restaurant visits and discussions with chefs
- Rich, insightful culinary experiences

kichigin19/Fotolia

Slide 6

⑥

Today's Itinerary

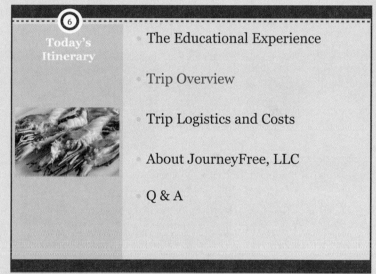

- The Educational Experience
- Trip Overview
- Trip Logistics and Costs
- About JourneyFree, LLC
- Q & A

augustcindy/Fotolia

Slide 7

Why France?

⑦

- The cooking capital of the world
- Each region offers new culinary wonders
- Less costly than one might think

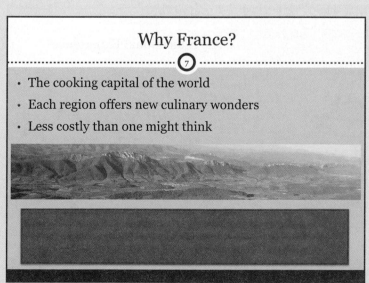

Oleksiy Drachenko/Fotolia

Slide 8

An Overview of the Trip
A Seven-Day Journey

⑧

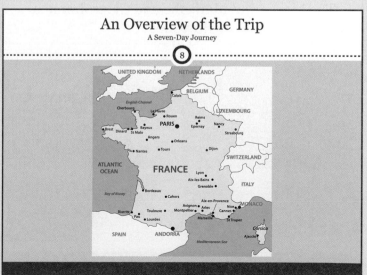

pavalena/123RF

Paris and the Cordon Bleu

9

Dan Breckwoldt/Fotolia (left); David Angel/Alamy (middle); Image Source/Alamy (top right)

Brittany's Fish Markets and Pastry Shops

10

stevanzz/Fotolia (top left); Fuse/Thinkstock/Getty Images (bottom left); bbsferrari/Fotolia (top right); Philippe Halle/123RF (bottom middle); Pixinoo/Fotolia (bottom right)

The Loire Valley Chateaus

11

philipimage/Fotolia (top left); lamio/Fotolia (bottom left); dusk/Fotolia (top middle); Radu Razvan/Fotolia (bottom right); wjarek/Fotolia (top right)

The Bordeaux Region and Its Vineyards

12

The Art Archive/Alamy (top left); Pictures news/Fotolia (bottom left); sablin/Fotolia (top middle); Shchipkova Elena/Fotolia (bottom right); Rostislav Sedlacek/Fotolia (top right)

The Markets of Marseille and Gastronomy of Provence

13

Valentinna/Fotolia (top left); Amy Goodchild/Shutterstock (bottom left); Alex Tihonov/Fotolia (top right); Monkey Business/Fotolia (bottom middle); Dorling Kindersley/Getty Images (bottom middle); fototehnik/Fotolia (bottom right)

14

Today's Itinerary

- The Educational Experience
- Trip Overview
- Trip Logistics and Costs
- About JourneyFree, LLC
- Q & A

WavebreakMediaMicro/Fotolia

Financing the Journey
Cost Efficiency at Its Best
(15)

- Tours and educational events.
  - Over $500 in discounts for group tours
  - Over $200 in educational tour discounts
- Travel to the country:
  - Round-trip from Pearson to Charles de Gaulle
- Travel within the country:
  - Coaches, shuttles, and EuroPass
- Lodging:
  - B&B, low-cost hotels
- Total cost: Approx. $3,000 per teacher

Cost Breakdown
(16)

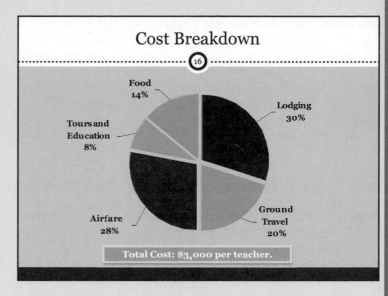

Food 14%
Lodging 30%
Tours and Education 8%
Airfare 28%
Ground Travel 20%

Total Cost: $3,000 per teacher.

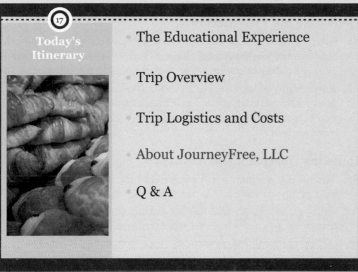

(17)

Today's Itinerary

- The Educational Experience
- Trip Overview
- Trip Logistics and Costs
- About JourneyFree, LLC
- Q & A

Eduard Zhukov/Shutterstock

About JourneyFree
Why us?
(18)

- Solid reputation, strong financials
  - 24 years in the industry
  - $46 million in annual revenue last year
  - Publicly traded, privately run

- A wide array of travel experiences
  - Many destinations served
  - Partnerships with local touring agencies

- A personal touch
  - The Corporate Rewards program
  - Private agencies around the world

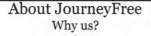

sorapop/Fotolia

Questions?

adisa/Fotolia

Questions for Reviewing the Culinary Adventure Tour Presentation

Analyzing Purpose and Audience

1. What is the purpose of this presentation? Is it primarily informative or persuasive?

2. The ideal outcome of the presentation is that teachers sign up for the trip, or school administrators agree to fund teachers for the trip. How should this "call to action" be delivered?
   - Should the slides end by asking for a "sale"?
   - Should the presenter do that orally?
   - Should the presenter skip this step and leave the audience to think about the content and sign up later?

3. Imagine yourself as the target audience: high school teachers and administrators. What questions do you think they will have? Does this presentation leave any important questions unanswered?

Reviewing the Structure and Composing Oral Content

4. The slides themselves do not begin with a compelling visual opening designed to capture the audience's attention. Brainstorm what Rachel could say as she begins her presentation.

5. The presentation is divided into five parts. Do you think this is an effective structure? If so, why? If not, why not?

6. Between each section of the presentation, a transition slide appears to indicate the new section. Are the transition slides effective?

7. The end of the presentation simply asks for questions and answers. Consider the advice for endings given in this chapter:

   - Summarize your main message.
   - Visualize the outcome for the audience.
   - Ask for what you want.
   - Make next steps clear.

   Brainstorm what Rachel could say at the end of the presentation in all four of these categories. What do you recommend that she say?

Evaluating the Presentation Slides

8. This presentation is not designed to stand alone. It needs a presenter. In this case, would a stand-alone presentation be a more appropriate idea? Explain your answer. Should Rachel bring handouts, brochures, or other written material to leave behind?

9. This presentation uses a consistent visual style and template. In your opinion, does it work well with this presentation? If so, why? If not, why not?

10. This presentation includes a number of bullet point slides. Are the bullets parallel? Are any slides too crowded? Are there any slides you would recommend revising?

11. This presentation includes only one data graphic: the pie chart on slide 16. Is that pie chart appropriate and easy to read? If so, what makes it effective? If not, how would you revise it?

12. Slides 9 through 13 present attractive pictures of the areas of France the tour will visit. To be effective, the pictures should be similar. All the headlines mention some food- or beverage-related term except for one. How could you revise that headline?

13. The final slide asking for questions features a picture of pastry. Assume that you'd like a picture that will help spark interesting questions. What picture(s) or text could the slide contain instead of a picture of pastry?

14. As Stephanie evaluates whether the slides will be easy to present, she considers using animation on various slides. Perhaps the bullets should come up one by one. Perhaps the pictures of the French regions should appear gradually, instead of all at once. Identify which slides, if any, would be effective if they revealed content gradually rather than all at once.

15. As a final step in reviewing, Stephanie should proofread all slides for correctness and consistency. Consider typing errors, spelling, font size, consistent punctuation, consistent heading sizes, and consistent bullet points. Do you see anything that needs to be changed?

Delivering the Presentation

16. Slides 9 through 13 include no text. Rachel will need to talk through the key points on these slides. What kinds of information should she provide when she projects these slides?

17. Rachel intends to serve regional food at this presentation. Should she serve it at the beginning of the presentation? At the end? Or as she discusses each region? What is the rationale for your answer?

Handling Questions and Answers

18. Should Rachel plan to take questions throughout the presentation or just at the end? What is the rationale for your answer?

19. What questions should Rachel anticipate? Should she address any of those questions in the presentation itself?

REVIEW QUESTIONS

1. Describe the difference between a persuasive presentation and a collaborative presentation.

2. What are two elements of "setting" that affect how you plan to present?

3. In addition to slides, what other communication tools can you use during a presentation?

4. What is the main difference between a visual aid presentation and a stand-alone presentation?

5. What are the main goals of a presentation opening?

6. Name three recognizable patterns you can use to organize a presentation.

7. Name three guidelines to follow when choosing or designing a slide template.

8. What are the advantages and disadvantages of animating bullet lists on slides?

9. What three things should you do when answering a question in a presentation?

10. What are the differences between a webinar, a webcast, and a podcast?

CRITICAL THINKING

1. Public speaking makes many people nervous. What do you think are the main reasons public speaking causes fear? What makes you nervous about making presentations? What tips in this chapter can help you feel more comfortable presenting?

2. Research has shown that public speaking ability is a key predictor of career success. Why do you think that is the case?

3. Imagine that you are presenting quarterly financial results at a meeting. You need to decide whether to present the key figures

in a handout that the audience can look at as you present, to project the key figures on slides, or do both. What are the advantages and disadvantages of each option? What would you decide?

4. Imagine that you are making a sales presentation and you brought a few examples of the product you are selling to share with the audience. You wonder whether there is any advantage to having images of the product in a slideshow presentation also. What would be the advantage of having projected images in addition to examples of the product to pass around?

5. During a presentation's question-and-answer session, it is a best practice to repeat a question to the entire audience before you answer it. Name at least three advantages you gain by repeating the question.

6. Imagine that you have a teammate who is a poor presenter. That person is required to participate in your team presentation. What are some options to ensure a valuable contribution from that presenter?

DEVELOPING YOUR COMMUNICATION SKILLS

 What do you analyze when planning a business presentation? *(pages 384–387)*

EXERCISE 1 Analyze your purpose and outcome: Why?

For each of the following scenarios, determine the purpose and intended outcome of the presentation:

a. A presentation to a group of potential customers explaining various types of investment instruments

b. A presentation to a group of potential customers explaining why they should use your company as an investment firm

c. A presentation to your supervisor explaining how to implement a process you have developed

EXERCISE 2 Analyze your audience: Who?

Select one of the following scenarios and identify a real person who could be the audience. For your chosen scenario, answer the audience analysis questions as shown in Figure 12.2 for the specific audience you identified. Be sure the audience is someone you know.

a. A professor you know well is the executive director of your school's Young Entrepreneurs Club. You and a few of your classmates have an idea for an entrepreneurial business you would like the club to fund. Funding is competitive, and this professor makes the funding decisions. Identify your entrepreneurial idea, and analyze this professor as your audience.

b. Your family members or friends are debating where to go for a group vacation. The group decided that each person with a preferred location would develop a brief presentation to persuade the others. Identify your preferred location and specific audience members, and answer the audience analysis questions as shown in Figure 12.2 for the specific audience members you identified.

c. Your business communication class is planning a fundraiser and is in the process of planning where to donate the money. Your instructor invites people who are interested in proposing a charitable organization to give a persuasive presentation in class. Using the questions in Figure 12.2, analyze your instructor and classmates as your audience.

EXERCISE 3 Analyze your message: What?

For each of the scenarios in Exercise 2, write a main message that meets the criteria for a main message listed on pages 386–387.

EXERCISE 4 Analyze your setting: Where?

Prepare a written response for each of the following scenarios:

a. Imagine you are planning to give a presentation in the same setting where you hold your business communication class or

some other specific classroom at your school. What key features of that setting should you keep in mind as you plan your presentation?

b. Imagine you are planning to give the same presentation over the Internet (via WebEx or some other technology), with each person looking at your slides on his or her own computer and listening to you via telephone. What are some key differences between this setting and the classroom setting? What will you do differently as you prepare your presentation?

c. Imagine that instead of giving your presentation live, you will be videorecording it and posting it as a video podcast on YouTube, Vimeo, or some other site for people to watch at their own convenience. What will you do differently for that setting?

d. Imagine that instead of videorecording your presentation, you will simply be posting your presentation slides for people to read. What will you do differently for that setting?

EXERCISE 5 Analyze your medium options: How?

For each of the scenarios in Exercise 2, explain which medium option(s) you would use and why. In addition, explain which medium options would not be appropriate and why.

 How do you compose the presentation? *(pages 388–407)*

EXERCISE 6 Organize the content: Planning an opening

Select one of the scenarios in Exercise 2 and plan two different openings using two of the following four techniques:

a. Cite a surprising fact or statistic.

b. Tell a relevant story or anecdote.

c. Quote an expert, someone well known, or a familiar saying.

d. Ask a question.

EXERCISE 7 Organize the content: Planning your ending

For each of the options in Exercise 1 and Exercise 2, choose one or more of the following as an appropriate ending. How would you justify your decision?

- Summarize your main message.
- Visualize the outcome for the audience.
- Ask for what you want.
- Make the next steps clear.

EXERCISE 8 Create a storyboard

Imagine that a prospective employer has asked you to submit a slide deck along with your application. In five slides, you are to demonstrate why you are the best candidate for the job. Prepare a storyboard for this slide deck. The storyboard will consist of five rectangles, each representing a slide. For each "slide," write a clear headline and sketch the content of the slide body or write notes about what you will include.

EXERCISE 9 Develop a template

a. Many websites offer downloadable PowerPoint templates. Conduct a search using the term "PowerPoint templates," and find at least one template that you believe would be appropriate for a business presentation and one that you believe is not appropriate. Be prepared to share your findings with the class.

b. Select a template that you believe is acceptable and create an alternative version of that template by changing key features on the slide master. Change the fonts, the font sizes, the shape of bullets, and the colours. Compare the two versions and write an email to your instructor explaining which you like best and why.

EXERCISE 10 Design individual slides

a. Select one slide from your storyboard in Exercise 8 and design two versions of the slide: one that uses bullets and one that does not.

b. Examine the slide below and offer three or more suggestions for improvement. Reference your suggestions with citations from this chapter.

EXERCISE 11 Evaluate your slides in a practice session

Publicly traded companies typically make their investor presentations available on their websites. These presentations are created as slides, which are often saved as PDF files. Go to the websites of the companies in the following list to find investor presentations, or search the Internet to find an investor presentation from any other company that interests you. (Hint: use a web browser and type in "Investor presentations [company name].") You may have to explore the company websites to find these presentations.

- Bank of Montreal
- Canadian Tire
- eBay
- Google
- Hudson's Bay Company (HBC)
- McDonald's
- Royal Bank of Canada
- ScotiaBank
- TD Canada Trust

Select a brief presentation of 10 to 15 slides, or select a portion of a longer presentation. Review and analyze the selected slides, answering the following questions:

a. Do the slides follow the principles of effective slide design presented in this chapter? Describe how the slides do or do not follow these principles.

b. Can you read and understand the slides as an independent document without a speaker? Why or why not?

Make sure you attach the presentation to your answers.

EXERCISE 12 Using hyperlinks in presentations [Related to the Technology feature on page 405]

Your company, Beautiful Hair, is planning to launch a new advertising campaign for its women's hair care products. Managers are considering two directions. One campaign features thin, young, glamorous models. The other features models that look like "real women." Your supervisor has asked you to research current attitudes toward portrayals of women in advertising and make a presentation recommending an approach to the marketing department. Your supervisor expects you to include images from competitive products' advertising campaigns in your presentation. She also expects you to document your research. Prepare a slide presentation supporting and explaining your recommendation. If useful, include hyperlinks to videos of competitive advertisements.

If your instructor asks you to make this presentation in class, practise in advance, working on all the delivery skills you learned in Section 12.3 of this chapter. Your instructor may ask classmates to provide you with feedback on your presentation delivery.

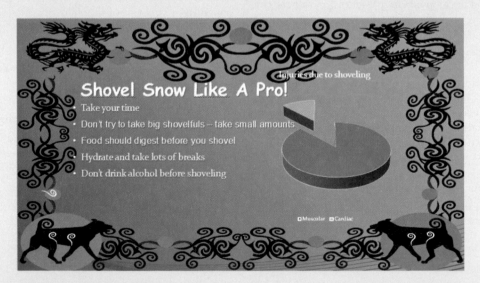

Accompanies Exercise 10

LO 12.3 **How do you deliver and evaluate the presentation?**
(pages 407–413)

EXERCISE 13 Set the stage

Think about the last slide presentation you delivered, either in a class or at your job. Explain how you used the following presentation techniques to set the stage for your presentation: practise, dress for the part, arrive early and warm up, set up all equipment and props, decide where you will stand, keep the lights on so that attention is on you, and have water available. If you did not use a technique, explain why not or whether it would have improved your presentation experience.

EXERCISE 14 Control your body

Many people are not aware of the body movements they make during a presentation. Use a webcam or video camera to record yourself making one of the impromptu presentations in Exercise 25. Play the recording and evaluate your body language, eye contact, and facial expressions. Summarize your evaluation in an email to your instructor.

EXERCISE 15 Use your voice effectively

Refer to Exercise 14. Evaluate your presentation recording based on the techniques outlined in this section. Did you speak to the back of the room? Did you speak slowly, especially at the beginning of the presentation? Did you modulate your voice and minimize verbal tics? Did you use pauses instead of *ers* and *ums*? Did you avoid upward inflection? Summarize your evaluation in an email to your instructor.

EXERCISE 16 Coordinate with your team

Think about the last team presentation you gave. In an email to your instructor, describe the context for the presentation (when, where, why, and what) and then explain how your team used the guidelines outlined in this section to coordinate your group effort. If your team did not integrate one (or more) of the guidelines, identify whether a negative result occurred.

EXERCISE 17 Avoiding plagiarism in presentation slides [Related to the Ethics feature on page 412]

Presentation slide sets are widely available on the Internet. You can find many professional presentations at slideshare.net. Alternatively, you can use your favourite search engine to search more widely for slide sets produced by people who are not professional communicators.

As directed by your instructor, prepare for a class by searching for six examples of slide sets. You should try to find:

a. three sets of slides that, in your opinion, fail some or all of the ethics criteria (see page 412)

b. three sets of slides that, in your opinion, pass most or all of the ethics criteria

Come to class prepared to discuss your choices and your reasoning with the class.

 LO 12.4 **How do you handle questions and answers?**
(pages 413–415)

EXERCISE 18 Answer questions skillfully

Imagine that Rachel Jones is giving the JourneyFree presentation (pages 422–425) discussed earlier in the chapter and she receives the following questions. Plan answers to the questions.

a. **A hostile question:** "You say the tour is only $3,000, but that is a huge amount of money for some of us. How can we afford that?"

b. **Question to which you do not know the answer:** "Where can we apply for external funding for these kinds of educational experiences?"

c. **An idea you have already rejected:** "Wouldn't Japan or China be a better location, considering the importance of those cuisines for today's cooking?"

d. **A question that gets the presentation off track:** "I'm glad you're organizing this trip to France because France is my favourite country. I've been there five times, and each time I learn something new. In fact, the last time I was there . . ."

EXERCISE 19 Meeting audience expectations [Related to the Culture feature on pages 408–409]

When you present to an audience in another culture, it is important to follow that culture's rules of business etiquette. On YouTube (or other video-sharing site), find a video about business etiquette in a country other than Canada. Show your video to the class and then facilitate a class discussion about how you would apply those etiquette principles if you were delivering a business presentation in that culture. Your instructor may ask you to do this exercise individually or as a team.

 LO 12.5 **How do you adapt your approach for online presentations?** *(pages 416–420)*

EXERCISE 20 In a live online presentation, manage the audience experience

Imagine that you are presenting the Rowland-Grey presentation (see Figure 12.17) online to Carolyn Reese, who is out of the office. Select one slide and plan how you would present that slide to her if she were viewing it on a computer in a different location.

EXERCISE 21 In a podcast, provide content that offers lasting value

Imagine that you work for JourneyFree (page 422), described earlier in the chapter, and that Rachel Jones has asked you to propose ideas for a series of audio or video podcasts that the company can produce and distribute on its website with links from JourneyFree's various social media outlets. The goal of the podcast is not to sell any products but to provide useful information that will keep people coming back to the JourneyFree sites. Develop ideas for three podcast episodes and present them persuasively in a three- to five-minute presentation with at least one visual aid.

EXERCISE 22 Evaluating your presentation delivery skills

Prepare a three-minute "icebreaker" presentation about yourself to deliver to your classmates. Focus on your life, your hobbies and interests, your job, your family, your travel, your recent reading, or any combination of these. Here are four ideas for how you can organize this presentation:

a. Chronological: Present three or four events in your life that have been important to you and made you the person you are today.

b. Topical: Provide a sample of your life, telling your audience a little bit about different topics such as your family, your education, and your hobbies.

c. Common thread: Identify a common thread that runs through several events in your life and provide examples.

d. Key event: Focus on one defining event that set your life on its current path.

If your instructor arranges for students' presentations to be videorecorded, watch the video and evaluate your presentation delivery skills based on the advice in Section 12.3. Submit to your instructor an email with your evaluation and a list of key presentation skills you will work on in the class.

EXERCISE 23 Evaluating the presentation skills of others

Evaluate the presentation skills of a business presenter based on a presentation or speech you find on the Internet. Where can you find such talks and presentations? Search YouTube, Vimeo, TED, and Talks@Google for your favourite politician, business leader, or thought leader. After you watch the presentation, write an email to your instructor answering the following questions:

a. Did the speaker read a speech or talk naturally?

b. Did the speaker use visual aids? If so, were they effective?

c. What was the speaker's main point? Summarize it in a few sentences.

d. How was the presentation organized?

e. What were the main claims of the presentation? Were the claims credible? Why or why not?

f. Do you consider this presenter to be an effective speaker? Provide evidence to support your point of view.

g. Do you have any recommendations for the presenter? Explain them.

EXERCISE 24 Distributing presentations through social media "channels"

Many businesses choose to consolidate their online presentations, slides, and podcasts on one or more dedicated social media "channels," such as a YouTube channel or a Slideshare Enterprise channel. On YouTube or SlideShare, find a social media channel of a company that interests you and review the archive of media on that channel. Choose one or two video presentations, slide decks, or podcasts, and prepare a five-minute presentation to your class. Explain how the company uses that social media channel, what kind of audio or video files are on that channel, and whether you believe these are useful and provide a positive image of the company. As part of your presentation, show a brief excerpt from one of the company's audio or video presentations.

EXERCISE 25 Impromptu speaking

In a one- to two-minute presentation, answer one of the following questions. Be sure to begin your presentation with the short version of the answer and then elaborate.

a. What advice would you give students graduating from your high school this year and planning to attend your college or university?

b. What is your ideal job when you graduate?

c. If you could travel anywhere, where would it be?

d. What is the most valuable course you have taken thus far in college or university?

e. What one change would you recommend to the president of your college or university?

Communicating Your Professional Brand: Social Media, Résumés, Cover Letters, and Interviews

LEARNING OBJECTIVES

(LO A.1) **How do you polish your professional presence for a job search?** *pages 431–437*

Examine your career goals, strengths, and skills

Define your brand message and create strategic social media content

Evaluate your virtual professional image

(LO A.2) **How do you compose effective résumés and cover letters?** *pages 437–442*

Examine your options for organizing your résumé

Compose customized résumé content

Compose persuasive cover letters

Evaluate your content and design

Create an effective follow-up method

(LO A.3) **How do you prepare for a job interview?** *pages 442–445*

Analyze how to benefit from different types of interviews

Compose good answers and good questions

Evaluate your professional appearance

Project a professional presence

Compose "thank you" messages

Introduction

Your professional presence is critical to your success during a job search. Employers will evaluate your character, your skills and abilities, your fit with the job, and your growth potential. To pass that evaluation, you need to communicate a strong **professional brand**: the image you present that makes you stand out compared with other applicants. This appendix helps you create a professional brand and communicate it through your social media presence, your résumé and cover letters, and your job interviews.

Professional brand The image you present of yourself that makes you stand out compared to other applicants.

(LO A.1) # How do you polish your professional presence for a job search?

When you are searching for a job, it is important that you project a professional presence, both online and in person. Craft your image so that employers will notice you and consider hiring you.

Examine your career goals, strengths, and skills

Analyze your goals, strengths, and skills and reflect on your most satisfying work-related activities. Key points for reflection include the following:

- Think about your participation in clubs and organizations related to your major, and your volunteer efforts for not-for-profit organizations.

ACE

Analyze

- Review your internships and summer jobs.
- Consider the factors that will make you happy in a job:
  - Do you prefer to work collaboratively or on your own?
  - Would you enjoy a creative position or a more procedural job?
  - Do you see yourself working for a large or small company? In a large or small city?
  - Do you want to start your own business to promote a new product or service?
- Target internships at specific companies where you think you'd like to work after graduation. Internships can help you and your potential employer determine if you are a good fit.
- Consider alternatives to working for a single employer, such as freelancing or entrepreneurship.

Identify your strengths and skills by creating a list like the one in **FIGURE A.1**. Analyzing your strengths and skills helps you accomplish two goals:

1. You can determine which jobs you are best qualified to pursue.
2. You can build evidence of your skills to use in your cover letters, résumés, and interviews to sell yourself to a potential employer.

Remember to update this "skill inventory" frequently to keep your list current and to help tailor your résumé to different jobs.

Compose

Brand message A statement that communicates the unique value you offer your employers.

Define your brand message and create strategic social media content

Your professional brand is established through your personal interactions, email messages, and social media content (Tom, 2014). At the core of a professional brand is a **brand message**: A statement that communicates the unique value you offer your employers.

Outline all your work experiences and create three to five bullet points that identify the specific skills you developed on the job and the specific results you achieved.

Identify areas of expertise you developed outside of work, which might come from coursework, extracurricular activities, and hobbies. Having a wide variety of talents will make you more marketable.

List your sellable qualities, which are the abilities that make you an asset to a company. Identify how, where, and to what extent you developed them.

Identify weaknesses so you can work on improving them, especially if they are often required for jobs in your field. Avoid applying for positions that require skills you do not have.

Experience:

Internship with a financial management company

- Gained problem-solving and interpersonal skills while providing personal customer service to a diverse client base
- Improved data management skills by organizing client records, inputting data, and designing reports in the client database
- Analyzed spreadsheets to create effective charts and graphs to support persuasive client presentations
- Gathered information, evaluated content, and wrote articles for a monthly newsletter that provided financial management advice to clients

Areas of Expertise:

- Programming Java applets (learned from computer class)
- Designing webpages (self-taught)

Sellable Qualities:

- Enhanced interpersonal skills through co-writing and presenting role-playing scenarios for Students Against Drunk Driving (SADD) awareness events at local high schools
- Developed leadership skills as president of the campus Business Club, and initiated two successful fundraising events, led meetings, and delegated duties
- Gained collaboration and negotiation skills working with parents and children as a youth soccer coach for four years

Weaknesses:

- Lack of experience preparing and delivering formal presentations
- Missing deadlines because of problems with time management

FIGURE A.1 How to Analyze Your Strengths and Skills

FIGURE A.2 How to Compose Your Brand Message

What should your brand message say?

- Explain who you are, what you do, what deeply interests you, and what value you offer a prospective employer.
- Stress your **unique selling proposition**: the skills or qualities that set you apart from other applicants.

> "As a new marketing and international business professional, I am passionate about bridging culture gaps that stand in the way of effective marketing. Just as products must be adapted to meet the needs of different cultures, working styles must be adjusted when working across borders. I am an enthusiastic collaborator who enjoys working with people from different cultures to better understand both market needs and different working styles."

What are you good at? Are you a marketing team player, a process improvement analyst, or a strategy alignment magician (Tom, 2014)? Note the example in **FIGURE A.2**.

Always include your brand message in your social media profiles and consider adding a tag line to your email signature block and business cards. You might also include your brand message below your contact information on your résumé or create a fact sheet as a "leave behind" at the end of an interview (Kennedy, 2014).

Don't forget to develop an **elevator pitch**! This short summary of your value to an employer will be critical to your networking success.

Create strategic social media content

You are a *social job seeker*, because you will use social media to find job opportunities, get job referrals, and learn employees' perspectives on a company (Jobvite, 2014). Employers are using social media for their own purposes:

- Ninety-four percent of employers use social media in their recruiting process (Jobvite, 2013).
- LinkedIn is the most popular social media site for employers.
- Employers use Facebook to get a feel for the personality of candidates.
- Employers use Twitter to announce jobs and to follow interesting candidates.
- Employers use a range of other outlets, such as Quora, GitHub, and Pinterest, to get a sense of candidates' expertise (Anders, 2012; Meister, 2014).
- Employers use social media to search for candidates and to evaluate candidates who apply (Doughtery, 2014).

As a result, you need to make yourself visible on social media by creating a professional social media presence and by engaging your **network**. The following sections provide advice to ensure that your social media content is both visible and valuable.

Make yourself visible and valuable

Create online content that anyone can access. Be visible and searchable: Create a blog, online résumé, e-portfolio, or video résumé, and link all your sites so employers can easily find your content (Augustine, 2014a). Ensure your content is up to date and that it effectively represents your professional brand.

If you choose to include a photo of yourself on these sites, select a head shot and ensure that any visible clothing looks like interview attire. Make sure the photo is clear and in focus. To present a consistent image, use the same photo in all of your online profiles, including your Facebook and Twitter accounts. **FIGURE A.3** outlines ways to use your Facebook, LinkedIn, and Twitter accounts during your job search.

FIGURE A.4 (page 436) identifies ways to increase your perceived value to a future employer through current and relevant social media content.

Unique selling proposition The skills or qualities that set someone or something apart from the competition.

Elevator pitch A concise statement designed to communicate the value of an idea, product, or job candidate; intrigue the audience; and initiate a deeper conversation.

Network The circle of people who are aware of your career goals and can help you learn about career opportunities.

FIGURE A.3 How to Target Specific Social Media Platforms During a Job Search

Facebook

Ensure your personal network is aware of your job search and reshape your site to communicate your professional brand and present a positive image to employers. According to employment experts, Facebook has become such a standard recruitment tool that employers who do not find a Facebook site for a candidate may assume that the candidate has something to hide (Schwabel, 2012).

Facebook page

- **Use a professional photo** of yourself as well as a cover photo that illustrates or helps define your brand.

- **Post recent activity updates** that highlight professional accomplishments. If you have attended conferences, read relevant books, or used your skills in volunteer work, make that information obvious.

- **"Like" companies that you want to work for** as well as professional groups and job sites. Interact with these sites by posting comments and asking questions.

- **Expand your connections** by sending friend requests to faculty, staff, and anyone you meet through professional contacts. Subscribe to sites of professionals who are in your desired job field.

Twitter

Use Twitter to broadcast content related to your job search, both professional information about yourself as well as content about your field of study.

Create a compelling bio:

- **Keep it short.** A Twitter bio can be no more than 166 characters.

- **Use your real name** rather than a "Twitter handle" to increase your credibility.

- **Use keywords from your brand message** to compose your bio. Think of your bio as an elevator pitch (a concise statement designed to communicate your value and initiate a deeper conversation) (Collamer, 2013).

- **Include your school's name, the year you will graduate, and any awards you have received.** Twitter is less formal than other platforms, so it's possible to add some personality and still be professional (van Bastelear, 2014).

Use Twitter as a job-search tool:

- **Subscribe to industry- or job-related lists** and participate in talks and discussions. Tweet about the topics.

- **Follow important people in your field.** Research industry leaders and follow new people each month to continuously expand your network.

- **Post updates on your job search.**

- **Retweet interesting posts** from important people in your target industry, and tweet links to interesting industry-related articles (Bortz, 2014).

Twitter bio

Shavon Alkins
@shavon-d-alkins
@CampusUniversity '15 with honors. Marketing and International business major. Obsessed with bridging cultures. Focused on tailored marketing. Craves Sriracha.

FIGURE A.3 *(continued)*

LinkedIn

Unlike Facebook, LinkedIn is primarily intended to be an interactive professional networking tool. During a job search, use LinkedIn to make yourself more visible to employers, to enlarge your network, and to complement your résumé. Your LinkedIn profile should not just copy your résumé content but expand upon it with more detailed career summary information, recommendations, and links to relevant publications and videos (Barrett-Poindexter, 2011; G. Hall, 2012).

LinkedIn profile

| Home | Profile | Contacts | Groups | Jobs | Inbox | Companies | More |

Shavon Alkins

Seeking an opportunity to help a Canadian or global company expand international markets

Saskatoon, Saskatchewan   Marketing and Advertising

Current   Sales Associate at Sears

Previous   Food Lion, Eastlawn Elementary, Campus University Language Lab

Education   Bachelor of Science (B.S.), Business Administration, Marketing, and International Business at Campus University

Improve your profile   Edit ▾   **151** connections

Summary

New marketing professional who is passionate about reaching international audiences and contributing to a creative marketing team.

I developed my interest in international work while studying abroad in the Philippines, Spain, and Italy. My passion for marketing stems from academic and work experiences—especially listening to the voice of the customer to improve marketing, sales, and customer service.

Key experiences and qualifications:

- Studied abroad in the Philippines, Spain, and Itlay
- Led student team in succesful international marketing project in the Philippines
- Returned to Manila to present at the Philippine Business Conference & Expo
- Developed deep understanding of customer needs as a sales and customer service professional
- Achieved honors in marketing at Campus University
- Speak fluent Spanish

Eager to be employed by a Canadian or global company to help expand international markets.

Experience

Sales Associate, 2015–Present
Sears Canada, Saskatoon, SK
Use interpersonal skills to greet and assist customers courteously and efficiently. Assist with cashier functions and other duties as assigned.

Cashier/Sales Associate 2014–2015
Food Lion, LLC, Saskatoon, SK
Interacted with customers, facilitated transactions, and maintained cash drawer.

Classroom Assistant, 2012–2015
Eastlawn Elementary, Saskatoon, SK
Worked with 5th grade children to develop their literacy skills and recognize word sets in English.

Language Lab Assistant, 2011–2012
Campus University, Saskatoon, SK
Prepared lab coursework activities.

Cashier/ Sales Associate, 2010–2011
Family Dollar Inc., Prince Albert, SK
Managed front-end sales and provided excellent customer service. Performed store setup tasks.

Skills & Expertise

Business Marketing   International Business   Accounting   Spanish
Leadership   Communication   Computer Skills

Education

Campus University, Saskatoon, SK
B.S., Business Administration, Marketing and International Business
2011–2015

Create a compelling profile:

- **Use a photo that presents you as a professional.** Research shows that professional recruiters who search LinkedIn spend the most time looking at a candidate's photo, education, and current job (Giang, 2012a).

- **Write a persuasive headline,** the statement that appears below your name. Tailor your headline to sell your strengths and persuade a recruiter to continue to read your profile.

- **Create a summary that serves as an advertisement** for you and sells your professional brand. Highlight your strengths and abilities.

- **Provide compelling details.** Include your education, current and past employment, and other experiences that demonstrate your professional skills. Use keywords that recruiters might search.

- **Showcase visual and written work** with links to your personal website, your YouTube channel, e-portfolios, and publications.

Take advantage of LinkedIn as a job-search tool:

- **Use LinkedIn's built-in applications** to pull feeds from your Twitter account and blog postings, and then tweet and blog about your job search and industry-related content.

- **Use LinkedIn's "People You May Know" section** to increase your network. Use the "View All" feature, and check the list each week to search for new connection possibilities.

- **Ask for recommendations** from those in your network who can write about your strengths and skills. Recommendations enhance your credibility, especially when they come from industry professionals.

- **Link to companies that you want to work for** and read their updates to stay current with information that you can use during employment interviews.

- **Participate in discussion groups** that are related to jobs or fields that interest you.

- **Update your status** weekly so people in your network are reminded about you and your job search.

FIGURE A.4 How to Highlight Your Value to Employers in Your Social Media Content

Post positive status updates	• Post about things that sell your strengths, including everything from the professional events you attend to your volunteer work. • Avoid posting negative comments or "liking" questionable content (such as inappropriate photos or offensive jokes).
Emphasize your accomplishments	• Post about your education, scholarships and awards, and your work experiences. • Include information about conferences or presentations you attend. • Comment about your volunteer work and other service-related activities.
Use *content marketing* techniques	• Provide valuable information without trying to "sell" anything. • Write about new trends in your industry to demonstrate your awareness. • Link to cutting-edge articles and comment about them. • Provide other examples that demonstrate your interest and knowledge.
Demonstrate positive work traits in your site profiles	• Demonstrate that you are organized and hardworking by organizing your site effectively and updating it with detailed posts. • Show that you are open to new ideas by posting comments about your travel, interesting articles and books, and new trends and concepts.

ACE

Evaluate

Evaluate your virtual professional image

As you develop a strategic social media presence, also consider the image you present across other communication mediums, including:

• business cards,
• email messages, and
• your telephone conversations.

Are you consistently communicating your brand message and your professionalism? Use the checklist in **FIGURE A.5** to analyze and evaluate your virtual professional image to ensure that it is polished, relevant, and current.

Review your telephone image

• **Record a professional greeting.** Be sure your recorded message clearly states your name, requests that callers leave their name and number, and assures them that you will return the call as soon as possible.
• **Evaluate your greeting.** Ensure it is clear, concise, and complete. Avoid distracting background music or cute sayings.
• **Smile when you talk.** This brightens the sound of your voice.
• **Check your voice mail messages every day.** Respond within 24 hours, if not sooner.

Review your online image

• **Clean up your social media sites** before launching a job search, and then continuously monitor them.
• **Remove unprofessional content**, such as pictures, negative comments, and other information you do not want a potential employer to see.
• **Ask your friends to remove content** about you (or at least your identification) from their social media sites if that content may be perceived as unprofessional.
• **Google yourself** and also search within social media sites to see what others can find about you online. Repeat this on a weekly basis.

FIGURE A.5 How to Evaluate Your Virtual Image

FIGURE A.5 *(continued)*

Review your email image

- Use a professionally worded personal **email address** rather than your school email account, which may be disabled a few months after you graduate. Consider the different images these email addresses communicate: "2cool4school@gmail.com" or "jon.swartz@gmail.com."
- Include a professional **email signature block** to provide your contact information. Make sure the contact information you list in your email signature block is consistent with your business card.
- Consider including a *tag line* to help sell your professional brand.

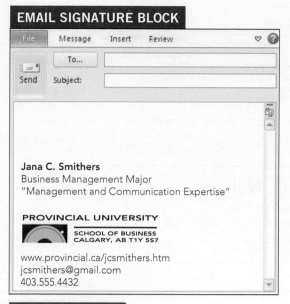

Review your business cards

- Keep the **design professional**, and list your contact information (phone number, email address, and your LinkedIn account).
- Include **URLs** if you have a web résumé, video résumé, or online portfolio to support your job search.
- List your **memberships**, especially those that relate to your degree, to enhance your professional networking possibilities.
- Consider including **bulleted skills**, highlights from your résumé, or a tag line on the back of your business card.

How do you compose effective résumés and cover letters?

LO A.2

Most employers spend only six seconds reviewing a résumé (The Ladders, 2012). Therefore, the best résumés communicate their main message quickly and clearly. Employers focus on a few critical data points:

- Your name
- Where you currently work, your start date, and your title
- Where you previously worked, your start and end date, and your title
- Your education (Giang, 2012b)

Once employers have narrowed the applicant pool, they spend much more time reviewing your details, so make sure your résumé doesn't include anything that will make it easy for the reviewer to throw it away, such as typos, bad formatting, and vague wording (Bowers, 2012).

Compose

Examine your options for organizing your résumé

The three standard ways to organize your résumé content are chronological, functional, and combined. All of them include some key features that are listed in **FIGURE A.6**.

- **Use a chronological résumé to emphasize work experience.** The **chronological résumé** is a traditional format that organizes the content sequentially, starting with

Analyze

Chronological résumé A traditional résumé style that lists content sequentially, starting with the most recent experience.

FIGURE A.6 How to Create a Chronological Résumé to Focus on Experience

> **WANTED: Head Lifeguard.** Supervise 15 guards, create schedules, oversee events, and maintain guard equipment inventory. Lifeguarding experience and certification required. Leadership and teamwork skills needed. We serve a diverse clientele, including international tourists, so global appreciation and cultural awareness a plus. Send your résumé to LakeFront Properties, 1 Lakefront Blvd., Winnipeg, MB R2C 0X9.

CHRONOLOGICAL RÉSUMÉ

Brendan G. Neilly

(204) 555-0210 | bgneilly@yahoo.com

www.linkedin.com/pub/brendan.neilly | Twitter@brendan.neilly

188 Birch Road Winnipeg MB R2C 8H3

OBJECTIVE

To provide effective leadership and model exceptional safety and customer service skills in the position of head lifeguard for Lakefront Properties.

EDUCATION

Bachelor of Science in Business Administration, May 2018

Concentration in Finance, Minor in Economics, GPA: 3.6

University of Manitoba

EXPERIENCE

Lifeguard

LakeFront Properties, Winnipeg, MB June–August 2015

- Fulfilled professional lifeguarding duties while maintaining an environment conducive to teamwork and safety
- Supervised weekly drills and assessments
- Communicated effectively with co-workers and diverse clientele

Sales Representative

Banana Republic, Winnipeg, MB, May 2011–May 2014

- Offered exceptional customer service as a shoe and accessory salesperson
- Processed financial transactions, including sales and returns

Shaw's Supermarket, Brandon, MB, November 2012–April 2013

- Greeted customers, bagged groceries, and maintained orderly working environment

SKILLS, ABILITIES, AND CERTIFICATIONS

- Lifeguard Management Certification, Canadian Red Cross, January 2016
- Waterfront Lifeguard Certification, Canadian Red Cross, May 2015
- Professional Rescuer CPR and First Aid Certification, YMCA, March 2015
- Leadership skills (cross-country captain, religious education instructor)
- Teamwork skills (intramural sports, group projects, Habitat for Humanity)
- Microsoft Word, Excel, PowerPoint; Internet research skills

EXTRACURRICULAR CLUBS AND ACTIVITIES

- Captain, University of Manitoba Water Polo Team, 2015–Present
- Habitat for Humanity, 2013–2015

SUMMER FOREIGN EXCHANGE PROGRAM

France, lived with an exchange family and was immersed in French culture, Summer 2014

For all résumés:

Select keywords from job advertisements and use them to describe your skills or your job duties. If your résumé doesn't include the right keywords, it will likely be one of the many résumés that are thrown away (Fertig, 2013).

Keep your résumé to one page if you are just starting your career.

Avoid copying résumé templates. You don't want your résumé to look like everyone else's.

Use contemporary fonts (Arial, Verdana, or Calibri) that are professional and easy to read.

Align content with tabs, not spaces, to ensure neatness

List one email address you are using for your job search and a phone number that has a professional voice mail greeting.

Include links to your professional social media sites, assuming they include professional content.

Compose a concise objective statement (if you choose to use one) that relates to the position you are applying for and outlines what you can do for the employer.

For chronological résumés:

List education near the top of your résumé.

List work experience in chronological order, beginning with the most recent position. Include internships even if they were volunteer jobs (K. R. Lewis, 2011).

List honours, awards, or scholarships if you didn't list them with your education.

Identify your skills below your work experience, with the most relevant qualifications for the position at the top of the list. Include additional skills that relate to the job rather than repeating skills listed under work experience.

Create a separate page of professional references that you can provide when it is requested, rather than including them on the résumé. Create the page with the same header as on your résumé. For each reference, list the name, company, title, and complete contact information. Be sure to ask your references for permission to list them (Olson, 2012).

the most recent and working backward. It highlights education and work experience as the applicant's primary assets.

- **Use a functional résumé to emphasize skills.** The **functional résumé** emphasizes the skills that qualify you for the position. This format is appropriate for applicants who have limited work experience related to the position, for example, students who are pursuing internships or professional positions immediately after graduation and who have no related work experience. Check out the example on **MyBCommLab** to see the résumé that Brendan Neilly designed to apply for a different summer job, an internship in financial management.

- **Use a combined résumé to balance experience and skills.** The **combined résumé** highlights the strengths of applicants who have both relevant experience and skills. This format is most appropriate for applicants who have worked in positions closely related to the one they are applying for and who also want to emphasize the advanced skill sets required for the new position. For example, assume Shavon Alkins is applying for a senior sales associate position. Shavon's résumé, shown on **MyBCommLab**, demonstrates a balance of skills and experience by highlighting the required skills listed in the job posting (leadership, communication, and computer skills) and also documenting sales experience with several companies.

Compose customized résumé content

Customize the content for the specific job you are seeking. The chronological résumé illustrated in Figure A.6 identifies design and content guidelines that apply to all résumés. Content guidelines for functional and combination résumés are provided on **MyBCommLab**.

Compose

Create plain-text versions of your résumé that you can use to cut and paste content into web-based databases, called *applicant tracking systems*, which companies often use to search and sort candidates' information. Check out the advice on **MyBCommLab** on how to create a plain-text version of your résumé.

A few specific sections of résumés are particularly challenging to compose. These include objective statements, work experience, and relevant skills:

- **Use an objective statement** to show how your goals can help an employer.
  - *To secure a challenging financial management position that requires strong analytical, interpersonal, and communication skills to help investors achieve their financial goals.*

- **Use a qualifications summary** if you have strengths and skills that qualify you for the job but little, if any, related work experience.
  - *Financial management major with experience*
    - *Analyzing detailed income and profit/loss statements*
    - *Explaining complicated tax requirements to clients*
    - *Managing Microsoft Dynamics, Quicken, and ERP application systems*

For advice about how to write these sections, look at the targeted recommendations in **FIGURE A.7**.

Compose persuasive cover letters

For each position you apply for, you need a customized **cover letter**, which is a persuasive message that highlights your relevant skills and persuades an employer to spend time reviewing your résumé. A cover letter typically introduces you and your résumé, specifies the position you are applying for, highlights your qualifications for that position, and requests an interview. A cover letter can take the form of a formal business letter, or it can be an email if you are submitting your résumé electronically. A cover letter allows you to do the following:

- Highlight the knowledge and experience that are most important to this position
- Direct the employer to pay attention to the key elements of your résumé
- Speak directly to an employer about your fit with the company
- Set yourself apart from the competition by conveying your professional personality and demonstrating your writing skills

Functional résumé A contemporary résumé style that emphasizes categories of skills rather than job experience.

Combined résumé A résumé style that takes advantage of both the chronological and functional methods of organizing content by highlighting work experience by date and skill sets by category.

Cover letter A persuasive letter or email sent to a prospective employer along with a résumé that "sells" your résumé to the employer.

FIGURE A.7 How to Compose Effective Work Experience and Skills and Abilities Sections

Work Experience

INEFFECTIVE	EFFECTIVE
• Responsible for the night crew at Arby's	• Supervised an eight-person night crew • Handled all customer and worker complaints
• Experience with general office duties	• Typed and filed confidential correspondence • Formatted flyers, brochures, and newsletters
• Worked as a packager on an assembly line	• Learned the value of precision and teamwork while working as a packager on a fast-paced assembly line • Received Employee-of-the-Month Award during first year
• Developed excellent communication skills	• Wrote a comprehensive policy and procedures manual for new interns
• Effective team player	• Collaborated on a successful client proposal, working with personnel from product design, marketing, and manufacturing
• Detail oriented	• Developed monthly and yearly sales and budget forecasts

Be specific about capabilities. Avoid vague, generic phrases.

Don't exaggerate your capabilities. If you include honesty as part of your brand, then inflating your capabilities would quickly damage that brand image.

Begin each item with an action verb, never with the personal pronoun "I," which would be repetitive.

Be consistent with verb tenses within each job you list. Use present tense verbs for current jobs and past tense verbs for previous jobs.

Skills and Abilities: Find and Use Keywords from Job Posting

Manager Needed

Sparrow Associates, a leading management consulting company in the Halifax area, seeks an enthusiastic and professional office manager to join our team. Effective collaboration is a must. Technical competencies in Microsoft Office software required. Analytical skills, especially as related to budget data, are highly valued. Online applications accepted through June 15 only at www.Sparrow.Associates.com.

Relevant Skills

Collaboration
• Participated in several committees and fundraising initiatives as an active member and treasurer of Young Acadians, a campus-based student organization

Technical Competence
• Skilled in Microsoft Office (Word, Excel, PowerPoint, and Outlook)
• Proficient in Microsoft Access and Adobe Dreamweaver

Analytical Skills
• Analyzed operating budget of a local not-for-profit organization and made recommendations for achieving cost savings and modifying a store's product line as part of a 60-hour service-learning requirement for a managerial accounting course

Analyze the position requirements

An effective cover letter will be tailored to meet the employer's needs by describing how you are qualified for the specific position. To determine how to customize your cover letter, use the words in the job posting or advertisement as you describe your experience, skills, and background. Indicate how you exemplify these traits or characteristics by describing how you gained the experience or mastered the skills.

Be persuasive

Recall the **AIDA** pattern (**A**ttention, **I**nterest, **D**esire, and **A**ction) to create or increase sales. You can use AIDA in your cover letter as well to sell yourself to an employer. For examples of both solicited and unsolicited cover letters, see **MyBCommLab**. The following guidelines (**FIGURE A.8**) will help you compose persuasive cover letters.

FIGURE A.8 How to Write a Solicited Cover Letter

To take advantage of the AIDA pattern, follow these steps for a solicited cover letter:

- Gain **attention** in the first paragraph by expressing a long-term interest in and knowledge about the company that goes beyond the information in the job advertisement.

- Build **interest/desire** by relating education and experience to the job requirements using keywords, but don't exaggerate your abilities. Provide examples that demonstrate skills.

- Motivate **action** by expressing enthusiasm, requesting an interview, including contact information, and mentioning a benefit to the employer.

To take advantage of the AIDA pattern, follow these steps for an unsolicited cover letter:

- Gain **attention** by including any or all of the following content: addressing the letter to a specific person, stating the purpose of the message, mentioning a mutual contact, and indicating a specific reason for interest in this company.

- Build **interest/desire** by demonstrating knowledge about the company and highlighting experience that relates to the company's focus.

- Also build **interest/desire** by highlighting your education and relating your coursework to skills and company needs.

- Motivate **action** by asking the recipient to contact you, even if no job openings exist. Express an interest in future job openings.

Evaluate your content and design

Before submitting your application materials to a potential employer, be sure you have someone who is not familiar with your school or work experience review your content to ensure clarity. Review the checklists in **MyBCommLab** to evaluate your résumés and cover letters to ensure that they communicate a professional image.

ACE

Evaluate

Create an effective follow-up method

If you have not heard from an employer 10 days after the application submission deadline, you can contact the employer to inquire about the status of your application. Follow up by phone or email, whichever medium you believe the employer would prefer, and use the opportunity to further sell your fit for the job. Here is an outline for an effective follow-up message:

- **Address the hiring manager** or contact person by name.
- **Indicate the position you applied for** and when you sent your résumé.
- **Briefly identify your knowledge of the company** and your interest in a long-term career with the company.
- **Ask if additional information is required.**
- **Request an interview** and provide your contact information.
- **Close on a positive,** forward-looking note.

How do you prepare for a job interview?

A job interview is a mutual learning experience. The employer will learn more about you to determine whether you are a good fit for the job, and you will learn more about the company and the position to determine whether the job is a good fit for you. You may get only one opportunity to persuade an employer that you are the best applicant, so it is important to develop professional interview skills.

Analyze

Analyze how to benefit from different types of interviews

Although traditional one-on-one interviews are still common, you may participate in several different kinds of interviews. For example, a company may ask you to participate in a campus interview or **virtual interview** before inviting you to visit the company. Once there, you may be involved in a one-on-one interview or a **panel interview** before meeting with a hiring manager. Each of these interview formats has a different goal, and **FIGURE A.9** outlines ways to maximize your benefit from each one.

Compose

Compose good answers and good questions

Interviewers use standard questions to help them learn about a candidate and assess that person's suitability for a job. As part of your interview preparation, develop clear, concise answers to these questions, along with details that allow you to elaborate on your strengths and sell your professional brand. Rather than bringing scripted responses with you, practise beforehand (and aloud) so your answers sound natural. A list of standard questions and suggested answer preparation found on **MyBCommLab** will help you respond.

You should also be prepared to address **behavioural question**, which are designed to determine how you would make decisions, solve problems, or respond to stressful situations (Resource Personnel Consultants, 2012). Your answers to these questions should demonstrate your collaborative skills, innovative thinking, and leadership abilities. One well-established method of responding to behavioural questions is to use the **STAR method**, which stands for Situation, Task, Action, and Result (Llarena, 2012). Develop a story that identifies a *situation* in which you completed a *task* (such as solving a problem or making a decision) by implementing a specific *action* that ended in a positive *result*. Research suggests that problem-solving stories are a powerful way to communicate competence (Blazkova, 2011). Here is an example of how STAR is used:

Question: Tell me about a time when you worked successfully under pressure.

Answer: (Start with the **situation**.) Last semester, I worked on a market research project for a small business near the university. Our team had difficulty

Virtual interview An interview conducted by telephone, Skype, or teleconference call, often used to narrow the candidate pool before scheduling an onsite visit.

Panel interview An interview format that involves several people, such as a search committee, who gather in a conference or seminar room with a job applicant to discuss the position.

Behavioural question A type of interview question designed to determine how you would make decisions, solve problems, or respond to stressful situations.

STAR method A method of answering a behavioural interview question by explaining a situation, task, and action that led to a positive result.

FIGURE A.9 How to Get the Most Benefit from Different Types of Interviews

For all interview formats	• Review the websites of the companies you want to meet with ahead of time so you are knowledgeable about their products or services, mission statements, and open positions. • Dress professionally, even if the job you are applying for is not an "office" position. • Adopt a confident and professional attitude. Be slightly more formal than you normally are. • Make a strong professional first impression by using a firm handshake, making eye contact, and smiling (practise greeting people ahead of time to feel confident about your body language). • Demonstrate your knowledge and interest in the company. • Speak clearly and at a normal pace. • Pause before speaking to gather your thoughts, then breathe deeply, articulate your words, and smile, even if you are on the telephone. • Ask for a business card and make notes on the back of the card to help you remember the interviewer who gave it to you. • Thank interviewers for taking the time to speak with you.
Virtual interviews: *Conducted by telephone or webcam to filter candidates before scheduling onsite interviews*	• Make or receive the call in a quiet location where you will not be disturbed. Remind anyone who might come into the room not to make any noise or distractions. Ideally, you should be near a writing surface with a pen and paper handy to write down names and other information you will need to recall quickly. • Begin the call professionally by identifying yourself before you ask for the person you're calling. • Write down the interviewers' names and job titles as they introduce themselves. If they don't provide their job titles, ask for them so you can ask specific questions that relate to people's positions. • Feel free to ask people to repeat or reword a question if you did not hear them clearly or are not sure what they are asking you. • Smile to brighten the tone of your voice. • Let the interviewer hang up first, both as a professional courtesy and to ensure that the interviewer has no final questions.
One-on-one interviews	• Establish that you have a natural fit with the organization and this person. • Ask questions about the supervisor's expectations, the challenges of the position, and daily activities expected in the position.
Panel interviews: *Several interviewers talking with one applicant*	• Take the initiative to approach each person and introduce yourself as you extend your arm to shake hands. • Begin your responses by first looking at the person who asked the question, make eye contact with the rest of the panel during your response, and conclude your answer by returning your eyes to the questioner. • When the interview concludes, thank each person for taking the time to meet with you.

collecting data. By the time we had collected it all, we had only one week to complete the project. (Describe the **task**.) In that one week, we needed to analyze all the data, develop a justified set of recommendations, and write a complete report for the client. (Describe the **action** you took.) Although I originally did not have a leadership role on the team, I took the lead and developed a work plan that delegated the work, set deadlines, and ensured that all the analysis was double checked by another member of the team. I also facilitated the team meeting when we developed recommendations. (Describe the **result**.) In the end, we not only completed our report on time, but our client agreed with our analysis and decided to implement three of our four recommendations.

Interviewers commonly ask candidates if they have any questions. Therefore, you must also be prepared to ask thoughtful questions. Not having good questions to ask is a common and detrimental interview mistake, according to employment specialists (Augustine, 2014b). Always ask three or four well-researched questions to demonstrate your interest in the job. Avoid asking questions that you could have easily researched on your own. For example, asking where the company's headquarters is located or how many employees they have tells the interviewer that you did not do your research. **DO NOT** ask questions that are more relevant once you have been offered a position. For example, asking any questions about benefits such as health insurance or perks such as travel will not impress the interviewers.

FIGURE A.10 provides some general questions that may be helpful to ask all potential employers. Toward the end of the interview, be sure to ask about the next steps (Green, 2012).

FIGURE A.10 Sample Questions to Ask during the Interview

Questions you can ask about the company:

1. The mission statement indicates that your goal is to . . . How does this organization fulfill this goal at an operational level on a day-to-day basis?
2. What are the company's plans for long-term growth? (only relevant to for-profit enterprises)
3. Can you tell me about the typical career paths for people in the position for which I'm interviewing?
4. What advice do you wish you'd received when you were starting here?

Questions you can ask about the position:

1. What is a typical day like in this job?
2. What are the greatest challenges of this position?
3. How would I be evaluated in this position, and by whom?
4. Who last had this position, and is he or she available if I have questions once I start the job?
5. Who would I be working most closely with on a daily basis?
6. When do you expect to make a hiring decision?

Prepare for virtual interviews

Employers are increasingly taking advantage of virtual meeting technologies to conduct virtual interviews with job candidates. The richer video interface offers employers a better chance to get a sense of their candidates (Blue, 2012). Here are some tips to ensure you present a professional image in a virtual interview (Backes, 2012; Stillman, 2011; Swanson, 2013):

- **Select a professional background.** What the interviewer sees behind you can be as important as what you are wearing. If possible, use a business office or a conference room. If you don't have access to a professional environment, position yourself in front of a neatly organized bookshelf or desk. Blank walls provide no visual interest, and busy backgrounds may be too distracting.

- **Use good lighting.** Choose natural light over fluorescent lights, which cast shadows or overilluminate your face. Your computer should be between you and a sunny window or table lamp so the interviewer can see you without shadows or glare.

- **Look at the camera, not the computer.** In a face-to-face interview, eye contact is important to make a positive impression. Eye contact is equally important in a virtual interview that includes video. Although looking at the interviewer's face on your computer monitor may seem like you're making good eye contact, you actually need to look at your camera lens to appear to be looking directly at the interviewer.

- **Ensure a good connection and equipment.** If possible, use a wired Internet connection on a computer that is fully charged or plugged into an electrical source. The combination of voice and video transmissions can significantly reduce your computer's resources. You don't want to lose your connection halfway through your interview.

- **Invest in and use a good-quality camera and microphone.** Any improvement you can gain in terms of sound and video quality will help you make a good impression.

- **Use good body language and "active listening" cues.** Studies show that it is more difficult to appear "likeable" on screen than it is in person (Sears, Zhang, Wisner, Hackett, & Yuan, 2013; Shellenbarger, 2014). Therefore, it is even more important that you sit up straight, smile, and lean in toward the computer and look engaged in the conversation. Sit at a comfortable distance so the interviewer can see more than your head, and use normal gestures. Make "active listening" noises such as "hmm" and "right" to demonstrate your attentiveness to the speaker. Remember to smile.

- **Practise.** Test your background, lighting, eye contact, and connection quality with friends and family to ensure you are presenting a professional image. Ask for feedback about your interview attire, the tone and volume of your voice, and any distracting background sights or sounds.

Evaluate your professional appearance

As part of your planning for an interview, evaluate your appearance and consider how best to project professionalism. You do not need to spend a fortune on new clothing, but you do need at least one good interview outfit and appropriate accessories.

Employers cite dressing inappropriately as one of the biggest mistakes job applicants make in interviews (J. Smith, 2013). Unsuccessful applicants dress much too casually, wearing street clothes such as jeans, low-slung pants, short skirts, gym shoes, or sandals. When dressing for interviews, follow one key rule: Even if you are interviewing in a more casual workplace, wear business formal attire to the interview. If you need more detailed information on the variations between business casual and business formal attire, check out **MyBCommLab**.

Wear a well-pressed professional business suit (jacket with matching slacks or skirt) in a conservative colour. To complete your professional look, be conservative in your grooming and makeup, bring a portfolio or business case, wear a watch, and turn off your cellphone. Your goal at an interview is not to express your personality through clothing and accessories but to *dress in a way that allows people to focus on what you say.*

Project a professional presence

Your goal during the interview is to be your best self and make a strong, positive impression. To achieve this goal, you need to act like a professional from the moment you arrive until the end of the interview, including during meals. If you need some detailed guidance on behaviour and etiquette during business meals and other special events, check out **MyBCommLab**.

You get just one shot at a first impression, and research suggests that employers may form their opinion of you within the first few seconds of meeting you (Smith, 2012). Body language and eye contact are strong influencers (Goman, 2012), but it is equally important to act like you are ready to be in the workplace. Starting from when you walk in the door, your professional presence can make a strong, positive, and lasting impression.

Arrive early.

- Know how long it will take you to get to the interview location. Research parking areas if you are driving. Know how long it will take to walk from the transit stop to the location. If you are concerned, check out the location one or two days ahead of time.
- Be ready and waiting in the reception area about 10 minutes before the interview time. Use the restroom before the interview begins.

Look ready to work

- Carry a pad of paper and nice pen. Do not try to take notes on a keyboard/tablet unless you can do so effectively with a stylus.
- Bring copies of your résumé printed on good paper.
- Have business cards handy with your name, email address, and phone number.
- Bring several copies of your list of references with complete contact information.
- Bring personal notes or website printouts about the company and the job for your reference.
- Bring a list of questions you plan to ask the interviewer.
- Ensure you have necessary personal items, such as tissues or bottled water.

Greet people professionally.

- Use people's names when you meet them.
- Use people's last names until they ask you to use their first names.
- Shake hands with everyone you meet, and practise your handshake ahead of time to ensure a firm, solid grip.

Treat support staff with courtesy and respect.

- Be polite and respectful to everyone you meet during your interview experience, including the receptionist who asks you to wait in an outer office and the assistant who offers you a cup of coffee.

Compose

Compose "thank you" messages

Within 24 hours of an interview, send a thank you message to offer your sincere gratitude for the time people took out of their busy schedules to meet with you (Quast, 2013; Slavina, 2013). Your thank you messages should reflect your conversations with the recipient and stress one or two key points: things you forgot to mention during the interview or points you want to highlight. Your thank you note may take the form of an email, a letter, or a handwritten note. Email provides a quick method of delivering your gratitude but is a casual method of communication. Typed business letters may seem more "official," but handwritten thank you notes may be the most effective medium for saying "thank you." From both professional and personal perspectives, people view a handwritten message as a sincere gesture that speaks volumes about your character and indicates a personal interest in the company or relationship. Here are some guidelines for writing thank you messages:

- **Keep the message short.** Just one or two short paragraphs is sufficient. Begin with a thank you followed immediately by the date of the interview and position.
- **Personalize the message** by mentioning something discussed during the interview, and emphasize a personal strength that contributes to the company.
- **Conclude with a positive, forward-looking statement** that encourages a response and includes contact information.

KEY TERMS

behavioural questions
  p. 442
brand message p. 432
chronological résumé p. 437

combined résumé p. 439
cover letter p. 439
elevator pitch p. 433
functional résumé p. 439

network p. 433
panel interview p. 442
professional brand p. 431
STAR method p. 442

unique selling proposition
  p. 433
virtual interview p. 442

Questions to Ask about Key Communications Technologies

For the purposes of this summary, *all* possible types of communications technology have been included: social media, software, web services, and mobile applications. This allows a comprehensive comparison of features and attributes. In all but a few cases, tools have been generically identified. This is not possible in the case of a few social media tools that have become so popular that they need to be identified specifically:

- Facebook
- Google
- LinkedIn
- Twitter
- YouTube

The most common technology tools have been categorized into three broad types:

- **Distribution tools:** for sharing information, either 1:1 or 1:many
- **Networking tools:** for discussing issues or expanding your business connections
- **Collaboration tools:** for virtual team work and productivity

Brief Explanation of the Questions Posed:

- **What resources do I need?** This question examines what resources are required beyond the use of an updated browser.
- **Is shared information searchable?** This question explores how publicly available posted or shared information may be.
- **Can I limit access?** This question examines how much control a user has over audience access.
- **Can shared information be easily reshared?** All digital information is sharable. If information within a specific tool can be reposted or shared with one or two clicks, then this information is "easily" reshared. The ease of sharing affects the size and scope of secondary distribution.
- **Is this tool synchronous or asynchronous?** An asynchronous tool allows users to collaborate or share without the need or expectation that the users are online at exactly the same time. A synchronous tool depends on participating users to be online and available at the same time.
- **Is there a monetary cost?** This question explores the typical monetary cost. Typically, tools that do not have a monetary cost will collect and sell the data gathered through the use of the tool to third parties. The implications of this business model are reviewed in Chapter 5.

KEY TECHNOLOGY TOOLS/TOOL TYPES

NAME/TYPE OF TOOL	POSSIBLE USES	WHAT RESOURCES DO I NEED?	IS SHARED INFORMATION SEARCHABLE?	CAN I LIMIT ACCESS?	CAN SHARED INFORMATION BE EASILY RESHARED?	IS THIS TOOL SYNCHRONOUS OR ASYNCHRONOUS?	IS THERE A MONETARY COST?
Blogs	**Distribution** of information, opinions, files, and/or graphics to a wide audience (e.g., training, product education and specifications, thought leadership)	An account with a blog host such as WordPress, Blogger, or Tumblr	Yes Comments made to blog posts are also searchable	Some platforms, like WordPress, allow posts to be password protected	Yes	Asynchronous	For most basic blog sites, no
Cloud Storage Tools (e.g., Dropbox, OneDrive, iCloud, Google Drive)	**Distribution** and storage of files to be shared with a limited audience **Collaboration** via shared files for editing	A user account Often a mobile app can be used	No	Yes. You can choose to share specific files or folders only with specific people	No	Asynchronous	A basic account is usually free Accounts with more storage come at a cost
Discussion Forums	**Distribution** of information/opinions to a wide or a limited audience (e.g., product education and customer service)	To post, you need an account with the specific discussion forum.	Usually searchable, depending on administrator settings	If you host a discussion forum, you can limit access to those with approved credentials	No	Asynchronous	Usually free to host or post
Email	**Distribution** of information, files, and/or graphics to a wide or a limited audience **Collaboration** by exchange of materials directly with recipients	An account with an email host, such as Gmail, Yahoo, or similar Most companies provide an email account to employees. Some such accounts require Outlook or similar email "client" software	Not publicly searchable Most email interfaces allow you to search your own received and sent messages	Yes. Emails are directed to specific recipients No. There is no way to control or monitor the size or scope of the secondary audience. Email can be easily forwarded, edited, copied, and shared without the original sender's knowledge	Yes	Asynchronous	Usually free or part of a web hosting account

(continued)

KEY TECHNOLOGY TOOLS/TOOL TYPES

NAME/TYPE OF TOOL	POSSIBLE USES	WHAT RESOURCES DO I NEED?	IS SHARED INFORMATION SEARCHABLE?	CAN I LIMIT ACCESS?	CAN SHARED INFORMATION BE EASILY RESHARED?	IS THIS TOOL SYNCHRONOUS OR ASYNCHRONOUS?	IS THERE A MONETARY COST?
Facebook	**Distribution** of current events (personal, professional, public) and/or graphics to a wide or a limited audience **Networking** possible by connecting with appropriate contacts **Collaboration** possible with near-synchronous exchange of messages directly with recipients	A Facebook account	This depends on each account's privacy settings and on Facebook's current sharing policies Most information posted is more searchable than users realize	To an extent This depends on each account's privacy settings and Facebook's current privacy policies	Yes	Adding items to the newsfeed is asynchronous Facebook Messenger has been redesigned to operate as more of a synchronous chat interface	It is free to use Advertising and data access come at a cost
Google Docs	**Collaboration** possible by "live" document editing directly within the application	A Google account	No	Yes	No	Asynchronous	Free
Instant Messaging (IM)	**Collaboration** possible with near-synchronous exchange of messages directly with recipients	To connect, each device needs the same instant messaging platform installed (e.g., Skype, WhatsApp, or similar)	No	Yes	No	Can be synchronous or asynchronous	Most basic IM apps are free
LinkedIn	**Distribution** of current events (personal, professional), opinion posts, and/or announcements to a limited audience **Networking** possible by connecting with appropriate contacts	A LinkedIn account	Names are searchable Profiles cannot be viewed without permission via a "connection"	Yes, by refusing a connection request	Yes	Asynchronous	A basic account is free Additional features come with a cost
Note-Sharing Applications (e.g., Evernote, OneNote)	**Collaboration** with virtual team members via chat, note, and document sharing/editing **Collaboration** with self by making notes, files, and materials available across platforms and devices	A user account Often a mobile app can be used	No	Yes	No	Asynchronous	Free

(continued)

KEY TECHNOLOGY TOOLS/TOOL TYPES

NAME/TYPE OF TOOL	POSSIBLE USES	WHAT RESOURCES DO I NEED?	IS SHARED INFORMATION SEARCHABLE?	CAN I LIMIT ACCESS?	CAN SHARED INFORMATION BE EASILY RESHARED?	IS THIS TOOL SYNCHRONOUS OR ASYNCHRONOUS?	IS THERE A MONETARY COST?
Twitter	**Distribution** of links and announcements (current events, personal, professional) and/or graphics to a wide audience **Networking** possible by connecting with others via common hashtag use	A Twitter account	Yes	No	Yes	Asynchronous	Free
Texting (SMS)	**Collaboration** possible with near-synchronous exchange of messages directly with recipients	Basic texting is native to most mobile devices Additional applications can add additional features (e.g., WhatsApp, Voxer, Viber, and similar)	No	Yes	No	Asynchronous	Depends on phone/usage plan
Videoconferencing/Online Meetings	**Collaboration** possible with audio, video, presentation, screen-sharing, and chat features in real time with two or more participants.	Requires specific software such as WebEx, GoToMeeting, Skype, Adobe Connect, or similar Requires consistent Internet bandwidth between all connected parties	No	Yes	No	Synchronous	Consumer-grade software is free for basic usage. Offers limited features and limited reliability More robust systems can be more expensive but offer more features and upgraded reliability
Voice over Internet Protocol (VoIP)	**Collaboration** possible with audio discussions in real time directly with single or multiple recipients	Requires specific software such as Skype, Viber, or similar Requires consistent Internet bandwidth between all connected parties	No	Yes	No	Synchronous	Most software is free for basic usage

(continued)

KEY TECHNOLOGY TOOLS/TOOL TYPES

NAME/TYPE OF TOOL	POSSIBLE USES	WHAT RESOURCES DO I NEED?	IS SHARED INFORMATION SEARCHABLE?	CAN I LIMIT ACCESS?	CAN SHARED INFORMATION BE EASILY RESHARED?	IS THIS TOOL SYNCHRONOUS OR ASYNCHRONOUS?	IS THERE A MONETARY COST?
Web Chat	**Distribution** of information to a single recipient (e.g., product education, service responses, or customer service)	To offer this service on a hosted website, special server-based software is required To use this service as a customer, no special software is required	No	Chat is limited to the service provider and the user/customer	No	Synchronous	The server-based software may not be free It is free to interface via web chat as a user/customer
Webinar	**Distribution** of information to a mass audience	Similar to requirements for videoconferencing	Depends on settings when a recording or archive is posted online.	Yes, it can be by registration only	Yes, by sharing a link to a webinar archive	Live event: Synchronous Archive: Asynchronous	Similar to videoconferencing
Wikis	**Collaboration** with virtual team members in a common shared space, allowing for discussions and document sharing	An account with a Wiki host such as PBworks, Wikia, or similar	Depends on access settings	Yes A Wiki can be set up to allow only specific people to participate	No	Asynchronous	Some hosting sites are free with advertising Some have a cost and no advertising
YouTube	**Distribution** of video (personal, professional) to a wide or a limited audience	A YouTube account Video files can be difficult to upload and stream if bandwidth is limited	Yes	Yes	Yes Access is dependent on privacy settings per video upload	Asynchronous	Free

Formats for Business Documents

Using standard formatting guidelines for basic business documents will help you ensure your written communications project a professional image. This appendix provides advice and annotated examples you can use to help you format your email messages and letters. See Chapter 11 for more complete report formatting directions.

If your instructor or employer requests formats that are different from the samples provided, keep in mind that your goal should always be to ensure a professional-looking document that effectively communicates your purpose.

EMAIL MESSAGES

Follow email formatting guidelines to ensure you include all the elements needed in business emails and that your content is easy to read on a computer or handheld device.

Email formatting guidelines

A professional business email message includes the following elements:

- **Email addresses.** When composing an email message, place the recipient's email address on the "To" line. If you want to send the same message to several recipients, separate their email addresses with commas. If you want to send a courtesy copy ("cc") to a secondary audience, add their email addresses on the "cc" line. The "bcc" line is for "blind courtesy copy" and is used to send a copy of the message to people without communicating that fact to the "To" and "cc" recipients.

- **Subject line.** Always include a short and meaningful subject line. The best subject lines clearly communicate the purpose of your message. For example, "Sales Meeting" is not a meaningful subject line for an email. The recipients would have to open your message to know whether you are trying to schedule a sales meeting or are following up after a meeting. If you are sending meeting minutes requiring no response, your subject line might be "Sales Meeting Minutes," which would indicate that the message is not urgent and recipients can read it when they have time. However, if you are trying to schedule a meeting and need their quick response, your subject line might be "Need Input for Meeting Date ASAP," which would prompt recipients to read the message right away.

- **Salutation.** The salutation or greeting addresses the message to the primary audience. How the message begins sets the tone for the rest of the document. Formal business emails frequently use "Dear" in the salutation, such as "Dear Mr. Smith." However, contemporary business writers are moving away from the traditional use of "Dear," especially in informal emails, often choosing instead to use a salutation such as "Hi, John" or "Hello, Mr. Smith." In some cases, you might simply use the person's name without any salutation, although some audiences may consider it rude to omit a salutation.

  Different salutations require different punctuation. In a formal email, a salutation like "Dear Mr. Smith:" ends with a colon. There is no other punctuation. In the less formal salutation, "Hello, John," a comma separates the greeting from the name, and the salutation ends with a colon or a comma. It is also common to see salutations formatted with *open punctuation,* which means neither the salutation nor the complimentary closing includes punctuation.

- **Name.** Whether you use a person's first or last name in the salutation depends on how you address the individual in face-to-face settings. If your boss has asked you to call him "John," address your email to him as "John" rather than "Mr. Smith." However, when emailing new clients or customers for the first time, do not assume they want you to use their first names. Practise better business etiquette by erring on the side of formality. Similarly, do not assume that a woman is a "Mrs." unless you know your recipient prefers "Mrs." It is better to use "Ms." or a professional title such as "Dr." or "Rev." when applicable.

- **Paragraphs.** Short email messages may include just a few lines of text. Longer messages should use effective paragraphing techniques to organize the content logically:

  - Keep the first paragraph short (50 words or less) and get to the point of the message. Imagine that your audience is reading the message on a smartphone or other handheld device. Make sure the main idea shows on the first screen so the reader doesn't have to scroll to find it. Do not begin with "This email is about . . ." Your subject line tells the recipient the topic of the email.

  - Begin the middle paragraph(s) with a topic sentence that identifies the main point of the paragraph. Keep the middle paragraphs relatively short: Average paragraphs are roughly 100 words in length.

  - End the message with a short paragraph requesting any action, indicating any deadlines, and maintaining goodwill with the audience.

- **Complimentary closing or signoff.** In formal situations, use a closing such as "Sincerely." In less formal messages, you may just write "Thanks" or "Regards." The closing is followed by a comma and your name on the next line. Using just your first name is fine for informal messages to people who will immediately recognize your email address. However, if you are writing to someone who does not know you, use your first name and last name. Do not use a personal title such as "Mr." or "Ms." with your name unless the recipient cannot identify your gender from your first name (such as Pat, Chris, or Rathi). In these cases, use your personal title so the recipient knows to address you as either Mr. or Ms. in a response to your message.

- **Signature block.** In formal emails, always include an electronic signature block that displays all relevant contact information, including your name, position title, department, company, email address, phone number, and fax number. Even in informal emails within your own organization using a signature block is a good practice. If someone wants to respond to your email by telephone, your telephone number will be immediately available. Further, if the recipient forwards your email or prints it, your contact information will remain with the message.

- **Attachments.** If you include attachments with an email, always identify the attachments within the body of the message to ensure that the recipient is aware of the attachments and knows what they include.

Informal and formal email formats

Here are two examples of email messages. **FIGURE C.1** provides an example of an informal email message, and **FIGURE C.2** provides an example of a formal email message. These can be used as templates when you craft your own business emails.

Email report format

You can compose informal email reports to share information with people within your organization. Email reports may also be appropriate for external audiences if the context is informal and you know the audience prefers email over other medium options. **FIGURE C.3** provides an example of an email report format. Notice that the salutation and complimentary closing are optional.

FIGURE C.1 Informal Email Message Format

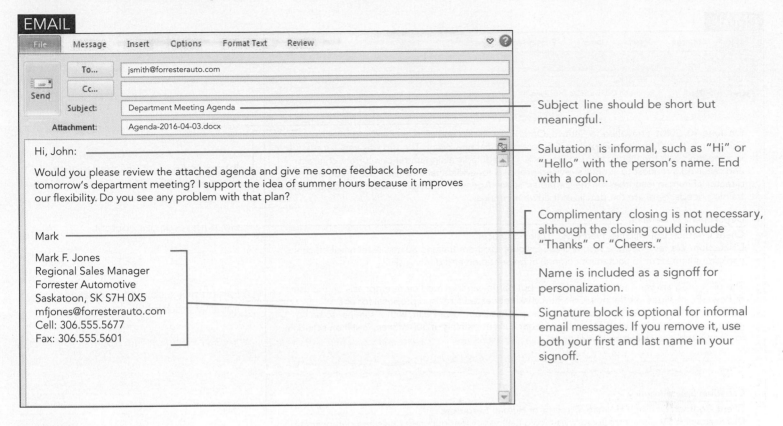

Subject line should be short but meaningful.

Salutation is informal, such as "Hi" or "Hello" with the person's name. End with a colon.

Complimentary closing is not necessary, although the closing could include "Thanks" or "Cheers."

Name is included as a signoff for personalization.

Signature block is optional for informal email messages. If you remove it, use both your first and last name in your signoff.

FIGURE C.2 Formal Email Message Format

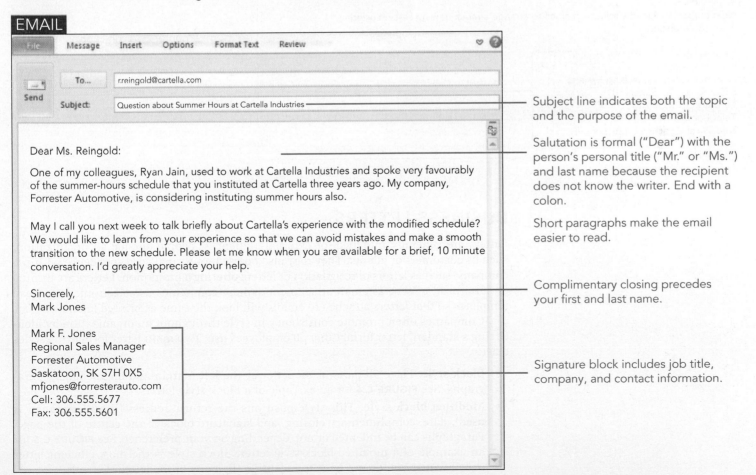

Subject line indicates both the topic and the purpose of the email.

Salutation is formal ("Dear") with the person's personal title ("Mr." or "Ms.") and last name because the recipient does not know the writer. End with a colon.

Short paragraphs make the email easier to read.

Complimentary closing precedes your first and last name.

Signature block includes job title, company, and contact information.

FIGURE C.3 Email Report Format

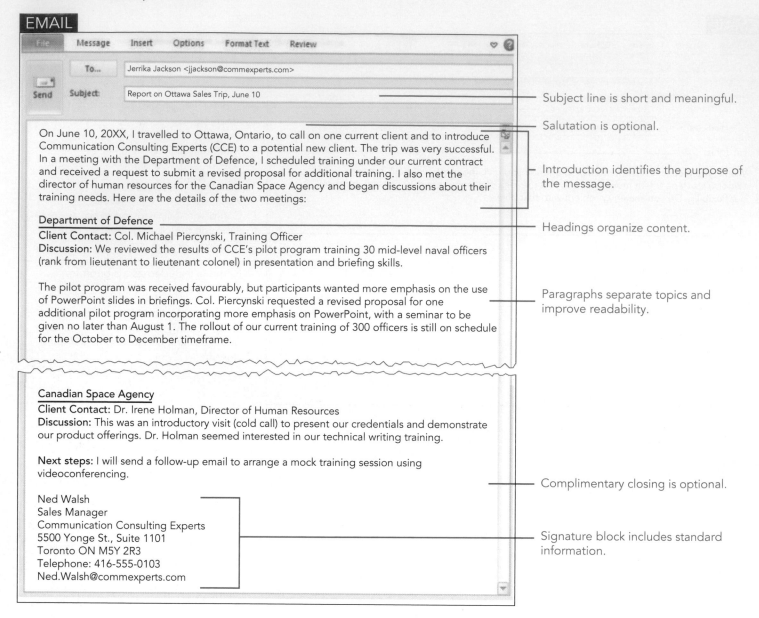

On June 10, 20XX, I travelled to Ottawa, Ontario, to call on one current client and to introduce Communication Consulting Experts (CCE) to a potential new client. The trip was very successful. In a meeting with the Department of Defence, I scheduled training under our current contract and received a request to submit a revised proposal for additional training. I also met the director of human resources for the Canadian Space Agency and began discussions about their training needs. Here are the details of the two meetings:

Department of Defence
Client Contact: Col. Michael Piercynski, Training Officer
Discussion: We reviewed the results of CCE's pilot program training 30 mid-level naval officers (rank from lieutenant to lieutenant colonel) in presentation and briefing skills.

The pilot program was received favourably, but participants wanted more emphasis on the use of PowerPoint slides in briefings. Col. Piercynski requested a revised proposal for one additional pilot program incorporating more emphasis on PowerPoint, with a seminar to be given no later than August 1. The rollout of our current training of 300 officers is still on schedule for the October to December timeframe.

Canadian Space Agency
Client Contact: Dr. Irene Holman, Director of Human Resources
Discussion: This was an introductory visit (cold call) to present our credentials and demonstrate our product offerings. Dr. Holman seemed interested in our technical writing training.

Next steps: I will send a follow-up email to arrange a mock training session using videoconferencing.

Ned Walsh
Sales Manager
Communication Consulting Experts
5500 Yonge St., Suite 1101
Toronto ON M5Y 2R3
Telephone: 416-555-0103
Ned.Walsh@commexperts.com

Callout labels:
- Subject line is short and meaningful.
- Salutation is optional.
- Introduction identifies the purpose of the message.
- Headings organize content.
- Paragraphs separate topics and improve readability.
- Complimentary closing is optional.
- Signature block includes standard information.

BUSINESS LETTERS

Letters are generally intended for external audiences: people outside an organization, such as customers or clients. They may also be used for formal correspondence within a company, such as letters of resignation or letters offering a promotion. Letters are printed on letterhead or sent as email attachments. Many companies use electronic letterhead templates so that letters attached to emails will look the same as printed letters.

Companies often promote consistency in style throughout an organization by identifying a standard letter format that all employees use. Two main letter formatting styles exist:

- **Block style.** Place all parts of the letter at the left margin and do not indent paragraphs. See **FIGURE C.4** for an example of a block-style letter.
- **Modified block style.** This style positions the return address (if no letterhead is used), date, complimentary closing, and signature block in the centre of the page. Paragraphs can be indented or not, depending on your preference. See **FIGURE C.5** for an example of a modified-block-style letter. Block style is the most efficient letter style because you do not have to indent or align any of the letter elements.

FIGURE C.4 Block-Style Letter

`LETTER`

CP CONSULTING PROFESSIONALS

233 Hamilton Avenue
St. John's, NL
A1E 1J7

O: (709) 555-5563
F: (709) 555-5564

queries@consultpro.com
www.consultpro.com

March 21, 20XX

Ms. Tonya Wyoll
Assistant Manager, Sales
ABC Communications, Inc.
253 O'Connell Drive
Corner Brook, NL
A2H 5N3

Dear Ms. Wyoll:

Thank you for your interest in our consulting services. I enjoyed our telephone conversation yesterday and am enclosing our proposal for the professional development workshop "Engaging Customers with Social Media."

The goal of this workshop is to help sales professionals harness the power of social media to increase sales. Participants in this workshop will learn to use social networks to find sales prospects, get past electronic gatekeepers, create a customer community, and drive customers to your website. Our clients report that the techniques they learn in the workshop are both easy to implement and effective.

Please contact me at r.nelson@consultpro.com or 555-5563 at your convenience to discuss the workshop in more detail or to schedule a session. I look forward to hearing from you.

Sincerely,

Regina Nelson

Regina Nelson
Training Director

Enclosure

Letterhead

Date line at left margin at least a half inch below the letterhead or centred vertically with the entire letter.

Three blank lines between date and inside address.

Inside address

Salutation

Paragraphs are single spaced and not indented.

Complimentary closing is followed by three blank lines to make room for the signature before the typed name and title.

Enclosure notation indicates that another document is enclosed in the same envelope.

FIGURE C.5 Modified-Block-Style Letter

LETTER

CONSULTING PROFESSIONALS

233 Hamilton Avenue
St. John's, NL
A1E 1J7

O: (709) 555-5563
F: (709) 555-5564

queries@consultpro.com
www.consultpro.com

March 21, 20XX ———————————— Date line begins at the centre point.

————————————— Three blank lines between
date and inside address.

Ms. Tonya Wyoll
Assistant Manager, Sales
ABC Communications, Inc.
253 O'Connell Drive
Corner Brook, NL
A2H 5N3

Dear Ms. Wyoll:

Thank you for your interest in our consulting services. I enjoyed our telephone
conversation yesterday and am enclosing our proposal for the professional
development workshop "Engaging Customers with Social Media."

The goal of this workshop is to help sales professionals harness the power
of social media to increase sales. Participants in this workshop will learn to use   Paragraphs are single
social networks to find sales prospects, get past electronic gatekeepers, create   spaced and not
a customer community, and drive customers to your website. Our clients report   indented.
that the techniques they learn in the workshop are both easy to implement and
effective.

Please contact me at r.nelson@consultpro.com or 555-5563 at your convenience
to discuss the workshop in more detail or to schedule a session. I look
forward to hearing from you.

Sincerely,

Regina Nelson   Complimentary closing, signed name,
                                    and typed name also begin at the
Regina Nelson   centre point.
Training Director

Enclosure

FIGURE C.6 Return Address

LETTER

Jon Raley
624 Shadyside Lane
Calgary, AB
T1Y 1E5
July 22, 20XX

Mr. Jacob Smithers
Precor Fabricating
200 Industrial Parkway
Edmonton, AB
T5A 0G8

Dear Mr. Smithers:

Letter formatting guidelines

When designing a letter, use the following guidelines to ensure that the letter projects a positive, professional image:

- **Letterhead or return address.** Most companies create custom-designed letterhead with their logo and/or company name and address at the top (or sometimes at the bottom or side) of the page. When sending letters for personal business, you might create your own letterhead to enhance the professionalism of your message. At a minimum, your personal letterhead should include your name and mailing address. You might also include your phone number and email address.

  If you are not using letterhead, provide your return address at the top of the page, starting either at the left margin (block style) or in the centre of the page (modified block style). The return address includes your street address on the first line and your city, province, and postal code on the next line. See **FIGURE C.6** and **FIGURE C.7** for examples.

- **Date.** Write out the date as month, day, and year (e.g., January 10, 20XX). At a minimum, place the date a half inch (usually three lines, depending on the font size) below the letterhead. Typically, letters should be centred vertically on the page. If

LETTER

JON RALEY
624 Shadyside Lane, Calgary, AB T1Y 1E5
(703) 555-2189 | jraley@att.net

July 22, 20XX

Mr. Jacob Smithers
Precor Fabricating
200 Industrial Parkway
Edmonton, AB
T5A 0G8

Dear Mr. Smithers:

FIGURE C.7 Personalized Letterhead

your letter is short, position the date several lines lower to balance the amount of blank space on the top and bottom of the page. If using a personal return address (with no letterhead), place the date on the line below your city, province, and postal code. Following the date, leave three blank lines (pressing the Enter key four times) between the date and inside address. If you are including a special notation, leave two blank lines between the date and the special notation.

- **Special notations.** If you are sending a letter by special delivery or certified mail, add these notations in ALL CAPS. If you are sending a letter to someone in a company but want to mark it as personal or confidential, add one of the following notations in ALL CAPS: "personal," "confidential," "private and confidential," or "strictly confidential." Align a special notation horizontally with the date, placing it two lines below the date and two lines above the inside address.

- **Inside address.** The inside address includes the name and address of the person to whom the letter will be sent. Follow these guidelines:
  - First line: Use "Mr." or "Ms." or some other courtesy title such as "Dr." or "Professor" in front of the person's name. If you include an employment title such as "Director of Marketing" after the name, capitalize it and separate it from the name with a comma.
  - Second line: Type the person's company name, if applicable.
  - Third line: Type the street address.
  - Fourth line: Type the city, province, and postal code. Use the provincial abbreviation (see the list of provinces and territories on page 462) and one space between all elements. Use a comma only between the city and province.
  - Leave one blank line between the inside address and the salutation.

- **Salutation.** The use of "Dear" in the salutation is traditional. However, it is not required in letters to people whom you know well. The salutation may consist of just the recipient's name. For formal letters, use the recipient's personal title (Mr. or Ms.) and last name. In informal situations and when you know the person well, use just the recipient's first name. If you do not know the name of the person who should receive your letter, create an attention line indicating a position title (such as "Attention: Human Resources Director" or "Attention: Sales Department") in place of the salutation. Leave one blank line between the salutation and the first paragraph.

- **Open/closed punctuation.** *Closed punctuation style* uses a colon (:) after the salutation and a comma after the complimentary closing. *Open punctuation style*, which is used less frequently, uses no punctuation at the end of the salutation or after the complimentary closing.

- **Subject line.** Subject lines are optional in letters. If you use them, use a short (three- to five-word) subject line to indicate the topic of your message. Depending on your company's preference, you may place it two lines above or two lines below the salutation.

- **Body.** Begin with a short first paragraph (two to three lines) that gets to the point (do not begin with "This letter is about . . ."). The middle paragraph(s) can be longer if necessary, up to 8 or 10 lines of text in each paragraph. Be sure each paragraph has a purpose and begins with a topic sentence. Use headings, bulleted lists, or enumerations as needed. The last paragraph should be short (two to three lines). In the closing, let the audience know what they should do next, include contact information, and reinforce goodwill.

- **Second (and subsequent) page headings.** Second page headings usually include the recipient's name, page number, and date of the message. This can be set flush left at the top of the second and subsequent pages.

- **Complimentary closing.** Start the signature block with a complimentary closing, such as "Sincerely" or "Best regards," followed by a comma (if using closed punctuation). Leave at least three blank lines between the closing and your typed name so you have enough room to sign your name.

- **Signed name.** On the printed copy, sign above your typed name. Your signature does not have to be legible, but it should fit neatly between the complimentary closing and your typed name. Flamboyant "celebrity-style" signatures do not project a professional image in business documents.

- **Typed name.** Position your typed name (as the author of the letter) three lines below the complimentary closing. Do not use a personal title, such as "Mr." or "Ms.," with your name unless the recipient cannot identify your gender from your first name (such as Pat, Chris, or Rathi). If you include your job title on the same line as your name, separate it with a comma. If your job title is long, place it on the line below your typed name (without a comma after your name).
- **Enclosure notation.** If you are including additional documentation with the letter, indicate that by typing "Enclosure" one line below your typed name.
- **Copy notation.** If you are sending a copy of the letter to someone else, indicate that by adding a "cc" notation below your typed name (or enclosure/attachment notation). The "cc" used to mean "carbon copy," but today it is commonly referred to as a "courtesy copy."
- **Postscript.** Commonly prefaced with "PS," postscripts are additional short content placed as an afterthought at the end of the message. They may be used in informal letters and sales letters (to retain the audience's attention) but should be avoided in most formal contexts. If the content is important, move it into the body of the message.
- **Vertical placement.** If the letter does not fill an entire page, centre the content vertically (top to bottom) on the page. You can do this manually by positioning the cursor at the date, zooming out to a full-page view, and then pressing the "Enter" key until approximately the same amount of space appears at the top (between the letterhead and the date line) and the bottom (between the last typed line and the bottom of the page). Alternatively, you can use your word processor's page setup feature to change the page's vertical alignment to centre. If you use this feature and plan to print your letter on company letterhead, first create a blank header and/or footer on your file that are the same size as any preprinted header and footer on the stationery. If you are writing your letter on "electronic" letterhead, be sure that the letterhead content is in the header portion of your page. Otherwise, the automatic centring feature will not work.

Envelope format

Most word processing programs include a mailing feature that helps you format envelopes. Use a format similar to that shown in **FIGURE C.8**. Place your return address on the front of the envelope in the upper left corner. If the company uses envelopes with a preprinted return address, you may add your name above the preprinted text. Begin the recipient's mailing address approximately in the centre of the envelope.

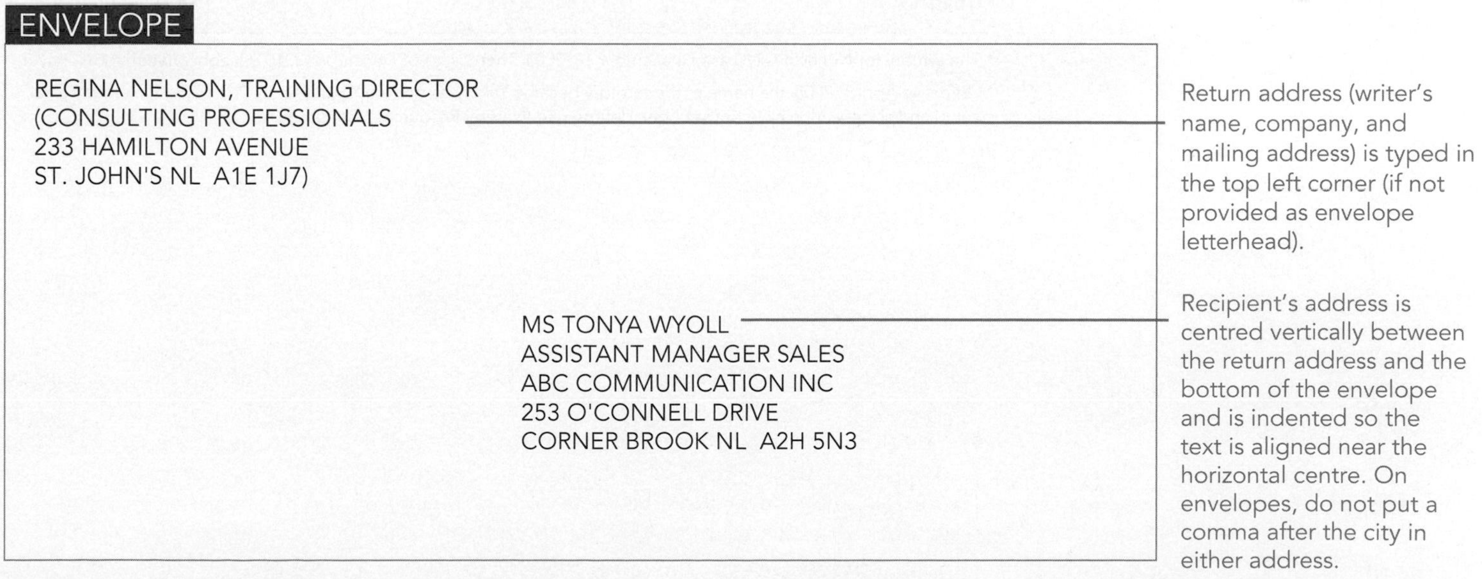

ENVELOPE

REGINA NELSON, TRAINING DIRECTOR
(CONSULTING PROFESSIONALS
233 HAMILTON AVENUE
ST. JOHN'S NL A1E 1J7)

MS TONYA WYOLL
ASSISTANT MANAGER SALES
ABC COMMUNICATION INC
253 O'CONNELL DRIVE
CORNER BROOK NL A2H 5N3

Return address (writer's name, company, and mailing address) is typed in the top left corner (if not provided as envelope letterhead).

Recipient's address is centred vertically between the return address and the bottom of the envelope and is indented so the text is aligned near the horizontal centre. On envelopes, do not put a comma after the city in either address.

FIGURE C.8 Envelope Format

Abbreviations of provinces and territories

Refer to the following list of abbreviations for addresses in letters and on envelopes. When addressing letters to international recipients, use the format shown in Figure C.8 and replace the province with the addressee's state or other principal subdivision. Add the country name in ALL CAPS in English on a line by itself at the end of the address block.

Canadian abbreviations and postal symbols

When shortened forms of the names of the provinces and territories are required for general-purpose use, such as within written documentation, abbreviations are recommended. The two-letter postal symbol is used in addresses, per the table below (Natural Resources Canada, 2014).

PROVINCE/TERRITORY	ABBREVIATION	ADDRESS/POSTAL SYMBOL
Alberta	Alta.	AB
British Columbia	B.C.	BC
Manitoba	Man.	MB
New Brunswick	N.B.	NB
Newfoundland and Labrador	N.L.	NL
Northwest Territories	N.W.T.	NT
Nova Scotia	N.S.	NS
Nunavut	—	NU*
Ontario	Ont.	ON
Prince Edward Island	P.E.I.	PE
Quebec	Que.	QC
Saskatchewan	Sask.	SK
Yukon**	Y.T.	YT

* The symbol for Nunavut is NU as of December 18, 2000. There is, as of December 2015, no abbreviation for Nunavut.

** Effective April 1, 2003, the name of the territory became Yukon, as per the Yukon Act (S.C. 2002, c. 7). A new postal symbol and abbreviation have not yet been determined (Natural Resources Canada, 2014).

APPENDIX D

Documentation and Reference Styles

Any time you quote, paraphrase, or use material from a source, you need to identify the source and provide enough information so your readers can find the source you reference. You do this by providing citations within the body of the text and a complete, alphabetized reference (or works cited) list at the end of the document. This is true whether you are writing a report, presentation, webpage, or blog.

Different fields of study use different reference styles, and your instructor, employer, or publisher will usually identify the style you are expected to use. Three styles are typical in academia:

1. APA style, found in the *Publication Manual of the American Psychological Association*
2. Chicago style (sometimes referred to as CMS), found in the *The Chicago Manual of Style*
3. MLA style from the Modern Language Association, found in the *MLA Handbook for Writers of Research Papers* and in updates on the MLA website

This appendix outlines the most common rules you will need to follow in two of these styles: APA, which is commonly used in business departments, and MLA, which is commonly used in English departments. The APA guidelines are based on the 6th edition of the *Publication Manual* and the *APA Style Guide to Electronic References*. The MLA guidelines are based on the *MLA Handbook for Writers of Research Papers*, 7th edition, as well as updates on the MLA website. For the rules of the Chicago style, see the online or print version of *The Chicago Manual of Style*.

APA IN-TEXT CITATIONS

Within your text, indicate the source of a citation by inserting authors' last names, the year of publication, and in some cases the page on which the material can be found (or the paragraph in an online source). Where you place this information depends on whether you paraphrase the original source or quote the source word for word.

Paraphrased content

Paraphrased content consists of information from a source presented in your own words. When paraphrasing or referring to another work, the citation can be part of the narrative or placed at the end of the sentence (inside the ending punctuation). Citations for paraphrases must include the author and date of the publication. In addition, APA guidelines encourage (but do not require) writers to include page or paragraph numbers to help readers find the paraphrased material in the original source.

For example, if the original source states "transparency is a popular reason for blogging, particularly for companies that want to be identified as mission-oriented or socially responsible" (Alboher, 2007, p. 3C), paraphrased content could be worded in one of the following three ways:

Single-author paraphrased source

In 2007, *New York Times* columnist Marci Alboher suggested that companies often use blogs to be transparent, especially those companies that want to be seen as fulfilling their stated mission or social responsibility initiatives.

The author's name and the publication date can be integrated into the text itself.

The author's name can be integrated into the text, with the date in parentheses immediately following the name. If the source has no date, use *n.d.* in the parentheses.

If the author's name is not integrated into the text, then the author's last name and the date, separated by a comma, appear in parentheses at the end of the sentence.

The first time you integrate authors' names into the text, use last names or full names. For six or more authors, use only the first author's name followed by "et al." Order the names as they appear in the original. Use "and" to separate the last author's name from the previous name. For subsequent references, use the first author's name followed by "et al."

When the authors' names are not integrated into the text, use only their last names in the parentheses and use "&" to separate the last author's name from the previous name.

When a cited work has no author, use the first few words of the reference list entry and the year. The first few words are usually the title. Note that the title is written differently than in the reference list: All words in the title are capitalized, and the title is enclosed in quotation marks.

List sources alphabetically by authors' names. Use semicolons to separate sources.

When the last names are the same, use first initials to determine the order of the sources.

Order the sources as they are ordered in the reference list, which assigns a letter after the date of sources written by the same author and published in the same year. Use that letter in the citation.

Identify personal communications with in-text citations only. APA style does not list personal communications on the reference page.

Or . . .

New York Times columnist Marci Alboher (2007) suggests that companies often use blogs to be transparent, especially those companies that want to be seen as fulfilling their stated mission or social responsibility initiatives.

Or . . .

Companies often use blogs to be transparent, especially those companies that want to be seen as fulfilling their stated mission or social responsibility initiatives (Alboher, 2007).

The following examples provide additional information about how to cite sources with multiple authors, sources with no identified author, and multiple sources.

Multiple authors of one paraphrased source

In the early days of blogging, prominent thinkers about blogging such as Rick Levine, Christopher Locke, Doc Searls, and David Weinberger (1999) prophesied the influence blogging could have on the corporate world.

Or . . .

In the early days of blogging, prominent thinkers about blogging prophesied the influence blogging could have on the corporate world (Levine, Locke, Searls, & Weinberger, 1999).

Works with no identified author

Many of the best business blogs are written by individuals, not corporations ("Best Business Blogs," 2011).

Multiple sources used to support one statement

Blogs also offer small businesses the opportunity to become completely transparent with their consumer base (Halzack, 2008; Mahon, n.d.; Rettberg, 2008; Scoble & Israel, 2006).

Multiple sources by authors with the same last name to support one statement

Corporate blogging is predicted to increase substantially in the next decade (Haffner, M., 2006; Haffner, R., 2008).

Multiple sources by the same author published in the same year

The medium options for corporate blogging vary widely, from standard blog applications to social media outlets (Jones, 2009a; Jones, 2009b).

Two types of sources require only in-text citations and are not included in the reference list: classical or religious works (such as the Bible) that are divided into the same sections in all editions, and personal communications.

Personal communication

Dr. Kenneth Darby, who studies corporate blogging, predicts social media will support new forms of industry blogging in the future (personal communication, November 2, 2012).

Experts predict that social media will support new forms of industry blogging in the future (K. Darby, personal communication, November 2, 2012).

Quoted content

Quoted content (used word for word) from a source uses a citation style similar to that for paraphrases. However, the quoted text must also be surrounded by quotation marks or set off as a block of text if it is more than 40 words long. In addition, the page or paragraph number for quotations must always be included. Just as with paraphrased content, the exact placement of these elements varies. Note the following examples.

Single-author quoted source

As *New York Times* columnist Marci Alboher (2007) points out, this "kind of transparency is a popular reason for blogging, particularly for companies that want to be identified as mission-oriented or socially responsible" (p. 3C).

Surround the quoted content with quotation marks. Put the date in parentheses after the author's name. Always place the page number after the quotation. Use a lowercase "p" followed by a period to abbreviate "page." If the quote spans more than one page, use "pp." Place the parentheses between the ending quotation mark and final period.

Or . . .

This "kind of transparency is a popular reason for blogging, particularly for companies that want to be identified as mission-oriented or socially responsible" (Alboher, 2007, p. 3C).

If all the citation elements appear in the parentheses, use commas to separate author, year, and page number.

Multiple-author quoted source

In The Cluetrain Manifesto, Levine, Locke, Searls, and Weinberger (1999) wrote:

The first time a source with up to five authors is used, list all authors' names. If the source has six or more authors, list only the first author's name followed by "et al."

A powerful global conversation has begun. Through the Internet, people are discovering and inventing new ways to share relevant knowledge with blinding speed. As a direct result, markets are getting smarter—and getting smarter faster than most companies. These markets are conversations. Their members communicate in language that is natural, open, honest, direct, funny and often shocking. Whether explaining or complaining, joking or serious, the human voice is unmistakably genuine. (p. 10)

When a quotation is longer than 40 words, do not enclose it in quotation marks. Instead, indent the content as a block quotation and place the page number after the final punctuation mark.

In *The Cluetrain Manifesto,* Levine et al. (1999) wrote: "A powerful global conversation has begun. Through the Internet, people are discovering and inventing new ways to share relevant knowledge with blinding speed. As a direct result, markets are getting smarter—and getting smarter faster than most companies" (p. 10).

The second and all subsequent times you refer to a source with three or more authors, list only the first author with "et al." to represent "and others." (Note: For two-author sources, such as Scoble & Israel, always list both authors.)

Quotations with words omitted

The Cluetrain Manifesto stated: "A powerful global conversation has begun. . . . Markets are getting smarter—and getting smarter faster than most companies" (Levine et al., 1999, p. 10).

Use ellipses (three spaced periods) to indicate you have omitted words from quoted text. If you have omitted words between two sentences, end the first sentence with a period and then provide the ellipsis (for a total of four spaced periods).

APA REFERENCE LIST

At the end of your paper, include a page titled "References" that presents an alphabetical list of all the sources you cited in your text. Reference list entries for most sources include four major elements in the following order: the author(s), year of publication, name of work, and publication information. The entire reference list is organized alphabetically according to the first word in the entry, usually the author's last name. If more than one source begins with the same word, then the order is determined by a different element (the date of publication or name of the work) as described in the following sections.

Authors

- List authors' last names first, use initials only for authors' first and middle names, and use one space between initials.
- Separate authors' names with commas, even when only two authors are listed. Use an ampersand (&) before the name of the final author.

- If an author has a hyphenated first name, include the hyphen and a period after each initial.
- List all authors in the order they appear on the publication.
- If the source lists more than seven authors, list the first six followed by an ellipsis (...) to indicate a break in the list and then the final author's name. In this instance, do not use an ampersand (&) before the final name.
- If the author is an organization, use a period at the end of the name to separate the author content from the next element of the reference.
- If a work has no author, begin the entry with the title of the work.

Examples:

Goins, T., & Robbins, D. R.

Jones, A. P., Baker, M.-A., & Cawfrey, G. L.

Pental, F., Raley, M., Meyer, R., Peterson, B., Boyd, L., Tobbin, E., . . . Jones, L. E. Clanton Corporation.

Year of publication

- Place the year the source was published in parentheses immediately after the author information. If a work has no author, put the year after the name of the work.
- If no date is available, put *n.d.* in the parentheses.
- For newspaper, magazine, and online articles (including blog posts and social media updates), include the month and day of publication *after* the year.
- If a reference list contains multiple sources for the same author, order the sources from oldest to newest.
- If a reference list contains multiple sources written by the same author and published the same year, use the titles to determine alphabetic sequence and differentiate the sources with lowercase letters added to the dates.

Examples:

Newspaper/magazine article. ⟶ Halzack, S. (2008, August 25).

Two articles by the same author with the same dates. ⟶ Albanese, A. R. (2006a). Google is not the net: . . .
Albanese, A. R. (2006b). The social life of books: . . .

Two articles by the same authors but with different dates. ⟶ Jones, A. P., Baker, M.-A., & Cawfrey, G. L. (2006).
Jones, A. P., Baker, M.-A., & Cawfrey, G. L. (2012).

Name of work

The format you use depends on the type of work. Complete works, such as books and websites, have just one title. By contrast, journal, newspaper, and magazine articles have article titles as well as publication titles. If your audience will need additional information to identify the type of publication, place that descriptive information in square brackets immediately after the title.

Articles and blog posts

- Use an unaltered font. Do not italicize, underline, or use quotation marks around the title.
- Use sentence case, capitalizing only the first word of the title and the first word of the subtitle, if it has one, and any proper nouns such as company names.
- Conclude with a period.

Books, videos, podcasts, and so on.

- Italicize the title. Do not underline.
- Use sentence case, capitalizing only the first word of the title and the first word of the subtitle, if it has one, and any proper nouns such as company names.
- Conclude with a period.

Journals and other periodicals

- Italicize the title of the journal or periodical. Do not underline.
- Use title case, beginning the first word and each word of four letters or more with a capital letter. Also capitalize any major words that are shorter than four letters as well as the first word after a colon, semicolon, dash, or period in a title.
- Conclude with a comma.

Examples:

Levine, R., Locke, C., Searls, D., & Weinberg, D. (1999). *The cluetrain manifesto: The end of business as usual. . . .* ◄─────────────── Book

Halzack, S. (2008, August 25). Marketing moves to the blogosphere: Business model shifts to engage customers online. *The Washington Post, . . .* ◄─────── Newspaper article

Goldman, S. (2009, August 7). For Honest Tea, Coke is it [Blog post]. Retrieved from www.honesttea.com/blog/category/from-seth-and-barry ◄────── Blog post

Publication information

How you list the publication information depends on the kind of source you reference. For example, journal articles usually require volume, issue, and page numbers. However, books list only the publishing company's location and name, and websites usually require only a "Retrieved from" web address.

Journal and other periodical articles

Following the title of the periodical itself, provide the volume number in italics immediately followed by the issue number in roman and in parentheses. No space separates the volume number from the issue number. Follow the issue number with a comma and page numbers. Page numbers do not use a page abbreviation ("p"), as was used for in-text citations. Indicate the range of page numbers with an en dash. End with a period.

Author, A. A., Author, B. B., & Author, C. C. (Year). Title of article. *Title of Periodical, volume*(issue), pages.

Thompson, L. (2009). Blogs: If used properly, an investor-friendly tool. *Compliance Week, 6*(62), 60.

Books and e-books

List the city and name of publisher separated by a colon. Include a period at the end.

Author, A. A., & Author, B. B. (Year). *Title of publication.* City, PR: Publisher's Name.

Levine, R., Locke, C., Searls, D., & Weinberg, D. (1999). *The cluetrain manifesto: The end of business as usual.* New York, NY: Basic Books.

Phibbs, B. (2011). *Groupon: You can't afford it—Why deep discounts are bad for business and what to do instead* [Kindle Edition]. Beyond the Page Publishing. Retrieved from http://amazon.com

> For an e-book, include the e-book version you read in brackets. Also provide the URL from which you downloaded the book.

Websites

If the name of the website is included in the URL or is obvious from the author's name, use "Retrieved from" followed by the URL. If the name of the website is not included in the URL or not obvious from the author's name, then include it as part of the retrieval statement. Remove the hyperlink (blue font color and underlines) format from web addresses and, when necessary, insert a space to allow long addresses to wrap effectively to the right margin. Do not use a period at the end of a web address.

Author, A. A., & Author, B. B. (Year). Title of article. Retrieved from http://xxxxx ◄─

Charman-Anderson, S. (2005). Dark blogs: The use of blogs in business. Retrieved from Strange Attractor website: www.suw.org.uk/files/Dark_Blogs_01 _European_Pharma_Group.pdf

> When the name of the website is not part of the URL, identify the website in the retrieval statement.

When an article on the web has no author, begin with the title of the article. → Best business blogs 2011. (2011). Retrieved from http://strategistnews.com/best-business-blogs.php

Other types of sources

Adapt the four-part citation elements to other types of reference sources. Here are some examples that may not fit the "normal" format. If it is not clear from the name what type of source it is, then provide descriptive information in brackets immediately after the title.

- **Annual report**

  Clanton Corporation. (2011). *2010 corporate annual report*. Retrieved from www.clantoncorp.com

- **Brochure**

  Montana State University Billings Career Services. (2009). *A polished interview* [Brochure]. Retrieved from www.msubillings.edu/careers/PDF/Polished%20Interview%20Brochure%209.pdf

- **Government publication**

  U.S. Bureau of Labor Statistics, U.S. Department of Labor. (2012). *Occupational outlook handbook*, 2012–13 edition. Washington, DC: U.S. Government Printing Office. Retrieved from www.bls.gov/ooh

- **Online encyclopedia or dictionary**

  Johnson, C. (2010). Communication in organizations. In *Encyclopedia of business* (2nd ed.). Retrieved from www.referenceforbusiness.com/encyclopedia/Clo-Con/Communication-in-Organizations.html

- **Blog post**

  Mahon, T. (2011, July 11). Nearly perfect suit [Blog post]. Retrieved from http://englishcut.com

- **Podcast**

  Wildhaber, J. (Writer), & Fogarty, M. (Producer). (2010, July 1). *Understanding voice and tone in writing* [Audio podcast]. Retrieved from http://grammar.quickanddirtytips.com/understanding-voice-and-tone-in-writing.aspx

- **Slide presentation (found online)**

  Baer, J. (2010). *11 must-dos for the serious blogger* [Online presentation]. Retrieved from www.slideshare.net/jaybaer/11-must-dos-for-the-serious-blogger-2512783

- **Online video (YouTube)**

  Krueger, B. (Producer). (2007). *Interview tips—Avoiding three common video resume errors* [Video file]. Retrieved from www.youtube.com/watch?v=R3t9ysT0A_U

Use the writer's real name, followed by the screen name in brackets. If you know only the screen name, provide it without brackets. Include the entire text of the tweet in the citation. →

- **Tweet or Twitter update**

  Scoble, R. [Scobleizer]. (2012, August 30). Our book, "The Age of Context" is underway and @shelisrael posted an excerpt from it: http://t.co/npCEkpHQ. . . Would love to know what you think [Tweet]. Retrieved from https://twitter.com/Scobleizer

For Facebook pages, put the author's first name in parentheses to make the page easier to retrieve. Spell out the full name of organizations. Include a retrieval date when the publication date is unknown. →

- **Facebook page**

  Tufte, E. [Edward]. (n.d.). Timeline [Facebook page]. Retrieved August 30, 2012, from www.facebook.com/EdwardTufte

  AACSB International. (n.d.). BizSchoolJobs [Facebook page]. Retrieved September 1, 2012, from www.facebook.com/AACSB/app_106877302704651

For a Facebook update, no retrieval date is necessary because all updates have publication dates. →

- **Facebook update**

  APA Style. (2012, August 14). Frequently asked question: Should hyperlinks be used in APA style papers? [Facebook status update]. Retrieved from www.facebook.com/APAStyle/posts/432784353427030

APA SAMPLE REFERENCE PAGE

To indent second and subsequent lines of a reference citation, use your word processor's "hanging indent" paragraph format feature rather than manually tabbing or spacing the text.

References

Albanese, A. R. (2006a). Google is not the net: Social networks are surging and present the real
service challenge—and opportunity—for libraries. *Library Journal, 131*(15), 32–34.

Albanese, A. R. (2006b). The social life of books: Write, read, blog, rip, share any good books lately? A
conversation with Ben Vershbow. *Library Journal, 131*(9), 28–30.

Best business blogs of 2011. (2011). Retrieved from http://strategistnews.com/
best-business-blogs.php

Charman-Anderson, S. (2005). Dark blogs: The use of blogs in business. Retrieved from Strange
Attractor website: http://www.suw.org.uk/files/ Dark_Blogs_01_European_Pharma_Group.pdf

Financial Times. (2009). FT ComMetrics blog index. Retrieved from http://ftindex.commetrics.com/

Goldman, S. (2008, August 25). For Honest Tea, Coke is it [Blog post]. Retrieved from
http://www.honesttea.com/blog/category/from-seth-and-barry/

Halzack, S. (2008, August 25). Marketing moves to the blogosphere; Business model shifts to engage
customers online. *Washington Post,* p. D1.

Levine, R., Locke, C., Searls, D., & Weinberg, D. (1999). The *cluetrain manifesto: The end of business
as usual.* New York, NY: Basic Books.

Mahon, T. (n.d.) *English cut.* Retrieved from http://englishcut.com

Rettberg, J. W. (2008). *Blogging.* Malden, MA: Polity Press.

Rosenberg, S. (2009). *Say Everything: How blogging began, what it's becoming, and why it matters.*
New York, NY: Crown Publishers.

Scoble, R., & Israel, S. (2006). *Naked conversations.* Hoboken, NJ: John Wiley & Sons, Inc.

Thompson, L. (2009). Blogs: If used properly, an investor-friendly tool. *Compliance Week, 6*(62), 60.

Two journal articles with the same author and year: use "a" and "b" after the year to identify the source in in-text citations. Note that the words after the em-dashes are not capitalized here because the dashes set off a phrase rather than a subtitle.

Online article—no author. Note that the name of the website is not needed because the name—Strategist News—is included as part of the URL.

Article published on the web. Note that the name of the website is included in the retrieval statement because that name is not obvious from either the URL or the author name.

Webpage—corporate author

Blog post

Newspaper article

Book, multiple authors

Website, no date

Book, single author

Journal article. The volume number is italicized and the issue number is in parentheses separated from the page number with a comma and space.

SAMPLE APA DOCUMENTATION IN PRESENTATION FILES

Whether you're creating a traditional presentation file or a report deck, cite your in-text sources on the slides, either immediately after the content or in the corner of the slide, as shown on page 470. Add a reference page to the end of report deck files or presentation handouts so your audience can refer to the original sources, if necessary.

THE MILLENNIAL APPROACH TO PROBLEM SOLVING

"Rather than insisting on solving society's challenges using the inherited, but inevitably limited wisdom of experts, Millennials would prefer to share their ideas and let the group find the right answer through their combined experiences."

EDHAR/Shutterstock

Source: Winograd & Hais (2009)

Source is added to the page where the original content appears. Use standard in-text citation formats.

REFERENCES

Best business blogs of 2011. (2011). Retrieved from http://strategistnews.com/best-business-blogs.php

Charman-Anderson, S. (2005). Dark blogs: The use of blogs in business. Retrieved from Strange Attractor website: http://www.suw.org.uk/files/Dark_Blogs_01_European_Pharma_Group.pdf

Rosenberg, S. (2009). *Say everything: How blogging began, what it's becoming, and why it matters.* New York, NY: Crown Publishers.

Scoble, R., & Israel, S. (2006). *Naked conversations.* Hoboken, NJ: John Wiley & Sons, Inc.

Thompson, L. (2009). Blogs: If used properly, an investor-friendly tool. *Compliance Week, 6*(62), 60.

Winograd, M., & Hais, M. D. (2009, November 9). Who needs critical thinking skills when we've got Facebook? [Blog post]. Retrieved from http://blog-jenniferlindsay.com/2009/11/09/who-needs-critical-thinking-skills-when-weve-got-facebook/

The complete reference citation is included in a reference page at the conclusion of the report deck (or presentation handout).

MLA IN-TEXT CITATIONS

MLA uses a simple and consistent style for all references to a source, whether the content is paraphrased or quoted. Provide enough information in the citation to help your audience find the correct work on the Works Cited page and find the cited material in the source itself. Typically, this means that citations include the author's last name and the page number for the cited material. If you are referring to an entire work and not a specific passage, no page number is needed. MLA documentation never includes publication dates in the parentheses.

The following examples correspond with the APA examples on pages 463–465 but are formatted as MLA-style citations. Fewer examples are provided because MLA uses the same format for quoted content as it does for paraphrased content.

Paraphrased content

When paraphrasing content (using original information in your own words) or even just referring to a source, cite the original work by including the author's name within the narrative or in an in-text citation at the end of the sentence (before the ending punctuation).

For example, if the original source states "transparency is a popular reason for blogging, particularly for companies that want to be identified as mission-oriented or socially responsible" (Alboher 3C), paraphrased content could be worded in either of the following ways:

Single-author source

In 2007, *New York Times* columnist Marci Alboher suggested that companies often use blogs to be transparent, especially those companies that want to be seen as fulfilling their stated mission or social responsibility initiatives (3C).

Or . . .

Companies often use blogs to be transparent, especially those companies that want to be seen as fulfilling their stated mission or social responsibility initiatives (Alboher 3C).

> If the author's name is used in the narrative, include only the page number in the parenthetical reference. Place the parentheses at the first natural pause, usually at the end of the relevant passage.

> If the author's name is not used in the narrative, both the author and page number(s) appear in parentheses (with no comma separating them).

Works with no identified author

Many of the best business blogs are written by individuals, not corporations ("Best Business Blogs").

> When a cited work has no author, use the first few words of the reference list entry. The first few words are usually the title.

Multiple authors of one source

In the *Cluetrain Manifesto*, Rick Levine, Christopher Locke, Doc Searls, and David Weinberger prophesied the influence blogging could have on the corporate world.

Or . . .

In the early days of blogging, prominent thinkers about blogging prophesied the influence blogging could have on the corporate world (Levine, Locke, Searls, and Weinberger).

Or . . .

In the early days of blogging, prominent thinkers about blogging prophesied the influence blogging could have on the corporate world (Levine et al.).

> If the authors' names are used in the narrative and you are referring to an entire work, rather than content from a specific page of the source, no parenthetical reference is necessary.

> When including multiple authors' names in the parenthetical reference, separate the last name with "and."

> Whether in the narrative or in parentheses, texts with more than three authors can be cited with the name of the first author followed by "et al."

Multiple sources used to support one statement

Blogs also offer small businesses the opportunity to become completely transparent with their consumer base (Halzack D1; Mahon; Rettberg; Scoble and Israel).

> When citing multiple sources in one reference citation, list sources alphabetically and separate them with semicolons. When citing websites without page numbers or books in their entirety, no page numbers are needed.

Multiple sources by the same author to support one statement

Corporate blogging is predicted to increase substantially in the next decade (Haffner, *Blogs* 26; Haffner, *Corporate* 2).

> To differentiate between two works by the same author, include the first word or an abbreviated form of the title after the author's name (with comma) and before the corresponding page number (no comma).

Personal communication

In contrast to APA style, in MLA personal communications such as interviews, letters, and emails are listed in the Works Cited list, so the in-text citation does not need to indicate that the source is a personal communication.

Dr. Kenneth Darby, who studies corporate blogging, predicts social media will support new forms of industry blogging in the future.

Experts predict that social media will support new forms of industry blogging in the future (Darby).

> A personal communication is treated exactly like a written source. The full reference information is included in the Works Cited list.

Quoted content

Quoted content (used word for word) from a source uses a citation style similar to that for paraphrases. However, the quoted text must also be surrounded by quotation marks or set off as a block of text if it is more than four lines long. In addition, the page or paragraph number for quotations must always be included. Note the following examples.

Single-author quoted source

Surround the quoted content with quotation marks. Always place the page number after the quotation. The number is not preceded by the word "page" or abbreviation "p." Place the parentheses between the ending quotation mark and final period.

As *New York Times* columnist Marci Alboher points out, this "kind of transparency is a popular reason for blogging, particularly for companies that want to be identified as mission-oriented or socially responsible" (3C).

Or . . .

If the author's name is not used in the narrative, both the author and page number(s) appear in parentheses (with no comma separating them).

This "kind of transparency is a popular reason for blogging, particularly for companies that want to be identified as mission-oriented or socially responsible" (Alboher 3C).

Multiple-author quoted source

When a source has two or three authors, list all their names in the citation. When a source has more than three authors, you may either list all their names or the name of the first author followed by "et al." ("and others") in roman not italics.

When a quotation is longer than four lines, do not enclose it in quotation marks. Instead, indent the content as a block quotation and place the page number after the final punctuation mark.

In *The Cluetrain Manifesto*, Levine, Locke, Searls, and Weinberger wrote:

> A powerful global conversation has begun. Through the Internet, people are discovering and inventing new ways to share relevant knowledge with blinding speed. As a direct result, markets are getting smarter—and getting smarter faster than most companies. These markets are conversations. Their members communicate in language that is natural, open, honest, direct, funny and often shocking. Whether explaining or complaining, joking or serious, the human voice is unmistakably genuine. (10)

Or. . .

In *The Cluetrain Manifesto*, Levine et al. wrote: "A powerful global conversation has begun. Through the Internet, people are discovering and inventing new ways to share relevant knowledge with blinding speed. As a direct result, markets are getting smarter—and getting smarter faster than most companies" (10).

Quotations with words omitted

Use ellipses (three spaced periods) to indicate you have omitted words from quoted text. If you have omitted words between two sentences, end the first sentence with a period and then provide the ellipsis (for a total of four spaced periods).

The Cluetrain Manifesto stated: "A powerful global conversation has begun. . . . Markets are getting smarter—and getting smarter faster than most companies" (Levine, Locke, Searls, and Weinberger 10).

MLA WORKS CITED LIST

At the end of your paper, include a "Works Cited" list: a double-spaced alphabetical list of all the sources you cited in your text.

Entries for most sources include four major elements in the following order: the author(s), name of work, publication information, and medium of publication (print or web). In addition, some sources require supplemental information to help a reader find the material. These major elements are separated by periods. The entire Works Cited list is organized alphabetically according to the first word in the entry, usually the author's last name. If more than one source begins with the same word, then the order is determined by a different element (author's first name or name of the work) as described in the following sections.

Authors

- List the first author's last name first, followed by his or her full first name (and middle initial or name if available).
- For an entry with one author, follow the first name with a period.
- For entries with two or three authors, list all the authors in the order they appear on the publication. Use a comma to separate names (even when only two authors are listed), and list the remaining authors with their first names before their last names. Use "and" before the last author's name.
- For entries with more than three authors, you may either list all the authors as described above or give the first author's name only, followed by "et al." ("and others") in roman not italics.
- If the author is an organization, use a period at the end of the name to separate the author name from the next element of the reference.
- If a work has no author, begin the entry with the title of the work.
- If you have cited more than one work by a specific author, order the entries alphabetically by title. For every entry after the first, use three hyphens in place of the author's name.

    Examples:

    Clanton Corporation.

    Smith, John.

    Smith, John, and Mary Jones.

    Smith, John, Mary Jones, and Tom Baker.

    Smith, John, Mary Jones, Tom Baker, and Lenore Kaplan.

     Or Smith, John, et al.

Name of work

In MLA style, all titles use title case: The first letter of every word is capitalized, except for *a, an, the,* and short prepositions. Put quotation marks around titles of short works, such as articles in periodicals, book chapters, and specific pages on a website. Follow the title with a period inside the closing quotation mark. If the title itself concludes with different punctuation, such as a question mark, that punctuation serves as the final punctuation mark. Use italics for titles of long works, such as books, plays, encyclopedias, and entire websites. Follow the title with a period or other end punctuation if the title itself includes it.

Examples:

Levine, Rick, Christopher Locke, Doc Searls, and David Weinberg. *The Cluetrain* ← Book
 Manifesto: The End of Business as Usual. . . .

Halzack, Sarah. "Marketing Moves to the Blogosphere: Business Model Shifts to ← Newspaper article
 Engage Customers Online." . . .

Goldman, Seth. "For Honest Tea, Coke Is It." . . . ← Blog post

Publication information and medium of publication

After the title of the work, include additional publication information to identify the source. The format will depend on the kind of source you cite.

Journal or other periodical articles

For journal articles, include the following publication information, in this order:

- **Journal title.** Put the journal name in italics. Do not use punctuation at the end of the journal name.

- **The volume and issue numbers.** Cite them as a single number sequence separated by a period. For example, "2.3" indicates the article can be found in the third issue of the second volume. In cases where issues are combined, such as the third and fourth, use a hyphen to separate the numbers (e.g., "2.3-4"). Use no punctuation after the issue number. Leave one space before the date.
- **Date of the publication.** For a scholarly journal, put the year of publication in parentheses followed by a colon. For other periodicals, do not place the date in parentheses, but do include the day, month, and year if they are available, followed by a colon. Leave one space before the page numbers.
- **Inclusive page numbers.** List the page numbers from the beginning of the article to the end using hyphens to separate page spreads and commas to indicate page breaks (such as 12-16, 20). Do not repeat hundreds or thousands. Use a concise form such as, 167-89 or 1125-30.
- **Medium of publication.** Indicate the medium of the publication you are referencing, beginning with a capital letter, for example Print, Web, or Kindle file.

Example

Scholarly journal

Last name, First name, and First name Last name. "Title of Article." *Title of Periodical* Volume.Issue (Year): pages. Medium of publication.

Goins, Tamara, and David R. Robbins. "An Analysis of Corporate Blogging." *The Delta Pi Epsilon Journal* 53.3 (2012): 38–48. Print.

Newspaper

Halzack, Sarah. "Marketing Moves to the Blogoshpere: Business Model Shifts to Engage Customers Online." *Washington Post* 25 August 2008: D1. Print.

Books and e-books

For books, include the following publication information, in this order:

- **Editions or series numbers.** When applicable, provide the series number, version, or edition of the publication after the book's title.
- **City of publication.** List the city where the book was published, which can generally be found on the book's title page or copyright page. If the book lists several locations, include only the first. Use a colon between the city of publication and the publisher.
- **Publisher.** You may abbreviate the name of the publisher, if it is long. For example, Cambridge University Press can be written as Cambridge UP. Use a comma between the publisher's name and year of publication.
- **Year of publication.** Use the latest copyright date listed on the copyright page. Follow the date with a period.
- **Medium of publication.** Indicate the medium of the book's publication you are referencing, beginning with a capital letter, for example Print, Web, or Kindle file.

Format the reference as you would for a printed book. Provide the place of publication, if it is available on the book. Some publishers of electronic books do not provide location information. End the reference with medium of publication (the type of electronic file you read).

Example

Last name, First name, First name Last name, and First name Last name. *Title of Book.* City: Publisher, Year. Medium.

Levine, Rick, Christopher Locke, Doc Searls, and David Weinberg. *The Cluetrain Manifesto: The End of Business as Usual.* New York: Basic Books, 1999. Print.

Phibbs, Bob. *Groupon: You Can't Afford It—Why Deep Discounts Are Bad for Business and What to Do Instead.* Beyond the Page Publishing, 2011. Kindle file.

Web-based sources

For web-based sources, include the following publication information in the following order. All items are followed by a period except for publisher, which is followed by a comma.

- **Website title.** If a website has a title that is distinct from the article or page you are citing, include the website's title, italicized.

- **Publisher's name.** Include the company, sponsor, or publisher name if one is listed. If none exists, use "N.p." to document "No publisher." Use a comma to separate the publisher's name from the date that follows.
- **Date of publication.** If a date of publication (or last updated date) is present, cite it, placing the day before the month and then the year (e.g., 4 Sept. 2009). Do not use commas, but use periods for the month abbreviation. Do not abbreviate May, June, or July. If no date is available, use "n.d."
- **Medium of publication.** Include the word "Web" to indicate this is an online source.
- **Date of access.** Identify the date you accessed the website using the same date format (day before abbreviated month followed by year).
- **Web address.** The URL is optional. The MLA 7th edition suggests that readers can more easily access websites by searching for author or title names, rather than keying in the complete URL. However, if you think that the document may be difficult to find through a search, include the url, enclosed in angle brackets (< . . .>) followed by a period.

Example

Last name, First name, First name Last name, and First name Last name. *Title of Website.* Name of Publisher, Date of Publication. Medium. Date of Access.

Charman-Anderson, Suw. "Dark Blogs: The Use of Blogs in Business." *Strange Attractor.* Corante, 13 June 2005. Web. 23 Apr. 2009.

"Best Business Blogs 2011." *Strategist News.* Strategist News, n.d. Web. 2 Apr. 2012.

← Do not include the url unless you think the document may be difficult to find through a search.

← When an article on the web has no author, begin with the title of the article.

Supplemental information

This content can include additional information that will help the audience identify the source. Such content may include parts in a series (such as, "Pt 2 of a series") followed by the name of the series or the name of a musical score. This information usually comes at the end of the entry. However, if you are providing supplemental information about the form that a source takes, MLA recommends putting that information directly after the title of the source.

Other types of sources

Apply the four-part citation elements to other types of reference sources. Here are some examples that may not fit the "normal" format. If it is not clear from the name what type of source it is, then provide descriptive information immediately after the title.

- **Annual report**

  Clanton Corporation. *2010 Corporate Annual Report.* n.d. Web. 1 July 2010.
- **Brochure**

  Montana State University Billings Career Services. *A Polished Interview.* Montana State University, 2009. Web. 1 Aug. 2009.
- **Government publication**

  U.S. Bureau of Labor Statistics, U.S. Department of Labor. *Occupational Outlook Handbook,* 2010–11 ed. Washington: U.S. Government Printing Office, 2010. Web. 15 July 2010.
- **Online encyclopedia or dictionary**

  Johnson, Clint. "Communication in Organizations." *Encyclopedia of Business,* 2nd ed. Reference for Business, 2010. Web. 15 July 2010.
- **Blog post**

  Mahon, Thomas. "Nearly Perfect Suit." Blog Post. *English Cut,* Savile Row Tailor Thomas Mahon, 11 July 2011. Web. 15 Aug. 2012.
- **Podcast**

  Wildhaber, Julie. "Understanding Voice and Tone in Writing." Podcast. *Grammar Girl.* Quick and Dirty Tips, 1 July 2010. Web. 15 July 2010.
- **Slide presentation (found online)**

  Baer, Jay. "11 Must-Dos for the Serious Blogger." Slide Presentation. *SlideShare.* Slideshare, Inc., n.d. Web. 15 July 2010.

Use the writer's real name, followed by the screen name in parentheses. If you know only the screen name, provide it without parentheses. Include the entire text of the tweet in the citation, using the same capitalization as in the original tweet. Include the date and the time of the tweet.

Until MLA publishes a specific resource on how to cite a Facebook page, treat it as a regular webpage.

Facebook updates will always have a publication date.

- **Online video (YouTube)**

  Krueger, Brian. "Interview Tips—Avoiding Three Common Video Resume Errors." Video. *YouTube.* YouTube, 10 Apr. 2007. Web. 15 July 2010.

- **Tweet or Twitter update**

  Scoble, Robert. (Scobleizer). "Our book, 'The Age of Context' is underway and @ shelisrael posted an excerpt from it: http://t.co/npCEkpHQ. . . Would love to know what you think." 30 Aug. 2012, 5:43 p.m. Tweet.

- **Facebook page**

  Tufte, Edward. "Timeline." *Facebook,* n.d. Web. 30 Aug. 2012.

  AACSB International. "BizSchoolJobs." *Facebook,* n.d. Web, 1 Sept. 2012.

- **Facebook update**

  APA Style. "Frequently Asked Question: Should Hyperlinks Be Used in APA Style Papers?" *Facebook,* 14 Aug. 2012. Web. 1 Sept. 2012.

- **Interview**

  Hodge, Elizabeth. Personal interview. 22 July 2009.

  Hodge, Elizabeth. Telephone interview. 31 August 2009.

- **Email**

  Hodge, Elizabeth. "Re: Additional Blogging Information." Message to the author. 24 July 2009. Email.

SAMPLE MLA WORKS CITED PAGE

Double space throughout the Works Cited page. To indent lines following the first line, use your word processor's hanging indent paragraph format feature rather than manually tabbing or spacing the text.

Works Cited

Albanese, Andrew Richard. "Google Is Not the Net: Social Networks Are Surging and Present the Real
  Service Challenge—and Opportunity—for Libraries." *Library Journal* 131.15 (2006): 32-34. Print.

--- "The Social Life of Books: Write, Read, Blog, Rip, Share Any Good Books Lately? A Conversation
  with Ben Vershbow." *Library Journal* 131.9 (2006): 28-30. Print.

Two sources by the same author: use "—" rather than repeating the name the second (and subsequent) time(s).

"Best Business Blogs 2011." *Strategist News.* Strategist News, n.d. Web. 2 Apr. 2012.

Online article, no author

Charman-Anderson, Suw. "Dark Blogs: The Use of Blogs in Business." *Strange Attractor.*
  Corante, 13 June 2005. Web. 23 Apr. 2009.
  <http://www.suw.org.uk/files/ Dark_Blogs_01_European_Pharma_Group.pdf>

Article published on the web

Financial Times. "Financial Times ComMetrics Blog Index." *ComMetrics: Tools for Benchmarking
  Social Media.* ComMetrics, 2009. Web. 15 July 2009.

Webpage, corporate author

Goldman, Seth. "For Honest Tea, Coke Is It." Blog Post. *Honesttea.com.*Honest Tea, Inc., 25 Aug. 2008.
  Web. 10 Aug. 2009.

Blog post

Halzack, Sarah. "Marketing Moves to the Blogosphere; Business Model Shifts to Engage Customers
  Online." *Washington Post* 25 August 2008: D1. Print.

Newspaper article

Levine, Rick, Christopher Locke, Doc Searls, and David Weinberg. *The Cluetrain Manifesto: The End of
  Business as Usual.* New York: Basic Books, 1999. Print.

Book, multiple authors

Mahon, Thomas. *English cut.* N.p. n.d. Web. 15 July 2009.

Webpage, no date

Rettberg, Jill Walker. *Blogging.* Malden: Polity Press, 2008. Print.

Book, single author

Rosenberg, Scott. *Say Everything: How Blogging Began, What It's Becoming, and Why It Matters.*
  New York: Crown Publishers, 2009. Print.

Scoble, Robert, and Shel Israel. *Naked Conversations.* Hoboken: John Wiley & Sons, Inc., 2006. Print.

Book, two authors

Thompson, Louis. "Blogs: If Used Properly, an Investor-friendly Tool." *Compliance* Week 6.62 (2009):
  60. Print.

Journal article

SAMPLE MLA DOCUMENTATION IN PRESENTATION FILES

When citing sources in presentation files or report decks, use an in-text citation on the slide where the content is presented and add a "Works Cited" page at the conclusion of the file.

THE MILLENNIAL APPROACH TO PROBLEM SOLVING

"Rather than insisting on solving society's challenges using the inherited, but inevitably limited wisdom of experts, Millennials would prefer to share their ideas and let the group find the right answer through their combined experiences."

EDHAR/Shutterstock

Source: Winograd and Hais

Source is added to the page where the original content appears. Use standard in-text citation formats.

WORKS CITED

"Best Business Blogs 2011." *Strategist News.* Strategist News, n.d. Web. 2 Apr. 2012.

Charman-Anderson, Suw. "Dark Blogs: The Use of Blogs in Business." *Strange Attractor.* Corante, 13 June 2005. Web. 23 Apr. 2009. <http://www.suw.org.uk/files/ Dark_Blogs_01_European_Pharma_Group.pdf>

Rosenberg, Scott. *Say Everything: How Blogging Began, What It's Becoming, and Why It Matters.* New York: Crown Publishers. 2009. Print.

Scoble, Robert, and Shel Israel. *Naked Conversations.* Hoboken: John Wiley & Sons, Inc. 2006. Print.

Thompson, L.ouis. "Blogs: If Used Properly, an Investor-friendly Tool. *Compliance Week,* 6.62 (2009): 60. Print.

Winograd, Morley, and Michael D. Hais. "Who Needs Critical Thinking Skills When We've Got Facebook?" *Jennifer Lindsay Digital.* Jennifer Lindsay Digital, 9 Nov. 2009. Web. 10 Jan. 2010.

The complete reference citation is included in a Works Cited list at the conclusion of the report deck (or presentation handout).

GLOSSARY

1:1 One-to-one distribution, as in a conversation or exchange between two people.

1:many One-to-many distribution, as in posting an article online for many people to view or sending an email to a wide distribution list.

A

Abstract One or two paragraphs often included at the beginning of a formal informational report that either (1) describe the content of the report so that a reader can decide whether to read the report or (2) briefly summarize the report, including the main points, conclusions, and recommendations.

Abstract wording Language that refers to broad concepts that an audience can interpret in multiple ways.

Active listening A process of focusing attentively on what a speaker says, actively working to understand and interpret the content, and then responding to acknowledge understanding.

Active voice A sentence structure in which the subject performs the action of the verb.

Affective conflict A conflict that results from differences in personalities and relationships. If affective conflicts remain unstated and unaddressed, they can lead to tension, stress, and dysfunctional work processes.

Agenda A detailed plan or outline of the items to be discussed at a meeting.

AIDA An acronym used in marketing to suggest the organization of sales communication: Attention, Interest, Desire, Action.

Ambiguous Having many possible interpretations or meanings.

Analytical report A report that analyzes information to solve a problem or support a business decision. Recommendation reports and evaluation reports are types of analytical reports. Proposals are a type of persuasive analytical report.

Analyzing The process of looking critically at four elements of your message: purpose, audience, content, and medium.

Anecdotal evidence Information you can get from a subjective report that may not be scientifically valid or representative but that may provide insight into your topic.

Anecdote A short, usually true, story that serves as an example or metaphor.

Animations Visual effects that control when and how elements appear on your slide when you present.

Announcement A message that publicly notifies people of information they need or want to know.

Antonyms Words that have opposite meaning.

Appendix A section (or multiple sections, called appendices) included at the end of a formal report or proposal that provides supplementary information.

Archive An organized collection of documents or materials that can be referenced or accessed when needed.

Asynchronous Refers to communication that takes place with a time gap between the sending of the message, the receiving of the message, and the response (e.g., email, regular mail, or text messaging).

Attachment A document that is included with a letter or email report to provide supplementary information.

Audience Anyone who receives a message and for whom a message is intended. The audience can be one person or many, depending on the number of recipients.

Audience benefits Advantages the recipient gains from agreeing with or acting on your message.

Audience or receiver benefits The positive outcomes your audience will experience by responding favourably to your request.

B

Badwill Negative press or public relations that result from a poor business practice on the part of a company or organization. It can affect the behaviour of investors and shareholders and can result in decreased revenues, loss of investors and customers, and decreased market share. Once incurred, badwill can require a company to invest time and money in "damage control" and thus experience a reduction in productivity as resources previously assigned to operational work are now assigned to resolving the badwill issue.

Barrier An obstacle that gets in the way of effective communication.

BCC An acronym that stands for blind courtesy copy or blind carbon copy. Email addresses entered into the BCC field will be hidden from all recipients, allowing a copy to be sent to additional recipients without the named recipient knowing it.

Behavioural question A type of interview question designed to determine how you would make decisions, solve problems, or respond to stressful situations.

Blog (derived from the term "web log") A regularly updated webpage run by an individual or group, either independently or as part of a larger organization, that is usually written in a conversational style and often comments on topics current to the individual or organization.

Brand message A statement that communicates the unique value you offer your employers.

Buffer An introductory sentence or paragraph that leads up to and softens a bad news message.

Bullet point list A vertically formatted list with each item preceded by a dot or other simple shape.

Business case A justification for a proposal showing that the recommended course of action benefits an organization and makes business sense.

C

CC An acronym that stands for courtesy copy. An email feature that allows a copy of a message to be sent to additional recipients.

Channel The method you use to deliver your message (e.g., telephone, face-to-face meeting, email, text message, website, or other). Also called *medium*.

Chronological résumé A traditional résumé style that lists content sequentially, starting with the most recent experience.

Clarity The quality of being unambiguous and easy to understand. Clear communication uses relatively simple words in well-constructed sentences and well-organized paragraphs.

Clichés Commonplace and often overused phrases that have lost their force and meaning.

Clipboard manager Software that allows a user to copy, organize, edit, save, and quickly reuse text excerpts, graphics, and other digital assets.

Cloud computing A general term for the storage of data and services in a central location, accessible via the Internet.

Cognitive conflict A conflict that results from differences in understanding content or tasks. Working through a cognitive conflict often leads to better decisions and work products.

Collaboration The process of working together to achieve a common goal.

Collectivist culture A culture that puts the welfare of the group or organization before people's individual interests.

Combined résumé A résumé style that takes advantage of both the chronological and functional methods of organizing content by highlighting work experience by date and skill sets by category.

Comfort zone A term that describes preferred behavioural, cultural, or attitudinal characteristics that are familiar and known.

Communication The process of planning, creating, delivering, and interpreting messages both verbally (through writing and speaking) and nonverbally (through gestures and symbols).

Communication strategy A plan for what and how you are going to communicate to ensure your message achieves your purpose.

Communication style The manner in which people interact with each other. The messages a person sends, intentionally and unintentionally, through spoken, written, and nonverbal communication.

Competitive proposal A proposal that will compete with other proposals for the same sale, funding, or opportunity.

Composing The process of drafting content, organizing it so that it is understandable from the audience's perspective, putting it into coherent sentences and logical paragraphs, and then designing a format or delivery approach that is professional and makes the communication easy to follow.

Comprehension Understanding what you hear or read.

Concede To admit that the opposing point of view has merit but does not invalidate your argument.

Conciseness Using no more words than necessary for a message to accomplish its purpose.

Concrete wording Language that is specific, making it likely that everyone will interpret it the same way.

Conditional Something that occurs only under certain conditions.

Condolences Another term for *sympathy message*.

Confirmation An acknowledgment that you have received information or understood a message correctly.

Confirmation email An email message sent shortly after a verbal exchange to verify the details discussed. The sender will expect a short reply of agreement or a longer reply to alter the details within the email.

Congratulatory message Communication sent to recognize someone's achievements or important events.

Content The substance of your message.

Content management system (CMS) A web-based application for creating, managing, and updating the content of a website to allow the website content to be managed easily by nontechnical content experts.

Content marketing A technique for persuading customers by providing them with valuable information without trying to sell them anything.

Context A set of circumstances that influences the purpose of communication, the best medium to use to communicate the message, and how receivers interpret a message.

Context (cultural) A term that describes how people in a culture deliver, receive, and interpret messages. Low-context cultures rely on explicit language to communicate. High-context cultures derive meaning not just from words but from everything surrounding the words.

Convenience sample A survey population selected because you have easy access to that group.

Cover letter A persuasive letter or email sent to a prospective employer along with a résumé that "sells" your résumé to the employer.

Cover message A letter, memo, or email accompanying a formal report or proposal, designed to explain the document and persuade the audience to read it.

Credentials A term that refers to the user ID and password combination that is usually required to access online services.

Credibility An audience's belief that you have expertise and are trustworthy based on your knowledge, character, reputation, and behaviour.

Cultural intelligence A person's ability to adapt successfully when exposed to new cultural expectations.

Culture The learned and shared attitudes and behaviours that characterize a group of people. People demonstrate their culture through values, ideas, and attitudes.

Curator Someone who selectively organizes material on a specific topic using a social media tool such as a blog, podcast, Pinterest, or Scoop.it, and then shares this collection of material with interested parties using social media tools such as Twitter, Facebook, or Google+.

Currency Can either mean (1) a system of money/legal tender, usually within a defined geopolitical area, or (2) the quality of being up to date, current, in use, or generally accepted.

D

Data graphics Visual representations of data in tables and graphs that allow you to see relationships and trends much more clearly than in text alone.

Decode To interpret the words, images, and actions of a message and attach meaning to them.

Degree of richness (in MRT, or media richness theory) Describes the amount of information transmitted in a particular medium, including nonverbal and subtextual information.

Deliverables The items or services you agree to deliver to your audience.

Desktop search tool A search engine designed to search for files on your computer or file server that contain specific words or that were produced within a specific time period.

Digital assets Electronic files containing data, information, or intellectual property that have monetary value to the legal owner.

Direct message A message structure that states the main point first before providing additional details, such as the background or rationale for a recommendation.

Direct organization Stating the main idea of the message before the supporting details.

Diversity Any dimension that can be used to differentiate groups and people from one another, such as ethnicity, gender, gender identity, age, marital status, education, income, national origin, disability, sexual orientation, or religion.

Drafting A creative process that involves getting information on the paper or computer screen before revising and editing it.

E

Elevator pitch A concise statement designed to communicate the value of an idea, product, or job candidate; intrigue the audience; and initiate a deeper conversation.

Emoticons The series of characters used to represent facial expressions in emails and texts.

Encode To translate the meaning of the message into words, images, or actions.

Enterprise social collaboration (ESC) The use of social media and other communications technologies (integrated voice, mobile apps, video, instant messaging, SMS texting, and others) to foster increased teamwork and knowledge sharing for the purpose of improving business outcomes.

Ethics The principles used to guide decision making and lead a person to do the right thing.

Ethnocentrism A belief that your own culture is superior to all others.

Evaluating The process of reviewing your communication to ensure it is complete, accurate, clear, concise, easy to understand, and error free. When you are evaluating someone else's communication, it is the practice of critically reviewing and judging communication.

Executive summary A separate, stand-alone mini-report included at the beginning of a formal analytical report that completely summarizes the main ideas and recommendations of the report and may be read instead of the main report.

Exit interview A survey or interview conducted with an individual who is leaving an organization or business relationship.

Explanatory text Written explanations that offer additional useful detail.

External audiences People outside your organization (clients, suppliers, partners).

External benefits Advantages that someone else (i.e., a third party) gains when your audience complies with a request.

F

Fallacy A violation of logical reasoning that leads to a flawed argument.

Feedback Any form of verbal or nonverbal response to a message.

Firewall A network tool that examines network traffic and allows or disallows information to pass based on the rules provided by the network administrator.

First Nations A term used to refer to the peoples who inhabited Canada from the earliest times, before colonization. There are currently over 630 recognized First Nations governments or bands across Canada, roughly half of which are in the provinces of Ontario and British Columbia. As of 2011, the total population was nearly 700,000 people.

Flash mob A seemingly spontaneous public performance, usually a dance, that appears to begin out of nowhere and then quickly disperses. These are often organized through the use of social media and used to promote other events, charities, companies, ideas, or movements.

For-your-information (FYI) message A message written as an act of kindness to pass along information you think someone will appreciate knowing.

Forming A stage of team development in which members get to know each other.

Functional résumé A contemporary résumé style that emphasizes categories of skills rather than job experience.

G

Goodwill The positive relationship between you (or your company) and your audience.

Goodwill message Any message that gives you the opportunity to establish and sustain a positive relationship with your audience.

Graph A visual representation of data that illustrates the relationship among variables, usually in relationship to x- and y-axes.

Gravitas An attitude of dignity, seriousness, and gravity.

Groupthink A behaviour exhibited by a group that values conformity and avoids conflict. Team members will state they are in agreement when, in fact, they are not. It can result in one strong team member making most of the decisions while the creativity and individualism of other team members are suppressed.

H

Hacker A person who uses computers to gain unauthorized access to systems and data.

Halo effect A type of unconscious bias when receiving information in which a past impression of the speaker (or writer) influences the perception of his or her message. For example, if you like and respect a person, you will unconsciously perceive his or her messages in a positive light. On the other hand, if you dislike a person, you will perceive his or her messages in a negative light.

Hard skills Specific, "teachable" abilities that are usually measurable. Professional knowledge, tools, and techniques, such as driving skills, words per minute on a keyboard, accounting, math, or computer programming, are examples.

Headline test A quick method of assessing the ethical impact of a communication choice by visualizing the action and its outcome as part of a publicly accessible news story featuring the individual who made the choice and the organization he or she is employed by.

HTML HyperText Markup Language. One of the foundational languages of the Internet that allows the user to insert formatting and images into text that will be viewed in a browser or email program.

I

Idiom An expression that means something other than the literal meaning of its words.

Impromptu speaking Speaking without advance knowledge of the topic or question.

Inclusiveness The quality or characteristic of including everyone and excluding no one.

Indirect message A message structure that builds up a case for a main point, providing details, background, and rationale, before stating the main point of the message.

Indirect organization Building up to the main idea of the message after the supporting details.

Individualistic culture A culture that values an individual's achievements, satisfaction, and independent thinking.

Informational report A report that provides readers with facts that they can easily understand and refer to when necessary. Progress reports, travel reports, and summary reports are types of informational reports.

Internal audiences People with whom you communicate inside your organization.

Internal benefits Advantages that your audience will directly receive from complying with your request. These may include reduced workload, increased professional recognition, or financial gains.

Interpretation Analyzing the meaning of what you hear, read, or see to determine its intention.

Interview A research method involving a structured discussion between two or more people, usually in a question-and-answer format.

Inuit A member of the Indigenous people of northern Canada. May also refer to the family of languages of the Inuit, also known as Inuktitut.

Iterative process A process or cycle that repeats, often with additional elements or improvements.

J

Jargon The specialized language of a specific field.

K

Killer app A feature, function, or application that becomes highly valued or indispensable and thus becomes pervasive in use.

L

Letters Formal correspondence, generally intended for external audiences. Letters can be sent through postal mail or by email attachment for quicker delivery.

Limitations The characteristics of the research that prevent you from generalizing your findings more broadly.

M

Mean The average derived by adding all responses and dividing the sum by the number of responses.

Median The number that represents the middle number in a distribution or the most central number.

Medium The method you use to deliver your message (e.g., telephone, face-to-face meeting, email, text message, website, or other). Also called *channel*.

Message headlines Slide headlines that summarize the key point or message of each slide.

Métis Mixed-race descendants of First Nations women and French men who self-identify as Métis and are accepted into the Métis Nation.

Milestone A "mini-deadline" for completion of a small task that contributes to the overall completion of a larger project.

Minutes Notes that describe what was discussed at a meeting, what was decided, and what actions will follow.

Mode The number that most frequently appears in a distribution.

Monochronic culture A culture that values punctuality and efficiency.

Monologue A lengthy speech delivered by one person.

N

Network The circle of people who are aware of your career goals and can help you learn about career opportunities.

Noncompetitive proposal A proposal that has no competition because your audience will not be considering any offers other than yours.

Nonverbal communication Messages conveyed through means other than words, for example, tone of voice, facial expressions, gestures, and body language.

Norming A stage of team development in which team members learn how to manage conflict and work with each other effectively.

O

Observational research A research method that involves watching people perform relevant activities and recording details about what you observe.

Organizational culture The values and behaviours that contribute to the unique social and psychological environment of an organization (BusinessDictionary.com, n.d.).

Outcome The result of your communication. What you want the recipients of your message to know, do, or feel about the subject of your message.

P

Panel interview An interview format that involves several people, such as a search committee, who gather in a conference or seminar room with a job applicant to discuss the position.

Parallel phrasing Using the same grammatical form for each item in a list.

Parallel structure Writing that features a series of ideas in identical grammatical structure, making it easier to read and understand.

Paraphrase A version of what someone else says, but in your own words and with your own emphasis.

Paraphrasing Restating someone else's message in different words.

Passive listening Hearing the words being spoken without actively paying attention to their meaning.

Passive voice A sentence structure in which the subject is passive and receives the action expressed by the verb.

Performing A stage of team development in which team members work collaboratively and achieve a high level of productivity.

Persuasion The process of influencing your audience to agree with your point of view, recommendation, or request.

Plagiarism Intentionally or unintentionally failing to acknowledge others' ideas in your work by presenting other people's work as your own.

Plain text Digital text that has no special formatting or code attached to it. It is often saved in a *.txt file.

Platform agnostic A term that describes software and applications that are able to fully function across all operating systems and devices. Most web-based tools are platform agnostic since they can be accessed by most devices regardless of their operating system.

Podcast An audio or video presentation or program that is recorded, posted on a website or a social media site such as YouTube or Vimeo, and distributed through links.

Polychronic culture A culture that has a relaxed attitude toward time and punctuality.

Polysyllabic Having more than one syllable.

Portable document format (PDF) A file format that provides an image of a document that is usually readable across multiple platforms and can be saved in editable and noneditable formats.

Power distance A characteristic of cultures that describes how that culture perceives inequality and authority.

Primary audience The person or people to whom your message is directly addressed.

Primary research Collecting your own original data.

Primary sources Sources from which you collect your own raw data.

Process An explicit or implicit set of operations or actions, usually aimed toward a specified outcome.

Productivity The rate, quality, or effectiveness of effort. A measure of the efficiency of a person, machine, factory, system, and so on in converting inputs into useful outputs (BusinessDictionary.com, 2015b).

Professional brand The image you present of yourself that makes you stand out compared to other applicants.

Professionalism The qualities that make you appear businesslike in the workplace.

Progress report A report that updates supervisors on the status of a long-term project.

Proofreading A systematic process of reviewing writing for errors.

Proposal A communication, often in report form, designed to persuade a business decision maker to adopt a plan, approve a project, choose a product or service, or supply funding.

Purpose The reason for communicating.

Push technology Communications technology that delivers messages directly to an account or device.

Q

Qualitative research Research that provides insight into the attitudes, values, and concerns of research subjects through interviews and observation.

Quantitative research Research that relies on numerical data, such as that gathered from structured survey responses to which you can assign numbers.

Quotations Any phrases, sentences, paragraphs (even single, distinctive words) that you take from any of your sources.

R

Random sample A population selected broadly from all available members of the population you want to study.

Range The span between the highest and lowest values.

Receiver's perspective An approach to communication that presents the information from the audience's point of view. The receiver's perspective focuses on what the audience needs and wants. It also considers how the audience benefits from your message.

Recommendation A business message that suggests a solution to a business problem.

Recommendation report A report that analyzes options and recommends a course of action.

Redundancy Unnecessary repetition of an idea.

Reference list A list of secondary research sources used in a research report.

Refute To respond with the intention of proving that an objection is wrong.

Repurpose To change something so that it can be used for a different purpose.

Request for proposal (RFP) An invitation for suppliers to competitively submit proposals to provide a product or service.

Return on investment (ROI) The benefits to be experienced after investing a resource, such as time or money. It is most effectively expressed in terms of profitability, but can be expressed in terms of time saved or efficiencies gained.

Revising A logical process that involves evaluating the effectiveness of your message in relation to your audience and purpose and then making changes in content, organization, or wording, as necessary.

Routine business message A short, nonsensitive, straightforward communication that asks questions, answers questions, provides information, or confirms agreements.

S

Sample A representative portion of your population.

Scope The range of your research. A broad scope includes a wide range of content, whereas a narrow scope focuses on specific aspects of the topic.

Secondary audience People whom the primary audience may communicate with or influence, based on the content, format, or tone of your message. The secondary audience may receive a copy or hear about your message without you knowing.

Secondary research Searching published reports, articles, and books for information other people have collected.

Secondary sources The results of other people's research that you consult as part of your research.

Self-awareness Understanding who we are and how we are similar to and different from others. How we see our various personality traits, values, attitudes, and behaviours. Understanding how consistent or inconsistent our self-view is compared with how other people see us.

Slang Nonstandard, informal language that may communicate well within a certain group but often excludes people from different countries, cultures, and social groups. This type of casual and colourful language tends to confuse others when translated.

Slide deck A common term used to refer to a set of projected slides that support or guide a presentation.

Slide master A tool within presentation software that allows you to select design features that will apply to all slides.

Social media Web-based applications, such as blogs, Facebook, and Twitter, designed to promote social interaction.

Soft skills Skills that usually relate to one's ability to interact productively with others. Interpersonal skills, social skills, etiquette, and communication are examples.

Software as a service (SaaS) Similar to *cloud computing*. Companies can offer services (email, data processing, database management, word processing, collaboration tools, and thousands of others) by providing the processing and software at a central location and allowing users to sign in and access services via the Internet.

Solicited proposal A proposal that your audience has requested.

Solicited sales communication A response to a request for sales information.

Stand-alone presentation A slide deck that makes sense without the benefit of a presenter.

STAR method A method of answering a behavioural interview question by explaining a situation, task, and action that led to a positive result.

Stereotype A perception about an individual or group based on a belief that all people in a given group behave the same way.

Storming A stage of team development in which teams experience conflict and begin to confront differences.

Storyboard A slide-by-slide sketch of the presentation that is used as a tool for organizing the flow of the presentation.

Style How you express yourself.

Subject line The line in the header of an email that communicates what the message is about and influences whether the audience will read the message.

Summary A brief version of someone else's text using your own words.

Survey A predetermined list of questions used to collect a structured set of information from a selected audience.

Survey population The audience from whom you want to collect survey responses.

Sympathy message A message that expresses compassion and understanding when someone experiences a loss. Also called *condolences*.

Synchronous Refers to communication that takes place in "real time," such as a phone conversation, meeting, or instant messaging exchange.

Synonyms Words that have the same or similar meaning.

T

Table A graphic that arranges data in columns and rows, allowing you to read down or across to see different relationships.

Talking Stick In some First Nations cultures, a stick or other symbolic item is held in turn by each speaker in a gathering. Only the person with the Talking Stick is permitted to speak, and they may continue to hold the item for as long as required to finish speaking.

Targeted sample A sample that consists of only specific people from the group you are studying.

Team Two or more people who recognize and share a commitment to a specific, common goal and who collaborate in their efforts to achieve that goal.

Team charter A document that describes a team's agreed-upon style of working together and their commitment to specific standards and expectations. It is most effective when it is created with the participation of each team member.

Template A prototype or example of how a document can be organized, structured, or formatted.

Tertiary sources Books and articles that synthesize material from secondary sources.

Textspeak Text-based word usage that has been shortened to accommodate communications that are limited to 140 characters. It often features the absence of vowels and lowercase "i" instead of uppercase "I," and it is regarded as extremely poor form in any context.

Thank you message An expression of appreciation when someone has done something for you.

Thesaurus A reference tool that offers alternative words, specifically synonyms and antonyms.

Time sensitive Information that is relevant to a particular, defined timeframe. The relevance expires after the timeframe has passed.

Title page The first page of a formal report, which includes identifying information such as the report's title, the name of the person or organization for whom the report was written, the author's name, position, and organization, and the date of submission.

Tone The image your language projects about you based on how the message "sounds" to the audience. Tone in writing is similar to your tone of voice (e.g., friendly, angry, positive, negative, formal, casual, professional, unprofessional, courteous, rude).

Topic sentence A sentence that identifies the main point or overall idea of the paragraph. It is usually the first sentence in a paragraph.

Topic-specific headings Section or paragraph titles that are short but include key ideas. They are often in the form of a short sentence and include a verb.

Travel report A report that documents activities on a business trip and presents accomplishments and issues.

U

Unambiguous Having only one clear interpretation or meaning.

Uncertainty avoidance A measure of how comfortable a culture is with ambiguity, risk, and change.

Unique selling proposition The skills or qualities that set someone or something apart from the competition.

Unsolicited proposal A proposal that your audience is not expecting.

Unsolicited sales communication Sales messages you send to audiences who did not request the information. Also called "cold-call sales messages."

Upward inflection A rising intonational speech pattern on the final syllables of a sentence, often indicating a question.

URL Uniform Resource Locator. Also called a "link," "hyperlink," or "web address."

V

Virtual interview An interview conducted by telephone, Skype, or teleconference call, often used to narrow the candidate pool before scheduling an onsite visit.

Visual aid presentation A presentation in which the speaker's words carry the main story of the presentation and the slides provide illustration and backup.

Voice over Internet protocol (VoIP) A connectivity platform that allows users to send voice data over the Internet, using Internet networks as the transmission medium. It is gradually replacing conventional telephone transmissions. VoIP tends to make moderately high bandwidth demands.

W

Webcast A web-based presentation that is broadcast over the Internet but is typically not very interactive.

Webinar An interactive web-based seminar that is broadcast over the Internet to a live audience.

White paper A report produced by a company or organization to educate readers about a complex business issue, product, or technology.

Wiki (derived from the Hawaiian word for "quick" as well as an acronym for "What I Know Is . . .") A type of online collaborative site that allows for all contributors/team members to edit both content and structure.

Writer's block An inability to begin or continue writing, often as a result of procrastination. The stress of shortened deadlines can block creative writing skills.

REFERENCES

Ackerman, E. (2015, January 9). New research shows Facebook still king of social networks. *Forbes*. Retrieved from http://www.forbes.com/sites /eliseackerman/2015/01/09/new-research-shows-facebook-still-king-of -social-networks

Adichie, C. N. (2009a, July). The danger of a single story. TED Talks. Retrieved from http://www.ted.com/talks/chimamanda_adichie_the _danger_of_a_single_story?quote=561

Adichie, C. N. (2009b, July). TED Quotes. Retrieved from http://www.ted .com/quotes?q=Chimamanda+Ngozi+Adichie+

Agnes, M. (2012a, May 10). 4 steps to preventing a social media crisis. Social Media Crisis Management. Retrieved from http://www.melissaagnes .com/4-steps-to-preventing-a-social-media-crisis

Agnes, M. (2012b). Lessons shared from a real live social media crisis. Retrieved from http://www.melissaagnes.com

Agnes, M. (2012c, May 31). When should a brand apologize? PR Daily.com. Retrieved from http://www.prdaily.com/Main/Articles/When_should_a _brand_apologize_11782.aspx

Amirtha, T. (2014, December 15). A map of scientific plagiarism around the world. *Fast Company*. Retrieved from http://www.fastcolabs.com/3039921 /a-map-of-scientific-plagiarism-around-the-world

Anders, G. (2012, March 12). Smart social media helps jobs find you. *Harvard Business Review: HBR Blog Network*. Retrieved from http://blogs.hbr.org /cs/2012/03/smart_social_ media_helps_jobs.html

Andrew-Gee, E. (2015, January 9). Facebook most popular, Instagram most loved in social media survey. *Toronto Star*. Retrieved from http://www .thestar.com/business/2015/01/09/facebook_most_popular_instagram _most_loved_in_social_media_survey.html

Aristotle & Kennedy, G. A. (2006). *On rhetoric: A theory of civic discourse* (2nd ed.). New York, NY: Oxford University Press.

Associated Press. (2015, March 10). Blurred Lines case: Robin Thicke, Pharrell Williams plagiarized Marvin Gaye song, jury finds. *CBC News*. Retrieved from http://www.cbc.ca/news/arts/blurred-lines-case-robin-thicke -pharrell-williams-plagiarized-marvin-gaye-song-jury-finds-1.2989642

Augustine, A. (2014a, March 4). How to tap into the hidden job market. *The Ladders*. Retrieved from http://info.theladders.com/your-job-search /hidden-job-market

Augustine, A. (2014b, May 27). 9 signs you didn't land the job. *The Ladders*. Retrieved from http://info.theladders.com/yourjob-search/job-interviews -gone-wrong?et_id=4256344196

Backes, L. (2012, May 31). 5 tips to a great Skype interview [Blog post]. Retrieved from http://blog.simplyhired.com/2012/05/5-tips-to-a -great-skype-interview.html

Baddeley, A. (2010). Working memory. *Current Biology, 20*(4), R136–140.

Baird, C. H., & Parasnis, G. (2011). From social media to social CRM: What customers want. IBM Global Business Services. Retrieved from http:// www-935.ibm.com/services/us/gbs/thoughtleadership/ibv-social-crm -whitepaper.html

Baldoni, J. (2013, July 15). How Edward Burkhardt is making the Lac Megantic accident even worse. *Forbes*. Retrieved from http://www.forbes.com/sites /johnbaldoni/2013/07/15/how-edward-burkhardt-is-making-the-lac -megantic-accident-even-worse

Bannerman, S. (2013). Crowdfunding culture. *Wi: Journal of Mobile Media*, 7(1). Retrieved from http://wi.mobilities.ca/crowdfunding-culture

Bariso, J. (2014, December 18). Why your email sign-off is more important than you think. *Inc*. Retrieved from http://www.inc.com/justin-bariso/ why-your-email-sign-off-is-more-important-than-you-think.html

Barnlund, D. (1970). A transactional model of communication. In K. K. Sereno & C. D. Mortensen (Eds.), *Foundations of Communication Theory* (pp. 83–102). New York, NY: Harper & Row.

Barrett-Poindexter, J. (2011, November 17). The value of writing a LinkedIn profile that's different from your résumé [Blog post]. Retrieved from http://www.glassdoor.com/blog/writing-linkedin-profile-resume

Beall, M. L. (2010). Perspectives on intercultural listening. In A. D. Wolvin (Ed.), *Listening and human communication in the 21st century* (pp. 141–157). Chichester, UK: Wiley-Blackwell.

Beltrame, J., & Paddon, D. (2013, April 11). RBC publicly apologizes to employees affected by outsourcing arrangement. *Financial Post*. Retrieved from http://business.financialpost.com/2013/04/11/rbc-apology-outsourcing/

Bippus, A., & Young, S. (2005). Owning your emotions: Reactions to expressions of self- versus other-attributed positive and negative emotions. *Journal of Applied Communication Research, 33*(1), 26–45.

Bismilla, V. (2011, Winter). Is there a place for students' mother tongue in college classrooms? *Global Citizen Digest*. Retrieved from http://www .centennialcollege.ca/pdf/global_citizen_digest/Winter-2011.pdf

Blankenship, K., & Holtgraves, B. (2005). The role of different markers of linguistic powerlessness in persuasion. *Journal of Language and Social Psychology, 24*(1), 3–24.

Blazkova, H. (2011). Telling tales of professional competence: Narrative in 60-second business networking speeches. *Journal of Business Communication, 48*(4), 446–463.

Blue, G. M. (2012, March 31). 4 tips for conducting a job interview using Skype. *Inc*. Retrieved from http://www.inc.com/guides/201103/4-tips-for -conducting-a-job-interview-usingskype.html

Bolchover, D. (2012) Competing across borders: How cultural and communication barriers affect business. *The Economist Intelligence Unit*. Retrieved from http://www.economistinsights.com/countries-trade-investment/analysis /competing-across-borders

Booth, W., Colomb, G., & Williams, J. (2008). *The craft of research* (3rd ed.). Chicago, IL: University of Chicago Press.

Bortz, D. (2014, February 6). Tweet yourself to a new job. *CNNMoney*. Retrieved from http://money.cnn.com/2014/01/01/pf/twitter-job .moneymag

Bowers, T. (2012, June 5). 10 resume mistakes to avoid. Retrieved from http://www.techrepublic.com/blog/career/10-resume-mistakes-to -avoid/4355

Bozorgian, H. (2012, July 10). Listening skill requires a further look into second/foreign language learning. *ISRN Education, 2012*. doi:10.5402/2012/810129

Brake, T. (2013). *Cultural intelligence: People building productive relationships in a world of difference*. London, UK: Transnational Management Associated Ltd. Retrieved from http://ebooks.tmaworld.com/ci

British Gas Twitter. (2013, October 17). Retrieved from https://twitter.com /BritishGas/status/390813129279823873/photo/1

Brock, S. (2012, May 20). Why can't our new workforce communicate? What can we do about it? [Blog post]. Retrieved from https://hcexchange .conference-board.org/blog/post.cfm?post=656

Brody, L., & Hall, J. (2008). Gender and emotion in context. In M. Lewis, J. Haviland-Jones, and L. Barrett (Eds.), *Handbook of emotions* (pp. 395–408). New York, NY: Guildford Press.

Brownell, J. (2010). The skills of listening-centered communication. In A. D. Wolvin (Ed.), *Listening and human communication in the 21st century* (pp. 141–157). Chichester, UK: Wiley-Blackwell.

Bryant, A. (2010, March 12). Three good hires? He'll pay more for one who's great. *New York Times*. Retrieved from http://www.nytimes.com /2010/03/14/business/14corners.html?scp=1&sq=tindell&st=cse

Bryant, A. (2011, April 1). You've passed the interview. Now give us a presentation. [Interview with Chris Cunningham]. *New York Times*. Retrieved from http://www.nytimes.com/2011/04/03/business/03corner .html?_r=1

Bryant, A. (2012, March 10). The memo list: Where everyone has an opinion. *New York Times.* Retrieved from http://www.nytimes.com/2012/03/11 /business/jim-whitehurst-of-red-hat-on-merits-of-an-open-culture .html?pagewanted=allm

Business meeting etiquette [Blog post]. (2008). Retrieved from http://www .chinatrade.com/blog/business-meeting-etiquette

BusinessDictionary.com. (2015a). Organizational culture. Retrieved from http://www.businessdictionary.com/definition/organizational-culture .html#ixzz3AwHYWKBA

BusinessDictionary.com. (2015b). Productivity. Retrieved from http://www .businessdictionary.com/definition/productivity.html#ixzz3kAgeJQ7i

Buttle, F. A. (2011). Word of mouth: Understanding and managing referral marketing. *Journal of Strategic Marketing, 8*(3), 241–254.

Canadian Council of Chief Executives. (2014, January). Preliminary survey report: The skill needs of major Canadian employers. Retrieved from http://www.ceocouncil.ca/wp-content/uploads/2014/01/Preliminary -report-on-skills-survey-Jan-20-2014-2.pdf

Canadian Press. (2009, January 2). Maple Leaf Foods CEO business newsmaker of the year. *The Telegram.* Retrieved from http://www.thetelegram.com /Living/2009-01-02/article-1451726/Maple-Leaf-Foods-CEO-business -newsmaker-of-the-year/1

CareerBuilder.com. (2012, April 18). Thirty-seven percent of companies use social networks to research potential job candidates, according to new CareerBuilder survey. Retrieved from http://www.careerbuilder.ca/share /aboutus/pressreleasesdetail.aspx?id=pr691&sd=4%2F18%2F2012&ed =4%2F18%2F2099

Carroll, D. (2012). *United breaks guitars: The power of one voice in the age of social media.* Retrieved from http://www.davecarrollmusic.com/book

Casey, K. (2012, April 30). 5 tips for handling complaints on social media. *Information Week.* Retrieved from http://www.informationweek.com/news /smb/ebusiness/232901141

Cassidy, J. (2011, July 25). Mastering the machine: How Ray Dalio built the world's richest and strangest hedge fund. *The New Yorker,* 56–65.

Catalyst. (n.d.). Infographic: The 2015 Canadian smartphone market. Retrieved from http://catalyst.ca/infographic-2015-canadian-smartphone-market

CBC Sports. (2008, June 19). *Hockey Night in Canada* theme contest opens. Retrieved from http://www.cbc.ca/sports/hockey/hockey-night-in-canada -theme-contest-opens-1.748296

Central Desktop. (2011, March 23). The state of social collaboration [Blog post]. Retrieved from http://cdblog.centraldesktop.com/2011/03/the-state -of-social-collaboration

Chain Store Age. (2015, January 16). Analysis: Target's Canadian lessons. Retrieved from http://www.chainstoreage.com/article/analysis-targets -canadian-lessonsf

Chui, M., et al. (2012, July). The social economy: Unlocking value and pro- ductivity through social technologies. McKinsey Global Institute. Retrieved from http://www.mckinsey.com/insights/high_tech_telecoms_internet /the_social_economy

Cialdini, R. (2001, October). Harnessing the science of persuasion. *Harvard Business Review,* 72–79.

Cialdini, R. (2009). *Influence: Science and practice* (5th ed.). Upper Saddle River, NJ: Pearson Education.

Citizenship and Immigration Canada. (2012, October 19). Canadian multicul- turalism: An inclusive citizenship. Retrieved from http://www.cic.gc.ca /english/multiculturalism/citizenship.asp

Clark, R. C., & Mayer, R. E. (2008). *E-learning and the science of instruction: Proven guidelines for consumers and designers of multimedia learning* (2nd ed.). Hoboken, NJ: Wiley.

Clarke, D., & Henry, D. (2012, June 10). Mr. Dimon goes to Washington. Reuters. Retrieved from http://www.reuters.com/article/2012/08/10 /us-jpmorgan-loss-senate-idUSBRE85908J20120810

Colao, J. (2012, September). With 60 million websites, Wordpress rules the web. So where's the money? *Forbes.* Retrieved from http://www.forbes .com/sites/jjcolao/2012/09/05/the-internets-mother-tongue

Collamer, N. (2013, February 4). The perfect elevator pitch to land a job. *Forbes.* Retrieved from http://www.forbes.com/sites/nextavenue /2013/02/04/the-perfectelevator-pitch-to-land-a-job

Collier, M. (2011). Social media crisis management: A no-nonsense guide. MackCollior.com. Retrieved from http://www.mackcollier.com/social -media-crisis-management

Communicaid Group, Ltd. (2009). Doing business in Mexico: Mexican social business and culture. Retrieved from http://www.communicaid.com /access/pdf/library/culture/doing-business-in/Doing%20Business%20in %20Mexico.pdf

Community Foundations of Canada. (n.d.). Diversity at work: Elements of a diverse workforce. Retrieved from http://hrcouncil.ca/hr-toolkit/ diversity-workforce.cfm

The Conference Board. (2008). New graduates' workforce readiness: The mid-market perspective. Retrieved from http://www.conference-board.org /Publications/describe.cfm?id=1422

Conference Board of Canada. (2015, February 5). British Columbia economy losing billions due to skills shortage. Retrieved from http://www .conferenceboard.ca/press/newsrelease/15-02-05/british_columbia _economy_losing_billions_due_to_skills_shortage.aspx

Conger, J. (1998, May–June). The necessary art of persuasion. *Harvard Business Review,* 84–95.

Content Marketing Institute. (2013). What is content marketing? Retrieved from http://contentmarketinginstitute.com/what-is-content-marketing

Cooper, P. (2013, August 28). How to be a good listener. Panel discussion hosted by *Huffington Post.* Retrieved from http://live.huffingtonpost.com/r /segment/how-to-actually-be-a-good-listener-/521caaef02a7605390000036

Corporate Valley. (2013, July 13). Barack Obama inspirational speech [Video file]. Retrieved from http://www.youtube.com/watch?v=CzII3W2MLYY

CorpU TV. (2008, July 3). Aaron's—Selecting an LMS vendor. [Video file]. For an example of a testimonial video on a learning management system. Retrieved from http://www.youtube.com/watch?v=n_Cx7qZjSdQ

Cosh, C. (2009, August 21). A man and his guitar. *Financial Post.* Retrieved from http://www.financialpost.com/scripts/story.html?id=f9065720 -c55a-4612-84eb-e168fd37ed1f&k=15437

Courville, R. (2009). *The virtual presenter's handbook.* Troutdale, OR: 1080 Group LLC.

Covey, S. R. (n.d.). Habit 2: Begin with the end in mind. Retrieved from http://www.stephencovey.com/7habits/7habits-habit2.php

Cowan, N. (2001). The magical number 4 in short-term memory: A reconsid- eration of mental storage capacity. *Behavioral and Brain Sciences, 24*(1), 87–114.

CPP, Inc. (2008, July). Workplace conflict and how businesses can harness it to thrive. Retrieved from http://img.en25.com/Web/CPP/Conflict_report .pdf

CreateSurvey. (2012). Guideline for branching. Retrieved from http://www .createsurvey.com/docs/guideline_for_branching.html

Creelman, V. (2012). The case for "living" models. *Business Communication Quarterly, 75*(2), 178–191.

CSM. (2011, March 9). Customer research shows bad news travels fast. *Customer Service Magazine.* Retrieved from http://www.customerservice manager.com/customer-research-shows-bad-news-travels-fast.htm

Darics, E. (2010). Relational work in synchronous text-based CMC of virtual teams. In R. Taiwo (Ed.), *Handbook of research on discourse behavior and digital communication: Language structures and social interaction* (pp. 830–851). Retrieved from http://www.academia.edu/1369298/Relational_work_in _synchronous_text-based_CMC_of_virtual_teams

Davis, H. (2013) Down with uptalk. Insight @ Guelph [Blog post]. Retrieved from http://www.uoguelph.ca/atguelph/02-02-13/insight.html.

DeKay, S. H. (2012). Where is the research on negative messages? *Business Communication Quarterly, 75*(2), 173–175.

Dell Computer. (2012). Idea Storm. Retrieved from http://www.ideastorm.com

DeWitt, J. (2014, September 22). 5 Tips for new team leaders. *Harvard Business Review.* Retrieved from https://hbr.org/2014/09/5-tips-for-new-team-leaders

DIALOG. (2014). DIALOG named one of Canada's 50 engaged workplaces. Retrieved from http://www.dialogdesign.ca/open-dialog/dialog-named -one-canadas-50-engaged-workplaces

Diana, Princess of Wales. (1997, June 12). Responding to landmines: A modern tragedy and its consequences. Keynote speech delivered at a seminar co-hosted by the Mines Advisory Group and the Landmine Survivors Network, London, UK. Retrieved from http://gos.sbc.edu/d/diana.html

Dierdorff, E., & Rubin, R. S. (2015, March 12). Research: We're not very self-aware, especially at work. *Harvard Business Review*. Retrieved from https://hbr.org/2015/03/research-were-not-very-self-aware-especially-at-work

Dietrich, G. (2012, January 13). FedEx customer video turned good PR. *Social Media Today*. Retrieved from http://socialmediatoday.com/ginidietrich/427273/fedex-customer-video-turned-good-pr

Direct Marketing Association. (2012, June 14). DMA releases 2012 response rate report. DMA. Retrieved from http://newdma.org/2012responseratereport

Dlugan, A. (2010, January 24). Ethos, pathos, logos: 3 pillars of public speaking. Six minutes: Speaking and presentation skills. Retrieved from http://sixminutes.dlugan.com/ethos-pathos-logos

Donnelly, T. (2011, January 14). How to deliver bad news to employees. *Inc.* Retrieved from http://www.inc.com/guides/201101/how-to-deliver-bad-news-to-employees.html

Doughtery, J. (2014, January 25). Job recruiters use social to vet prospects rather than find them [Infographic]. *Social Media Today*. Retrieved from http://socialmediatoday.com/leaderswest/2107916/infographic-job-recruiters-use-socialvet-prospects-rather-find-them

Dwyer, A. (2010). Customer-service gaffes can pay off. *Globe and Mail*. Retrieved from http://www.theglobeandmail.com/report-on-business/small-business/sb-marketing/customer-service-gaffes-can-pay-off/article4258796

Dyer, P. (2013). 50 top tools for social media monitoring, analytics and management. *Social Media Today*. Retrieved from http://socialmediatoday.com/pamdyer/1458746/50-top-tools-social-media-monitoring-analytics-and-management-2013

The Economic Times. (2015, February 3). India to have 651 million smartphones, 18.7 billion tables by 2019. Retrieved from http://articles.economictimes.indiatimes.com/2015-02-03/news/58751662_1_networking-index-mobile-users-population

The Economist. (2010, June 10). Stay on target. Retrieved from http://www.economist.com/node/16295664

Edison Research. (2012). The podcast consumer 2012. Retrieved from http://www.edisonresearch.com/home/archives/2012/05/the-podcast-consumer-2012.php

Ekman, P. (2007). *Emotions revealed: Recognizing faces and feelings to improve communication and emotional life* (2nd ed.). New York, NY: Henry Holt & Co.

Elliott, T. (2013, October 21). Naheed Nenshi wins Calgary election. *Global News*. Retrieved from http://globalnews.ca/news/916467/naheed-nenshi-wins-calgary-election

Emanuel, R., Adams, J., Baker, K., Daufin, E., Ellington, C., Fitts, E., & Okeowo, D. (2008). How college students spend their time communicating. *International Journal of Listening, 22*(1), 13–28.

eMarketer. (2010, March 6). Social fans more likely to buy. Retrieved from http://www.emarketer.com/Article.aspx?R=1007568

Environmental Paper Network. (2007). The state of the paper industry: Monitoring the indicators of environmental performance. Retrieved from http://www.environmentalpaper.com/documents/StateOfPaperIndSm.pdf

Experian. (2013). *Data Breach Response Guide: 2013–2014 Edition*. Retrieved from http://www.experian.com/assets/data-breach/brochures/response-guide.pdf

Farrington, J. (2008). Customer complaints: The income multiplier effect. CRM-Daily.com. Retrieved from http://www.crm-daily.com/story.xhtml?story_id=122002AUBP0I&full_skip=1

Faville, K., & List, A. (2011, August 30). Cone releases the 2011 online influence trend tracker. Cone Communications. Retrieved from http://www.coneinc.com/negative-reviews-online-reverse-purchase-decisions

Fenn, D. (2010, August 31). 10 ways to get more sales from existing customers. *Inc.* Retrieved from http://www.inc.com/guides/2010/08/get-more-sales-from-existing-customers.html

Ferrazzi, K. (2012, November 19). How to manage conflict in virtual teams. *Harvard Business Review*. Retrieved from https://hbr.org/2012/11/how-to-manage-conflict-in-virt

Ferrazzi, K. (2013, September 17). New people rules in a virtual world. Technomy. Retrieved from http://technomy.com/conf/13-detroit/job-creation/the-new-people-rules-in-a-virtual-world/

Ferrazzi, K. (2015, March 27). How to run a great virtual meeting. *Harvard Business Review*. Retrieved from https://hbr.org/2015/03/how-to-run-a-great-virtual-meeting

Fertig, A. (2013, October 22). Ensuring your résumé avoids applicant tracking system pitfalls. *US News*. Retrieved from http://money.usnews.com/money/blogs/outside-voicescareers/2013/10/22/ensuring-your-resume-avoids-applicanttracking-system-pitfalls

Few, S. (2010, May 26). BP oil collection: Is the effort really improving? [Blog post]. Retrieved from http://www.perceptualedge.com/blog/?p=790

Fields, M. (2012). Fourteen thought provoking social media quotes and resources. Retrieved from http://socialmediachimps.com/2012/14-thought-provoking-social-media-quotes-resources

Fiorella, S. (2011, July 30). Bringing the sales organization into the social relationship [Blog post]. Retrieved from http://www.thesocialcmo.com/blog/2011/07/bringing-the-sales-organization-into-the-social-relationship

Flynn, J., Valikoski, T., & Grau, J. (2008). Listening in the business context: Reviewing the state of research. *International Journal of Listening, 22*(2), 141–151.

Formula for success. (1992, December). *Financial World, 161*(24), 40.

Francis, W. (2013, September 18). As quoted in Twitter complaints: Companies respond more quickly. *BBC: Consumer knowledge and learning*. Retrieved from http://www.bbc.co.uk/consumer/24149289

Gabrielle, B. (2010). *Speaking PowerPoint: The new language of business*. Kirkland, WA: Insights Publishing.

Gambles, I. (2009). *Making the business case: Proposals that succeed for projects that work*. Surrey, UK: Gower Publishing, Ltd.

Gartner Newsroom. (2012, April 11). Gartner says worldwide PC shipments grew 1.9 percent in first quarter of 2012. Retrieved from http://www.gartner.com/it/page.jsp?id=1981717

Gartner Newsroom. (2013, January 29). Gartner says 80 percent of social business efforts will not achieve intended benefits through 2015. Retrieved from http://www.gartner.com/newsroom/id/2319215

Geddes-Soltess, Z. (2012, December 6). How to simplify your social media content [Blog post]. *Salesforce Marketing Cloud Blog*. Retrieved from http://www.salesforcemarketingcloud.com/blog/2012/12/how-to-simplify-your-social-media-content/

Giang, V. (2012a, May 23). This heatmap proves that looks are the most important thing on your LinkedIn profile. *Business Insider*. Retrieved from http://www.businessinsider.com/should-you-include-a-picture-on-your-linkedin-profile-2012-5

Giang, V. (2012b, April 9). What recruiters look at during the 6 seconds they spend on your résumé. *Business Insider*. Retrieved from http://www.businessinsider.com/heres-what-recruiters-look-at-during-the-6-seconds-they-spend-on-your-resume-2012-4

Gibson, R. (2014, February). An interview with a passionate interculturalist in the business world. *SIETAR EUROPA Journal*. Retrieved from http://www.sietareu.org/images/stories/newsletters/sietar_journal_dec-feb_2014.pdf

Glover, P. (2012, March 12). Team conflict: Why it's a good thing. *Fast Company*. Retrieved from http://www.fastcompany.com/1824515/team-conflict-why-its-a-good-thing

Goman, C. K. (2012, May 7). 10 body language tips to help you land that first job. *Forbes*. Retrieved from http://www.forbes.com/sites/carolkinseygoman/2012/05/07/10-tips-to-help-you-land-that-first-job

Gong, K. (2011). Cultural difference effects on business: Holding up Sino-U.S. business negotiation as a model. *Cross-Cultural Communication, 7*(2), 101–104.

Goodwin, J. (2010, August 17). Malpractice suits drop when doctors admit mistakes, fewer malpractice suits result, study says. *BusinessWeek*. Retrieved from http://www.businessweek.com/lifestyle/content/healthday/842158.html

Gordon, J. (2006). *Presentations that change minds*. New York, NY: McGraw-Hill.

Government of Canada. (1985a). Access to Information Act. Revised Statues of Canada (1985, c. A-1). Retrieved from http://laws-lois.justice.gc.ca/eng/acts/A-1/page-1.html#h-2

Government of Canada. (1985b). Copyright Act. Revised Statues of Canada (1985, c. C-49). Retrieved from http://laws-lois.justice.gc.ca/eng/acts/c-42

Government of Canada. (2015, January 23). The Canada 150 logo design contest. Retrieved from http://www.canada150.gc.ca/eng/1407417717020

Graham, S. (2011, August 2). Using social media to improve employee communication, collaboration, and even compensation. *Fast Company*. Retrieved from http://www.fastcompany.com/1770955/using-social-media-improve-employee-communication-collaboration-and-even-compensation

Grant, M. (2014, February 26). Twitter got your tongue? How social media ruined my interview skills. *USA Today—College*. Retrieved from http://college.usatoday.com/2014/02/26/twitter-got-your-tongue-how-social-media-ruined-my-interview-skills/

Green, A. (2012, April 18). The 10 best interview questions to ask. *US News & World Report*. Retrieved from money.usnews.com/money/blogs/outside-voices-careers/2012/04/18/the-10-best-interview-questions-to-ask

Grohmann, K. (2009, October 2). Olympics-FIFA's blatter moved by Lula's Rio 2016 bid speech. Reuters. Retrieved from http://www.reuters.com/article/olympicsNews/idUSL257623920091002

Guimaraes, T. (2015, February 9). The top demographic trends for every major social network. *Business Insider*. Retrieved from http://www.businessinsider.com/2015-social-network-demographic-trends-2015-2

Guppta, K. (2014, December 15). Dave Pell of NextDraft: Email is still a killer app, and newsletters are hot again. *Forbes*. Retrieved from http://www.forbes.com/sites/kavigupta/2014/12/15/dave-pell-of-nextdraft-email-is-still-a-killer-app-and-newsletters-are-hot-again

Gupta, N. (2013, March 11). Texting: The great untapped business resource. *Fast Company*. Retrieved from http://www.fastcompany.com/3006745/texting-great-untapped-business-resource

Hackos, J., & Winstead, J. (1995). Finding out what users need and giving it to them: A case study at Federal Express. *Technical Communication 42*(2), 322–327.

Hall, E. (n.d.). Quotlr. Retrieved from http://quotlr.com/author/edward-t-hall

Hall, G. (2012, May 12). 6 things on your LinkedIn profile that shouldn't be on your résumé. Mashable. Retrieved from http://mashable.com/2012/05/12/linkedin-profile-resume

Halperin, J. (2012, February 13). Presentation tip: Communicating bad news. *Forbes*. Retrieved from http://www.forbes.com/sites/propointgraphics/2012/02/13/presentation-tip-communicating-bad-news

Hargie, O. (2011). Communicating without words: Skilled nonverbal behavior. In O. Hargie, *Skilled interpersonal communication: Research, theory and practice* (5th ed., pp. 43–82). New York, NY: Routledge.

Harris, S. (2014, August 20). How Gregg's turned Google logo disaster into a PR positive. *Daily Express*. Retrieved from http://www.express.co.uk/news/uk/501209/Offensive-Greggs-logo-appears-on-Google-profile

Harris, T. E., & Sherblom, J. C. (2011). *Small group and team communication*. Upper Saddle River, NJ: Pearson.

Harte, B. (2009, December 10). Introducing "The state of social media marketing" report. MarketingProfs. Retrieved from http://www.mpdailyfix.com/introducing-the-state-of-social-media-marketing-report/

Hedderich, N. (1999). Review of Richard D. Lewis, *When Cultures Collide: Managing Successfully Across Cultures. Global Business Languages, 4*, article 12.

Hill, K. (2012, January 24). When a hashtag becomes a bashtag. *Forbes*. Retrieved from http://www.forbes.com/sites/kashmirhill/2012/01/24/mcdstories-when-a-hashtag-becomes-a-bashtag

Hocutt, M. A., Bowers, M. R., & Donavan, D. T. (2008). The art of service recovery: Fact or fiction? *Journal of Services Marketing, 20*(3), 199–207.

Hofstede, G., & Minkow, M. (2010). *Cultures and organizations: Software of the mind* (3rd ed.). New York, NY: McGraw-Hill.

Holmes, R. (2013, September 9). Will social media help kill bad customer service? LinkedIn. Retrieved from http://www.linkedin.com/pulse/20130909170326-2967511-will-social-media-help-kill-bad-customer-service

Hu, J. (2001). An alternative perspective of language re-use: Insights from textual and learning theories and L2 academic writing. *English Quarterly, 33*(1), 52–62.

Huang, L. (2010). Cross-cultural communication in business negotiations. *International Journal of Economics and Finance, 2*(2), 196–199.

Hudson, L. (2009, September 19). Fitting in, and rising to the top: An interview with Adam Bryant. *New York Times*. Retrieved from http://www.nytimes.com/2009/09/20/business/20corner.html

Humber, T. (2012, June 11). Warming up to flex time. *Canadian HR Reporter*. Retrieved from http://www.hrreporter.com/blog/Editor/archive/2012/06/11/warming-up-to-flex-time

Hume, T. (2012, February 3). The secrets of doing business in India. CNN.com. Retrieved from http://edition.cnn.com/2012/02/03/business/doing-business-india

Hupert, A. (2009, April 30). Chinese negotiation: Doing the business vs. doing the deal. *Chinese Negotiation*. Retrieved from http://www.chinesenegotiation.com/2009/04/chinese-negotiation-%E2%80%93-doing-the-business-vs-doing-the-deal

Indigenous Corporate Training Inc. (2015). Retrieved from http://www.ictinc.ca/team

INSEE. (2015). National Institute of Statistics and Economic Studies. Retrieved from http://www.insee.fr/en/default.asp

Intel. (2012). Intel social media guidelines. Retrieved from http://www.intel.com/content/www/us/en/legal/intel-social-media-guidelines.html

International Energy Agency. (2014). WEO 2014 electricity database. [Excel spreadsheet]. *World Energy Outlook*. Retrieved from http://www.worldenergyoutlook.org/resources/energydevelopment/energyaccessdatabase

ITIM International. (2009). *Geert Hofstede: Cultural dimensions*. Retrieved from http://www.geert-hofstede.com/hofstede_united_states.shtml

Jack, R. E., Blais, C., Scheepers, C., Schyns, P., & Caldera, R. (2009). Cultural confusions show that facial expressions are not universal. *Current Biology, 19*, 1543–1548.

Jansen, F., & Janssen, D. (2010). Effects of positive politeness strategies in business letters. *Journal of Pragmatics, 42*(9), 2531–2548.

Janusik, L., & Wolvin, A. (2009). 24 hours in a day. *International Journal of Listening, 23*(2), 104–120.

Jobvite. (2013). 2013 Social recruiting survey results. Retrieved from http://web.jobvite.com/rs/jobvite/images/Jobvite_Social Recruiting2013.pdf

Jobvite. (2014). 2014 Jobvite job seeker nation study. Retrieved from http://web.jobvite.com/rs/jobvite/images/2014%20Job% 20Seeker%20Survey.pdf

Jordan, J. (2013, April 8). Emails opened on mobile? Start designing for fingers and thumbs [Blog post]. Retrieved from https://litmus.com/blog/emails-opened-on-mobile-start-designing-for-fingers-and-thumbs

Joseph, B. (2015, January 20). First Nation talking stick protocol [Blog post]. Retrieved from http://www.ictinc.ca/blog/first-nation-talking-stick-protocol

Joseph, B. (n.d.). 23 tips on working effectively with Aboriginal peoples: Tips on what not to say or do. Retrieved from http://www.ictinc.ca/23-working-effectively-with-aboriginal-peoples-tips-on-what-not-to-say-or-do

JPMorgan Chase. (2012a, May 10). Business update. Retrieved from http://i.mktw.net/_newsimages/pdf/jpm-conference-call.pdf

JPMorgan Chase. (2012b, May 10). Investor presentations. Retrieved from http://investor.shareholder.com/jpmorganchase/presentations.cfm

Karim, K. (2009). Pundits, pachyderms and pluralism: The never-ending debate on multiculturalism. *Canadian Journal of Communication, 34*, 701–710.

Katz, L. (2008, March). Negotiating international business: Italy. In L. Katz (Ed.), *Negotiating international business: The negotiator's reference guide to 50 countries around the world*. Retrieved from http://www.globalnegotiationresources.com/cou/Italy.pdf

Katz, L. (2011, August). Negotiating international business: Brazil. In L. Katz (Ed.), *Negotiating international business: The negotiator's reference guide to 50 countries around the world*. Retrieved from http://www.globalnegotiationresources.com/cou/Brazil.pdf

Katzenbach, J., & Smith, D. (1993). *The wisdom of teams: Creating the high performance organization*. Boston, MA: Harvard Business School Press.

Kauffman, C. (2014, August 12). Set the tone for trust [Video]. *Harvard Business Review*. Retrieved from http://hbr.org/video/?bcpid=2072970314001&bckey=AQ~~,AAAB4mHtenE~,_rixfzbq5sX3kYRD-76PJa-Z8t5PlMpq&bctid=3117517466001

Kawasaki, G. (2010, March 19). Just give him 5 sentences, not "War and Peace." Interview by Adam Bryant. *New York Times*. Retrieved from http://www.nytimes.com/2010/03/21/business/21corner.html

Kelly, N. (2012, May 10). 5 ways social media can increase your revenue from existing customers. *Social Media Examiner*. Retrieved from http://www.socialmediaexaminer.com/turn-customers-into-increased-revenue

Kennedy, J. L. (2014). How to create a personal brand for your job search. Dummies.com. Retrieved from http://www.dummies.com/how-to/content/how-to-create-a-personal-brand-for-your-job-search.html

Kenrick, D. T., Goldstein, N. J., & Braver, S. L. (Eds.). (2012). *Six degrees of social influence: Science, application, and the psychology of Robert Cialdini*. New York, NY: Oxford University Press.

Kerkhof, P. (2012, June 2). Talking to customers: Characteristics of effective social media conversations. Conference presentation at the 11th European Conference of the Association for Business Communication.

Kerkhof, P., Schultz, F., & Utz., S. (2011, May). How to choose the right weapon. Social media represent both a catalyst for and weapon against brand crises. *Communication Director*, pp. 78–79.

Kerpen, D. (2011). *Likeable social media*. New York, NY: McGraw-Hill.

Kilmann, R. H. (2011, April). Celebrating 40 years with the TKI assessment. *CPP Author Insights*. Retrieved from http://www.cpp.com/PDFs/Author_Insights_April_2011.pdf

Kirchner, Z. (2011, August 31). Research report: Be prepared by climbing the social business hierarchy of needs. Altimeter Group. Retrieved from http://www.altimetergroup.com/2011/08/research-report-be-prepared-by-climbing-the-social-business-hierarchy-of-needs.html

Knapp, M., & Hall, J. (2009). *Nonverbal communication in human interaction* (7th ed.). Belmont, CA: Wadsworth Publishing.

Kovach, S. (2014, November 27). Facebook's privacy policy is changing and you're going to get a long email about it. *Business Insider*. Retrieved from http://www.businessinsider.com/facebook-privacy-policy-change-2014-11

Krakovsky, M. (2009). National poker face. *Psychology Today, 42*(1), 20.

Kwintessential. (2014). Doing business in . . . Etiquette and protocol guidelines. Retrieved from http://www.kwintessential.co.uk/etiquette/doing-business-in.html

The Ladders. (2012). Keeping an eye on recruiter behavior: New study clarifies recruiter decision-making. Retrieved from http://cdn.theladders.net/static/images/basicSite/pdfs/TheLadders-EyeTracking-StudyC2.pdf

LaFasto, F., & Larson, C. (2001). *When teams work best: 6,000 team members and leaders tell what it takes to succeed*. Newbury Park, CA: Sage.

Langley, M. (2012, May 18). Inside JPMorgan's blunder. *Wall Street Journal*. Retrieved from http://online.wsj.com/article/SB10001424052702303448404577410341238847980.html

Lapowsky, I. (2013, April 8). Don't multitask: Your brain will thank you. *Inc.* Retrieved from http://www.inc.com/magazine/201304/issie-lapowsky/get-more-done-dont-multitask.html

Lewin, K., Llippit, R., & White, R. K. (1939). Patterns of aggressive behavior in experimentally created social climates. *Journal of Social Psychology, 10*, 271–301.

Lewis, K. R. (2011, October 26). Should you include volunteer work on a résumé? *CNNMoney*. Retrieved from http://management.fortune.cnn.com/2011/10/20/should-you-include-volunteer-work-on-a-resume

Lewis, R. (2006). *When cultures collide: Leading across cultures* (3rd ed.). Boston, MA: Nicholas Brealey Publishing.

Lewis, S. (2010). Reading for the love of it (Part 1) [Video file]. Retrieved from http://www.youtube.com/watch?v=TsU6C46msvI

Lewis, S. (2013). Interview. TVO's *The Agenda with Steve Paikin* [Video file]. Retrieved from http://www.youtube.com/watch?v=IqxXtAH6I94

Litmus Email Analytics. (2015). Email client market share. Retrieved from http://emailclientmarketshare.com

Llarena, M. (2012, April 12). R.A.T.S. is how employers prioritize the S.T.A.R. method. Retrieved from http://melissallarena.com/news/r-a-t-s-how-employers-prioritize-s-t-a-r-method

Llopis, G. (2013, May 20). 6 ways effective listening can make you a better leader. *Forbes*. Retrieved from http://www.forbes.com/sites/glennllopis/2013/05/20/6-effective-ways-listening-can-make-you-a-better-leader/

Loomer, J. (2012, May 6). Detailed history of Facebook changes, 2004–2012 [Blog post]. Retrieved from http://www.jonloomer.com/2012/05/06/history-of-facebook-changes

Luckerson, V. (2013, September 3). Man spends more than $1,000 to call out British Airways on Twitter. *Time*. Retrieved from http://business.time.com/2013/09/03/man-spends-more-than-1000-to-call-out-british-airways-on-twitter

MacLachlan, M. (2010, April 6) Becoming a cultural chameleon: Adaptability skills essential for cross cultural success. Communicaid Cross-Cultural Training Blog. Retrieved from http://www.communicaid.com/cross-cultural-training/blog/becoming-a-cultural-chameleon-adaptability-skills-essential-for-cross-cultural-success/#.U-OW1GMh231

Managing People at Work. (2005). Making room for emotions at work. Retrieved from http://www.managingpeopleatwork.com/Article.php?art_num=3902

Maoz, M. (2012, January 31). Social CRM for customer support—Peer Power [Blog post]. Michael Maoz: Gartner Blog Network. Retrieved from http://blogs.gartner.com/michael_maoz/2012/01/31/social-crm-for-customer-support-peer-power

March, J. (2012, February 27). How to turn social feedback into valuable business data. Mashable Social Media. Retrieved from http://mashable.com/2012/02/27/social-data-insights/

Masuda, T., & Nisbett, R. (2001). Attending holistically versus analytically: Comparing the context sensitivity of Japanese and Americans. *Journal of Personality and Social Psychology, 81*(5), 922–934. Retrieved from http://www.ualberta.ca/~tmasuda/index.files/Masuda&Nisbett2001.pdf

McAbee, S. (2010, February 3). Turn your employees into social media ambassadors [Blog post]. Steve McAbee: iMedia Connection. Retrieved from http://www.imediaconnection.com/content/25812.asp

McCarthy, D. (2009, September 15). Managing across cultures. Great Leadership. Retrieved from http://www.greatleadershipbydan.com/2009/09/managing-across-cultures.html

McDonnell, A. (2010, August 21). How 35 percent of companies are using social media, and what turns workers on—and off—to companies [Blog post]. Retrieved from http://thehiringsite.careerbuilder.com/2010/08/21/how-35-percent-of-companies-are-using-social-media-and-what-turns-workers-on-and-off-to-companies/

McHugh, M., & Hambaugh, J. (2010). She said, he said: Gender, language and power. In J. Chrisler & D. McCreary (Eds.), *Handbook of gender research in psychology* (Vol. 1, pp. 379–410). New York, NY: Springer.

Mediacorp. (2014). Canada's best diversity employers. Retrieved from http://www.canadastop100.com/diversity

Meister, J. (2014, January 6). 2014: The year social HR matters. *Forbes*. Retrieved from http://www.forbes.com/sites/jeannemeister/2014/01/06/2014-the-year-social-hr-matters/

Meyer, E. (2014, April 3). Are you a holistic or specific thinker? *Harvard Business Review*. Retrieved from https://hbr.org/2014/04/are-you-a-holistic-or-a-specific-thinker/

Meyer, J. (2012, May 6). How to launch Facebook offers in minutes. *Social Media Today*. Retrieved from http://socialmediatoday.com/james-meyer/502007/launch-facebook-offers-minutes

Microblogging. (n.d.). *Oxford Concise English Dictionary (Online)*. Retrieved from http://oxforddictionaries.com/definition/english/microblogging

MIT Center for Collective Intelligence. (n.d.). Measuring collective intelligence. Retrieved from http://cci.mit.edu/mciresearchpage.html

Mitchelmore, S., & Rowley, J. (2010). Entrepreneurial competencies: A literature review and development agenda. *International Journal of Entrepreneurial Behavior & Research, 16*(2), 92.

Morgan, J. (2010, November 3). What is social CRM? *Social Media Examiner*. Retrieved from http://www.socialmediaexaminer.com/what-is-social-crm/

Morgan, J. (2013, July 30). The 12 habits of highly collaborative organizations. *Forbes*. Retrieved from http://www.forbes.com/sites/jacobmorgan/2013/07/30/the-12-habits-of-highly-collaborative-organizations

Morrison, T. (2004, December 21). Global business basics: The problem of proxemics. *IndustryWeek*. Retrieved from http://www.industryweek.com/articles/global_business_basics_1907.aspx

Moss, C. (2014, April 14). US Airways tweeted an extreme pornographic image and left it up for a long time. *Business Insider*. Retrieved from http://www.businessinsider.com/us-airways-pornographic-tweet-2014-4

Mueller, M. P. (2012, May 4). A stunning, new social media tactic: Handwritten notes [Blog post]. Retrieved from http://boss.blogs.nytimes.com /2012/05/04/a-stunning-new-social-media-tactic-handwritten-notes /?BU-D-E-AD-OB-TXT-BUS-ROS-0512-NA=

Munter, M. (2012). *Guide to managerial communication* (9th ed., p. 54). Upper Saddle River, NJ: Prentice Hall.

Murphy, S., Hobbs, A., Rose, Z., Madden, S., & Irwin, J. (2015). *Policy paper: LGBTQ+ Students.* Ontario Undergraduate Student Alliance. Retrieved from http://www.ousa.ca/wordpress/wp-content/uploads/2015/04 /LGBTQ-Students.pdf

Nass. C. (2012, November 13). Multitasking: How it is changing the way you and your children think and feel [Video file]. *Stanford Alumni Association.* Retrieved from http://www.youtube.com/watch?v=9VEjK4BS2js

National Forum on Education Statistics. (2010). *Forum guide to data ethics* (NFES 2010–801). U.S. Department of Education. Washington, DC: National Center for Education Statistics.

Natural Resources Canada. (2014, August 22). Abbreviations and symbols for the geographical names of the provinces and territories. Retrieved from http://www.nrcan.gc.ca/earth-sciences/geography/place-names/useful -material-translators/9237

NewsWire. (2008, June 6). CBC'S *Hockey Night in Canada* to introduce $100,000 search for new theme song. Retrieved from http://www .newswire.ca/en/story/226457/cbc-s-hockey-night-in-canada-to -introduce-100-000-search-for-new-theme-song

Nielsen. (2012, April 10). Global consumers' trust in "earned" advertising grows in importance. Retrieved from http://nielsen.com/us/en/insights/press -room/2012/nielsen-global-consumers-trust-in-earned-advertising-grows .html

Nielsen Insights. (2015). Reputation's role in unlocking brand value. Retrieved from http://www.nielsen.com/ca/en/insights/news/2015/reputations-role -in-unlocking-brand-value.html

NM Incite. (2011). State of the media: The social media report Q3 2011. Retrieved from http://cn.nielsen.com/documents/Nielsen-Social-Media -Report_FINAL_090911.pdf

Northwestern University Information Technology. (2012). Information security news. [Podcast]. Retrieved from http://www.it.northwestern.edu/security /podcast.html

O'Leary, M. (2008, April). New portals enrich STM menu. *Information Today.* Retrieved from http://www.deepwebtech.com/talks/InfoTodayReprint.pdf

Office of the Privacy Commissioner of Canada. (2015, July 7). Legal information related to PIPEDA. Retrieved from https://www.priv.gc.ca/leg_c /leg_c_p_e.asp

Olson, L. (2012, January 12). The ins and outs of providing references [Blog post]. Retrieved from http://money.usnews.com/money/blogs/outside -voices-careers/2012/01/12/the-ins-and-outs-of-providing-references

Ontario Ministry of Community and Social Services. (2015, January). About the Accessibility for Ontarians with Disabilities Act, 2005 (AODA). Retrieved from http://www.mcss.gov.on.ca/en/mcss/publications/accessibility /aoda2005.aspx

Palomares, N. (2009). Women are sort of more tentative than men, aren't they? How men and women use tentative language differently, similarly, and counter stereotypically as a function of gender salience. *Communication Research, 36*, 538–560.

Parks, N. (2013, May). The respectful question. Respectful Workplace. Retrieved from http://www.respectfulworkplace.com/2013/05/30/the -respectful-question

Patel, A., & Reinsch, L. (2003). Companies can apologize: Corporate apologies and legal liability. *Business Communication Quarterly, 11*(1), 9–25.

Pentland, A. (2008). *Honest signals.* Cambridge, MA: MIT Press.

Peters, S. (2012, February 27). How to give your blog a conversational tone. Remarkable Blogger.com. Retrieved from http://remarkablogger .com/2012/02/27/how-to-give-your-blog-a-conversational-tone/

Pew Research Center. (2014, February 13). Emerging nations embrace internet mobile technology. Retrieved from http://www.pewglobal.org /2014/02/13/emerging-nations-embrace-internet-mobile-technology /#texting-most-popular-use-of-cell-phones

Pew Research Center. (2015, April 15). Cell phones in Africa: Communication Lifeline. Retrieved from http://www.pewglobal.org/2015/04/15/cell -phones-in-africa-communication-lifeline

Princeton Language Institute (Ed.). (n.d.). Benefit. *Roget's 21st century thesaurus* (3rd ed.). Retrieved from http://thesaurus.reference.com/search?r =20&q=benefit

Quast, L. (2013, October 26). Job seekers: No, the interview thank you note is not dead. *Forbes.* Retrieved from http://www.forbes.com/sites/lisaquast /2013/08/26/job-seekersno-the-interview-thank-you-note-is-not-dead

Rabe, C. B. (2006). *The innovation killers: How what we know limits what we can imagine—and what smart companies are doing about it.* New York, NY: AMACOM.

Radicati, S. (2014, January). Email statistics report, 2014–2018. Retrieved from http://www.radicati.com/wp/wp-content/uploads/2014/01/Email -Statistics-Report-2014-2018-Executive-Summary.pdf

Radicati, S. (2015, March). Email statistics report, 2015–2019. Retrieved from http://www.radicati.com/wp/wp-content/uploads/2015/02/Email -Statistics-Report-2015-2019-Executive-Summary.pdf

Reiche, S. (2013, June 20). Managing virtual teams: Ten tips. *Forbes.* Retrieved from http://www.forbes.com/sites/iese/2013/06/20/managing-virtual -teams-ten-tips/

Resource Personnel Consultants. (2012, February 24). "Tell me about a time when . . ." Be ready for behavioral interview questions. Retrieved from http://www.rpc.us.com/2012/02/tell-me-about-a-time-when-be-ready -for-behavioral-interview-questions

Richmond, V. P., & McCroskey, J. (2000). *Nonverbal behaviour in interpersonal relations.* Boston, MA: Allyn and Bacon.

Ries, R. (2012, May 30). The 10 commandments for delivering bad news. *Forbes.* Retrieved from http://www.forbes.com/sites/forbesleadership forum/2012/05/30/10-commandments-for-delivering-bad-news

Robertson, C., & Krauss, C. (2010, August 2). Gulf spill is the largest of its kind, scientists say. *New York Times.* Retrieved from http://www.nytimes .com/2010/08/03/us/03spill.html?_r=1&fta=y

Rosenblatt, D. (2011, September 13). Maple Leaf Foods apology [Video file]. Retrieved from http://www.youtube.com/watch?v=zIsN5AkJ1AI

Sanchez, T. (2010). *The hidden energy crisis: How policies are failing the world's poor.* London: Practical Action Publishing.

Sapountzis, T. (2012, April 25). You just deployed a social media listening platform, now what? *Social Media Today.* Retrieved from http:// socialmediatoday.com/node/495904

Satov, J. (2013). Institutions, ethics, and social media. Presentation at the Breakfast Seminar Series of The Centre for Ethics and Corporate Policy, Toronto.

Schroth, H. A., Bain-Chekal, J., & Caldwell, D. F. (2005). Sticks and stones may break bones and words can hurt me: Words and phrases that trigger emotions in negotiations and their effects. *International Journal of Conflict Management, 16*(2), 102–127.

Schuster, C. (2004, November 1). How to manage a contract in China. *Agency Sales Magazine.* Retrieved from business.highbeam.com/19/article-1G1 -125067432/manage-contract-china

Schwabel, D. (2012. March 1). How to shape your Facebook profile to help you land a job. *Time.* Retrieved from http://moneyland.time.com/2012/03/01 /how-to-shape-your-facebook-profile-to-help-you-land-a-job

Sears, G. J., Zhang, H., Wiesner, W., Hackett, R., & Yuan, Y. (2013). A comparative assessment of videoconference and face-to-face employment interviews. *Management Decision, 51*(8), 1733–1752.

Selling Power TV. (2010, April 4). How Kodak leverages social media [Video file]. Retrieved from http://www.youtube.com/watch?v=GlE8_mKjPnQ

Shellenbarger, S. (2014, March 25). Why likeability matters more at work: Likability is more important—and harder to pull off—on video. *Wall Street Journal.* Retrieved from http://online.wsj.com/news/articles /SB10001424052702303725404579461351615271292?mod=ITP _personaljournal_1&mg=reno64-wsj

Slater, M. (2011, August 5). Dolce & Gabbana tries to silence Facebook activists. Change.org. Retrieved from http://news.change.org/stories /dolce-amp-gabbana-tries-to-silence-facebook-activists

Slavina, V. (2013, June 17). Why women must ask (the right way): Negotiation advice from Stanford's Margaret A. Neale. *Forbes*. Retrieved from http://www.forbes.com/sites/dailymuse/2013/06/17/why-women-must-ask-the-rightway-negotiation-advice-from-stanfords-margaret-a-neale

Smith, A. (2015, April 1). U.S. smart phone use in 2015. Pew Research Center. Retrieved from http://www.pewinternet.org/2015/04/01/us-smartphone-use-in-2015

Smith, J. (2013, February 21). The 13 most outrageous job interview mistakes. *Forbes*. Retrieved from http://www.forbes.com/sites/jacquelynsmith/2013/02/21/the-13-most-outrageous-job-interview-mistakes

Smith, P., & Lam, M. (2013). 2013 Campus Recruitment Report: Educator Summary. Canadian Association of Career Educators and Employers. Retrieved from http://www.cacee.com/_Library/Campus_Recruitment_Docs/2013_CACEE_Campus_Recruitment_Report_-_Career_Educator_Summary.pdf

Smith, R. (2012, June 5). Interview first impressions—The most crucial 2 seconds in your net job interview [Blog post]. Retrieved from http://blog.randstad.ca/Blog/bid/132650/Interview-First-Impressions-The-Most-Crucial-2-Seconds-In-Your-Next-Job-Interview

Socialbakers. (2015a). Socialbakers Builder—Social media management tool. Retrieved from http://www.socialbakers.com/products/builder

Socialbakers. (2015b). Socially devoted: The standard of customer care in social media. Retrieved from http://sociallydevoted.socialbakers.com/?ref=socially-devoted-banner-q3-2014

Solomon, C. (2012). *The challenges of working in virtual teams: Virtual teams survey report*. New York, NY: RW³ CultureWizard.

Sousa, D. (2011). *How the brain learns* (4th ed.). Thousand Oaks, CA: Corwin Press.

Spahn, J., & Purses, J. (2012, March/April). 3 steps to empathic active listening. Practice Management Center [Blog post]. Retrieved from http://www.fpanet.org/professionals/PracticeManagement/PracticeSolutionsMagazine/MarchApril2012/3StepstoEmpathicActiveListening/

Spencer-Oatey, H., & Franklin, P. (2009). Intercultural interaction: A multi-disciplinary approach to intercultural communication. In E.T. Hall (Ed.), *Beyond culture* (pp. 22–24). London, UK: Palgrave Macmillan.

Statista. (2015a). Leading social networks worldwide as of August 2015, ranked by number of active users (in millions). Retrieved from http://www.statista.com/statistics/272014/global-social-networks-ranked-by-number-of-users

Statista. (2015b). Number of monthly active Twitter users worldwide from 1st quarter 2010 to 2nd quarter 2015 (in millions). Retrieved from http://www.statista.com/statistics/282087/number-of-monthly-active-twitter-users

Statista. (2015c). Number of monthly active international Twitter users from 2nd quarter 2010 to 2nd quarter 2015 (in millions). Retrieved from http://www.statista.com/statistics/274565/monthly-active-international-twitter-users

Stiff, J. B., & Mongeau, P. A. (2002). *Persuasive communication* (2nd ed.). New York, NY: The Guilford Press.

Stillman, J. (2011, June 7). How to nail your video interview. *Inc.* Retrieved from http://www.inc.com/guides/201103/4-tips-forconducting-a-job-interview-using-skype.html

Stockdale, V. (2014, April 28). Children to become illegal: The week in Twitter gaffes. *Huffington Post*. Retrieved from http://www.huffingtonpost.co.uk/verity-stockdale/children-to-become-illegal-the-week-in-twitter-gaffes_b_5225232.html?just_reloaded=1

Storti, C. (2007). *Speaking of India: Bridging the communication gap when working with Indians*. Boston, MA: Intercultural Press.

Stuckey, J., & Munro, D. (2013, June). *The need to make skills work: The cost of Ontario's skills gap*. Conference Board of Canada. Retrieved from http://www.collegesontario.org/Need_to_Make_Skills_Work_Report_June_2013.pdf

Sussman, S., & Sproull, L. (1999). Straight talk: Delivering bad news through electronic communication. *Information Systems Research, 10*(2), 150–188.

Swanson, D. (2013, September 9). 7 tips to nail a Skype interview. *Forbes*. Retrieved from http://www.forbes.com/sites/learnvest/2013/04/09/7-tips-to-nail-a-skype-interview

Tannen, D. (1991). *You just don't understand: Women and men in conversation*. London, UK: Virago.

Taylor, J. (2010, December 13). Technology: Be focused, be happy [Blog post]. Retrieved from http://www.psychologytoday.com/blog/the-power-prime/201012/technology-be-focused-be-happy

Taylor, J. (2011, April 8). Multitasking is out, single tasking is in. *Huffington Post*. Retrieved from http://www.huffingtonpost.com/dr-jim-taylor/single-tasking_b_845809.html

Telegraph staff. (2009, October 3). Brazil's weeping President Luiz Inácio Lula da Silva revels in 2016 Olympics vote. *The Telegraph*. Retrieved from http://www.telegraph.co.uk/sport/othersports/olympics/news/6257463/Brazils-weeping-President-Luiz-Inacio-Lula-da-Silva-revels-in-2016-Olympics-vote.html

Thompson, D. (2015, January 18). The secret to smart groups: It's women. *The Atlantic*. Retrieved from http://www.theatlantic.com/business/archive/2015/01/the-secret-to-smart-groups-isnt-smart-people/384625

Thompson, L. L. (2011). *Making the team: A guide for good managers* (4th ed.). Upper Saddle River, NJ: Pearson.

Tobin, J. (2011, August 26). Analysis: How often brands post to Facebook, and the impressions they generate [Blog post]. Retrieved from http://www.ignitesocialmedia.com/social-media-measurement/analysis-how-often-brands-post-to-facebook-and-the-impressions-they-generate/

Toller, C. (2015, January 13). Women now hold one in five corporate board seats in Canada. *Canadian Business*. Retrieved from http://www.canadianbusiness.com/innovation/women-on-boards-catalyst-global-survey-2015/

Tom, A. (2014, September 12). Brand yourself to stand out during a job search. Career Professionals of Canada. Retrieved from http://careerprocanada.ca/brand-stand-job-search

Towers Watson. (2011). Clear direction in a complex world: How top companies create clarity, confidence and community to build sustainable performance. *2011/2012 Communication ROI Study™*. Retrieved from http://www.towerswatson.com/assets/pdf/5995/Towers-Watson-ROI-Survey.pdf

Tran, M. (2009, July 23). Singer gets his revenge on United Airlines and soars to fame. *The Guardian News Blog*. Retrieved from http://www.theguardian.com/news/blog/2009/jul/23/youtube-united-breaks-guitars-video

Tran, M. (2014, April 23). #myNYPD Twitter callout backfires for New York Police Department. *The Guardian*. Retrieved from http://www.theguardian.com/world/2014/apr/23/mynypd-twitter-call-out-new-york-police-backfires

Tuckman, B. W. (1965). Developmental sequence in small groups. *Psychological Bulletin, 63*, 384–399.

Tufte, E. (1983). *The visual display of quantitative information*. Cheshire, CT: Graphics Press.

Turkle, S. (2012, April 22). The flight from conversation. *New York Times*. Retrieved from http://www.nytimes.com/2012/04/22/opinion/sunday/the-flight-from-conversation.html?_r=1

TurkReno, Inc. (2011, November 11). Twitter best practices learned with hard knocks. Retrieved from http://www.turkreno.com/web-blog/2011/11/twitter-best-practices-learned-with-hard-knocks/

Turner, L. H., & West, R. (2010). *Introducing communication theory: Analysis and application* (4th ed.). New York, NY: McGraw-Hill.

UK Trade and Investment. (2010, February 29). Doing business in the Netherlands. Retrieved from http://www.invest.uktradeinvest.gov.uk/download/107212_100410/Doing%20Business%20in%20Netherlands.html

University of Twente. (n.d.). Media richness theory. Retrieved from http://www.utwente.nl/cw/theorieenoverzicht/Theory%20Clusters/Mass%20Media/Media_Richness_Theory

University of Victoria. (2015, January). Style guide. Retrieved from http://communications.uvic.ca/publications/style/section-5.html

van Bastelaer, S. (2014, January 2). How to write a professional bio for LinkedIn, Twitter, and more. *Huffington Post*. Retrieved from http://www.huffingtonpost.com/her-campus/how-towrite-a-profession_b_4644730.html

Van Grove, J. (2009, July 15). United breaks guitars surpasses 3 million views in 10 days. Mashable. Retrieved from http://mashable.com/2009/07/15/united-breaks-guitars

Vandelay Design. (2008, June 11). Designing and formatting blog posts for readability. Retrieved from http://vandelaydesign.com/blog/design/formatting-blog-posts-readability/

Voice Council Magazine. (2014, October 26). Is a singing flash mob legal? Retrieved from http://voicecouncil.com/is-a-singing-flash-mob-legal

W³Techs. (2015, January). Usage of content management systems for websites. Retrieved from http://w3techs.com/technologies/overview/content _management/all/

Wakefield, J. (2013, September 3). Promoted tweet used to complain about British Airways. *BBC News: Technology*. Retrieved from http://www.bbc .co.uk/news/technology-23943480

Wall Street Journal. (2013, November 29). President Obama delivers Thanks-giving address [Video file]. Retrieved from http://www.youtube.com /watch?v=ay6KfudiBws

Wallace, E. (2009, May–June). *Business relationships that last*. Austin, TX: Green-leaf Book Group Press.

Wasserman, T. (2013, September 2). Man buys promoted tweet to complain about British Airways. Mashable. Retrieved from http://mashable.com /2013/09/02/man-promoted-tweet-british-airways

Watkins, M. (2013, June 27). Making virtual teams work: Ten basic principles. *Harvard Business Review*. Retrieved from https://hbr.org/2013/06/making -virtual-teams-work-ten

Wells, K. (2010, May 24). Technical briefing [Video]. Retrieved from http:// bp.concerts.com/gom/kentwells_update24052010.htm

Wilson, G. (2013, April 15) Quoted in The multi-tasking myth. *The Age*. Retrieved from http://www.theage.com.au/executive-style/management /blogs/performance-matters/the-multitasking-myth-20130404-2h828 .html#ixzz2VnQz6Fgx

Wilson, T. (2011, February 1). The best legal advice is often an apology. *Globe and Mail*. Retrieved from http://www.theglobeandmail.com/report-on -business/small-business/sb-growth/day-to-day/the-best-legal-advice-is -often-an-apology/article626797

Wolfe, J. (2010). *Team writing: A guide to writing in groups*. New York, NY: Bedford/St. Martins.

Wolvin, A. D. (Ed.). (2010). *Listening and human communication in the 21st century*. Chichester, UK: Wiley-Blackwell.

Wong, D. (2010). *The Wall Street Journal guide to information graphics: The dos and don'ts of presenting data, facts, and figures*. New York, NY: W.W. Norton.

Wood, J. (2013). *Gendered lives: Communication, gender, & culture* (10th ed.). Boston, MA: Wadsworth.

Woolley, A., & Malone, T. (2011, June 1). Defend your research: What makes a team smarter? More women. *Harvard Business Review*. Retrieved from https://hbr.org/2011/06/defend-your-research-what-makes-a-team -smarter-more-women/ar/1

World Wind Energy Association. (2014). Small wind world report 2014 update. Retrieved from http://small-wind.org/wp-content/uploads/2014/03/2014 _SWWR_summary_web.pdf

Young, R. O. (2011). *How audiences decide: A cognitive approach to business communication*. New York, NY: Routledge.

Yusof, D. (2009). A different perspective on plagiarism. *Internet TESL Journal, 15*(2). Retrieved from http://iteslj.org/Articles/Yusof-Plagiarism.html

Zhou, H., & Zhang, T. (2008). Body language in business negotiation. *International Journal of Business and Management, 3*(2), 90–96. Retrieved from http://journal.ccsenet.org/index.php/ijbm/article/view/1680/1588

Zillman, M. P. (2012). Deep web research 2012. Retrieved from http://www .deepwebresearch.info

Zuber, J. (2012, June 11). Is it legal? Getting fired via text message. *KFox14 News*. Retrieved from http://www.kfoxtv.com/news/news/it-legal-getting -fired-text-message/nPQ7k

Zupeck, R. (2008, January 2). Six tips to managing workplace conflict. CNN.com/living. Retrieved from http://www.cnn.com/2008/LIVING /worklife/01/02/cb.work.conflict/index.html

INDEX

Key terms and the page number on which they are defined appear in **boldface**; *f* indicates figure; *t* indicates table; *n* indicates note.

A

abbreviations for provinces and territories, 462
Aboriginal peoples, 109–110
About.com, 68*n*
absolutes, 84
abstract, 330
abstract wording, 47
AC Nielson, 312
academic research, 287, 288*f*
    see also research
academic writing, 49
Academy of Management Executive, 131*n*
access, 135, 146
Access to Information Act, 133
Accessibility for Ontarians with Disabilities Act, 111
accommodation, 174
accurate hearing, 75–78
accusatory language, 83, 83*f*
accusatory statement, 195
accusing tone, 267
ACE model, 27*f*, 119–120, 197, 223
    see also analyzing; composing; evaluating
    bad news, effective delivery of, 258–270
    bad news messages, 260*f*
    blogging business, 153
    business presentations, 419*f*, 420
    business reports, 328–331, 370, 371
    case study, 58–59
    communication issues, resolving, 86
    communication technologies, 152
    diverse and intercultural situations, 119–120, 119*f*
    example of use of ACE model, 55*f*, 56
    information research, use of, 316*f*
    interpersonal communication skills, support of, 84*f*, 85
    negative messages, 277*f*
    persuasion, 224–229
    persuasive messages, 248*f*, 249
    proposals, preparation of, 370
    research reporting, 317–318
    routine and positive messages, 212*f*
    routine communications, professionalism in, 213
    and single tasking, 36
    teams, 182*f*, 183
action, 245
active listening, 14, 67, **74,** 75*f*, 444
active voice, 50, 51*f*, 267
ad hominem attack, 234*f*
adaptability, 16–17, 17*f*, 70–73, 72*f*, 98
    adapting your style, 66, 70, 72–73
    of communication styles, 66–67, 67*f*
Adfluent Media, 129, 153
Adichie, Chimamanda Ngozi, 95, 95*f*, 98
Adobe, 145, 146
affective conflict, 170
affective personality conflicts, 173
agenda, 164, 166, 167*f*
The Agenda, 82
AIDA (Attention, Interest, Desire, and Action), 24*f*, **240**
air kiss, 104
Alfred, 296*f*
Alt-J: Research in Learning Technology, 298
Altima Healthcare Canada Inc., 27, 56
Altimeter Group, 275

Amazon, 257, 312
Amazon.ca, 296*f*, 299
ambiguity, 104
ambiguous, 81
American English, 107
American Psychological Association (APA), 313, 369
    see also APA style
Amirtha, Tina, 292
analytical report, 328
analyzing, 27, 28–34
    see also ACE model
    audience, 27, 30–32, 31*f*, 328–329, 385
    audience's needs, 225–226
    bad news messages, 258–262
    business presentation, 384–387
    business reports, 328–329
    business result, 225
    content, 27, 31–32, 226
    desired outcome, 28–29, 225
    medium, 27, 32–33, 226–227, 387
    message, 386–387
    outcome, 385
    and persuasive messages, 224–227
    purpose, 27, 28, 225, 328, 385
    questions to develop content, 258–260
    setting, 387
    stakeholders' needs, 225–226
    strategic time management, 35*f*
    strengths and skills, 432*f*
    survey results, 305–306
anecdotal evidence, 310
anecdote, 390
animations, 399, 400*f*
announcements, 199, 199–200
antonyms, 54
APA in-text citations, 313*f*, 463–465
    multiple-author quoted source, 465
    multiple authors of one paraphrased source, 464
    multiple sources by authors with same last name, 464
    multiple sources by same author published in same year, 464
    multiple sources used to support one statement, 464
    paraphrased content, 463–464
    personal communication, 464
    quotations with words omitted, 465
    quoted content, 465
    single-author paraphrased source, 463–464
    single-author quoted source, 465
    works with no identified author, 464
APA reference list, 465–468
    annual report, 468
    articles, 466
    authors, 465–466
    blog posts, 466, 468
    books, 466, 467
    brochure, 468
    e-books, 467
    Facebook page, 468
    Facebook update, 468
    government publication, 468
    journals, 467
    name of work, 466–467
    online encyclopedia or dictionary, 468
    online slide presentation, 468
    online video, 468

other sources, 468
periodicals, 467
podcasts, 466, 468
publication information, 467–468
publication year, 466
sample reference page, 469
tweet or Twitter update, 468
videos, 466
websites, 467–468
APA style, 313, 369, 463
    APA citation in graphics, 369*f*
    formal reports, 347*f*
    in-text citation, 313*f*, 463–465
    reference list, 347*f*, 465–468
    reference page citation, 313*f*
    sample documentation in presentation files, 469–470
apology, 260
appeal to popular opinion, 234*f*
appendix, 330, 348–349, 348*f*
Apple, 137, 230, 296*f*
appropriate to the situation, 14
Appsavvy, 383
archive, 203
ask, 205, 390
    see also O-A-R (observe, ask, research)
assertiveness spectrum, 68*f*
Association for Training and Development (ATD), 291
assumptions, 111, 114, 117, 146
asynchronous, 45, 135
attachment, 137, 330
attention, 243, 390
ATutor, 288
audience, 7
    analysis of, 27, 30–32, 31*f*, 385
    audience benefits, 30, 47, 193–195, 225
    audience oriented, 11
    bad news, reaction to, 259
    benefits, 225
    business presentation, 389–390, 391, 408, 413
    business reports, 328–329, 349
    concede, 226
    concerns and needs, identify, 290–291
    emotional needs, 236
    emotions, 234–236
    expectations, and business presentations, 408–409
    external audience, 42
    focus on your audience, 80–81
    information needs, 225, 226
    internal audience, 42
    knowing your audience, 230
    mass audience, 151
    mobile devices, 132
    motivation, 225, 226, 391
    multiple audiences, 9
    needs of, 9, 47
    objection, 226
    online presentations, 416–417
    potential resistance, 225–226
    primary audience, 30, 31*f*, 225, 291
    proposals, non-Canadian audience, 359
    psychological needs, 236
    receiver's perspective, 193–195
    refute, 226
    relevance of, 27

audience (*continued*)
return on investment (ROI), 225
secondary audience, 30, 31*f*, 225, 291
social media messages, 44
audience benefits, 30, 47, 193–195, **194**
audience-related criteria, 227*f*, 261*f*, 387*f*
audio recording, 70, 71–72
authentic questions, 83
avoid narrative, 330–331
avoidance, 174
Aw, A., 68*n*

B

backgrounds, 395
bad news messages, 257
ACE model, 260*f*, 277*f*, 278
acknowledgment of mistakes or problems, 272–273
apology, 260, 273
audience reaction, 259
audience's point of view, 269
buffer, 266–267, 267*f*
common business messages, 271–274
cultural assumptions, 269–270
denial of customer claims, 271–272
direct organization, 263*f*, 264*f*
effective strategies, 263–268
effective *vs.* ineffective phrasing, 266*f*
elements of, 272–273
evaluate, 268–269
example of, 259*f*
explanation, 259–260, 272
"first and follow up" strategy, 268
fixing the problem, 272–273
goodwill, sense of, 268–269
indirect organization, 263*f*, 265*f*
intercultural perspective, 270
justification, 259–260
medium, 260–262, 261*f*
message, 267–269
negative change, communication of, 273–274, 274*f*
neutral language, 267
passive voice, 267
planning of, 258–262
positive language, 267
reoccurrence, 272–273
responsibility, 272
social media, 275–277
soften the bad news, 260, 266–268
solution, proposal of, 267
state clearly, 266
technology, 262
where to state, 263–266
badwill, 197
BAE Systems, 204
Baker, Katrina, 299, 311
Baldoni, John, 230
ballroom presentations, 242
bandwidth, 132–133
bar chart, 361*f*
Bariso, Justin, 147
barriers, 7
to hearing, 75
team communications, 162
types of, 7–8
basic elements of persuasion, 229–238
BBC, 210
BCC (blind carbon copy *or* **blind courtesy copy),** 137–**138, 199,** 201
Beaucoup.com, 297
Beaver Tails, 20*f*
behavioural questions, 442
Belding, Shaun, 277
benefits, 225
best interests, 116–117
biased language, 83, 113*f*

bibliography, 330, 369–370
Bies, Robert, 262
Bing, 295, 296*f*, 297
Birds and Beans, 6
Bismilla, Vicki, 102
BizBrief, 408
Biznar.com, 296*f*
Blackboard, 288
Blair, Tony, 238
blame, 50
blind carbon copy. *See* BCC
blind courtesy copy. *See* BCC
block style, 42–43, 456, 457*f*
blogs, 33*f*, 45, 45*f*, **134,** 136, 153, 246, 448*t*, 466, 475
boardroom presentations, 242
body language, 77, 81, 444
body slides, 396*f*
Boolean operators, 297
brainstorming, 177
Brake, Terence, 96
branching questions, 304–305
brand message, 432–436, 433*f*
Bridgewater Associates, 170
British English, 107
British Gas, 275
Brock University, 161, 183
buffer, 263
bullet point list, 42, 43*f*
bullet slide, 397*f*
burden of proof, 234*f*
Burkhardt, Ed, 230
business case, 354
business communication
characteristics of successful communicators, 10–20, 10*f*
communication skills, and success, 5–7
complex process, 7–8
effective business communication, 4–5
business culture, 51
Business Insider, 142
business letters. *See* letter formatting guidelines; letters
business presentation
analysis when planning, 384–387
APA sample documentation, 469–470
attention, capturing, 390–391
audience expectations, 408–409
audience response, 413
body control, 410
composition of, 388–407
conclusion, 393
delivery of, 407–413
evaluation of, 407–413
framework or map, 391
handouts, 405–407, 406*f*
main points, limiting, 391–393
middle content, organization of, 391–393
MLA sample documentation, 478
motivate audience to care, 391
online presentations, 416–419
opening, 389–391
organization of content, 388–393
organizational patterns, 392*f*, 393
practice session, 398–405
presentation techniques, 407–411
prioritization of points, 391
question-and-answer (Q&A) sessions, 413–415
rapport, 389–390
slide presentation, 388*f*
slides. *See* slides
storyboard, 393–395
teamwork, 411–413
template, 395–396
type of presentation, identification, 388
visual aid presentations, 411
vocalization, 410–411
business purpose, 44

business reports
see also formal reports
ACE model, 328–331
appendices, 348–349, 348*f*
audience, 349
body, 335
composition, 329–331
discussion, 330, 340–346*f*
electronic format, 349
email report format, 454, 456*f*
executive summary, 334, 337*f*
formal reports. *See* formal reports
introduction, 335, 339*f*
list of figures, 336
list of tables, 336
online distribution, 349
organization of, 332–350
preview, 330, 334–335
progress reports, 332, 333*f*
purpose, 349
references, 347–348, 347*f*
structure, 332–350
supporting information, 330, 347–349, 347*f*
table of contents, 334–335, 338*f*
title page, 334, 336*f*
travel reports, 332
trip report, 334
visuals, integration of, 360–367
business research, 287, 320–321
see also research
business result, 225

C

"c factor," 178–180
call for action, 195–196
Call My Bluff, 73–74
call waiting, 148
CamScanner, 295*f*
Canada Post, 309
Canadian abbreviations and postal symbols, 462
Canadian Association of Career Educators and Employers, 4, 5*n*
Canadian Broadcasting Corporation (CBC), 311
Canadian Business, 117, 298
Canadian Business & Current Affairs (CBCA), 296*f*
Canadian Business Journal, 298
Canadian Cancer Society, 366
Canadian Council of Chief Executives (CCCE), 4, 4*n*
Canadian English, 107
Canadian HR Reporter, 32
Canadian Journal of Learning and Technology, 291
Canadian Network for Innovation in Education (CNIE), 291
Canadian Press, 273
Carey, Mariah, 95
Carleton University, 98
Carnegie Mellon University, 178
Carroll, Dave, 142
case studies
Culinary Adventure Tour Presentation, 422–426
A Day's Worth of Routine Messages, 215–216
Developing Better Interpersonal Communication Skills, 87–89
Making the Best of Bad News, 279–281
Managing Conflict in a Virtual Cross-Cultural Team, 184–185
Reporting Results to a Client, 373–374
Researching to Answer Business Questions, 320–321
Selecting Tools and Channels, 154–155
Starting a New Business, 250–251
Using ACE to Improve Communication Results, 58–59
Working as a Cross-Cultural Team, 121–123

categorization, 392f
CBCA, 312
CBCA Complete, 298
cc (courtesy copy), 199
channel, 7
Chapters.Indigo.ca, 296f, 299
Chicago Manual of Style. See Chicago style
Chicago style, 313, 348, 369
  in-text citation, 313f
  reference page citation, 313f
Chief Learning Officer, 299
chronological order, 392f
chronological résumés, 437–439, 438f
Chrysler Corporation, 97
Chui, Michael, 177
Cialdini, Robert, 236, 238n, 248
CIBC, 223, 249
Cisco Systems Inc., 132
Citation Manager, 313f
citations, 369
CJNI Radio, 273
claim requests, 193, 199f
clarity, 14–**15**, **47**, 47f, 81, 270
Clark, Ruth C., 291
Clarke, Liz, 65, 86, 392
The Clean Clothes Campaign, 276
clear wording. *See* clarity
clichés, 50–51, 51f
Clipboard Magic, 204
clipboard manager, 204
ClipMate, 204
closed punctuation style, 460
cloud computing, 131, 133, **313**
cloud storage tools, 136–137, 143, 448t
CMS. *See* Chicago style
CNET Forums, 312
coaching, 180–181
Cobb, Jeff, 301f
cognitive conflict, 170
cold-call sales messages, 244
collaboration, 20, 175
collaboration tools, 142–146
  cloud storage tools, 143
  email, 143
  Facebook, 144
  instant messaging, 144
  note-sharing applications, 144–145
  online meetings, 145
  texting (SMS), 145
  videoconferencing, 145
  voice over internet protocol (VoIP), 145
  wikis, 145
collaborative working environment, 168
collectivist culture, 101, 104
College of the North Atlantic iLINK, 296f
colour, 395
combined résumé, 439
comfort zone, 66, 67–68
  getting out of your comfort zone, 70, 72–73
  reflective practices, 70
  self-assessment tools, 67
common courtesies, 148
common errors, 52–53, 52f
common language, 106–107
Communicaid, 66
communicating negative change, 274f
communication, 3
  changes in, 17
  context, 9
  face-to-face interactions, 73
  failure to communicate, 65
  intercultural communication. *See* intercultural communication
  mobile communications. *See* mobile communications

nonverbal communication. *See* nonverbal communication
oral communication, 46
  richest form, 73
  study of, 3, 4–7
  study of business communication, 4–7
  team. *See* team
  verbal and nonverbal, conflicts between, 8
  written communication, 46
communication skills, 5–7
communication strategy, 10
communication styles, 66
  adaptability of, 66–67, 67f
  adapting your style, 66
  comfort zone, 67–68
  and culture, 69–70, 105–106
  gender-specific communication styles, 84–85
  learn to adapt, 70, 72–73
  in the Lewis model, 106f
  preferred communication style, 66, 72
  understanding communication styles, 66–74
communications technologies
  see also specific communication tools
  ACE model, 152
  bandwidth, 132–133
  basics of, 131–134
  best practices, 146–151
  cloud computing, 133
  collaboration tools, 142–146
  distribution tools, 136–140
  evolution and change, 134
  main function of, 136–146
  media richness theory (MRT), 130–131
  mobile devices, uses of, 132
  networking tools, 140–142
  platform agnostic tools, 133
  privacy, 133–134
  questions about, 134–135, 447–451
  security, 133–134
  selection of tools (case study), 154–155
  software as a service (SaaS), 133
  understanding of, 130–135
Community Foundations of Canada, 388, 389n
company information, 32
compelling evidence, 238
competing goals, 171–172
competition, 174
competitive edge, 4–5
competitive proposal, 351
complaints, 142
completeness, 47
compliments, 267f
component parts, 392f
composing, 28, 34–46
  business presentation, 388–407
  business reports, 329–331
  content of message, 37
  drafts, 34–35
  email messages, 41–42
  instant messages, 44–46
  letters, 42–43
  main point, 38
  mobile messages, 44–46
  organization of message, 37
  outline, 37–38, 37f, 38f, 41
  persuasive messages, 228, 228f
  professional format and delivery, 41–43
  questions and requests, 192–196
  social media messages, 44–46
  strategic time management, 35–37, 35f
  voice mail messages, 43
comprehension, 76–79
compromise, 175
concede, 226
conceptual order, 392f
conciseness, 14–**15**, **48**, 48f

concrete wording, 47
conditional, 201
condolences, 208
Conference Board of Canada, 5, 5n
conference calls, 148–150
confirmation, 199
confirmation email, 147
conflict management, 170–175
  accommodation, 174
  avoidance, 174
  cause of conflict, 171
  collaboration, 175
  competition, 174
  compromise, 175
  cross-cultural teams, 184–185
  giving in, 174
  techniques, 174–175
conflict style, 68f
confusing questions, 193f
congratulatory messages, 207–208, 208f
consistency, 238f
Container Store, 6
content, 11, **27**, 31, 37
content errors, 52–53
content management system (CMS), 134
content marketing, 246
Content Marketing Institute, 246
content-related criteria, 227f, 261f, 387f
context, 7, 9, **100**, 116
convenience sample, 302
conversation games, 73
  Call My Bluff, 73–74
  free phone time, 74
  Twenty Questions, 73
  Two Truths and a Lie, 73
conversational style, 49–50, 50f
Cooper, Pamela, 75
Copyright Act, 133
Corbis Images, 412
Corporate Valley, 82
cost, 135
Cottage Life, 246
Cottagelife.com, 247n
courtesy copy. *See* cc (courtesy copy)
cover letter, 439–441, 441f
cover message, 355
Covey, Steven, 385
credentials, 133
credibility, 230, 230–231
CRM-Daily.com, 233n
cross-cultural teams, 121–123
crowdsource, 311
cultural identity, 98, 99
cultural intelligence, 98–100
  improvement of, 100–109
  mindset of, 98–100
  understanding how cultures differ, 100–104
cultural norms, 100–104
culture, 19, 96
  see also intercultural communication
  assumptions and access, 146
  assumptions in questions, 117
  audience expectations and business presentations, 408–409
  bad news, perspective on, 270
  in business communications, 51
  business culture, 51
  "c factor" team culture, 179
  collectivist culture, 101, 104
  and common language, 106–107
  and communication styles, 69–70, 105–106
  differences among cultures, 100–104
  expectations, 108
  high-context culture, 100–101, 101f
  holistic culture, 104
  individualistic culture, 101

culture (*continued*)
  intercultural communication. *See* intercultural
    communication
  low-context culture, 100–101, 101*f*
  monochronic cultures, 104
  multiculturalism, 18–19
  organizational culture, 97
  persuasive appeals, 231
  and plagiarism, 292–293
  polychronic cultures, 104
  power distance, 103
  proposals for non-Canadian audience, 359
  routine messages and corporate culture, 205
  specific culture, 104
  touch, 104
  uncertainty avoidance, 103–104
  Western cultures, 104
  working with many cultures, 18–19
Cunningham, Chris, 383
curator, 417
currency, 138
customer service representative (CSR), 139
customers, 18

D

Daft, Richard L., 130, 131*n*
Daimler-Benz AG, 97
Dalio, Raymond, 170
Darics, Erika, 144, 177
data, ethical representation of, 365–366
data displays, 365–366
data graphics, 360
data slides, 398
Dave Carroll Music, 142*n*
Davenport, Ruth, 273
Davis, Hank, 82
Davis-Ali, Susan, 73
decision making, 163
decode, 7
deep web portals, 296*f*, 297
DeeperWeb.com, 297
defensiveness, 415
degrees of richness (in MRT), 130–131
deliverables, 162, 351
delivery of business presentation, 407–413
Dell Computers, 211
denial of customer claims, 271–272, 271*f*
desire, 98, 244
Desire2Learn, 288
desktop search tool, 295, 296*f*
diagram slide showing relationships, 398*f*
DIALOG, 178
Diana, Princess of Wales, 238
Dierdorff, E., 181*n*
differences of opinion, 172
different locations, 262
digital assets, 143
Dimon, Jamie, 272–273
direct answer, 197
direct message, 192–193, **239**
direct organization, 38–40, 39*f*, 192*f*, 263
disabilities, 110–111
discussion elements of report, 340*f*–346*f*
discussion forums, 137, 448*t*
dismissiveness, 415
distribution tools, 136–140
diversity, 109
  ethnicity, 111
  gender identity, 111–113
  impact of culture on communication, 97
  and inclusiveness, 109–119
  Indigenous peoples of Canada, 109–110
  people with disabilities, 110–111, 111*f*
  physical impairments, 110–111, 111*f*
  respectful inquiry, 116–119

sexual identity, 111–113
  sexual orientation, 113–116
  study of, 96
document versions, 143
documentation of research, 368–370
documentation styles. *See* APA style; Chicago style;
    MLA style
Dolce & Gabbana, 276
downward inflection, 82
drafting, 40
drafts, 34–35
Dropbox, 142, 314, 314*f*, 314*n*, 319
Dunne, David, 273
Dyer, Pam, 210

E

E-Learning 24/7, 301*f*
Eastman Kodak, 18
easy for your audience to understand, 11
edit, 49
Edwards, Marc, 3, 21
ego issues, 173
Elder, Amy, 161, 183
Element K, 301*f*
elevator pitch, 433
email, 33*f*, 137, 143, 329, 330, 448*t*
  appropriate *vs.* inappropriate responses, 115*f*, 116*f*
  attachments, 454
  best practices, 146–148
  bullet point lists, 43*f*
  closing or signoff, 454
  as collaboration tool, 143
  composing email messages, 41–42
  confirmation messages, 199
  confirmation of information, 200*f*
  effective *vs.* ineffective, 12*f*
  email addresses, 453
  email report format, 454, 456*f*
  first paragraph, 43*f*
  formal formats, 454, 455*f*
  formatting, 453–456
  identification information, 329
  informal formats, 454, 455*f*
  name, 454
  negative change, follow-up, 274*f*
  paragraphs, 454
  persuasive recommendation, 241*f*
  poor *vs.* excellent email form, 149*f*
  poorly designed *vs.* professionally designed, 42*f*
  preview elements, 330
  problems, 137–138
  proofreading, 148
  salutation, 453
  signature block, 454
  signature files, 147–148
  signoff, 147
  subject line, 40, 453
  topic-specific heading, 43*f*
  trip report, 334
email image, 437*f*
email surveys, 303*f*
emoticons, 77
emotional commitment, 236–238
emotional content, 76
emotions, 234–236, 247
empathy, 76, 267*f*
emphasis, 50, 76
employee satisfaction, 18
employees
  communication skills, 6
  firing employees, 262
  opinions and perceptions, 32
  social recruiting, 18
  support and education, 18
  valuable employee, 6

Employment and Social Development Canada, 309
Employment Equity Act, 111
encode, 7
EndNote, 312
enterprise social collaboration (ESC), 145
envelope format, 461, 461*f*
Environment Canada, 309
errors
  common errors, 52, 52*f*
  content errors, 52–53
  email, 137–138
  margin of human error, 137–138
  reducing, with templates, 203
  systematic check for, 53–54
ethics, 15–16, 34
  apologize or not apologize, 273
  audio recording, 71–72
  BCC, 201
  business presentation, 412
  data, representation of, 366–367
  ethical challenges, 16
  ethical researcher, how to be, 309–310
  interview questions, assumptions in, 117
  medium, choice of, 32–34
  O-A-R. *See* O-A-R (observe, ask, research)
  persuasion, and dishonesty, 235
  photography, 71–72
  plagiarism and repurposing, 412
  preservation of language, 102–103
  teams, 165
  video recording, 71–72
  visual aids, 412
ethnicity, 111
ethnocentrism, 96–97
ethos, 229
evaluating, 28, 46–55, **79**
  bad news messages, 268–269
  business presentation, 407–413
  business reports, 331
  clarity, 47
  completeness, 47
  credibility of sources, 299–300
  edit, 49
  feedback, 54–55
  interview results, 308
  and listening, 79
  persuasive messages, 228–229
  primary research, 300–310
  research sources, 295–300
  revising, 46–49
  slides in practice session, 398–399
  strategic time management, 35*f*
  survey results, 305–306
  virtual professional image, 436–437, 436*f*
Evernote, 143, 144, 177
Everything, 296*f*
examples, 233
executive summary, 330, 334, 337*f*
exit interviews, 384
expert authority, 232
explanatory text, 201
external audience, 42
external benefits, 194
external proposal, 351
external source, 31, 32
external stakeholders, 141
eye contact, 78*f*, 81

F

face to face, 33*f*, 176, 195–196
face-to-face surveys, 303*f*
Facebook, 3, 6, 10, 17, 18, 27, 33*f*, 36, 45, 45*f*, 133,
    134–135, 136, 136*f*, 138, 140–141, 143,
    144, 210, 246, 257, 275, 276, 311, 417,
    449*f*, 468, 476

FaceTime, 153
facial expressions, 76–77, 77*f*, 81
facts, 114, 232, 267*f*, 390
fallacy, 234, 234*f*
false analogy, 234*f*
false cause, 234*f*
false dilemma, 234*f*
Farrington, Jonathan, 232
Fast Company, 292
faulty assumptions, 172
Federal Express (FedEx), 6, 276
Federal Food and Drug Administration (FDA), 95
Federman, Mark, 287, 317
feedback, 8, 54–55, 177
  instructor feedback, 70
  and intercultural communications, 108–109
  peer coaching model, 180–181
  peer feedback, 70
  teams, 163
Ferrazzi, Keith, 175–176
Ferrazzi Greenlight, 175
Field, M., 418*n*
file attachments, 132
file folder organization, 314*f*
file names, 314
file sharing, 177
file size restrictions, 137, 143
file types, 297
Financial Post, 296*f*, 298
firewalls, 133
First International Courier Systems Inc., 95, 120
First Nations, 97, 109–110, 179–180
first paragraph, 42, 43*f*
First Peoples, 109–110
flash mob, 140
flexibility, 117
follow-up, 442
fonts, 395–396, 396*f*
Food Banks Canada, 191, 213
for-your-information (FYI) messages, 208–209, 209*f*
Forbes, 230
formal reports, 330, 332–350
  see also business reports
  APA style, 348
  appendix, 348–349, 348*f*
  audience, design for, 349
  Chicago style, 348
  discussion, 340–346*f*
  executive summary, 334, 337*f*
  formatting, 335
  identification information, 329
  introduction, 335, 339*f*
  list of figures, 335
  list of tables, 335
  manuscript-style reports, 349
  MLA style, 348
  online distribution, electronic format for, 349–350
  preview, 330, 337–339*f*
  purpose, 349
  references, 347–348, 347*f*
  request for proposal (RFP), 354–355
  software features, format with, 335
  supporting information, 347–349, 347*f*
  table of contents, 334–335, 338*f*
  title page, 334, 336*f*
formality, 108
format errors, 53
format for business documents
  abbreviations for provinces and territories, 462
  business letters, 456–462
  email messages, 453–456
  envelope format, 461, 461*f*
forming, 164
framework, 391

Francis, Will, 210
free phone time, 74
free writing, 40–41, 40*f*
French language, 107
functional résumés, 439

G

Garage Technology Ventures, 48
Garcia, Enrique, 313*f*
Gartner Inc., 177
gay, 114*f*
Gaye, Marvin, 292
gender identity, 111–113
gender-specific communication styles, 84–85
general accepted truths, 267*f*
general search engine, 296*f*
generalizations, 111
Georgetown University, 262
Gersho, Marzena, 191, 213
gestures, 77, 81
Getty Images, 412
Gibson, Robert, 103
giving in, 174
globalization, 102
Globe and Mail, 296*f*, 298
GlobeInvestorGold, 296*f*, 298
Glover, Paul, 170
Glover, Ron, 96
Gmail, 133
goals and deliverables, 163
Gonzalo, Frédéric, 276–277
good news, 267*f*
goodwill, 28, 197–199, 205, **258,** 260
goodwill messages, 191, 204–209
  congratulatory messages, 207–208
  for-your-information (FYI) messages, 208–209
  quick responses, 210–211
  real-time goodwill, 211
  on social media, 210–211
  sympathy messages, 208
  thank you messages, 206–207
Google, 134, 142, 153, 210, 290, 295, 296, 296*f*, 297, 298
Google+, 417
Google Docs, 133, 136*f*, 142, 143, 177, 449*t*
Google Drive, 142, 314, 319
Google Scholar, 298–299, 300, 312
Google Talk, 417
GoToMeeting, 145, 416
Government of Canada, 311
Government of Ontario, 111
grammatical errors, 53
Grant, McKenna, 73
graph, 360, 360*f*, 361–363*f*, 361*f*, 369
  bar chart, 361*f*
  design checklist, 363–364
  histogram (step-column), 362*f*
  histograph (frequency polygon), 362*f*
  horizontal bar chart, 361*f*
  line chart, 362*f*
  100% bar chart, 361*f*
  paired bar (tornado) chart, 362*f*
  pie chart, 361*f*
  scatter plot, 363*f*
  terminology, 364*f*
graphics, 132, 369, 369*f*
gratitude, 195–196
gravitas, 82
Greggs, 142
Groupon, 332, 334–335, 347
groupthink, 174
Gueldenzoph Snyder, Lisa, 392
Gupta, Naveen, 45

H

hackers, 133
Hadfield, Chris, 246
Hall, Edward T., 100, 102, 104
halo effect, 79
handouts, 405–407, 406*f*
handshake, 104
hard skills, 73
Harvard Business Review, 181*n*
Harvard Medical School, 82
hasty generalizations, 234*f*
headline test, 15–16, 16*f*
headlines, 396
hearing accurately, 75–78
hearing impairment, 111*f*
hedge, 84
Heijn, Albert, 276
Hernandez, Jodie, 262
hesitation, 84
heterosexism, 114*f*
high-context culture, 100–101, 101*f*
high-performance teams, 175–182
  "c factor," 178–180
  peer coaching model, 180–181
  productivity, 175–177
  virtual best practices, 175–177
Hip + Urban Girl's Guide (HUG), 129, 153
histogram (step-column), 362*f*
histograph (frequency polygon), 362*f*
Hockey Night in Canada, 311
Hofstede, Geert, 101, 103
holistic culture, 104
honesty, 415
Hoover's, 296*f*, 298
horizontal bar chart, 361*f*
host, 151
hostile question, 415
HR Council for the Voluntary/Non-Profit Sector, 109
hrreporter.com, 32
HTML, 147
Hudson, Linda, 204–205
humour, 108

I

I language, 83
"I" *vs.* receiver's perspective, 195*f*
IBIS World, 296*f*
IBM, 16–17, 17*f*, 96
identification information, 329
idiom, 108
IMA Management and Technology, 68*n*
impersonal statement, 195
impromptu speaking, 414
in-text citation
  APA style, 313*f*, 463–465
  Chicago style, 313*f*
  MLA style, 313*f*, 470–472
inclusive terms, 112*f*
inclusiveness, 109–119
Indigenous Corporate Training Inc., 179
Indigenous peoples of Canada, 108, 109–110
indirect message, 192–193, **239**
indirect organization, 38–40, 39*f*, 192*f*, 193*f*, 263
individual differences, 76
individualistic culture, 101
Industry Canada, 71–72, 72*n*, 296*f*
ineffective request, 224*f*
informal style, 14
information needs, 225, 226, 288–295
informational messages, 30*f*, 197–204
  announcements, 199–200
  confirmation, 199
  direct answer, 197
  follow up, 198–199

informational messages (*continued*)
goodwill, creation of, 197–199
instructions, 200–202
reply to questions, 197
templates, 203
informational report, 328
instant messages, 33*f*, 44–46, 46*f*, 144, 449*t*
Institute of Coaching, 82
Institute of Ismaili Studies, 98
Institute of Performance and Learning, 291
instructions, 200–202, 202*f*
instructor feedback, 70
intercultural communication
see also culture
bad news, perspective on, 270
common language, 106–107
communication styles in the Lewis model, 106*f*
cultural intelligence. *See* cultural intelligence
delivering bad news, 269–270
impact of culture on communication, 97
Lewis model of cultural types, 105–106, 105*f*
respectful inquiry, 116–119
strategies for, 107–109
study of, 96
interest, 243–244
internal audience, 42
internal benefits, 194
internal proposal, 351
internal source, 31
International Listening Association, 75
International Olympic Committee, 236
Internet Public Library, 297
interpersonal communication skills, 5–7.
interpretation, 76–79
intersex, 112
interview, 300, 306, 307*f*
see also research, interview; specific types of
interviews
conducting of, 306–308
evaluating results, 308
planning of, 307
introduction, 335, 339*f*
Inuit, 109–110
ipl2.org, 297
Isherwood, Carol, 140
ISI Science Citation Index, 300
iterative process, 8
iTunes, 10

J

jargon, 8, 108
job interview, 442–446, 443*f*
job search
cover letter, 439–441, 441*f*
follow-up, 442
job interview, 442–446
professional appearance, 445
professional presence, 431–437, 445
résumés, 437–439, 438*f*, 440*f*, 441
social job seeker, 433
social media, 434–435*f*
thank you messages, 446
job skills, 4*f*, 5*f*
job titles, 114
Jobs, Steve, 230
Joseph, Bob, 179–180
Journal of International Business Studies, 298
JPMorgan Chase, 272–273
jump to conclusions, 79

K

Kantar Retail, 97
Karim, Karim H., 98
Kauffman, Carol, 82

Kawasaki, Guy, 48
Keirsey Temperament Sorter (KTS-II), 67
Keynote, 395
killer app, 143
KLM, 210
know your audience, 244

L

Lam, M., 5*n*
landline, 148
Landmines Survivors Network, 238
language acquisition, 102–103
language barriers, 8
language basics, 107, 108*f*
language preservation, 102–103
LaRose, Cathy, 113
layouts, 132
Le Massif, 276–277
leadership skills, 169–175
conflict management, 170–175
create a supportive climate, 169–170
key leadership fundamentals, 169–170
overcommunicate, 169
reinforce team objectives, 169
Leadhership1, 73
leaning forward, 78*f*
Learning Circuits, 291
Lengel, Robert H., 130, 131*n*
lesbian, 114*f*
Leslie, Kathleen, 257, 278
letter formatting guidelines, 456–462
block style, 456, 457*f*
body, 460
closing, 460
copy notation, 461
date, 459–460
enclosure notation, 461
inside address, 460
letterhead, 459, 459*f*
modified block style, 456, 458*f*
open/closed punctuation, 460
page headings, 460
postscript, 461
return address, 459, 459*f*
salutation, 460
signed name, 460–461
special notations, 460
subject line, 460
typed name, 461
vertical placement, 461
letters, 33*f*, 42–43, 329, 330
see also letter formatting guidelines
Lewis, Richard, 96, 105–106, 105*f*, 105*n*, 106*f*, 106*n*
Lewis, Stephen, 82
Lewis model of cultural types, 105–106, 105*f*
LexisNexis, 296*f*, 298
LGBTQ, 114*f*
Librarian's Internet Index, 297
Library & Archives Canada AMICUS, 296*f*
library online catalogue, 296*f*
Likert (agreement) scale, 304*f*
liking, 238*f*
limitations, 291
line chart, 362*f*
linear-actives, 105
LinkedIn, 18, 33*f*, 45, 45*f*, 134, 136, 136*f*, 138,
140–141, 141, 311, 312*n*, 319, 449*f*
list of figures, 335
list of tables, 335
Listening Pro, 211
listening skills, 68*f*, 74–80
accurate hearing, 75–78
active listening, 14, 67, 74, 75*f*
comprehension, 76–79
evaluating, 79

and intercultural communication, 107
interpretation, 76–79
nonverbal, 76–77
paraphrase, 77–78
passive listening, 74
questions, 77–78
responding, 79–80, 80*f*
Litmus Email Analytics, 132
Little, Bob, 301*f*
Liviero, Flavio, 176
logical argument, 231–234, 232*f*, 233*f*
logical fallacies, 234
logos, 229
love and belonging, 236
low-context culture, 100–101, 101*f*
Lula da Silva, Luiz Inácio, 236, 238

M

MacLachlan, Matthew, 66–67
MacRumors, 312
mail surveys, 303*f*
main point, 38, 47
Manage Your Online Reputation (McCain), 273
Managerial Science, 131*n*
manuscript-style reports, 349
map, 391
Maple Leaf Foods, 273
Marcy, Wendy Kam, 129, 153
marital status, 112
Maslow, Abraham, 236
Mawani, Farzana, 27, 56
Mayer, Richard E., 291
McCain, Michael, 273
McDonald's, 275
McDonough School of Business, 262
McKinsey, 177
mean, 306
media richness theory (MRT), 130–131, 131*f*
Mediacorp, 109
median, 306
medium, 7, 27
analysis of, 32–33
audience-related criteria, 227*f*
bad news messages, 260–262
business reports, 329, 329*f*
choices, 27, 226–227, 387
content-related criteria, 227*f*
response-related criteria, 227*f*
selection of, 33*f*
social media, effect on, 32
meeting, 33*f*
see also online meetings
memo, 33*f*
memo-style progress report, 333*f*
Mendeley, 312
message headlines, 242, 388
messages
see also specific types of messages
business presentation, 386–387
clarity of, 268–269
cold-call sales messages, 244
content, 37
direct message, 39*f*, 192, 239
emotional content, 76
goodwill, sense of, 268–269
honesty of, 268–269
indirect message, 39*f*, 192, 239
organization of message, 37
routine messages. *See* routine business messages
sales messages, 240–245
Métis, 109–110
Meyer, Erin, 104
microblogs, 33*f*, 44–45, 45*f*
Microsoft, 137, 230, 314*n,* 405*n*
Microsoft Word, 54, 334–335

milestones, 164
Mines Advisory Board, 238
minutes, 164, 166, 167*f*
MIT Center for Collective Intelligence, 178
mixed messages, 8
MLA in-text citations, 313*f*, 470–472
  multiple-author quoted source, 472
  multiple authors of one source, 471
  multiple sources by same author, 471
  multiple sources used to support one statement, 471
  paraphrased content, 470–471
  personal communication, 471
  quotations with words omitted, 472
  quoted content, 472
  single-author quoted source, 472
  single-author source, 471
  works with no identified author, 471
MLA style, 313, 348, 369
  in-text citation, 313*f*, 470–472
  reference page citation, 313*f*
  sample documentation in presentation files, 478
  works cited list, 472–476
MLA works cited list, 472–476
  annual report, 475
  authors, 473
  blog post, 475
  books, 474
  brochure, 475
  e-books, 474
  email, 476
  Facebook page, 476
  Facebook update, 476
  government publication, 475
  interview, 476
  journals, 473–474
  medium of publication, 473–475
  name of work, 473
  online encyclopedia or dictionary, 475
  online slide presentation, 475
  online video, 476
  other types of sources, 475–476
  periodicals, 473–474
  podcast, 475
  publication information, 473–475
  sample works cited page, 477
  supplemental information, 475
  tweet or Twitter update, 476
  Web-based sources, 474–475
mobile communications
  business use of, 44
  composing mobile messages, 44–46
  face-to-face interactions, impact on, 73–74
mobile devices, 132
mobility issues, 111*f*
mode, 306
moderate effectively, 150
moderating strategy, 68*f*
moderator, 151
Modern Language Association (MLA), 313, 369
  see also MLA style
modified block style, 42–43, 456, 458*f*
monochronic cultures, 104
monologue, 81
Moodle, 288
motivating question, 243
motivation, 225, 226, 246–248
Mowatt, Jeff, 277
MTV, 10
multi-actives, 105
multiculturalism, 18–19
multiple choice questions, 304*f*
multitasking, 35–36, 75
Munro, D., 5, 5*n*
Munter, Mary, 388
mute button, 148
Myers-Briggs Type Indicator (MBTI), 67

N
names, 113
narrative, 330–331
Nass, Clifford, 36
National Geographic, 10
National Institute of Statistics and Economic Studies (INSEE), 369
national norms, 105
National Post, 298
native file, 349
needs, 98, 236
negative messages. *See* bad news messages
network, 433
networking sites, 45, 45*f*
networking tools, 140–142
networking websites, 33*f*
neutral, 267
New Directions Learning and Development, 116
New York Police Department, 275
newsletter, 33*f*
NextDraft, 143
NM Incite, 312
Noe, R. A., 131*n*
nonbiased language, 113*f*
noncompetitive proposal, 351
noninclusive terms, 112*f*
nonverbal communication, 8, **76–77**, 78*f*, 81
  and intercultural communication, 107–108
  support your message, 81
nonverbal tendencies, 68*f*
norming, 164, 166
Northwestern University, 417
note-sharing applications, 144–145, 449*f*
numerical data, 232
Nymi Inc., 327, 371

O
O-A-R (observe, ask, research), 34
  assumptions and access, 146
  assumptions in interview questions, 117
  audience expectations and business presentations, 408–409
  bad news perspective, 270
  BCC, 201
  "c factor" team culture, 179
  culture, and communication style, 69–70
  ethical researcher, 309–310
  language acquisition for employment, 102–103
  persuasive appeals, 231
  plagiarism, 293, 412
  proposals, non-Canadian audience, 359
  repurposing, 412
  routine messages and corporate culture, 205
  team ethics, 165
Obama, Barack, 82
objection, 226
objective, 331
objective statement, 439
objectivity, 331
observational research, 300, **308–310**
  see also research
observe, 34, 70, 205
occupation-specific language, 101
1:1, 132
100% bar chart, 361*f*
one-on-one interviews, 443*f*
OneDrive, 142
1:many, 132
OneNote, 143, 144
online article database, 296*f*
online bookstore, 296*f*
online business research tools, 296*f*
online databases, 296*f*, 312
online image, 436*f*
online indices, 312

online meetings, 145, 150–151, 176, 416, 450*t*
online presentations, 416–419
online publication site map, 296*f*
online survey format, 304–305
online surveys, 303*f*
Online Women's Business Center, 68*n*
ooVoo, 145, 416
open ended questions, 304*f*
open punctuation style, 460
opening of presentation, 389–391
opportunity/action, 392*f*
oral communication, 46
organization, 47
organization of message, 37
organizational culture, 97
outcome, 11, 28–29, 29*f*, 225, 385
outcome statements, 28, 29*f*, 30*f*
outline, 37–38, 37*f*, 38*f*, 41

P
P. F. Chang, 211, 211*f*
Paikin, Steve, 82
paired bar (tornado) chart, 362*f*
panel interview, 442, 443*f*
parallel phrasing, 201
parallel structure, 42
parallelism, 397, 397*f*
paraphrase, 368, 463
paraphrasing, 77–78, 78*f*
Parks, Ned, 116
partial sentences, 41
partner, 114*f*
passive listening, 74
passive voice, 50, 51*f*
PasteItIn, 204
pathos, 229
PBworks, 145
PDF (Portable Document Format), 112, 349
peer coaching model, 180–181, 181*f*
peer feedback, 70
Pell, Dave, 143
people with disabilities, 110–111, 111*f*
people with physical impairments, 110–111, 111*f*
PepsiCo, 101
performing, 164, 166
personal conflict, 173
personal experience, 233
Personal Information Protection and Electronic Documents Act (PIPEDA), 133
personal life, 6–7
persuasion, 12, 29–30, **223**, 238–248
  ACE model, 224–229
  audience's emotions, 234–236
  competing needs, 223
  composing persuasive messages, 228, 228*f*
  culture, and persuasive appeals, 231
  and dishonesty, 235
  emotional appeals, 237*f*
  fallacies, 234
  indirect, social media, 246
  logical argument, 231–234
  motivating others, 246–248
  recommendation, 241*f*
persuasive appeals, 231
persuasive messages. *See* persuasion
Peter V. Gustavson School of Business, 273
Pew Research Center, 146
photographs, 71–72, 369
physical impairments, 110–111, 111*f*
physiological barriers, 8
pie chart, 361*f*
Pijls, Bert, 275
Pinterest, 417
plagiarism, 292–293, **368**, 412
plain text, 147

platform agnostic, **131**, 133
Plotnikoff, Jeff, 383, 420
podcast, 416, 417–419, 466, 475
point form, 41
polychronic cultures, 104
polysyllabic, 54
portable document format (PDF), 132, 349
positive image, 260
positive response, 197
positive wording, 49, 49*f*
postal symbols, 462
posture, 77
potential resistance, 225
power distance, 103
powerful language, 238
PowerPoint, 395, 397, 405, 407
prejudgment, 79
presentation. *See* business presentation
presentation software, 242
presentation storyboard, 394*f*
preservation of language, 102–103
preview, 330
    email, 330
    executive summary, 334
    formal reports, 330, 337–339*f*
    introduction, 335
    letters, 330
    list of figures, 335
    list of tables, 335
    table of contents, 334–335
primary audience, 30, 31*f*, **225**, 291
primary research, 32, 232, 300–310
primary sources, 292
Pritchard, David, 6
privacy, 133–134, 137, 143
problem/solution, 392*f*
process, 162
productivity, 161, 175–177
professional appearance, 445
professional brand, 431–437
    brand message, 432–436, 433*f*
    career goals, strengths, and skills, 431–432, 432*f*
    evaluation of virtual professional image, 436–437, 436*f*
    social media, 432–436
    value, 433, 436*f*
    visibility, 433
professional format, 41–43
professional image, 49
professional presence, 445
professionalism, 12, 14, 15*f*, 213
progress reports, 332, 333*f*
proofreading, 52–54
    checking for errors, 53–54
    common errors, 52, 52*f*
    emails, 148
    tools for, 54
proposal, 350
    external proposal, 351
    internal proposal, 351
    non-Canadian audience, 359
    preparation of, 350–354
    problem, understanding of, 351
    proposal-writing software, 358
    request for proposal (RFP), 354–359, 356*f*
    RFP structure as formal report, 354–355
    solicited proposal, 352*f*–353*f*
    solution, propose, 351
    type, appropriate, 351–354
ProQuest LLC., 298*n*
provinces, abbreviations for, 462
provocative questions, 83
psychological barriers, 8
purpose, 11, **27**, 28, 44, 225, 328, 349, 385
purpose-related criteria, 387*f*
purpose statements, 28, 29*f*, 30*f*
push technology, 143

Q
qualifications summary, 439
qualitative research, 292
quality of work, 163
quantitative data (table and graph), 398*f*
quantitative research, 292
Queen's University QCAT, 296*f*
question-and-answer (Q&A) session, 413–415
    anticipation of questions, 414
    planning for, 414–415
    setting up, in introduction, 414–415
    short, clear answers, 414
    skillful answers, 415
    teams and, 414
    three-part answer, 415
questions, 77–78
    about key communications technologies, 447–451
    about technology tools, 134–135
    assumptions in, 117
    authentic questions, 83
    background research questions, 289*f*
    behavioural question, 442
    branching questions, 304–305
    in business presentation, 390
    business reports, 328*f*
    composing messages with questions, 192–196
    to develop content, 258–260
    hostile question, 415
    job interview questions, 442–444, 444*f*
    long and complex questions, 415
    multiple choice questions, 304*f*
    open ended questions, 304*f*
    provocative questions, 83
    question-and-answer (Q&A) sessions, 413–415
    reply to questions, 197
    survey questions, composition of, 303–305
    tag question, 84
    yes/no questions, 304*f*
QuickClip, 204
quotation marks, 296
quotations, 368, 390
    APA style, 465
    MLA style, 472

R
The Radicati Group, 137
Radio Shack, 262
Rail World, 230
random sample, 302
range, 305
rapport, 389–390
rating scale, 304*f*
reactives, 105
readability tool, 54
reading levels, 54*f*
real-time collaborative writing, 177
real-time goodwill, 211
reason for the request, 193
receiver benefits, 194
receiver's perspective, 193–195, **194**, 273
reciprocity, 238*f*
recommendation, 13*f*, **239**–240, 239*f*, 242
recommendation report, 332
Red Hat, 32
red herring, 234*f*
RedFlagDeals, 312
redundancy, 48, 48*f*
reference list, 312–313, **330**, 369–370
    see also APA reference list
reference styles. *See* APA style; Chicago style;
        MLA style
references, 347–348, 347*f*
reflective practices, 70
RefME, 312
refute, 226

RefWorks, 312, 313*f*, 313*n*
Regional Municipality of Peel, 3, 21
relational issues, 173
relationship status, 114*f*
reports. *See* business reports; formal reports
repurpose, 140, 412
request for assistance, 117–119
request for information, 198*f*
request for proposal (RFP), 354–358, 356*f*
requests, 192–196
    audience benefits, 193–195
    call for action, 195–196
    claim requests, 193
    direct *vs.* indirect, 192–193
    gratitude, 195–196
    receiver's perspective, 193–195
research, 32, 107, 205
    see also interview; O-A-R (observe, ask, research);
        observational research; survey
    academic research, 287, 288*f*
    accuracy of source, 300
    ACE model, use of, 316*f*
    analyze question and topic, 289–290
    anecdotal evidence, 310, 312
    audience concerns, 290–291
    audience needs, 290–291
    authorship, credibility of, 299–300
    background research questions, 289*f*
    books, 299
    branching questions, 304–305
    business research, 287, 288*f*, 320–321
    cloud information, organization of, 313–314
    computer notes, organization of, 313–314
    convenience sample population, 302
    credibility of sources, 299–300
    current information, 300
    define activities, 291–293
    determination of information, 288–295
    documentation, 368–370
    documents, organization of, 313–314
    electronic files, collection of, 295
    ethical researcher, 309–310
    experts in social media, 311
    identify potential criteria, 290*f*
    information sharing, 311–312
    interview, 306–308
    leads in reliable sources, 299
    Likert (agreement) scale, 304*f*
    multiple choice questions, 304*f*
    observational research, 300
    online database, 298–299
    online index, 298–299
    online source evaluation, 295–300
    online survey format, 304–305
    open ended questions, 304*f*
    people to survey, choice of, 302
    primary research, 32, 232, 300–310
    primary sources, 292
    print files, collection of, 295
    print source evaluation, 295–300
    qualitative research, 292
    quantitative research, 292
    questions, post to, 311
    random sample population, 302
    rating scale, 304*f*
    reference list, 312–313
    relevance of information, 300
    results, organization of, 312–316
    sample population, 302
    scope of, 291
    search tips, 296–297
    secondary research, 32, 232
    secondary sources, 292
    social media, use of, 310–312
    surveys, 302–306, 303*f*
    targeted sample population, 302

tertiary sources, 293
tools for finding research sources, 296f
web search, 295–297
work plan, 293–295, 294f, 315f
yes/no questions, 304f
research mode, 287
reshared information, 135
resources, 134
respect, 108
respectful inquiry, 116–119
response, 79–80
response-related criteria, 227f, 261f
résumés, 437–439, 438f, 440f, 441
return on investment (ROI), 225
revising, 40, 46–48
RingCentral, 45
Rivington, Courtney, 327, 371
Romero, Cristobal, 313f
Rosen, Adrienne, 95, 120
routine business messages, 191
ACE model, use of, 213
case study, 215–216
and corporate culture, 205
informational messages, 197–204
questions and requests in, 192–196
routine informational announcement, 202f
Royal Bank of Canada (RBC), 110, 273
Rubin, R. S., 181n
RW3 CultureWizard, 130

S

Saba, 288
safety, 236
Safian, Roger, 417
Sakai, 288
salary, 6
sales messages, 240–245
"same language, different culture," 106–107
sample, 302
Scania, 176
scarcity, 238f, 244
scatter plot, 363f
scholar.google.ca, 300
Schwom, Barbara, 392
Scoop.it, 417
scope, 291
Scotiabank, 350f, 350n
Scott, E., 68n
search online database, 298f
search tips, 296
searchable information, 134–135
second opinion, 54
secondary audience, 30, 31f, **225**, 291
secondary research, 32, 232
secondary sources, 292
security, 133–134, 137, 143
selecting the best medium for persuasive
messages, 227f
self-actualization, 236
self-assessment tools, 67
self-awareness, 181, 181f
self-esteem, 236
self-identity, 98
semantic barriers, 8
sensitive information, 118f, 119
sentence style, 331
setting, 387
setting-related criteria, 387f
sexual identity, 111–113
sexual orientation, 113–116, 114f
shared information, 135, 140
Sherman, R., 68n
Shopify, 18, 19n
Siemens AG, 103
significant other, 114f

silver lining, 268
simplified style, 42–43
"single story" perspective, 95–98
skills, 5–7
communication skills, 5–7
job skills, 4f, 5f
leadership skills, 169–175
listening skills. See listening skills
skill gaps, 5f
Skype, 46f, 145, 153, 416, 417
Slack, 416
slang, 50–51, **108**
slide deck, 388
slide master, 395, 396f
slide-sharing sites, 311–312
slides, 388f
animations, 399–405
APA style, 468
data slides, 398
design of individual slides, 397–398
ease of presentation, 399
evaluation, 398–405
online slide presentation, 475
slide numbers, 396
text slides, 397
SlideShare, 311, 312f, 416
slow speech, 108
smartphones, 132, 312
smile, 109
Smith, P., 5n
social collaboration systems, 177
social identity, 98, 99
social media, 6, 33f, 257, 311
anecdotal evidence, gathering of, 312
audience, 44
bad news, spread of, 275–277
best practices, 151
business use of, 44
communication, effect on, 10
community, creation of, 211
composing social media messages, 44–45
crisis plan, 275–277
early warning monitoring, 276
environmental scan, 276
exclusive perks, 211
experts in, 311
face-to-face interactions, impact on, 73–74
Facebook, 33f
goodwill, creation of, 210–211
hashtag to bashtag, 275
indirect persuasion, 246
information sharing, 311–312
LinkedIn, 33f
medium options, effect on, 32
negative comments, 276
networking tools, 140–142
networking websites, 33f
peer-to-peer support, 211
professional brand, 432–436
questions, post to, 311
quick responses, 210–211
real-time goodwill, 211
research, role in, 310–312
response, 276–277
stakeholder scan, 276
staying current with, 17–18
strategic use of, 18
surveys, 211
Twitter, 33f
social network, 133–134
social proof, 238f, 244
social recruiting, 18
Social Sciences Citation Index, 300
Socialbakers, 210
SocialSearcher.com, 312
Sociological Abstracts, 296f

soft skills, 73
software as a service (SaaS), 131, 133
solicited proposal, 351
solicited sales communications, 244
SolutionsIQ, 210
Spartan, 204
Speaking of India (Storti), 269
speaking strategies, 80–85
focus on your audience, 80–81
gender-specific communication styles, 84–85
negative response, avoiding, 82–84
nonverbal communication, use of, 81
share the conversation, 81
upward inflection, 82
Special FX, 257
specific culture, 104
specific data, 368
specific facts, 368
spelling errors, 53
spoken or emailed request for a favour, 195f
spouse, 114f
stages of team development, 165f
stand-alone presentations, 388
Standard and Poor's, 296f, 298
STAR method, 442–443
startling fact, 243
statistic, 390
Statistics Canada, 366n
Steele, Celisa, 301f
stereotypes, 96–97, 100, 111
storming, 164
Storti, Craig, 269
storyboard, 393
straight posture, 78f
strategic communicators, 10–11
strategic time management, 35–37, 35f
Stuckey, J., 5, 5n
study of business communication, 4–7
see also communication
style, 49
subject line, 40
subject matter experts, 306
SuccessFactors, 288
successful business communicator, 10–20
summary, 368
survey, 300, 302, 302–306
see also research
analyze results, 305–306
branching questions, 304–305
convenience sample population, 302
evaluate results, 305–306
interpret results, 305–306
medium, choice of, 302–303
online survey, 304–305
population, choice of, 302
questions, 304f
questions, composition of, 303–305
random sample population, 302
sample population, 302
survey population, 302
targeted sample population, 302
survey population, 302
Sutherland, Tom, 178
Swadron, Carolyn, 223, 249
sympathy message, 208, 209f
synchronous, 46, 65, 135
synonyms, 54, 297

T

table, 360, 364–365, 369
table of contents, 334–335, 338f
tablets, 312
tag question, 84
Tagoras, Inc., 301f
Talking Stick, 179

Tannen, Deborah, 84
Target, 97
targeted sample, 302
team, 161
 barriers to team communications, 162
 business presentation, 411, 413
 "c factor," 178–180
 calendar review, 164
 collaborative working environment, 168
 and communication, 163–164
 contact information, 163
 decision making, 163
 development stages, 164–166
 division of work, 163
 effective meetings, 166–167
 ethics, 165
 feedback, 163
 function of, 163–164
 goals and deliverables, 163
 high-performance teams, 175–182
 leadership skills, development of, 169–175
 meetings, 164
 member's emotions, 247
 milestones, 164
 online social collaboration, 177
 performance expectations, 163
 persuasion and, 247
 roles and responsibilities, 163
 special roles, 166
 team charter, 162–164, 178–180
 team decisions, 168–169
 valued team member, 167–169
 virtual team, 171
team charter, 162–164, 178–180
techniques for appealing to emotion, 238f
technology
 see also communications technologies
 bad news, communication of, 262
 clipboard manager software, 204
 deep web portals, 297
 face-to-face interactions, impact on, 73–74
 formal report format, software features, 335
 formal reports, formatting, 335
 hashtag to bashtag, 275
 hyperlinks in PowerPoint, 405
 proofreading tools, 54
 recommendations, and presentation software, 242
 single tasking, 36
 social collaboration, 177
 staying current with, 17–18
 tools grouped by use, 136f
 when complaints go viral, 142
TED.com, 408
telephone, 33f
telephone image, 436f
telephone surveys, 303f
templates, 203
territories, abbreviations for, 462
tertiary sources, 293
text messaging, 33f, 45–46, 45f
text references, 369
text slides, 397
text to explain graphics, 366f
texting (SMS), 145, 450t
textspeak, 147
thank you messages, 206–207, 206f, 207f, 267f, 446
thesaurus, 54
Thicke, Robin, 292
thinking aloud, 41

though-provoking story, 243
time orientation, 104
time sensitive, 138
Tindell, Kip, 6
title page, 334, 336f
title slide, 396f
TMA World, 96
tone, 30, 49, 76, 107, 331
tools for finding research sources, 296f
topic sentence, 41, 47
topic-specific heading, 42, 43f
touch, 104
Training Journal, 301f
transgender, 112
travel reports, 332
tree chart, 38, 38f
trigger words, 84
TripAdvisor, 257, 275
True Colors, 67
trust, 270
truth, 16
Tuckman, Bruce W., 164
Tufte, Edward, 363
Turnitin, 293, 293n
TVO, 82
Twenty Questions, 73
Twitter, 6, 27, 33f, 36, 44, 45f, 134–135, 136, 136f, 138–139, 140–141, 141f, 141n, 142, 210, 246, 257, 273, 275, 417, 450t, 468, 476
Two Truths and a Lie, 73

U

unambiguous, 81
unbiased language, 83
uncertainty, 104
uncertainty avoidance, 103–104
Unicorn, 18, 19f
unique identity, 98, 98f
unique selling proposition, 433, 433f
United Airlines, 142
"United Breaks Guitars" (Carroll), 142
University of Alberta NEOS, 296f
University of Guelph, 82
University of London, 36
University of Victoria, 273
unsolicited proposal, 354
unsolicited sales communications, 244
unsolicited sales message, 245f
upspeak, 82
uptalk, 82
upward inflection, 82
URLs, 135
US Airways, 142
US Army, 236
USA Today, 73
usage errors, 53

V

Ventura, Sebastian, 313f
verbal tendencies, 68f
verbal tics, 410–411
video recording, 70, 71–72
videoconferencing, 132, 145, 150–151, 450t
Vimeo, 416
virtual interview, 442, 443f, 444
virtual meetings. *See* online meetings
virtual professional image, 436–437, 436f

virtual team, 171
visible minority, 111
visual aid presentations, 388, 411
visual impairment, 111f
visuals
 business reports, 360–367
 graph design, 363–364
 graphs, 360, 360f, 361f–363f
 integration of data displays, 365–366
 table design, 364–365
 tables, 360
 visual aid presentations, 388, 411
voice, 50
voice mail, 15f, 43, 44f
voice over internet protocol (VoIP), 145, 450t
volume, 107

W

Wall Street Journal, 82
web-based documents, 329
web chat, 139, 451t
web format, 349
webcast, 416
WebEx, 145, 416, 417
webinar, 132, 139, 151, **416**, 451t
website, 33f
Weiss, Craig, 301f
Western cultures, 104
When Cultures Collide (Lewis), 105
white paper, 300, 349
Whitehurst, Jim, 32
Whole Foods Market, 210
Wikipedia, 145, 290, 293, 297, 309
wikis, 33f, 145, 177, 451t
wildcards, 296–297
Williams, Pharrel, 292
Wilson, Glenn, 36
Wilson, Tony, 273
Windows Search, 296f
Woolley, Anita, 178
Word, 349
wordiness, 48f
wording, 245
Wordpress, 134
work plan, 315f
workplace diversity. *See* diversity
works cited list. *See* MLA works cited list
World Health Organization, 111
WorldWideScience.org, 297
wrinkled forehead, 78f
writer's block, 40
written communication, 46
written request for information, 196f

Y

Yahoo, 295, 296f
Yahoo Pipes, 210
Yelp, 257, 275
yes/no questions, 304f
YouTube, 18, 134, 136, 136f, 139–140, 142, 273, 275, 276, 408, 409, 416, 451t, 468, 476

Z

Zite, 210